Farm Managerial Economics

The Authors

Dr. K. Nirmal Ravi Kumar is presently working as Professor and Head (Agricultural Economics) in Agricultural College, Mahanandi in Acharya N.G. Ranga Agricultural University. He has a brilliant academic career and he specialized in 'Agricultural Marketing' both in his post-graduate and doctoral programmes. He is actively involved in agricultural research and teaching activities during the past thirteen years in the University. He published 55 articles in popular agricultural journals. He also contributed two technical bulletins on economic aspects of irrigation water management highlighting the research priorities in major irrigation commands of Andhra Pradesh and need based technological interventions to address the same during his active stint in "Andhra Pradesh Water Management Project", an international project funded by The Royal Netherlands Embassy. His interest areas include International trade of Indian agriculture, Farming systems approach, Irrigation water management *etc*. The following are the other major contributions (books) by the same author:

- ☆ Indian Agriculture in the 21st Century - Challenges and Opportunities
- ☆ World Trade Agreement and Indian Agriculture - Implementation Experience
- ☆ Microeconomic Analysis in Agriculture
- ☆ Objective Agricultural Economics (Two Editions)
- ☆ Farmers Indebtedness in India - An Economic Analysis
- ☆ Research Methodology for Agricultural Economics
- ☆ Methodology for Social Sciences Research in Agriculture
- ☆ Agricultural Marketing
- ☆ Agricultural Production Economics
- ☆ Encyclopedia of Rural Management

Kalyan Chakravarthy Guntuboyina is a "Senior Researcher" with Wageningen UR and his main area of expertise is in public-private-partnership (PPP) framework development for sustainable agri-business projects. He has been project leader for the Agro-park projects of Wageningen UR in Mexico and China and is also leading the "India Water Initiative" project, which involves the framework development for enabling implementation of climate-smart irrigation solutions in India.

With a Master's degree in Genetics and Plant breeding and PG Diploma in Agribusiness Management, he has worked with some leading organizations such as BASF, Rabobank International, YES Bank and IFFCO in senior management and leadership positions before joining Wageningen UR. Kalyan has authored several industry reports prominent among which are "Developing Globally Competitive Fruit & Vegetable Value Chains" (published by the Confederation of Indian Industry and released at the International F&V Summit in 2008) Report on Indian Agriculture: Winds of Change (published by Federation of Indian Chambers of Commerce (FICCI) and released by the Honourable Prime Minister of India at the FICCI National Agribusiness Summit - October 2006) and "The Indian Seed Industry" (published by Rabobank International-2002).

Kalyan's scientific publications include "Indo-US Collaborations: The Agribusiness Opportunity" (published by Indian Council of Research in International Economic Relations, April 2007) "Agricultural Debt Waiver and Debt Relief Scheme: What it means for Banks?" (published by The Institute of Chartered Financial Analysts of India, ICFAI University Press - October 2008) and "Transition Strategies for Metropolitan Food Clusters" (published by the International journal of Arts and Sciences, 2011). Other publications of Kalyan include: "Sino-Dutch Shenxian New City of Agro Eco and Health" Conceptual Master Plan for the development of the Agropark" Wageningen, Wageningen UR, 2014; "Metropolitan Food Cluster Chiapas, Mexico, Feasibility Study", Wageningen, Wageningen UR 2014.

Kalyan has held several honorary positions which include, Member of Planning Commission's working group on Animal Husbandry and Livestock (2011) and Convenor of Agri-business sub-committee of Indian Banks Association (2009 -2010). He is presently a Member of the Advisory Committee of Post Graduate Diploma programme of National Institute of Agriculture Extension Management, (MANAGE) India.

Farm Managerial Economics

K. Nirmal Ravi Kumar

Kalyan Chakravarthy Guntuboyina

2017

Daya Publishing House®

A Division of

Astral International Pvt. Ltd.

New Delhi – 110 002

Cataloging in Publication Data—DK
Courtesy: D.K. Agencies (P) Ltd. <docinfo@dkagencies.com>

Ravi Kumar, K. N. (Kotamraju Nirmal), 1969- **author.**
Farm managerial economics / K. Nirmal Ravi Kumar, Kalyan Chakravarthy Guntuboyina.
pages cm
Includes bibliographical references.

ISBN 978-93-86071-17-0 (International Edition)

1. Farm management. 2. Agriculture Economic aspects. I. Title.

S561.R38 2017 DDC 630.68 23

Published by : **Daya Publishing House®**
A Division of
Astral International Pvt. Ltd.
– ISO 9001:2015 Certified Company –
4736/23, Ansari Road, Darya Ganj
New Delhi-110 002
Ph. 011-43549197, 23278134
E-mail: info@astralint.com
Website: www.astralint.com

– Dedicated to –

Late K. RAMA CHANDRA RAO

ACHARYA N.G. RANGA AGRICULTURAL UNIVERSITY
ADMINISTRATIVE OFFICE, RAJENDRANAGAR,
HYDERABAD-500030

Dr. K. Raja Reddy
Director Research

Phone (O): 040-24015078
Mobile: 8008896185
E-mail: dr_angrau@yahoo.co.in

Foreword

Managing a farm is a responsibility. Managing farms on a sustainable basis, while making a profit is one of the biggest challenges facing agriculture. Successfully managing a farm business is certainly the goal of farm owners. To ensure profitability on the farms, the farmers must apply certain basic economic principles of farm production. The quality of the decisions made by manager is an important component in determining the longevity of the farm business. So, understanding the farm managerial decisions and their underlying economic principles will enable the students to familiarize with the microeconomic concepts of farm production and do some basic research related to farm production, resources and product combinations, farm cost structure, farm planning, risk analysis *etc.* Keeping in view of these aspects, this text book entitled 'Farm Managerial Economics' was designed, so as to enable the students to learn the applicability concepts of basic economic principles on farm production and management. This textbook equally serve the Agricultural Officers and other stakeholders in understanding the applicability aspects of farm managerial principles and in turn, facilitate them to guide the farmers to plan for proper enterprises combination, cost-effective production and in maximizing their profits. I complement the sincere efforts of Dr. K. Nirmal Ravi Kumar in bringing out this volume duly considering the latest syllabi, as prescribed by the Vth Deans' Committee recommendations appointed by the Indian Council of Agricultural Research. I hope this book will also be of immense use for the Academicians, as it harbours standard and updated material pertaining to the basic concepts of Farm Managerial Economics.

(K. RAJA REDDY)

Authors' Note

We consider this as a bold attempt to present a comprehensive text material on the fundamental aspects of Farm Managerial Economics. We will not dare enough to make a tall claim regarding the originality of the material incorporated in this text book entitled, 'Farm Managerial Economics', but we certainly admit that, the concepts are dealt in-detail in a lucid form, so as to enable the students and Academicians to learn, understand and conceptualize the same. The present volume can serve as a standardized text book for the graduates, post-graduates and doctoral students, who wish to pursue their career in the field of Agricultural Economics in different State Agricultural Universities.

This task of writing and publishing the text book on the basic aspects of 'Farm Managerial Economics' has been one of the most challenging and satisfying experiences for us. We sincerely thank our parents and gratefully dedicate this piece of work to them, as they motivated us at an early age about the importance of education and the value of hard work.

(K.Nirmal Ravi Kumar)
Professor & Head, Dept. of Agricultural Economics, Agril. College, Mahanandi
Acharya N. G. Ranga Agricultural University (ANGRAU)

(Kalyan Chakravarthy Guntuboyina)
Senior Researcher & Business Coordinator
Agroparks and Metropolitan Food Clusters
Wageningen University and Research Centre
6700 AA, Wageningen, The Netherlands

Contents

Function) – Assumptions - Explanation of the law - Shapes of TPP, MPP and APP curves - Relationship between TPP, MPP and APP - Reasons for increasing MRs - Reasons for constant MRs - Reasons for diminishing MRs - Reasons for negative MRs - Differences between three stages of LVP – Limitations of LDR - Applicability of LDR - Differences between Traditional approach and Modern approach of Returns to a variable factor - Cost Principle - Different types of costs - Explicit costs - Implicit costs - Opportunity cost - Limitations of opportunity cost - Social cost - Short run and Long Run Costs - Short run Absolute costs – TFC - SRTVC – SRTC – Short run per unit costs - AFC – SRAVC – SRATC – SRMC – Opportunity cost vs MC - Relation between SRMC and MPP in the short run production programme - Relation between SRMC and SRTC - Relation between SRMC and SRAVC - Relationship between SRMC and SRATC curves - Effects of taxes on cost structure of a firm - Effect of specific tax - Imposition of license fees - B. Long Run Costs - Absolute Cost - Long Run Total Cost – Long run per unit costs – Long Run Average Total Cost – Long Run Marginal cost - Cost analysis in the short run and long run production programmes - Recovery of costs - Equilibrium conditions of the firm - Applicability of Cost Principle - Cost function vis-à-vis Production function - Principle of Factor Substitution - LCC of factors or Optimum factor combination or Producer's Equilibrium or Optimal Combination of factors - Marginal Product Approach - Isoquant - Isocost Approach - Tabular method - Algebraic method - Graphical method - Cost minimization for a given level of output - Output maximization for a given cash outlay and prices of the two resources - Inequality between MRTS and Price ratio of resources - Limitations of LCC - Types of resources and their relationships – Substitutes – Complements - Good substitutes - Perfect substitutes - Constant rate of substitution of resources - Decreasing rate of substitution of resources - Increasing rate of substitution of resources - Applicability of Principle of Factor Substitution - Special Cases of Substitution - Principle of Product Substitution - Optimum Products Combination - Opportunity cost approach - PPC and Iso-revenue line approach - Tabular method - Algebraic method - Graphical method - Inequality between MRPS and Price ratio of products - Types of enterprise combinations - Joint products - Complementary product relationship - Supplementary product relationship - Competitive product relationship - Constant rate of substitution of products - Decreasing rate of substitution of products - Increasing rate of substitution of products - Antagonistic relationship - Applicability of Product Substitution Principle - Principle of Equi-Marginal Returns – Assumptions - Explanation of the Principle - Practical Applicability - LDR vis-à-vis Principle of Equi-Marginal Returns - Principle of Comparative Advantage - Absolute Advantage - Comparative Advantage - Practical Applicability - Time Comparison Principle - Discounting – Compounding - Discount rate – Opportunity Cost of Capital - Social Discount Rate - Net Present Value - Criteria for selection of projects based on NPV - Merits of NPV - Benefit Cost Ratio - Criteria for selection of projects based on BCR - Limitation of BCR analysis - Internal Rate of Return - Procedure to compute IRR - Criteria to use IRR - Merits of IRR - Limitations of IRR - Comparison between NPV and IRR - Similarities in results of NPV and IRR - Conflict between NPV and IRR in

Acronyms

AC: Average Cost
AFC: Average Fixed Cost
AFC_X: Average Factor Cost
AE: Allocative Efficiency
AFC_X: Average Factor Cost
AMS: Aggregate Measurement of Support
APP: Average Physical Product
AR: Average Revenue
ARC: Average Revenue Curve
ARP: Average Revenue Product
ATC: Average Total Cost
AVP: Average Value Product
BCR: Benefit Cost Ratio
BEP: Break Even Point
CACP: Commission for Agricultural Costs and Prices
CCPC: Comprehensive Scheme for Study of Cost of Cultivation of Principal Crops
CI: Cropping Intensity

CMR: Contribution Margin Ratio
COP: Cost of Production
CPM: Critical Path Method
CVP: Cost-Volume-Profit
CYI: Crop Yield Index
DES: Directorate of Economics and Statistics
DMP: Domestic Market Price
EE: Economic Efficiency
EFT: Earliest Finishing Time
E_p: Elasticity of Production
EST: Earliest Start Time
FAO: Food and Agriculture Organization
GC: Gini Coefficient
GDP: Gross Domestic Product
GFI: Gross Farm Income
GM: Genetically Modified
HYV: High Yielding Varieties
ICAR: Indian Council of Agricultural Research
IDC: Indifference Curve
INM: Integrated Nutrient Management
IPM: Integrated Pest Management
IRR: Internal Rate of Return
IWRM: Integrated Water Resources Management
KVKs: Krishi Vigyan Kendras
LCC: Least Cost Combination
LCM: Least Cost Method
LDR: Law of Diminishing Returns
LEMR: Law of Equi-Marginal Returns
LFT: Latest Finishing Time
LP: Linear Programming
LRAC: Long Run Average Cost
LRATC: Long Run Average Total Cost
LRMC: Long Run Marginal Cost
LRS: Long Run Supply

LRTC: Long Run Total Cost
LST: Latest Start Time
LVP: Law of Variable Proportions
MC: Marginal Cost
MES: Minimum Efficient Size
MFC_x: Marginal Factor Cost
MGNREGA: Mahatma Gandhi National Rural Employment Guarantee Act Scheme
MIRR: Modified Internal Rate of Return
MODI: Modified Distribution
MPP: Marginal Physical Product
MR: Marginal Returns or Marginal Revenue
MRC: Marginal Revenue Curve
MRP: Marginal Revenue Product
MRPS: Marginal Rate of Product Substitution
MRS: Marginal Rate of Substitution
MRTS: Marginal Rate of Technical Substitution
MSPs: Minimum Support Prices
MU: Marginal Utility
MVP_x: Marginal Value Product of a factor
MWD: Man Working Days
NB: Net Incremental Benefits
NBIR: Net Benefit Investment Ratio
NFI: Net Farm Income
NGOs: Non-Governmental Organizations
NPV: Net Present Value
NPW: Net Present Worth
NWC: North West Corner Rule
NWS: Net Worth Statement
OCC: Opportunity Cost of Capital
OPC: Optimum Product Combination
OPMR: Operating Profit Margin Ratio
PBP: Pay Back Period
PERT: Programme Evaluation and Review Technique

PPC: Production Possibility Curve
PPF: Production Possibility Frontier
PWB: Present Worth of Benefits
PWC: Present Worth of Costs
P_X: Price of the variable input 'X'
P_Y: Price of the output or product 'Y'
PWU: Productive Man Work Units
R and D: Research and Development
RCN: Replacement Cost New
ROA: Rate of Return on Assets
ROE: Rate of Return on Farm Equity
RTS: Returns to Scale
SAUs: State Agricultural Universities
SDR: Social Discount Rate
SFCI: State Farms Corporation of India
SRATC: Short Run Average Total Cost
SRAVC: Short Run Average Variable Cost
SRD: Social Rate of Discount
SRMC: Short Run Marginal Cost
SRS: Short Run Supply
SRTC: Short Run Total Cost
SRTVC: Short Run Total Variable Cost
SS: Social Surplus
TC: Total Cost
TCOC: Total Cost of Cultivation
TE: Technical Efficiency
TFC: Total Fixed Cost
TFC_X: Total Factor Cost
TPP: Total Physical Product
TR: Total Returns
TRC: Total Revenue Curve
TU: Total Utility
TVC: Total Variable Cost
TVP: Total Value Product

VAM: Vogel's Approximation Method
VAP: Value of the Average Product
VMP: Value of Marginal Product
VOP: Value of Production
WTO: World Trade Organization

1

Introduction to Farm Management

Agricultural sector in India is changing rapidly since the mid-sixties with the advent of 'Green Revolution' (boost in food grains production). Later, the agricultural sector also witnessed a number of revolutions in terms of boosting production with reference to oilseeds (Yellow Revolution), milk (White Revolution), fish (Blue Revolution), and fruits and vegetables (Golden Revolution), non-conversational energy (Black/Brown Revolution), eggs (Silver Revolution), potatoes (Round Revolution), tomatoes and meat (Red Revolution) and fertilizers (Grey Revolution). Presently, the country is marching ahead towards 'Rainbow revolution' comprising all the above revolutions. An important fact behind these revolutions is the economic consideration. Farmers have been adopting the new technologies in different fields of agricultural sector, as they contribute higher outputs in their respective production programmes. With gradual market orientation of Indian agricultural sector, emphasis on cost-effective production of enterprises has gained momentum. This led to the increased importance on various aspects of crop production programme like cost analysis, profitability analysis, strategies to combat various risks and uncertainties in farm business, optimization of resource use and output *etc*. Thus, the focus of Agricultural Economics has shifted towards 'Farm Management', as it deals with all the above aspects at the micro (farm) level. In the recent period, irrespective of the sector, the term 'management' has become a catchword. This is not an exception regarding the economic issues of a farm and since then, the concepts of farm management have gained rapid significance in the Indian agricultural sector.

However, unlike other sectors, in agricultural sector, there are no specialized institutions to train the farmers or scientific personnel exclusively on the issues pertaining to farm management. This calls for giving a specialized emphasis to the discipline of farm management, so as to make the farmers vibrant in understanding the various aspects like farm decision making, farm planning, resource planning (land, labour and capital), farm costing, farm accounting, profitability analysis *etc.* To analyze these farm managerial aspects, the scientific personnel in the field of Agricultural Economics in general and Agricultural Production Economics in particular should be specially trained enough with statistical tools such a production function, Linear Programming (LP) *etc.*, as farm management basically involves the application of scientific and technical principles of Agricultural Production Economics to a particular farm. Thus, farm management is a specialized branch of Agricultural Production Economics to attend and solve for day to day problems regarding the management of the farm. The farm management has been elevated as a separate discipline in view of the gaining importance for cost minimizing and profit maximizing concepts on the farm. Further, several modern economists transferred the basic principles of economics in relevance to agriculture with special reference towards managing the farm. We practically see farmers are being affected by profound changes in the demand for agricultural commodities, rising costs of production, risk and uncertainties in the farm business, changes in governmental programmes and policies *etc.* Added to these, farmers often face labour shortage problems in the villages, fluctuations in farm output, price volatility of commodities *etc.* All these issues faced by the farmers are often complex and hence, suitable management strategies and practices must keep pace with them. In view of this, the specialized discipline of farm management aims at making the farmers to keep up with the latest production techniques, so as to make better management decisions for improving the profitability of farm businesses. Though this discipline is of the recent origin, it is being viewed with different meanings. Some Agricultural Economists view it as a specialized branch of Agricultural Production Economics, some view it as an art that explains how the farmer has to draw and supervise his farm production activity in the context of making profits and some others view it as a branch of Agricultural Economics that deals with the application of economic principles to individual farm units regarding the rational allocation of scarce resources in the context of wealth earning and wealth spending activities of the farmer. Considering these divergent views, farm management is defined in different ways by the economists as given here under.

Farm management is the study of the business principles of farming. It may be defined as the science of organization and the management of the farm enterprise for the purpose of securing the greatest continuous profits.

– (Warren)

Farm management is concerned with, how can the individual farmer so organize the factors of production - land, labour and capital - on his farm, so adapt practice to his particular environment, and so dispose of his product, as to yield him the largest net return, while still maintaining the integrity of his land and equipment'

– (Butterfield)

Farm management, as the subdivision of economics which considers the allocation of limited resources within the individual farm, is a science of choice and decision making.

– (Heady and Jensen)

Farm management is concerned with the organization and deployment of the resources put into a farm business - the land, the capital, the labour and that item of over-riding importance, the ability and skills of the individual farmer

– (Dexter and Barber)

Farm management is concerned with the organization of resources, with planning their use, both within and between enterprises, and with the control of plans both during their implementation and afterwards.

– (Barnard and Nix)

Farm management is the process by which resources and situations are manipulated over time by the manager of the farm system in trying, with less than full information, to achieve his or her goals.

– (Dillon)

Farm management is concerned with the decisions which affect the profitability of the farm business.

– (Castle, Becker and Nelson)

Farm management can be thought of as being a decision-making process. It is a continual process. The decisions are concerned with allocating the limited resources of land, labour, and capital among alternative and competing uses. This allocation process forces the manager to identify goals to guide and direct the decision making.

– (Kay and Edwards)

Farm management is a branch of agriculture economics, which deals with wealth earning and wealth spending activities of the farmer in relation to organization and operation of farm in relation to organization and operation of farm business for securing maximum possible net income.

– (Bradford and Johnson)

Farm management is defined as a science which deals with organization and operation of farm business in the context of resource use efficiency and continuous profits.

– (Efferson)

Farm management as the method is the utilization of sound principles in the selection, organization and conduct of an individual farm business for tile purpose of obtaining the greatest possible profits.

– (Adams)

On going through the above definitions, it is clear that, they share a common point *i.e., 'farm management involves decision making regarding rational allocation of resources in the production programme'*. They further emphasize that, farm management is the science of organizing and combining people and resources like natural and material resources for the purpose of production of crops and allied enterprises on the farm. It is an applied science of Agricultural Production Economics that deals with the decision making process, whereby limited resources are allocated to a number or production alternatives to organise and operate the business in such a way as to attain the desired goals like minimization of costs and maximization of profits. Thus, these definitions also emphasize that economics is the core of farm management, since the key task of farm management is making choice between two or more alternatives. Among the definitions cited earlier, the definition given by Prof. Dillon emphasized *'farm management is what farmers do'* and this definition is a more succinct one compared to other definitions. This definition highlighted the following aspects in the context of defining farm management:

- ✰ Dynamic nature of farm system, environment and hence, management.
- ✰ Subjective judgements by the farmer in taking decisions towards the achievement of his goals.
- ✰ Uncertainties and consequent risks present in the farm manager's decision.
- ✰ Plan the level of resources usage over time.
- ✰ Dynamic role of farm manager in managing the farm in accordance with the changing conditions (Figure 1.1) rather than assuming passive role by merely organizing and controlling the farm activities.
- ✰ Goal seeking behavior rather than only profit making. That is, even non-profit goals say, farm family satisfaction is recognized in taking up enterprises on the farm.

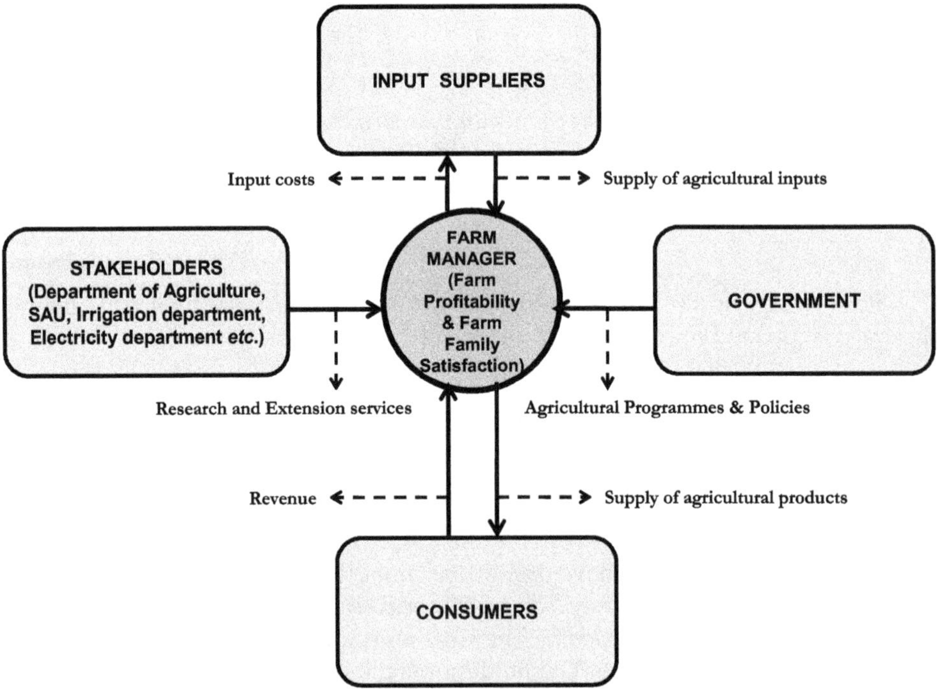

Figure 1.1: Farmer and his Environment in Managing the Farm.

Considering the above aspects, the definition given by Prof. Dillon is considered to be more meritorious and contrastingly different from other definitions. Further, if the word 'farm' is removed from Dillon's definition, it can even serve as an excellent definition of management in general. In general, all the above definitions share a common view that, farm management is a science of decision making, which deals with judicious decision making regarding the use of scarce farm resources, having alternative uses to obtain maximum profit and family satisfaction on a continuous basis from the farm as a whole. So, farm management mainly aims at maximization of net profits from the farm as a whole. Note that, considering the dynamic view of farm management, as defined by Prof. Dillon, the decision making by the manager on the farm should be consistent with the agricultural programmes and policies formulated by the Government from time to time.

I. Basic Elements in Farm Management

Figure 1.1 depicts the basic elements of farm management. They include: farm manager, Government, input suppliers, stakeholders and consumers.

- ☆ *Farm manager:* He was the central element, as he manages all the activities on the farm. He executes all the production activities on the farm, so as to achieve the broad goals like minimization of costs and maximization of profits. He was faced with dynamic decision-making environment within which he has to make all production decisions. These decisions, however, are somewhat complex with many limitations imposed by the unique environment and consequently, he faces several risks and uncertainties in the farm business (such as weather, insect pests, fluctuating market prices etc). Though some farm decisions can be changed frequently (tactile decisions), some can be changed with greater difficulty and some cannot be changed at all that are relevant to 'biological' and 'physical' laws of nature. Examples like, the gestation period of mango orchard cannot be shortened by the farm manager, amount of feed the livestock can consume per day, sowing seasons of crops *etc.* So, the farm manager must carry out all the activities on the farm knowing his limitations placed by the biological and physical laws of nature. Due to his limitations, the farm manager faces a lot of problems regarding what to produce, how to produce, how much to produce *etc.* Knowing his limitations, the farm manager should be continuously on the alert to identify problems of any type as quickly as possible and define them concisely. Good problem identification will minimise time it takes to complete the remainder of the decision making steps. Of course, the competence with which the farm manager is able to recognize and define conditions or problems depend on various factors like farming experience, level of education (exposure to ideas and approaches to problem solving) and his willingness to take risks.
- ☆ *Government:* Farm manager must be vigilant regarding the programmes and policies being implemented by the Government and he should plan the production programme in relevance to them. This fetches higher income to the farmer, as the programmes and policies being implemented by the

Government highlight the priorities of crop production. For example, the Government of Andhra Pradesh advocates the farmers not to go for tobacco cultivation (being a neglected crop in the State) and not go for paddy again in rabi season because of acute power and water shortages. If the farmers still goes against the Government's recommendations, they will not get safeguarded by the Government at times of price fall after the harvesting season. So, the farm manager must be vigilant about the various Government's programmes and policies like fertilizer subsidy, subsidy on drip irrigation, increased Minimum Support Prices (MSPs) for the crops, subsidy for purchasing machinery, subsidy for using bio-fertilizers *etc.*

- ☆ ***Input suppliers:*** These are the agencies (like fertilizer dealers, pesticide dealers, seed firms, firms selling machinery, implements etc) that supply requisite inputs to the farmers for taking up crop production programmes. The quality of the inputs supplied by them counts much in boosting the productivity of the crops. As input prices are not under the control of farmers, the farm manager generally aims at using the most efficient productive process and to achieve this, he uses expensive resource in smaller quantity relative to a cheaper resource. Sometimes, the farm manager aims at proper resources combination (manures and fertilizers, labour and capital etc) that ensures cost minimization in the production prrogramme.
- ☆ ***Stakeholders:*** These are the agencies that contribute to the agricultural development process. They include agencies like Department of Agriculture, State Agricultural Universities (SAUs), Department of Animal Husbandry, Department of Irrigation, Department of Electricity, Non-Governmental Organizations (NGOs), Krishi Vigyan Kendras (KVKs) *etc.*, and they offer requisite guidance to the farm managers in the execution of crop production programmes. Some of the agencies like Department of Agriculture, Department of Animal Husbandry, Department of Irrigation, Department of Electricity *etc.*, even offer the inputs to the farmers at subsidized rates to be employed in the production programmes.
- ☆ ***Consumers:*** Note that, the consumers of farm production are not only the end users of the produce, but may also include the processing agencies, who purchase raw produce from the farmers for further processing it and makes it suitable for direct consumption. Further, the farm family satisfaction will be given due recognition in managing the farm by the farm manager. That is, besides cultivating the crops that fetch higher price from the consumers, the farm family consumption interests should also be taken into consideration in planning the crop production programme. This is where the concept of farm management is different from the profit motive concept of Agricultural Production Economics. For example, if the farmer possesses four acres of land, he will go for cultivating a food crop (say, paddy or wheat) in part of his operational holding considering the food requirements of his farm family, though cultivation of commercial crops like cotton or chillies will fetch him still a higher remunerative price than a food crop. Thus, under farm management science, farm family satisfaction will be given due recognition.

Above all these elements, farm production is the only occupation in which living and working are closely associated. This association ensures the following advantages:

- ☆ A portion of fresh produce produced on the farm can be used for family consumption.
- ☆ Offer employment to the farm family members.
- ☆ Farmer's wife normally prefers farming operations to other occupations because, she is more acquainted with her husband's work and business.
- ☆ All members of farm family collectively take the farm managerial decisions.

II. Objectives of the Study of Farm Management

Farm management as the science deals with the organization of people, natural and material resources for the purpose of crop and livestock production in order to maximize the profits, while optimizing the input use. Thus, managing the farm means, to plan it, organize it, supervise the activities, and coordinate the functioning of factors of production, buying and selling activities and analyzing the financial efficiency of the farm. This management of farm is not something done once for all, but it is to be done season by season and year by year. The management of the farm is best examined and understood under the whole farm situation. The subject of economics serves as the core of farm management, since the key task of farm management involves making choice between two or more alternatives. With the tools of general economic theory forming the base and looking at the farm structure as a whole, the study of farm management encompasses the following objectives:

- ☆ To analyze the existing use of resources like land, labour, capital, management and the production pattern on the farm.
- ☆ To analyze the factors responsible for the deviation of resources usage from their optimum level.
- ☆ To explain the means and procedure for moving the resources usage from the existing combination to their optimum use for profit maximization.
- ☆ To outline conditions that would simultaneously obtain its objectives of profit maximization and family satisfaction through optimum use of resources and judicious income distribution.
- ☆ To ensure Least Cost Combination (LCC) of resources by planning proper resources combination in the production programme.
- ☆ To study the optimum combination of enterprises on the farm considering the relationship that exists between them.
- ☆ To maximize the resource use efficiency in the production programme and to find out ways and means for increasing the efficiency of use of farm resources through analyzing input-output relationship.
- ☆ To analyze cost structure of various crops and allied enterprises, so as to minimize the losses in the production programme.

- ☆ To plan the crop production programme with due recognition to the comparative advantage the products enjoy both in domestic and international markets.
- ☆ To analyse the best means of employing the limited resources usage in the production programme such that, the resource usage is economically efficient.
- ☆ To analyze how profitable the long term investment is considering long gestation period of the enterprise.
- ☆ To analyze, how the most likely future returns on the capital invested in the business can be improved.
- ☆ To study the comparative economics of different enterprises practiced on the farm.
- ☆ To determine the relation of size of farm to land utilization, cropping pattern, capital investment, labour employment *etc.*
- ☆ To study the impact of technological changes on farm business.
- ☆ To estimate the incremental income from the enterprises due to additional investments or planning scientific changes on the enterprises.
- ☆ To analyze the changes in the net worth of the farm business over a period of time
- ☆ To plan the crop production programme considering various risks and uncertainties that the farmer may encounter in the business and plan the strategies accordingly.
- ☆ To analyze, how best the farmer will cope up with various risks and uncertainties in the farm production.
- ☆ To prepare and implement alternate farm plans that contribute to higher incremental income to the farmer
- ☆ To find out the optimal solution to economic decisions (say, maximization of profits and minimization of costs) under a given set of (linear) resource constraints.
- ☆ To analyze the rate of return derived from both owned capital invested and total capital invested in the production programme.

III. Types of Farm Management Decisions

Farm management can be defined as a science of decision making. Innumerable decisions which a farmer will take in the farm business are related with either cost minimization or production (profit) maximization concepts, as the farm profits depend upon the total costs incurred in the production of enterprises on the farm. The various decisions taken in the farm business can be conveniently categorized into three types *viz.*, Organizational management decisions, Administrative management decisions and Marketing management decisions (Figure 1.2). These decisions made on the farm is a continuous process.

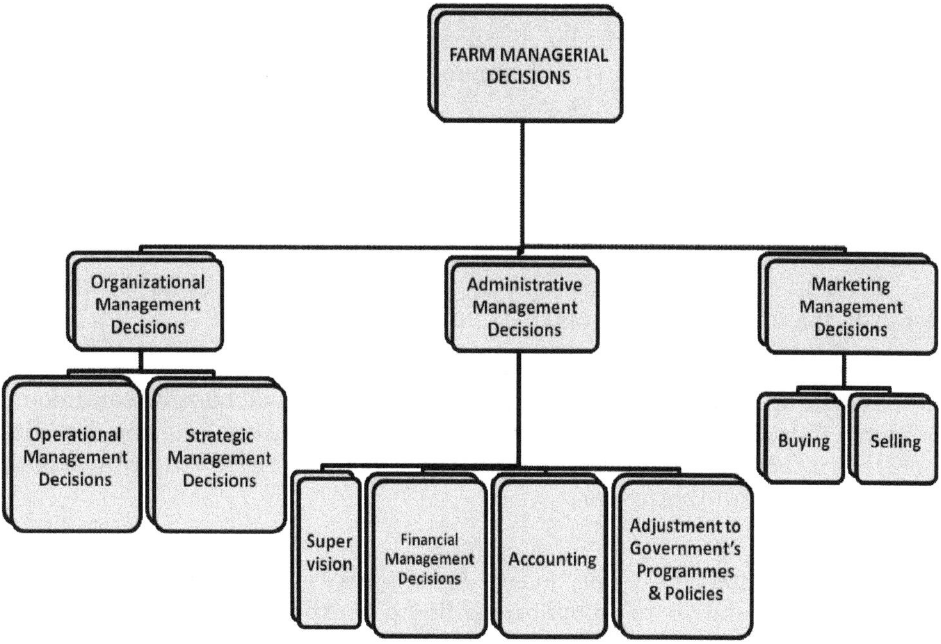

Figure 1.2: Classification of Farm Managerial Decisions.

A. Organizational Management Decisions

These decisions mainly aim at better organization of farm business. They can be conveniently divided into Operational management decisions and Strategic management decisions.

i. Operational Management Decisions

These are the decisions taken by the farmer very frequently regarding day to day operations on the farm. The frequency of these operational management decisions is more as compared to strategic management decisions. These decisions will generally involve less amount of investment. So, these decisions are also called as Tactile decisions. The farmer can reverse these decisions once taken very quickly and with less investment or with no investment. For example, if the farmer wishes to perform weeding operation by engaging 20 casual labour and if the labour costs are very high due to their scarcity, he can immediately change the decision towards application of a post-emergence herbicide. Similarly, the decisions taken by the farmer regarding how to produce, what to produce, how much to produce *etc.*, all fall under operational management decisions.

ii. Strategic Management Decisions

These are the decisions taken less frequently by the farmer in the farm business and these decisions involve huge amount of investment compared to operational management decisions. The farmer has to undergo critical thinking before making these decisions. Once the decision is taken and implemented, it is difficult to reverse the decision. For example, if the farmer purchases machinery or land, it is difficult to reverse the decision. Similarly, the decisions relating to digging of bore well, land reclamation, soil conservation, type of farming to be taken up *etc.*, all fall under strategic management decisions.

B. Administrative Management Decisions

These decisions are mainly related to:

i. Supervision

The farmer has to supervise the day to day farm operations in the business towards minimization of costs and maximization of profits.

ii. Financial Management Decisions

To take up various activities on the farm, the farmer will borrow loan amount from the financial institutions or from private money lenders. So, farm decisions generally include: when to borrow, where to borrow, how much to borrow, at what interest rate he has to borrow *etc.*

iii. Accounting

Farm accountancy also falls under administrative management decisions. The farmer has to maintain an account regarding cost expenditure incurred by him, quantity of output sold in the market, prices received, gross returns derived and profits realized in the business. Such accounting of information pertaining to costs and returns is useful to the farmer to analyze the progress of farm business and it also indicates his credit worthiness.

iv. Adjustment to Government's Programmes and Policies

Generally, in taking up enterprise on the farm, the farmer has to adjust himself to Government's programmes and policies being implemented. For example, the Government of Andhra Pradesh often advocate the farmers to go for pulse crops in rabi season, keeping in view of the acute power and water shortages. Further the farmers are also advocated to go for micro-irrigation in view of acute water scarcity.

Other decisions relating to accounting and book-keeping and production for home consumption and the market also fall under administrative management decisions.

C. Marketing Management Decisions

These decisions deal with both buying and selling activities of the farmer.

i. Buying

It includes the decisions related to purchase of inputs such as what to buy, where to buy, when to buy, how much to buy, from when to buy, at what price the farmer has to buy *etc.*

ii. Selling

It includes the decisions related to sale of farm output such as what to sell, where to sell, when to sell, how much to sell, for whom to sell *etc.*

Note that, the decision pertaining to buying and selling activities are very important in the context of profitability of farm business. This is because, a farmer may be a good manager in planning, organizing, controlling and coordination of different farm operations, but these may not show positive influence on the Net Worth Statement (NWS) or Balance sheet of farm business because, he pays too much for buying and sells at low prices. Thus, a farmer may enjoy good managerial skills in performing the farm operation, but he is poor in applying basic business (economic) principles. So, the farmer must possess both managerial skills and business attitude in performing farm business.

Besides above, other important farm managerial decisions include:

- ☆ What is the best size of the farm or enterprise can the farmer can manage?
- ☆ What kinds and sizes of buildings the farmer should use?
- ☆ What kind of soil conservation programme the farmer should implement?
- ☆ What type of machinery and equipment to be used on the farm?
- ☆ What farm practices are to be employed in the farm?
- ☆ What composition of inputs (say, fertilizer doses, pesticide dosages) to be used?

All the above decisions, regarding management of farm cannot be considered separately from each other. Rather, they should be seen on integrated business, which gives cohesion to the farm business. Once these farm management decisions are made, they can be translated into activities or a series of activities, which may be grouped into technical, commercial, financial and accounting categories (Table 1.1).

- ☆ ***Technical activities:*** These activities are related to all physical production activities. For example, the activities relating to what to produce, how to produce and how much to produce all can be categorized under technical activities.
- ☆ ***Commercial activities:*** These activities include all buying and selling activities of the farm manager in conducting the farm business. So, they are related to purchase of inputs and employing them at LCC to ensure cost-effective production. They are also related to storage, handling, marketing of commodities produced on the farm.
- ☆ ***Financial activities:*** These are the activities related to acquisition and use of capital, repayment plans, rate of interest at which the loan is to be borrowed *etc.*, by the farmer in the farm business. It also includes analysis of the farm manager for future capital investments.
- ☆ ***Accounting:*** These activities are related to the maintenance of farm records, including records of buying, selling, payment of labour wages *etc.* This activity will enable the farm manager to prove his credit worthiness before the banker.

Table 1.1: Different Activities to be Performed in Farm Management

Activity	*Nature of Activity*	*Examples*
Technical activity	Production of enterprises on the farm	What to produce, how to produce and how much to produce *etc.*, related production problems
Commercial activity	Purchase of inputs and sale of output	***Inputs:*** When to purchase, where to purchase, from whom to purchase, at what price to purchase, quantity to purchase, quality of inputs to purchase *etc.* ***Output:*** When to sell, where to sell, for whom to sell (*i.e.*, in domestic market or international market), at what price to sell, quantity to sell etc.
Financial activity	Acquisition and use of capital	Amount of capital to be borrowed, rate of interest, repayment plan *etc.*
Accounting	Maintenance of farm records	Physical Farm Records Financial Farm Records Supplementary Farm Records

No doubt, 'profits' is the immediate goal of making farm managerial decisions. However, this is not the final goal, as the farmer ultimately aims at maximization of family satisfaction. So, 'good family living' is the ultimate goal of farm management study. If profit is the ultimate goal, farm manager and farm family need not work for 12 hours per day, 7 days per week and 365 days per year on the farm. So, farm living, working and satisfaction derived through working on farm are important than mere profitability. This does not mean profitability is having less importance in farm management, but it is equally important in the following contexts:

- Higher net income from the farm influences the standard of living of farm family.
- Higher net income contributes more productive investment on the farm.
- Higher net income enables the farmer to meet his family living expenses.

Thus, farm profitability is the means of achieving the farm family satisfaction thereby, the latter is the ultimate end or goal of the farm management. If we see the practical world, many farm mangers, who succeeded in managing the farm also succeeded in home management and thus, there exists direct relationship between farm management and home Management. It is essential to note that, managerial decisions on the farm varies from farm to farm, as no two farms are exactly alike in respect of soil and other basic resources. So, common recommendations cannot be given for all the farms though all farm managerial decisions are provided by the background principles of agricultural production economics.

IV. Factors Influencing Farm Managerial Decisions

We already know that, the decisions taken by the farm manager will guide the farm business towards achieving the two major goals *viz.*, cost minimization and profit maximization. Note that, the farmer cannot decide and implement one decision straight away to address the problem under consideration, as he faces with several alternative courses of action both in terms of allocation of resources and selection of enterprise combinations. In view of this, several factors will influence the decision making regarding their implementation in the farm business and they include:

- ✰ ***Size of the farm:*** This is the most influential factor, as for deciding and implementing the farm management decisions, first the size of land holding should be sufficiently large enough or preferably of economic size. That is, if the land holding size is too small or uneconomic, it is not feasible to implement the decisions efficiently.
- ✰ ***Availability of different combinations of resources:*** We know some of the farm resources substitute each other such that, without affecting the level of output, cost minimization can be achieved in the production programme. For example, manure and fertilizer resources are good substituites and if the farmer increases the dosage of manure, he will substitute the use of fertilizer without affecting the level of output and achieves the LCC of these two resources. Similarly, machinery and human labour are good substitutes. So, the rate of substitution of two resources determines the level of resources combination in the production programme and this influences the decision making of the farm manager.
- ✰ ***Level of resource usage:*** According to the concept of Law of Diminishing Returns (LDR), the continuous increase in the quantity of one resource (keeping the level of other resources constant) does not increase the output in the same proportion after a certain level of output. So, the farmer's decision regarding the level of resource usage depends upon its Marginal Physical Product (MPP) and he will go on using the resource up to the point of its zero MPP (if it is available free of cost) or up to the point of Marginal Cost (MC) = Marginal Returns (MR) for that resource (if it is priced). Further, if the resources combination is technically efficient (on the isoquant), it may not be allocatively efficient (*i.e.*, the combination of resources at the point of LCC). So, the farmer has to take a fruitful decision considering the economic efficiency of resources usage in the production programme.
- ✰ ***Extent of use of fixed and variable resources:*** A farmer continues to employ the use of a variable resource in the production programme, till its MPP is equal to zero or as long as the Marginal Value Product of resource (MVP_X) is equal to Marginal Factor Cost (MFC_X). However, regarding the use of fixed resource or durable resource, which render service for a fairly longer period of time, its under-utilization leads to high fixed cost on a farm. A farmer, therefore, needs planning and ensuring full use of his fixed resources, so as to minimize the fixed cost per unit of output and realize higher profits.
- ✰ ***Selection of enterprises:*** In case, if the farmer prefers to go for individual crop enterprise, his decision depends upon the season and agro-ecological situation. If the farmer prefers to have enterprises combination, his selection depends upon the relationship between the enterprises such as competitive or supplementary or complementarity *etc.*

- ☆ ***Efficiency of resource usage:*** Resource use efficiency counts much towards maximization of profits in the production programme, when compared to the net income earned or declined costs in absolute terms. So, farmer's decision will revolve around the maximization of resources use efficiency.
- ☆ ***Adoption of technology:*** Technology contributes higher output for the same level of inputs or same level of output at lower levels of inputs applied in the production programme. Depending upon the circumstances prevailing, the farmer may go for labour saving technology or capital saving technology or both. In case, if the labour scarcity is severe in the village, the farmer goes for labour saving or capital intensive technology and if the labour supply is plenty, the farmer goes for capital saving or labour intensive technology in the production programme. That is, the choice of farm manager's decision depends upon the relative availability of these two (labour and capital) resources.
- ☆ ***Recovery of costs:*** The decision whether to continue the production programme or not depends upon, how far the gross returns cover the total costs or variable costs in the short run and long run production programmes. As discussed through Table 2.14, if the Total Returns (TR) cover only the Short Run Total Variable Cost (SRTVC) and not the Short Run Total Cost (SRTC), then the farmer can continue the production programme in the short run. If the TR could not cover the STRVC in the short run, the farmer will take the decision to stop the production programme temporarily with the expectation that the price of the produce will gradually rise and cover the Short Run Average Variable Cost (SRAVC). In case of long run production programme, if the gross returns cover the Long Run Total Costs (LRTC), then the farmer can continue the production programme. On the other hand, if the gross returns could not cover LRTC in the long run, the farmer will take the decision to stop the production programme permanently. So, analyzing cost structure of farm business is essential for planning farm managerial decisions.
- ☆ ***Risk and uncertainties in the farm business:*** Right from the initiation of a crop production programme to till the transaction of its produce in the market, the farmer has to face various types of risks and uncertainties. So, to combat these, the farmer will implement various managerial decisions such as selection of crop enterprises that are less prone to risk, crop diversification, crop insurance, futures trading *etc.*
- ☆ ***Types of farming:*** Considering the extent of income generation, the farmer also makes the decisions regarding the type of farming to be adopted on the farm. If the single enterprise alone contributes more than 50 per cent share in the annual income of the farmer, he prefers to go for specialized farming. If no single enterprise alone contributes more than 50 per cent share in the annual income of the farmer, he prefers to go for diversified farming. If the farmer wishes to utilize the by-products on the farm effectively, he prefers to go for mixed farming.

- ☆ ***Systems of farming:*** To enjoy the benefits of large scale marketable surplus of commodities, the farmers especially small and marginal farmers, prefer to involve in different systems of farming like cooperative farming, collective farming *etc.*
- ☆ ***Planning and budgeting:*** When the farmer wishes to bring desirable changes on the farm, he may go for simple farm planning and even complete farm planning. Accordingly, he takes up partial budgeting and complete budgeting respectively and based on the incremental income he derives, he will implement the decisions on the farm.
- ☆ ***Farm-Family needs:*** Farm-family satisfaction and managing the farm are inter-related. This is because:
  - ❑ Farm contributes several materials to the farm-family like food, fuel and even clothing in many parts of the world. If the farmer had to purchase these items, it would cost or burden him.
  - ❑ From the produce harvested, the farmer can retain a part for seed purpose in the ensuring season.
  - ❑ Farm also provides boarding and lodging for the farm-family members and even for hired labour.
  - ❑ Automobiles and other vehicles of the farm can be used by farm-family members.
  - ❑ Above all, a scientifically managed farm provides recreation, health, comforts and leisure to all the members of the farm-family.
- ☆ ***Government policies:*** Above all, the farm decisions to be taken by the farmer are influenced by the programmes and policies being implemented by the Government. The farmer takes the enterprises on the farm based on the input subsidies, MSPs, marketing infrastructure *etc.*, offered by the Government.

Considering all the above considerations between farm business and farm family living, it can be summed up to state that, 'farming is a mode of life as well as a business'. Note that, the farm family satisfaction on the farm does not mean mere consumption of food items produced, but the pleasure the farm family members derive by contributing their services on the farm.

V. Complexity of Farm Managerial Decisions

The decisions taken by the farm manager are not concrete and they are frequently changing keeping in view of the following complexities involved in the farm business:

- ☆ Fluctuating income of the farm manager
- ☆ Fluctuating credit worthiness and credit requirements
- ☆ Fluctuating prices of farm inputs and products
- ☆ Frequent changes in technology of production of farm enterprises
- ☆ Changing policies of the Government

- Risks and uncertainties involved in the farm business
- Non-availability of requisite inputs in sufficient quantity and quality

In view of the above complexities, the farm managers with good technical background and experience about the enterprises will respond correctly to the situations, while some managers with poor technical background and low experience will respond incorrectly to the complexities.

VI. Importance or Need of the Study of Farm Management

The importance of farm management can be easily understood by going through the objectives listed earlier. It covers a wide range of issues that are to be addressed by the farm manager in the farm business towards the attainment of two major goals *viz.*, minimization of costs and maximization of profits. Thus, in marching towards addressing these goals, he employs certain economic principles, which forms the basis for the science of farm management. Farm Management is considered both an art and a science because, it involves the skillful practice and use of scientific knowledge to solve various problems on the farm using the problem solving approach. The tools and techniques of basic economic theory like concept of LDR, Cost principle, Principle or Law of Equi-Marginal Returns (LEMR), time value of money *etc.*, are applied to the practical situation to analyze the profitability of the farm business. In fact, farm management is the only science, which deals with the profitability aspect of farm business and this differentiates from other agricultural sciences. This science deals with the application of business principles of farming from the point of view of an individual farm. Its field of study is limited to an individual farm as a unit in achieving two major goals *viz.*, cost minimization and profit maximization in the farm business. In dealing with the issues of profitability, farm manager has to take several fruitful decisions regarding the employment of factors of production in the farm business. In this context farm management is otherwise designated as Science of decision making. It is also called as Science of choice, as the farm manager will make the best choice in choosing the right combination of resources and in the production of right combination of enterprises. As a science of choice making, it deals with the efficient utilization of the available limited farm resources among competing ends. Thus, the farm management as an applied science tends to suggest solutions to the various issues that farmer dealt in managing his farm. It involves the application of business principles and practices to the farming with an objective of obtaining the maximum possible returns from the farm as a unit under a sound farming programme. It also deals with optimal decision making in the organization and operation of a farm business. This applied science encompasses the following topics:

- Appraising the level of resources with the farmer and resource relationships.
- Possible enterprise combinations on the farm
- Production function relationship dealing with resource use efficiency on the farm
- Analyzing the cost structure and profitability decisions on the farm
- Allocation of scarce resources across the enterprises on the farm

- ☆ Comparative advantage in taking up enterprises on the farm
- ☆ Profitability in taking up long term investments on the farm that have long gestation period
- ☆ Farm planning and budgeting
- ☆ Risks and uncertainties involved in taking up enterprises on the farm
- ☆ Managing farm business offers an unusual opportunity for combining farm business and farm family living.
- ☆ Managing farm business ensures better living on the part of the farmer.
- ☆ Farm business also promotes group life among the farmers and this is essential to human beings.

Note that, the above listed areas are so inter-linked such that, a systematic study of all of them will facilitate to understand thoroughly about the farm business. Further, the farm management investigations give thrust and direction to farm business improvement by providing useful information to planners, farmers and extension workers. The research studies conducted on various issues of farm management like land reclamation, irrigation and drainage, input-output relationship, optimal dosage of fertilizers on various crops *etc.*, serves as an aid to formulate various programmes and policies by the Government. Further, these research studies can be used to plan the growth of farm resources in the future, keeping the macroeconomic objectives of the nation in view. Hence, there lies the importance of farm management studies in promoting the nations' economy. The importance of farm management can also be viewed from its microeconomic scope *i.e.*, it considers 'farm' as a single unit. As a science of decision making, it address various production problems like what to produce, how to produce, how much to produce *etc.* It covers all aspects of farming, which have bearing on the economic efficiency of farm resources. Farm management also plays an important role in establishing a favourable economic relationship between the rural and urban population. When the farmers practice scientific management of enterprises on the farm, it contributes more income to them and thereby, their standard living will improve. It also contributes to the rise in standard of living of the non-farm population, as they enjoy consumption of good quality and standardized farm products. So, the quality farm production contributes to rise in standards of living of both farm and non-farm population. In the same way, if the farm production is adversely affected due to poor management and other reasons, the standards of living of both farm and non-farm populations gets affected. Further, the survival of agro-based industries also gets affected, as they exclusively depend upon the raw material supplied from the agricultural sector. This infers that, farm management practices influences the level of living of both rural and urban population. Rural prosperity is reflected in urban progress, whereas rural poverty and misery are the two sides of an inefficient farm management.

The importance of the farm management and how it differs from other fields of science can be examined from its following distinguishing characteristics:

- ☆ Farm management is basically a practical science in addressing various farm problems at micro level.

- Farm management as a science deals with economic efficiency of resources rather than just physical efficiency. This implies, farm management science is profit oriented.
- In analyzing the managerial aspects of the farm, it requires collabouration with other sciences. So, farm management is considered as an integrating science and hence, the scope of farm management is much broader than other sciences.
- Every farm is treated as an independent unit in terms of available resources and hence, it is microeconomic in its perspective.

VII. Characteristics of a Good Farm Manager

Considering the objectives and importance of farm management discipline, the farm manager must possess the following characteristics to execute the activities on the farm on scientific lines:

- He must have a prior goal or objective in performing the activities on the farm.
- He must possess a keen sense of observation.
- He must possess an enquiring mind.
- He must have the capacity to analyze the activities on the farm.
- He must be innovative in accepting and adopting modern technologies on the farm.
- He must be risk taking in the business.
- He must be a good leader and motivate other workers on the farm.
- He must be technically competent, *i.e.*, he must know what to do and how to do the activity.
- He must be time bound in accomplishing the tasks on the farm.
- He must be able to define the problem clearly without any ambiguity.
- He must be able to plan the corrective steps for the activities with the available resources.
- He must have an alternative plan to combat various risks and uncertainties that he faces in the farm business.

VIII. Farm Management in Relation to Other Sciences

As discussed earlier, farm management as an applied science deals with all the aspects (physical, chemical and biological aspects) of taking up enterprises on the farm and thus, it draws the basic information provided by other agricultural sciences (Figure 1.3). Compared to other fields of agricultural science, farm management study is more practical oriented. Besides dealing with all the aspects of agricultural science, farm management study put all these facts with reference to a farm and thereby, more interested in analyzing its profitability. The following are the relations between farm management and other agricultural sciences:

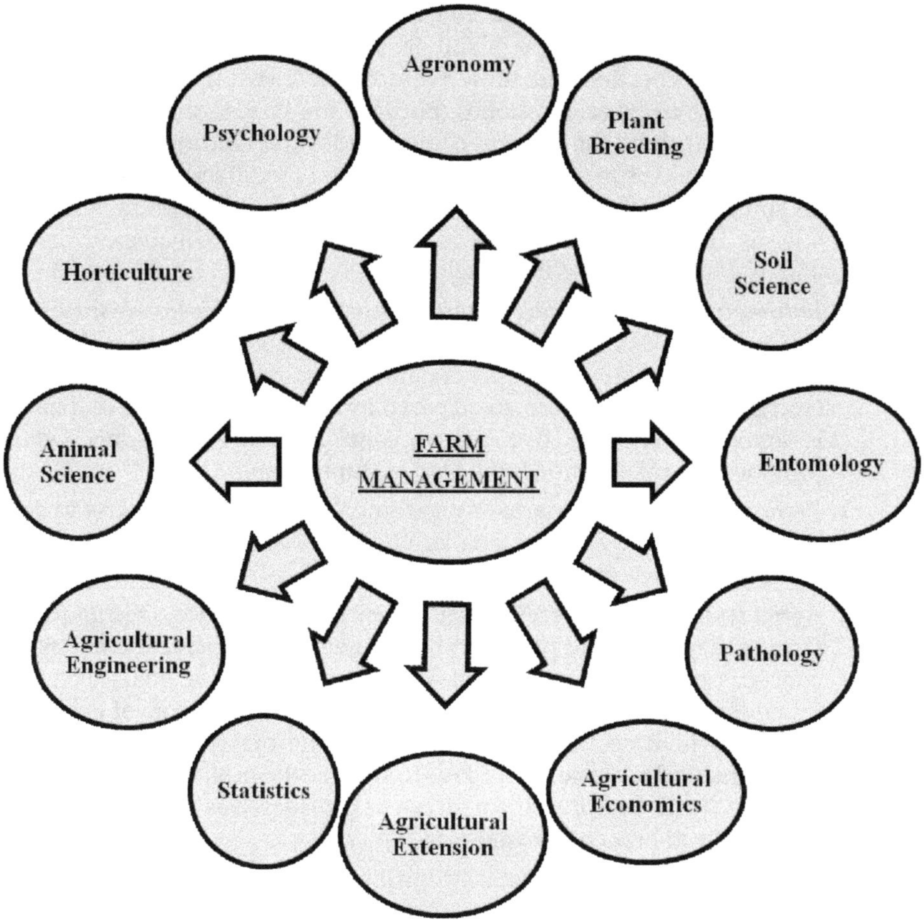

Figure 1.3: Farm Management in Relation with other Sciences.

- ☆ ***Agronomy:*** We know, in taking up crop enterprises on the farm, first the farmer should have thorough knowledge about the scientific package of practices of different enterprises, varieties of the crops suitable for the given agro-ecological situation, critical stages of crop growth, quality of seed to be used in the production programme, meteorological information of that area, irrigation and drainage facilities *etc*. Thus, the knowledge pertaining to these agronomical aspects is essential for the farmer to have scientific farm management.
- ☆ ***Plant breeding:*** The farmer should be aware of the traits of different plant varieties such as disease tolerance, high yielding ability, drought tolerance, salinity resistance *etc*., and this facilitate him to select the crop varieties in relevance to the agro-ecological situation. This knowledge also enables the farmer to obtain higher returns over the same level of inputs usage.

☆ ***Soil Science:*** Before sowing the crop(s), first the farmer should have thorough knowledge about the type of soil, its structure, texture and its physico-chemical properties and these features have strong influence on the selection of crops and varieties. Further, the farmer should have prior information about the nutrient content and water holding capacity of the soil. He should be aware of different dosages of fertilizers to be used based on soil testing. The science which provides this information is the Soil science. The knowledge of Soil science is also essential to manage irrigation and drainage problems in the fields.

☆ ***Entomology:*** In cultivating the crops, some produce losses are inevitable due to pests infestation. In this context, knowledge of the farmer about the type of pest, its life cycle, nature of damage, symptoms of damage, stage of crop growth for infestation, plant part damaged *etc.*, is essential so that, the losses can be minimized by practicing control measures. The science which provides this information is the field of entomology.

☆ ***Pathology:*** It guides the farmers regarding the causal organisms for various diseases (say, fungal or bacterial or viral diseases), symptoms, plant part infected and their management strategies.

☆ ***Agricultural Economics:*** As discussed earlier, the tools and techniques of farm management are provided by the general economic theory, as the concepts of farm management addresses two major goals *viz.,* cost minimization and profit maximization. The basic concepts of economic theory like LDR, cost analysis, LEMR, time value of money *etc.*, are applied to the practical farm situation, so as to analyze the profitability of the farm business. Thus, farm management can be considered as an applied science or specialized branch of economics.

☆ ***Agricultural Extension:*** In cultivating the crops, the farm manager aims at two major goals *viz.*, cost minimization and profit maximization. To achieve these two goals, farmer should have adequate technical knowledge regarding the use of inputs and technology in the production programme. In this context, Agricultural Extension as a subject provides the requisite technical information to the farmers, as the dissemination of modern technology to the farmer counts much in boosting the productivity of crops on the farm.

☆ ***Statistics:*** Statistics is another science that has been used extensively by the other disciplines like Agricultural Economics, Agronomist, Entomologist, Agricultural Engineering *etc.* This science is helpful in providing methods and procedures by which data regarding specific farm problems can be collected, analyzed and evaluated.

☆ ***Agricultural Engineering:*** To boost the agricultural production on cost-effective basis, farmers resort to mechanized farming compared to labour intensive farming. In such cases, the farmers should have adequate knowledge regarding different types of implements and machinery available, their uses, their cost structure, repairs and maintenance *etc.*, for their employment in the production programme. Further, the farmers should be well aware about irrigation and drainage water management, soil conservation, micro irrigation *etc.* The knowledge pertaining to these aspects and their applicability on the farm is supplied by Agricultural Engineering and hence, the farm manager should have thorough knowledge on these aspects for effective farm management.

- ☆ ***Animal Science:*** In the farm, farm manager exclusively takes up livestock enterprises like cattle, sheep, goat, poultry, sericulture, apiculture *etc.* Sometimes, he may go for mixed farming combing crops with a significant portion of livestock enterprise. Under Indian conditions, mixed farming is a rule and hence, the farmers will often take up a livestock enterprise that enjoys either supplementary or complementary relationship with the crop enterprise. In such cases, the knowledge of the farmer pertaining to the production of livestock enterprises is essential and hence, farm management as an applied science will enjoy the relationship with animal science.
- ☆ ***Horticulture:*** This science deals with the production of fruits and vegetables on the farm. In hilly areas, where farming of agricultural crops is not profitable, the farmers depends upon the cultivation of fruits and vegetable crops due to extreme climatic conditions. Even on the farms located near to the cities, the farmers cultivate fruits and vegetables and they enjoy more profits than the cultivation of agricultural crops. In such cases, the knowledge of the farmer pertaining to Horticulture science provides important information regarding the cultivation practices of horticultural crops.
- ☆ ***Psychology:*** This science provides information of human motivations and attitudes. We know, the attitude of the farmer towards risk taking depends on his psychological strength. So, the knowledge of psychology guides the farmer in facing various risks and uncertainties in the production programme.

Thus, physical and biological sciences like Agronomy, Animal husbandry, Soil Science, Horticulture, Plant Breeding, Agricultural Engineering *etc.*, provide information regarding what and how much can be produced by the farmer in his farm. Psychological science guides the farmer in making choices regarding the use of resources and selection of enterprise combinations. So, farm management as a science integrates and synthesizes diverse pieces of information from physical, biological and psychological sciences. Hence, the scope of farm management is much broader than the other branches of Agricultural Economics because, it uses information from all of them as well as from other disciplines. It requires information from Agricultural Marketing, Agricultural Production Economics, Financing, Sociology, Psychology, Mathematics and Government Policy for the purpose of taking decisions. Thus, farm management involves knowledge of both arts and sciences, unlike the other branches of Agricultural Economics. So, farm management could be called as a *'Jack of all trades'* discipline involving the knowledge of the arts and sciences and harmonizing them into a useful amalgam for the purpose of solving a specific problem. Note that, though farm management involves more of a practical study about the farm, it considers not only the profitability of farm business, but also the farm family satisfaction. Sometimes philosophy and religion forbid the farmers to grow certain enterprises, though they are highly profitable. For example, Islam prohibits Muslim farmers to take up piggery, while Hinduism prohibits Hindu farmers in taking up beef production.

IX. Farm Management Problems in India

Management of farms in India is difficult, as it involves various issues or problems to be addressed by the farm managers. The following are the important problems the farm managers generally encounter in managing the farms:

- ☆ Illiteracy on the part of the farmers, especially with regard to adoption of modern technologies on the farm.
- ☆ Majority of the farmers are small and marginal farmers because of sub-division and fragmentation of land holdings and hence, they enjoy only small scale marketable surplus. As a result, farming is mostly subsistence oriented rather than market oriented.
- ☆ The small sized land holdings will not permit the farmers to enjoy the economies of large scale farming and the adoption of mechanized farming. On account of their small size, they remain uneconomical for the adoption of modern technologies.
- ☆ Farmers play four roles simultaneously in conducting the farm business *viz.*, entrepreneur, farm manager, agricultural labour and financer. He takes decisions in two capacities as an entrepreneur and farm manager.
- ☆ Inadequacy of capital with the farmers and hence, there is slow adoption of modern technology on their farms.
- ☆ Production on the farms is largely dictated by the monsoon rains. Any vagaries of monsoon rains cause wide fluctuations in the output.
- ☆ Lack of adequate training to the farmers on the adoption of modern technologies in the farms. Though the Government offers modern technologies to the farmers at subsidized rates, the farmers could not use them efficiently on the farms due to lack of adequate training.
- ☆ Cost structure of inputs, prices of outputs, marketing facilities *etc.*, varies across the regions in the country and this leads to variations in agricultural income of the farmers across the regions.
- ☆ Location specific or farming situation based technologies are not available to the farmers. Though modern technologies are available to the farmer for each and every operation, they may not suitable to a farmer under a given farming situation.
- ☆ Farmers being largely illiterate are not maintaining farm records and accounts. This poses difficulty in establishing their credit worthiness before the banker in accessing institutional credit. So, they mainly depend on

non-institutional credit at higher rates of interest, which reduces the profitability of farm business.

- ☆ Unlike produce marketing, input marketing enjoys no strict regulation by the Government. This results in cheating on the part of the farmers regarding the quality supply of inputs like seeds, fertilizers, pesticides *etc.*, by the private traders.
- ☆ Farmers receive no training for improving their managerial skills in performing the farm business. They were not trained enough in facing various risks and uncertainties in the farm business. Whatever trainings they receive from the Government and other stakeholders, they are meant only for performing an operation on efficient scale.
- ☆ Facilities like transport, communication, storage *etc.*, are not developed on scientific lines in the villages and this poses greater difficulty in accessing and implementing the modern technologies on the farm.
- ☆ Due to weather aberrations, farming may not be continuous on the farm and hence, it leads to unemployment and under employment of labour in performing farm operations.
- ☆ For promoting export competitiveness, cost-effective production of commodities is gaining more and more significance in the era of globalization and trade liberalization. Hence, there is a shift from labour intensive production technologies to capital intensive production technologies on the farm.

X. History of Farm Management in India

At the time of Indian Independence, agriculture was the major venture and it was easy to become a farmer. But, the farmers used to follow primitive methods of cultivation thereby, productivity of crops was low. Farming was mostly subsistence oriented and most farmers are nearly totally self-sufficient. They produced most of the inputs they needed for production such as seeds, draft animals, feed and simple farm equipment. The small amount of output left over after consumption needs was sold for cash to the non-farm population. With gradual commercialization of agriculture, now the farmers found it increasingly profitable to concentrate on production and began to purchase inputs they formerly made themselves. This trend enabled others to build business that focused on meeting the need for inputs used in production agriculture such as seed, fertilizers, pesticides, machinery *etc.* These farms transformed into the industries that make up the 'agricultural inputs sector'. Input farms are major part of agri-business and produce variety of technologically based products that account for approximately 75 per cent of all the inputs used in production agriculture. At the same time when the agriculture input sector was evolving, a similar evolution was taking place in the form of commodity processing and food manufacturing. The form of most commodities (wheat, rice, milk, livestock etc) must be changed to make them more useful and convenient for consumers. These changes were hastened because of the advancement of production and processing technologies and in the present day, even most farm families use purchased food and fiber products rather than doing the processing themselves. It is apparent that, these drastic changes in the agricultural sector are due to the growth of 'farm management' as a specialized discipline that makes the farmers to manage their farm businesses on scientific note. From advocating the concepts of managerial practices to be practiced by the farmers in the farming, the role of farm management had increased up to the application of economic principles to the farming in the contexts of realizing cost minimization and profit maximization. This also infers that, farm management as a specialized discipline of agriculture is of recent origin. However, it is very difficult to say, when the fruits of farm management science have been first harvested, but it can be stated that, the present form of farm management has come to its own very recently. A brief history of farm management work in India is reviewed here under.

- ☆ First organized study in the field of farm cost accounting was initiated in 1923-24 by the Punjab Board of Economic Inquiry. The studies conducted by the Board provided useful information regarding the variations in cost structure, returns and resource use pattern in different crops. This study covered 29 villages with different socio-economic characteristics in different districts of the Punjab province. These surveys were aimed at collecting basic data on farming rather than at a *'scientific interpretation of the financial position of farming business as a whole in the area'* (ISAE, 1953, p. 31). The relevance of these studies lay in the fact that, till 1923, there was no organized effort of this kind to study the financial aspects of farming business in India. These surveys continued for a period of five years and the results were published by the Board of Economic Enquiry in Punjab in 1929. Information on various aspects of the farm economy was collected by the case-study method. From the information gathered, estimates of expenses for cultivation for various inputs and net profits were calculated. These village studies conducted by Punjab Board of Economic Enquiry moved a step forward in that they used an almost uniform methodology and classification of costs and returns to analyze the farm economy across villages.
- ☆ In eastern India, Jack (1927) studied Faridpur district of West Bengal province and gave estimates of net value per acre (by deducting the cost of cultivation from the gross value of produce) from the cultivation of rice, oil seeds, jute, betel and sugar cane, grasses, fruits and garden produce. Neither the total cost of cultivation nor the methodology used for calculating cost of cultivation to derive net value was specified in this study.
- ☆ An exhaustive study on farm management was made by Prof. P.C. Patil, Professor of Agricultural Economics, Poona, during 1928-30. The investigations were carried out in six districts of Bombay Presidency. Under the leadership of P. C. Patil, the Department initiated an attempt at exhaustive farm-cost studies in which opportunity costs were calculated using cost accounting principles (ISAE, 1953, p. 32). According to Shah (1971), Patil's study was a breakthrough in understanding the concept of gross income from farming. He included the part of the produce consumed

by the family in gross income. In previous studies, gross income had been taken to be equal to the quantity sold by the producer.

- ☆ The first *'All-India Study of Costs and Returns on Farmers Holdings'* was conducted by the Indian Council of Agricultural Research (ICAR) during 1933-36. This study was limited to the costs of production of sugarcane and cotton and some other important crops in the principally sugarcane growing tracts of India. The data and the findings were published under the title *'Report on the cost of the production crops in principal sugarcane and cotton tracts in India, 1939'.*
- ☆ In 1935-36, the Imperial Council of Agricultural Research, on request from the Indian Sugar Committee and Central Cotton Committee, conducted an inquiry into the costs of cultivation of cotton, sugarcane and other crops grown in rotation. The study was conducted in Lyllapur, Jullundur and Gurdaspur districts in Punjab using cost accounting methods (Singh, 1940, p. 103).
- ☆ During the same period, in 1936, the Gokhale Institute of Politics and Economics worked in selected villages of Wai taluk in Satara district on an application of survey methods to farm business studies in India. The study was aimed at evolving a methodology to study the economic aspects of cultivation of crops and farm economy in line with methods and techniques adopted in western countries (Gadgil and Gadgil, 1940a). Out of the 39 villages in the *taluk*, 23 villages were selected for detailed study, a range considered representative of the diversity of the region and crops grown. From the selected villages, cultivators with farms of various sizes (in terms of area operated) were selected. In order to evaluate the performance of farms in the study area, scholars estimated 'farm income' per farm by subtracting all farm expenses from farm receipts. Farm income was defined in the study as 'the difference between receipts and expenses, that is, what the operator received for his own and his family's labour for the year and for the use of the capital invested by him" (Gadgil and Gadgil, 1940b). Farm expenses and farm receipts were calculated by attributing money values to all expenses whether paid in cash or kind, retained or sold, or used for own consumption or farm production (Gadgil and Gadgil 1940b; Thorner, 1980). The main achievement of this study was that it provided estimates of labour utilised, total expenditure, gross value of output, and net profits for farms of different sizes and of different tenurial arrangements.
- ☆ In the South, in 1937, Thomas and Ramakrishnan resurveyed the villages studied by Slater in Madras Province and the State of Cochin (Thomas and Ramakrishnan, 1940). The resurveys of the "Slater villages" provided detailed estimates of the farm accounts of cultivators operating different size of farms in terms of operational holdings and of the costs of cultivation and net returns from different crops in the villages studied.
- ☆ In 1939, Huque (1939) gave estimates of cost of cultivation for crops in different districts in Bengal province.

- Sayana (1949), while dealing with problems of the then Madras Province, gave estimates of various items of costs incurred in cultivation and net incomes from wet paddy in Bhimavaram taluk in West Godavari district and tobacco in Guntur taluk. While discussing the limitations in estimating the production costs and returns, he wrote that, '*the accuracy of the estimates of production costs may be vitiated for various reasons. In the first place, the agriculturists, illiterate as they are, do not keep accounts and even the few who do, do not keep detailed costs for all items. Contribution of one's own labour and the help rendered by and to neighbours are seldom recorded...Even where some kinds of accounts are kept, no account is kept between the family and the field. The farm is not debited with the value of the family labour, not is it credited with the value of farm products consumed by the family*' (Sayana, 1949, p. 218).
- The Research Programme Committee, Planning Commission, Government of India, initiated studies in the economics of farm management in six regions for the country, namely Punjab, Uttar Pradesh, Madhya Pradesh, Madras, Bombay and West Bengal during 1954-55 to 1956-57 *i.e.*, for a period of three years. The studies were extended to Andhra Pradesh, Bihar and Odisha in 1957-58. The reports on these studies gave a deep insight into the agricultural economy of the country.
- The Agro-Economic Research Centres established in 1954-55 for different regions are working on various aspects of rural economy as well as on price movements and fair price shops. The reports provided good material for policy decisions.
- In 1966-67, Punjab Agricultural University, Ludhiana initiated a programme of farm management extension education with the Extension Specialists located in all the districts of the State. This scheme was considered remarkable in rendering extension education to the farmers on the managerial aspects of the farm.
- The Comprehensive Scheme for studying the Cost of Cultivation of Principal Crops in India is being implemented since 1970-71 as a 100 percent Central Sector Plan Scheme on the basis of recommendations made by the Standing Technical Committee on Indices of Input Costs constituted in 1967 under the Chairmanship of Dr. Ashok Mitra. The main objectives of the scheme are as follows:
  - Collection and compilation of field data on cost of cultivation and cost of production in respect of 29 crops.
  - Estimation of crop-wise and state-wise costs of cultivation and production, and
  - Computation of the indices of terms of trade between agriculture and non-agriculture sectors.

  The estimates of cost of Cultivation are used by Commission for Agricultural Costs and Prices (CACP) for recommending MSPs of 25 crops. Directorate of Economics and Statistics (DES) in the Ministry of Agriculture gets this study conducted through 16 Agricultural/General Universities/Colleges besides the Directorate of Tobacco Development. Under this scheme, the field data pertaining to the cost of cultivation/cost of production are collected, compiled and tabulated by different Implementing Agencies. The data are checked, corrected, validated and analysed to generate crop-wise and state-wise cost estimates by DES before these are passed on to the CACP to be used as data base for recommending the MSPs of various agricultural commodities to the Government of India. The cost estimates generated under the scheme are also used for policy formulation by the Central Government and State Governments, and others including Agricultural/General Universities, Government/Non-Government Research Organizations, and individual researchers. In addition, the data are also used for working out the Index Numbers of Terms of Trade between Agriculture and Non-agricultural Sectors. The scheme is being implemented in 16 states, namely, Andhra Pradesh, Assam, Bihar, Gujarat, Haryana, Himachal Pradesh, Karnataka, Kerala, Madhya Pradesh, Maharashtra, Odisha, Punjab, Rajasthan, Tamil Nadu, Uttar Pradesh and West Bengal. The scheme covers 29 crops,namely, paddy, wheat, jowar, bajra, maize, ragi, barley, moong, urd, arhar, gram, masur, groundnut, rapeseed/ mustard, nigerseed, soyabean, sunflower, sesamum, cotton, jute, sugarcane, VFC tobacco, onion, potato, ginger, tapioca, areacanut, coconut and black pepper.

☆ Since it began, the *Comprehensive Scheme for Study of Cost of Cultivation of Principal Crops* (CCPC) was reviewed twice by committees of experts. The first review was done by the Special Expert Committee on Cost of Production Estimates (referred as the First Review Committee) in 1979-80. The major recommendation of the committee that was accepted and implemented from 1981-82 onwards was to shift from a single crop approach to a crop-complex approach, that is, an approach in which all the crops in the selected sample holdings would be studied instead of the principal crop alone. In 1990, the Government of India constituted the Second Review Committee under the Chairmanship of C. H. Hanumantharao (GOI, 1990). The major recommendations of the Committee were:

- ❑ that the crop complex approach be supplemented with a single-crop approach to ensure that aspects of cultivation of minor crops are also studied;
- ❑ that family labour be valued on the basis of actual wages paid to casual labourers rather than on the basis of the wage rates of attached farm servants; and
- ❑ that management costs be calculated by taking 10 per cent of the paid out cost (Cost A2).

The Government of India accepted these recommendations with some modifications. Sen and Bhatia (2004) have shown that many of the methodological shortcomings of the CCPC scheme are because other recommendations of the two Review Committees remained unimplemented.

- ✰ Presently, various SAUs and Social Science Research Institutions are also engaged on research in farm management problems and farm cost studies in different locations. In all SAUs, 'Farm management' is taught as a specialized course for B.Sc (Ag) students. At M.Sc (Ag) and Ph.D levels in the department of Agricultural Economics, farm management studies on different issues are assigned to the students for conducting research studies.
- ✰ The State Department of Agriculture in collabouration with the scientific personnel of SAUs and ICAR institutes are organizing training programmes to the farmers on various aspects of farm management, especially in boosting the crop productivity with due emphasis on cost-effectiveness in the context of globalization and trade liberalization.

Considering the above pattern of developments over a period of time, farm management as a specialized (applied) science in agriculture has gained momentum after fifties and this infers that, this science is fast developing in India. Regarding the future development of farm management as a specialized discipline, it calls for identification and analysis of farm production problems farming situation-wise and thereby, giving situation specific recommendations to the farmers and to the Government to overcome the same. That is, the farm management studies must be microeconomic in their scope with well framed specific objectives. For example, studies on the economics of paddy production, maize production *etc.*, do not clearly indicate, how they will be used to correct the situation at the farmer's level. So, it is important to pinpoint the problem and make it more specific to provide the answer that was sought in the study. Further, since the number of marginal and small holdings is increasing largely as a result of the sub-division of holdings due to the growth of population, it calls for conducting more studies that are relevant to the problems of these holdings. Thus, the focus of farm management studies must be shifted towards addressing the problems of small and marginal farmers. Further, noticing the importance of globalization and trade liberalization, the farm management studies should keep in mind the crops that enjoy comparative advantage in the international market. Above all, farm management studies should focus on bringing integrated area development in the context of programmes and policies framed by the Government.

XI. Farm Management vis-à-vis Agricultural Production Economics

As discussed earlier, farm management is a specialized branch of Agricultural Production Economics, as the tools and techniques studied under Agricultural Production Economics are applied to a single farm unit in addressing the farm managerial concepts. The following are the important differences between Agricultural Production Economics and Farm management (Table 1.2):

Table 1.2: Comparative Picture between Agricultural Production Economics and Farm Management

Agricultural Production Economics	*Farm Management*
Agricultural Production Economics deals with the principles of choice that are applied to the use of land, labour, capital and management in the farming industry.	Farm management deals with organization and operation of farm business with a view to get continuous profits.
Mainly deals with allocative efficiency of resources.	Mainly deals with economic efficiency of the resources.
Macro in its scope *i.e.*, it studies the decision making behaviour of farmers in the aggregate business activities	Micro economic in its scope *i.e.*, its study is restricted individual farm business unit.
It is an inter-farm study	It is intra-farm study.
Agricultural Production Economics is a specialized branch of Agricultural Economics.	Farm management is an integral part of Agricultural Production Economics because, the principles of latter are applied to the farm business. So, tools and techniques for farm management analysis are supplied from general economic theory.
The main objectives in Agricultural Production Economics include cost minimization, profit maximization and optimization of output through enhancing resource use efficiency.	All are objectives of Agricultural Production Economics are equally applicable to farm management science, but due emphasis is given regarding farm family satisfaction in taking up crops and allied enterprises.

XII. Basic Terms and Concepts in Farm Managerial Economics

i. Farm

The best definition that can be given for a 'farm' involves the following three propositions:

- ☆ First, it must be a producing unit. That is, the activities performed on the farm must result in the production of output.
- ☆ Second, it is a 'business' unit. That is, business (economic) principles are applied on it, so as to enjoy economic benefits by the farmer.
- ☆ Third, it is a 'legal' unit. That is, farming can be carried as a peasant farming, cooperative farming, partnership mode *etc.* The piece of land can be subdivided among the farm family members *i.e.*, father to sons and daughters.

Another popular definition of farm is *'any tract or tracts of land operated under one management upon which agricultural operations are conducted'*. Depending upon the activity taken up on the farm, there are different types of farms as given here under.

- ☆ ***Crop–Specialty farms:*** These farms practice crop production programme either on specialization or diversification mode.
- ☆ ***Animal specialty farms:*** There farms mainly emphasize the output production from livestock enterprises.

- ☆ ***Ranch farm:*** These farms are meant for cultivating pastures on which livestock grazes and multiplies.
- ☆ ***Self Sufficing Farms or Subsisted Farms or Family Living Farms:*** These farms are meant for producing output that was consumed by the farm family and not for the sake of market. Family living and working are more closely associated with these farms.
- ☆ ***Family farms:*** These farms are similar to family living farms in the sense that, farm organization is mainly determined by the farmer and family members and do not employ any hired labour for executing the farm operations.
- ☆ ***Family- size farms:*** These farms are also similar to family living farms, but unlike family farms, these family size farms engage hired (extra) labour for the short peak load periods, but regular work is done by the farm family force.

ii. Cropping System

Cropping system is an important component of farming system. It represents cropping pattern used on a farm and their interaction with resources, other farm enterprises and available technology, which determine their makeup.

iii. Cropping Pattern

Cropping pattern means the proportion of area under various crops at a point of time in a unit area. It indicates the yearly sequences and spatial arrangement of crops and fallow in an area.

Table 1.3: Cropping Pattern in India (Area in million hectares)

Year	*1990-91*	*2003-04*	*2009-10 (p)*
Total area under crops	185.74	189.67	192.2
Net area sown	143.00	140.71	140.02
Cropping intensity (per cent)	129.89	134.8	137.26
Area under food crops	141.03	142.12	141.06
Area under non-food crops	44.71	47.55	51.14
Net irrigated area	48.02	57.05	63.23
Total/Gross irrigated area	63.20	78.07	86.42

Source: Agriculture Census (2010-11).

iv. Crop Rotation

Crop sequence and crop rotation are generally used synonymously. Crop rotation is the practice of growing a series of dissimilar types of crops in the same area in sequential seasons for various benefits such as to avoid the buildup of pathogens and pests that often occurs when one species is continuously cropped. It also seeks to balance the fertility demands of various crops to avoid excessive depletion of soil

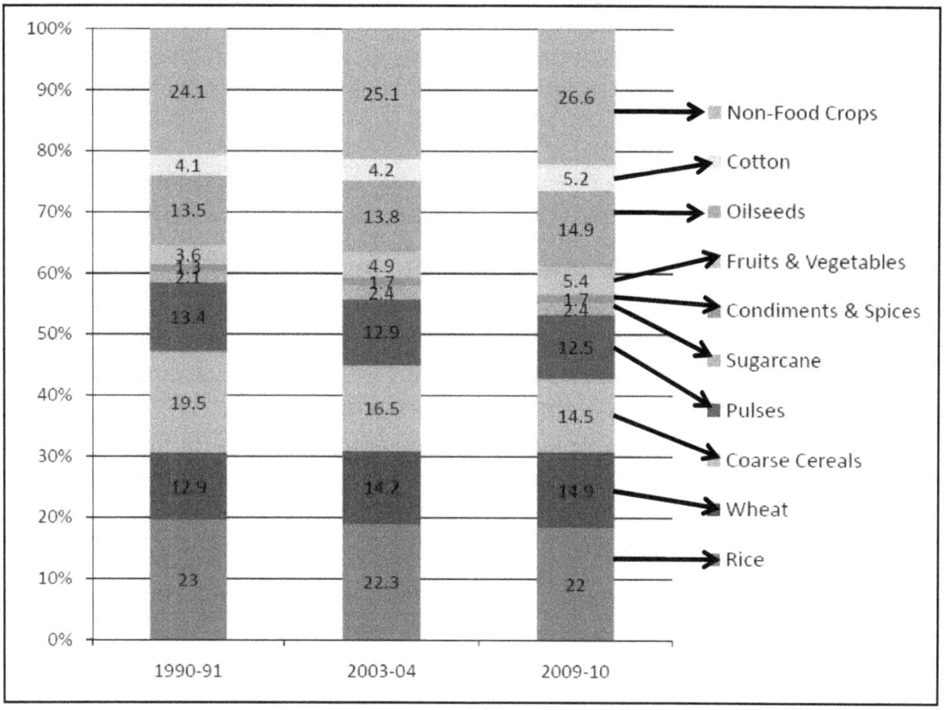

Figure 1.4: Crop-wise Share (per cent) in Area.
Source: Agriculture Census (2010-11).

nutrients. A traditional element of crop rotation is the replenishment of nitrogen through the use of green manure in sequence with cereals and other crops. Crop rotation is a type of cultural control that is also used to control pests and diseases that can become established in the soil over time. The changing of crops in a sequence tends to decrease the population level of pests.

v. Cropping Scheme

Cropping scheme is the plan according to which crops are grown on individual plots of a farm with an object of getting maximum returns from each crop without impairing the soil fertility. Cropping scheme provides an idea beforehand about the following:

- ☆ What crop is to be cultivated in a farm?
- ☆ What amount of area is allotted for a particular crop?
- ☆ The relative claim for acreage of the competitive crop.
- ☆ Selection of crops as per the facilities available for power, irrigation, inputs, labour transport *etc.*
- ☆ Utilization of inputs and other resources available on the farm without wastage.
- ☆ Preparation of budget for each crop.

vi. Mixed Cropping

Growing of two or more crops simultaneously and intermingled without row arrangements, where there is significant amount of intercrop competition.

vii. Intercropping

Growing of two or more crops simultaneously in alternate rows or otherwise in the same area, where there is significant amount of inter-crop competition.

viii. Farm Entrepreneur and Farm Business manager

- *Farm Entrepreneur:* Farm entrepreneur is the person, who runs, organizes and supervises the business effectively. He will take more risk in the production programme and he is solely responsible regarding outcome of the business *i.e.*, either profit/losses he will bear.
- *Farm business manager:* He is the person employed by the farm entrepreneur to run and supervise his business. Farm business manager will be responsible for running the business efficiently. He will get a fixed salary from the entrepreneur, but he will not bear any risk regarding the outcome of business.

ix. Efficiency

It refers to the best use of resources employed in the production programme such that, output derived per unit of resource employed will be the maximum or highest. So, there is no wastage of the use of resources in the production programme.

- *Economic efficiency of resource usage:* It refers to increasing output without using more conventional inputs. That is, economic efficiency refers to the use of resources, so as to maximize the production or output. A production technology is said to be more economically efficient than another (in relative terms), if it can produce more output without using more or extra resources or with existing resources only. In absolute terms, a production programme can be called economically efficient if:
  - No additional output can be obtained without increasing the amount of inputs.
  - Production proceeds at the lowest possible per-unit cost.

  Thus, the central idea of economic efficiency is that, in a production programme, nothing more can be achieved given the resources available. Economic efficiency can be classified in two: Technical efficiency and Allocative efficiency.
  - *Technical efficiency:* Also called Physical or Operational or Organizational efficiency. Measuring technical efficiency is to use inputs and output quantity without introducing their prices. The concept of Average Physical Product (APP) indicates the technical efficiency of a variable resource usage in the production programme. This implies that, technical efficiency refers to realizing the maximum output (in physical terms) with given resources and obtainable technology. That

is, this efficiency refers to the extent to which inputs usage can be reduced, while output levels are either maintained or even increased. So, technical efficiency can be attained in the following three possible ways:

- Producing same output at minimum possible inputs usage.
- Producing more output at the same level of resource usage.
- Both quantity of output produced and resource level are on the rise, but the increase in quantity of output produced is more compared to the rise in resource level.

Considering the above aspects, a farmer is not technically efficient, if he does not follow the best practices which are available. Thus, the emphasis of technical efficiency is on using the level of resources by keeping the resources level to the least possible. The lower the resource usage, the higher is the technical efficiency. So, efficiency is said to have increased, when resource level is reduced for performing an operation in the farm. This can be brought out by reducing physical losses or through change in technology in the production programme. A change in the technique of production may also result in the reduction of resource usage and thereby, reduces wastage of resources on the farm. Examples of technical efficiency gains would be the introduction of a less expensive weeding method, fertilizer application, irrigation *etc.*

- ***Allocative (Pricing) efficiency:*** This efficiency tries to capture farmer's ability to apply the inputs in optimal proportions with respective prices (Farrell 1957; Coelli *et al.* 2005). Inefficiencies arise, when factor market contain monopoly elements, collusion among input supply firms *etc.* The concepts of technical efficiency, allocative efficiency and economic efficiency can be well-explained through the Figure 1.5.

Assume that, a farmer employs two resources X_1 and X_2 to produce an output Y on an isoquant, I_1I_1 under the assumption of constant RTS. This isoquant of a firm will allow the measurement of technical efficiency. If the farmer uses quantities of inputs at the point *'A'* to produce a unit of output, the technical inefficiency of that firm could represent as the distance *'AB'*. It is the amount by which both the inputs need could be proportionally reduced without a reduction in output. This is usually expressed in percentage terms by the ratio *BA/OA*, which represents the percentage by which the inputs usage that can be reduced to achieve technically efficient output on isoquant at point 'B'. So, the Technical Efficiency (TE) of a firm is measured by the ratio: TE= *OB/OA*. The value of TE ranges between 0 and 1, and represents the degree of technical efficiency. Technical efficiency of resource usage is equal to 1 at point *B* because, it lies on the isoquant curve.

Assume IC is the iso-cost line. From this, we can derive the inputs price ratio. This guides to compute the Allocative Efficiency (AE) at point A

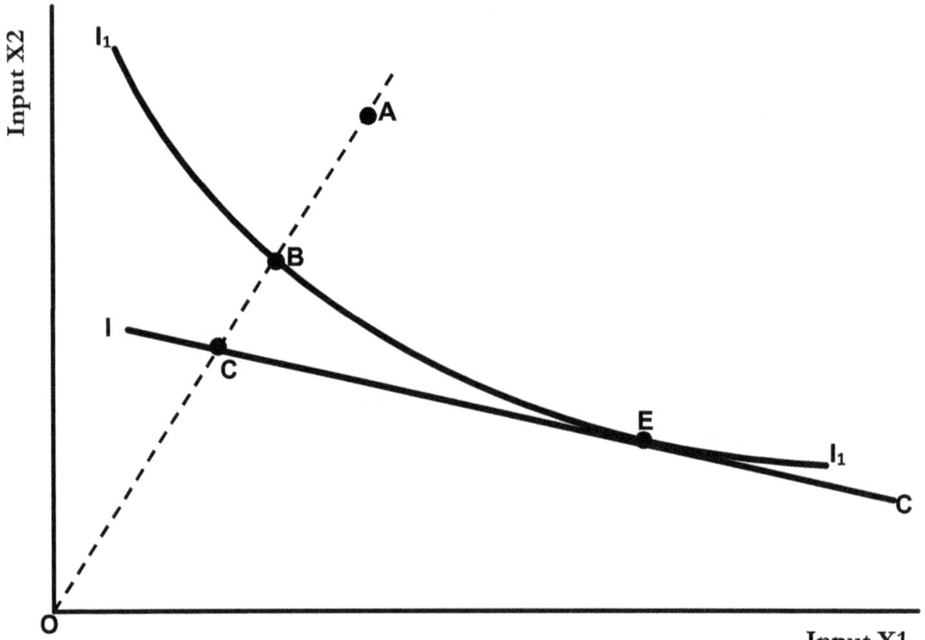

Figure 1.5: Technical, Allocative and Economic Efficiencies of Resources Usage.

and it is given by the ratio: AE= *OC/OB*. The decrease in production costs with the distance from *B* to *C* would happen, if production is performed at both the allocatively and technically efficient point *E* (point of LCC) instead of at the only technically efficient, but not allocative efficient point *B*.

The total economic efficiency (EE) is defined to be the ratio: EE= *OC/OA*. The distance from *A* to *C* also represents the cost cut in production, if a firm produces at the point C with both technical efficiency and allocative efficiency, instead of at the point *A* with both technical inefficiency and allocative inefficiency. Thus, economic efficiency is the product of both technical efficiency and allocative efficiency. So, economic efficiency includes technical efficiency (along with allocative efficiency) and expresses it in monetary terms. So, Y/X *i.e.*, APP indicates technical efficiency, and $Y.P_Y/X.P_X$ indicates economic efficiency. So, the economically efficient method of production is that method that produces a given level of output at the lowest possible cost. It is the least-cost technically efficient process.

The above two types of efficiencies *i.e.*, technical and allocative efficiencies are mutually reinforcing in the long run, and one without the other is not enough. Frequently, there are conflicts between these two varieties of efficiency. Among these two, allocative efficiency is more desirable because, it considers the value of resources and not just their quantity.

- ☆ ***Cost of cultivation and Cost of production:*** We know, for the use of resources and resource services in the production programme, the farmer incurs costs. The two terms 'Cost of cultivation' and 'Cost of production' are used synonymously in the cost theory, but there exist nice distinction between these two.

  - ❑ ***Cost of cultivation:*** It refers to the expenditure incurred by the farmer on all the resources and resource services in a production programme for a crop on area basis. For example, cost of cultivation of paddy is Rs.35,000/ha. Cost of cultivation per hectare can be calculated by using the formula: Total cost of cultivation for the crop/Land area in hectares

  - ❑ ***Cost of production:*** It refers to the expenditure incurred by the farmer on all the resources and resource services in a production programme for a crop on per unit output basis. For example, the cost of production of paddy is Rs. 1200/quintal. Cost of production of a commodity (Rs./quintal) can be calculated by using the formula:

    (Total cost – Value of by product)/Quantity of main produce in quintals.

    Since, cost of production involves expressions of cost in terms of output, it normally associated with both fixed and variable resources. However, cost of cultivation expresses cost in terms of per unit land area and land itself is a variable resource. Unlike cost of production, cost of cultivation is not useful for making production decisions. Cost of production of commodities guides the Government in deciding MSPs and cost of cultivation guides in deciding scale of finance for agricultural crops. In general, cost of cultivation includes factor costs up to the stage of gathering the harvest and that cost of production to include factor costs up to the stage of marketing the produce. The revenue earned by the farmer must cover the cost of cultivation, so as to continue the farm business. Similarly, in terms of cost of production, the price the farmer realizes for the output produced must cover the cost of production. Of course, these aspects are discussed in-detail in the Chapter 5.

2

Economic Principles of Farm Management

We know, economics is the study of the allocation of scarce resources among unlimited wants and needs. It is concerned with how best and what efficient way to allocate limited resources to various alternative uses. As discussed in the earlier Chapter 1, the farm is a production sub-system in an economy, and normally identified as a business venture, The farmer employs various resources in the production programme and the important farm managerial decision is to boost the economic efficiency of resources. The ability of a farmer to organize, allocate and achieve economic efficiency of resources mainly depends upon their managerial capacity. So, management is concerned with decision making. Like in any business venture, the farmer is the manager of a farm business and he decides how best to use his limited resources. The basic principles that guide the farm managerial decisions are provided by the general economic theory. Applying these basic production economic principles in the art of managing a farm business is known as Farm management. The managerial decisions taken by the farmer through employing the basic economic principles on the farm enable the farmer to organize resources and manipulate them to his advantage, so as to control and determine the relationship between input and output when the exact conditions of the farm production environment is not fully known. The exact and full knowledge about a farm situation is not always possible. However, the farmer must make decisions, even if it may turn out to be wrong. The art of management involve, minimizing (or reducing) the possibility of getting the wrong results by using past information, experiences, getting advises from experts or extension advisors *etc.* A good manager is flexible and responsive to changes in order to avoid getting wrong results. In general, farm managerial decisions are mainly meant towards achieving profit maximization in the business. But, the achievement of this objective is constrained by various factors and hence, the application of basic economic principles of production counts much for providing increased level of food and fibre from the farm. Besides profit-maximization objective, it is equally important on the part of the farmer to select the enterprises on the farm with a view to meet consumption habit of the family. So, at times, the farmer has to include some enterprises on the farm that are less profitable from the economics point of view. So, in a farm business, non-monetary factor(s) may over-ride the profit maximization assumption. Above these factors that guide the farm business, it is essential to note that, farm managerial decisions are dynamic and they keep on changing depending upon the resources availability with the farmer, risks and uncertainities in the business environment, fluctuations in prices of both inputs and output, production for the current period and also for the future, short term and long term investments, resources combination to be employed, products combination to be produced, opportunity cost of selecting a particular enterprise on the farm, level of resource usage on a particular enterprise *etc.* To meet these influences on the farm, farmers employ various economic decisions that are guided by the following seven basic principles:

1. Law of Diminishing Returns (LDR) or Law of Variable Proportions (LVP)
2. Cost Principle or Minimum Loss Principle
3. Principle of Factor Substitution
4. Principle of Product Substitution
5. Principle of Comparative Advantage
6. Law of Equi-marginal Returns
7. Time Comparison Principle

Note that, the above general economic principles can be applied to any enterprise on the farm and there are no separate principles for each part of the business rather, each principle applies to all parts. The application of these principles enhances the farmer's judgement in taking fruitful decisions on the farm and thus considered as *sine qua non* for successful farm management. Let us now discuss in-detail about the applicability of these seven economic principles towards the management of the farm.

1. Law of Diminishing Returns (LDR)/Law of Variable Proportions (LVP)

This law implies Short run production function or Proportionality relationship. Here, 'short run' refers to short-period of time. This is the period of time for which two conditions hold good *viz.*, there is at least one fixed input in the production programme and firms can neither enter nor exit the industry. So, in the short run, the farmer cannot vary all the factors. Some of the factors are fixed and some are variable. So, in order to vary the output level, the farmer has to vary only the variable factors, but the size or scale of the firm remains fixed. The factors that remains fixed are called the

Fixed factors, whereas the other factors, which the farmer can vary are called the Variable factors. For example, in a short run production programme, the farmer cannot vary factors like land, machinery *etc.*, and hence, they are fixed factors and other factors like seed, fertilizer, pesticides *etc.*, are variable factors. Fixed factors are not related with the level of output. That means, irrespective of the level of output, the level of fixed factors remains same. So, when the output is increased or decreased or even zero, the level of fixed factors remains same. Conversely, with reference to variable factors, their level of usage is directly related to the output level produced in the production programme. That means, if the output level increases, the level of variable factors also increases and *vice versa*. So, when there is no production programme (*i.e.*, zero output), the level of variable factors is also zero. However, the distinction between fixed factors and variable factors arises only in the short run, as in the long run all the factors/resources are variable. Thus, 'short run' is a short period of time, in which there is no possibility for the farmer/firm to vary the plant size. In LDR, we will study the influence of variability of one factor on the output of the production programme, keeping the other (fixed) factors constant and it is shown mathematically as,

$$Y=f(X_1,/X_2,X_3,X_4,X_5,X_6................X_n)$$

where, Y=Output from the enterprise, X_1 is the variable factor, X_2,X_3,X_4,X_5,X_6 ....X_n are fixed factors,/denotes the separation of variable factors from fixed factors. Thus, short run is the period in which the farmer cannot vary the fixed inputs. Nevertheless, the short run is long enough to allow variation of the variable inputs. The concept of short run production function can be explained through LDR.

To understand different parameters like TPP, MPP, APP, isoquants, MRTS, isoclines and ridge lines of the short run (cubic) production function, it is essential to gain enough background about these basic concepts and they are discussed here under.

i. TPP

It is, otherwise, called as Total product. It is the output realized by the farm-firm expressed in physical terms. It is the sum total of MPPs. For example, 40 quintals of output of paddy produced by the farmer infers TPP. Note that, the production function itself is sometimes referred to as TPP function. This TPP is indicated by 'Y'.

ii. APP

It is the ratio between total output (TPP) and a variable input employed in the production programme. So, APP=Y/X and it indicates the technical efficiency of a variable resource. So, APP is the total output resulting on the average from each unit of the variable input, *i.e.*, the TPP divided by the amount of variable input. For any level of input use (X), APP represents the average amount of output per unit of X being used. If you imagine to increase input use one unit at the time, then the APP is the average output from each unit of variable input. APP for a selected point on the TPP can be calculated by drawing a line (ray) from the origin to the selected point on the TPP curve. The slope of the line gives APP *i.e.*, Y/X. The same is discussed through Figure 2.1. APP also enjoys relation with MPP and it is popularly called as Marginal-Average relation and the same is discussed in the ensuing pages.

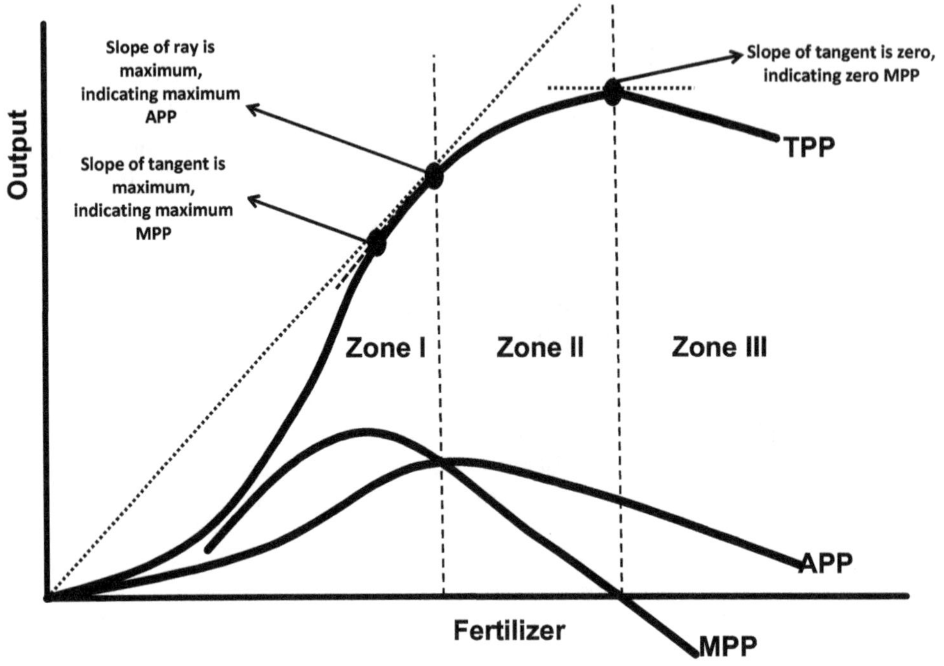

Figure 2.1: Measuring APP and MPP from TPP in a Single Input Production Function.

iii. MPP

The term 'marginal' is frequently used in economics. It has the same meaning as 'added'. It is the additional output produced in a production programme due to additional or incremental usage of one unit of input. It is, otherwise, expressed as the change in total output due to one more or one less unit of a variable input. Note that, if you imagine to increase the variable input use one unit at the time, then the MPP is the output (TPP) derived from the last unit of variable input. The rate of change of APP as output changes is indicated by MPP. It is given by, MPP=$\Delta Y/\Delta X$ or MPP = $TPP_n - TPP_{n-1}$. The MPP of input Xi might be referred to as MPP_{Xi}. This MPP_{Xi} represents the rate of change or slope of the given production function and is obtained by drawing a tangent on the TPP curve and measuring its slope (Figure 2.1). For a discrete change, $MPP_{Xi} = \Delta Y/\Delta Xi$. For an infinitesimal change, $MPP_{Xi} = \Delta Y/\Delta Xi$ (= the slope of the TPP curve at the relevant point). Notice that, MPP representing the incremental change in TPP, can be either positive or negative. This MPP is analogous to concept of marginal utility in consumer theory except that, MPP is a cardinal number measured on the ratio scale and is not an ordinal number.

Suppose, the given single input production function is Y = f(X). One way of expressing MPP is by the expression $\Delta Y/\Delta X$, where Δ denotes change. This expression of MPP as $\Delta Y/\Delta X$ can be read as 'change in output realized due to change in the variable input X'. For the above production, APP is given by: 'Y/X' or 'f(X)/X' and this can be read as 'average output produced for given level of variable input'. Assume the given production function as: Y = 5X. From this equation, MPP is given as 5 units. This is because, if X = 1, then Y = 5; and if X = 2, Y = 10. So, the change in output realized due to change in one unit of the variable input X (*i.e.*, MPP) is equal to 5 units. That is, each additional or incremental unit of X (ΔX) produces 5 additional or incremental units of Y (ΔY). So, for each additional unit of X employed in the production programme, TPP increases by 5 units. In this example APP equals to Y/X *i.e.*, 5X/X = 5. So, for this single input production function (without intercept), MPP = APP = 5 units for all positive values for X. MPP and APP are calculated for the tabular data presented in Table 2.1 based on the above definitions.

Table 2.1: APP and MPP of a Variable Factor

Variable Input Fertilizer, X (Units)	*TPP (Output, Y) (Units)*	*APP (Y/X)*	*ΔX*	*ΔY*	*MPP (ΔY/ΔX)*
5	2	0.40	–	–	–
10	5	0.50	5	3	0.60
15	9	0.60	5	4	0.80
20	14	0.70	5	5	1.00
25	20	0.80	5	6	1.20

However, the procedure described above calculating both MPP and APP is tedious and time consuming. So, let us look at a quicker and more accurate means for calculating MPP and APP, if the production function is given. As discussed earlier, the MPP (ΔY/ΔX) represents the rate of change or slope of the production function. It is to be noted that, the production function itself is referred to as TPP and MPP function refers to the rate of change in the TPP function. So, if the slope of the TPP function is computed, it implies MPP function *i.e.*, representing the rate of change in the TPP. Assume the above production Y = 5X. Given this TPP function (or production function), the MPP function is given by: ΔY/ΔX = 5. So, the incremental increase in output Y associated with for every one unit increase in the use of X is 5 units. In this case, the MPP function is represented by (ΔY/ΔX) and is equal to the constant 5, as it does not depend upon the value of X. Another way of finding the MPP of the input is done through graphically, by drawing a tangent on the TPP curve from the Y-axis. That is, at any point on the TPP curve, MPP can be computed by simply drawing the tangent from the Y-axis and measuring the ΔY and ΔX (Figure 2.2). Suppose, let us measure MPP at point A on the TPP curve. That is, we have to measure the slope of TPP curve at point A. To get this, draw a tangent through this point A from Y-axis originating at B. Then slope of TPP curve can be measured by the ratio: BC/OE or RS/MN. In this fashion, we can work out MPP at different points on TPP. But, this is a cumbersome procedure, as we have to draw several tangents on the TPP curve.

So, the best procedure to compute MPP is by taking first derivative of the given production function. The first derivative of the production function is defined as the limit of the expression ΔY/ΔX, as ΔX approaches zero. As ΔX becomes smaller and

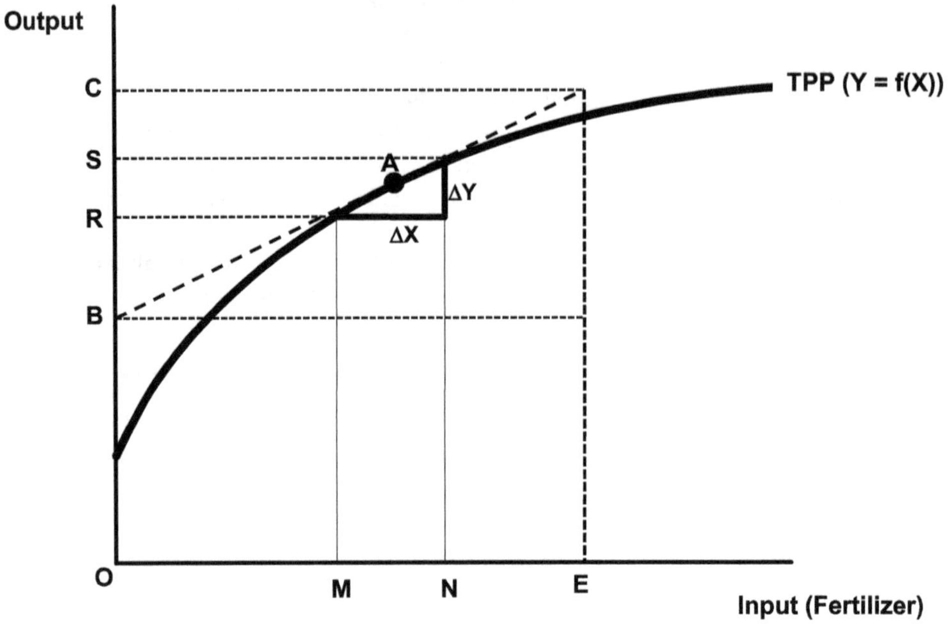

Figure 2.2: Measurement of MPP - Graphical method.

smaller, ΔY/ΔX becomes a better and better approximation for the true slope of the production function. The first derivative, dY/dX, represents the exact slope of the production function at a particular point. Assume, the production function, Y=f(X) and its first derivative can be written as: dY/dX = f1 = d(TPP)/d(X) = MPP. Now, let us consider the above single input production function: Y=5X. So, for this function, MPP = dY/dX = 5. Since, the first derivate of the function is without any X variable, this slope (MPP) remains constant at any point on the TPP curve. That is, the MPP remains same for all values of X. So, in this case, dY/dX is same as ΔY/ΔX, as the slope of the function (MPP) is a constant number (*i.e.*, 5) and is not dependent on the value of X. However, assume another production function as: $Y = 70 + 2.67X^{0.5}$. So, the first derivative of this function (General Rule: $Y = bX^n$ can be found by the rule dY/dX $= bnX^{n-1}$) is given by: MPP = dY/dX = $2.67 * 0.5X^{-0.5} = 1.335X^{-0.5}$. In this case, MPP varies with X value and hence, it is not the same for all values of X. So, to calculate the MPP, not only the first derivative is sufficient, but we also need the value of X. In the given production function, $Y = 70 + 2.67X^{0.5}$, the constant 70 indicates the intercept of the TPP and we know, the derivative of any constant value in a function is '0'. So, in solving for MPP, the derivative of 70 is '0'. So, a constant in the production function does not affect the slope of the function. Since, MPP (dY/dX = $1.335X^{-0.5}$) depends upon the value of X applied by the farmer *i.e.*, as X appears in the first derivative, only dY/dX will provide the exact MPP, but will not be the same as the approximation calculated by ΔY/ΔX. As discussed earlier with reference to the MPP computed under Linear production function (Y=a+bX), MPP = ΔY/ΔX = dY/dX = b. Considering only response part of the linear production function, APP = b. So, $E_P = 1$. Similarly in Cobb-Douglas production function, $Y = aX^b$,

$$MPP = dY/dX = baX^{b-1}$$

$$APP = aX^b/X = aX^bX^{-1} = aX^{b-1}$$

$$So,\ E_P = (baX^{b-1})/(aX^{b-1}) = b$$

So, E_P for the above production (power) function is always equal to the constant '*b*'. Let us look at another example assuming the production function: $Y = a\sqrt{X}$.

$$So,\ MPP = dY/dX = 0.5aX^{-0.5}$$

$$APP = (a\sqrt{X})/X = (aX^{0.5})/X = aX^{0.5}X^{-1} = aX^{-0.5}$$

$$So,\ E_P = (0.5aX^{-0.5})/(aX^{-0.5}) = 0.5$$

So, E_P for the above (non-linear Cobb-Douglas) production function is always equal to the constant '0.5'. However, this is not the same as the relationship that exists between MPP and APP for the neoclassical production function in which the ratio (*i.e.*, E_P) is not constant, but continually changing as the use of X increases in the production programme.

iv. Total Value Product (TVP)

It is the expression of output or TPP in monetary terms. It is given by, $TVP=TPP*P_Y$, where, P_Y is price per unit of output.

v. Average Value Product (AVP)

It is the product of APP and price per unit of output, given by

$$AVP=APP*P_Y = (Y/X)*P_Y = TVP/X$$

vi. Marginal Returns or Marginal Revenue (MR)

It refers to additional returns or revenue generated due to production of an additional unit of output. It is given by, $MR=(\Delta TR/\Delta Y)$.

vii. Marginal Cost (MC)

It is the additional cost incurred in producing an additional unit of an output. It is given by, MC= Change in Short Run Total Cost ($\Delta SRTC/\Delta Y$) = Change in Short Run Total Variable Cost ($\Delta SRTVC/\Delta Y$), (where, SRTC = Short Run Total Cost, SRTVC = Short Run Total Variable Cost).

viii. Marginal Factor Cost (MFC_X)

It is the additional cost incurred in using an additional unit of an input in the production programme. This MFC_X is equal to the factor price. It is given by,

$$MFC_X = \text{Change in TC/Change in input usage} = \Delta TC/\Delta X = \Delta TVC/\Delta X$$

ix. Marginal Value Product of a factor (MVP_X) or Value of Marginal Product (VMP)

It refers to additional returns or revenue derived from using an additional unit of an input in the production programme. It is given by,

MVP_X or VMP= Change in Total Returns/Change in input usage = $\Delta TR/\Delta X$ or $MPP * P_Y$

Thus, the product between MPP and P_Y is called VMP. Similarly, as mentioned earlier, multiplying the amount of APP by P_Y, we obtain the AVP. So, AVP = APP * P_Y. The graphical representation of the VMP and of the AVP is the same as MPP and APP, but in value terms.

Note that, the optimal use of the variable input, is when the VMP is equal to the factor price (P_X) or price of extra unit of input (MFC_X) employed in the production programme. That is, increasing the employment of a variable factor by one unit is profitable, as long as the increase in the MVP_X (or VMP) is higher than the MFC_X (or price of extra unit of factor). So, the point of optimality is when MVP_X (or VMP) = MFC_X (or P_X). So, the level of employment of a variable factor depends upon two important economic aspects *viz.*, price of the variable input (P_X) and price of the product (P_Y).

Production Function with One Variable Factor (Returns to a Variable Factor)

Let us discuss the short run (cubic) production function involving one variable factor influencing the output. Returns to a variable factor refers to the relation between a variable factor employed in the production programme and output realized, when all other factors are held constant. That means, when one factor is continuously varied in the production programme, keeping other factors constant, it exerts an influence on the output and this influence is known as Returns to a variable factor. There are two approaches to study the returns to a variable factor *viz.*, Traditional approach and Modern approach.

The Classical Economists are of the opinion that, there are three possible influences of varying a factor on the output viz.,

- ☆ Increase in output at an increasing rate (Increasing (marginal) returns to a variable factor or Law of increasing (marginal) returns)
- ☆ Increase in output at a constant rate (Constant (marginal) returns to a variable factor or Law of constant (marginal) returns)
- ☆ Increase in output at a diminishing rate (Diminishing (marginal) returns to a variable factor or LDR)

This traditional explanation of the behaviour of returns *viz.*, at increasing rate, constant rate and diminishing rate was explained by Alfred Marshall. Besides these, the production also experiences negative (marginal) returns *i.e.*, each unit of a variable factor contributes negative additional output to total output and this negative contribution is in increasing magnitude.

i. Increasing (Marginal) Returns to a Variable Factor or Law of Increasing (Marginal) Returns

In law of increasing (marginal) returns, each additional unit of a variable input when applied to a fixed level of other inputs, it will add more amount of additional output to the total output than the preceeding unit of an additional input. Due to increase in total output (TPP) at an increasing rate, both MPP and APP also increases for every unit of an additional input. Inversely, from cost point of view, it is termed as 'Law of decreasing (marginal) costs', as the MC goes on decreasing for every additional unit of an input. This is because, each and every additional unit of an input is accompanied by more than proportionate increase in output and thereby, the MC of each unit of an input goes on decreasing. In the words of Marshall, *'an increase of labour and capital leads generally to improved organization, which increases the efficiency of the work of labour and capital. Therefore, in those industries, which are not engaged in raising raw produce, an increase of labour and capital generally gives a return increase more than in proportion and further this improved organization tends to diminish or even override any increased resistance which nature may offer to raise increased amounts of raw produce'*. This definition given by Alfred Marshall highlights two important aspects *viz.*, increasing (marginal) returns in the firm is due to better organization and this is common in manufacturing industries, which do not engage in producing its own raw material. Benham stated the law *'as the production of one factor in the combination of factors is increased upto a point, the marginal product of the factor will increase'*. In the words of Joan Robinson, *'when an increased amount of any factor of production is devoted to certain use, it is often the case that improvement in organization can be introduced which will make natural units of the factor (men, acres or money capital) more efficient, so that, an increase in output does not require a proportionate increase in the physical amount of the factor. This law or rather tendency, like the law of diminishing (marginal) returns, may apply equally to all the factors of production, but, unlike the law of diminishing (marginal) returns, it does not apply in every case. Sometimes an increase of the factors will lead to improvements in efficiency and sometimes it will not'*. The important features of this definition includes, increasing (marginal) returns in the firm is due to better organization (as explained by Alfred Marshall), increasing (marginal) returns can be seen irrespective of the production activity *i.e.*, either industry or agriculture, provided the level of the factor or factors are increased and the increasing (marginal) returns is not 'inevitable' unlike diminishing (marginal) returns. So, the definition given by Joan Robinson also highlights the significance of diminishing (marginal) returns, as its operation is always inevitable in a production programme, but the law of increasing (marginal) returns may be exhibited, but it is not a must always. The law of increasing (marginal) returns is explained through the following Table 2.2.

Table 2.2: Increasing (Marginal) Returns to a Variable Factor

Fixed Input, Land (Units)	*Variable Input Fertilizer, X (Units)*	*TPP (Output, Y) (Units)*	*APP (Y/X)*	*ΔX*	*ΔY*	*MPP (ΔY/ΔX)*
2	5	2	0.40	–	–	–
2	10	5	0.50	5	3	0.60
2	15	9	0.60	5	4	0.80
2	20	14	0.70	5	5	1.00
2	25	20	0.80	5	6	1.20

It is clear from the Table 2.2 that, if the variable input, fertilizer is increased continuously keeping other inputs like land fixed in the production programme, the output increases at an increasing rate, as indicated by the increase in MPP. Since, output (TPP) increases at an increasing rate, the APP also increases. The diagrammatic representation of the Table 2.2 infers that, the production function is convex to origin (Panel A of the Figure 2.3) and the slope of production function *i.e.*, MPP is increasing (Panel B of the Figure 2.3). However, this law is not applicable to agriculture and applies mostly to manufacturing industries that too, upto the point of optimality, beyond which, the constant and diminishing MRs will operate. The MPP for law of increasing (marginal) returns is given by, $(\Delta_1 Y/\Delta_1 X)<(\Delta_2 Y/\Delta_2 X)<(\Delta_3 Y/\Delta_3 X)<$ — $<(\Delta_n Y/\Delta_n X)$.

ii. *Constant (Marginal) Returns to a Variable Factor or Law of Constant (Marginal) Returns*

This law represents the transition from increasing (marginal) returns to diminishing (marginal) returns and *vice versa* in a production programme. In law of constant (marginal) returns, each additional unit of a variable input when applied to a fixed level of other inputs, it will add same amount of additional output to the total output, as the preceding unit of an additional input. Due to increase in total output at constant rate, both MPP and APP remains constant for every additional unit of an input. Inversely, from cost point of view, it is termed as 'Law of constant (marginal) costs', as the MC remains same for every additional unit of an input. This is because, each and every additional unit of an input is accompanied by same proportionate increase in output and thereby, the MC of each unit of an input remains same. In the words of Marshall, '*the stage of constant (marginal) returns comes at that point, where the effects of increasing (marginal) returns and diminishing (marginal) returns balance each*

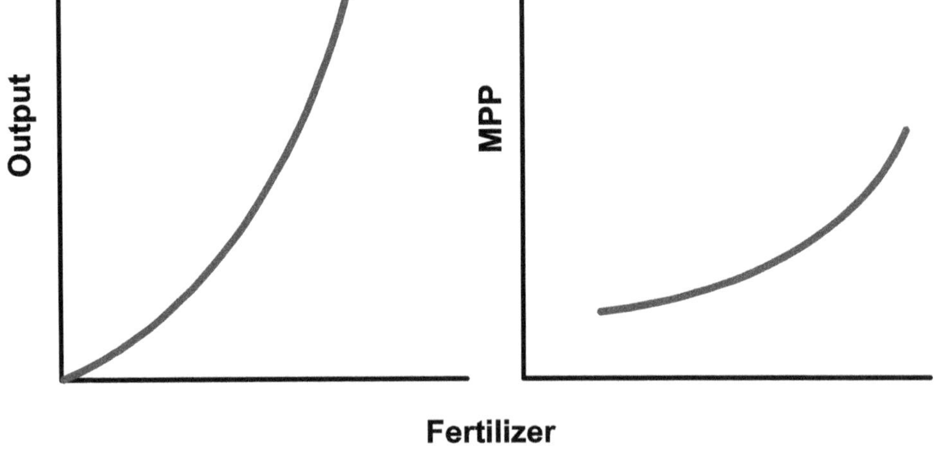

Figure 2.3: Increasing (Marginal) Returns to a Variable Factor.

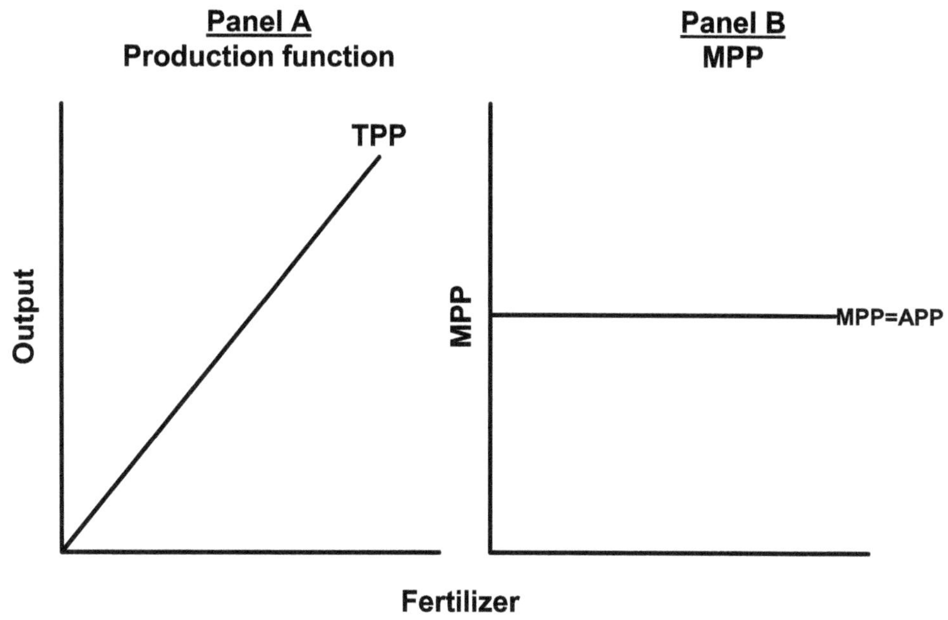

Figure 2.4: Constant (Marginal) Returns to a Variable Factor.

other'. According to Prof. Stigler, *'when all of the productive services are increased in a given proportion, the product is increased in the same proportion'*. The law of constant (marginal) returns is explained through the following Table 2.3.

Table 2.3: Constant (Marginal) Returns to a Variable Factor

Fixed Input, Land (Units)	*Variable Input Fertilizer, X (Units)*	*TPP (Output, Y) (Units)*	*APP (Y/X)*	*ΔX*	*ΔY*	*MPP (ΔY/ΔX)*
2	5	2	0.40	–	–	–
2	10	4	0.40	5.00	2.00	0.40
2	15	6	0.40	5.00	2.00	0.40
2	20	8	0.40	5.00	2.00	0.40
2	25	10	0.40	5.00	2.00	0.40

It is clear from the Table 2.3 that, if the variable input, fertilizer is increased continuously keeping other inputs like land, fixed in the production programme, the output increases at constant rate, as indicated by the constancy of MPP. Since, output is increased at constant rate due to constancy of MPP, APP is also constant. The diagrammatic representation of the above Table 2.3 infers that, the production function is a straight line sloping upwards from the origin (Panel A of the Figure 2.4) and the slope of production function *i.e.,* MPP is constant and equal to APP, thereby, lies parallel to X-axis (Panel B of the Figure 2.4). However, this law is also not applicable to agriculture. The MPP for law of constant (marginal) returns is given by, $(\Delta_1 Y/\Delta_1 X)=(\Delta_2 Y/\Delta_2 X)=(\Delta_3 Y/\Delta_3 X)$ = ——$=(\Delta_n Y/\Delta_n X)$.

iii. Diminishing (Marginal) Returns to a Variable Factor or LDR

In LDR, each additional unit of a variable input when applied to a fixed level of other inputs, it will add less amount of additional output to the total output than the preceding unit of an additional input. Due to increase in total output at diminishing rate, both MPP and APP also decreases for every additional unit of an input. Inversely, from cost point of view, it is termed as 'Law of increasing (marginal) costs', as the MC goes on increasing for every additional unit of an input. This is because, each and every additional unit of an input is accompanied by less than proportionate increase in output and thereby, the MC of each unit of an input goes on increasing. This concept of LDR was first proposed by Turgot, but Malthus and Ricardo have refined this concept. In the words of Marshall, *'keeping the fixed factors constant, when marginal product diminishes with the increase in the quantities of a variable factor, it is called law of diminishing (marginal) returns'*. According to Boulding, *'as we increase the quantity of one input which is combined with a fixed quantity of other inputs, the marginal physical productivity of the variable input must eventually decline'*. In the words of Joan Robinson, *'the law of diminishing (marginal) returns states that, with a fixed amount of any one factor of production, successive increases in the amount of other factors will, after a point, yield a diminishing increment of the product'*. The LDR is explained through the following Table 2.4.

Table 2.4: Diminishing (Marginal) Returns to a Variable Factor

Fixed Input, Land (Units)	*Variable Input Fertilizer, X (Units)*	*TPP (Output, Y) (Units)*	*APP (Y/X)*	*ΔX*	*ΔY*	*MPP (ΔY/ΔX)*
2	5	5.00	1.00	–	–	–
2	10	8.50	0.85	5	3.50	0.70
2	15	10.80	0.72	5	2.30	0.46
2	20	12.60	0.63	5	1.80	0.36
2	25	13.00	0.52	5	0.40	0.08

It is clear from the Table 2.4 that, if the variable input, fertilizer is increased continuously keeping other inputs like land, fixed in the production programme, the output increases at diminishing rate, as indicated by the decline in MPP. Since, output increased at diminishing rate, the APP also decreased. The diagrammatic representation of the above Table 2.4 infers that, the production function is concave to origin (Panel A of the Figure 2.5) and the slope of production function *i.e.*, MPP is diminishing (Panel B of the Figure 2.5). This law is more common in agriculture and equally applies to other sectors *viz.*, industry, mining *etc.*, as well. The MPP for LDR is given by, $(\Delta_1 Y/\Delta_1 X)>(\Delta_2 Y/\Delta_2 X)>(\Delta_3 Y/\Delta_3 X)>$ —$>(\Delta_n Y/\Delta_n X)$.

This concept of three different laws of returns *i.e.*, increasing, constant and diminishing (marginal) returns is a classical or traditional approach. However, Modern Economists discarded this view and opined that, the returns to a variable

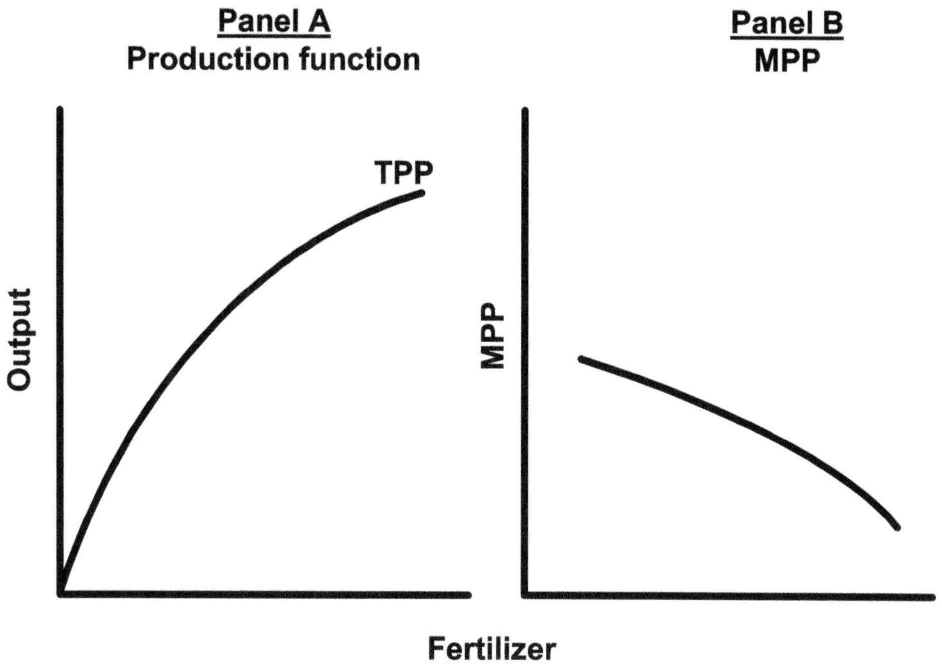

Figure 2.5: Diminishing (Marginal) Returns to a Variable Factor.

factor *i.e.*, increasing, constant and diminishing (marginal) returns are not three distinct laws, but they are different phases of a single law called 'LVP'. Further, Marshall opined that, the LDR applies to 'agriculture' sector only, because of the following special features:

- ☆ In agriculture, nature plays a very vital role in the production programme compared to human element. So, due to this excess dependence on natural and climatic factors, there is less control on the part of the farmer to execute the production programme.
- ☆ There is less scope for division of labour because, farmer himself has to play four important roles such as, farm entrepreneur, farm manager, capitalist and labour.
- ☆ Less scope for mechanization due to sub-division and fragmentation of land holdings.
- ☆ Bringing inferior lands into cultivation is another important reason for the early operation of LDR. This is because, to meet the food security needs for mounting population, inferior lands will be brought into cultivation and for such lands, the productivity is very low.
- ☆ Due to continuous cultivation of crops on the same piece of land, soil fertility gets exhausted.

- There is less scope for efficient planning of the production programme because of excess dependence on natural factors on one side and limited capital availability to the farmer on other side.
- The agricultural labour are less skilled and hence, their efficiency is low.
- Agricultural operations are spread over a larger area and hence, supervision may not be effective.
- Availability of a specialized machinery to perform a particular operation is limited.

This clearly infers that, in the production programme, where nature plays a crucial role or there is less control by the human element, this LDR sets in early. But in the sectors, where there is more human element involved in controlling production programme compared to natural factors, the operation of this law can be delayed. It is wrong to say that, this law will not apply in industry because, if the industry is greatly expanded, it is difficult to supervise on the part of the manager and hence, cost per unit of output increases indicating that, this law is in operation.

In the words of Alfred Marshall, '*an increase in capital and labour applied in the cultivation of land, causes, in general, a less than proportionate increase in the amount of produce raised, unless it happens to coincide with the improvement in the arts of agriculture*'. He believed that, production is governed by three different laws of returns and the LDR is particularly applicable to agricultural sector. This is because, had the LDR

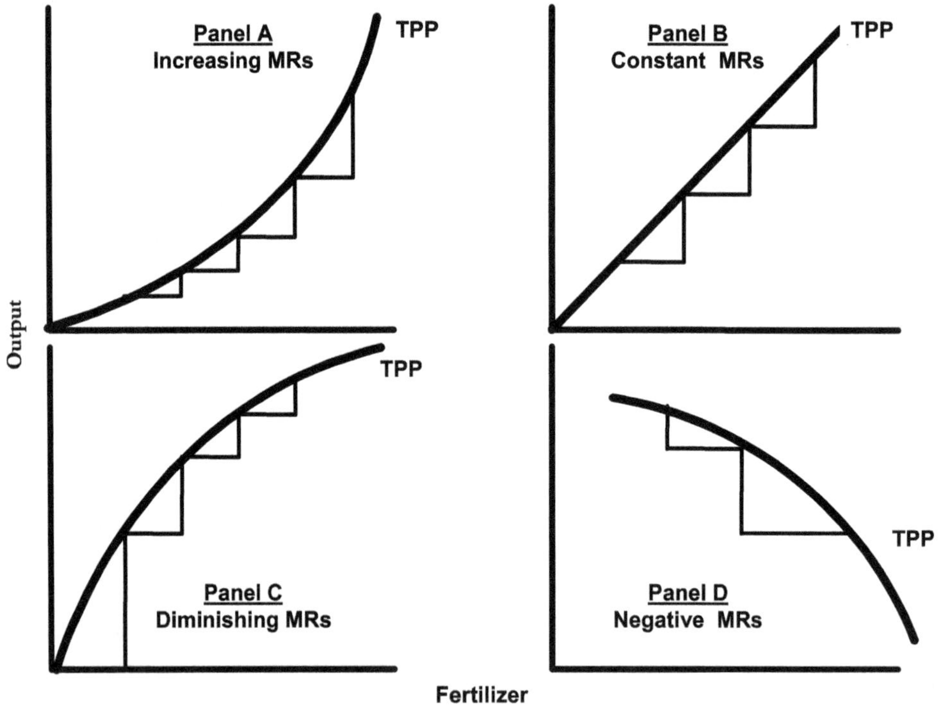

Figure 2.6: Laws of Returns in a Single Input Production Function.

not applies to agricultural sector, the farmers would have produced significant output on the farm for the whole of the world. In this context, this law is also called the Flower pot law. This is because, if it did not hold true, the world's entire food supply could be grown in a single flower pot. So, the operation of LDR in agriculture contributes less additional output to total output compared to increments made in the variable factor. He further opined that, the law of increasing (marginal) returns applies to industrial sector and stated that, *'the part played by the nature confirms the diminishing (marginal) returns, while the part that man plays confirms to increasing (marginal) returns'*. So, according to Marshall, law of increasing (marginal) returns, law of constant (marginal) returns and LDR are three separate laws of returns to a variable factor. Note that, if the employment of a variable factor is still increased beyond the occurrence of diminishing marginal returns, the production also experiences negative (marginal) returns *i.e.,* each unit of a variable factor contributes negative additional output to total output and this negative contribution is in increasing magnitude. Thus, the TPP curve starts falling downward, as MPP turns negative (Panel D of the Figure 2.6).

According to Modern Economists, all the three laws of returns *i.e.,* law of increasing (marginal) returns, law of constant (marginal) returns and LDR operate as separate phases in a single law called as 'LVP'. So, the concept of diminishing (marginal) returns applies not only to agriculture, but also to industries as well. That means, if one input is continuously varied, keeping other inputs constant, the diminishing (marginal) returns will set in irrespective of the sector. So, LVP is a universal law according to the Modern Economists. This law (LVP) is so called because, the proportion among the inputs used is different *i.e.,* other inputs are held constant and only one input is continuously increased to study the influence on the output. Hence, LVP falls under short run production function. This law is also called as 'Law of non-proportional returns' because, returns are not proportionately increased, as the increase in input usage. This law is also called as, 'Law of Added cost and Added returns' because MC=MR is the output optimizing criterion in the production programme. This LVP is also considered as 'Fundamental law of Economics'. Note that, this law is an empirical generalization, not a deduction from physical or biological laws. The following are the popular definitions of LVP:

'When total output or production of a commodity is increased by adding units of a variable unit, while the quantities of other inputs are held constant, the increase in total production becomes, after some point, smaller and smaller'.

(Watson)

'As the proportion of one factor in a combination of factors is increased, after a point, first the marginal and then the average product of that factor will diminish'.

(Benham)

'As equal increments of one input are added, the inputs of other productive services being held constant, beyond a certain point the resulting increments of product will decrease i.e., the marginal products will diminish'.

(G. Stigler)

'An increase in some inputs relative to the other fixed inputs will, in a given state of technology, causes output to increase, but after a point the extra output resulting from the same addition of extra inputs will become less'.

(Paul Samuelson)

'The law of variable proportions states that, if the input of one resource is increased by equal increments per unit of time while the inputs of other resources are held constant, total product (output) will increase, but beyond some point the resulting output increases will become smaller and smaller'.

(Leftwitch)

'If, with the same methods of production, successive physical units of an input are added to a constant physical quantity of another input (or fixed combinations of other inputs), the total physical output obtained would vary in magnitude through three distinct phases'.

(J. M. Cassels)

The above definitions explain that, all the three laws of returns *viz.*, increasing (marginal) returns, constant (marginal) returns and diminishing (marginal) returns will operate in the production programme, if we go on increasing one input continuously, keeping other inputs constant. That means, first the (marginal) returns will increase at increasing rate, then at constant rate, then at diminishing rate and finally decreases at increasing rate, if one factor is continuously increased, keeping other inputs constant in the production programme. This law can be better explained by studying the patterns of TPP, MPP and APP in different stage or stages of LVP.

Assumptions

This law holds true under the following assumptions:

- Quantity of input that is to be varied is given.
- Only one input should be varied keeping other inputs constant, as this facilitates to study the effect of changes of one input on the output or production. So, this law does not apply to cases, where all inputs are variable. Thus, this law assumes short run production function, as in the long run, all the inputs are variable.
- Factors of production are clearly classified as fixed and variable. For example, fertilizer is the variable factor, and capital and land are fixed factors.
- All the units of a variable input should be homogeneous. For example, same type of nitrogen fertilizer (say, urea) should be employed as a continuous variable factor.
- There should not be any change in the state of technology or methods of production. Thus, the LDR cannot predict the effect of an additional unit of input, when technology is allowed to change.
- The output *i.e.*, TPP, APP and MPP should be measured in terms of physical units only. They should not be considered in monetary terms because, even if the output falls due to operation of LDR, but total returns may increase, if price of the output increases in the market and *vice versa*.

- ☆ There should be possibility of varying the proportions of factors, so as to produce the output. That means, the factors involved in the production programme should not be perfect complements, as we vary only one factor keeping other factors constant. That is, it is possible to combine the factors of production is variable proportions. The production function is not of fixed proportions type.
- ☆ This law is applicable in terms of costs, only if the prices of variable inputs as well as output remain same.

Explanation of the Law

The concept of LVP explained through Table 2.5 and Figure 2.7 reveals that, if we go on increasing one input, keeping other inputs constant, first the output increases at increasing rate, then increases at constant rate, then increases at diminishing rate and finally decreases at an increasing rate. It is also evident that, as long as MPP is positive, TPP increases, when MPP is zero, TPP is maximum and when MPP is negative, TPP starts declining. Considering the behaviour of these three curves *viz.*, TPP, MPP and APP curves, Cassels classified the entire production process into three stages or stage (Figure 2.7). These three stage have a special significance in analyzing the efficiency with which the resource is used and the features of these stage are discussed here under.

Table 2.5: Different Stage of Short Run Production Function (LVP)

Fixed Input Land – (Acres)	*Variable Input Fertilizer (X)*	*Output or TPP (Y)*	*ΔX*	*ΔY*	*MPP (ΔY/ΔX)*	*APP (Y/X)*	*Returns to a Variable Factor*
1	1	2	1	2	2	2.00	Increasing (marginal) returns
1	2	6	1	4	4	3.00	
1	3	11	1	5	5	3.67	
1	4	17	1	6	6	4.25	Constant (marginal) returns
1	5	23	1	6	6	4.60	
1	6	28	1	5	5	4.67	Diminishing (marginal) returns
1	7	32	1	4	4	4.57	
1	8	33	1	1	1	4.13	
1	9	33	1	0	0	3.67	Zero (marginal) returns
1	10	32	1	–1	–1	3.20	Negative (marginal) returns
1	11	29	1	–3	–3	2.64	

i. First Zone or Stage

This stage starts from the point of origin up to the point, where MPP is equal to APP or APP is maximum. The important features of this stage include:

- ☆ In this stage, the E_p (MPP / APP) is more than one because, MPP is higher than APP throughout the stage.

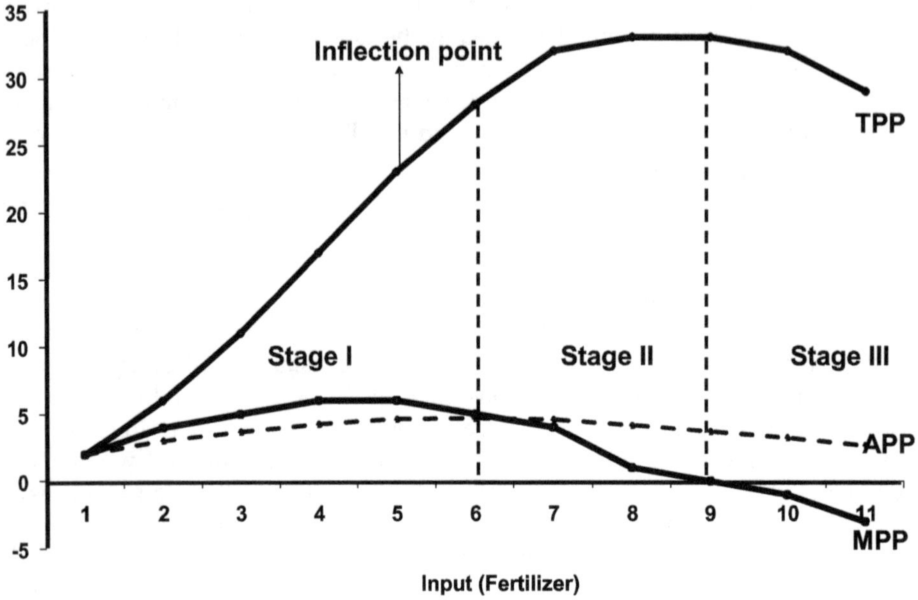

Figure 2.7: Three Stages of LVP.

- At the end of first stage, MPP=APP. So, E_p is equal to one, implying that percentage change in output is equal to percentage change in input. At the point of E_p equal to one, the TPP is increasing at diminishing rate or MPP is positive, but falling at diminishing rate. Note that, when MPP is falling in this stage, APP is rising and this implies that, though MPP is falling, it is sufficiently higher than APP and this contributes to rising TPP at diminishing rate.
- When MPP is maximum, its corresponding point on TPP curve indicates 'Inflection point', which indicates that, TPP is now increasing at diminishing rate and there is change in curvature of TPP from convex to concave. This inflection point marks the end of increasing MPP and the start of diminishing MPP.
- In this stage, TPP increases at an increasing rate up to the point of inflection, then at constant rate and after inflection point, TPP increases at diminishing rate because, MPP first increases, becomes constant and finally decreases in this stage. Hence, the curvature of TPP changes from convex to concave and this is indicated by the inflection point. This further indicates that, all the three laws of returns will be experienced in the first stage thereby, the LDR starts operating in the first stage itself after employing five units of fertilizer *i.e.,* after inflection point on the TPP curve.
- APP continuously increases and reaches maximum at the end of this stage, where it equals to MPP.

- ☆ In this stage, though MPP falls, APP still rises between fifth and sixth units of fertilizer, as MPP is more than APP.
- ☆ In this stage, both APP and TPP will rise continuously whereas, MPP rises, reaches maximum and then starts falling (Figure 2.8). The MPP would be greater than the APP of the variable input. In this stage, the relative rate of increase in the output would be greater than the relative rate of increase in the variable input. At the end of this stage, the two rates would be the same indicating the point of equality between MPP and APP. This point represents the 'Extensive margin of production'.
- ☆ The quantity of fixed factor in this stage is too much relative to the use of variable factor such that, if we even withdraw some of the fixed factor, TPP will not fall. So, in this stage, the MPP of fixed factor is negative.

This stage of increasing (marginal) returns starts, when the quantity of a fixed factor is abundant relative to the quantity of the variable factor. As more and more units of the variable factor are added to the constant quantity of the fixed factor, it is more intensively and effectively used. This causes the production to increase at a rapid rate. Another reason of increasing (marginal) returns is that, the fixed factor initially taken is indivisible. As more units of the variable factor are employed to work on it, output increases greatly due to fuller and effective utilization of the variable

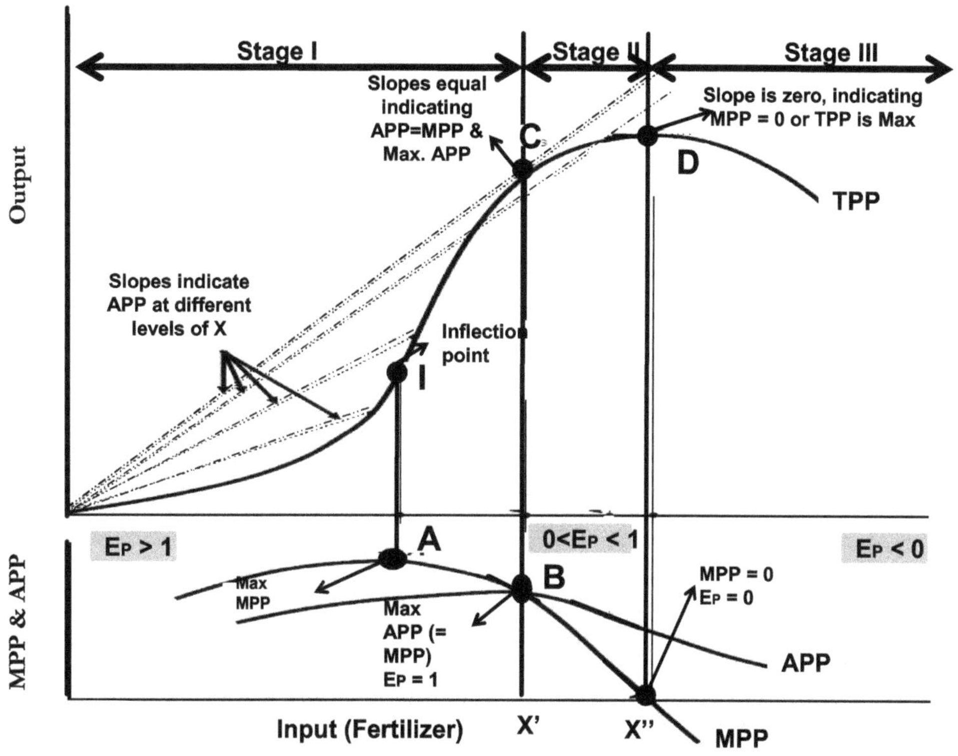

Figure 2.8: Three Stages of a Neo-Classical Production Function.

factor. However, this stage is called as 'Irrational stage' or 'Sub-optimal stage' because, the farmer will not optimize the output in this stage, as TPP is still increasing in the second stage (diminishing rate) and in the second stage, though MPP and APP are falling, but they are positive. This implies that, if the farmer increases the input dosage, he can still increase the output (TPP) and thereby, he definitely moves to second stage.

ii. Second Zone or Stage

This is the most important stage in the production function. This stage starts from the point, where MPP is equal to APP and ends, where MPP is equal to zero or TPP is maximum. The important features of this stage include,

- ☆ The boundaries of this stage are the points at which the technical efficiency of the variable resource is maximum (*i.e.*, APP is maximum) at the starting point of this stage and the technical efficiency of the fixed resource is maximum (*i.e.*, TPP is maximum) at the end point of this stage.
- ☆ In this stage, E_p is less than one, as MPP is less than APP implying that, the percentage change in output is less than the percentage change in input.
- ☆ At the end of this stage, the E_p is zero, as MPP is zero indicating that, ninth unit of fertilizer will contribute nothing to the output (Figure 2.8).
- ☆ In this stage, TPP increases at diminishing rate, as MPP is falling. That is, the relative increase in TPP would be less than the relative increase in the quantity of the variable input.
- ☆ Both MPP and APP decreases in this stage and APP is always higher than MPP. This downward slope of the (diminishing) MPP curve illustrates the background and importance of this principle.
- ☆ At the end of this stage MPP becomes zero and TPP becomes maximum. This point is known as the 'Intensive margin of production'.
- ☆ In this stage, the average product of fixed inputs (not shown) is still rising, because output (TPP) is rising while fixed input usage is constant.
- ☆ The employment of additional variable input increases the output per unit of fixed input, but decreases the output per unit of the variable input.
- ☆ The optimum input or output combination for the (price-taking) farmer will be in this stage.
- ☆ At the boundary between Stage II and Stage III, the highest possible output is being obtained from the fixed input.

This Stage II occurs, when the fixed factor becomes inadequate relative to the quantity of the variable factor. As more and more units of a variable factor are employed, the marginal and average products decline. Another reason of diminishing (marginal) returns in the production function is that, the fixed indivisible factor is being worked too hard. It is being used in non-optimal proportion with the variable factor. According to Mrs. J. Robinson, the diminishing (marginal) returns occur because the factors of production are imperfect substitutes of one another. This stage is called as 'Rational stage' or 'Optimal stage' because, there is a possibility of optimization of output. This is so because, in this stage, MPP is less than APP, TPP continues to increase, but at a diminishing rate. Both MPP and APP are decreasing. The ratio of the variable input to fixed inputs is higher, hence adjustments is possible between the two margins (*i.e.*, MPP = APP and MPP = 0). The maximum APP of a fixed inputs occurs at MPP = 0, while that of variable input occurs at MPP = APP. Therefore, Stage II is the rational stage to produce. Note that, no profit-maximizing farmer would produce in Stages I and III. In Stage I, by adding one more unit of fertilizer, the farmer can increase the TPP (output) and APP of all units. Thus, it would be unwise on the part of the farmer to stop the production in this Stage I. Regarding Stage III, it does not pay the producer, as for each additional unit of input, TPP decreases and further, the use of additional inputs in this stage is not advisable, as MPP turns negative. So, a rational producer will always seek to produce in Stage II, where MPP and APP of the variable factor are positive, but diminishing. At which particular point, the farmer will decide to produce depends upon the various factors like, output he would like to produce, price of the factor he has to pay, price of the product in the market *etc.* The criteria to optimize the output in this stage are given below.

1. ***MC=MR (From output side):***
2. ***MPP=Factor-Product price ratio:*** [$MPP=(P_X/P_Y)$]

   $= MPP * P_Y = P_X$

So, MVP_X or VMP = P_X (where P_X = Price of factor, Fertilizer). This equation can also be written as: MVP_X or VMP = MFC_X (where MFC_X gets equal to P_X as shown through Table 2.6).

In the above formula (MVP_X or VMP = $MFC_{X)}$, the left side component (MVP_X or VMP) denotes the increase in revenue and the right side component (MFC_X or $P_{X)}$ denotes the increase in the cost of adding one more unit of fertilizer or price of fertilizer. As long as the increment in revenues exceeds the increment in costs, the profit of the producer will increase. So, we can increase the dosage of fertilizer and thereby, its MPP will decreases. So, the VMP will decrease. Since, under the assumption of perfect market competition, price of fertilizer and product do not change. So, finally, at one point of dosage of input, the increase in revenue equals the increase in cost *i.e.*, VMP = P_X. At this point, the farmer will stop adding more units of input. With further addition of units of fertilizer, MPP declines thereby, the additional revenue (VMP) would be less than the additional costs (P_X), and this reduces the profits of the farmer. As shown through Figure 2.9, the point of profit maximization can be determined, where the factor-product price ratio line (P_X/P_Y) lie tangent to the TPP (the tangent drawn on TPP implies MPP). The above formulae further infer that, 'marginal' concept guides the farmer to know to what extent he can push the output to maximize the profits or to how much level, the input should be used to minimize the costs in the production programme and not the 'average' concept.

Thus, the level of input usage within Stage II at which the farmer can maximize the profits is all depends upon how many units of output the farmer can sell, the price of the product, and the monetary costs of employing the variable input. A close look at the Table 2.6 reveals that, at eighth unit of fertilizer, MR=MC, $MPP=(P_X/P_Y)$, VMP

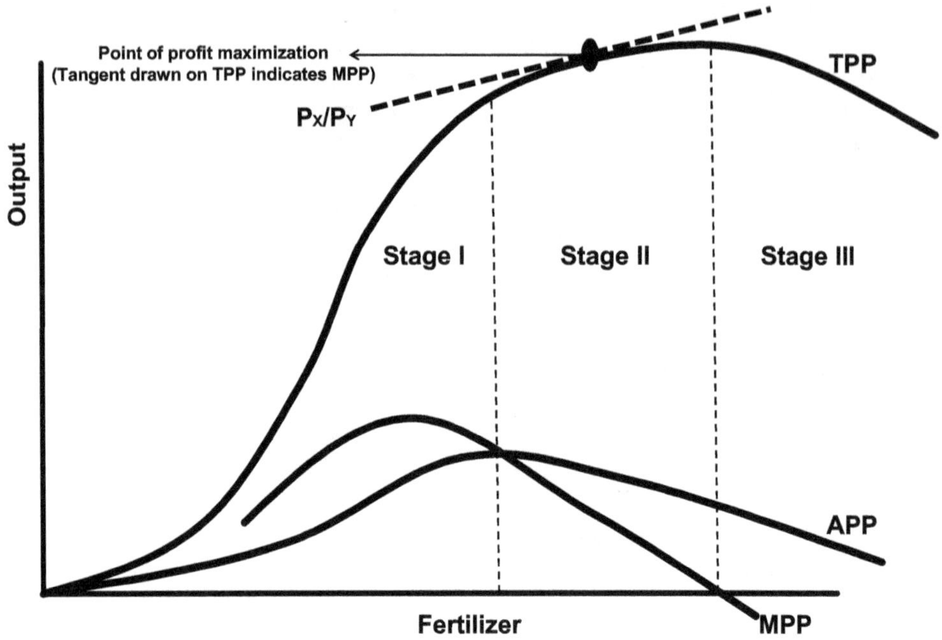

Figure 2.9: Point of Profit Maximization: MPP = (PX/PY).

= P_X or MFC_X thereby, the output is optimized in the production programme at eighth unit of fertilizer. So, at this level of input usage, the farmer will maximize net returns or profits (Rs.250/-). Even at seventh unit of fertilizer, the farmer maximizes the net returns (Rs.250/-) as in eighth unit of fertilizer, but at seventh unit of fertilizer, the optimality conditions *viz.*, MC(Rs.2.50/-)≠MR(Rs.10/-), MPP(4)≠P_X/P_Y(1), VMP(Rs.40)≠P_X(Rs.10) or ≠MFC_X(Rs.10) are not fulfilled and more over, it is advisable for the farmer to increase the input usage up to eighth unit of fertilizer because, total output in quantity terms increases from 32 units to 33 units. This maximization of net returns is seen even at 7th unit of fertilizer because, in this case discrete data are assumed. Had the data are continuous, profit maximization will occur only at 8th unit of fertilizer.

Inequality between MR and MC or MVPx (VMP) and MFCx (or P_X)

Case1: MR>MC or MVPx (VMP)>MFCx (or P_X)

This case is observed in the first stage of production function and the farmer is advised to increase the input usage, so that MC or MFC_X increases and becomes equal to MR or MVPx (VMP) respectively to attain optimality in the production programme. Similarly, with increase in input usage, MPP decreases thereby, MVPx (VMP) falls and gets equal to P_X and this optimality is achieved in Stage II.

Case 2: MR<MC or MVPx (VMP)<MFCx (or P_X)

This case is observed in the third stage of production function and the farmer is advised to reduce the input usage so that, MC or MFC_X decreases and becomes equal to MR or MVPx (VMP) respectively to attain optimality in the production programme.

Table 2.6: Profit Maximization in Short Run Production Function (LVP)

Input X (Fertilizer)	*Physical Relationships*					*Economic Relationships (Costs, Returns and Profits)*								
	TPP Y	*MPP ($\Delta Y/\Delta X$)*	*APP (Y/X)*	*ΔX*	*ΔY*	*SRTVC ($X * P_X$) (Given P_X=10/-)*	*ΔSR TVC*	*MC (ΔSR TVC/ΔY)*	*TR ($Y^* P_Y$) (Given P_Y=10/-)*	*ΔTR*	*MR ($\Delta TR/\Delta Y$)*	*MFCx (ΔSR TVC/ΔX)*	*VMP or MVPx = ($\Delta TR/\Delta X$) or (MPP * Py)*	*NR* (TR-SRTVC)*
1	2	2	2.00	1	2	10	10	5.00	20	20	10	10	20	10
2	6	4	3.00	1	4	20	10	2.50	60	40	10	10	40	40
3	11	5	3.67	1	5	30	10	2.00	110	50	10	10	50	80
4	17	6	4.25	1	6	40	10	1.67	170	60	10	10	60	130
5	23	6	4.60	1	6	50	10	1.67	230	60	10	10	60	180
6	28	5	4.67	1	5	60	10	2.00	280	50	10	10	50	220
7	32	4	4.57	1	4	70	10	2.50	320	40	10	10	40	250
8	**33**	1	4.13	1	1	80	10	**10.00**	330	10	**10**	**10**	**10**	**250**
9	33	0	3.67	1	0	90	10	0.00	330	0	0	10	0	240
10	32	–1	3.20	1	–1	100	10	–10.00	320	–10	10	10	–10	220
11	29	–3	2.64	1	–3	110	10	–3.33	290	–30	10	10	–30	180

Note: *: Net Returns.

Similarly, with decrease in input usage, MPP increases thereby, MVPx (VMP) rises and gets equal to P_X and this optimality is achieved in Stage II.

Assume, if the input price decreases in the market, it is profitable to increase input use, as now a one unit increase in input has a lower cost, lower than the increase in revenue. This applies up to the amount for which the new input price is equal to the VMP. So, the new optimal input use will be larger than before. On the contrary, if input price increases in the market, it is profitable to decrease input use, as now the decrease in costs resulting from a one unit decrease in input is larger than the decrease in revenue resulting from the lower production. This applies up to the amount for which the new input price is equal to the VMP. So, the new optimal input use will be smaller than before. Note that,

- ✰ If the input price (P_X) becomes higher than the AVP, where AVP=VMP, no extra input use is profitable, as the cost for using each unit of input exceeds the revenue that results from each unit of input. This defines the farmer's demand curve for that input (= the amount of that input that is bought by the farmer for each input price, holding all other things constant). The point of equality of AVP and VMP corresponds to the declining part of the VMP curve. As mentioned earlier, AVP and VMP curves enjoy the same relation like APP and MPP curves (Panel A of Figure 2.10).
- ✰ If output price (P_Y) decreases, the VMP and AVP curves shift downward (MPP and APP remain unchanged, but they are multiplied by a lower

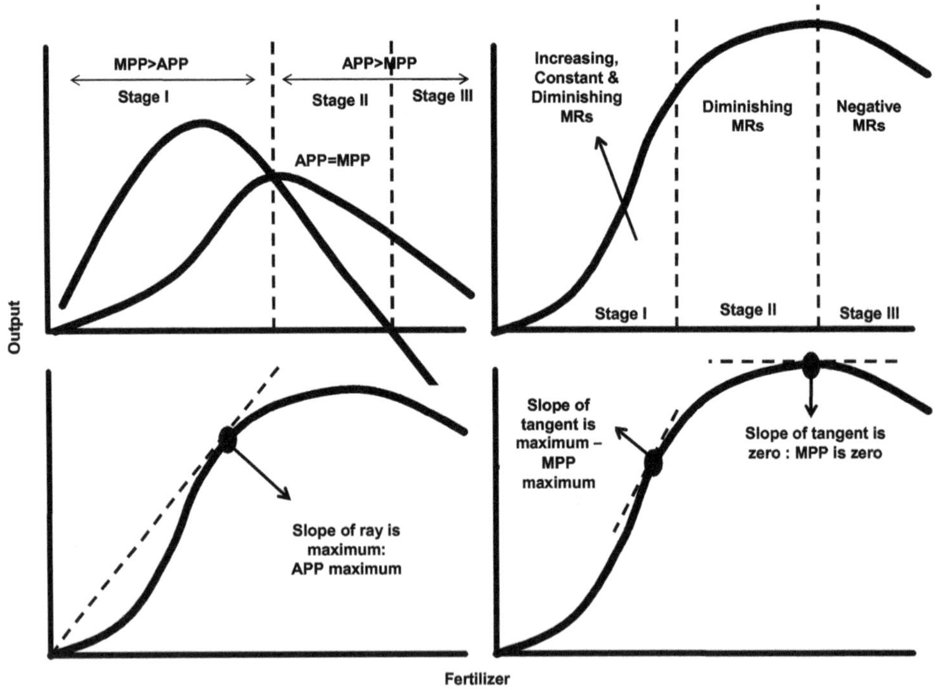

Figure 2.10: Behaviour of TPP, MPP and APP in Three Stages of Single Input (Cubic) Production Function.

output price). So, it is profitable to use less input (now the decrease in costs resulting from a one unit decrease in input is larger than the decrease in revenue resulting from the lower production). This applies up to the amount for which the input price is equal to the new VMP. So, the new optimal input use will be smaller than before. Hence, the farmer's demand curve for that input shifts to the left.

- ☆ If output price (P_Y) increases, the VMP and AVP curves shift upward (MPP and APP remain unchanged, but they are multiplied by a higher output price). So, it is profitable to use more input (now the increase in revenue resulting from a one unit increase in input is higher than the additional cost of that unit). This applies up to the amount for which the input price is equal to the new VMP. So, the new optimal input use will be larger than before. Hence, the farmer's demand curve for that input shifts to the right. Therefore, the farmer's demand for that input is negatively related to its own price, but positively related to output price. For example, farmer's demand for fertilizers decreases, it their price increases, but the demand for fertilizers increases, if the price of crop output increases.

iii. Third Zone or Stage

This stage starts from the point, where MPP is equal to zero or TPP is maximum and continue till the end of production programme. The important features of this stage include:

- ☆ At the beginning of third stage, E_P is zero because, MPP is zero and in the third stage, E_P turns negative or less than zero because, MPP is negative.
- ☆ TPP is maximum at the beginning of this stage and later it falls at an increasing rate because, MPP turns negative and decreases at an increasing rate. Hence, this stage is also called 'Stage of negative returns'.
- ☆ APP still falls when compared to second stage due to fall in TPP, but remains positive. It will not become zero or negative, as long as TPP is positive.
- ☆ The level of fixed factor is very low compared to level of variable factor. Since, the level of variable factor is too high relative to fixed factor, the MPP of variable factor is negative.
- ☆ The output per unit of both the fixed and the variable input declines throughout this stage.

This stage is also called as 'Irrational stage' or Supra-optimal stage' because, farmer cannot optimize the output in this stage and more over, if he operates in this stage, he experiences 'double loss' in terms of a greater fall in output on one hand and increase in the cost expenditure on the resource on the other hand. So, from a technical point of view, it can be excluded to use the variable factor in the third stage, as TPP declines at an increasing rate for every one unit increase in the variable factor.

So, Stage I and Stage III are called 'Irrational stages', as the farmer cannot optimize the output in these two stages and hence, they are completely symmetrical. In Stage I, the level of fixed factor is too high relative to variable factor thereby, the MPP of fixed factor is negative. However, in stage III, the level of variable factor is too high relative to fixed factor thereby, the MPP of variable factor is negative. So, a rational producer will never choose Stage III to produce the output, as he experiences 'double loss' in this stage. Even if the input (fertilizer) is offered at free of cost, he will not enter the stage III and he will produce the output, where MPP is equal to zero or TPP is maximum. On the other hand, if the input is priced, he will try to optimize the output based on the criteria discussed earlier with reference to both output side and input side. It is interesting that, the farmer will not stop in Stage I in producing the output, as in Stage II, we see the TPP is increasing (but at diminishing rate) and though APP and MPP are falling, but remain positive. So, the farmer should operate in second stage to optimize the output. Hence, second stage is otherwise called as Rational stage or Optimal stage. That is, between the points of Extensive margin and Intensive margins of production, the farmer has to optimize the output. This law is also called as LDR because, in the stage II, the optimization of output is possible, when the TPP increases at diminishing rate. But, it is important to note that, LDR is only one phase of the more comprehensive LVP.

Reasons for Increasing MRs

The concept of increasing MRs is seen in the first stage of production function and the reasons for this increasing MRs are given below.

- ☆ ***Effective supervision of less variable factor:*** In first stage, the farmer employs more of fixed factor and less of variable factor, so that, he can effectively supervise the variable factor, thereby, the efficiency of variable factor will be increased (indicated by the rise in MPP).
- ☆ ***Division of labour:*** The farmer can go for specialization or division of labour with the variable factor he employs at the initial stage of production function and due to better organizational methods, increasing MRs can be experienced. However, this is not possible, if the scale of production is small. If the scale of production is considerably large, specialization or division of labour can be introduced in the production programme, leading to economies of scale, implying increasing MRs.
- ☆ ***Efficient use of fixed factor:*** When more and more of a variable factor is added to the fixed factor, the fixed factor can be effectively utilized and this leads to rise in production at rapid pace. This is because, at the initial stage of production, the large quantities of fixed factor remain unutilized (say, machinery) and when variable factor is increased, it ensures fuller utilization of fixed factor and this leads to rise in TPP.
- ☆ ***Indivisibility of fixed factor:*** It is difficult to employ the fixed factor in requisite quantity suiting the levels of variable factor employed in the production programme, because of 'indivisibility' of the fixed factor. This means that, the allocation of fixed factor cannot be divided in accordance with the level of variable factor and level of output to be produced and hence, a certain quantity of fixed factor has to be employed irrespective of the level of output. For example, processing machinery in a sugar factory is capable of processing say, 1000 units of sugar cane in a day. But, it is

actually utilized to process only 700 units of sugar cane due to less availability of raw material. So, certain capacity of the processing machinery remains idle and this is due to indivisibility of the machinery. Similarly, certain costs are fixed in a business unit, whether the production is more or less or even nil, such as, rent of factory, wages or salaries of permanent employees *etc.*, and this infers the indivisibility of the fixed factor in the production programme. So, by adding more and more of a variable factor, the fixed factor will be better utilized and the increase in production will lead to decline in fixed cost per unit of product produced from the factory.

- ☆ ***Economies of scale:*** Both internal and external economies of scale result in the increasing MRs in the production programme. Internal economies are those, which arise in a particular firm as a result of expansion of output and large scale operation. It includes indivisibility of machinery, employment of skilled labour (specialization of labour), efficient management *etc.* External economies arise for the industry as a whole, as a consequence of the expansion of that industry and are shared by all the firms in that industry.

Reasons for Constant MRs

The concept of constant MRs is seen in stage I and it is a transition phase from increasing MRs to diminishing MRs. The reasons for this constant MRs are given below.

- ☆ ***Optimum utilization of variable factor:*** The allocation of variable factor in the production programme is at optimum level and this ensures its efficient utilization in proper combination with the fixed factor.
- ☆ ***Ideal factor ratio:*** There is an ideal combination between the variable factor and fixed factor employed in the production programme and this combination leads to constancy of MRs in increasing the returns in the business.

The constancy of MRs is common in industries like sugar industry growing its own raw material (sugar cane), cotton industry growing its own raw material (cotton), jute industry growing its own raw material (jute) *etc.* In such industries, the production of raw materials experiences diminishing (marginal) returns, whereas the manufacturing of products experiences increasing (marginal) returns, thereby, one neutralizes the other. So, we can say, constant MRs is the simultaneous working of law of increasing MRs and law of diminishing MRs. So, the concept of constant MRs is the case of an optimum firm. Below the point of optimality, the firm experiences increasing MRs and beyond the point of optimality, the firm experiences diminishing MRs. So, the point of optimality is the ideal combination of factors of production and it is the equilibrium point of man's ingenuity and nature's niggardliness.

Reasons for Diminishing MRs

The concept of diminishing MRs starts in stage I and continues through out in stage II and the reasons for this diminishing MRs are given below.

- ☆ ***Less supervision:*** As farmer employs more of a variable factor compared to fixed factor in the production programme, the supervision of variable factor on the part of farmer will be difficult and hence, MPP starts falling, thereby, TPP increases at diminishing rate. However, there is scope for profit maximization even when the farm-firm experiences diminishing MRs because, even MPP is falling, it is still positive and TPP is still increasing, but at diminishing rate.
- ☆ ***Imbalance between variable and fixed factors:*** Continuous increase of a variable factor leads to total imbalance between the excess amount of variable factor and less amount of fixed factor. As a result, the technical efficiency of both these factors gets affected leading to diminishing MRs from the variable factor. This is because, the continuous increase of one variable factor makes the fixed factor inadequate relative to the quantity of variable factor and thereby, the additional units of variable factor will have less and less units of fixed factor to work with. So, the excess of variable factor receives less and less aid from the scarce fixed factor and this contributes to diminishing MRs.
- ☆ ***Certain factors remain fixed:*** In a production programme, some factors like land, machinery *etc.*, are fixed in short run and some are variable, thereby, the adjustment and judicious combination of these two factors is not possible and hence, the MRs gets affected.
- ☆ ***Indivisibility of fixed factor:*** The indivisibility of fixed factor contributes to diminishing MRs like that of increasing MRs. When the variable factor is increased continuously, a stage will be reached in the production programme, such that, there will optimum combination of fixed factor and variable factor. If still the variable factor is increased beyond that optimum combination, the MRs will decline because, the optimal combination of fixed factor and variable factor is disturbed and fixed factor is subjected to intensive usage, as it is indivisible. For example, if a machinery in a sugar factory is capable of processing 1000 units of sugar cane and if more raw material is available to the factory due to bumper harvest of sugar cane in that area, then the machinery (fixed factor) is subjected to intensive usage. Likewise, the fertility of land is fixed and if it is subjected to continuous cultivation, the MRs will decrease, as the fertility gets exhausted in due course of time. This indivisibility of fixed factor compared to variable factor leads to diseconomies in large scale production.
- ☆ ***Certain variable factors become scarce:*** In a production programme, even all the variable factors cannot be varied as desirable, because of their scarcity. For example, labour availability, especially skilled labour may not be available in plenty to boost the MRs. So, due to scarcity of certain factors, the combination of factors in the production programme gets disturbed and hence, the diminishing MRs sets in.
- ☆ ***Lack of perfect substitutes:*** The absence of perfect substitutes for the factors further aggravates the problem of judicious combination of factors in the production programme. For example, there is no perfect substitute for skilled

labour to execute the technical works in a sugar factory. Similarly, if the electricity supply to a sugar factory is affected, it will affect the production, as there is no perfect substitute to this factor, thereby, leading to diminishing MRs from the factory. So, since the elasticity of substitution between the factors is not infinite, the diminishing MRs operate in the production programme. According to Joan Robinson, *'the law of diminishing (marginal) returns operates due to imperfect substitutes'.*

- ☆ ***Wrong combination:*** Scarcity of some variable factors and imperfect substitutability of factors lead to wrong combination of factors. The fixed factor becomes less compared to variable factor and this wrong combination leads to diminishing MRs. Further, the units of a variable factor employed may differ in their efficiency.

Reasons for Negative MRs

The following are the reasons for the negative MRs:

- ☆ If still the variable factor is increased indiscriminately, the MRs will decline and turns negative, as it is relatively difficult on the part of the farmer to supervise the excess quantity of variable factor relative to fixed factor.
- ☆ The excessively large variable factor relative to fixed factor also impairs the efficiency of fixed factor due to over exploitation of fixed factor, thereby, the efficiency of both fixed and variable factors will be affected.

Thus, in the Stage III, when there is negative MPP, an increase in the quantity of fertilizer decreases the TPP. For example, by applying fertilizer to an unfertilized field, it will increase crop yields. But, too much fertilizer will burn out the crop, and output will be zero. Thus, any excess of a variable input over and above its optimum is detrimental to the total output. Had the fixed factor is perfectly divisible, there is no possibility of having either increasing MRs or diminishing MRs. This is because, even at the beginning of production programme, the fixed factor is employed in requisite quantity such that, it will have optimal combination with the variable factor. So, the possibility of having large quantity of fixed factor against small quantity of variable factor will not arise at all, even at the beginning of production programme. So, at every output level, there will be optimum combination of fixed and variable factors to ensure constant MRs on sustained basis. In the words of Prof. Bober, *'let divisibility enter through the door, law of variable proportions rushes out through the window'.* The reduction in the level of fixed inputs would result in the entire set of physical product curves shift towards left (Panel B of Figure 2.11) *i.e.,* all the three stages ends at lower levels of output compared to Panel A of the Figure 2.11.

To sum up the above discussion, the operation of LVP is due to the fact that, as we continuously increase one variable factor, keeping the other factors fixed in the production programme, initially, the factor proportions become more and more suitable for the production and MPP increases. But, after a certain level of employment of resources, the production process becomes too crowded with the variable input and the factor proportions become less and less suitable for the production. It is from this point that, the MPP of the variable input starts falling. This production function

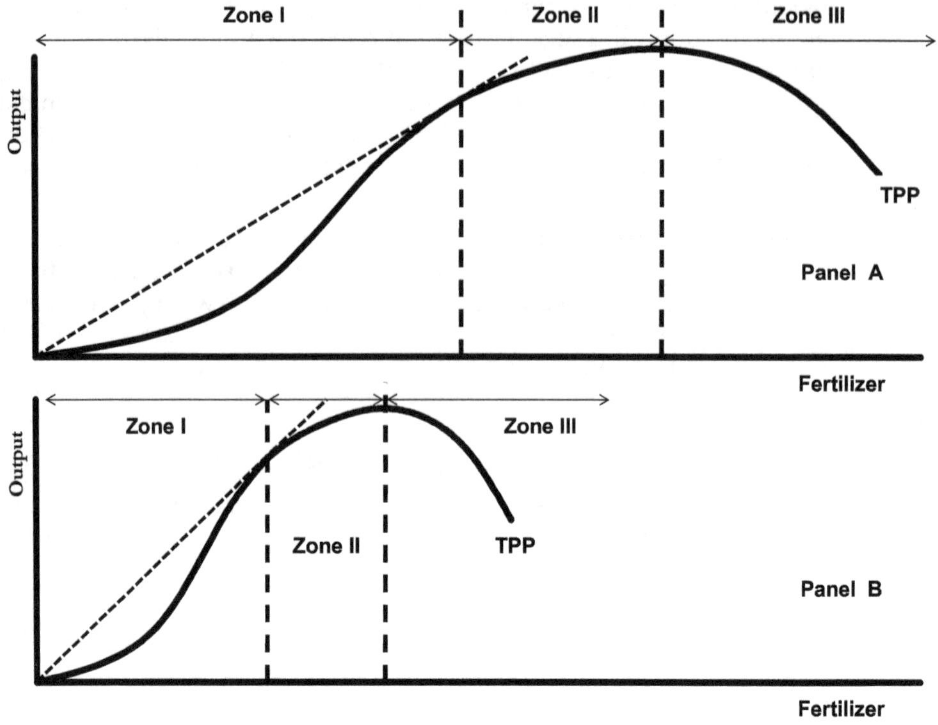

Figure 2.11: Shifts in Stages of Production with a Reduction in the Level of Fixed Inputs.

with all four 'shape' types in the described order, like the one shown through Figure 2.8 is referred to as the Neo-Classical Production Function. This type of production function has especially been used to describe production relationships within agriculture.

Limitations

This law will not be applicable,

- When new soils are brought into cultivation
- If there is change in technology adopted by the farmer. For example, if the farmer employs modern technology, the output will increase continuously and the operation of LDR will be delayed.
- If the farmer is having insufficient resources or capital.
- If the farmer goes for scientific management practices like selection of good quality seed, seed treatment, judicious use of manures and fertilizers, use of modern implements, deeper tillage, provision of good irrigation and drainage facilities *etc.*, the operation of LDR can be delayed.
- In the context of globalization and the increased access of the farmers to import modern technology and inputs from foreign nations, the concept of LDR is less relevant as a concept.

Applicability of LVP/LDR

This LDR has both theoretical as well practical applications and they are discussed here under.

- ☆ The LDR forms the basis for Malthusian Theory of Population. According to Thomas Robert Malthus, the growth of food production is at slow pace compared to population growth mainly because of the operation of the LDR in the food production process.
- ☆ This law will guide the farmer that, the point of optimality is crossed, once the operation of LDR is witnessed in the production programme. So, invariably at the point of equality of MC and MR from a variable factor, the producer must continue the production programme.
- ☆ This law is helpful in understanding clearly the process of production through explaining the input output relations. It also tells us that the tendency of diminishing returns is found in all sectors of the economy, which may be agriculture or industry.
- ☆ The concept of LDR helps to explain the disguised unemployment in developing countries like India. We know, capital is a scarce factor in farming and hence, the farmer employs more labour-intensive methods in the production process. As the labour input is too intensive against the scarce capital factor, the MRs we derive from the labour is zero or almost equal to zero. This infers that, even if some labour are removed from the farming, the fall in output is zero. Such type of unemployment, where MPP of labour is zero refers to Disguised unemployment or Concealed employment. So, the concept of LDR guides to withdraw labour from the farming, when their MPP is equal to zero and to allocate these labour services in other productive works such as irrigation works, constructing roads *etc.*, where they contribute higher MPP to the total output in different sectors.
- ☆ The LDR also explains the secular stagnation in developed countries, which leads to slow growth of the economy. This is because, the new investments made on the capital equipment will lead to diminishing MRs, thereby, the new investors in the economy are discouraged, till the new capital investments contribute to production.
- ☆ This LDR also forms the basis for LDMU in the theory of demand and diminishing marginal productivity theory of distribution.
- ☆ LDR forms the basis for Ricardian theory of rent. According to this theory, a superior (fertile) land will earn differential rent because, in the inferior lands, the concept of LDR will be in operation, as the MRs will decline with the increased applications of labour and capital.
- ☆ The LDR not only applies to land, building sites, mining, fisheries, plantations *etc.*, but also to other types of production. For example, in the use of machinery, if we employ more and more of raw material (say, sugarcane in a sugar factory), initially the machinery may yield higher levels of output (sugar). But, sooner or later, the additional doses of raw

material will increase the total output only at a diminishing rate, implying the operation of LDR. So, the concept of LDR is in operation in all types of production programmes irrespective of the sector. But, in the production programme, where more influence of natural factors is there compared to human element, the LDR operates rather quickly (agriculture). Conversely, when the influence of human element is more compared to natural factors, the operation of LDR is delayed in the production programme (manufacturing industries).

- ✰ Helps the farmer in identifying rational and irrational stage of operation.
- ✰ This law guides the farmers regarding the level of resource usage in the production programme at which he can maximize the profits.
- ✰ It also indicates to what extent the output level should be increased, so as to maximize the profits.
- ✰ It also guides the farmer in deciding the size of the farm he can operate with given level of resources.

So, the LDR is a universal law and in the words of Wicksteed *'LDR is as universal as the law of life itself'*. So, the universal validity of this law has elevated the subject of Economics to the realm of pure science. Being the operation of LDR is inevitable in any production activity, it is essential to formulate the strategies to delay the operation of this law. It is understood from the limitations of the LDR that, new technological inventions and innovations is the only remedy to delay the operation of LDR in any production activity. The practical experience of farmers closely follows the concept of marginal analysis. Farmers tend to apply the variable input in small steps. They might test the application of fertilizer (or any input) over a number of years, gradually trying out the level of factor, where optimization of output is attained. As more experience is gained over the years through demonstrations or trials an optimal allocation of fertilizer can be reached. This often differs from recommendations that are given by agricultural extension workers. It is up to the farmers to test the combinations and arrive at their own decisions as to the most profitable input application.

Differences between Traditional Approach and Modern Approach of Returns to a Variable Factor

- ✰ As per Traditional approach, the production programme is subjected to three different laws of returns due to a variable factor *i.e.*, law of increasing return, law of constant returns and LDR. But, according to Modern approach, there is one law called LVP in which, the above three laws of returns operate.
- ✰ The Traditional approach proposed that, the law of increasing returns operate in manufacturing industries and LDR operates in agriculture sector. But according to Modern approach, all the three laws of returns operate as separate phases in any production programme irrespective of the sector.
- ✰ In Traditional approach, land alone is considered as a fixed factor. But, according to Modern approach, any factor can be fixed in the production programme.

2. Cost Principle or Minimum Loss Principle

We know, a farmer employs several resources to produce the output and he tries to minimize the cost in the production programme. He takes into consideration the resources relationships in allocating them in the enterprise or among the enterprise combinations. This concept will be discussed in the ensuing pages through analyzing the Least Cost Combination (LCC) of resources or Optimum factor combination. The other important way that guides the farmer to conduct the farm-business is to analyze the cost structure both in the short run and long run production programmes. We know, production is the result of resources and resource services employed in the business. The farmer has to make payments for these resources and resource services employed in the production programme. From the point of view of the factor supplier, it is called as 'Factor income', while from the farmer or firm point of view, it is 'Factor payment' or 'Cost of inputs'. So, 'cost' refers to the money expenditure incurred by the farmer in his production programme. The determinants of cost of production (COP) include, the size of farm-business, the level of production, the nature of technology used, the quantity of resources and resource services used, labour efficiency *etc.* Thus, the cost of production of a commodity is the aggregate of prices paid for the factors of production used in producing a commodity.

Generally, the term 'COP' refers to the money expenses incurred in the production of a commodity. In the words of Gulhrie and Wallace, '*in Economics, cost of production has a special meaning. It is all of the payments or expenditures necessary to obtain the factors of production of land, labour, capital and management required to produce a commodity. It represents money costs which we want to incur in order to acquire the factors of production*'. In the words of Campbell, '*production costs are those, which must be received by resource owners in order to assume that, they will continue to supply them in a particular time of production*'. But money expenses are not the only expenses incurred in the production of a commodity and there are number of factors and services such as, entrepreneurship, land, capital *etc.*, which are offered by the farmer himself without charging any price or receiving any payment for them. So, while computing the total cost of production, allowance should be made for such expenses. This allocation and use of resources in the farm will influence the supply of output. The supply of output along with demand in the market determines the price of the commodity. So, we can say, cost of the resources indirectly influences the price of the commodity. It is, therefore, essential to have clear understanding about different types of costs that influence the output or production of the farm.

I. Different Types of Costs

There are different types of production costs widely used in the production programmes and they are discussed here under.

A. Explicit Costs

In the production programme, the farmer employs various resources and resource services such as seed, manures, fertilizers, pesticides, hired labour, bullock labour, machinery labour *etc.* To employ these resources, the farmer has to purchase them or their services through paying cash outlay from his pocket. Such costs incurred by the farmer are called explicit costs or out of pocket costs.

B. Implicit Costs

Implicit costs refer to costs of self-owned and self-employed resources. They are also called as imputed costs. Examples include, wages of farmer's own labour, wages of farm family labour, interest on owned fixed capital, rental value of owned land *etc.* These implicit costs are also important to compute the cost of production of a commodity because, had the farmer not employed these owned resources, he has to depend upon hired resources to use them in the production programme. The implicit costs consist of the opportunity costs of using the own resources without receiving any explicit compensation for those resources. For example, the farmer himself works along with hired labour, but does not receive any wages, thereby, he forgoes the opportunity to earn a wage working for someone else. These implicit costs are considered as costs in an economic sense, as they are a part of the firm's costs of doing business.

The structure of farm costs depends on how farm inputs are defined. Farm inputs are either purchased (explicit costs) or farmer-owned (implicit or imputed costs) from previous year's produce (in case of seeds/planting materials) or sourced within the farm household (in case of family labour). The cost of producing one unit of output will depend on the prices of the inputs used, the size and scale of the producing enterprise and the efficiency of resource usage. So, the farm cost structure is the summation of the market prices of all purchased inputs and the imputed costs of the farmer-owned inputs. The implicit (imputed) costs are calculated at what the inputs could have earned in alternative uses.

C. Opportunity Cost

It is other wise called as Alternative cost. Since, it is difficult to measure the real cost, as it deals with troubles and sacrifices of different factors employed in the production programme, the concept of Opportunity cost was introduced. This concept of opportunity cost was based on scarcity and versatility (alternative applicabilities) features of the resources. We know, nearly, all decisions taken in the agri-business involve trade-offs. When a farmer chooses something, he has to give up some other. So, every action and choice made by the farmer is associated with advantages and disadvantages, costs and gains. For example, if the farmer wants to apply fertilizer on one crop (paddy), he has to forego its application on other crop (maize). So, some amount of net revenue that could be generated in the next best use of fertilizer must be given up (maize) or sacrificed due to its employment on the most profitable use (paddy). The net revenue which we forego, when making a choice or decision is called the Opportunity cost of the decision. This concept of opportunity cost was proposed by John Stuart Mill. It is otherwise called as Economic opportunity loss. According to Leftwitch, *'opportunity cost of a particular product is the value of the foregone alternative product that resources used in its production could have produced'*. In the words of Ferguson, *'the alternative or opportunity cost of producing one unit of the commodity X is the amount of commodity Y that must be sacrificed in order to use resources to produce X rather than Y'*. In the words of Lipsay, *'opportunity cost of using any factor is what is currently foregone by using it'*. So, it is the cost equivalent to the returns from the next best alternative foregone. That means, it refers to the returns from the next best missed alternative. This also implies that, the cost of using a resource in a particular venture is the benefit foregone by not using it in the next best alternative use. This is because, in general, the resources are very scarce and hence, they cannot be used simultaneously to produce several products. If we use a resource on one enterprise, its service is missed on other enterprise. The foregone opportunity is also taken as cost and is termed as opportunity cost. So, opportunity cost of this resource is the returns foregone from the next best alternative use. Hence, this concept of opportunity cost arises only when there are alternatives for the use of resources *i.e.*, it is a relative concept. This opportunity cost includes both explicit costs and implicit costs. The concept of opportunity cost differs from implicit costs in the sense that, it is more comprehensive, as it relates to all the resources (both borrowed and owned) whereas, the concept of imputed cost applies only to the self-use of the self-owned resources. Similarly, the concept of opportunity cost differs from outlay costs in the sense that, outlay costs are the explicit costs, which are entered into the record books of an account, but opportunity costs relate to sacrificed alternatives and they are not entered into the record books of an account. The following are the examples to illustrate the concept of opportunity cost:

- For example, a farmer who is producing paddy can produce maize with the same factors. Therefore, the opportunity cost of a quintal of paddy is the amount of output of maize given up.
- Suppose, a person is having Rs.500 and he can invest on shirt, pant, dhoti and short. If the price of pant is Rs.500, shirt is Rs.400, dhoti is Rs.390 and short is Rs.275, then the opportunity cost of purchasing a pant is not Rs.400 of shirt, but the satisfaction he misses from purchasing and wearing the shirt. This is because, opportunity cost is not equal to the cost of next best alternative fore gone, but equal to the returns (satisfaction in this case) missed from the next best alternative. Further, the opportunity cost is the satisfaction he misses from the shirt alone, as opportunity cost is the cost equivalent to returns from the next best alternative only and not all the commodities.
- If a sugar factory owns the land, there is no cost of using the land (*i.e.*, the rent) to the entrepreneur. But, the factory has an opportunity cost of using this land, which is equivalent to the rent forgone by not letting the land out on rent.

Limitations of Opportunity Cost

The following are the important limitations of the concept of opportunity cost:

- The concept of opportunity cost will arise only when there are alternatives for resource usage. If alternatives are absent, there is no opportunity cost for that resource.
- In case, if the resource is not willing to move to other occupations, the concept of opportunity cost will not arise. For example, a skilled labour working in a sugar factory may not show willingness to move to other occupation, thereby, the opportunity cost of that labour resource will not exist.

- Sometimes, it is very difficult to measure the opportunity cost. For example, if a smoky factory is located in an area and it offers significant employment to the people living there, but causing pollution hazards to the people living in that area. Taking the health hazards of the people into consideration, it is difficult to compute the opportunity cost of the establishment of that factory.
- In case of highly specialized capital equipment such as rice mill, mango processing unit, groundnut decorticator etc, the concept of opportunity cost will not arise because, these capital equipments have no alternative uses.
- The concept of opportunity cost assumes perfect competitive market situation, which implies that, the nature of commodity is homogenous. But in realistic situation, imperfect competition is more common.

So, the concept of opportunity cost is subjective. Only the chooser can determine the most attractive alternative for itself from its special point of view. Every farmer will have a different list of things valued in decline from top to bottom due to different priorities. Even for the same activity or enterprise, different farmers take it with different opportunity cost.

D. Social Cost

Economic costs can be calculated at two levels *viz.*, micro-level and macro-level. The micro-level economic costs relate to functioning of a firm as a production unit, while the macro-level economic costs are the ones that are generated by the decisions of the firm, but are paid by the society and not the by firm. For example, if the decision of a pesticide firm is to expand its output, it leads to increase in its costs and these costs are called Private costs. But, these private costs also leads to certain costs to the society, may be in the nature of greater pollution, greater congestion *etc.* These costs which are external to the firm are called external costs or externalities from society's point of view. Thus, private costs are those which are actually incurred by a firm in the business activity to produce the product and these private costs do not always equate with the total cost to society. Social costs, on the other hand, are the total costs to the society on account of production of a product. That means, they are not borne by the producing firm, but are incurred by others in the society. In manufacturing the pesticides say, the firm discharges its wastes into the nearby river and this leads to the following negative implications or externalities to the society:

- The people in that locality have to purchase water purifiers to have safe drinking water.
- The recreation use of this river gets affected.
- Farmers practicing aquaculture are affected.
- Pollution results in tremendous health hazards, which involve costs to the society as a whole.

These problems are mainly due to firm's or producer's negligence. Even consumers' actions can further aggravate the social cost like using the same river water for irrigation purposes, livestock maintenance *etc.* All these costs are called External costs arising out of a firm and directly associated with a production of a product or a service. But, the producer will not bear these external costs, but are experienced by the society as a whole. So, social cost is the sum of private costs and external costs and the difference between social costs and private costs is called an External cost. The sum of both private costs and social costs constitute Economic costs. So, we can write,

Social costs = Private costs + External costs

External costs = Social costs - Private costs

Economic costs = Private costs - Social costs

So, if external costs > 0, then social costs > private costs. Then society tends to:

- ☆ Price the good or service too low, and
- ☆ Consume too much of the good or service.

The Social cost can also be referred to as the Total cost. It should be noted that, these costs are not exclusively monetary, as externalities such as pollution negatively affect the air quality of everyone around the polluted area. It is important that, the externalities may be negative or positive.

Negative Externalities

When social costs of production are greater than that of the private cost of production, it is a case of negative externality of production. These negative externalities will arise when the firm externalizing their costs onto the society, in order to reduce its own total cost. As a result of negative externalities, we see that, the society will be negatively influenced by the actions of the firm. The above cited example of a pesticide firm is the case of a negative externality.

Positive Externalities

In some cases, the externalities may be positive. When social costs of production are less than that of the private cost of production, it is a case of positive externality of production. A good example of a positive externality is say, an establishment of educational institution or a yoga centre in a locality. In the beginning, few people learn healthy habits in a yoga centre. These people, in turn, disseminate these healthy habits among the people within locality and outside the locality. So, this positive externality when added to the private benefit will lead to higher social benefits.

Short Run and Long Run Costs

The costs incurred by the farmer can be conveniently categorized as given below with reference to ***Short run and Long Run production programmes.***

A. Short Run Costs

i. ***Absolute Costs:*** They include: Total Fixed Cost (TFC), SRTVC and SRTC.

ii. ***Per Unit Costs:*** They include: Average Fixed Cost (AFC), Short Run Average Variable Cost (SRAVC), Short Run Average Total Cost (SRATC) or Short Run Average Cost (SRAC) and Short Run Marginal Cost (SRMC).

B. Long Run Costs

i. Absolute Cost: It include: Long Run Total Cost (LRTC).

ii. Per Unit Costs: They include: Long Run Average Total Cost (LRATC) or Long Run Average Cost (LRAC) and Long Run Marginal Cost (LRMC).

A. Short Run Costs

i. Absolute Costs

a. TFC

It is the cost incurred by the farmer in the production programme irrespective of the level of output. That means, whatever may be the level of output or even at zero output level, TFC remains same. So, when there is zero production, TC is equal to TFC. These fixed costs are the costs related to fixed resources only. The distinction between fixed costs and variable costs will arise only in short run because, in the long run, all the resources are variable and hence, all costs are variable costs in the long run. But, the recovery of the fixed costs is considered important in the long run and not in the short run. Hence, fixed costs are also called as long run costs. To an Economist, the fixed costs are Overhead costs and to an Accountant, they are Indirect costs. Firms have no control over fixed costs in the short run. For this reason, fixed costs are sometimes called as Sunk costs. They are also called as On-costs or Supplementary costs. TFC curve is a straight line parallel to X-axis because, irrespective

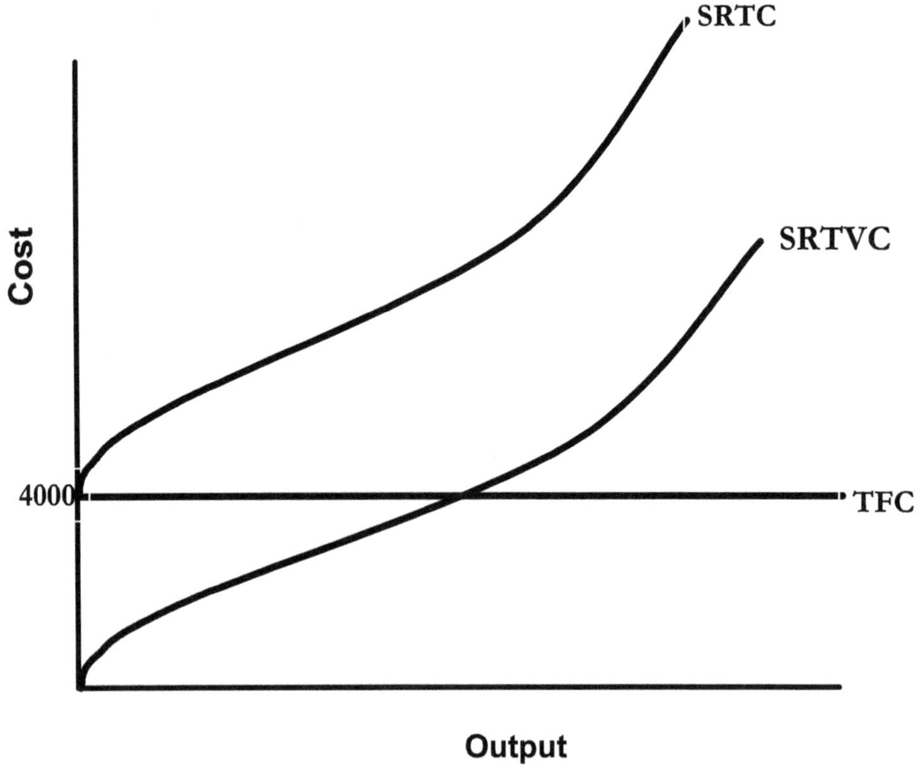

Figure 2.12: Traditional Theory – Short Run Absolute Cost Curves in Production of Paddy.

of the level of output, TFC remains same (Figure 2.12). When the output goes up, the fixed cost per unit of output comes down, as the TFC is then divided between larger number of units of output. Examples include, depreciation, interest on loan amount, land revenue *etc.*

b. SRTVC

As the name indicates, this cost varies with the level of output. So, when output is zero, variable cost is also zero and when output increases, variable cost also increases. These costs are related to variable resources only and they increase, but not necessarily in the same proportion as the increase in output. In order to increase output, the farmer must increase the quantity of variable factors of production that he employs. Therefore, as farm output increases, the farm's variable costs must also increase. The degree of proportionality between the variable cost and output depends upon the utilization of fixed factors during the process of production. The SRTVC curve is an inverted S shaped curve passing through the origin because, when output is zero, SRTVC is zero (Figure 2.12). At the beginning of production programme SRTVC curve rises rather slowly because at the initial levels of output, the production programme comprises of more of fixed factors and less of variable factors. So, when there is less amount of variable resource, they are properly managed by the farm manager leading to higher resource use efficiency. So, due to internal economies of scale, increasing returns or decreasing costs is experienced, thereby, the curve rises slowly. But with the gradual increase in output, the proportion of variable factors in relation to fixed factors will be more leading to diseconomies of scale, which results in diminishing returns or increasing costs and hence, the curve rises steeply at higher levels of output thus, giving an S shape to the SRTVC curve.

SRTVC are considered in the short run because, in a short period, the output of the production programme can be increased by increasing the variable factors only and not of fixed factors. So, the farmer has to recover these costs from the returns in the short run production programme. So, variable costs are also called as short run costs. They are, otherwise, called as direct costs or prime costs. Examples include, pesticide cost, seed cost, fertilizer cost, human labour wages *etc.* But, if the period under consideration is long enough to allow the necessary adjustments in the capacity of the farm, the fixed costs no longer remain fixed and they can also be varied. That means, all the costs are variable in the long run, as all the factors are variable in the long run and no factor is fixed.

It is usually assumed by the Economists that, the variable costs continuously vary with the output. But, there are some cases, where costs remains fixed for each of range of output, but the movement from one range of output to another only, the costs will increase. This is common in case of electricity bills paid by the farmer, as up to a certain units of electricity consumption, the tariff remains same, but beyond certain units of electricity consumption, the tariff changes. Similar is the case of telephone bills, over time wage rates of workers in fertilizer companies *etc.* So, these costs consist of a fixed portion and a variable portion and are, therefore, known as Semi-variable costs.

In normal cases, as we see in the crop production programmes, the variable cost increases as output increases, but this increase need not be equally proportionate. Its proportion first declines, becomes constant and then starts rising. SRAVC also behaves in a similar way. Accordingly, the variable costs are of three types,

- ☆ ***Progressive variable costs:*** If the variable costs increase faster than the output is increased, it is referred as Progressive variable costs. Say, if output is increased by one per cent, variable costs increase by more than one per cent.
- ☆ ***Proportional variable costs:*** If the variable costs increase in the same proportion as output is increased, it is referred as Proportional variable costs. Say, if output is increased by one per cent, variable costs also increase by one per cent.
- ☆ ***Regressive variable costs:*** If the variable costs increase at slower pace than the output is increased, it is referred as Regressive variable costs. Say, if output is increased by one per cent, variable costs increase by less than one per cent.

Note that, the categorization of a cost into fixed or variable does not have a clear cut meaning. For example, seed, manures, fertilizers, pesticides *etc.*, which the farmer applies to the crops are generally considered as variable costs, but once they are applied in the field, they now become sunk (fixed) costs, as the farmer cannot recover their purchase price by selling them. Similarly, the depreciation on machinery is considered as a fixed cost, but in the long run, the farmer may sell away that machinery thereby, he will not incur that fixed cost. Same is the case in case of hired labour. If the labour are paid on annual basis, he may be regarded as permanent labour and hence, the wages paid to him by the farm manager falls under fixed costs. On the other hand, if the labour are hired for a specific purpose for only a limited period of time, they fall under casual labour and their wage payment falls under variable costs. These examples clearly indicate that, the categorization of a particular input as a fixed cost or variable cost is thus closely intertwined with the particular period involved. In the long run, since all the factors are variable (machinery example as quoted above), there are only variable costs and fixed costs are completely absent. However, in short run say, 4-6 months, some factors are fixed (land, machinery etc) and some are variable (fertilizers, pesticides etc).. Over a very short period of time, say, in about two to three weeks, *i.e.,* within a single production season, all costs can be considered as fixed. Thus the categorization of costs of the inputs into fixed cost or variable-cost can be made only with reference to the length of the production period. The greater is the production period, the lower is the distinction between fixed and variable costs; and the shorter is the production period, the greater is the distinction between fixed and variable costs or the proportion of fixed costs to variable costs increases. That is, the proportion of fixed costs to variable costs decreases, as the length of the production period increases.

c. SRTC

It is also called as Production cost. It refers to the total expenditure incurred in the production programme to produce a certain level of output. SRTC is the sum of

TFC and SRTVC *i.e.*, SRTC = TFC + SRTVC. SRTC curve will have the same shape (inverted 'S' shaped) and slope like SRTVC curve, as the behavior of SRTC curve is similar to that of SRTVC curve. This is because, the variation in SRTC is due to the variation in SRTVC only because, TFC always remains constant at all levels of output and hence, they are placed at equi-distance at all levels of output. So, the difference between SRTC and SRTVC at any point is TFC. To illustrate the concepts of TFC, SRTVC and SRTC, consider the example of a single farm operating in the short-run with fixed factors *viz.*, land and machinery and variable factors as shown through Table 2.7. The same data are depicted graphically (Figure 2.12) and they are referred to as Absolute cost curves. As shown in the Figure 2.12, total output units have been measured along the X-axis and costs have been shown on the Y-axis. At a distance of Rs. 4000, we find TFC curve as a line parallel to X-axis. This shows that, even at zero output level, SRTC is equivalent to TFC. From here onwards, SRTC curve rises continuously and in the same proportion as SRTVC.

SRTVC increases with increase in output, but at the initial levels of output *i.e.*, up to 11 units of output, SRTVC increases at diminishing rate, but between 11 and 18 units of output, the SRTVC increases at constant rate and beyond 18 units of output, the SRTVC increases at increasing rate. Both SRTC and SRTVC curves have the same shape and slope, as the changes in SRTC is due to changes in SRTVC only and there is no change in TFC due to changes in output. So, both SRTVC and SRTC are parallel curves and SRTC curve is just the vertical summation of the TFC and SRTVC curves. The vertical distance between SRTC and SRTVC curves is the same at all output quantities. The reason, of course, is that, this vertical distance is TFC. Since, TFC is constant, the vertical distance is constant, thereby, the SRTVC and SRTC remain parallel and they do not intersect each other. In other words, the SRTC and SRTVC curves are essentially the same curves, but the SRTC curve will be higher than SRTVC curve, as it includes the TFC component. This further implies that, the slopes of both SRTC and SRTVC curves are identical at each and every output quantity. So, both SRTC and SRTVC indicate the SRMC of producing additional quantity of output. That means, the slopes of both SRTC and SRTVC curves indicates the additional cost incurred in the production programme to produce an additional unit of output (SRMC). This further indicates that, any quantity-induced change in SRTC must come from SRTVC only, as TFC is fixed at all levels of output.

ii. Per Unit Costs

They include, AFC, SRAVC, SRATC and SRMC. All the per unit cost curves both in short run and long run are 'U' shaped, but in long run, the curves are more flatter than in the short run. In Figure 2.13, short run per unit cost curves are shown considering varying output units on the X-axis and different cost amounts on the Y-axis. All the four per unit cost curves have been drawn on the basis of respective values in the Table 2.7. The column I shows output of the production programme. In column 5, we computed AFC, which is a ratio of TFC to total output. Column 6 reads SRAVC. It is a ratio of SRTVC to total output. In column 7, we computed SRATC for different units of output. It is a ratio of SRTC to total output or AFC + SRAVC. In column 8, SRMC is computed as a ratio between ΔSRTVC/ΔY or differences between successive SRTVC values or as a ratio between ΔSRTC/ΔY or differences between

Table 2.7: Short Run Absolute Costs, per Unit Costs and MPP in the Production of Paddy

Output, Y (Units)	*TFC*	*SRTVC*	*SRTC*	*AFC*	*SRAVC*	*SRATC*	*SRMC*	*Rate of Change of SRMC*	*MPP*	*Rate of Change of MPP*
0	400	0	400.00	–	0	–	–	–	–	–
4	400	250.00	650.00	100.00	62.50	162.50	250.00	Diminishing MC	4	Increasing MPP
11	400	392.86	792.86	36.36	35.71	72.08	142.86	Constant MC	7	Constant MPP
18	400	535.72	935.72	22.22	29.76	51.98	142.86		7	
23	400	735.71	1135.71	17.39	31.99	49.38	200.00	Increasing MC	5	Diminishing MPP
25	400	1235.71	1635.71	16.00	49.43	65.43	500.00		2	
26	400	2235.71	2635.71	15.38	85.99	101.37	1000.00		1	

successive SRTC values. The behaviour of these per unit costs is an interesting and important part of cost analysis. From both Table 2.7 and Figure 2.13, we can better explain the behaviour of these short run per unit cost curves.

a. *AFC*

The AFC is the fixed cost per unit of output. It is obtained by dividing the TFC by the quantity of the commodity produced or output *i.e.*, AFC = TFC/Y. Alternatively, AFC can also be computed by subtracting SRAVC from SRATC, given by, AFC = SRATC – SRAVC.

It is generally referred as 'Spreading the over heads' because, TFC is same irrespective of the level of output and hence, AFC will spread over different levels of output in terms of TFC incurred per each unit level of output. From the above formula, it is clear that, since TFC remains same at different levels of output, the AFC decreases continuously with increase in level of output (Table 2.7). Hence, AFC is a continuous falling curve from left to right giving a shape of rectangular hyperbola (Figure 2.13) implying that, AFC decreases with increase in level of output. But, TFC curve is parallel to X-axis indicating that, TFC remains same irrespective of the level of the output (Figure 2.12). From the Table 2.7 and Figure 2.13, we can also have the following inferences:

- ☆ AFC is based on the values of TFC. AFC curve is seen to be continuously falling from Rs. 100 to Rs. 15.38. However, initially it falls sharply and then with a slower tempo because, at the beginning output rises fastly (due to increasing MRs) and later slowly (due to diminishing MRs).
- ☆ AFC is high at relatively small output quantities and low at relatively large output quantities. That means, with increase in output, TFC is spread more thinly over a larger quantity.
- ☆ AFC remains positive, it never reaches a zero value and never turns negative. It is asymptotic *i.e.*, it won't touch either of the two axes. If AFC curve touches the X-axis, it implies that, for that given level of output, AFC is zero. But, this is not possible because, TFC will not be zero even at zero level of output. It won't touch the Y-axis also, as it implies, AFC is infinity (TFC/Y = TFC/0 = infinity). So, AFC curve will not touch either of the axes.
- ☆ AFC curve will have negative slope through out *i.e.*, slopes downward from left to right. This declining AFC curve is a major reason that the SRATC curve is negatively sloped for relatively small output quantities. In fact, firm that employs a lot of fixed factors relative to variable factors (TFC has a substantial share in SRTC), enjoys a downward falling SRATC.

We can also derive AFC from both SRATC and SRAVC curves. At the initial levels of output, the gap between the SRATC curve and the SRAVC curve is relatively more. But, as the firm expands the output, the gap between SRATC curve and SRAVC curve continuously decreases, indicating that, there is continuous decline in AFC with increase in output. So, from the gap between SRATC curve and SRAVC curve, we can easily compute the AFC. So, the AFC curve need not be indicated in the family of 'U' shaped per unit cost curves, as the gap between SRATC and SRAVC curves

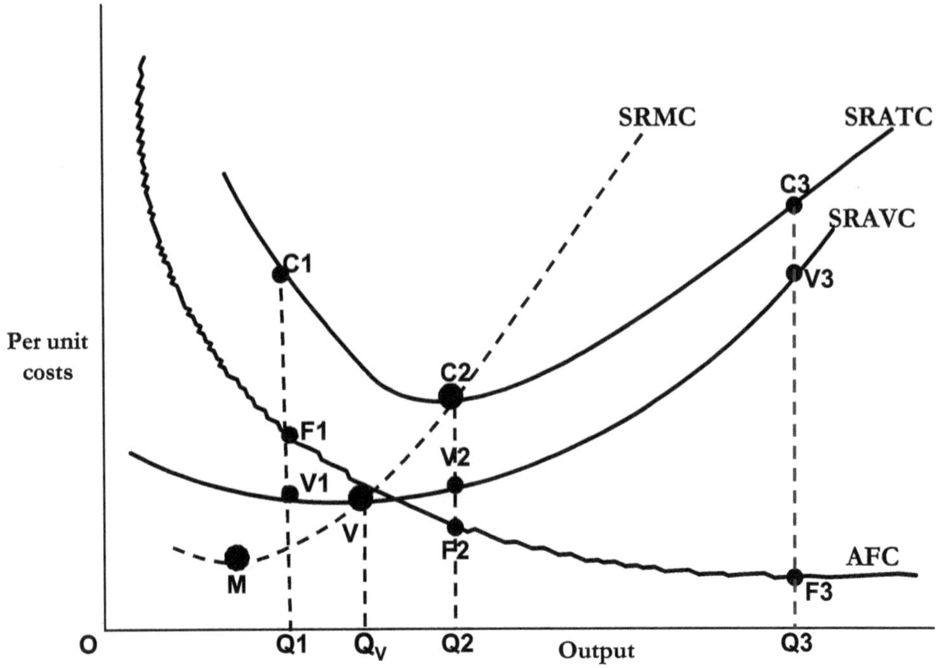

Figure 2.13: Traditional Theory – Short Run per Unit Cost Curves in Cultivation of Paddy.

itself indicates the behaviour of AFC curve. The rise in SRAVC curve further suggests that, it is solely responsible for the positive slope of SRATC curve. On the other hand, the negative slope of SRATC is mainly contributed by the negative slope of AFC curve, though SRAVC also contributed to some extent. From the given formula above, TFC can be computed from AFC by multiplying it with the given level of output (Figure 2.14).

AFC when compared with price of the commodity, indicates whether or not the farmer should shut down production in the short run. If price is greater than AFC, then the farmer is able to cover, at least, fixed expenses. Even though, the farmer might be incurring an economic loss, he will lose less by producing than by shutting down the production. However, if price is less than AFC, then it is better for the farmer to shut down the production.

b. SRAVC

It is the variable cost per unit of output. So, SRAVC = SRTVC/Y = (X.Px)/Y = Px/(Y/X) = Px/APP.

From the above formula, we can say that, SRAVC is inversely related to APP (Figure 2.15). As shown in the Figure 2.15, when APP is rising, it implies technical efficiency of variable factor is increasing and thereby, SRAVC decreases. Similarly, when APP is maximum, SRAVC is minimum. When APP declines, it implies decline in technical efficiency of variable resource, thereby, SRAVC rises. An alternative

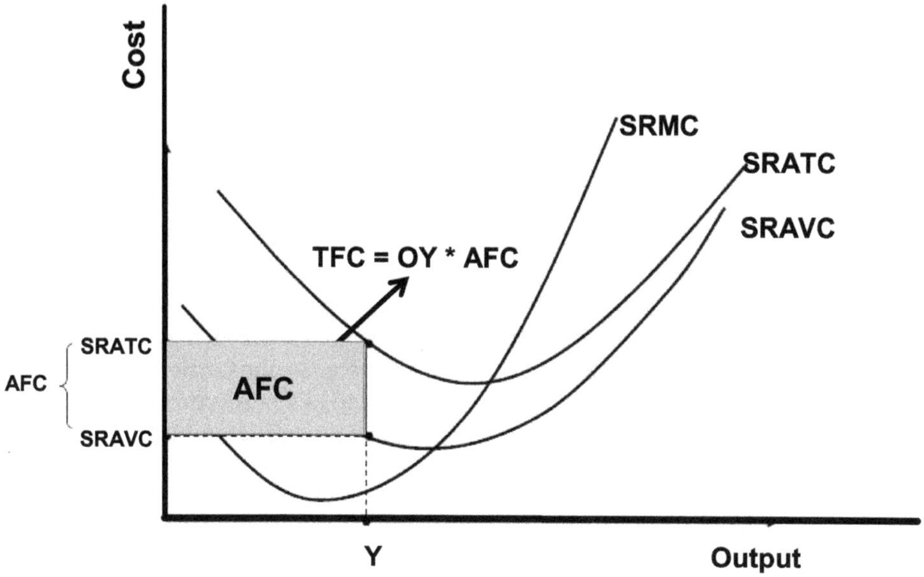

Figure 2.14: Computation of TFC from AFC.

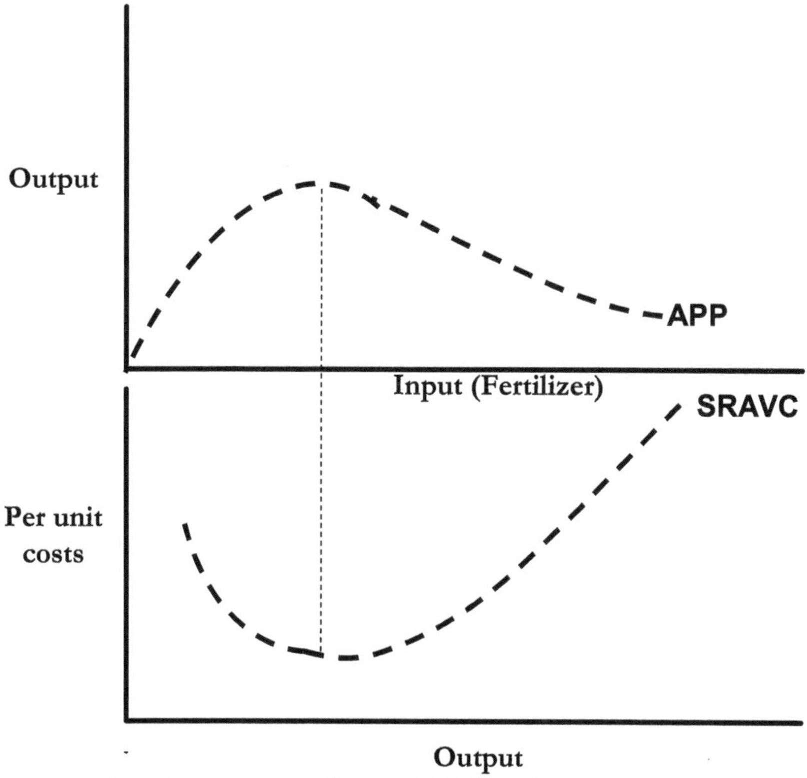

Figure 2.15: Relation between APP and SRAVC Curves in Short Run Production Programme.

specification for computation of SRAVC is by subtracting AFC from SRATC, given by, SRAVC = SRATC – AFC.

From the Figure 2.13 it is clear that, SRAVC curve first falls, reaches a minimum point 'V' and later rises. When it reaches the minimum point 'V', SRAVC = SRMC curve. That means, SRMC curve cuts the SRAVC curve at its minimum point. SRAVC is a U-shaped curve indicating that, it has a negative slope for small quantities of output, reaches a minimum value, then has a positive slope for larger quantities of output. This U-shape is indirectly attributable to the LDR. The negatively-sloped portion of SRAVC is attributable to increasing MRs and the positively-sloped portion is attributable to diminishing MRs. The SRAVC curve falls first because, at the beginning of production programme or when the output is small, there is more amount of fixed resources and less amount of variable resource. So, the farmer can efficiently manage this less amount of variable resource leading to higher resource use efficiency. So, due to internal economies of scale, increasing returns/diminishing costs are experienced leading to fall in SRAVC curve. This is up to 18 units of output and at 18th unit of output, the SRAVC reaches minimum (Rs. 29.76). But, beyond 18 units of output, the SRAVC curve rises at an increasing rate. This is because, at higher levels of output, the production programme comprises of more amount of variable resources and comparatively less amount of fixed resources. Hence the production programme experiences diseconomies of scale regarding management of labour and other variable resources, thereby, leading to diminishing returns or increasing costs. Hence, the SRAVC curve starts rising upwards, thus giving a U shape. It is also clear that, SRAVC remains positive, it never turns negative. It may be zero, when no production programme is taken up by the farmer because, SRTVC = 0. The behaviour of SRAVC depends on the behaviour of SRTVC *i.e.*, if SRTVC are progressive, SRAVC increases, if SRTVC are proportional, SRAVC is constant, if SRTVC are regressive, SRAVC decreases.

The SRAVC curve is most important to the analysis of a farmer's decision to shut down production in the short run. If price of output is greater than SRAVC, then the farmer may or may not be receiving an economic profit, but it is better to continue the production in the short run rather than shutting down the production. Shutting down production entails a loss equal to TFC. When price is greater than SRAVC, sufficient revenue is generated to pay all variable costs and some TFC, making the operating loss less than TFC. On the other hand, if price is less than SRAVC, then the farmer incurs a loss greater than TFC by producing the output. The farmer's loss includes both TFC plus part of the SRTVC not covered by the returns. As such, it is better for the farmer to shut down the production programme, if price falls below SRAVC and await for better times. Like TFC from AFC, SRTVC can be obtained by multiplying SRAVC with the given level of output (Figure 2.16).

c. *SRATC*

It is also called as Short Run Average Cost. SRATC is the ratio between SRTC to output or it is the sum of AFC and SRAVC. So, SRATC = SRTC/Y = (TFC/Y + SRTVC/Y) = AFC + SRAVC.

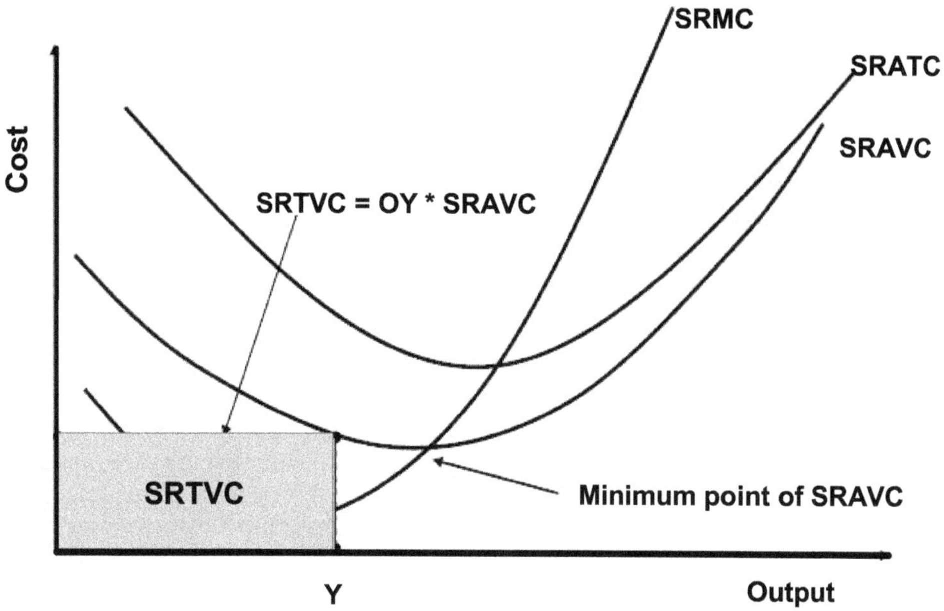

Figure 2.16: Computation of SRTVC from SRAVC.

As discussed earlier, SRTC curve is the vertical summation of the SRTVC curve and the TFC curve. This also holds true for the SRATC curve, which is just the vertical summation of the SRAVC curve and the AFC curve. SRATC curve is a U- shaped curve. It implies that, the SRATC has a negative slope for small quantities of output, reaches a minimum value, then has a positive slope for larger quantities of output. This U-shape is indirectly attributable to the concept of LDR. When the output level is low, there is more of fixed factor and less of variable factor in the production programme. Hence, the farmer can efficiently supervise the variable factor, thereby, the resource use efficiency is increased. This implies that, there is internal economies of scale leading to increasing returns/diminishing costs. Besides these, the fixed resources like machinery, equipment *etc.*, are used efficiently. Hence, SRATC curve starts falling downwards. When the output is reached to a certain level, the SRATC curve will be at minimum. This is because of two reasons:

- There is a proper balance between the levels of both fixed and variable factors.
- The variable resources are used efficiently and fixed resources like equipment and machinery are used up to the normal capacity, thereby, the firm experiences constant returns/constant costs leading to minimum of SRATC. This minimum SRATC implies the optimum normal capacity of business firm or cost of production at minimum level.

With gradual increase in the level of output, beyond optimal normal capacity of the production of enterprise, there is more amount of variable factor compared to fixed factor. Hence, it leads to diseconomies of scale thereby, leading to diminishing returns/increasing costs. Similarly, the fixed resources like equipment and machinery are over-utilized in the production programme (working for more number of hours), thereby, leading to diminishing returns/increasing costs and hence, SRATC rises upwards and thus giving a 'U' shape to SRATC curve. Thus, increasing MRs is indirectly responsible for negatively sloped portion of SRATC curve, the constant MRs is indirectly responsible for minimum portion of SRATC curve and diminishing MRs (which overwhelms the continuing decline of AFC curve) is indirectly responsible for the positively-sloped portion of the SRATC curve.

The behaviour of SRATC curve can also be explained from the behaviour of both AFC and SRAVC curves (Figure 2.13). At the beginning of production programme, the SRATC curve is initially at high level because, there is more of fixed cost and less of variable cost. As explained earlier, initially, SRAVC curve starts falling due to efficient utilization of variable resources. AFC also falls because, TFC remains same at all levels of output. Hence, SRATC curve starts falling downwards. But, with gradual increase in level of output, SRAVC curve starts rising (larger variable factor compared to fixed factor), but still AFC falls. The fall in AFC is more or outweighs the rise in SRAVC curve and hence, SRATC curve continues to fall. This is upto a certain level of output and beyond that, the SRAVC rises more than the fall in AFC. That means, now SRAVC outweighs AFC and hence, SRATC starts rising upward and thus, giving a 'U' shape to SRATC curve. SRTC can be obtained by multiplying SRAVC with given level of output (Figure 2.17).

As shown through Figure 2.13, SRATC curve shows three distinct phases. Between C_1C_2, the SRATC curve slopes downward. At C_2 the curve reaches a minimum point. From C_2 to C_3 the curve starts continuously rising upwards. Thus, two

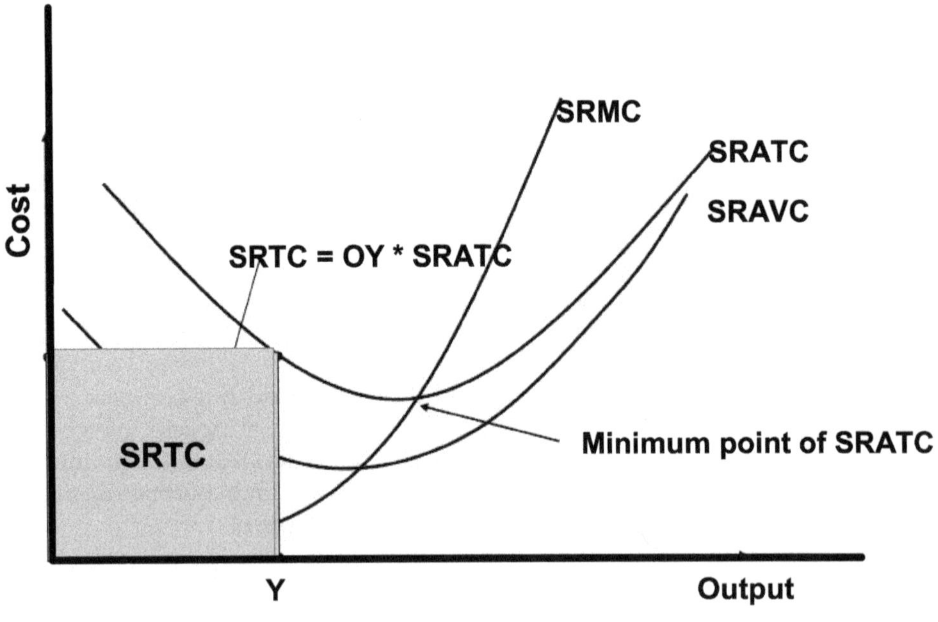

Figure 2.17: Computation of SRTC from SRATC.

components of SRATC are noticeable. At output level Q_1, the value of SRATC = C_1Q_1, which is equal to the sum of F_1Q_1, the fixed cost component and V_1Q_1, the variable cost component. So, $C_1Q_1 = F_1Q_1 + V_1Q_1$. The lowest point on SRATC is C_2. Around this point SRATC remains constant for a moment. At output level Q_2, the value of SRATC = C_2Q_2, which is equal to the sum of F_2Q_2, the fixed cost component and V_2Q_2, the variable cost component. So, $C_2Q_2 = F_2Q_2 + V_2Q_2$. At output level Q_3, the value of SRATC = C_3Q_3, which is equal to the sum of F_3Q_3, the fixed cost component and V_3Q_3, the variable cost component. So, $C_3Q_3 = F_3Q_3 + V_3Q_3$. So, to the left of C_2, SRATC falls (C_1C_2) and to its right SRATC rises (C_2C_3). SRATC, thus, shows the three phases of cost behaviour, namely, the diminishing, the minimum (constant) and the increasing cost phases. In the beginning of production programme, when there is diminishing MCs, the SRATC slopes downward *i.e.*, between C_1C_2. This diminishing MCs is due to efficient utilization of less quantity of variable resources and given fixed resources. So long as fixed and indivisible factors are not used to their fullest capacity, the SRATC keeps on falling. Once the fixed resources are utilized at their fullest capacity and there is proper combination with variable resources, the MCs are at minimum/ constant, thereby, the SRATC reaches a minimum point (C_2). This is the point of optimum utilization of fixed resources. If the output continues to increase beyond this point (OQ_2), the fixed resources get over utilized and the variable resources are in excess (leading to increasing MCs), thereby, they have improper combination with less quantity of fixed resources and coupled with improper management cause SRATC to rise. From the Table 2.7 and Figure 2.13, we can also have the following inferences:

- ☆ SRATC remains positive, it never reaches a zero value and never turns negative.
- ☆ Each SRATC value consists of two average costs *viz.*, AFC and SRAVC. For example, when SRATC is Rs. 162.50, Rs. 100 is AFC and Rs. 62.50 is SRAVC at four units of output.
- ☆ At low levels of output, the share of AFC is more (compared to SRAVC) in SRATC, but at higher levels of output, the share of SRAVC is more (compared to AFC) in SRATC.

It is important to note that, the minimum point of SRATC represents Break Even Point (BEP) because, this point represents the summation of AFC and SRAVC and the equality of Average Revenue Curve (ARC) with the minimum point of SRATC ensures no profit and no loss to the farmer. Further, note that, if the farmer operates at the point of break even, he can continue the production programme, as at BEP, price=SRATC and hence, price > SRAVC (as discussed under Table 2.14. The farmer is not interested in covering AFC from the price of output, as TFC will be there, whether the farmer produces or not.

d. SRMC

It is the additional cost incurred by the farmer to produce additional unit of output. SRMC includes only variable cost because, it is an additional cost made in the production programme. No fixed cost forms a component of SRMC because, it remains same at different levels of output. Thus, SRMC is defined as the change in

SRTC or SRTVC resulting from an incremental change in output. For an incremental change in output, SRMC is given by:

SRMC = ΔSRTC/ΔY = ΔSRTVC/ΔY = ΔX.Px/ΔY = Px/MPP [since, ΔY/ΔX = MPP]

In the above formula, it is clear that, SRMC is inversely related to MPP. That means, when MPP increases, SRMC decreases *vice-versa*. When MPP is maximum, SRMC is minimum. When MPP is zero, SRMC is maximum and it is vertical and lies parallel to Y-axis (Figure 2.19). SRMC can also be computed from the following formulae:

SRMC = $(SRTC_n - SRTC_{n-1})$ or $(SRTVC_n - SRTVC_{n-1})$

where, $SRTC_n$ = SRTC at n^{th} level of output, $SRTC_{n-1}$ = SRTC at n-1th level of output, $SRTVC_n$ = SRTVC at n^{th} level of output, $SRTVC_{n-1}$ = SRTVC at n-1th level of output.

SRMC indicates the slope of the SRTC and SRTVC functions at a given level of output. SRMC can be defined in terms of derivatives. That is,

SRMC = dSRTC/dy = dSRTVC/dy

For example, a value for SRMC of Rs.10 indicates that, the last or incremental unit of output, cost an additional Rs.10 to produce. Thus, the concept of deriving SRMC from SRTC curve (Figure 2.18) is similar to the derivation of MPP from TPP curve of Figure 2.2. Also note that, we can derive the SRMC curve from SRTVC curve, as SRMC includes only variable costs, as no fixed costs can be varied in the short run production programme. Now, let us derive, SRMC from the following cases:

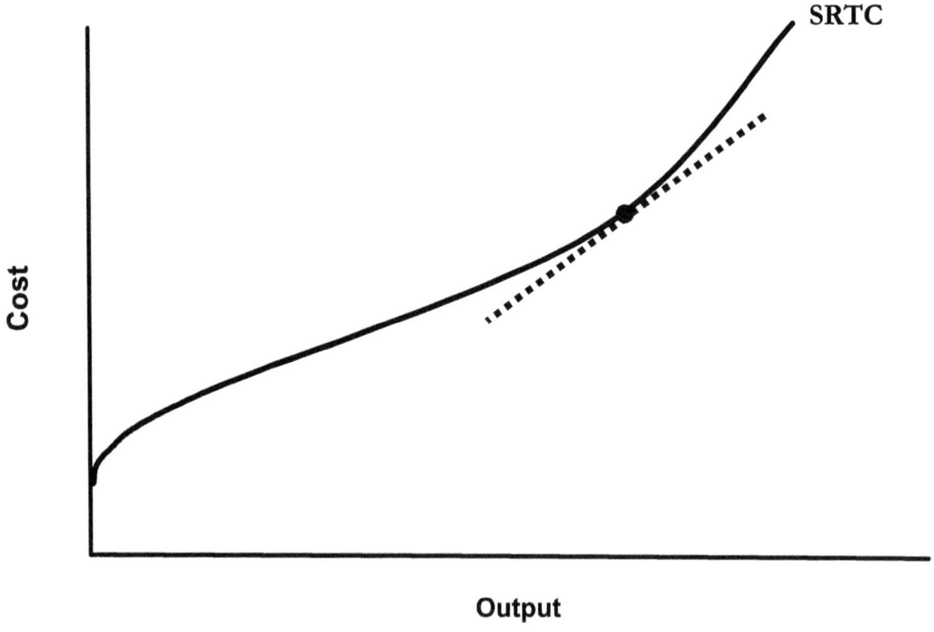

Figure 2.18: Derivation of SRMC from SRTC in a Short Run Production Function.

Case 1: SRTC (C) = $10Y - 4Y^2 + Y^3$, then SRMC is given by:

$$SRMC = \frac{\Delta C}{\Delta Y} = 10 - 8Y + 3Y^2$$

Case 2: SRTC (C) = $420 + 2Y + Y^2$, then SRMC is given by:

$$SRMC = \frac{\Delta C}{\Delta Y} = 2 + 2Y$$

Case 3: Given, SRTC = $1000 - 50Y + 10Y^2$

So, SRATC = (1000/Y) - 50 + 10Y

SRMC = - 50 + 20Y

Considering the above SRTC function, if fixed costs are considered in the production programme, then SRTC, SRATC and SRMC are upward sloping curves. On the other hand, if only variable costs are considered in the production programme say, SRTVC (C_1)=10Y, then both SRATC and SRMC are equal (=10) and they both curves join with each other and lie parallel to axis.

Opportunity Cost vs MC

The following points highlights the differences between opportunity cost and MC:

- ☆ Opportunity cost expresses the relationship between scarcity and choice, while MC represents the cost of producing an additional unit of output.
- ☆ MC always has a monetary value, while opportunity cost can have a monetary value or not.
- ☆ Opportunity cost includes the value of lost time, output, utility and the benefits that might have been enjoyed, if the other choice is made, while MC does not.
- ☆ MCs are visible, while opportunity costs are not.
- ☆ MC is the cost incurred during the production of a unit output, while opportunity cost is the cost incurred during the producer's or consumer's choice of which resource to use or product to buy respectively.

Relation between SRMC and MPP in the Short Run Production Programme

From the Table 2.7, it is interesting that, SRMC behaviour shows three phases of change *i.e.*, diminishing SRMC, constant SRMC and increasing SRMC. Initially, up to 11 units of output, the SRMC decreases from Rs.250 to Rs. 143. Then, between 11 to 18 units of output, SRMC remains constant at Rs. 143. Finally, above 18 units of output, SRMC continuously increases from Rs.143 to Rs.1000. These three phases are marked as diminishing SRMC, constant SRMC and increasing SRMC respectively and they exactly correspond with increasing MPP or MRs, constant MPP or MRs and diminishing MPP or MRs on the output or returns side. This infers that, when returns diminish, costs increase and both are constant for the same units of output.

Regarding the shapes of SRMC and MPP curves, the U-shape of the SRMC curve is closely related to the hump-shape of the MPP curve (Figure 2.19). The increasing portion of the MPP curve corresponds with the decreasing portion of the SRMC curve. This is because, each additional unit of an input is increasingly more productive, thereby, a given quantity of output can be produced with lesser quantity of variable input. The decreasing portion of the MPP curve corresponds with the increasing portion of the SRMC curve. This is because, each additional unit of an input is less and less productive, thereby, a given quantity of output can be produced only with higher quantity of variable input. The peak of the MPP curve corresponds with the minimum of the SRMC curve. So, the variable cost is associated with the cost of employing a variable unit in the short run production programme and this guides to form the relationship between MPP and SRMC curves. As shown through Figure 2.19:

- ☆ The MPP curve in the Panel A has a distinctive hump-shape, with MPP rising, reaching a peak, then falling. The rising portion of the MPP curve is the result of law of increasing MRs. The falling portion is attributable to diminishing MRs.

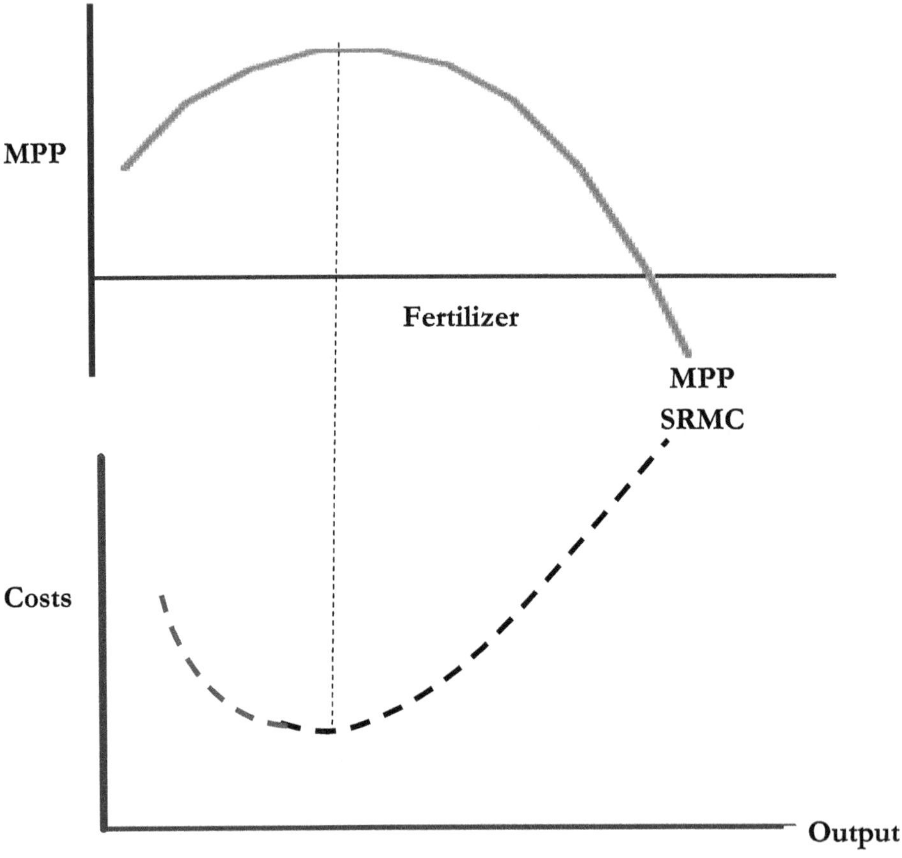

Figure 2.19: Relation between MPP and SRMC Curves in Short Run Production Programme.

- ☆ The SRMC curve in the Panel B has a distinctive U-shape, with SRMC initially falling, reaching a minimum and then rising. The falling portion of the SRMC curve is the result of increasing MRs. The rising portion is attributable to diminishing MRs.
- ☆ The quantity of output at which SRMC of additional input is minimum is the same quantity of output produced by variable input when the MPP of that variable input is at a maximum.
- ☆ Over the range of output, in which MPP increases, then the variable input experiences increasing MRs, thereby, SRMC declines.
- ☆ Over the range of output, in which MPP falls, then the variable input experiences diminishing MRs, thereby, SRMC rises.

The above relationships infer that, the correspondence between the MPP and SRMC of a variable input is guided by the concept of LDR.

Relation between SRMC and SRTC

As the shape of the SRMC curve is influenced by the concept of LDR, the same concept also influences the shape of the SRTC curve (as the slope of SRTC is SRMC). The flattening slope of the SRTC curve for small quantities of output is due to

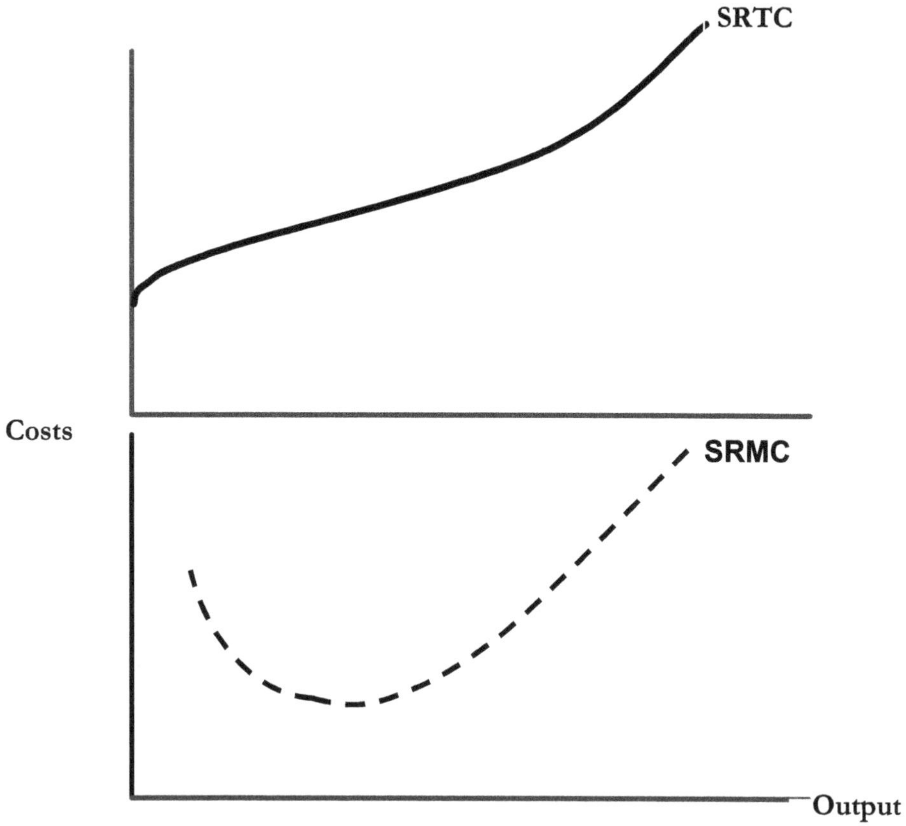

Figure 2.20: Relation between SRTC and SRMC Curves in a Production Programme.

increasing MRs (Figure 2.20). However, with the onset of the diminishing MRs causes the SRTC curve to rise steeply. Hence, SRTC curve rises less rapidly than output at output levels below Y and more rapidly at higher output levels *i.e.*, beyond Y (Figure 2.21). As a consequence, the SRMC and SRATC curves are U-shaped. We already know that, SRMC cuts SRATC at its lowest (minimum) point *i.e.*, at output level Y. The following are the conclusions from both the Figures 2.20 and 2.21:

- ☆ If the SRTC curve has a positive slope, then SRMC curve also show positive slope.
- ☆ If the SRTC curve has a positive and increasingly steeper slope, then the SRMC curve is positive and rising.
- ☆ If the SRTC curve has a positive and increasingly flatter slope, then the SRMC curve is positive, but falling.

It is important that, the above relation between SRMC and SRTC also holds good between SRMC and SRTVC. This is because, any change in SRTVC is due to change in SRMC and any change in SRTC is due to change in SRTVC, as TFC is fixed at all levels of output. This also infers that, the slopes of both SRTVC and SRTC indicates SRMC.

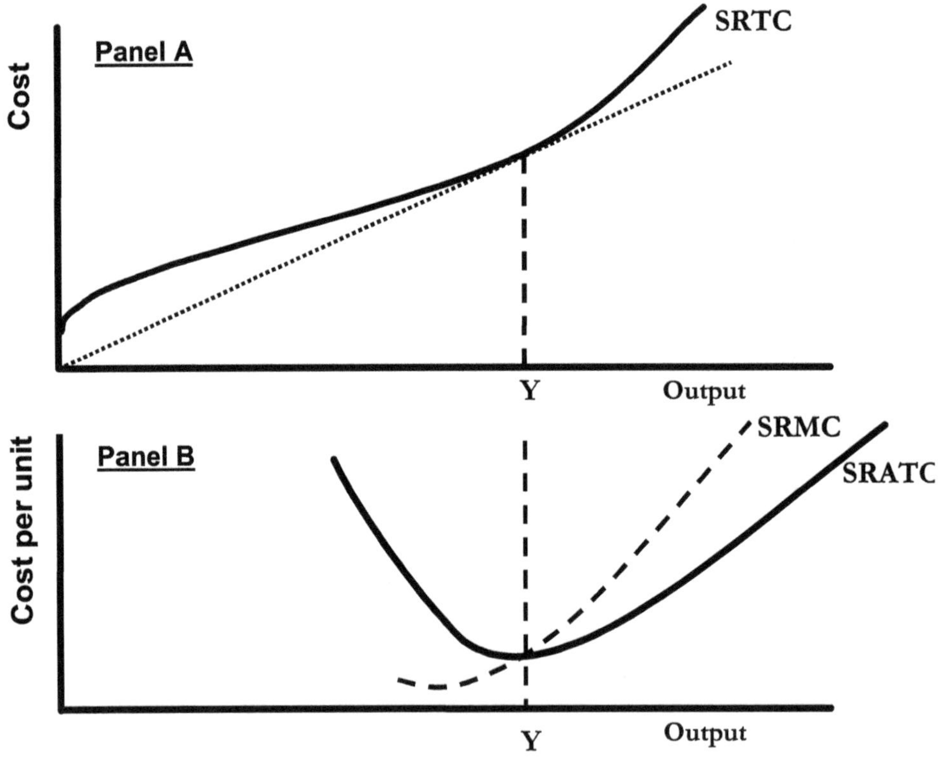

Figure 2.21: Relation between SRTC, SRMC and SRATC Curves.

Relation between SRMC and SRAVC

We know, SRMC can also be expressed as SRMC = $SRTC_n - SRTC_{n-1}$ or $SRTVC_n - SRTVC_{n-1}$. Since no fixed cost form a component of SRMC, marginal fixed cost is equal to zero. This can be well explained from the equations given below:

$SRMC = SRTC_n - SRTC_{n-1} \longrightarrow$ *Equation 2.1*

$SRTC_n = TFC + SRTVC_n \longrightarrow$ *Equation 2.2*

$SRTC_{n-1} = TFC + SRTVC_{n-1} \longrightarrow$ *Equation 2.3*

Substituting the equations 2.2 and 2.3 in 2.1, we get

$SRMC = (TFC + SRTVC_n) - (TFC + SRTVC_{n-1})$

$SRMC = TFC + SRTVC_n - TFC - SRTVC_{n-1}$

$SRMC = SRTVC_n - SRTVC_{n-1} \longrightarrow$ *Equation 2.4*

So, from the above Equation 2.4, we can say that, SRMC includes only variable cost and no fixed cost. Thus, SRMC is independent of fixed cost and an increase in SRMC is due to increase in SRTVC.

The behaviour of SRMC curve resembles the behaviour of SRAVC curve. This is because, SRMC includes only variable cost. The SRMC curve is U-shaped. It is relatively high at small quantities of output, then as the output increases, SRMC declines, reaches a minimum value, then rises. So, SRMC curve is constructed to study the relation between SRMC and the level of output, holding other variables, like technology and factor prices constant. The 'U' shape of SRMC curve is directly attributable to increasing and then diminishing MRs of the concept of LDR. That means, as the production programme experiences increasing MRs, the SRMC falls and when the production programme experiences diminishing MRs, the SRMC rises., thus giving a 'U' shape to the SRMC curve. So, the negatively-sloping portion of the SRMC curve coincides exactly with increasing MRs of stage I of production function and the positively-sloping portion of the SRMC curve coincides exactly with diminishing MRs of stage II of production function. As shown in the Figure 2.13,

- ☆ Below the SRAVC curve, SRMC curve first falls and then rises.
- ☆ As long as SRMC curve is below SRAVC curve, SRMC curve falls rapidly because, SRMC is related to only one additional unit of output whereas, SRAVC is related to all the units of output.
- ☆ While rising, SRMC curve intersects SRAVC curve at its minimum point 'V' and beyond that point, SRAVC curve starts rising.
- ☆ When SRMC curve is above SRAVC, SRMC rises rapidly because, SRMC is related to only one additional unit of output whereas, SRAVC is related to all the units of output.
- ☆ Thus, when SRAVC curve is declining or negatively sloped, the SRMC curve is below the SRAVC curve. But, when SRAVC curve is rising or positively sloped, the SRMC curve is above the SRAVC curve. This is in accordance with the marginal-average rule.

Relationship between SRMC and SRATC curves

The relation between SRMC and SRATC also follows the marginal-average rule. As shown in the Figure 2.13,

- The SRMC curve also intersects the SRATC curve at its minimum point.
- When SRATC curve falls, SRMC curve is below the SRATC curve. But, the fall in SRATC is less when compared to the fall in SRMC because, SRATC is related to all units of output, whereas, SRMC is related to only one additional unit of output. Hence, SRMC falls steeply when compared to SRATC. This is shown in the Figure 2.13 where, SRMC curve reaches the minimum point 'M' quickly and whereas, SRATC curves reaches the minimum point 'C_2' rather slowly. So, when SRMC falls, SRATC also falls and the fall in SRMC is faster than fall in SRATC. Thus, if the slope of SRATC is negative, SRMC must be less than SRATC.
- When SRMC increases, SRATC continues to fall up to a certain level of output *i.e.*, up to its minimum point 'C_2' and SRATC lies above SRMC. This is because, the fixed resources are used very efficiently to increase the output, but the SRMC or additional cost incurred is not productive enough in producing more of additional output, as indicated by the rise in SRMC curve. However, the rise in SRMC should not be above the SRATC of all the preceding units of inputs. So, this implies that, when SRMC is increased, still SRATC falls.
- At the minimum point of SRATC *i.e.*, 'C_2', SRMC intersects the SRATC curve. So, SRMC curve touches the SRATC curve at its minimum point implying that, at that minimum point of SRATC, both SRMC and SRATC are equal and SRATC remains constant. So, when SRATC is constant, SRMC must be constant. Thus, if the slope of SRATC is zero, SRATC is at its minimum and SRMC must equal to SRATC *i.e.*, SRMC intersects SRATC at its minimum from below.
- When SRMC rises above SRATC, SRATC also rises, but at a slower pace compared to SRMC *i.e.*, when SRMC is above SRATC, SRMC rises faster than SRATC. This is because, SRMC is related to only one additional unit of output whereas, SRATC is related to all the units of output. So, this implies that, SRMC rises at a faster pace, whereas, SRATC rises at slower pace. Thus, if the slope of SRATC is positive, SRMC must be greater than SRATC.
- It is not necessary that, SRMC must necessarily rise to rise SRATC. Even if SRMC falls, SRATC can be increased, but the SRMC should be greater than SRATC of all the preceding units of inputs.
- Since MC is an additional cost incurred in the production programme, we can write, $SRTC_{n+1}$ = SRTCn + SRMC. Thus,
  - if the SRMC of $(n+1)^{th}$ unit is less than SRATCn (SRATC of all the previous 'n' units) then, SRATCn+1 will be smaller the SRATCn.

- if the SRMC of (n+1)[th] unit is more than SRATCn (*i.e.*, SRATC of all the previous 'n' units), then SRATCn+1 will be more than SRATCn.

So the final the relationship between SRATC and SRMC is shown through the following diagram:

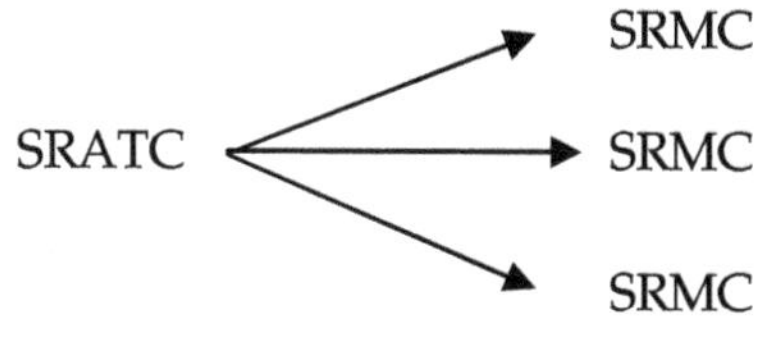

- When SRMC is below SRATC, SRATC falls *i.e.*, SRMC curve pulls the SRATC curve downwards. As long as SRMC is below SRATC curve, a rise or fall in SRMC will lead to fall in SRATC.
- When SRMC = SRATC, SRATC remains constant and SRATC is at minimum point. So, to have constant SRATC, we should have constant SRMC.
- When SRMC is above SRATC, SRATC rises upward. That means, SRMC curve pulls SRATC curve upwards. As long as SRMC curve is above SRATC curve, a rise or fall in SRMC will lead to rise in SRATC.

☆ It is important that, the minimum values of the SRAVC curve and SRATC curve occur at different quantities of output Q_V and Q_2 respectively. This is because of the following reasons:

- SRMC curve intersects each of the SRAVC and SRATC curve at their minimum points.
- At the point of intersection of SRMC curve with SRAVC curve, the SRMC curve has positive slope and this positive slope implies rise in SRMC, rise in SRTVC and thereby, the SRAVC quickly reaches the minimum compared to SRATC.
- Since SRATC includes SRAVC + AFC, the rise in SRMC above SRAVC though contributes to rise in SRAVC due to increase in SRTVC, but the greater fall in AFC outweighs the rise in SRAVC, thereby, the SRATC still continue to slope downwards. So, after a certain level of output *i.e.*, Q_VQ_2, SRMC intersects the SRATC at its minimum C_2 due to downward fall of AFC at a faster pace compared to rise in SRAVC.
- Since SRATC reaches minimum at larger output level (the slope of line drawn from origin to SRTC is minimum) compared to SRAVC (the slope of line drawn from origin to SRTVC is minimum), the SRMC cuts the minimum of SRATC at larger output level compared to the intersection between SRMC and SRAVC curves.

Thus, the family of short run per unit cost curves *viz.*, AFC, SRAVC, SRATC and SRMC have U-shapes. Each is U-shaped because, it begins with relatively high but falling cost for small quantities of output, reaches a minimum value, then has rising cost at large quantities of output. Although, the AFC curve is not U-shaped, it is occasionally included with the other three just for sake of completeness. The U-shapes of the SRAVC, SRATC and SRMC curves are directly or indirectly the result of increasing MRs for small quantities of output (Stage I of short run production function) followed by diminishing MRs for larger quantities of output (Stage II of short run production function). Among these three per unit cost curves, the SRMC curve is directly influenced by the concept of LDR. The U-shaped pattern for the SRMC curve that results from increasing and diminishing MRs is then indirectly responsible for creating the U-shape of the SRAVC and SRATC curves. So, between the three curves *i.e.*, SRAVC, SRATC and SRMC, the basic mathematical relation *viz.*, average-marginal relation exists. The advantage of analyzing the family of 'U' shaped cost curves is that, from these per unit cost curves, we can easily compute the total cost values *i.e.*, TFC, SRTVC and SRTC. This is because, SRTVC is the quantity times SRAVC, SRTC is the quantity times SRATC and TFC is the quantity times AFC. Otherwise, if we compute SRTC and SRTVC from SRATC and SRAVC curves, the difference between SRTC and SRTVC indicates TFC. These U-shaped per unit cost curves form the foundation for the cost and output analyses in short-run production programme, thereby, guide for profit-maximizing production in a firm.

The importance of SRMC curve is discussed in the ensuing chapters, as it takes a center stage in analyzing the point of optimality of short run production function and in the case of perfect competition, the portion of this SRMC curve above the SRAVC curve represents the supply curve of the firm in the short run (and the portion of the LRMC curve above LRATC curve represents supply curve of the firm in the long run). Besides these, it also indicates the efficient allocation of resources, as the decline in SRMC indicates efficient allocation of a variable resource and *vice versa*.

Effects of Taxes on Cost Structure of a Firm

2.1. Effect of Specific Tax

Assume the Government imposed a specific tax of Rs.10 on each product of a food processing firm. This imposition of specific tax will vary the SRTVC and hence, SRTC without affecting the TFC. Due to changes in SRTVC and SRTC of the firm, the per unit cost curves *viz.*, SRATC, SRAVC and SRMC also change, but there is no change in AFC. So, considering the rise in specific tax by Rs.10 per unit, at every unit of output, the $SRTVC_A$, $SRTC_A$, $SRAVC_A$, $SRATC_A$ and $SRMC_A$ rise by the full amount of the tax. On comparing the original cost structure (Table 2.8), the SRTVC, SRTC, SRAVC, SRATC and SRMC rise by the full amount of the tax *i.e.*, Rs.10 in Table 2.9 *i.e.*, after imposition of specific tax. For example, if the firm sells 5 units of output, its $SRAVC_B$ is Rs. 20.4 before imposition of specific tax by the Government and after imposition of tax, the $SRAVC_A$ rises to Rs. 30.4, as the firm must pay Rs.10 per unit in the form of tax to the Government. So, $SRAVC_A = SRAVC_B + 10$. So, when $SRAVC_A$ increases, $SRATC_A$ increases and hence, $SRMC_A$ also increases by Rs.10 per unit of product after imposition of tax. Since, SRAVC does not influence the AFC, there is no change in AFC even after imposition of tax, as the change in SRATC is only due to SRAVC.

Table 2.8: Cost Structure of a Food Processing Firm before Imposition of Specific Tax

Output, Y (Units)	*TFC*	*$SRTVC_B$*	*$SRTC_B$*	*$SRMC_B$*	*AFC_B*	*$SRAVC_B$*	*$SRATC_B$*
1	100	25	125		100.0	25.0	125.0
2	100	45	145	20	50.0	22.5	72.5
3	100	57	157	12	33.3	19.0	52.3
4	100	77	177	20	25.0	19.3	44.3
5	100	102	202	25	20.0	20.4	40.4
6	100	136	236	34	16.7	22.7	39.3
7	100	170	270	34	14.3	24.3	38.6
8	100	226	326	56	12.5	28.3	40.8
9	100	298	398	72	11.1	33.1	44.2
10	100	390	490	92	10.0	39.0	49.0

Note: $SRTVC_B$ and $SRTC_B$ are the absolute costs before imposition of specific tax.

$SRMC_B$, $SRAVC_B$ and $SRATC_B$ are the per unit costs before imposition of specific tax.

Table 2.9: Cost Structure of a Food Processing Firm after Imposition of Specific Tax

Output, Y (Units)	*TFC*	*$SRTVC_A$*	*$SRTC_A$*	*$SRMC_A$*	*AFC_A*	*$SRAVC_A$*	*$SRATC_A$*
1	100	35.0	135.0		100.0	35.0	135.0
2	100	65.0	165.0	30.0	50.0	32.5	82.5
3	100	87.0	186.9	21.9	33.3	29.0	62.3
4	100	117.0	217.0	30.1	25.0	29.3	54.3
5	100	152.0	252.0	35.0	20.0	30.4	50.4
6	100	196.0	295.8	43.8	16.7	32.7	49.3
7	100	240.1	340.2	44.4	14.3	34.3	48.6
8	100	306.0	406.0	65.8	12.5	38.3	50.8
9	100	387.9	487.8	81.8	11.1	43.1	54.2
10	100	490.0	590.0	102.2	10.0	49.0	59.0

Note: $SRTVC_A$ and $SRTC_A$ are the absolute costs after imposition of specific tax.

$SRMC_A$, $SRAVC_A$ and $SRATC_A$ are the per unit costs after imposition of specific tax.

A comparative picture of the per unit cost curves of the two situations *i.e.*, before imposition of specific tax and after imposition of specific tax, reveals the following interesting points (Figure 2.22):

- ☆ The imposition of specific tax shifts the $SRAVC_A$, $SRATC_A$ and $SRMC_A$ curves upward by the amount of the tax *i.e.*, Rs.10 per unit.
- ☆ The $SRMC_A$ intersects the $SRATC_A$ at its minimum in accordance with the Marginal-Average rule. This is because, both $SRMC_A$ and $SRATC_A$ shifted

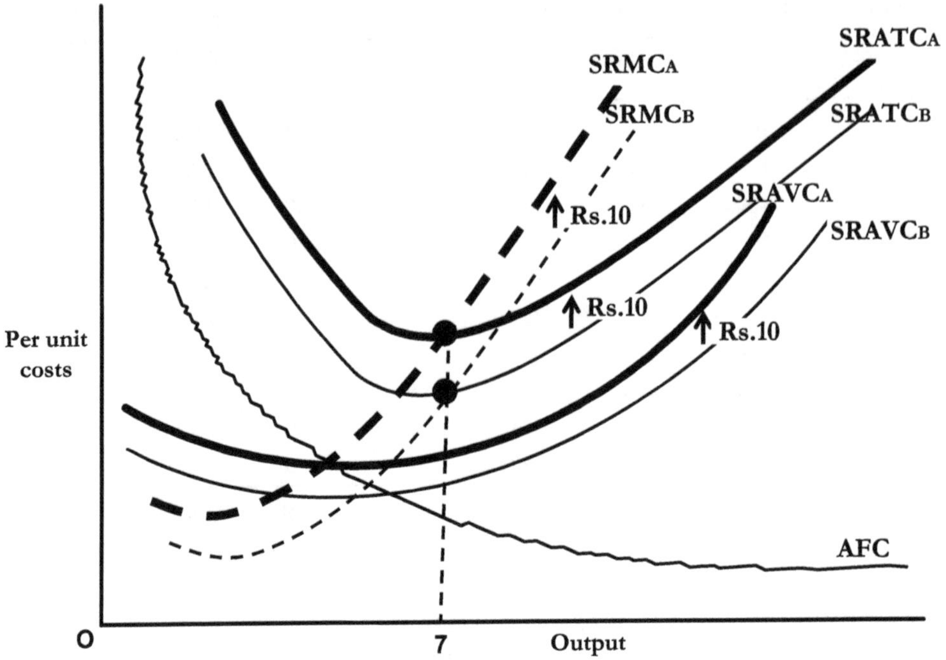

Figure 2.22: Effect of Specific Tax on Cost Structure of a Firm.

upward exactly by the same amount. As a result, the $SRATC_A$ reached minimum exactly at the same level of output (at 7th unit) as $SRATC_B$ at its minimum. At 7 units of output, the minimum of the $SRATC_B$ is Rs.38.6 and minimum of $SRATC_A$ is Rs.48.6. This implies that, by imposing specific tax, the $SRATC_A$ rises over $SRATC_B$ by Rs.10, but it does not affect the output at which average cost is minimized.

2. Imposition of License Fees

Assume the Government imposed license fee on the firm. This fee the firm must pay for the right to operate a business. Assume a lumpsum tax (license fee) of Rs.500 is imposed on a firm and this affects the firm's TFC only and not their SRTVC. On comparing the original cost structure of a firm (Table 2.10), with the change in imposition of license fee (*i.e.*, change in TFC), the $SRTC_A$, AFC_A and $SRATC_A$ will change and there is no change in SRTVC, SRAVC and SRMC (Table 2.11). It is important to note that, since the license fees does not vary with output, the more the firm produces, the less tax it pays per unit of output. That is, when the output is only one unit, tax paid per unit of output is Rs.500, but when the output is 10 units, tax paid is only Rs.50 per unit of output.

On comparing Table 2.11 with the original cost structure (Table 2.10) and through Figure 2.23, the following interesting points can be highlighted:

- ☆ TFC_A was increased by Rs.500 *i.e.*, to Rs.600 due to imposition of license fee (lumpsum tax) on the firm.

Table 2.10: Original Cost Structure of a Food Processing Firm before Imposition of License Fees

Output, Y (Units)	TFC_B	$SRTVC_B$	$SRTC_B$	$SRMC_B$	AFC_B	$SRAVC_B$	$SRATC_B$
1	100	25	125		100.0	25.0	125.0
2	100	45	145	20	50.0	22.5	72.5
3	100	57	157	12	33.3	19.0	52.3
4	100	77	177	20	25.0	19.3	44.3
5	100	102	202	25	20.0	20.4	40.4
6	100	136	236	34	16.7	22.7	39.3
7	100	170	270	34	14.3	24.3	38.6
8	100	226	326	56	12.5	28.3	40.8
9	100	298	398	72	11.1	33.1	44.2
10	100	390	490	92	10.0	39.0	49.0
11	100	507	607	117	9.1	46.1	55.2
12	100	654	754	147	8.3	54.5	62.8
13	100	836	936	182	7.7	64.3	72.0
14	100	1058	1158	222	7.1	75.6	82.7
15	100	1325	1425	267	6.7	88.3	95.0

Note: TFC_B, $SRTVC_B$ and $SRTC_B$ are the absolute costs before imposition of license fees.

AFC_B, $SRMC_B$, $SRAVC_B$ and $SRATC_B$ are the per unit costs before imposition of license fees.

Table 2.11: Cost Structure of a Food Processing Firm after Imposition of License Fees

Output, Y (Units)	TFC_A	$SRTVC_A$	$SRTC_A$	$SRMC_A$	AFC_A	$SRAVC_A$	$SRATC_A$	*Tax/ Output*
1	600	25	625		600.0	25.0	625.0	500.0
2	600	45	645	20	300.0	22.5	322.5	250.0
3	600	57	657	12	200.0	19.0	219.0	166.7
4	600	77	677	20	150.0	19.3	169.3	125.0
5	600	102	702	25	120.0	20.4	140.4	100.0
6	600	136	736	34	100.0	22.7	122.7	83.3
7	600	170	770	34	85.7	24.3	110.0	71.4
8	600	226	826	56	75.0	28.3	103.3	62.5
9	600	298	898	72	66.7	33.1	99.8	55.6
10	600	390	990	92	60.0	39.0	99.0	50.0
11	600	507	1107	117	54.5	46.1	100.6	45.5
12	600	654	1254	147	50.0	54.5	104.5	41.7
13	600	836	1436	182	46.2	64.3	110.5	38.5
14	600	1058	1658	222	42.9	75.6	118.4	35.7
15	600	1325	1925	267	40.0	88.3	128.3	33.3

Note: TFC_A, $SRTC_A$ is the absolute cost after imposition of license fees.

AFC_A and $SRATC_A$ are the per unit costs after imposition of license fees.

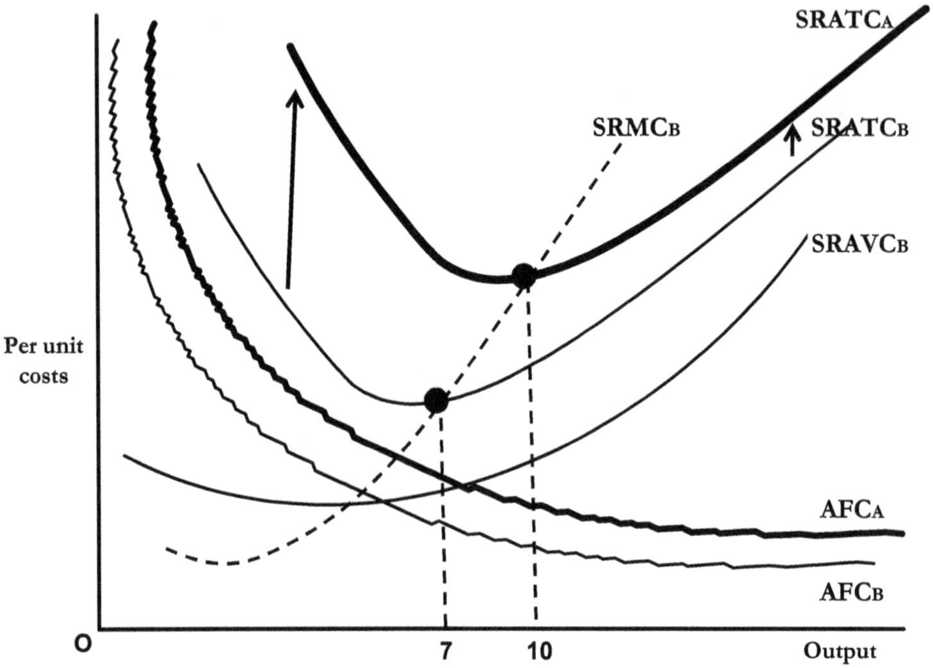

Figure 2.23: Effect of Imposition of License Fees on a Food Processing Firm.

- ☆ Due to increase in TFC_A, the $SRTC_A$ will increase.
- ☆ The AFC_A and $SRATC_A$ will also rise due to rise in their respective absolute costs.
- ☆ Because the average tax payment per unit falls with increase in output, the gap between the $SRATC_A$ curve and the $SRATC_B$ curve falls with increase in output (Figure 2.23).
- ☆ Since the license fees do not influence the $SRTVC_B$, there is no change in $SRTVC_A$ and $SRMC_A$.
- ☆ The $SRMC_B$ and $SRMC_A$ curves cuts their respective $SRATC_B$ and $SRATC_A$ curves at their minimum points. Because the $SRATC_A$ curve lies above the $SRATC_B$ curve, the quantity at which the $SRATC_A$ curve reaches its minimum *i.e.,* 10 units of output is larger than the quantity of 7 units of output at which the $SRATC_B$ is minimum.

Now let us summarize the seven types of costs (*i.e.,* three absolute costs and four per units costs) as shown through Table 2.12.

Table 2.12: Summary of Seven Costs

Sl.No.	*Type of Costs*	*Definitions*	*Relationship with other Costs*
1.	TFC	It is the cost incurred by the farmer in the production programme irrespective of the level of output and it is associated with fixed resources only.	TFC = SRTC – SRTVC
2.	SRTVC	It is the cost incurred by the farmer in the production programme, which varies with the level of output and it is associated with variable resources only.	SRTVC = SRTC – TFC
3.	SRTC	It refers to the total expenditure incurred in the production programme to produce a certain level of output. That is, this cost is associated with both fixed and variable factors in a production programme.	SRTC = TFC + SRTVC
4.	AFC	AFC is the fixed cost per unit of output produced.	AFC = SRATC – SRAVC or AFC = TFC/Y
5.	SRAVC	SRAVC is the variable cost per unit of output.	SRAVC = SRTVC/Y or SRAVC= Px/APP
6.	SRATC	SRATC is total cost per unit of output.	SRATC = SRTC/Y or SRATC = AFC + SRAVC
7.	SRMC	SRMC is the additional cost incurred by the farmer to produce additional unit of output.	SRMC = ΔSRTC/ΔY or SRMC = Px/MPP or SRMC = $SRTC_n – SRTC_{n-1}$ or SRMC = $SRTVC_n – SRTVC_{n-1}$

B. Long Run Costs

i. Absolute Cost

a. *Long Run Total Cost (LRTC)*

a. *LRTC*

It is the total cost incurred by the farmer in the long run production programme. The LRTC increases with increase in output in the production programme thereby, LRTC curve rise upward continuously. Like SRTC, LRTC also rises less rapidly than output up to certain level of output and later LRTC rises more rapidly at higher output levels. Since, all costs are variable in the long run, only LRTC prevails for the long run production programme, as fixed costs are totally absent. Hence, there is no need to distinguish between LRTC and Long Run Total Variable Cost (LRTVC). So, in the long run, LRTC is merely LRTVC.

ii. Per Unit Costs

a. LRATC

As discussed earlier, in the long run production programme, all the factors are variable and no or very few factors are fixed. So, to get the LRATC, the LRTC is divided by the quantity of output produced. So, LRATC is the per unit cost incurred by a firm in a long run production programme, when all the factors or inputs are variable. This LRATC is guided by the concept of RTS. Since, all the factors are variable in the long run, there are no fixed costs and hence, no AFC in the long run. Hence, there is no need to distinguish between LRATC and long run AVC (LRAVC). So, in the long run, LRATC is merely LRAVC. In the absence of fixed factors (as all the factors are variable) the laws of returns *i.e.*, increasing, constant and diminishing MRs are not relevant to LRATC. But, there are two similar influences *viz.*, economies of scale (or increasing RTS) and diseconomies of scale (or diminishing RTS). In explaining the behaviour of SRATC, we noticed that, the negative sloping of SRATC is due to increasing MRs and positive sloping is due to diminishing MRs in the short run production programme. But, in long run production programme, since all the factors are variable, the MRs or concept of LDR will not guide the production programme. Instead, the LRATC is guided by the increasing and diminishing RTS, which translates into economies of scale and diseconomies of scale respectively. Before going to analyze the concept of LRATC, it is essential for the students to have a clear cut idea about the concepts of economies of scale and diseconomies of scale, as they guide the LRATC behaviour in the long run production programme.

- ☆ ***Economies of scale:*** It implies increasing RTS in the long run production programme, where the proportionate increase in output is more than proportionate increase in all the factors, thereby, leading to fall in LRATC. For relatively small levels of output, a firm tends to experience economies of scale and increasing RTS.
- ☆ ***Diseconomies of scale***: It implies diminishing RTS in the production programme, where the proportionate increase in output is less than proportionate increase in all the factors, thereby, leading to rise in LRATC. For relatively higher levels of output, a firm tends to experience diseconomies of scale and diminishing RTS.

However, in terms of economies of scale and in terms of diseconomies of scale, the LRATC curve falls and rises comparatively at a slower peace than SRATC curves because, in the long run, all costs are variable costs and very few costs are fixed and hence, the firm has more control on the variable factors. That means, in the long run, the existing factors can be worked fully and more efficiently with long term planning. Hence, LRATC curve will be more flatter compared to SRATC curve.

b. LRMC

LRMC is the rate at which LRTC changes per unit change in output in the long run production programme. This is given by: $\Delta LRTC/\Delta Y$. Thus, LRMC equals the slope of LRTC curve with reference to a tangent drawn from Y-axis.

Now let us summarize the long-run costs (one absolute cost and two per unit costs) as shown through Table 2.13.

Table 2.13: Summary of Long Run Costs

Sl.No.	Type of Cost	Definitions	Relationship with other Costs
1.	**LRTC**	LRTC refers to the total expenditure incurred in the long run production programme to produce a certain level of output. Unlike SRTC, LRTC is associated with only variable factors, as all the factors are variable in the long run.	Sum of total costs
2.	**LRATC**	LRATC is the per unit cost incurred by a firm in a long run production programme	LRATC = LRTC/Y
3.	**LRMC**	LRMC is the rate at which LRTC changes per unit change in output in the long run production programme	LRMC = ΔLRTC/ΔY

i. Cost analysis in the short run and long run production programmes

It is important for a farmer to recover the costs incurred in short run (fixed costs and variable costs) and in long run (variable costs) production programmes. The following are the important aspects:

- *Recovery of costs:* As discussed earlier, in short run, the farmer incurs both fixed costs and variable costs. So, the farmer tries to recover these costs from the gross returns he derive from the business. But, in short run, due to price fluctuations, the gross returns may or may not recover the TC incurred by the farmer. At times of fall in market prices, the gross returns tend to be lower than TC incurred by the farmer. In such case, the distinction between fixed costs and variable costs in the short run production programme guides the farmer to plan the business. But, in long run, the farmer has to recover the TC incurred in the production programme, as all costs are variable costs in the long run. The Table 2.14 highlights the importance of recovery of costs from the gross returns derived by the farmer both in short run and long run production programmes.
- *Equilibrium conditions of the firm:* Since, in short run production programme, some factors are fixed and some are variable, thereby, the best possible combinations of factors is not obtained. So, only the proportion of variable factors has to be changed to increase the output. Hence, for a short run production programme, the point of equilibrium output or maximum profits is given by, SRMC= MR.

In long run production programme, the point of optimality is Long Run MC (LRMC) = MR. It is important that, the SRMC is influenced by variable costs only, whereas LRMC is influenced by both fixed costs and variable costs, as all costs are variable costs in the long run.

Applicability of Cost Principle

Having discussed the background about cost structure of the firm both in short run and long run production programmes, it is essential to look at their practical applicability and the same is discussed through the following examples:

Table 2.14: Recovery of Short Run and Long Run Costs in the Production Programme.

Period	*Absolute Terms*	*Per Unit Terms*	*Inferences*	*Recommendation to Farmer*
Short run production programme	Gross returns > SRTC	Price> SRATC	Gross returns from the output covers both TFC and SRTVC	Continue the business
	SRTVC< Gross returns <SRTC	SRAVC < Price < SRATC	Gross returns of the output cover SRTVC and part of TFC. So, loss is less than the amount of TFC.	Con tinue the business as long as MR>SRMC
	Gross returns < SRTVC	Price<SRAVC	Gross returns of the output could not even cover SRTVC. So, loss is more than the amount of TFC.	Stop the production programme temporarily. So, to continue the production programme in short run, gross returns (price of output) must at least cover SRTVC (SRAVC)
Long run production programme	Gross returns > LRTC	Price>LRATC	Gross returns of the output covers the LRTC	Continue the business
	Gross returns < LRTC	Price<LRATC	Gross returns of the output could not cover LRTC.	Stop the business permanently and plan for an alternate enterprise. So, to continue the production programme in long run, gross returns (price of output) must cover LRTC (LRATC)

Example 2.1

Assume, three farmers A, B and C plan to cultivate the same crop 'X' and they have the same cost structure. Farmer A incurred SRTVC of Rs. 4000, TFC of Rs. 1000 in his production programme (Table 2.15). He produced 20 quintals of output and he realized a market price of Rs. 500 per quintal. Regarding farmer B, he incurred the same expenses like farmer A in cultivating the crop, though he predicted the fall in prices in advance to Rs.225 per quintal. Farmer C also predicted the price fall in advance and he has not cultivated the crop 'X'. Now, indicate which farmer was adversely affected in the farm business and indicate the reasons. Suggest the measures to minimize the losses in the production programme.

Solution

Among the three farmers A, B and C, farmer 'C' is most affected because, he suffered a huge loss of Rs.1000 to the extent of TFC incurred in the business. This is so because, even when the output is zero (or when no production activity is taken up), the farmer C has to necessarily incur TFC, which is equal to Rs.1000. Farmer A is most benefitted, as he gained a profit of Rs. 5000. Regarding farmer B, he has applied cost principle to minimize the losses by taking up the programme and he has taken up the crop cultivation even when there is fall in price of output to Rs. 225 per quintal in the market. As a result, he incurred a loss to the extent of Rs. 500 which is less than TFC (Rs.1000). This on comparison with farmer C indicates that, the losses are minimized for Farmer B by cultivating the crop even under adverse price situation. So by applying cost principle, the losses are minimized by the farmer B to the extent of less than TFC. Hence, cost principle is also called as 'Minimum loss principle'. On the other hand, farmer C has not applied cost principle and hence, he suffered huge loss of Rs.1000 compared to farmer B, which is equal to TFC because, this cost must be incurred even when there is no production programme.

Table 2.15: Applicability of Cost Principle

Sl.No.	*Item*	*Farmer A*	*Farmer B*	*Farmer C*
1.	TVC	4000	4000	–
2.	TFC	1000	1000	1000
3.	TC	5000	5000	1000
4.	Output (Quintals)	20	20	–
5.	Price (Rs./qtl)	500	225	–
6.	Gross Income (Rs.)	500 * 20 = Rs.10,000/-	225 * 20 = Rs.4500	–
7.	Net Income (Rs.)	5000	500	1000
8.	Selling price per unit of output (Rs./qtl)	500	225	–
9.	SRAVC = SRTVC/Y(Rs.)	4000/20 =200	4000/20 = 200	–
10.	AFC = TFC/Y (Rs.)	50	50	–
11.	SRATC=SRTC/Y(Rs.)	250	250	–
12.	Strategy	Since gross returns (Rs.10000) is more than SRTC (Rs. 5000) or selling price per unit of output (Rs.500/qtl) is greater than SRATC (Rs.250/qtl) the farmer can continue the production programme and he can realize maximum profits at the point of optimality MC=MR	Since gross returns (Rs.4500) is less than SRTC (Rs. 5000), but more than SRTVC (Rs.4000) or selling price per unit of output (Rs. 225/quintal) is less than SRATC (Rs. 250 but more than SRAVC (Rs.200), the farmer can continue the production programme temporarily as long as MR > MC. When MC = MR. No doubt, farmer incurred a loss of Rs.500, but due to application of cost principle, the losses are reduced to the extent of less than TFC of Rs.1000.	The farmer incurred a huge loss of Rs. 1000 to the extent of TFC. So, he should apply Cost principle, so as to minimize the losses to the extent of less than TFC.

Example 2.2

Suppose a farmer is cultivating paddy in his one acre of land. He already incurred Rs.8000 in cultivating the crop. He has to harvest and thresh the crop for which he has to incur Rs.7000. Assume that, there is a cyclone and heavy rains damaged the crop badly and hence, the farmer could earn only Rs.10000 by selling the output. Whether, the farmer has to harvest the crop and leave the crop to the nature in such situation?

Solution

By applying cost principle or minimum loss principle, the farmer has to harvest the crop and sell it in the market. This is because, if the crop is not harvested by the farmer, the already incurred costs of Rs.8000 now becomes the sunk costs or fixed costs. So, the loss would be Rs. 8000. On the other hand, if the farmer had harvested the crop, his SRTC now will be Rs.8000 + Rs.7000 = Rs.15000, and net returns will be Rs.10000 – Rs.15000 = (- Rs.5000). So, by harvesting and selling the produce, the loss will be only Rs.5000, whereas if the crop was not harvested and left to the nature, the loss will be much higher *i.e.*, Rs.8000. So, by applying cost principle, he can minimize the losses. Let us assume that, the cyclone storm is so severe and the farmer could get TR Rs.3000 only by selling the produce. In such case, it is better for the farmer not to harvest the crop, as the loss is much more when the crop is harvested [3000-(8000+7000) = (-12000)] than when the crop is left to nature without harvesting it (*i.e.*, Rs.8000). So, the principle here is, when the expected returns are more than additional cost, it is economical for the farmer to cultivate and harvest the crop though SRTC > TR, as it reduce the losses to the extent of less than already incurred sunk costs. However, note that, consider the recovery of only SRTVC from TR is important in the short run production programme to continue the production programme.

Thus, the appplicability of Cost Principle include:

- ☆ Guides the farmer, whether to cultivate a crop in the season or not.
- ☆ Guide the farmer, how best he can minimize the losses to the extent of less than TFC.

Cost Function vis-à-vis Production Function

The following points highlight the differences between cost function and production function in producing an output:

- ☆ Cost function shows the relationship between cost and output *i.e.*, C=f(Y). Production function shows the relationship between output and input(s) *i.e.*, Y=f(X).
- ☆ In cost function, dependent variable is expressed in monetary terms (cost) and independent variable (output) in physical terms. In production function, both the dependent variable (output) and independent variable (input) are expressed in physical terms.
- ☆ In cost function, output is on X-axis and cost is on Y-axis. In production function, input is on X-axis and output is on Y-axis.
- ☆ SRTVC looks like a mirror image of production function (TPP).

- ☆ Slope of SRTVC function appears to be exactly the inverse of the slope of a production function.
- ☆ The production function (TPP) initially increases at increasing rate until the inflection point was reached and beyond this point, it increases at diminishing rate. The cost function first increases at a diminishing rate until the inflection point is reached and later increases at increasing rate.
- ☆ For both production function and cost function, inflection point coincides at the same level of output.
- ☆ When production function includes a range of increasing (marginal) returns, constant returns and diminishing returns, then the total cost function (and variable cost function) will have decreasing marginal cost, constant cost and an increasing cost respectively.
- ☆ It is important that, when output reaches maximum in the production programme, it is indicated by TPP curve at its peak in the production function (at the end of Stage II). When the farmer still applies the input beyond TPP maximum, it results in double loss to the farmer *i.e.,* output falls on one side and wastage of resource or excess cost on the part of the farmer by using resource that do not contribute to increase in output on the other side. So, TPP curve starts falling downwards and this represents Stage III of short run production function. The per unit cost curves (SRTVC and SRTC) with reference to this fall in output in Stage III of production function looks strange, as they turn backward (Panel A of Figure 2.24). This implies, costs on the additional variable input are incurred, even at output levels that could have been achieved with a much lower level of input usage. This portion of cost curves (turning backward) refers to Stage III of SRTC and SRTVC curves. Once SRTVC and SRTC turn backward, they are no longer considered technically as functions, as there will be two SRTVCs and two SRTCs for each level of output in Stage III of cost function. In such case, SRTVC and SRTC might be thought of as a cost correspondence rather than a cost function.

  Unlike SRTVC and SRTC curves, TFC curve returns along the exact same curve being a straight line parallel to X-axis. This Stage III behaviour of absolute cost curves can also be reflected with reference to their respective per unit cost curves (Panel B of Figure 2.24). Like TFC curve, AFC curve also returns along the exact same curve. Beyond the point of output maximization (*i.e.,* when MPP of resource turns negative in Stage III), since SRTVC and SRTC curves turn backward to represent the new higher SRTVC and SRTC associated with the reduction in output, when variable inputs are still employed, the respective SRAVC and SRATC curves also turn back themselves to represent the new higher SRAVC and SRATC associated with the reduction in output, when inputs are used beyond the point of output maximization. Because of AFC, SRATC is still higher than SRAVC even in Stage III and while returning back, SRATC curve crosses over SRAVC curve. At the end of Stage II *i.e.,* at the commencement of Stage III or rather we can say, when the output is maximum (MPP=0), both SRAVC and

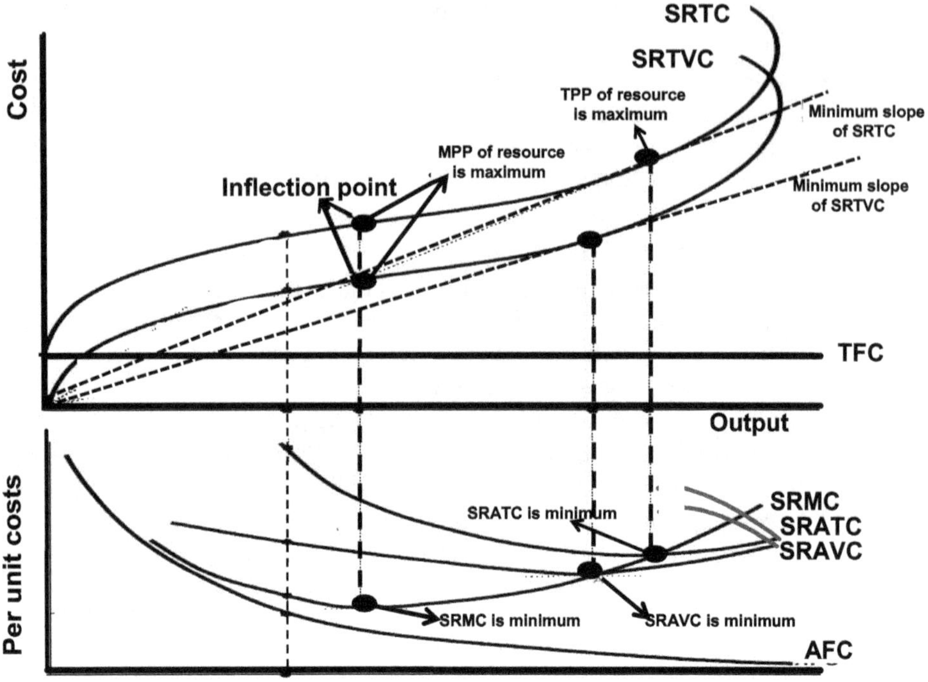

Courtesy: David L Debertin

Figure 2.24: Stage III of SRTVC and SRTC Curves.

SRATC curves are perfectly vertical *i.e.*, with an infinite slope. In stage III, SRMC goes into the negative quadrant as MPP is negative and forms a mirror image of its appearance in the positive quadrant (David L. Debertin).

☆ In (short run) production function analysis, the concept of LDR explains that, each additional unit of a variable input (say, fertilizer) when applied to a fixed level of other inputs, after a certain level of output, it will add less amount of additional output to the total output than the preceding unit of an additional input. That is, after a certain level of output, the incremental output from each additional unit of input gradually decreases. Thus, the (short run) production function explains the concept of LDR from the input side. The cost function explains the same concept of LDR, but from the output side. It states that, as the output is successively increased by one unit at a time, after a certain level of output, each incremental or additional unit of output requires more and more additional units of an input or one or more variable inputs. That is, if output is increased incrementally, after a point, each incremental or additional unit of output becomes more and more costly with respect to the use of inputs. So, an incremental unit of output is produced, but only at the expense of using more and more additional input. This difference between production function and cost function also explains, why SRTVC and TPP are mirror images to each other. The duality of production function and cost function can be well-explained from the following points (Figure 2.25).

- As mentioned earlier, SRTVC curve and TPP curve are mirror images to each other (Figure 2.26).
- The inflection point on TPP (implies maximum MPP) corresponds to minimum SRMC.
- The slope of TPP curve, where APP is maximum corresponds to minimum SRAVC.
- The point of maximum TPP corresponds to maximum TR and maximum SRTVC from that unit of variable input. The point of maximum SRTVC also correspond to maximum SRTC at a given level of output, as both SRTVC and SRTC curves lie parallel to each other, but the latter include TFC that is constant at all levels of output. However, the point of minimum SRAVC occurs at an output level smaller than the level at which minimum SRATC occurs.

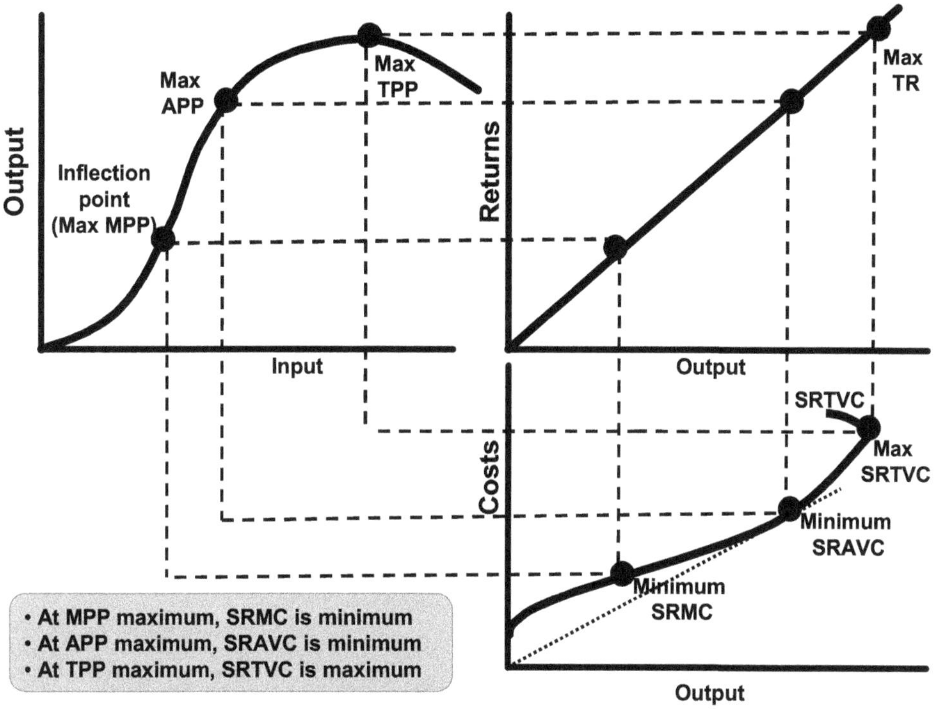

Figure 2.25: Duality of Cost Function and Production Function.

Figure 2.25 pertaining to SRTVC curve shows that, it turns back in Stage III *i.e.,* beyond the point of output maximization and this represents the higher SRTVC associated with the reduction in output, when inputs are used beyond the point of output maximization. This inverse in Figure 2.26 refers to correspondence and not a function.

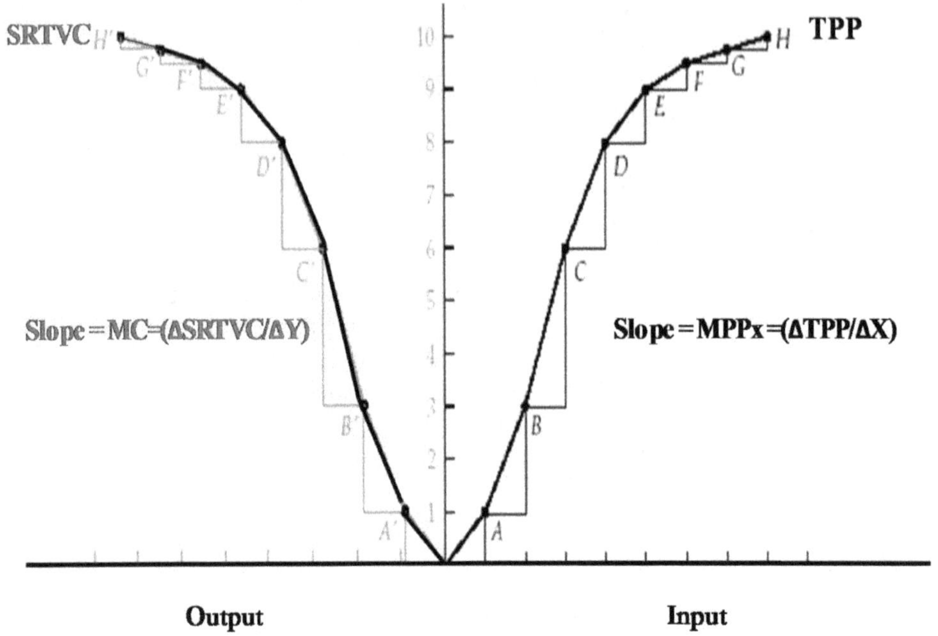

Figure 2.26: TPP and SRTVC Curves are Mirror Images.

From the above explanation, it is evident that, cost function is dual to the production function. Since in production function, we solve the functional relationship in terms of 'Y', in cost function, we solve the functional relationship in terms of the 'X'. Let us go through the following cases:

- *Case 1:* Given production function is: $Y = bX$. So, the corresponding inverse production function is: $X = Y/b$.
- *Case 2:* Given production function is: $Y = 2X$. So, the corresponding inverse production function is: $X = Y/2 = 0.5Y$.
- *Case 3:* Given production function is: $Y = X^{0.5}$. So, the corresponding inverse production function is: $X = Y^{1/0.5} = Y^2$
- *Case 4:* Given (Cobb-Douglas) production function is: $Y = aX^b$. So, the corresponding inverse production function or cost function is: $X = (Y/a)^{1/b}$.

Note that, in all the above cases, the inverse production function contains all the coefficients contained in the original production function and these inverse production functions can be converted into true variable cost functions by multiplying the physical quantities of inputs with their respective input price (P_X). If these functions were drawn on the Y-axis, it will be in monetary terms and not in physical terms. Further note that, not all production functions can have corresponding inverted function in order to obtain the corresponding dual cost function. The rule of thumb is *'any production function that includes both increasing and diminishing TPP will not have an inverse function, but only an inverse correspondence'*. The neoclassical production function *i.e.*, $Y = a + bX + cX^2 - dX^3$ is an example. The MPP for this equation is given by: MPP=dY/dX = $b + 2cX - 3dX^2$. Thus, TPP has both increasing and diminishing functions and hence, this neoclassical (cubic) production function does not have an inverse production function.

Thus, the production function can be converted into cost function by multiplying the inverse production function with price of input. That is,

Given production function Y= f(X)

Then, inverse production function is given by: $X=f^{-1}(Y)$. Now, multiply this inverse production function with price of input (P_X) to get (total) cost function. That is,

$P_X.X + TFC = TC = [P_X f^{-1}(Y)]$.

3. Principle of Factor Substitution

This principle guides the farmer to address the basic production problem *i.e.*, 'how to produce'. Cost minimization is one of the important aspects in a crop production programme. It is essential to note that, mere increasing the output will not contribute to higher profits in the farm business. This is because, market prices are totally uncertain and if increased output is associated with fall in prices, it will lead to declined profits and sometimes, even losses as well. In this context, cost effective production is one measure that will definitely lead to profits in the business. We know, farmer employs several resources in a production programme like manures, fertilizers, human labour, machinery, weedicides, human weeding *etc.* The farmer can employ the combination of these resources to produce an output in the production programme. This use of input combinations in a farm production programme to produce a given level of output constitute factor-factor relationship. The mathematical expression for factor-factor relationship is: $Y = f(X_1, X_2)$, if there are no more inputs in the production process. If there are more than two, or 'n' number of different inputs, the mathematical expression for factor-factor relationship might be written as $Y= f(X_1, X_2/X_3, X_4, X_5, \ldots\ldots\ldots\ldots X_n)$, where Y=Output, X_1, X_2 = Variable inputs, X_3, X_4, $X_5 \ldots\ldots X_n$ = Fixed inputs. That means, almost anything can be produced in many different ways by varying the factor combinations. So, this factor-factor relationship implies 'How to produce'. Determination of the cost-effective technique by employing different combinations of resources for production is an important issue the price system tries to handle. Every farmer aims at using the most efficient productive process. An economically efficient production process is one in which, the farmer uses expensive resource in smaller quantity relative to a cheaper resource. That is, in order to reduce cost of production, he substitutes cheaper resource for the more expensive one. For example, if capital is relatively cheaper than labour, the farmer will use a capital intensive production process. Contrary wise, if labour is relatively cheaper than capital, labour-intensive production system will be adopted. In under developed countries, where labour is relatively cheap, techniques involving more labour contribute to least cost, while in developed economies where labour is relatively expensive, capital-using and labour-saving techniques are employed to minimize costs. So, the feasible methods of producing any given output typically range from those that are very capital-intensive to those that are quite labour-intensive. So, the concept of factor-factor relationship revolves around the following important objectives *viz.*,

- ✰ Minimization of cost in the production programme through alternate resource use combinations.
- ✰ Achieving both technical and allocative efficiencies of resources.
- ✰ Determination of level of output to be produced in the production programme.
- ✰ Production of output with the given level of resources with due emphasis on cost-effectiveness.

In factor-factor relationship, the farmer has to make the choice among the resources that can be substitutable, so as to achieve cost-effective production. In the beginning of a production programme, the farmer poses some questions for himself like: which means of production (*i.e.*, which combination of resources) is best for taking up the production programme? On what basis the farmer has to make this decision? and what could cause a farmer to change the means of production he uses? These and other questions will be answered in the course of this chapter. Further, we know that, one price prevails for a single commodity in a free enterprise economy and hence, only economically efficient producers can continue in the industry. Those incapable of paying resources their minimum reward (factor prices) will either close down or shift to the production of some other commodity. The analysis of factor-factor relationship to ensure cost minimization objective is based on the following assumptions:

- ✰ Farmer produces a single product or output in the production programme.
- ✰ The two factors or productive resources are substitutable. This implies that, one resource can be used a little more and other factor a little less, without changing the level of output. That is, the proportions of factors are variable.
- ✰ Physical production conditions are given.
- ✰ The scale of operation is variable.
- ✰ The state of technology remains constant.
- ✰ Farmers employ two variable inputs; and other inputs are fixed. So, the production function can be expressed as: $Y = f(X_1, X_2 \mid X_3, X_4, \text{—}X_n)$.
- ✰ Farmer is a price taker in the market.

LCC of Factors or Optimum Factor Combination or Producer's Equilibrium or Optimal Combination of Factors

When the farmer can vary the level of more than one input in the production programme, he can usually choose to produce any given output level in different ways of input combinations. If such input combinations are possible to produce a given level of output, the farmer will generally opt for the cheapest way possible. This lowest possible cost on the part of the farmer in employing two resources to produce a given level of output in the production programme refers to the LCC of resources. Thus, LCC of resources or factors refers to optimum combination of factors that ensure minimum costs in producing the given level of output. To ensure the costs are minimum in the production programme, we should be aware of two basic concepts viz., isoquant and iso-cost line. The combination of isoquant and iso-cost lines helps to determine the least-cost technique ie., the combination of resources that minimizes the total cost of producing a given level of output. The farmer can achieve the optimum factor combination by choosing that combination of factors which will cost him the least. The choice is based on the prices of the two resources at a particular time. Based on the relative prices of the two resources, the farmer will decide the use of more of one resource and substitute the other resource. As discussed earlier, a given level of output on an isoquant can be produced using many different combinations of two variable resources. In choosing between the two competing resources, the saving in the resource replaced must be greater than the cost of resource added or the increase in cost due to employment of extra added resource must be less than reduced cost due to replacement of reduced resource. So, such combination of resources usage ensures LCC in the production programme. So, LCC refers to the optimum factors combination, which a farmer can employ to produce a specific quantity of output at the lowest possible cost. So, among different possible combinations of resources, the farmer has to choose, one combination which yields a given level of output with least possible outlay. This LCC can be achieved in two different ways:

A. Marginal Product Approach.

B. Isoquant - Isocost Approach.

A. Marginal Product Approach

As per the Equation 2.5, the slope of the isoquant is given by:

$MRTS_{MF} = (\Delta F)/(\Delta M) = (MPP_M/MPP_F)$ *Equation 2.5*

The slope of the isocost line is given by: $-(P_M/P_F)$ *Equation 2.6*

Putting these two together, we can achieve the LCC combination of resources for any output level, $MPP_M/MPP_F = -(P_M/P_F)$. In this equation, the term on the left-hand side is just the MRTS between manure and fertilizer ($MRTS_{MF}$). Finally, we can rearrange the equation $MPP_M/MPP_F = -(P_M/P_F)$ to get:

$MPP_M/P_M = -(MPP_F/P_F)$ *Equation 2.7*

The above Equation 2.7 can also be written as: $MC_F/MC_M = -(P_M/P_F)$, as MPP of a resource and its MC are inversely proportional as proved earlier.

The above Equation 2.7 gives us another insight. It says that, when you have found the least-cost input mix for any output level, then the MPP of manure divided by the price of manure will be equal to the MPP of fertilizer divided by the price of fertilizer. MPP of manure divided by the price of manure means that, the additional output the farmer derives from spending one more rupee on the manure. So, we can say, MPP_M/P_M as the 'MPP produced per rupee spent on manure'. Similar is the case for (MPP_F/P_F). Using this language, we can state the result as follows: *'When a farmer achieves the LCC of two resources viz., manure and fertilizer, the 'MPP produced per rupee spent on manure' must equal the 'MPP produced per rupee spent on fertilizer' or the $MRTS_{MF}$ (i.e., MPP_M/MPP_F) of two resources must equal to the ratio of input prices (P_M/P_F).* Say, in case of inequality *i.e.*, if $MPP_M/P_M \neq (MPP_F/P_F)$, then the farmer can always shift his spending from one input to another, lowering its cost while leaving its output unchanged. Assume that, $MPP_M/P_M = 2$ and $(MPP_F/P_F = 3$. Then, the farmer can easily save money (minimize the cost) by shifting money away from manure towards fertilizer. Each rupee shifted away from manure causes output to decrease by 2 units, while each rupee shifted toward fertilizer causes output to rise by 3 units. Thus, the farmer could shift money away from manure, and use to increase the amount of fertilizer, and still keep the output unchanged. By shifting more money towards fertilizer means purchasing and employing more fertilizer thereby, MPP_F will decrease and thereby, MPP_F/P_F gets equal to MPP_M/P_M. To generalize, *whenever the MPP per rupee is different for any two inputs, the farmer can always shift his spending from the input with the lower MPP per rupee to the input with the higher MPP per rupee thereby, achieving lower total cost with no change in output*. In other words, *a farmer can reduce the cost in the production programme, by using more of those factor with a high (MPP/Price) ratio and less of those with a low (MPP/Price) ratio, until they all become equal.*

The above explanation is so useful, as it can be generalized to the case of more than two inputs employed in the production programme. This is because, when a farmer employs more than two inputs, it is difficult to illustrate isoquants and isocost lines on a two-dimensional graph. So, the above Equation 2.7 can be used to generalize to any number of inputs. Suppose, the farmer employs 'N' inputs in a production programme, with MPPs: MPP_A, MPP_B, MPP_C, —, MPP_N and input prices P_A, P_B, P_C, ..., P_N. Then, for any given level of output, the LCC of all of these inputs will always satisfy:

$$MPP_A/P_A = MPP_B/P_B = MPP_C/P_C = — = MPP_N/P_N \longrightarrow \text{Equation 2.8}$$

As per the above Equation 2.8, when a farmer employs many variable inputs, the LCC of factors mix can be obtained, when the MPP per rupee of any factor will be equal to the MPP per rupee of any other factor. The economic meaning of the above optimal solution of LCC with reference to Equation 2.8 is as follows: *'if one rupee spent for purchasing resource A results in an increase in production i.e., MPP_A/P_A and is larger than the decrease in production resulting from spending one rupee less for purchasing resource B (MPP_B/P_B), it pays to shift of one rupee from purchasing resource B to resource A. By this shifting of money resource in continuous fashion i.e., with increased addition of resource A, MPP_A gradually decreases and MPP_B gradually increases and finally, the ratio of MPP_A/P_A and MPP_B/P_B becomes equal or $(MPP_A/MPP_B) = (P_A/P_B)$. This is exactly the point of tangency between isoquant and iso-cost line. By doing so, the total output and total cash outlay of the farmer will not change'*. Likewise, the equilibrium can be compared with other resources to be dealt by the farmer in his production programme. The above Equation 2.8 also refers to 'Last Rupee Rule', which states that, the farmer should select the combination of factors, where the last rupee spent on one factor gives as much extra output as the last rupee spent on any other factor. This implies that, cost is minimized, if a factor combination is chosen such that, the last rupee spent on one factor adds as much extra output as the last rupee spent on other factor.

B. Isoquant-Isocost Approach

Economic efficiency in factor–factor relationship is attained when the physical concept ($MRTS_{MF}$) is integrated with the economic concept (price ratio of factors). Thus, the LCC of factors combination can be determined by imposing the isoquant map on isocost line. This methodology is based on the following assumptions:

- ☆ There are two factors (manure and fertilizer) in the production programme.
- ☆ All the units of each factor (*i.e.*, manure and fertilizer) are homogeneous.
- ☆ The prices of factors (manure and fertilizer) are given and constants.
- ☆ The total cash or money outlay with the farmer is also given.
- ☆ There is perfect competition in the factor market.

The methodology employed through this approach can be explained in three ways:

i. Tabular method
ii. Algebraic method
iii. Graphical method

i. Tabular Method

In this method, we will study different resources combinations the farmer can employ at given market prices of two resources and thereby, we can work out the total costs incurred in employing them in the production programme (Table 2.16). The best resource combination is the one that incurs least cost to the farmer. It is clear that, by employing 5 units of X_1 (Manure) and 3 units of X_2 (Fertilizer) *i.e.*, at Combination E, the total cost incurred in the production programme can be minimized, which is equal to Rs.19. Any other combination of these two resources will lead to more cost on the part of the farmer than the above combination of 5 units of X_1 (Manure) and 3 units of X_2 (Fertilizer). So, this principle advocates the farmer to employ above Combination E of resources to minimize the costs in the production programme.

Table 2.16: LCC of Resources in the Production Programme

Combination	*X_1 (Manure)*	*X_2 (Fertilizer)*	*Cost Incurred*		*Total Cost Incurred by the Farmer (Rs.)*
			Price (X_1=2/unit)	*Price (X_2=3/unit)*	
A	1	13	2	39	41
B	2	9	4	27	31
C	3	6	6	18	24
D	4	4	8	12	20
E	5	3	10	9	19

ii. Algebraic Method

The principle of LCC states that, cost will be minimum in a production programme by employing two resources in such a way that, where MRTS of resources is inversely equal to their price ratio. We already know that, slope of isoquant indicates MRTS of two resources i.e, $MRTS_{MF}=\Delta F/\Delta M$, and the slope of iso-revenue line indicates the price ratio of these two resources *i.e.*, P_M/P_F. So, the point of LCC in the production programme is given by:

$$MRTS_{MF}=\Delta F/\Delta M = P_M/P_F \qquad \textit{Equation 2.9}$$

iii. Graphical Method

Generally, a farmer faces two choices of optimal factor combinations or LCC of factors *viz.*, cost minimization for a given level of output or output maximization for a given cash outlay and prices of the resources. In both cases the factors will have to be employed in optimal combination at which the total cost incurred will be minimum.

a. *Cost minimization for a given Level of Output*

Here, the farmer tries to minimize the cost to produce a given level of output in the production programme. Let us suppose, the money with the farmer is Rs. 60 and he has to allocate this money between the two resources *viz.*, manure (Rs. 5/unit) and fertilizer (Rs. 6/unit) and assume that, the farmer wishes to produce 100 units of output (100Y). The earlier discussion on isoquant and iso-cost line reveals two important aspects *viz.*, the isoquant infers 'what combination of resources the farmer is willing to buy' and the iso-cost line guides the farmer, 'what the farmer is able to buy', so as to attain the LCC of resources. So, when the isoquant and the iso-cost line are combined, we find the quantities of each resource the farmer is both willing and able to buy, so as to produce a desired level of output. So, the isoquant and iso-cost line for a given level of output helps the farmer to find out the combination of resources that will lead to LCC of resources. So, the LCC refers to the point of cost minimization in the production programme at a particular combination of resources, given outlay with the farmer and prices of the resources in the market.

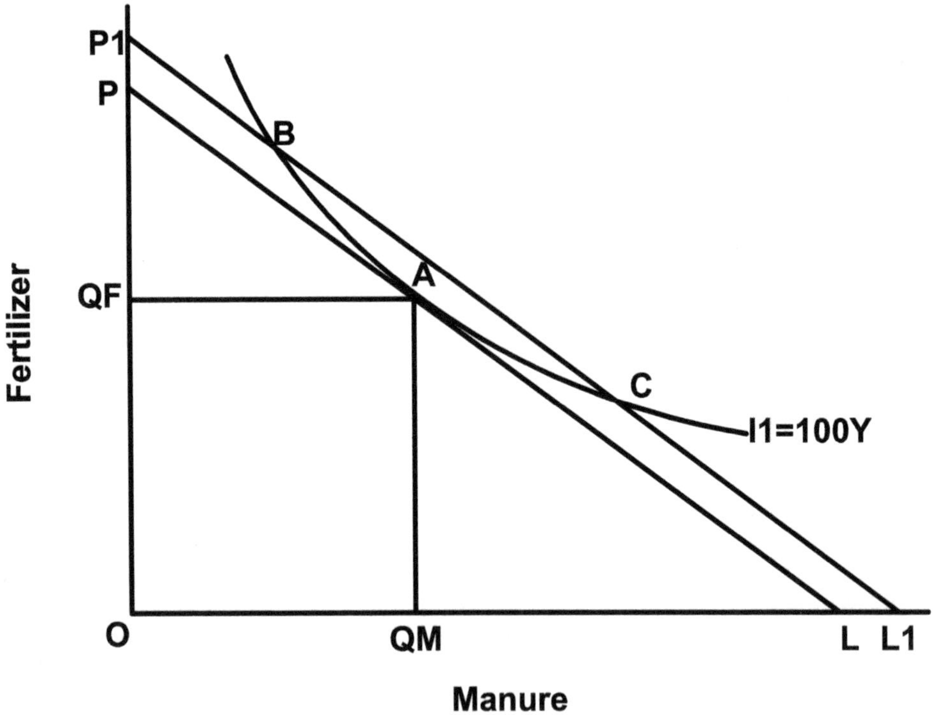

Figure 2.27: Farmer's Equilibrium – Iso-cost Line Tangent to Isoquant (Cost minimization for a given output).

From the Figure 2.27, it is clear that, the iso-cost line PL is tangent to the isoquant of 100Y at point 'A' and this indicates that, by allocating OQ_M units of manure and OQ_F units of fertilizer, the cost is minimum in the production programme. It is also important that, the farmer can allocate any combination of resources below PL iso-cost line, but 100Y cannot be achieved. Similarly, the iso-cost line P_1L_1 touches the isoquant at B and C, but to produce same 100Y, the farmer needs more cash outlay, as these points B and C are with reference to higher iso-cost line.

Thus, given the prices of two resources, resources bundle at points B and C clearly involves the highest total cost compared to resources bundle at point A. Note that, there is no iso-cost line lower than PL that would enable the farmer to produce output, Y=100 units. Thus, we say resources combination 'A' is the LCC for producing output, Y=100 units. Note also that, at point A, the isoquant and iso-cost line lie tangent to each other, meaning that, their slopes are equal. Recall now the values of the slopes of these two curves. The slope of isoquant indicates MRTS of these two resources *i.e.*, $MRTS_{MF} = \Delta F/\Delta M$. The slope of iso-cost line indicates prices ratio of manure and fertilizer *i.e.*, P_M/P_F. So, the point of LCC is given by:

$$MRTS_{MF} = \Delta F/\Delta M \; (= MPP_M/MPP_F) = P_M/P_F \qquad \textit{Equation 2.10}$$

Thus, the LCC of resources occurs at the point, where the MRTS of the resources is inversely equal to the ratio of their prices or the ratio of MPP of resources is directly equal to the ratio of their prices.

This simply tells the farmer that, the LCC of manure and fertilizer is such that, equal increments of output should be obtained for the last rupee spent on each of the inputs. (Note that, if we consider labour and capital are the two resources for studying LCC, P_K do not refer to the price of machine, but the implicit rental cost per unit time period (*i.e.*, the user cost of capital). This discussion infers the following three important conditions essential to achieve point of LCC of resources:

Condition 1: The iso-cost line should be tangent to the isoquant from below

Condition 2: Slope of the iso-cost line should be equal to the slope of isoquant

Condition 3: Isoquant should be convex to the origin

Condition 1: The Iso-Cost Line should be Tangent to the Isoquant from below

The farmer's equilibrium position is only at a point, where the iso-cost line is tangent to the isoquant from below. This is explained through the Figure 2.27, where an isoquant I_1 and PL iso-cost line are tangent to each other at point A to produce 100Y. That means, the farmer attains LCC of resources by allocating OQ_M quantity of manure and OQ_F quantity of fertilizer. Even though, the points B and C on the same isoquant yields 100Y, they are not the points of cost-minimization, as these points B and C are with reference to higher iso-cost line P_1L_1. To put it simply, cost-minimization cannot be ensured to produce a given level of output of 100Y either at B or C. So, we can infer that, at point A, where iso-cost line is tangent to isoquant I_1 from below, it is the point of LCC of resources *i.e.*, by employing OQ_M quantity of manure and OQ_F quantity of fertilizer resources. Note that, the point of tangency between the isocost line and an isoquant is an important, but not a necessary condition for producer's equilibrium. The essential condition is that, the slope of the isocost line must equal the slope of the isoquant. Thus, at a point of equilibrium MRTS or MPPs of the two factors must be equal to the ratio of their prices. Another important condition is that, the isoquant must be convex to the origin *i.e.,* the MRTS of manure for fertilizer ($MRTS_{MF}$) must be diminishing at the point of equilibrium. These two essential conditions are discussed here under.

Condition 2. Slope of the Iso-Cost Line should be Equal to the Slope of Isoquant

The second condition essential for arriving at the point of LCC is that, the slope of the iso-cost line should be equal to the slope of isoquant from below at the point of their tangency at an output level (100Y). As explained through Figure 2.28, the iso-cost line PL of the farmer is tangent to the isoquant I_1 of 100Y from below at point A. So, at point A on isoquant I_1, the slope of the iso-cost line is equal to the slope of the isoquant I_1, where the farmer employs OQ_M and OQ_F quantities of manure and fertilizer respectively. We know, the slope of isoquant indicates MRTS of manure for fertilizer and slope of iso-cost line indicates price ratio of two resources and the point of LCC is explained below.

Slope of the isoquant = $MRTS_{MF} = (\Delta F)/(\Delta M)$

Slope of the iso-cost line = (P_M/P_F)

So, the point of farmer's equilibrium (LCC) is when the slope of the isoquant is equal to the slope of the iso-cost line and this is given by,

$(\Delta F)/(\Delta M) = (P_M/P_F)$ or $MRTS_{MF} = (P_M/P_F)$ *As per the Equation 2.9*

The Equation 2.9 infers that, at point A, what the farmer is willing to pay *i.e.,* his physical exchange rate between manure and fertilizer resources ($MRTS_{MF}$) is equal to

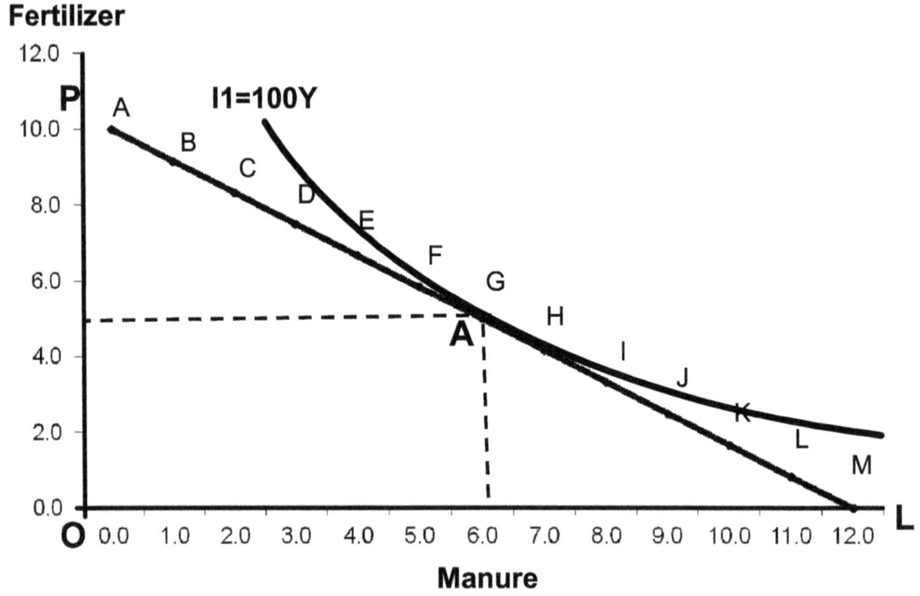

Figure 2.28: Farmer's Equilibrium for Manure and Fertilizer Combinations (Slope of isoquant = Slope of iso-cost line).

what he actually pays *i.e.*, the market exchange rate P_M/P_F. So, at the point of LCC, the slope of isoquant is equal to the slope of iso-cost line or the $MRTS_{MF}$ is inversely equal to the price ratio of the manure and fertilizer resources. The point of LCC can also be stated that, the rate at which the farmer is willing to substitute manure for fertilizer is inversely equal to the price ratio between manure and fertilizer resources.

Inequality between MRTS and Price Ratio of Resources

Case 1: When $MRTS_{MF}$ is Greater than Price Ratio of Resources

This is given by, $(\Delta F)/(\Delta M) > (P_M/P_F)$. So, to attain the point of LCC of resources, the farmer should employ more of added resource (manure) or less of replaced resource (fertilizer), such that, the equality between MRTS and price ratio of resources is ensured and thereby, the farmer is at the point of equilibrium (LCC).

Case 2: When $MRTS_{MF}$ is less than Price Ratio of Resources

This is given by, $(\Delta F)/(\Delta M) < (P_M/P_F)$. So, to attain the point of LCC of resources, the farmer should employ less of added resource (manure) or more of replaced resource (fertilizer), such that, the equality between MRTS and price ratio of resources is ensured and thereby, the farmer is at the point of equilibrium (LCC).

The following Table 2.17 summarizes the decision to be taken by the farmer based on the relationship between $MRTS_{MF}$ and price ratio of resources (P_M/P_F):

Table 2.17: Decision Rule for the Farmer to Achieve LCC of Resources

Rule	*$MRTS_{MF}$*	*Relation*	*Price Ratio*	*Decision to be taken by the Farmer to Achieve LCC*
1	$\Delta F/\Delta M$	>	(P_M/P_F)	Increase the use of added resource (manure) or reduce the use of replaced resource (fertilizer)
2	$\Delta F/\Delta M$	<	(P_M/P_F)	Decrease the use of added resource (manure) or increase the use of replaced resource (fertilizer)
3	$\Delta F/\Delta M$	=	(P_M/P_F)	This is the point of LCC and the farmer should not disturb this resources combination.

Condition 3. Isoquant should be Convex to the Origin

This is an essential condition to be fulfilled for arriving at the point of farmer's equilibrium (LCC). When the iso-cost line is tangent to the isoquant, at the point of tangency, the isoquant should be convex to origin and this is a necessary condition for farmer's equilibrium. In other words, the MRTS of manure for fertilizer must be diminishing at the point of equilibrium. The same is shown through the Figure 2.29, where at the point of farmer's equilibrium *i.e.*, at A, the shape of the isoquant I_2 is convex to origin.

In the Figure 2.29, the price line PL touches isoquant I_1 at point B and isoquant I_2 at point A. A close examination of the Figure 2.29 shows that, at the point of tangency of price line PL and isoquant I_1, at point B, the isoquant I_1 is concave to the origin, where it implies $MRTS_{MF}$ is increasing rather than diminishing. So, definitely the farmer moves away from point B and reaches the isoquant I_2 and attains LCC at point A, where he employs OQ_M and OQ_F quantities of manure and fertilizer respectively.

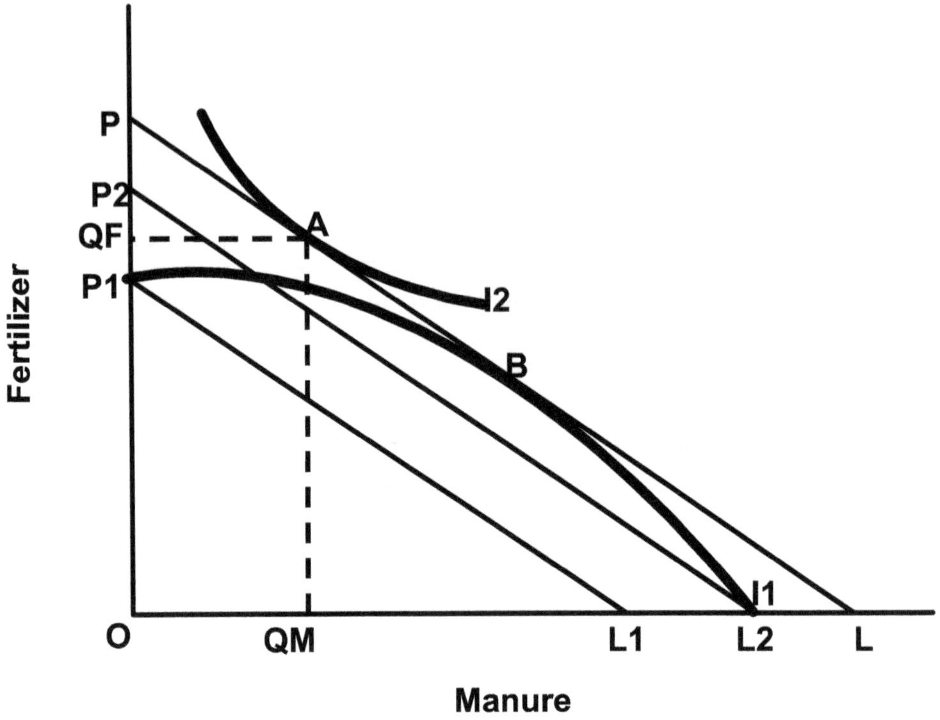

Figure 2.29: Farmer's Equilibrium – Iso-cost Line is Tangent to 'Convex' Isoquant from Below.

If the farmer moves along the same isoquant I_1, he can obtain the same output either at points P_1 or L_2, that too at lower cost. But, to attain LCC at P_1 or L_2, the farmer will have a corner solution *i.e.*, the farmer has to employ only one resource in the production programme (*i.e.*, at P_1 he employs only fertilizer and at L_2 he employs only manure). But, producing same output at P_1 or at L_2 on par at point B by employing only one of the resources violates the assumption of isoquants approach. So, this gives the information that, the farmer will be in equilibrium, when iso-cost line is tangent to the isoquant I_2 and that too, when that isoquant is convex to origin (*i.e.*, at point A), where it shows diminishing MRTS of resources. So, in the principle of factor substitution, the concept mainly revolves around the point, *'always be certain that the value of the resources replaced is greater than the value of the resource added'*.

The above explanation clearly infers that, at point A on the isoquant I_2 (Figure 2.29), all the above three conditions are fulfilled or satisfied and hence, we can conclude that, the farmer is in equilibrium at point A (LCC), through employing OQ_M and OQ_F quantities of manure and fertilizer respectively. So, we can define the farmer's equilibrium as a situation, where the farmer purchases a particular combination of two resources with a given level of cash outlay and at given prices of the resources, such that, he is not willing to move away from the attained equilibrium situation or show no tendency to re-arrange his purchases for the resources. So, in the principle of factor substitution, the concept mainly revolves around the point, *'always be certain that the value of the resources replaced is greater than the value of the resource added'*.

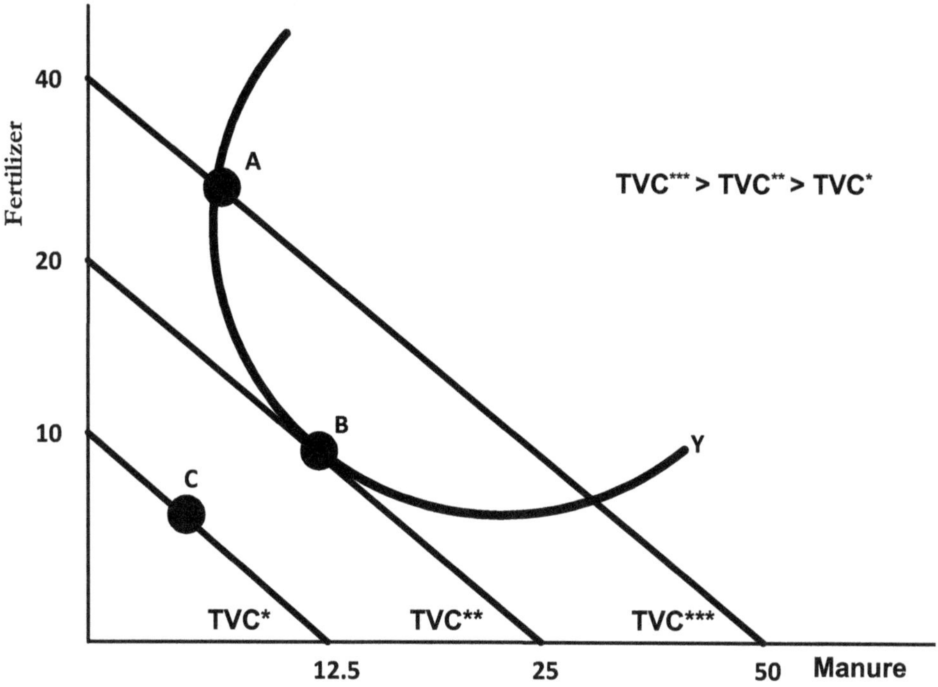

Figure 2.30: Constancy of Slope of Iso-cost Lines.

#: From this concept of TVC, the slope of iso-cost line can also be derived as given below. We know, TVC = f(M, F) = $(P_M * M) + (P_F * F)$. So, $(P_F * F) = TVC - (P_M * M)$. From this, $F = (TVC/P_F) - \{(P_M/P_F)*M\}$. Finally, $(\Delta F/\Delta M) = (dF/dM) = P_M/P_F$.

Figure 2.30 draws the comparative picture between the LCC of resources and other combinations of inputs with reference to isoquants and iso-cost lines. It is clear that, at point B, there is LCC of resources to produce output Y. At point A, the combination of two resources involves higher cost (compared to point B) to achieve the same level of output Y. At point C, the combination of two resources is not sufficient to produce output 'Y'. The Figure 2.30 also reveals that, Total Variable Costs (TVCs)# on the two resources are pre-defined iso-cost lines and as the iso-cost lines move away from the origin, TVC also increases *i.e.*, TVC*** > TVC** > TVC*.

b. *Output Maximization for a given Cash Outlay and Prices of the Two Resources*

The other way of attaining the optimal combination of factors is maximizing the output for a given level of outlay with the farmer and for the given prices of the two resources. Considering the given cash outlay with the farmer and given prices of the two resources, we can draw the iso-cost line PL (Figure 2.31). This PL line is tangent to the isoquant I_2 of 200Y at point A, which implies the farmer allocates OQ_M quantity of manure and OQ_F quantity of fertilizer to maximize the output of 200Y. The iso-cost line PL also touches the isoquant I_1 at points B and C, but the isoquant I_1 represent less level of output (100Y). So, the farmer prefers to allocate OQ_M quantity of manure and OQ_F quantity of fertilizer to maximize the output of 200Y. Further, at the point of

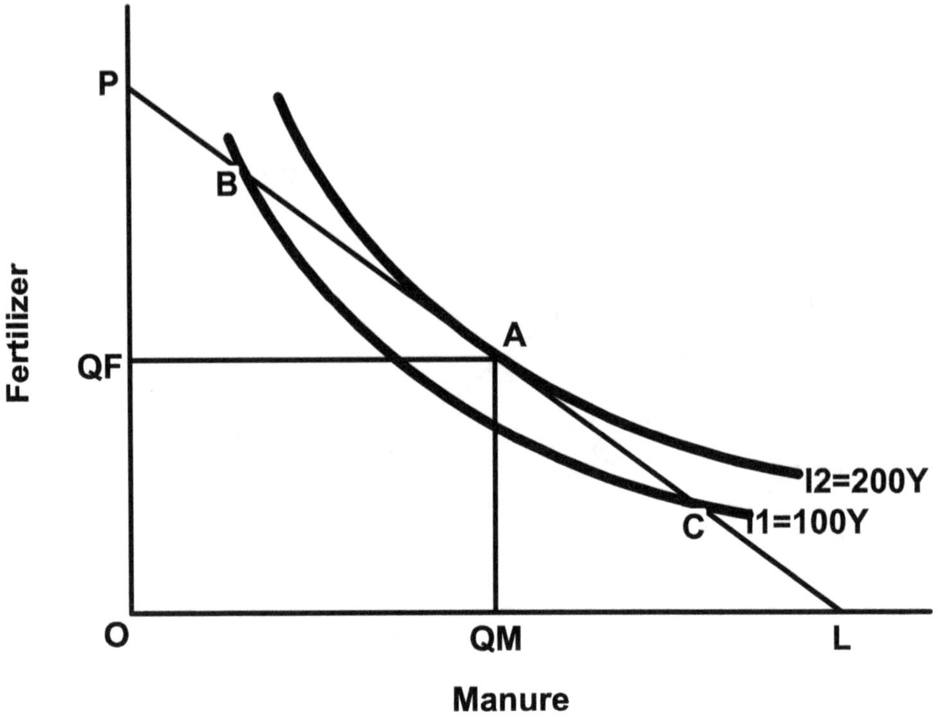

Figure 2.31: Farmer's Equilibrium – Output Maximization for a given Cash Outlay and Prices of the Resources.

tangency of iso-cost line and isoquant I_2 at point A, all the three necessary conditions discussed earlier are fulfilled.

What Happens if Prices of both Inputs Change

As discussed earlier, if the prices of both the inputs change in the same proportion (say, increased by 10 per cent each), the slope of the iso-cost line remains the same, but the new iso-cost line move towards the origin or shifts to the left. So, it will now become tangent to a lower isoquant. So, profits will now decrease, as less output will be produced. The opposite will be true, if prices of both inputs decrease by the same proportion

What Happens if Price of only one Input Changes

As discussed earlier, if price of only one input say, price of manure (P_M) increases, the slope of the iso-cost line changes and it becomes steeper now. The new iso-cost line will lie tangent to the lower isoquant. So, output decreases and hence, profits will decrease (due to same total cost for a lower production). Similarly, the *proportion* between the inputs will change *i.e.*, ratio of F/M will increase, as due to rise in P_M, the farmer substitutes fertilizer for manure. The opposite will be true, if price of one of the inputs will decrease. Note that, more generally, due to change in the relative prices of the inputs, the proportion of inputs (F/M) also changes. For example, if P_M increases by three percent and P_F increases by one percent, then F/M will increase, as the

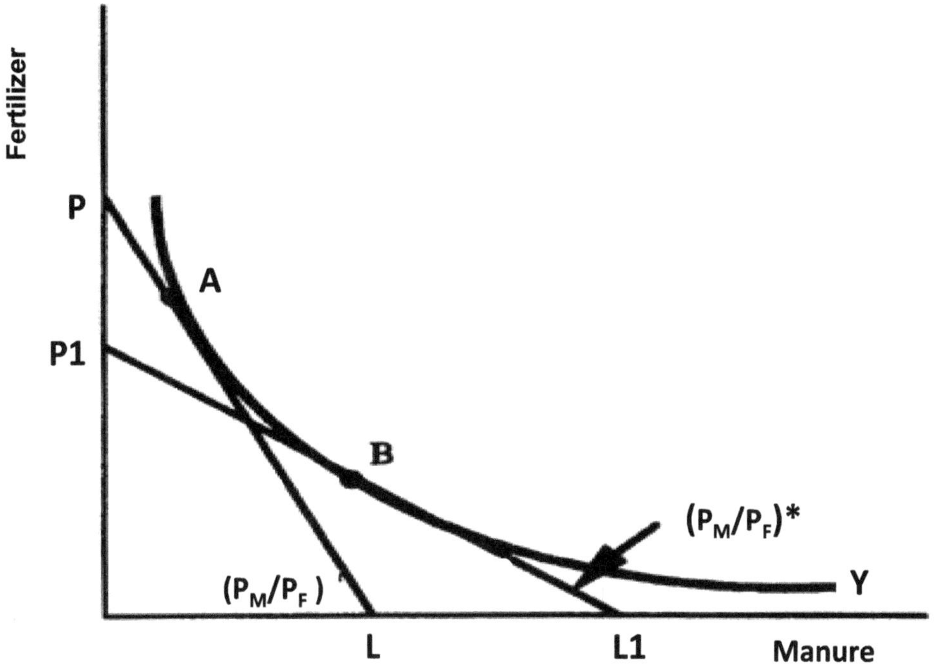

Figure 2.32: Shift in Farmer's Equilibrium Due to Change in Price of Manure Relative to Fertilizer.

farmer now substitute fertilizer for manure. So, the choice of resources combination in a production programme to ensure LCC clearly depends upon prices of the resources. Let us examine the case, where price of manure falls in the market and the shift in LCC of resources is discussed through Figure 2.32. PL is the initial iso-cost line, where the price ratio of the two resources *viz.*, manure and fertilizer is P_M/P_F. With reference to this iso-cost line PL and isoquant, LCC is obtained at point A. Imagine now that, the price of manure falls *relative* to the price of fertilizer. Thus, if the farmer wishes to produce the same output Y, he would face the new isocost line P_1L_1, with slope $(P_M/P_F)^*$. Note that, because the relative price of manure is now lower, the iso-cost line P_1L_1 for producing Y is flatter. As a result, the farmer achieves new LCC of resources at B, which involves more manure and less fertilizer. Thus, it may be concluded that, when the relative price of manure falls, the farmer will substitute toward a production technique that utilizes more manure and less fertilizer.

Limitations of LCC

They include:

- ☆ Some factors may not be exactly divisible, especially human labour, pesticides *etc.*, thereby, this method may not be suitable to minimize the cost.
- ☆ This LCC of resources may not be suitable in case of complementary resources.

VI. Types of Resources and their Relationships

Basically there are two types resource relationships *viz.*, Substitutes and Complements.

A. Substitutes

These are the resources, which can be reshuffled in the production programme. That means, if the level of one resource is increased, the level of other resource must be compulsorily decreased, so as to produce a given level of output. Substitutes may be Good substitutes and Perfect substitutes.

- ☆ ***Good Substitutes:*** For good substitutes, the shape of isoquant is convex to origin. For substitutes MRTS is always negative. Ex: Machinery and human labour, manure and fertilizer are good substitutes.
- ☆ ***Perfect substitutes:*** Some resources are perfectly substitutable, which means that these resources are completely interchangeable. Ex: Family labour and hired labour, owned bullock labour and hired bullock labour, farm produced manure and manure purchased from market, Brand A of N fertilizer and Brand B of N fertilizer *etc.* For perfect substitutes, isoquant is a straight line connecting two axes (Panel A of Figure 2.33).

In substitution relationship, the resources substitute either at constant rate or at decreasing rate or at increasing rate.

i. Constant Rate of Substitution of Resources

Constant rate of substitution occurs, when the rate of replacement of one resource by the other resources does not change or remains same, as the added resource is increased in its magnitude. That means, if added resource is increased by 1 unit, it replaces the replaced resource by the same magnitude as that of preceding added unit of added resource. In constant rate of resources substitution, isoquant is a straight line connecting two axes (Panel A of Figure 2.33). $MRTS_{X1X2}$ equation of constant rate of resources substitution is given by: $\Delta_1X_2/\Delta_1X_1 = \Delta_2X_2/\Delta_2X_1 = \Delta_3X_2/\Delta_3X_1 =$ .... $= \Delta nX_2/\Delta nX_1$ (Table 2.18). This constant rate of resource substitution occurs only in case of perfect substitutes. Ex: Family labour and hired labour, owned bullock labaour and hired bullock labour, farm produced manure and manure purchased from market, Brand A of N fertilizer and Brand B of N fertilizer *etc.* But, this constant rate of resources substitution is not common in agriculture. In case of constant rate of resources substitution, the decision to use the level of resource usage is based on two aspects:

- ☆ Instead of using two resources, it is better for the farmer to use only one resource, so as to minimize the cost.
- ☆ The farmer prefers to use low priced resource instead of high priced resource.

ii. Decreasing Rate of Substitution of Resources

This occurs, when rate of replacement of one resource by other resource decreases, as the added resource is increased in its magnitude. That means, if the added resource is increased by 1 unit it replaces less amount of replaced resource, when compared to the preceding unit of added resource. In decreasing rate of substitution of resources, isoquant is convex to origin (Panel B of the Figure 2.33). Ex: Machinery and human labour, manure and fertilizer, labour and capital *etc.* This rate of substitution of resources is more common in agriculture.

Table 2.18: Constant Rate of Resources Substitution in the Production Programme

X_1	ΔX_1	X_2	ΔX_2	$MRTS_{X1X2} = \Delta X_2/\Delta X_1$
1		10		
	1		–2	–2
2		8		
	1		–2	–2
3		6		
	1		–2	–2
4		4		
	1		–2	–2
5		2		

In decreasing rate of resource substitution, if we go on increasing added resource (X1), it will substitute less and less of replaced resource (X_2), as MPP of added resource will gradually decrease due to its increasing magnitude and hence, it substitutes less and less of replaced resource. The level of resources usage in a production programme experiencing decreasing rate of substitution depends upon the relationship between

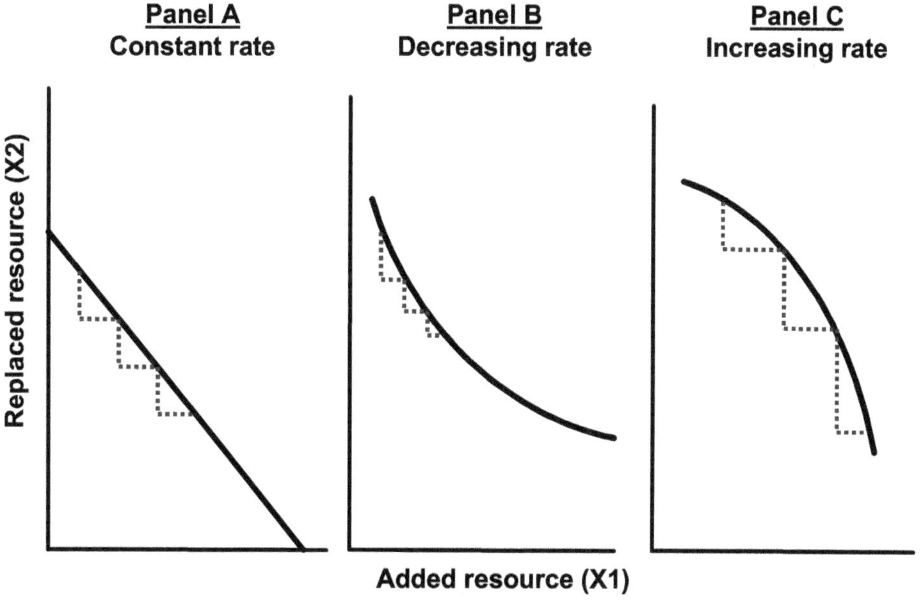

Figure 2.33: Types of Resources Substitution – Shapes of Isoquants.

MRTS and price ratio of inputs, as discussed through Table 2.19. $MRTS_{X1X2}$ equation for decreasing rate of resources substitution is given by: $\Delta_1X_2/\Delta_1X_1 > \Delta_2X_2/\Delta_2X_1 > \Delta_3X_2/\Delta_3X_1 > \ldots\ldots\ldots\ldots\ldots > \Delta nX_2/\Delta nX_1$ (Table 2.19).

Table 2.19: Decreasing Rate of Resources Substitution in the Production Programme

X_1	ΔX_1	X_2	ΔX_2	$MRTS_{X1X2} = \Delta X_2/\Delta X_1$
1		15		
	1		–5	–5
2		10		
	1		–3	–3
3		7		
	1		–2	–2
4		5		
	1		–1	–1
5		4		

iii. Increasing Rate of Substitution of Resources

This occurs, when rate of replacement of one resource by other resource increases, as the added resource is increased in its magnitude. That means, if the added resource is increased by 1 unit, it replaces more amount of replaced resource, when compared to the preceding unit of added resource. In increasing rate of substitution of resources, isoquant is concave to origin (Panel C of the Figure 2.33). This rate of resources substitution is not common in agriculture. $MRTS_{X1X2}$ equation for increasing rate of substitution is given by: $\Delta_1X_2/\Delta_1X_1 < \Delta_2X_2/\Delta_2X_1 < \Delta_3X_2/\Delta_3X_1 < \ldots\ldots\ldots\ldots\ldots < \Delta nX_2/\Delta nX_1$ (Table 2.20).

Table 2.20: Increasing Rate of Resources Substitution in the Production Programme

X_1	ΔX_1	X_2	ΔX_2	$MRTS_{X1X2} = \Delta X_2/\Delta X_1$
1		15		
	1		–1	–1
2		14		
	1		–2	–2
3		12		
	1		–3	–3
4		9		
	1		–5	–5
5		4		

B. Complements

Complements are the resources, which combine in a fixed proportion thereby, they are used together in production programme. When price of one resource or input

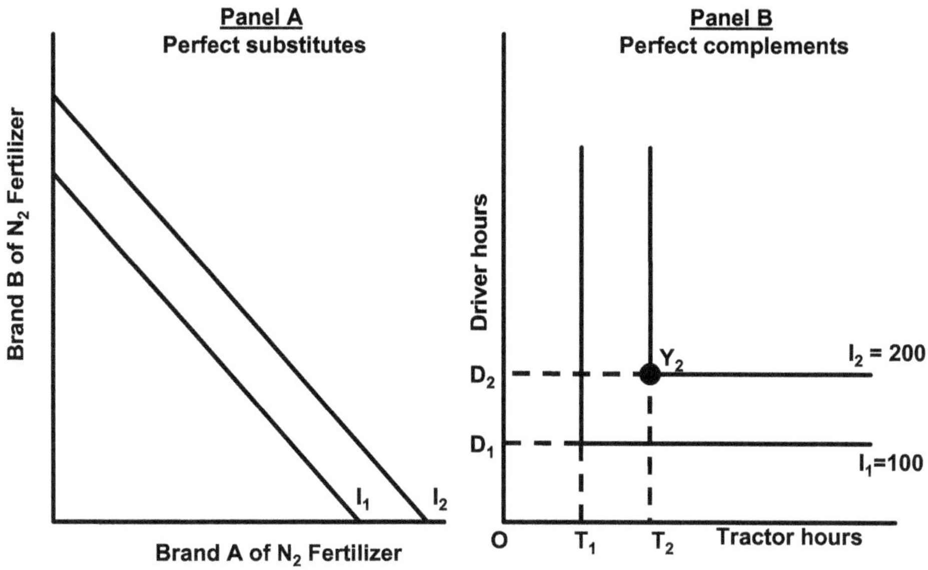

Figure 2.34: Different Shapes of Isoquants Depending Upon Resources Relationships.

is increased, the demand for both the resources will be decreased and *vice-versa*. Examples include: tractor hours and driver hours, a pair of bullocks and farmer ploughing the land, for preparation of one water molecule, we require two atoms of hydrogen and one atom of oxygen *etc.* When wage rate of tractor driver was increased, to save the cost, the farmer will reduce both the tractor hours and driver working hours. No question arises on the part of farmer regarding the level of one resource usage over the other because, both the resources will combine in a fixed proportion. MRTS = 0, for complements because, the inputs combine in fixed proportion and they does not substitute each other. The shape of isoquant for complements is 'L' shape (Panel B of Figure 2.34). It is clear that, to produce 100 units of output on isoquant I_1, the farmer should employ OT_1 tractor hours and OD_1 driver hours. If the output is to be increased to 200 units on isoquant I_2, the farmer should employ more of both the resources *i.e.*, OT_2 of tractor hours and OD_2 of driver hours. Simply increasing the level of one input (say, tractor hours up to OT_2) without increasing level of other input (*i.e.*, keeping the driver hours at OD_1), it is not possible to achieve higher level of output on isoquant I_2. This is because, the inputs must combine only in fixed population to increase the output.

Thus, note that, when the production function offers limited input substitution opportunities, the $MRTS_{MF}$ changes substantially, as we move along an isoquant. In this case, the isoquants are nearly L-shaped (*i.e.*, the inputs are good complements). On the other hand, when the production function offers abundant input substitution opportunities, the $MRTS_{MF}$ changes gradually, as we move along an isoquant and in this case, the isoquants are nearly straight lines, as in case of near perfect substitutes.

Applicability of Principle of Factor Substitution

As discussed above, the farmer employs several resources like land, labour, capital, machinery, seeds, fertilizers, pesticides *etc.* These resources are usually scarce with him, but enjoy alternative uses. So, the farmer substitute one resource for other resource and sometimes, he resort for resources combinations depending upon two important aspects *viz.*, availability of resources and prices.

- ☆ ***Availability of resources***: Depending upon the availability of resources, the farmer will plan the resource usage. For example, if labour availability is scarce, the farmer employs more of machinery and if labour availability is plenty, he employs more of labour to machinery. Similarly, if land resource is scarce, the farmer goes for intensive cultivation and if the land availability is plenty, the farmer goes for extensive cultivation. Sometimes, the farmer uses combinations of both the resources depending upon their relative availability.
- ☆ ***Price:*** In general, the farmer prefers a cheap resource to a costlier or dearer resource with the main objective of minimization of cost in the production programme. This principle factor substitution has two propositions:
  - ❑ The farmer generally substitutes one resource for another resource as long as one resource is cheaper than another resource. Generally the farmer substitutes a cheaper resource in place of costlier resource.
  - ❑ The farmer goes on substituting the resource as long as the increase in additional cost incurred in using added resource (say, machinery) is less than decrease in cost due to saving of replaced resource (hired labour). This is explained below.

Increase in additional cost of Added Resource < Decrease in cost due saving of Replaced resource

(Say, Machinery ⟶ Rs. 1000) < (Say, Hired Labour ⟶ Rs. 1500)

$$(\Delta X_1 * PX_1) < (\Delta X_2 * PX_2)$$

So, we can write the above expression as

$$(PX_1/PX_2) < (\Delta X_2/\Delta X_1)$$

The right hand expression implies $MRTS_{X1X2}$ and thereby, $MRTS_{X1X2}$ is greater than Price ratio of two factors. To attain LCC of factors, as discussed earlier, the farmer should increase the use of added resource, machinery (X_1) and replace more and more of replaced resource, hired labour (X_2). Reverse is the case, when $MRTS_{X1X2}$ is less than Price ratio of two factors and hence, the farmer should increase the use of replaced resource, hired labour (X_2) and replace more and more of added resource, machinery (X_1). This concept of LCC is applicable, when the factors substitute each other at decreasing rate. However, if the inputs substitute each other at constant rate or increasing rate, the farmer should use only one input depending upon the relative prices of the input. As mentioned above, the farmer will employ more of cheaper resource relative to dearer resource. In case of factors which combine in fixed proportion (i.e, complements), there is no other alternative for the farmer as he has to employ both the factors because, only that combination of factors are needed to produce the output.

For example, to prepare a water molecule, we need to combine two atoms of hydrogen and one atom of oxygen.

Special Cases of Substitution

In the above discussion, we noted that, the farmer substitutes cheaper resource for the dearer resource with the sole objective of minimizing the costs, but maintaining the same level of output in the production programme. However, there are certain cases, where resources substitution also leads to increase in the output and at the same reduces the cost in the production programme. For example, if the farmer prefers to use a HYV seed of paddy instead of local variety seed, the total output will increase significantly. Though HYV seed may be costlier than local variety seed, the output produced from the former is much higher than from the local variety seed and thereby, the added value from the HYV seed outweighs the added cost incurred in using it. Thus, the increase in output value due to the use of HYV seed outweighs the increase in cost in employing it in the production programme. The superiority of this substitute is established not only by the cost of the new practice, but also by the value of the added yield. In estimating the profitability of such practices, budgeting technique becomes more useful. It is a case of shift in the production function.

4. Principle of Product Substitution

This principle mainly aims at addressing the basic production problem 'What to produce'. So far, we discussed about the production programme, where resources combination (factor-factor relationship) is considered important in the context of cost minimization, by keeping output level constant. When a farmer decides to take up production programme in the farm, first he has to plan about what type of enterprises he has to produce. This can be decided only after taking into consideration the stock of the resources available with him. The farmer then has to decide, how much and how he should produce the enterprises or products. In general, farmer practices more than one enterprise in his farm. In such a case, the farmer faces the problem of resource allocation across the selected enterprises. This is because, the resources available with the farmer are usually limited, but they have alternative uses in the production programme. So, with the available limited resources, the farmer should plan the production programme *i.e.*, whether he has to go for a single enterprise (specialization) or for enterprise combinations (diversification) with the ultimate objective of achieving profit maximization in the farm business. This concept of production problem refers to 'what to produce' by the farmer with the given level of resources. So, the product-product relationship deals with resources allocation among the competing enterprises by considering the constancy of resources level with the farmer, while products (outputs) are varied. We know, production function of enterprise Y_1 is given by, $Y_1 = f(X_1, X_2, X_3/X_4, X_5, X_6 — Xn)$. Similarly, production function of enterprise Y_2 is given by, $Y_2 = f(X_1, X_2, X_3/X_4, X_5, X_6 — Xn)$. So, with the given resources, the farmer can produce only Y_1 or only Y_2 or can produce a combination of Y_1 and Y_2. When the farmer desires to produce the combination of two products, we can write the functional relationship as, $Y_1 = f(Y_2)$. If the farmer deals with more than two enterprises, we can write the same as $Y_1 = f(Y_2, Y_3, — Yn)$. The enterprises combination, so selected by the farmer at a given level of resources should ensure maximization of profits in the production programme. The following are the objectives of product-product relationship:

- ☆ Maximization of profits for the given level of resources.
- ☆ Determination of the best combination of enterprises for the given level of resources.
- ☆ Determination of level of resources usage *i.e.,* allocation of resources on each enterprise.
- ☆ Determination of level of output to be produced from each enterprise.

Optimum Product Combination (OPC)

Generally, the farmer has to optimize the product combination for the given level of resources. This OPC can be achieved in two different ways:

A. Opportunity cost approach.

B. PPC – Iso-revenue line approach.

A. Opportunity Cost Approach

We know, the slope of the PPC is given by:

$$MRPS_{PM} = (\Delta M)/(\Delta P) = (MPP_P/MPP_M) \qquad \textit{Equation 2.10}$$

We also know, the slope of the iso-revenue line is equal to $-(P_P/P_M)$. Putting these two together, we can find the OPC combination for a given resources level and this is given by, $MPP_P/MPP_M = -(P_P/P_M)$. In this equation, the term on the left-hand side is just the MRPS between paddy for maize ($MRPS_{PM}$). Finally, we can rearrange the equation $MPP_P/MPP_M = -(P_P/P_M)$ to get:

$$MPP_P/P_P = -(MPP_M/P_M) \qquad \textit{Equation 2.11}$$

Since, MPP and MC are inversely proportional, the above Equations 2.10 and 2.11 can be written as follows:

$$MRPS_{PM} = (\Delta M)/(\Delta P) = (MPP_P/MPP_M) = (MC_M/MC_P) \qquad \textit{Equation 2.12}$$

Since, $(MPP_P/MPP_M) = (MC_M/MC_P)$

$$(P_P/P_M) = (MC_M/MC_P) \qquad \textit{Equation 2.13}$$

$$MC_P \times P_P = MC_M \times P_M$$

So, the point of OPC is given by,

$$MRPS_{PM} = [(\Delta M)/(\Delta P) = (MPP_P/MPP_M) = (MC_M/MC_P)] = (P_P/P_M) \qquad \textit{Equation 2.14}$$

The above Equation 2.14 gives us another insight. It says that, when you have found the optimum product mix for any resources level, the marginal product of paddy divided by the price of paddy (MPP_P/P_P) will be equal to the marginal product of maize divided by the price of maize (MPP_M/P_M). Marginal product of paddy divided by the price of paddy (MPP_P/P_P) means that, the additional paddy output the farmer derives for every one unit increase in price of paddy in the market. Similar is the case for (MPP_M/P_M).

Case 1: Assume $MRPS_{PM} > (P_P/P_M)$

This implies,

$MRPS_{PM} = [(\Delta M)/(\Delta P) = (MPP_P/MPP_M) = (MC_M/MC_P)] > (P_P/P_M)$. But, we know, at the point of OPC:

$MRPS_{PM} = [(\Delta M)/(\Delta P) = (MPP_P/MPP_M) = (MC_M/MC_P)] = (P_P/P_M)$.

To ensure OPC, increase the output of maize by allocating more resources so that, MPP_M will decrease and MC_M will rise. Since, MPP_M will fall, it ensures the equality between $MRPS_{PM}$ and (P_P/P_M).

Case 2: Assume $MRPS_{PM} < (P_P/P_M)$

This implies,

$MRPS_{PM} = [(\Delta M)/(\Delta P) = (MPP_P/MPP_M) = (MC_M/MC_P)] < (P_P/P_M)$. But, we know, at the point of OPC:

$MRPS_{PM} = [(\Delta M)/(\Delta P) = (MPP_P/MPP_M) = (MC_M/MC_P)] = (P_P/P_M)$.

To ensure OPC, increase the output of paddy by allocating more resources so that, MPP_P will decrease and MC_P will rise. Since, MPP_P will fall, it will ensures the equality between $MRPS_{PM}$ and (P_P/P_M).

Note that, the above concept can be explained in terms of opportunity cost of producing two products. For example: a farmer is producing two products A and B (Figure 2.35). If he transfer one unit of labour away from Product B production to Product A production, he must give up 30 units of Product B and gain 25 units of

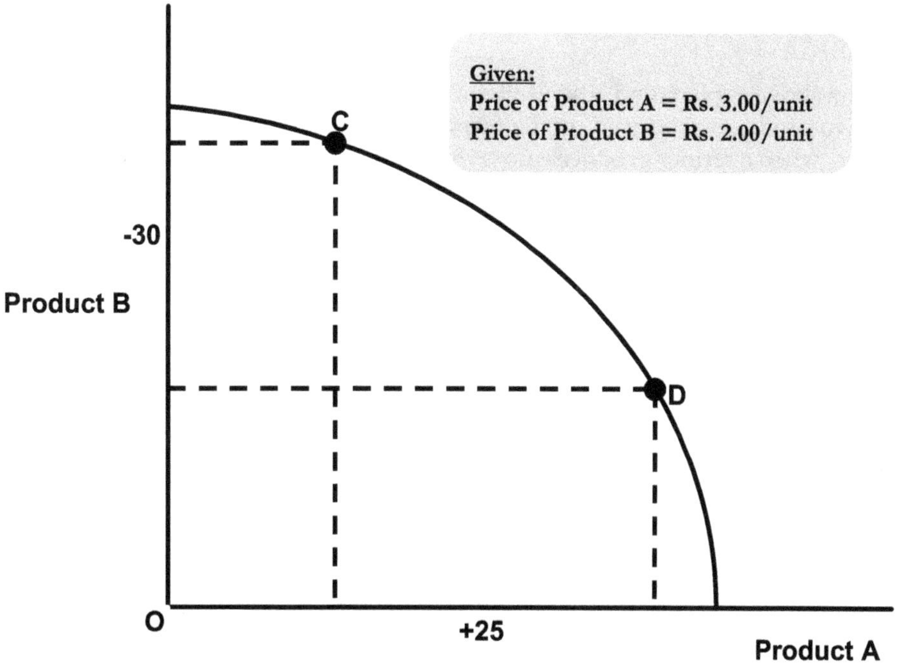

Figure 2.35: Estimation of OPC Based on Opportunity Cost Concept.

Product A. So, the $MRPS_{AB}$ or Marginal Opportunity Cost of product A for Product B is given by: $\Delta B/\Delta A = (30/25)$. That is, the opportunity cost of each unit of Product A is 6/5 or 1.20 of Product B. Bringing relative prices into the picture, we might find that, the price of Product A is Rs. 3.00/unit and price of Product B is Rs. 2.00/unit. So, $P_A/P_B = 3.00/2.00 = 1.50$. Stated differently, (as a *Terms of Trade*), the farmers is willing to trade 1 unit of Product A for Rs.3.00 and with that Rs.3.00, he could then acquire 1.5 units of Product B. That is, one unit of Product A is worth equal to 1.5 units of Product B *given these prices.*

If we compare the relative price of Product A with the opportunity cost of Product A, we find that, the value (price) of Product A in terms of Product B is greater than the opportunity cost of producing Product B. This is given by:

- ✰ One unit of Product A is worth 1.50 units of Product B (*i.e.*, Price ratio)
- ✰ One unit of Product A costs 1.20 units of Product B ($MRPS_{AB}$ or Marginal Opportunity Cost of each unit of Product A in terms of each unit of Product B)

So, $MRPS_{AB} < P_A/P_B$

So, $(\Delta B/\Delta A) < P_A/P_B$

So, considering the equilibrium under OPC, the farmer should allocate more resources towards Product A production and away from Product B production. With the reallocation of resources, the opportunity cost of Product A production will rise. This reallocation should continue until the following is true:

$MRPS_{AB} = P_A/P_B$

$(\Delta B/\Delta A) = P_A/P_B$

The above explanation is so useful, as it can be generalized to the case of more than two products produced by the farmer in his production programme. This is because, when a farmer produces more than two products, it is difficult to illustrate PPCs and iso-revenue lines on a two-dimensional graph. So, the above Equation 2.14 can be used to generalize to any number of products. Suppose, the farmer produces 'N' products in a production programme, with MPPs *viz.*, MPP_A, MPP_B, MPP_C, - - - -, MPP_N and product prices P_A, P_B, P_C, ..., P_N. Then, for any level of resources usage, the OPC of all of these products will always satisfy:

$$MPP_A/P_A = MPP_B/P_B = MPP_C/P_C = \text{---} = MPP_N/P_N \qquad \textit{Equation 2.15}$$

As per the above Equation 2.15, when a farmer produces more than two products, the OPC of products mix can be obtained, when the extra output (MPP) derived from a product per rupee of that product will be equal to the extra output (MPP) derived from any other product per rupee of that product.

B. PPC – Iso-revenue Line Approach

The earlier discussion on PPC and iso-revenue line reveals two important aspects *viz.*, the PPC infers 'what combinations of products the farmer is willing to produce' and the iso-revenue line guides the farmer, 'what quantities of products the farmer will sell', so as to maximize the profits in the production programme. So, when the

PPC and the iso-revenue line are combined, we find the quantities of each product the farmer is both willing and able to sell for the given level of resources. So, the PPC and iso-revenue line helps the farmer to find out the optimum combination of products, where he can maximize the profits. So, the OPC refers to the point of profit maximization in the production programme at a particular combination of products for the given level of resources. This approach involves three ways of explaining the attainment of OPC in the production programme. They are:

i. Tabular method
ii. Algebraic method
iii. Graphical method

i. Tabular Method

In this method, we will study the output levels of two products for different combinations and based on the information pertaining to the market prices of two products, we can work out the total revenue or income from the two products (Table 2.21). The OPC is the one that yields maximum total revenue to the farmer. It is clear that, by producing 2 units of output of Y_1 (paddy) and 20 units of output of Y_2 (maize) *i.e.*, at Combination A, the total revenue of the enterprises combination can be maximized, which is equal to Rs.240. Any other combination of two enterprises will lead to less amount of total revenue than the above combination of 2 units of output of Y_1 (paddy) and 20 units of output of Y_2 (maize). So, this concept advocates the farmer to allocate more area under Y_2 (maize) enterprise and comparatively less area under Y_1 (paddy) enterprise, so as to maximize the profits in the production programme.

Table 2.21: Optimum Combination of Enterprises through Estimation of Total Revenue

Combination	*Y_1 (Paddy)*	*Y_2 (Maize)*	*Returns*		*Total income from the Enterprise Combination(Rs.)*
			Price (Y_1=20/unit)	*Price (Y_2=10/unit)*	
A	2	20	40	200	240
B	4	10	80	100	180
C	6	8	120	80	200
D	8	3	160	30	190
E	10	2	200	20	220

ii. Algebraic Method

The principle of OPC states that, profits will be maximum in a production programme in producing two products in such a way that, where MRPS of products is inversely equal to their price ratio. We already know that, slope of PPC indicates MRPS of two products i.e, $MRPS_{PM}=\Delta M/\Delta P$, and the slope of iso-revenue line indicates the price ratio of two products *i.e.*, P_P/P_M. So, the point of OPC in the production programme is given by:

$$MRPS_{PM}=\Delta M/\Delta P = P_P/P_M$$

iii. Graphical Method

Economic efficiency in product-product relationship is attained when the physical concept ($MRPS_{PM}$) is integrated with the economic concept (price ratio of products). Thus, the OPC can be determined by imposing the PPC map on iso-revenue line. This methodology is based on the following assumptions:

- The farmer produces only two products *viz.,* paddy and maize in the production programme.
- The prices of products are given and constant.
- The total revenue the farmer expects is given.
- There is perfect competition in the product market.

Three important conditions must be fulfilled to arrive at the point of optimum combination of products. They include,

a. The iso-revenue line should be tangent to the PPC from above
b. Slope of the iso-revenue line should be equal to the slope of PPC
c. PPC should be concave to the origin

a. The Iso-Revenue Line should be Tangent to the PPC from Above

The point of OPC is where, the iso-revenue line is tangent to the PPC from above. Figure 2.36 shows that, iso-revenue line PL is tangent to the PPC at point A, where the farmer attains OPC by selling OQ_P quantity of paddy and OQ_M quantity of maize. Any point other than A *i.e.,* at M_1 or N_1 will not contribute to maximum profits, as these points touch the lower iso-revenue line P_1L_1. Moreover, at these points, the iso-revenue line is not tangent to the PPC. Note that, the point of tangency between the PPC and iso-revenue line is an important, but not a necessary condition for achieving OPC. The essential condition is that, the slope of the iso-revenue line must equal the slope of the PPC. Thus, at the point of equilibrium, MRPS of the two products must be equal the ratio of their prices. Another important condition is that, the PPC must be concave to the origin *i.e.,* the MRPS of paddy for maize ($MRPS_{FM}$) must be increasing at the point of equilibrium. These two essential conditions are discussed here under.

b. Slope of the Iso-revenue Line should be Equal to the Slope of PPC

The second condition essential for arriving at the point of OPC is that, the slope of the iso-revenue line should be equal to the slope of PPC from above for the desired combination of products. As explained through Figure 2.36, the iso-revenue line PL of the farmer is tangent to the PPC from above at point A. So, at point A on PPC, the slope of the iso-revenue line is equal to the slope of the PPC, where the farmer produces OQ_P and OQ_M quantities of paddy and maize respectively. We know, the slope of PPC indicates MRPS of paddy for maize and slope of iso-revenue line indicates price ratio of two products and the point of OPC is explained below.

Slope of the PPC= $MRPS_{PM} = (\Delta M)/(\Delta P)$

Slope of the iso-revenue line = (P_P/P_M)

So, the point of profit maximization is when the slope of the PPC is equal to the slope of the iso-revenue line and this is given by,

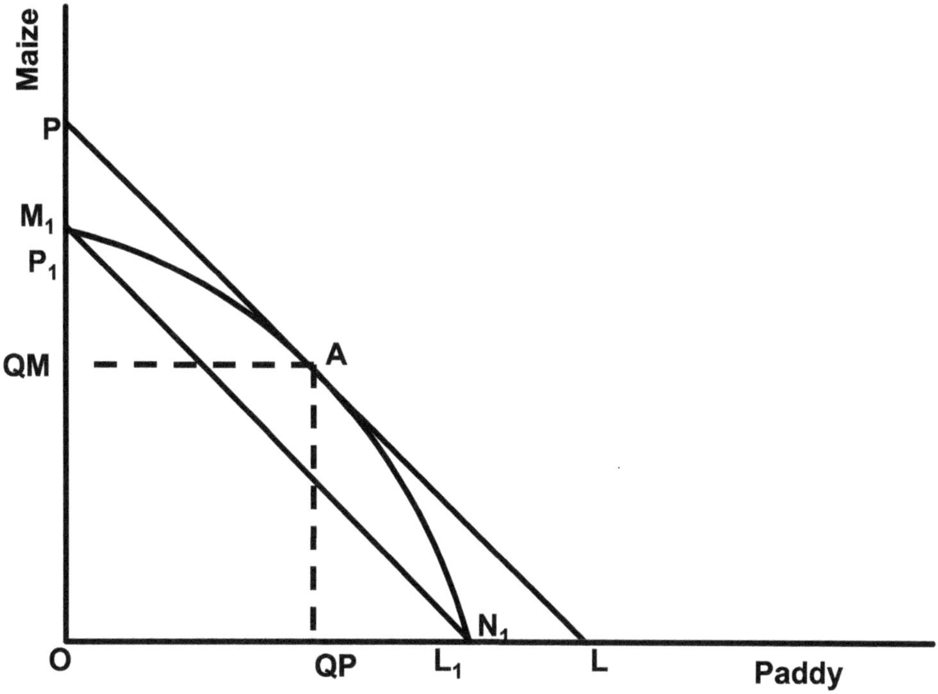

Figure 2.36: Farmer's Equilibrium – Iso-Revenue Line Tangent to Production Possibility Curve from Above.

$(\Delta M)/(\Delta P) = (P_P/P_M)$ or $MRPS_{PM} = (P_P/P_M)$ *Equation 2.16*

So, at the point of OPC, the slope of PPC is equal to the slope of iso-revenue line or the $MRPS_{PM}$ is inversely equal to the price ratio of paddy and maize. The point of OPC can also be stated that, the rate (MRPS) at which the farmer is willing to substitute paddy for maize is inversely equal to the price ratio between paddy and maize.

c. PPC Should be Concave to the Origin

This is an essential condition to be fulfilled for arriving at the point of OPC. When the iso-revenue line is tangent to the PPC, at the point of tangency, the PPC should be concave to the origin. In other words, the MRPS of paddy for maize must be increasing at the point of equilibrium. The same is shown through the Figure 2.36, where at the point of OPC *i.e.*, at A, the shape of the PPC is concave to origin. If at the point of tangency, PPC is convex to origin (Figure 2.37), it is not the point of profit maximization, as the movement from B towards either M_1 or N_1 will yield more revenue. In such a situation, the farmer will produce either at M_1 or N_1 rather than at B. But, the farmer will definitely operate at M_1, where PPC touches higher iso-revenue line P_1L_1. So, this gives the information that, the farmer will attain maximum profits, when the iso-revenue line is tangent to the PPC from above and that too, when that PPC is concave to origin, where it shows increasing MRPS.

The above explanation clearly infers that, at point A on the PPC (Figure 2.36), all the above three conditions are fulfilled or satisfied and hence, we can conclude that,

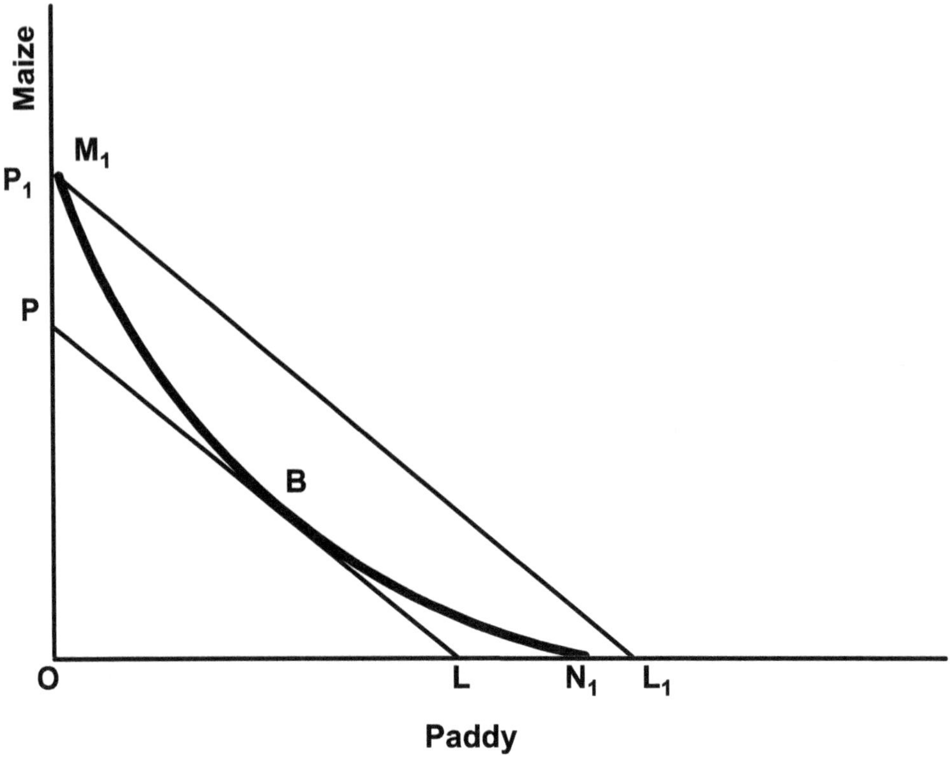

Figure 2.37: Farmer's Equilibrium – Production Possibility Curve should not be Convex at the Point of Tangency.

the farmer attains maximum profits at point A, through selling OQ_P and OQ_M quantities of paddy and maize respectively. Now, we know that, at the point of tangency, $MRPS_{PM}$ is inversely equal to the slope of the iso-revenue line. That is, $\Delta M/\Delta P = P_P/P_M$. We can write the same as $(\Delta M*P_M) = (\Delta P*P_P)$. The economic meaning of this optimal solution is as follows: *'if producing less of maize i.e., by ΔM, results in a decrease in revenue $(-\Delta M*P_M)$, but allows an increase in production of paddy i.e., by ΔP, results in an increase in revenue $(\Delta P*P_P)$ and if the additional revenue from paddy $(\Delta P*P_P)$ is greater than decrease in revenue from maize $(\Delta M*P_M)$, i.e. $(\Delta P*P_P) > (\Delta M*P_M)$ or $(\Delta M/\Delta P) < (P_P/P_M)$, then it is profitable to shift resources from producing maize to producing paddy (the cost is the same, the revenue increases). By doing so, $MRPS_{PM}$ gradually decreases: i.e., for a further equal decrease in maize output (ΔM), the increase in paddy output (ΔP) is smaller, and the shift of resources is less profitable and at one point, $(\Delta P*P_P) = (\Delta M*P_M)$ and thereby, no further shift is profitable and this point corresponds to the tangency point'.*

Inequality between MRPS and Price Ratio of Products

Case 1: When $MRPS_{PM}$ is Greater than Price Ratio of Products

This is given by, $(\Delta M)/(\Delta P) > (P_P/P_M)$. So, to attain the point of OPC, the farmer should produce more of replaced product (maize) or less of added product (paddy). From the Table 2.22, it is clear that, $MRPS_{PM} > P_P/P_M$

(2.25) > (2)

$\Delta M/\Delta P > P_P/P_M$

So, to achieve OPC in the production programme, the farmer should increase the output of maize (*i.e.*, replaced product) from 26 to 44 units or reduce the output of paddy (*i.e.*, added product) from 24 to 16 units.

Table 2.22: OPC of Two Products, Paddy and Maize

Combination	*Land Area (Units)*		*Output (Units)*				*$MRPS_{PM}$ ($\Delta M/\Delta P$)*	*P_P/P_M*
	Paddy	*Maize*	*Paddy*	*ΔP*	*Maize*	*ΔM*		
A	0	4	0		75			
				8		15	1.88	2
B	1	3	8		60			
				8		16	**2**	**2**
C	2	2	16		44			
				8		18	2.25	2
D	3	1	24		26			
				8		26	3.25	2
E	4	0	32		0			

Case 2: When $MRPS_{PM}$ is less than Price Ratio of Products

This is given by, $(\Delta M)/(\Delta P) < (P_P/P_M)$. So, to attain the point of OPC, the farmer should produce less of replaced product (maize) or more of added product (paddy). From the Table 2.22, it is clear that, $MRPS_{PM} < P_P/P_M$

(1.88) < (2)

$\Delta M/\Delta P < P_P/P_M$

So, to achieve OPC in the production programme, the farmer should increase the output of paddy (*i.e.*, added product) from 8 to 16 units or reduce the output of maize (*i.e.*, replaced product) from 60 to 44 units.

Table 2.23: Decision Rule for the Farmer to Achieve OPC of Two Enterprises

Rule	*$MRPS_{PM}$*	*Relation*	*Price Ratio*	*Decision to be taken by the Farmer to Achieve OPC*
1	$\Delta M/\Delta P$	>	P_P/P_M	Allocate more resources to produce more of replaced product (maize) or allocate less resources to produce less of added product (paddy)
2	$\Delta M/\Delta P$	<	P_P/P_M	Allocate less resources to produce less of replaced product (maize) or allocate more resources to produce more of added product (paddy)
3	$\Delta M/\Delta P$	=	P_P/P_M	This is the point of OPC and the farmer should not disturb the output and acreage under the two enterprises.

The Table 2.23 summarizes the decisions to be taken by the farmer based on the relationship between $MRPS_{PM}$ and price ratio of products (P_P/P_M):

It is essential to note that, prices of the products fluctuate in the market and hence, it is essential to analyze, how the products combination varies due to changes in prices of the products.

What Happens if Prices of Both Products Change

As discussed earlier, if the prices of both the products change in the same proportion (say, increased by 10 per cent each), the slope of the iso-revenue line remains the same, but the new iso-revenue line shifts away the origin or shifts to the right side, as now the revenue with the farmer increases (because, the farmers are price conscious). So, it will now become tangent to a higher PPC. So, profits will now increase, as more output of both the products will be produced coupled with rise in prices of both the products. The opposite will be true, if prices of both products decrease by the same proportion. The above concept can be explained in a different way, if the farmer has inelastic cash requirements. That is, if the prices of both the products increase in the market, now the farmer gets the same revenue as earlier, only by producing and selling less amounts of both the products. In such case, iso-revenue line shifts towards left, but the profits will increase, as the costs can be reduced by producing less quantities of both the products. However, the former version (farmers are price conscious) is more valid than the latter.

What Happens if Price of Only One Product Changes

As discussed earlier, if price of only one product, say price of paddy (P_P) increases, the slope of the iso-revenue line changes, as it becomes more flat now and it will lie tangent to the higher PPC. So, output of paddy increases and hence, profits will increase (same total cost and a high revenue). Similarly, the *proportion* between the products will change *i.e.,* ratio of M/P will decrease, as due to rise in P_P, the farmer substitutes paddy for maize. The opposite will be true, if price of one of the products will decrease. Note that, more generally, due to change in the relative price of the products, the proportion of products also changes. For example, if P_P increases by one percent and P_M increases by three percent, then M/P will increase, as the farmer now substitute maize for paddy. This is why, the supply of a product (say, maize) is inversely related to the price of substitute product (paddy). That is, if price of paddy increases in the market, the farmers will produce more of paddy and the supply of maize will decrease.

Types of Enterprises Combinations

The PPC as discussed earlier helps to illustrate the relationship, which could exist between the products produced on the farm. We know, products or enterprises compete for limited resources such as land, labour, capital and others. So, the farmer must ensure that the resources are allocated among these enterprises, so as to achieve maximization of profits. There are five types of enterprises relationships:

A. Joint products

B. Complementary product relationship

C. Supplementary product relationship
D. Competitive product relationship
E. Antagonistic products

A. Joint Products

These are the products, which are produced simultaneously through a single or same production process. That is, we cannot produce one product in the absence of another product and the production of one implies the production of the other. These two products combine in a fixed proportion or ratio. That is, the level of production of one product decides the level of production of another product. Hence, there is no problem of decision making on the part of farmer regarding, which product should be produced more and which should be less in the short run. In the long-run, however, changes in the relative prices of the two products may necessitate a change in the products combination. For example, a continued increase in the price of wool compared to the price of mutton may necessitate a change in the sheep breeds, which would produce a higher proportion of wool. Once this happens, again the proportions of the two products become fixed. The PPC curve for joint products is inverted 'L' shape (Panel A of the Figure 2.38) and MRPS = '0' for joint products. All farm commodities are mostly joint products. Examples include: Paddy grain + Straw, Cotton seed + Lint, Sheep wool + Mutton, Cattle and Manure, Butter and Buttermilk *etc.* However, with the advances in technology of agriculture like application of bio-technology, genetic engineering *etc.*, the proportion of one product over the proportion of other product can be slightly varied. Examples include: seedless grapes, seedless papaya *etc.* Similarly, there are some varieties of oil palm, which produce more palm oil than kernel. So, the farmer could take the advantage of this type of scenario in deciding on what to produce. When the demand for palm oil for example, is on the increase and price is increasing, the farmer can decide to go for the variety which yields more palm oil. Switching from variety however, may take some time.

B. Complementary Product Relationship

Two enterprises are said to be complementary, when an increase in the production of one enterprise or product, it leads to increase in production of other enterprise at a given level of resource usage. This complementary relationship between two enterprises exists, when with a change in the level of production of one, the other also changes in the same direction. The two enterprises do not compete for resources, but contribute to the mutual production by providing an element of production required by each other. That is, this relationship occurs, when one of the products supplies input(s) to the production of the other. So, complementarity between the products exists, when an increase in the production of one product through the transfer of more resource to its production leads to increase in the production of the other product. For example, in groundnut + red gram intercropping system, red gram crop fixes nitrogen from the atmosphere and it will be utilized by the groundnut crop. So, the yields of groundnut increase with increase in production of red gram. So, this relationship exists only, when one enterprise produces an element which is required in the production of another enterprise. However, these two enterprises are complementary only up to a certain level of resource usage, but later they start competing each other for the limited (money) resources available with the farmer. That means, if more resources are devoted to one enterprise (say, groundnut) the production of groundnut will increase and the production of red gram is affected. Thus, the two enterprises do not remain complementary over all possible combinations. They become competitive at some stage. When both complementary and competitive relationships occur, the complementary relationship occurs first and then is followed by the competitive relationship. So, when these two relationships (complementary followed by competitive) exist, the farmer can increase the outputs of both the enterprises as long as they are complementary to each other *i.e.,* he can produce both the enterprises up to the end of the complementarity stage without reference to the prices of the two products. When they enter the competitive stage, the substitution ratio and the price ratio of the two products should be considered and the OPC has to be determined as in the case of competitive enterprises. MRPS for complementary enterprises is more than zero *i.e.,* positive (Case I of Table 2.24). As long as the two enterprises are complementary, the farmer need not draw the price comparison between the two enterprises. But, when the two enterprises turn competitive for the use of resources, prices become a determining factor in deciding for which enterprise the resources should be diverted.

From Panel B of the Figure 2.38, it is clear that, up to AB portion of PPC, production of Y_1 enterprise is complementary with Y_2 enterprise. Similarly, up to CD portion of PPC, production of Y_2 is complementary with Y_1 enterprise. That means, between AB and CD portions of PPC, the two enterprises are complementary to each other. But, between B and C portion of PPC, the enterprises start competing with each other for limited resources with the farmer. That means, between B and C portion of PPC, if the

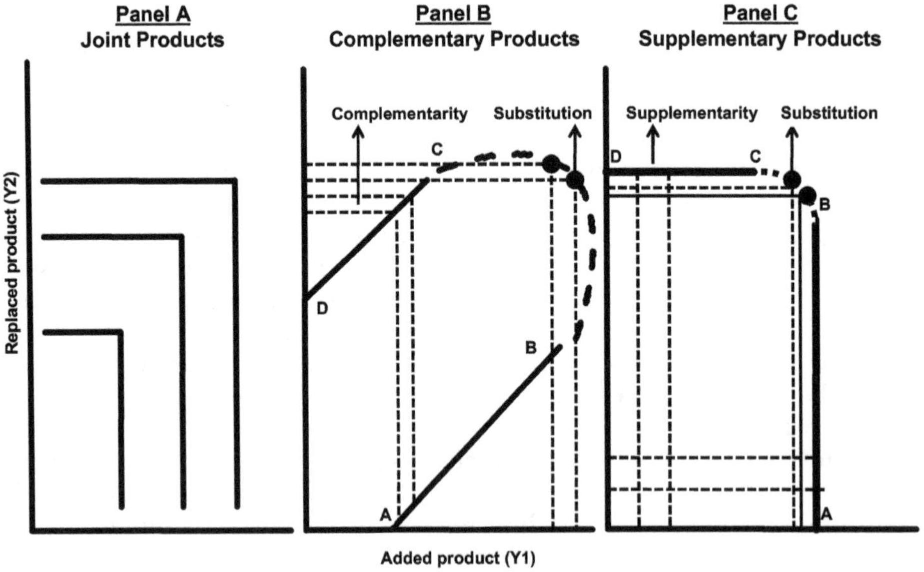

Figure 2.38: Types of Enterprise Combinations and Shapes of PPCs.

production of Y_1 is increased, production of Y_2 is decreased. All complementary relationships should be taken advantage by producing both enterprises up to the point, where they become competitive.

Table 2.24: Complementary, Competitive and Supplementary Enterprises Relationships

Y_1	Y_2	ΔY_1	ΔY_2	$MRPS_{Y1Y2}$ $(\Delta Y_2/\Delta Y_1)$	*Nature of Enterprise Relationship*
Case I					
10	35	–	–	–	Since $MRPS_{Y1Y2}$ is positive (>0), the relationship between the enterprises is Complementary.
15	41	5	6	1.20	
18	43	3	2	0.67	
Case II					
21	20	–	–	–	Since $MRPS_{Y1Y2}$ is negative (<0), the relationship between the enterprises is Competitive *i.e.*, they substitute each other.
32	13	11	–7	–0.64	
39	9	7	–4	–0.57	
Case III					
15	13	–	–	–	Since $MRPS_{Y1Y2}$ is zero, the relationship between the enterprises is Supplementary.
19	13	4	0	0.00	
26	13	7	0	0.00	

C. Supplementary Product Relationship

Two enterprises are said to be supplementary, when an increase or decrease in the production of one enterprise will not have any influence (*i.e.*, neither increase nor decrease) on the level of production of another enterprise, but adds to the total income of the farm. That is, in case of supplementary enterprises, one enterprise can be added without contracting the other. These supplementary enterprises employ labour, feed, capital and buildings not used by other enterprises, which otherwise go as waste. So, supplementary enterprises do not influence each other but, add to the total income of the farm. That is, supplementarity exists between enterprises, when the output levels of two enterprises are independent of each other. Example include: paddy + apiculture. Similarly, production of cocoa and oil palm using labour and some implements can be said to be complementary, but the use of pressing machinery for extracting palm oil does not affect the production of cocoa, as it is not needed in cocoa production. We practically see on many small farms, a small dairy enterprise or a poultry enterprise or a small bee-keeping enterprise may be supplementary to the main crop enterprise because, they utilize surplus family labour and even some feeds, which would otherwise go to waste. An expansion of say, poultry enterprise up to this size or below it, does not necessitate a change in other enterprises on the farm. The farmer can expand the production of these allied enterprises as long as they remain supplementary to the main crop enterprise(s) and when they are expanded far, they become competitive for the inputs. So, the farmer can go for diversification of enterprises on the farm, up to the end of the supplementary stage. As long as the returns added by each enterprise are greater than its costs, the relative prices of two products are not important. So, the supplementary enterprises can be practiced, till they will not compete for resources. From Panel C of the Figure 2.38, it is clear that, Y_1 is supplementary to Y_2 up to AB portion and Y_2 is supplementary to Y_1 up to CD portion of PPC. But, between B and C portion of PPC, these two enterprises will compete with each other. If two enterprises have supplementary relationship, it is better for the farmer to take up both the enterprises, unless they compete for limited resources. These two enterprises upto the supplementary stage do not compete for resources, but make use of resources when they are not being utilized by one enterprise. So, MRPS=0 for supplementary relationship (Case III of Table 2.24). In some cases, enterprises enjoy supplementary relationship for one resource, but competitive for another. In such cases, the relationship between the enterprises should be treated as 'competitive', as the resource for which the enterprises are competitive might be crucial for each of its production. Note that, as long as the relationship between the two enterprises is supplementary, the farmer need not compare the prices of the two enterprises and he can operate both the enterprises as long as MR (Price) > MC. If the level of a supplementary enterprise is pushed up further, then the two enterprises under consideration become competitive for the resources thereby, price relationship between the two enterprises become the important deciding factor. That is, the principle of opportunity cost becomes operative (discussed in-detail in the ensuing pages of this Chapter).

D. Competitive Product Relationship

Two enterprises are said to be competitive, when an increase in production of one enterprise leads to decrease in the production of another enterprise and *vice-versa*. That is, when the production of one enterprise is increased, with resources held constant, there is compulsory sacrifice or reduction in the output of another enterprise. So, this competitive relationship exists, when an increase or decrease in the production of one enterprise will influence the production of other enterprise inversely. This is because, these two enterprises compete for the same resources. So, MRPS for competitive enterprise is less than zero or negative (Case II of Table 2.24). Examples like groundnut and sunflower, paddy and maize *etc.*, if cultivated in the same season, they compete for land resource. In competitive relationship, enterprises or products substitute each other and the substitution may be at a constant rate or increasing rate or decreasing rate.

i. Constant Rate of Product Substitution

This substitution occurs, when the rate of replacement of one product by the other product does not change or remains same, as the added product increases in its magnitude. That means, if added product is increased by 1 unit, it replaces the replaced product by the same magnitude as that of preceding added unit of added product. So, in constant rate of product substitution, with each one unit increase or gain in one product, a constant quantity of another product must be decreased or sacrificed. In constant rate of product substitution, PPC is a straight line connecting the two axes *i.e.*, it is linear negatively sloped (Panel A of Figure 2.39). $MRPS_{Y1Y2}$ equation for constant rate of product substitution is given by: $\Delta_1 Y_2/\Delta_1 Y_1 = \Delta_2 Y_2/\Delta_2 Y_1 = \Delta_3 Y_2/\Delta_3 Y_1$ $= \ldots\ldots\ldots\ldots\ldots = \Delta n Y_2/\Delta n Y_1$ (Table 2.25). This constant rate of product substitution occurs only in case of perfect substitutes. Even two varieties of paddy are good substitutes, but not perfect substitutes. Hence, this constant rate of product substitution is not common in agriculture. In case of this substitution, the decision to produce the products is based on two aspects:

- Instead of producing two products, it is better for the farmer to produce only one product, so as to maximize the profits.
- The farmer prefers to produce high priced product instead of low priced product. That is, when the two products substitute each other at constant rate, it is better for the farmer to take up any one enterprise, depending upon their relative prices in the market. That means, we advocate the farmer to go for specialization in production programme.

Table 2.25: Constant Rate of Product Substitution in the Production Programme

Y_1	ΔY_1	Y_2	ΔY_2	$MRPS_{Y1Y2} = \Delta Y_2/\Delta Y_1$
1		10		
	1		–2	–2
2		8		
	1		–2	–2
3		6		
	1		–2	–2
4		4		
	1		–2	–2
5		2		

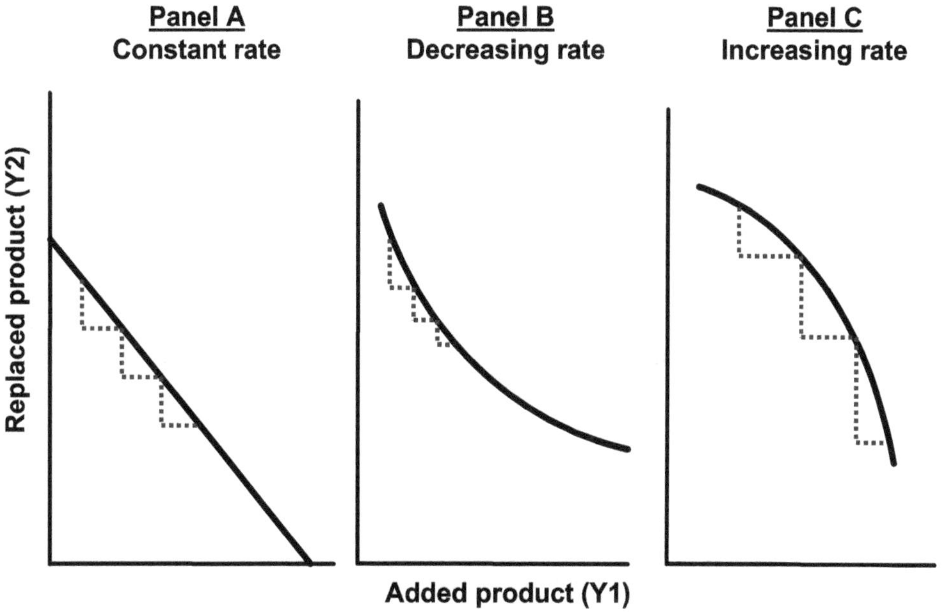

Figure 2.39: Types of Product Substitution – Shapes of Production Possibility Curves.

Note that, constant rate of product substitution occurs, when one product exhibits increasing (marginal) returns (Figure 2.3) and another product exhibits diminishing (marginal) returns (Figure 2.5) in their production programme. That is, one of the production functions has an elasticity greater than one (increasing returns), the other has an elasticity of less than one (diminishing returns). Thus, both the production functions have stages of increasing and diminishing returns.

ii. Decreasing Rate of Product Substitution

This substitution occurs, when the rate of replacement of one product by the other product decreases, as the added product increases in its magnitude. That means, if added product is increased by 1 unit, it replaces the replaced product by a lesser magnitude than that of preceding added unit of added product. That is, each unit increase in the output of one enterprise is accompanied by lesser and lesser decrease in the production of another enterprise. In decreasing rate of product substitution, PPC is convex to origin (Panel B of Figure 2.39). $MRPS_{Y1Y2}$ equation of decreasing rate of product substitution is given by: $\Delta_1 Y_2/\Delta_1 Y_1 > \Delta_2 Y_2/\Delta_2 Y_1 > \Delta_3 Y_2/\Delta_3 Y_1 > \ldots\ldots\ldots\ldots > \Delta n Y_2/\Delta n Y_1$ (Table 2.26). This rate of product substitution also is not common in agriculture.

Table 2.26: Decreasing Rate of Product Substitution in the Production Programme

Y_1	ΔY_1	Y_2	ΔY_2	$MRPS_{Y1Y2} = \Delta Y_2/\Delta Y_1$
1		15		
	1		–5	–5
2		10		
	1		–3	–3
3		7		
	1		–2	–2
4		5		
	1		–1	–1
5		4		

Note that, decreasing rate of product substitution occurs, when both the products exhibit increasing MRs in their production programme. But, this increasing MRs is not common in agriculture. Even though both the products are experiencing increasing MRs in case of decreasing rate of product substitution, it is advocated to the farmer to go for specialization i.e, taking up only one enterprise depending upon their relative prices. This is because, increasing MRs of an enterprise in its production programme is seen in only in first zone of neo-classical production function (Figure 2.7). But, in this Stage I, farmer cannot maximize the profits and he has to move to second zone to maximize the profits. But, if the farmer takes up both the enterprises, the limited resources will be utilized on both the enterprises and he will remain only in Stage I only, where he cannot maximize the profits. Hence, we advocate the farmer to take up only one enterprise so that, the limited resources that can be allotted to another enterprise can be utilized for the selected enterprise and hence, the farmer can move to Stage II, where he can realize maximum profits at least from one enterprise. In case of this substitution, the decision to produce the products is based on two aspects:

- Instead of producing two products, it is better for the farmer to produce only one product, so as to maximize the profits.
- The farmer prefers to produce high priced product instead of low priced product. That is, when the two products substitute each other at decreasing rate, it is better for the farmer to take up any one enterprise, depending upon their relative prices in the market. That means, we advocate the farmer to go for specialization in production programme.

iii. Increasing Rate of Product Substitution

This substitution occurs, when the rate of replacement of one product by the other product increases, as the added product increases in its magnitude. That means, if added product is increased by 1 unit, it replaces the replaced product by more than that of preceding added unit of added product. So, the increase in the level of one enterprise decreases the level of other enterprise substantially. In increasing rate of product substitution, PPC is concave to the origin (Panel C of the Figure 2.39). $MRPS_{Y1Y2}$ equation for increasing rate of product substitution is given by: $\Delta_1 Y_2/\Delta_1 Y_1 < \Delta_2 Y_2/\Delta_2 Y_1 < \Delta_3 Y_2/\Delta_3 Y_1 < \ldots\ldots\ldots\ldots\ldots < \Delta n Y_2/\Delta n Y_1$ (Table 2.27). This rate of product substitution occurs only, when the products are good substitutes. For example, paddy and maize, groundnut and sunflower *etc.*, are good substitutes, but not perfect substitutes. This increasing rate of product substitution is more common in agricultural production. In case of this substitution, it is better for the farmer to produce both the products, so as to maximize the profits. This is because, both the products experience diminishing MRs in their production programme (Figure 2.5). So, we advocate the farmer to go for diversification in production programme, if the products substitute each other at an increasing rate. That is, profits are maximized by producing both the products.

Table 2.27: Increasing rate of product substitution in the production programme

Y_1	ΔY_1	Y_2	ΔY_2	$MRPS_{Y1Y2} = \Delta Y_2/\Delta Y_1$
1		15		
	1		–1	–1
2		14		
	1		–2	–2
3		12		
	1		–3	–3
4		9		
	1		–5	–5
5		4		

The above discussion infers that, when enterprises are competitive, three things determine the exact combination of the products which would be most profitable to the farmer viz.,

- ✰ The rate at which one enterprise substitutes for the other,
- ✰ The prices of the products, and
- ✰ The cost of producing the products.

E. Antagonistic Relationship

It is opposite to complementarity relationship. Two enterprises are said to have antagonistic relationship, when both the enterprises are taken up simultaneously, both of their production functions gets affected. For example, if bhendi and brinjal are cultivated in neighbouring plots or fields, both the crops are affected by fruit sucking pests and diseases. So, both the enterprises are affected adversely.

Considering the above types of enterprises relationships, the farmers have to take advantage in allocating the resources among the enterprises or in choosing the crop varieties that contribute to maximization of farm profits. Prices of both factors and products can be the determinants for choosing the enterprises combination.

Applicability of Product Substitution Principle

The above discussion infers that, if the farmer is having unlimited resources, he need not worry about the product substitution or product combination, because straight away he can select the enterprises which will fetch him more returns. But, in general, the farmer will have limited resources and he has to allocate these limited resources on the enterprise he selects or among the enterprise combinations he prefers. So, the principle of product substitution mainly aims at studying the resource allocation among the enterprise or enterprise combinations taken up by the farmer. This principle revolves around the following two propositions:

- ✰ Resource level being constant, the farmer substitutes the product with higher returns in place of the product with low returns. That means, if the level of one product is increased, the level of other product will decrease, because the resource level with the farmer is constant.
- ✰ The farmer goes on substituting one product for another product as long as the increasing returns of added product is greater than decreasing returns of replaced product. That is,

  Increasing returns from added product > Decreasing returns of replaced product

  $\Delta Y_1 * PY_1 > \Delta Y_2 * PY_2$

  $PY_1/PY_2 > \Delta Y_2/\Delta Y1$

  Price ratio of products > MRPS

From the above equation, it is clear that, to earn more profits, the farmer has to increase production of more of added product or decrease production of replaced product. Reverse is the case, when $MRPS_{Y1Y2}$ is more than Price ratio of two products and hence, the farmer should increase the production of more of replaced product or decrease production of added product. This concept of optimum product combination is applicable, when the products substitute each other at increasing rate. That is, if the products substitute at increasing rate (which is very common in agriculture), then the farmer has to go for diversification. That means, he has to produce both the enterprises and the point of optimality is when MRPS is inversely equal to price ratio of products. However, if the products substitute each other either at constant rate or decreasing rate, the farmer should go for specialization *i.e.,* production of only one product that enjoys higher price in the market.

5. Principle of Equi-Marginal Returns

We have already seen that, the focus of Economics is to utilize the limited resources efficiently among unlimited or prioritized wants. In this context, the Principle of Equi-Marginal Returns will guide the farmers in deriving maximum profits from the available limited resources. This principle of Equi-Marginal Returns is an extension to the LDR to two enterprises or more than one enterprise. This law explains the behaviour of a farmer in allocating his limited resources among various enterprises, so as to derive maximum profits. This law closely follows the Robbins's definition of Economics in various aspects *viz.,* the resources are scarce with the farmer, resources have alternative uses, resources can be allocated among different enterprises or products, the farmer has scale of preferences among unlimited wants, farmer aims to derive maximum profits from limited resources *etc.* So, this law is more realistic compared to LDR. In a production programme, if the farmer is having unlimited resources, he need not worry about the enterprise selection, enterprise combinations, resource use efficiency *etc.,* and the point of optimality he can achieve where, SRMC = MR in producing a particular enterprise. This is the case of LDR principle. But, in practical situation, the resources available with the farmer are limited and he has to use the resources very efficiently. Hence, generally the farmer prefers substituting one enterprise for another enterprise or taking up enterprise combinations, so as to achieve maximum resource use efficiency across the enterprises. He can maximize returns, where the MRs derived from the last unit of resource spent is equal or almost equal across the enterprises he selects. So this principle states that returns will be maximum in a production programme by using the limited resources in such a way that, the MRs derived from the last unit of resource spent is equal or almost equal across the enterprises he selects. This principle of Equi-Marginal Returns is also known by various names *viz.,* the Law of Substitution, the Law of Maximum Profits, Law of opportunity costs *etc.* This law is known as the Law of Maximum Profits because, the farmer tries to derive maximum profits from his limited resources in such a way that, the MRs derived from one enterprise is the same as the MR of enterprise on another use. It is also known as the Law of Substitution because, farmer substitutes one enterprise for the other till he gets the maximum profits from his limited resources. So, this principle guides the farmer in making choices out of many given enterprises on which he can spend his limited amount of money. It is also called the Law of opportunity cost because, the allocation of resources across the enterprises is based on the concept of opportunity cost. This makes the farmer indifferent to re-adjust his expenditure unless some change takes place in his income, the prices of the commodities *etc.* It is also called Proportionality Rule because, it is the Principle of Proportionality that guides the farmer to derive maximum profits from the limited resources available with him. This principle can be defined as 'a farmer tends to regulate his production of different enterprises in such a way that, the MRs derived from them are equal'. In other words, 'the farmer maximizes his income by allocating the resources between the enterprises such that, the MRs of the last resource spent on each item is equal'. So, we can infer that, the farmer will be in equilibrium, when he distributes his resources among various enterprises in such a way that, the MRs derived from the last rupee spent on each enterprise is the same. To put it in simple words, profits will be maximum by using the limited resources in such a way that, the MRs derived from the last unit of money resource spent on each enterprise is more or less equal. It is essential to note that, when the farmer has limited resources, he must aim to realize the greatest returns from the resource that is scarcest. Say, for example, if the farmer has plenty of labour and feed resources but with limited capital outlay, he should aim at maximizing the returns from each rupee invested on the enterprise(s). However, some farmers enjoy more capital but suffer from limited labour resource and in such case, he must aim at maximizing labour returns on the selected enterprise(s).

Assumptions

Since this law is based on the LDR, some of the assumptions of LDR coincide with assumptions of Principle of Equi-Marginal Returns. The main assumptions of the Principle of Equi-Marginal Returns are as under.

- ☆ The MRs of different enterprises are independent of each other and diminishes with more and more allocation of resources.
- ☆ Every farmer will act rationally in selecting the enterprises with his limited resources.
- ☆ The farmer has limited resources to allocate on the enterprises under consideration.
- ☆ Input and output prices should remain constant and known to the farmer.
- ☆ There should be more than one enterprise, as the farmer tries to substitute one enterprise for the other, so as to derive maximum profits with the available limited resources.

Explanation of the Principle

The equi-marginal principle was originally associated with consumption theory and the law is called 'the law of equi-marginal utility'. The law of equi-marginal utility states that a utility maximizing consumer distributes his limited consumption expenditure between various goods and services he/she consumes in such a way that, the marginal utility derived from each unit of expenditure on various commodities is the same. The pattern of consumer's expenditure maximizes a consumer's total utility. The same equi-marginal principle has been applied to the allocation of limited resources between their alternative enterprises with a view to maximizing profit in case a firm carries out more than one enterprise. This principle suggests that available resources (inputs) should be so allocated between the alternative options such that the MRs from the various enterprises are equalized. The concept of Principle of Equi-Marginal Returns in production theory is similar (analogous to) the Law of Equi-Marginal Utility of consumption theory. This concept of Principle of Equi-Marginal Returns can be explained with the help of following hypothetical example (Table 2.28). Suppose, a farmer is having Rs.5000 and he wishes to allocate this limited money among three enterprises A, B and C. If the farmer allocates Rs.5000 on only one enterprise say, either on A or B or C, he derives the rate of return as 2.20 or 2.88 or 2.32 respectively. Let us apply the concept of Principle of Equi-Marginal Returns *i.e.,* spending the limited resources in accordance with higher MRs he can derive from each unit of resource. Considering the MRs across the preferred enterprises, the farmer will invest first unit of Rs.1000 on enterprise B, because it yields higher MRs of Rs.3500. The farmer spends second unit of Rs.1000 on enterprise B again because, it yields a MR of Rs.3400. Similarly, he will spend third unit of Rs.1000 on enterprise B again and he derives Rs.3000 MRs. But, regarding fourth unit of Rs.1000, the farmer prefers to spend on enterprise C because, it yields MRs of Rs.2700, which is comparatively higher than enterprises A and B. Similarly, fifth unit of Rs.1000 is spent on enterprise A because, MRs he derive *i.e.,* Rs.2600 is higher compared to B and C enterprises. So by following the Principle of Equi-Marginal Returns, the farmer prefers to spend Rs.3000 on enterprise B, Rs.1000 each on enterprises C and A and by doing so, he can maximize Total Returns (TRs) to Rs.15,200 at a rate of return of 3.04 and no other combination of resource (money) allocation across the enterprises will yield higher TR than Rs.15,200 or with a rate of return of 3.04.So, this principle guides the farmer in efficient allocation of resources across the enterprises, so as to maximize the profits with the given limited resources. The above concept illustrated through Figure 2.40 reveals that, spending Rs.3000 on enterprise B and Rs.1000 each on enterprises A and C will maximize the profits, as indicated by the equal slopes of MR curves of all the three enterprises.

Table 2.28: Allocation of Resources Across the Enterprises Based on the Concept of Opportunity Cost

Capital	*MRs*		
	Enterprise A	*Enterprise B*	*Enterprise C*
1000	2600	3500	2700
1000	2500	3400	2400
1000	2400	3000	2300
1000	2000	2500	2200
1000	1500	2000	2000
TR	11,000	14,400	11,600
Rate of Return by allocating limited money on a single enterprise	= 11,000/5000= 2.20	=14,400/5000= 2.88	= 11,600/5000= 2.32
Rate of Return by allocating limited money in accordance with the Principle of Equi-Marginal Returns	[(3500+3400+3000+2700+2600)/5000] = (15200/5000) = 3.04		

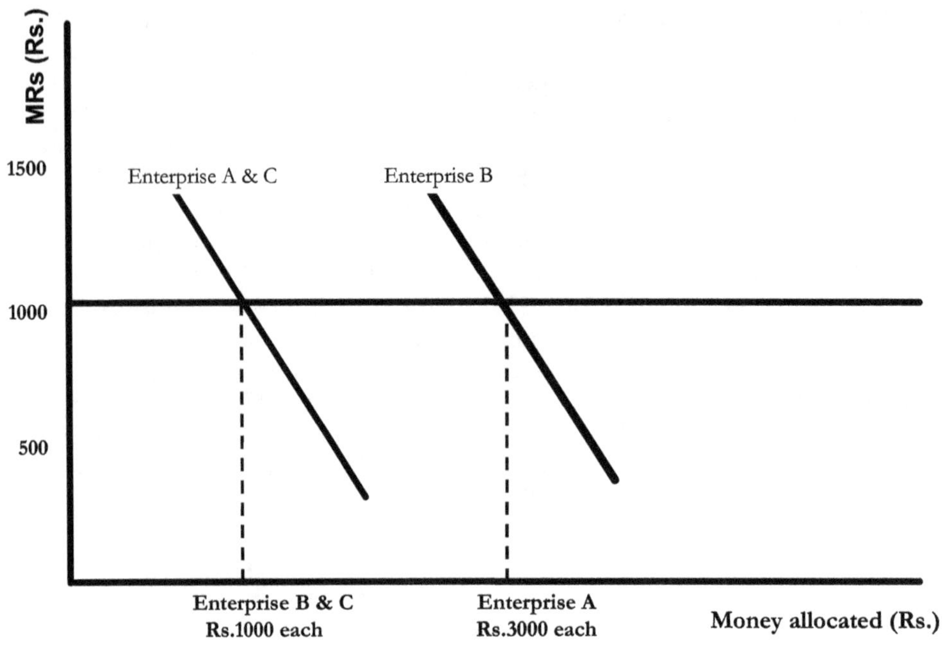

Figure 2.40: Allocation of Resources Across the Enterprises in Accordance with the Principle of Equi-Marginal Returns.

This Principle of Equi-Marginal Returns is also called as Opportunity cost principle because, the farmer allocates his limited resources across the selected enterprises based on the opportunity cost concept. As discussed earlier, opportunity cost refers to cost equivalent to the returns from the next best missed alternative. We know, when resources are put to one use opportunities of other alternatives are lost. In the above example, for the first unit of resource *i.e.*, Rs.1000 spent on enterprise B yields a MR of Rs.3500. The opportunity cost of this first unit of Rs.1000 is MR of Rs.3,400 of the same enterprise B. Hence, the second unit of Rs.1000 is again spent on enterprise B for which MR is Rs. 3,400. For the second unit of Rs. 1000, the opportunity cost is MR of Rs.3000 of enterprise B again. Hence, the third unit of Rs.1000 is again spent on enterprise B, which gives a MR of Rs.3000. The opportunity cost of this third unit of Rs.1000 is MR of Rs.2700 of enterprise C. Hence, the fourth unit of Rs.1000 is spent on enterprise C for which MR is Rs.2700. For this fourth unit of Rs.1000, the opportunity cost is MR of Rs.2600 of enterprise A. Hence, the fifth unit of Rs.1000 is spent on enterprise A for which MR is Rs.2600. Thus, the procedure of allocating resources across the selected enterprises depends on the opportunity cost concept. Thus, the Principle of Equi-Marginal Returns can be applied only where

- ☆ Farmer have limited resources
- ☆ resources have alternative uses and
- ☆ investment in various alternative uses is subjected to diminishing MRs.

Thus, the Principle of opportunity cost (LEMR) infers that, the resources should always be used, where they bring in the greatest MR and not the greatest average returns. That is, for each addition of resource in the production programme, we compare, not average returns, but the MR across the enterprises under consideration. Thus, the concept of principle of opportunity cost states that, *'a farmer can have the best combination of enterprises from this limited resources, when they are so organized such that, we cannot change the use of single unit of a resource without reducing the income'.*

Practical Applicability

The following points highlight the practical importance of this principle:

- ✰ It will guide the farmer to plan his budgetary requirements in advance regarding investment on different enterprises.
- ✰ It also helps the farmers to study the different enterprise relationships. *i.e.,* whether enterprises selected are supplementary or complementary or competitive in nature.
- ✰ It also guides the farmers to maximize the resource use efficiency in the production programme.
- ✰ It also guides the farmers, whether he has to go for diversification or specialization in the farm business.

LDR vis-à-vis Principle of Equi-Marginal Returns

Table 2.29: Differences between LDR and Principle of Equi-Marginal Returns.

Sl.No.	*LDR*	*Principle of Equi-Marginal Returns*
1.	This principle is applicable in the production programme, when the resource level with the farmer is unlimited	Principle of Equi-Marginal Returns is applicable in the production programme, when the resource level with the farmer is limited
2.	In LDR, we deal with only one enterprise	Principle of Equi-Marginal Returns deals with more than one enterprise if the farmer goes for diversification in the farm business.
3.	The point of profit maximization in LDR principle is MC=MR because, the resources with the farmer are unlimited.	Since the resources are limited, the point of profit maximization is when MR is equal across all the enterprises for the last unit of rupee spent on them. Since the resources are limited, the farmer cannot go up to MC=MR criterion.
4.	This principle advocates the farmer to maximize profit in a specialized production programme.	This principle advocates the farmer to go either for specialization or diversification of farm business depending upon the MRs the farmer derives from each rupee spent on the enterprises.
5.	New soils, new technology *etc.*, can limit the operation of LDR principle	There are no such limitations in case of LEMR.
6.	The concept of substitution of one enterprise by another will not arise in LDMU.	The concept of substitution of one enterprise by another will arise in LEMU, so as to maximize the TR from limited resources.

Contd...

Table 2.29–*Contd...*

Sl.No.	*LDR*	*Principle of Equi-Marginal Returns*
7.	The TR derived through application of LDR concept is lower compared Principle of Equi-Marginal Returns, as the farmer will not substitute one enterprise for another.	The consumer derives higher satisfaction through the application of LEMU concept, as he substitutes one commodity with higher MU in place of another commodity with lower MU.
8	LDR concept aims at maximization of TR through production of a single enterprise.	Principle of Equi-Marginal Returns ensures twin objectives *viz.*, efficient utilization of resources and maximization of TRs.

6. Principle of Comparative Advantage

This principle will guide the farmer to go for regional specialization of crops and allied enterprises in an area. We know that, farmers cultivate a wide variety of crops and practice different allied enterprises under diversified climatic conditions. But, some enterprises in some areas will have some additional advantages either in terms of yields or costs or prices or quality of output or marketing facilities *etc.* Taking these advantages into consideration, the farmer prefer to take up the enterprises. For example, in Andhra Pradesh in East and West Godavari districts, farmers practice paddy cultivation, in Duggirala area of Guntur district, farmers prefers turmeric cultivation, in Srikakulam district mesta, in Chittoor district farmers prefer mango cultivation, in Visakhapatmam district sugarcane *etc.* Similarly, in Southern parts of India - paddy cultivation, in Northern parts of India – wheat cultivation, in Himachal Pradesh – Apples, in Rajasthan - sheep rearing, in Karnataka - sericulture *etc.*, are practiced. This specialization of enterprises is mainly due to various advantages the farmer will reap in terms of yields or costs or prices or quality of output or marketing facilities *etc.* These advantages can be classified into two types *viz.*, Absolute Advantage and Comparative or Relative Advantage.

i. Absolute Advantage or Arithmetic Advantage

It is the ability of a region or a country to produce a commodity with lowest absolute cost or with lesser amount of resources than any other region or country in the world. This concept of absolute advantage was proposed by Adam Smith. This absolute advantage is, otherwise, defined as the arithmetic size of the margin between costs in using resources and returns from the resources. If this margin is larger for the product in one area than in another area, the first area has an absolute advantage in producing that commodity (Heady and Jensen, p 46). If a country possess absolute advantage with reference to any commodity, it is better for the country to go for specialization in the production of that commodity, as it will enjoy trade advantage in the market. So, in studying absolute advantage, we compare the economics of enterprises across the regions or across the countries. But, to gain more from trade, a country need not enjoy absolute advantage rather, comparative advantage for a commodity is sufficient.

ii. Comparative Advantage or Relative Advantage or Percentage Advantage

It refers to the ability of a region or country to produce a commodity at lower opportunity cost than any other commodity in the same region. So, in comparative advantage, we compare the economics of enterprises within the same region or within the same country. This concept of comparative advantage was given by David Ricardo and Robert Torrens. This advantage also infers that, if farmers want the greatest profit, they should produce those things considering yields, costs and prices, in which their relative or percentage returns are greatest, it doesn't dictate production in line only with absolute advantage (Heady and Jensen, p 47). Thus, comparative advantage exists, when a country has a margin of superiority in the production of a commodity *i.e.*, where the opportunity cost of production is lower. David Ricardo in his book *'Principles of Political Economy and Taxation'* emphasized this concept of comparative advnantage and its role in explaining the international trade of commodities. So, this theory of comparative advantage is also called Comparative cost theory, is regarded as the classical theory of international trade.

These two advantages *i.e.*, absolute and relative advantages can be well-explained with help of following examples:

Example 2.3

Assume there are five countries producing a commodity X in the world with the following cost structure:

- ☆ Country A: Rs.1050/unit
- ☆ Country B: Rs.1000/unit
- ☆ Country C: Rs.1200/unit
- ☆ Country D: Rs.1210/unit
- ☆ Country E: Rs.1150/unit

From the given cost structure, it is evident that, Country B enjoys Absolute Advantage in the world in the production of commodity X over all other countries, as it enjoys lowest cost of production. However, Country E enjoys comparative advantage over countries C and D in producing commodity X, as Country E can export the commodity to these two countries C and D. For the same reason, Country A also enjoys comparative advantage over Country C, D and E and Country C enjoys comparative advantage over Country D.

Example 2.4

Let us suppose, there are two countries C_1 and C_2. If all the factors of production and technology are diverted towards food production in C_1 and C_2 countries, the output is 100 units in C_1 and 400 units in C_2. Similarly, if all the factors of production and technology are diverted towards clothes production both in C_1 and C_2 countries, the output is 100 units in C_1 and 200 units in C_2 (Table 2.30).

Table 2.30: Absolute Advantage and Comparative Advantage in Production of Commodities

Countries	*Food*	*Cloth*	*Food: Cloth*
C_1	100 units	100 units	1:1
C_2	400 units	200 units	2:1

☆ ***Absolute advantage:*** From the Table 2.30 it is clear that, country C_2 enjoys absolute advantage over C_1 with reference to the production of both food and clothes. So, this appears that, there will not be any mutual trade between two countries taking absolute advantage into consideration.

☆ ***Comparative advantage:*** Though absolute advantage of country C_1 indicate the absence of mutual trade between the two countries, the opportunity cost of producing both the commodities show otherwise. To analyze the opportunity cost of producing these two commodities, compute the ratio between food and clothes production in each country *i.e.*, in country C_1 it is 1:1 and in country C_2 it is 2:1.From these ratios, the following are the important findings:

❑ *Country C_1:*

- The opportunity cost of producing one unit of clothes is one unit of food. That means, if we increase the cloth production by one unit, one unit of food production should be sacrificed.
- The opportunity cost of producing one unit of food is one unit of clothes. That means, if we increase the food production by one unit, one unit of clothes production should be sacrificed.

❑ *Country C_2:*

- The opportunity cost of producing 1 unit of clothes is 2 units of food. That means, if we increases the clothes production by 1 unit, 2 units of food production should be sacrificed.
- The opportunity cost of producing 1 unit of food is 0.5 units of clothes. That means, if we increase the food production by 1 unit, only 0.5 units of clothes production should be sacrificed.

From the above findings, regarding the production ratios of both the commodities in both the countries, we can say that, country C_1 has comparative advantage with reference to clothes production because, if we increase the clothes production by 1 unit, only 1 unit of food production should be sacrificed, whereas in case of country C_2 if we increase clothes production of 1 unit, 2 units of food production should be sacrificed. Hence, it is better for the country C_1 to specialize in clothes production. Reverse is the case for country C_2, where it enjoys comparative advantage in terms of food production. This is because, if we increase food production by 1 unit in country C_2 only 0.5 units of clothes production is sacrificed, whereas in country C_1 if we increase food production by 1 unit, 1 unit of clothes production should be sacrificed. Hence, it is better for the country C_2 to specialize in food production. To conclude that, to have mutually gainful trade between the two countries, C_1 and C_2 should specialize in the production of clothes and food respectively and country C_1 exports clothes to country C_2 and country C_1 exports food to country C_2. So, this comparative advantage based on opportunity cost for the production of commodities ensures mutually beneficial trade between the two countries.

It is to be noted that, if the exchange rates or ratios between the countries is same *i.e.,* 1:1 and 1:1 or 2:1 and 2:1; then none of them will benefit by entering into international trade. The students must note that, comparative advantage is a dynamic concept *i.e.,* it can and does change over time. That means, a region or a country can enjoy comparative advantage over a period of time and after some period, it may lose its competitiveness. This can be better understood from the following examples:

Example 2.5: Maize

Avg. of 1993-94 to 1997-98: MSP : Rs. 265.00/qtl, IP : Rs. 294.48/qtl

Avg. of 1998-99 to 2002-03: MSP : Rs. 490.00/qtl, IP : Rs. 411.25/qtl

Example 2.6: Turmeric

Avg. of 1993-94 to 1997-98: MP : Rs. 1912.52/qtl, IP : Rs. 2320.21/qtl

Avg. of 1998-99 to 2002-03: MP : Rs. 1866.50/qtl, IP : Rs. 3039.31/qtl

It is evident that, in case of maize, though it is export competitive during the first period *i.e.,* Avg. of 1993-94 to 1997-98, but during the second reference period *i.e.,* Avg. of 1998-99 to 2002-03, the commodity is not export competitive, as the average MSP is higher than international price. However, in case of turmeric, the export competitiveness was increased, as the average MSP was declined and international price was increased during the selected reference periods. Thus, the comparative advantage for a commodity is not a static picture and it varies depending upon the production subsidies, qualitative production, cost of production, movements in exchange rates, import duties, inflation, non-price competitiveness of producers such as product design, reliability *etc.*

Practical Applicability

This principle guides the farmer in going for regional specialization of production of commodities taking into consideration the relative advantages in terms of of yields or costs or prices or quality of output or marketing facilities *etc.* In accordance with the concept of comparative advantage, all countries produce and export those commodities in which they have cost advantages and import those commodities in which they have cost disadvantages.

7. Time Comparison Principle

There are two ways of spending financial resources in the farm-business:

- ☆ Money spent on working capital like seeds, fertilizers, pesticides *etc.* These costs will be recovered immediately in the production programme in the same accounting year. The only criterion the farmer should follow is MC = MR to maximize the profits.

- Investment made to create capital assets like machinery, technology, infrastructure, establishment of orchards like mango, citrus *etc.* These investments cannot be recovered in the same accounting year. Moreover, in these investments, there will be a gestation period between the investment and accrual of returns into the business. That means, considerable time gap is indispensible between the investment made and accrual of returns. So, during gestation period money resource gets locked up in the business. In making long-term investments on the farm, the farmer has to take important decisions pertaining to the time of accrual of returns into the business. So, time decisions come into farm management in many ways.
  - Should the farmer go for cultivation of annual crops like paddy, wheat, vegetables *etc.*, that yield returns in the same accounting year or should he go for plantation crops like mango, citrus, apple *etc.*, that produce output and yield returns after a long gestation period?
  - Should the farmer go for purchasing a second hand machinery that cost him Rs.25000 and lasts for 5 years or should the farmer purchase a new machinery that cost him Rs.6000 and that lasts for 20 years?
  - Should the farmer go for cash-grain cropping system, which will give higher returns now and declining returns in the future or should go for establishing vermi-composting unit that contribute low returns now and increasing returns in the future?

Such questions can be answered by applying this Time comparison principle.

There is a popular phrase that, '*A dollar today is worth more than a dollar a year from now*'. The same concept applies in choosing between investment in a farm-business. Those investments that promise earlier returns are preferable to those that promise later returns. A dollar received now is more valuable than a dollar received a year from now, because of the simple reason that, if you have a dollar today, you can put it in the bank and can have more than a dollar a year from now due to earning interest. In general, people prefer benefits or cash now to benefits or cash later for reasons which include:

- They desire to consume goods now rather than delay their enjoyment
- They can invest the cash now in other lucrative opportunities *i.e.*, say on other enterprises or simply save the money in the bank
- The expectation of future benefits may have various risks and uncertainties
- Inflation will reduce the value of future benefits.

Discounting and Compounding

Discounting

Since, the dollar in hand today is more worth than dollar in the future, we need some means of weighing cash inflows that are received at different times so that, they can be compared. By discounting technique, we can adjust the value of a dollar received any number of years from now to its present value so that, it can be compared with the value of a dollar in hand today. Thus, in discounting technique, we estimate the present value of future money. By discounting the future values of cash inflows to the present value, it will enable the farmer to compare the present investment with other competing investments *i.e.*, helps to ascertain the Opportunity Cost of Capital (OCC).

Compounding

The opposite of discounting technique is compounding technique, where we compute the future value of present worth of money in its future date so that, it can be compared with the value of a dollar in hand today. Thus, in compounding technique, we estimate the future value of present money. Assume that, if a bank pays 5 per cent interest on a deposit of Rs.100 today, it will worth Rs.105 in one year from now. This can be expressed in mathematical terms by means of the following formula or equation:

$$F_1 = P\,(1 + i)^1$$

Where, F_1 = Balance at the end of one year period, P = Amount saved/invested in the current period, and 'i' = Rate of interest per year (per cent).

Example 2.7

If a saving is made now of Rs. 100 deposited in a bank, to earn interest at 5 percent, then P = Rs.100 and i = 0.05. Under these conditions, F_1 = Rs.105, the amount to be received in one year. The amount of Rs.100 is the present value of money saved and its future value is Rs.105 after one year due to earning interest. This Rs.105 is also known as the compounded value of the present value of money saved in the bank (Rs.100) or Rs.100 is known as the discounted value of the future Rs.105 receipt. So, Rs.100 represents the value in present terms of Rs.105 to be received a year from now, when the interest rate is 5 percent. When, if Rs.105 is left in the bank for a second year, then at the end of the second year, the original Rs.100 deposit will have grown to Rs.110.25 by the following way:

Original deposit	Rs.100.00
Interest for the first year (Rs.100 × 0.05)	5
Balance at the end of the first year	105
Interest for the second year (Rs.105 × 0.05)	5.25
Balance at the end of the second year	Rs.110.25

Notice that, the interest for the second year is Rs.5.25, as compared to only Rs.5.00 for the first year. The reason for the greater interest earned during the second year is that, during second year, interest is being paid on *interest*. That is, the Rs.5.00 interest earned during the first year has been left in the account and has been added to the original Rs.100 deposit, when computing interest for the second year. This is known as the compound interest. In this case, the compound is annual. Interest can also be compounded on a semi-annual, quarterly, monthly, or even more frequent basis. The more frequently compounding is done, the more rapidly the balance will grow. So, we can determine the future value of present money balance in an account after 't' periods of compounding using the following formula:

$$Ft = P\,(1 + i)^t$$

where t = number of periods.

If t = 2 years and the interest rate is 5 percent per year, then the balance in two years will be as follows: $F_2 = 100\ (1 + 0.05)^2$ = Rs.110.25.

The above discussion on compounding can be viewed from the reverse direction, which implies the discounting technique *i.e.*, we estimate the present value of future income. That means, in the earlier example, if we receive Rs.110.25 after two years from now at an interest rate of 5 percent, its present value will be Rs. 100. We use the following formulae for discounting:

$P = Ft/(1 + i)^t$

Considering another example, assume that, you are going to receive Rs.200 two years from now from an investment. That means, the future value of the sum is Rs.200. Since, this is the amount that you will be receiving after two years, its present value is computed as follows (assume i=5 per cent):

In this example, Ft = Rs.200 (the amount to be received in future), i = 0.05 (the annual rate of interest), and t=2 (the number of years in the future that the amount is to be received)

$P = Ft/(1 + i)^t$

$P = 200/(1 + 0.05)^2$

P = Rs.200/1.1025

P = Rs.181.40

As shown by the computation above, the present value of Rs.200 to be received two years from now is Rs.181.40, if the interest rate is 5 percent. In effect, Rs.181.40 received right now is equivalent to Rs.200 received after two years, if the rate of interest is 5 percent. That is, Rs.181.40 and Rs.200 are just two ways of looking at the same thing. This process of finding the present value of a future cash flow is called discounting. This concept of present value is of central importance in economic analysis. We know that, benefits and costs from long term investments (projects) may not accrue immediately, but rather over a period of time. Since a dollar received today is worth more than a dollar received in the future, future streams of costs and benefits must be reduced to a present-day value. The difference between present and future dollar values is dependent upon the interest or discount rate. For example, the higher the interest rate, the more a dollar will return in the future, if loaned with interest. This logic can also be reversed so that, if future costs and benefits are known, and the interest rate is given, their present value can be calculated by the process of discounting. The concept of discounting is exemplified through Table 2.31. It is clear that, with increase in discount factor, the Present Worth of Costs (PWC) in a project will decline. Since, no discounting is followed, the undiscounted cost structure lie parallel to the X-axis *i.e.*, remains same for the entire life of the project (Figure 2.41). From the above discussion, it is clear that, 'i' refers to interest (discount) rate, (1+i) refers to compounding factor and 1/(1+i) refers to discounting factor.

Table 2.31: Relation between Discount Factor and Present Worth

Year	Actual Value of Costs	Discount Factor 10 per cent= $(1/(1.10)^t)$	PWC	Discount Factor 15 per cent= $(1/(1.15)^t)$	PWC
1	1000	0.909	909.091	0.870	869.565
2	1000	0.826	826.446	0.756	756.144
3	1000	0.751	751.315	0.658	657.516
4	1000	0.683	683.013	0.572	571.753
5	1000	0.621	620.921	0.497	497.177
6	1000	0.564	564.474	0.432	432.328
7	1000	0.513	513.158	0.376	375.937
8	1000	0.467	466.507	0.327	326.902
9	1000	0.424	424.098	0.284	284.262
10	1000	0.386	385.543	0.247	247.185

Discount Rate

In the above example, we have discounted Rs.200 to its present value of Rs.181.40, when the rate of interest is 5 percent. This 5 percent interest that we have used to find the present value is called the Discount rate. This employment of discount factor to estimate the future value of present cash flows (Compounding) and present value of future cash flows (Discounting) is a common practice in appraising long term

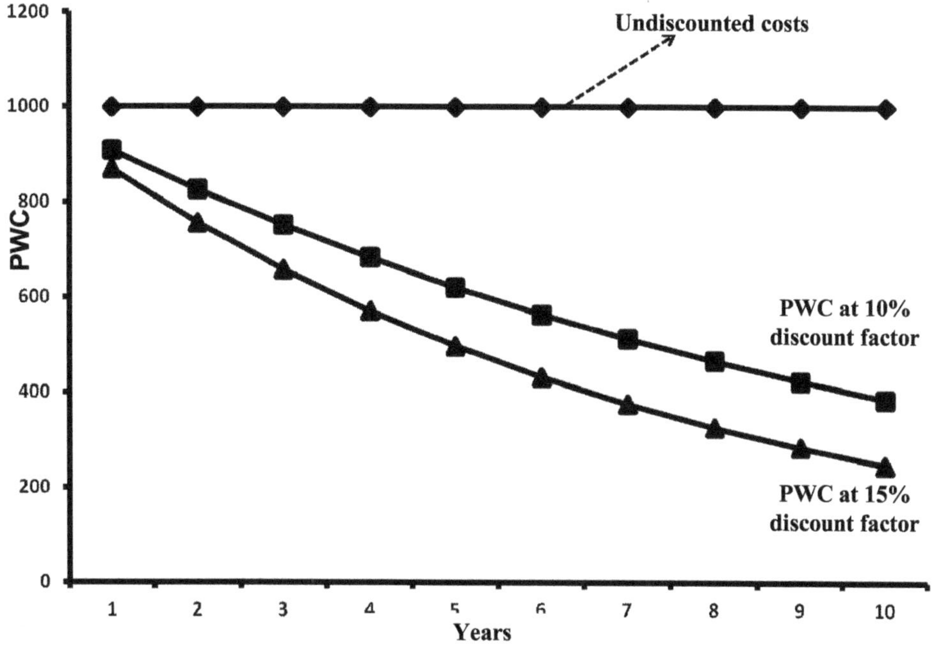

Figure 2.41: Relation between Discount Factor and Present Worth.

investment decisions. Note that, the basic formula for discounting can be applied regardless of the length of the time horizon. Selection of an interest or discount rate greatly influences the economic viability of the long term investment. So, there has been considerable controversy regarding the selection of appropriate discount rate. Lower interest rates will make projects appear more worthwhile and will favour long-lived projects over short-lived ones. In fact, there is no simple rule for choosing a discount rate. Two main approaches are used in selecting proper discount rates for project investments *viz.*, OCC and Social Discount Rate (SDR) or Social Rate of Discount (SRD) of time preference.

- ✰ ***OCC:*** The OCC approach suggests that, the discount rate should reflect the cost of funds withdrawn from the private sector of the economy. OCC also corresponds to the rate of return on investment elsewhere in the economy. Therefore, the discount rate should be equivalent to current market interest rate.
- ✰ ***SRD or SDR:*** This is the interest rate at which a section of the society will save the money in economy or the society prefers present consumption over future consumption. SDR of 12 per cent is widely used for discounting measures. However, the popular choice of discount factor in some countries ranges from 8 – 15 percent. Generally, the SDR is lower than the OCC.

The rate of discounting varies with the amount of capital with the farmers. It will be lower for a farmer with unlimited capital and higher for a farmer with limited capital. For farmers with unlimited capital, market rate of interest is taken as the discount factor, whereas for farmers with limited capital, the rate of returns from the next best opportunity is the discount factor. For example, a farmer possesses only a limited capital of Rs. 5000 and wishes to buy a milch cow. If he does not purchase milch cow with this available limited capital, he would have spent in purchasing fertilizers for applying on his crops, where, he gets an additional return of Rs. 1000/-. So the rate of return in the next best opportunity is (1000/5000) *100 = 20 per cent. So, the discounting rate to be employed is 20 percent for computing the present worth of cash flows regarding the investment on milch cow. Thus concept can be better understood from the following examples:

Example 2.8

A farmer wants to purchase a machinery to carry out farm operations. He has two options before him:

- ✰ He can purchase a new machinery at Rs. 25000/- with an estimated life of 10 years.
- ✰ He can purchase an old machinery worth of Rs.16000/- and replace it after 5 years with another old machinery worth of Rs.16000 which will also provide service for 5 years.

Now suggest the appropriate course of action:

i. if the farmer has unlimited capital (market rate of interest of 10 per cent).

ii. if the farmer has limited capital (the rate of returns he can derive from the next best missed alternative of investing purchasing milch cow is 25 per cent).

Note that, the quality of service rendered, salvage value and annual expenses on repairs and maintenance *etc.*, are same in case of both the options. Suggest him the appropriate course of action.

Solution

i. Farmer with Unlimited Capital

Alternative 1: (i) Present cost of new machinery =Rs.25,000

Alternative 2: (i) Present cost of first hand machinery =Rs.16,000

(ii) Present value (Present Cost) of second hand machinery at a market interest rate of 10 percent will be:

Present Value = $[16{,}000/(1+0.10)^5]$ = Rs.9938

Total present cost of two old machinery = Rs.16,000+Rs.9938 = Rs.25938

In this case, the farmer should purchase a new machinery because, the cost of purchasing a new thresher (Rs.25000) is less than the total present cost of two old machinery (Rs.25938).

ii. Farmer with Limited Capital

The farmer has the opportunity to invest money in dairy enterprise where he can earn 25 percent returns every year. So, here, discounting rate will be the opportunity cost *i.e.*, the rate of returns he can derive from the next best missed alternative of investing purchasing milch cow is 25 percent.

Alternative 1: (i) Present cost of new machinery = Rs.25,000

Alternative 2: (i) Present cost of first old machinery = Rs.16,000

(ii) Present cost of second hand machinery at the rate of return of 25 percent in its next best use:

Present Value = $[16{,}000/(1+0.25)^5]$ = Rs.5246

Total present cost of two old machinery = Rs.16,000+Rs.5246 = Rs.21246

In this case, it is economical to purchase two old machinery instead of one new machinery because, total present cost of two old machinery (Rs.21246) is less than the present cost of one new machinery (Rs.25000).

Note that, if the (discounted) rate of return of the investment is higher than the OCC, then we can advise the farmers to go for current investment. So, in discounting techniques, discounted cash flows *i.e.*, discounted cash inflows or discounted benefits or discounted returns or PWB and discounted cash outflows or discounted costs or discounted costs or PWC will be taken into consideration rather than absolute cash flows into the project during its life time.

Since costs and benefits occur during the life time of a long term investment and money has time value, it is essential to place current and future costs and benefits on an equal basis for comparison. This is done by assuming a discount factor to estimate the present values of future costs and benefits. Thus, discounting technique take into account the time-value of money or Principle of time preference. By this technique, we can 'reduce' the future benefits and costs to their present worth. So, this technique permits us to determine, whether to accept or reject the long term investment for implementation that have cash outflows and cash inflows during its life time. The various measures under this discounted technique include:

i. Net Present Value (NPV)/Net Present Worth (NPW)

NPV of an investment is defined as sum of discounted net benefits of a project over a period of time. That is, it is simply the summation of differences between PWB and PWC during each year of the project. NPV is also called as Discounted net cash flow method, as it uses the discounting method of analysis. This method considers the time value of money and the stream of cash flows over the entire life of the investment. The word 'net' in NPV is a reminder that, there is a cash flow at time t=0. Hence, 'net' means 'net of the cost *now*'. The following are the formulae employed to compute NPV:

$$NPV = \sum_{t=1}^{n} (B_t - C_t)/(1+i)^t$$

$$NPV = \sum_{t=1}^{n} N_t/(1+i)^t$$

$$NPV = \sum_{t=1}^{n} [(B_t - C_t) * \{1/(1+i)^t\}]$$

$$NPV = [N_1/(1+i)^1] + [N_2/(1+i)^2] + [N_3/(1+i)^3] + \text{———} + [N_t/(1+i)^t]$$

where, Bt : Discounted benefits or cash inflows or PWB

Ct : Discounted costs or cash outflows or PWC

Nt : Discounted Net benefits

i : Market rate of interest

t: Time period of project (1,2,3 – n years)

Note that, the NPVs of the project are additive. Additive in the sense, to compute NPV of an investment of 5 years period, the NPV of cash flows will be added for the five years period and that cumulative value indicates the NPV of the investment. Similarly, if the firm has two projects A and B, then the NPV of the combined investment is: $NPV_A + NPV_B$.

Criteria for Selection of Projects Based on NPV

- For a single project, a positive NPV indicates acceptability. For multiple (competing) projects, the project with the highest NPV should receive highest priority. Thus, NPV must be positive for making the project investment (Table 2.32). If NPV is negative, it is better to drop the project. That is, projects with negative NPV values should be rejected because, the present value of the stream of benefits is insufficient to recover the present value of stream of costs of the project. So, do not accept any project unless it generates a positive NPV, when discounted by the OCC.

Table 2.32: Decision about Project Selection Based on NPV Value

NPV	*Meaning*	*Decision*
NPV > 0	Investment would add value to the firm	Project may be accepted
NPV < 0	Investment would subtract value from the firm	Project should be rejected
NPV = 0	No gain-No loss to the firm	Project is break even and hence, the project manager will be indifferent in his decision, whether to accept or reject the project. This project adds no monetary value.

☆ Higher the NPV value is desirable. That is, project with highest NPV value should be selected. If there are several independent and mutually exclusive projects (if, among a number of projects, the firm can only choose one, then the projects are said to be mutually exclusive. For example: Suppose you have the choice of modifying an existing machine or replacing it with a brand new one. You could not do both and produce the desired amount of output. So, the acceptance of one project precludes accepting the other. Similarly, the option of a firm is to (a) expand its existing plant or (b) build a new one on a separate site in order to increase production capacity. In such mutually exclusive projects, the project that offers the higher NPV and Internal Rate of Return (IRR) would be picked. Since a firm usually has limited financial resources with substantial opportunity cost, it is not feasible to do both. Hence, these projects are considered mutually exclusive. In case of mutually exclusive projects, the economic decision is to go with NPV and not IRR. The NPV measure will rank projects in order of descending NPV values. Note that, regarding independent projects, they are evaluated as if you can invest in both projects. Therefore, a project with a positive NPV will also have an IRR higher than the OCC. The decision rule for independent projects is the same regardless of the measure used to evaluate profitability. That is, for independent investments (and if cash flows are conventional), then both the IRR and NPV methods lead to the same accept and reject decisions. However, as mentioned above in case of mutually exclusive projects, you can't take on both projects and you can choose only one. When deciding to pick between these two mutually exclusive projects, the NPV and IRR decision rules (assuming both all are profitable) can be in conflict because of time horizon and cash flow differences between the two projects. For example, if two projects are mutually exclusive, a short project (Project B) might have IRR=19 per cent and NPV=Rs.13,000 and a long project (Project A) might have IRR=14 percent and NPV=Rs.22500. So, the decision between these projects may be complicated, but as a general rule, you should pick the project with the higher NPV thereby, maximizing firm value.

- NPV is an absolute measure and not a relative measure and hence, we cannot compare one project with another project based on NPV values because, it does not give or indicate the rate of return earned from the each rupee investment. So, no ranking of acceptable projects is possible with the NPV criterion, being an absolute measure and not relative measure. In this context, the next discounted measure *i.e.*, BCR gives the rate of return earned from the each rupee investment in the project (Table 2.33).
- The selection of the discount rate affects the result of the investment appraisal. When a higher discount rate is used, the NPV decreases and *vice versa*. At some higher discount rate, the NPV values would be zero, and at an even higher rate, it could become negative.
- Compared to other investment appraisal techniques such as the BCR and IRR (discounting measures), the NPV is viewed as the most reliable measure to support investment decisions. As discussed above, in choosing between two projects A and B, the NPV measure may suggest that, project A is preferable, while the IRR measure may suggest project B is preferable. In such case, the result indicated by the NPV measure is more reliable. But, in some cases, a smaller project with a lower NPV may be more attractive due to a higher BCR. So, it is essential to use other discounting measures, which also yield useful additional information to assess the economic viability of the project.
- When the implementation agency faces a budget constraint *i.e.*, it has to select the project(s) within the limit of a fixed budget, choose that subset of the available projects, which maximizes the NPV.

Merits of NPV

- The NPV is the most widely accepted criterion for selecting between projects
- The value of NPV suggests, how much a project is adding in value terms to an existing entity or how much value the project is creating.
- A positive NPV means that, the project is expected to add value to the firm and will therefore, increase the wealth of the owners.
- Since the goal of project is to add value or increase owner's wealth, NPV is a direct measure of how well this project will meet the goal.
- Unlike BCR, NPV has units of currency such as Rupees or Dollars. So, one is able to know the impact in terms of value that the project would create.
- NPV is a single measure, which takes the amount and timing of cash flows into account.
- NPV measure is the superior method for mutually exclusive projects.
- The NPV method has the advantage that the end result of the computations is expressed in Rupees and not in a percentage.
- It can be used in situations, where the required rate of return varies over the life of the project.

But, NPV suffers from the limitations that, it is only an absolute measure (not a relative measure like BCR and IRR) and only comparable between projects, if the initial investment is the same.

Example 2.9

Assume a project with the following costs and benefits (Figures in Rs. Crores). Compute the NPV of the investment, assuming discount factor: 10 per cent.

Year	Incremental Costs (Rs.)	Incremental Benefits (Rs.)	df 10 per cent(1/ 1/(1.10)^t	Method 1		Method 2	
				PWC (Rs.)	PWB (Rs.)	Net (incremental) Benefits (NB)(Rs.)	PW of NB or NPV (Rs.)
1	2.840	0.000	0.909	2.582	0.000	–2.840	–2.582
2	10.250	0.000	0.826	8.471	0.000	–10.250	–8.471
3	11.460	0.000	0.751	8.610	0.000	–11.460	–8.610
4	8.370	0.000	0.683	5.717	0.000	–8.370	–5.717
5	4.210	0.000	0.621	2.614	0.000	–4.210	–2.614
6	2.090	0.000	0.564	1.180	0.000	–2.090	–1.180
7	2.140	6.440	0.513	1.098	3.305	4.300	2.207
8	2.510	12.320	0.467	1.171	5.747	9.810	4.576
9	3.750	16.740	0.424	1.590	7.099	12.990	5.509
10	2.910	15.450	0.386	1.122	5.957	12.540	4.835
11	1.060	30.710	0.350	0.372	10.764	29.650	10.392
12	1.030	70.260	0.319	0.328	22.387	69.230	22.059
			TOTAL	**34.855**	**55.259**		
			NPV	**55.259-34.855= Rs.20.404**			**20.404**

Example 2.10

Suppose, there are two project investments A and B. The first pays the net benefits of Rs.210 in the first year, but nothing in next year. The second investment B pays the net benefits of Rs.100 in the first year, and Rs.115 in next year (*i.e.*, a total of Rs.215). Now, among these two investments, the second investment appears to be better. But, the NPV of investments (projects) show otherwise, as it all depends upon the discount rate. If the discount rate is 5 percent, then computing NPV will give:

NPV of Investment A: = $[210/(1+0.05)^1] + [0/(1+0.05)^2]$ = Rs.200

NPV of Investment B: = $[100/(1+0.05)^1] + [115/(1+0.05)^2]$ = Rs.199.5

Thus, though the second investment B pays out a greater sum, after discounting, the first investment looks like a better choice.

Example 2.11

Assume the following projects with their NPVs. Which projects are rejected for investment?

Project A: NPV (+ Rs.70,000)

Project B: NPV (– Rs.50,000)

Project C: NPV (+ Rs.100,000)

Project D: NPV (- Rs.25,000)

Solution: Only projects A and C are acceptable and projects B and D are rejected. Among A and C, project C is more preferred, as it enjoys higher NPV.

Example 2.12

Following are the four projects along with their NPVs. If budget constraint is Rs.4 lakhs, choose that subset of the available projects.

Project E: NPV (+ Rs.60,000)

Project F: NPV (+ Rs.400,000)

Project G: NPV (+ Rs.150,000)

Project H: NPV (+ Rs.225,000)

Solution: Since budget constraint is Rs.4 lakhs, combinations EF, FG and FH are impossible, as they cost too much. Combinations GH, EG and EH are within the budget. GH combination with NPV of Rs.375,000 is more preferred, as its NPV is highest.

Example 2.13

Assume the following projects are mutually exclusive and select the project for investment.

Project I: NPV Rs.300,000

Project J: NPV Rs.700,000

Projects K: NPV Rs. 600,000

Solution: Projects J should be chosen because, it has the largest NPV.

ii. Benefit Cost Ratio (BCR)

BCR of an investment is the ratio between PWB to PWC in a project during its life time. That is, BCR is obtained, when the present worth of the benefit-stream is divided by the present worth of the cost-stream. So, BCR measures the relative size of the benefits to the costs of a project. As mentioned earlier BCR is a relative measure for selecting the projects, unlike NPV. This can be better understood from the following example (Table 2.33):

A close perusal of the Table 2.33 reveals that, considering the NPV values, it will be recommended to select Project 1, as its NPV value is higher over Project 2. However, BCR indicates otherwise *i.e.*, it guides to select Project 2 over Project 1, as the former yields higher rate of return from the investment compared to Project 2. Thus, for the

Table 2.33: Selection of Projects Based on NPV and BCR Measures

Projects	*Discounted Benefits (Rs./-)*	*Discounted Costs (Rs./-)*	*Net Benefits (Rs./-)*	*BCR*
1	8000	5000	3000	0.600
2	7420	4520	2900	0.642

selection of projects, BCR measure outweighs NPV, as the former being a relative measure. Of course, this is true, if initial investment in the projects is more or less same and are of the same duration and that too, if the projects are independent projects. The following is the formula employed to compute BCR:

$$BCR = \sum_{t=1}^{n} B_t/(1+1)^t / \sum_{t=1}^{n} C_t/(1+1)^t$$

$$BCR = \frac{\text{Sum of the PWB}}{\text{Sum of the PWC}}$$

where, Bt : Discounted benefits or cash inflows or PWB

Ct : Discounted costs or cash outflows or PWC

Nt : Discounted Net benefits

i : Market rate of interest

t: Time period of project (1,2,3 – n years)

Criteria for Selection of Projects Based on BCR

- ☆ For a single project, BCR greater than 1 indicates its acceptability (if BCR > 1 then, NPV > 0). For multiple (competing) projects, the project with the highest BCR (greater than 1) should receive highest priority. Thus, BCR must be greater than one for suggesting the project investment (Table 2.34).

- ☆ Higher the BCR is desirable *i.e.*, selection of project should be based on the highest magnitude of BCR value. Note that, the value of BCR will vary depending on the discount (interest) rate chosen. If higher discount factor is considered, the smaller the resultant BCR and if the discount rate is further increased, it can even make BCR to one or even less than one. So, the

Table 2.34: Decision about Project Based on BCR Value

BCR	*Meaning*	*Decision*
BCR > 1 or NBCR > 0	Investment would add value to the firm	Project may be accepted
BCR < 1 or NBCR < 0	Investment would subtract value from the firm	Project should be rejected
BCR = 1 or NBCR = 0	No gain-No loss to the firm	Project is break even and hence, the project manager will be indifferent in his decision, whether to accept or reject the project. This project adds no monetary value.

BCR criterion suggest to accept all independent projects with a BCR of greater than one, when the cost and benefit streams are discounted at the OCC. In case of mutually exclusive projects, go with NPV rather than BCR in selecting the project.

- ☆ BCR is a relative measure and hence, we can compare one or more projects based on BCR values. This is because, BCR indicates the rate of return from each rupee invested in the project.
- ☆ BCR measure is widely used in economic analysis of social projects and not in private investment analysis.

After computing the BCR, we can work out the Net BCR (NBCR) as follows: NBCR = BCR-1. For example, if the BCR of a project is 1.585 (Example 2.14), then the NBCR =1.585-1 = 0.585. This implies that, for every one rupee invested in the project, the gross returns derived are Rs.1.585 and net returns derived are Rs.0.585. If BCR is 1.585 and if it is to be declined to 1.000 (*i.e.*, to make the project break-even), then the benefits of the project could fall in terms of percentage is calculated by the following formula:

$[1-(1/BCR)] \times 100$

If BCR is declined from 1.585 to 1.000, then the percent fall in benefits to make the project break-even will be 36.925 percent.

Example 2.14

Assume a project with the following costs and benefits (Figures in Rs. Crores). Compute the BCR and NBCR of the investment, assuming discount factor: 10 per cent.

Year	*Incremental Costs (Rs.)*	*Incremental Benefits (Rs.)*	*Discount Factor @ 10 per cent $1/(1.10)^t$*	*BCR*	
				PWC	*PWB*
1	2.840	0.000	0.909	2.582	0.000
2	10.250	0.000	0.826	8.471	0.000
3	11.460	0.000	0.751	8.610	0.000
4	8.370	0.000	0.683	5.717	0.000
5	4.210	0.000	0.621	2.614	0.000
6	2.090	0.000	0.564	1.180	0.000
7	2.140	6.440	0.513	1.098	3.305
8	2.510	12.320	0.467	1.171	5.747
9	3.750	16.740	0.424	1.590	7.099
10	2.910	15.450	0.386	1.122	5.957
11	1.060	30.710	0.350	0.372	10.764
12	1.030	70.260	0.319	0.328	22.387
			TOTAL	**34.855**	**55.259**
			BCR	**1.585**	
			NBCR	**0.585**	

The above Examples 2.9 and 2.14 of NPV and BCR analyses clearly infer the following points:

- ☆ NPV measures totals, indicates the amount by which PWB exceed (or do not exceed) PWC.
- ☆ BCR measures the ratio (or rate) by which PWB do or do not exceed PWC.
- ☆ Both BCR and NPV are clearly similar, but not identical.

Example 2.15

Assume the following data (Figures in Rs. Millions) regarding PWC and PWB of two mutually exclusive projects of different sizes. Select the project for investment.

Project A: PWC = Rs. 5.0, PWB = Rs.7.0

Project B: PWC = Rs.20.0, PWB = Rs.24.0

Solution

From the given data,

For Project A: NPV_A = Rs.2.0 $BCR_A = 7/5 = 1.4$

For Project B: NPV_B = Rs.4.0 $BCR_B = 24/20 = 1.2$

So, according to the BCR criterion, project A should be chosen over project B because, $BCR_A > BCR_B$. But, the NPV of project B is greater than the NPV of project A. Since, the projects are mutually exclusive, project B should be chosen with higher NPV.

Limitations of BCR Analysis

The advantage of this measure is its simplicity. However, it suffers from some difficulties regarding its application. They include:

- ☆ It demands the analyst to assign monetary values to all benefits and costs. However, there are numerous benefits and costs that are intangible and therefore, difficult to value. Especially, for projects with an environmental impact, it can be difficult to place a rupee value on the benefits and also on costs. The value of a product can be easily estimated, but the exact value of social costs like environmental pollution cannot be easily estimated.
- ☆ The result of BCR is very sensitive to the choice of the discount rate.
- ☆ It is difficult to account for benefits and costs that can be realized from the project. In common, while most benefits and costs that arise in the present are known, many that arise in the future are unknown. So, the information will be limited to get the realistic BCR for the project. So, the concept of uncertainty plagues the exact measurement of BCR.
- ☆ Using the BCR to rank projects can lead to sub-optimal decisions. This is because, a project with a slightly higher BCR ratio will be selected over a project with a lower BCR even though, the latter project has the capacity to generate much greater economic benefits because, it involves greater scale.

- ☆ NPV measures in absolute or totals, indicates the amount by which PWB exceed (or do not exceed) PWC. But, BCR measures the ratio or rate by which, PWB do or do not exceed PWC. So, BCR measures the resource use in terms of efficiency.
- ☆ The BCR does not adjust for mutually exclusive projects of different sizes (Example 2.15).
- ☆ The BCR criterion is sensitive to the classification of project effect as a cost rather than a benefit or *vice versa*, unlike NPV criterion. This is because, BCR criterion will affect the magnitudes, which are entered as denominator and numerator. Let us look at this example: Assume the project's PWBs as: 10, 20 and 30 units and PWCs as: 10 and 20. So, the BCR= 60/30=2.0. But, if the PWC=10 units is treated as negative benefits, then the BCR becomes 50/25 =2.5. On the other, hand, NPV remains same in both the cases *i.e.*, 30 units regardless of the transfer.

iii. IRR

It is the discount factor at which, NPV is equal to zero. We already know that, there exists inverse relationship between the NPV and discount factor. So, by increasing the discount factor, NPV gradually decreases and at one level of discount factor, NPV becomes zero. That particular discount factor at which NPV=0 is called IRR. So, at IRR discount factor, the project breaks even, as PWB equals to PWC or NPV=0 or BCR=1. As the name suggests, the IRR of an investment measures its rate of return, whereas NPV measures the size of the return. If a farmer invests Rs.10000 in a project with an IRR of 20 per cent is exactly equivalent to investing the same Rs.10000 in an interest-earning bank account at an interest rate of 20 percent. Note that, IRR assumes re-investment of cash inflows at IRR.

It is shown through Figure 2.42, as the discount factor increases, NPV gradually decreases and at 40 per cent discount factor, NPV becomes zero. This discount factor (*i.e.*, 40 per cent) at which NPV=0 is called IRR. That is, at IRR discount factor (R), NPV= 0 and this means that, at IRR, the PWB equals the PWC in a project indicating that, it is just break even at 40 per cent discount factor. This 40 per cent IRR implies that, for every one rupee investment in a project, it earns Rs.1.40 gross returns or Rs.0.40 net returns from the date of investment of the project. Having estimated the IRR to be 40 percent, the rule will be to ACCEPT the investment at any interest rate less than 40 percent per annum and to REJECT the investment at any interest rate that exceeds 40 per cent per annum. Thus, IRR indicates the earning capacity of the project right from the investment period. IRR is, otherwise, called as Marginal Efficiency of Capital (MEC). The students must note that, at IRR=40 per cent, even if the project earns net returns by Rs.0.40 from the date of initial investment of the project, the project finally breaks even by the end of the project period. This is because of the presence of gestation period during which the gross returns are nil or net returns are negative in the project. The negative net returns of the project during gestation period is compensated by the actual net returns of Rs.0.40 right from the initial investment of the project and this lead to break even of the project by the end of the project period.

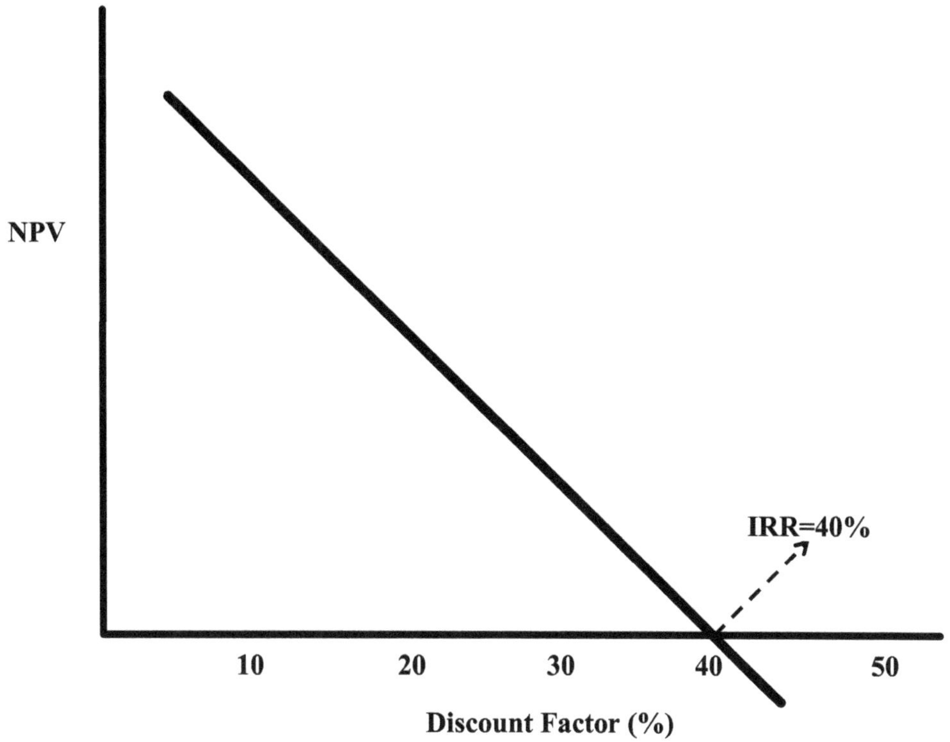

Figure 2.42: Inverse Relation between NPV and Discount Factor.

We can write the formulae for IRR in terms of above formulae discussed under NPV and BCR as follows by employing IRR discount factor (R).

$$NPV = \sum_{t=1}^{n} (B_t - C_t)/(1+R)^t = 0$$

$$BCR = \sum_{t=1}^{n} (B_t/(1+R)^t / \sum_{t=1}^{n} (C_t/(1+R)^t = 1$$

Procedure to Compute IRR

We already know, there exists inverse relationship between the NPV and discount factor. The IRR discount factor is computed by a trial and error procedure and it involves the following steps:

- ☆ First, an arbitrary discount factor is assumed and NPV is computed.
- ☆ If NPV is positive, it implies, the IRR is still higher and hence, a still higher discount factor will be considered to compute NPV again.
- ☆ If again NPV is positive, a still higher discount factor will be considered.
- ☆ This procedure is continued till NPV will become negative.
- ☆ So, between the last two successive NPVs *i.e.*, one positive NPV and one negative NPV, there is zero NPV. So, compute the discount factor at which the NPV=0, by interpolation method through employing the following formula:

$$\text{IRR (R)} = \text{Lower discount rate} + \text{Difference between two discount rates} \times \frac{\text{Present worth at lower discount rate}}{\text{Absolute difference between NPVs at two discount rates}}$$

The above trial and error procedure to compute IRR represent a mathematical method called 'Linear Interpolation' (Interpolation is simply finding the intermediate value between too discount rates we have chosen). As given in the formula, it is necessary to work out two NPV values. One of these calculations must give a positive NPV and the other calculation must give a negative NPV. The most difficult aspect of this trial and error procedure is making the initial estimates. If the estimate is too far from the final result, then several trials will have to be made to find two discount rates close enough together to permit accurate interpolation. In practice, it is better not to interpolate between intervals greater than about five percent because, the wider intervals can easily introduce an interpolation error. Note that, IRR is a mathematical concept, not an economic or financial criterion.

Criteria to Use IRR

- For the project to earn profits, IRR must be greater than OCC of investment.
- The relationship between an NPV, IRR and OCC is given below:
  - *Case 1:* If NPV >0 then, BCR>1 and IRR is greater than OCC. Then, it is advised to take up the project.
  - *Case 2:* If NPV = 0, then BCR=1 and IRR is equal to OCC. This is the point of indecision.
  - *Case 3:* if NPV < 0, then BCR<1 and IRR is less than OCC. Then, it is better to drop the project.

Example 2.16

Assume a project with the following costs and benefits (Figures in Rs. Crores). Compute the IRR of the investment, assuming discount factor: 10 per cent.

Year	*Incr Costs (Rs.)*	*Incr Benefits (Rs.)*	*Discount Factor 10 per cent $1/(1.10)^t$*	*Net (incremental) Benefits (NB)*	*PW of NB (or) NPV (Rs.)*	*15 per cent df $1+(1.15)^t$*	*NPV at 15 per cent (Rs.)*	*20 per cent df $1+(1.20)^t$*	*NPV at 20 per cent (Rs.)*
1	2.840	0.000	0.909	–2.840	–2.582	0.870	–2.470	0.833	–2.367
2	10.250	0.000	0.826	–10.250	–8.471	0.756	–7.750	0.694	–7.118
3	11.460	0.000	0.751	–11.460	–8.610	0.658	–7.535	0.579	–6.632
4	8.370	0.000	0.683	–8.370	–5.717	0.572	–4.786	0.482	–4.036
5	4.210	0.000	0.621	–4.210	–2.614	0.497	–2.093	0.402	–1.692
6	2.090	0.000	0.564	–2.090	–1.180	0.432	–0.904	0.335	–0.700
7	2.140	6.440	0.513	4.300	2.207	0.376	1.617	0.279	1.200

Contd...

Year	Incr Costs (Rs.)	Incr Benefits (Rs.)	Discount Factor 10 per cent $1/(1.10)^t$	Net (incremental) Benefits (NB)	PW of NB (or) NPV (Rs.)	15 per cent df $1+(1.15)^t$	NPV at 15 per cent (Rs.)	20 per cent df $1+(1.20)^t$	NPV at 20 per cent (Rs.)
8	2.510	12.320	0.467	9.810	4.576	0.327	3.207	0.233	2.281
9	3.750	16.740	0.424	12.990	5.509	0.284	3.693	0.194	2.518
10	2.910	15.450	0.386	12.540	4.835	0.247	3.100	0.162	2.025
11	1.060	30.710	0.350	29.650	10.392	0.215	6.373	0.135	3.991
12	1.030	70.260	0.319	69.230	22.059	0.187	12.940	0.112	7.765
			TOTAL	**NPV**	**20.404**	NPV	5.39092		–2.7655
			NPV			IRR (R)	18.3047		

Having estimated the IRR to be 18.31 percent, the rule will be to ACCEPT the investment at any interest rate less than 18.31 percent per annum and to REJECT the investment at any interest rate that exceeds 18.31 per cent per annum. This IRR also implies the maximum interest that a project could pay for the resources used, if the project is to recover its investment and operating costs and still break even. An IRR of 18.31 percent also means that, with a discount rate of 18.31 per cent, the project breaks even. This IRR approach is usually associated with a discount rate or OCC, against which the IRR is compared. If the IRR exceeds the OCC, the project is accepted (Table 2.35). In the above example, since IRR (18.31 per cent) is greater than the OCC (10 per cent), it is suggested to accept the project. Note that, although IRR of different projects will vary, a project manager cannot say with confidence that, the projects can be ranked on the basis of IRR. Only in a general way, the IRR will tell that, one project is better than another, in the sense that, it contributes more national income relative to resources used. For example, if the discount rate remains at 10 percent, then we cannot know with certainty that the project with 25 percent IRR contributes relatively more to national income than another project with 15 percent IRR and hence, we cannot say with confidence that, we should implement the former project with 25 percent IRR first. If the opportunity cost is raised to 18 percent, then the project with 15 percent IRR drops out of the investment and judgement will be easy to favour the investment of the project that yield 25 percent IRR.

Table 2.35: Decision about Project Based on IRR Value

IRR	*Meaning*	*Decision*
IRR > OCC	Investment would add value to the firm	Project may be accepted
IRR < OCC	Investment would subtract value from the firm	Project should be rejected
IRR = OCC	No gain-No loss to the firm.	Project is break even and hence, the project manager will be indifferent in his decision, whether to accept or reject the project. This project adds no monetary value.

There are some disadvantages associated with the IRR as a performance indicator. It is not suitable for the ranking of competing projects. It is possible for two projects to have the same IRR, but have different NPV values due to differences in the timing of costs and benefits. This implies, applying different appraisal techniques to the same basic data may yield contradictory conclusions.

Merits of IRR

Among the above three discounted measures, IRR is most widely used because of following reasons:

- ☆ It is a clear estimate indicating the rate of return from the initial period of investment.
- ☆ The estimate is unique in nature, as it cannot be compared with NPV and BCR.
- ☆ It has got wider applicability.
- ☆ The estimate is much consistent.
- ☆ This measure serves as the most important alternative to NPV.
- ☆ It is often used in practice and is intuitively appealing.
- ☆ It is based entirely on the estimated cash flows and is independent of interest rates found elsewhere.
- ☆ Results are expressed as a simple percentage and hence, are more easily understood than other measures.
- ☆ It indicates how sensitive investment decisions are to a change in interest rates.
- ☆ It is considered to be the most useful measure of project worth and used by almost all the institutions including World Bank in economic and financial analyses of the project.
- ☆ It represents the average earning power of the money used in the project over the project life. Hence, it is also sometimes called Yield of the investment.

Limitations of IRR

However, there are many problems with IRR as a criterion for project evaluation (Cary and Dunn, 1997; Anonymous, 2004). Some of them are:

- ☆ Can produce multiple answers. That is, IRR is unreliable in the situation of non-conventional net cash flows (Net cash flow sign changes more than once *i.e.*, a negative net cash flow after a positive one). That is, in the case of positive net cash flows followed by negative ones and then by positive ones, the IRR may have multiple values. With reference to the cash outflow and cash inflow in a project given through Table 2.36, there are multiple IRRs, as NPV is zero at two discount factors *i.e.*, 25 and 400 per cent (Figure 2.43). Among these two IRRs, which is correct IRR? We can't say. So, there is no unambiguously correct answer. This implies, the occurrence of multiple IRRs for a project and in such case, the IRR rule breaks down.

Table 2.36: Project with Multiple IRRs

Year	*Incr Costs (Rs.)*	*Incr Benefits (Rs.)*	*Net Incremental Benefits (Rs.)*	*IRR*			
				25 per cent df	*NPV at 25 per cent (Rs.)*	*400 per cent df*	*NPV at 400 per cent (Rs.)*
1	160000	0	–160000	0.8	–128000	0.2	–32000
2		1000000	1000000	0.64	640000	0.04	40000
3	1000000	0	–1000000	0.512	–512000	0.008	–8000
				NPV	**0**		**0**

☆ IRR discount factor is misleading is case of mutually exclusive projects. For the data given through Table 2.37, Project A enjoys lower NPV, (Rs. 7015), but higher IRR (100 per cent) when compared to Project B with higher NPV (Rs. 15147) but lower IRR (50 per cent). Since, higher NPV contributes more to the value of the project, go with NPV rather than IRR in ranking mutually exclusive projects (*i.e.*, select Project B for investment), or we can say, IRR measure is misleading in case of mutually exclusive projects.

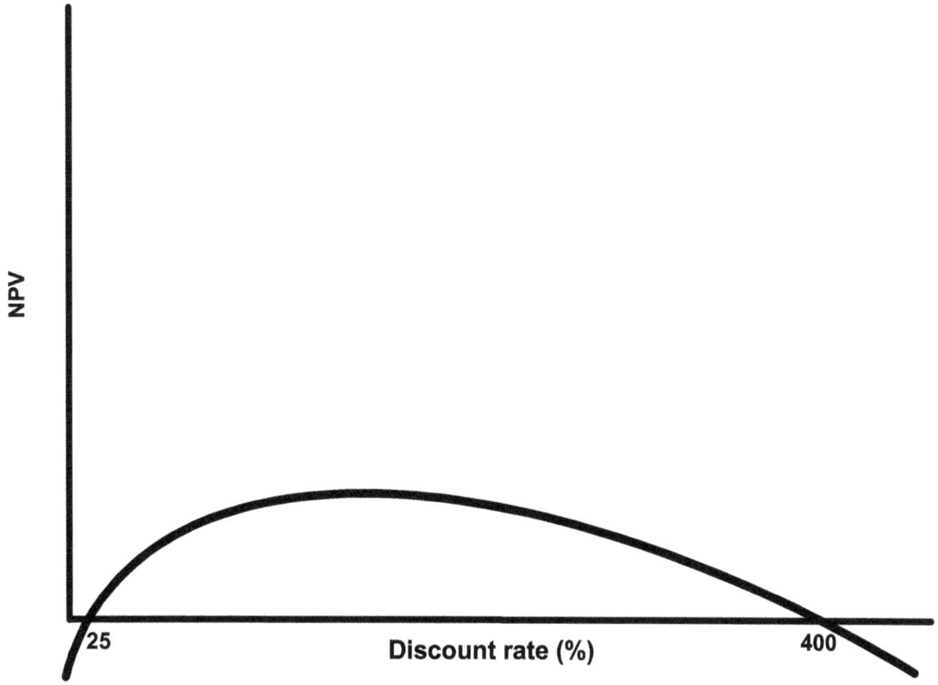

Figure 2.43: Project with Multiple IRRs.

Table 2.37: IRR is Misleading for Mutually Exclusive Projects

Year	*Incr Costs (Rs.)*	*Incr Benefits (Rs.)*	*df 12 per cent*	*Net Incremental Benefits (Rs.)*	*NPV (Rs.)*	*IRR*	
						100 per cent df	*NPV at 100 per cent df (Rs.)*
				Project A			
1	10000	0	0.893	–10000	–8929	0.50	–5000
2	0	20000	0.797	20000	15944	0.25	5000
				NPV	**7015**	**NPV = 0**	
Year	*Incr Costs (Rs.)*	*Incr Benefits (Rs.)*	*df 12 per cent*	*Net Incremental Benefits (Rs.)*	*NPV (Rs.)*	*IRR*	
						50 per cent df	*NPV at 50 per cent df (Rs.)*
				Project B			
1	50000	0	0.893	–50000	–44643	0.67	–33333
2	0	75000	0.797	75000	59790	0.44	33333
				NPV	**15147**	**NPV = 0**	

Table 2.38: IRR cannot Distinguish between Lending and Borrowing

Year	*Incr Costs (Rs.)*	*Incr Benefits (Rs.)*	*df 10 per cent*	*Net Incremental Benefits (Rs.)*	*NPV (Rs.)*	*IRR*	
						50 per cent df	*NPV at 50 per cent df (Rs.)*
				Project A			
1	4000	0	0.909	–4000	–3636.364	0.667	–2666.667
2		6000	0.826	6000	4958.678	0.444	2666.667
				NPV	**1322.314**	**NPV= 0**	
Year	*Incr Costs (Rs.)*	*Incr Benefits (Rs.)*	*df 12 per cent*	*Net Incremental Benefits (Rs.)*	*NPV (Rs.)*	*IRR*	
						75 per cent df	*NPV at 75 per cent df (Rs.)*
				Project B			
1	0	4000	0.909	4000	3636.364	0.571	2285.714
2	7000	0	0.826	–7000	–5785.124	0.327	–2285.714
				NPV	**–2148.760**	**NPV= 0**	

☆ Another important demerit of IRR is that, it cannot distinguish between lending and borrowing and hence, a higher IRR need not necessarily be a desirable thing. For the data given through Table 2.38, IRR is higher for Project B (75 per cent) compared to project A (50 per cent). But, project B is not an attractive project, as project A involves investment of Rs.4000 at a rate of return of 50 per cent, but project B involves borrowing Rs.4000 at a rate of return of 75 per cent. Even, if we go by NPV, Project A is more attractive over project B.

- ☆ IRR does not consider cost of capital and hence, it should not be used to compare projects of different duration. However, MIRR does consider cost of capital and provides a better indication of a project's efficiency in contributing to the firm's discounted cash flow.
- ☆ If cash flows are conventional and project is independent, then NPV and IRR lead to same accept and reject decisions. But, IRR measure can lead to erroneous rankings of mutually exclusive projects (taking one project means another is not taken), as the highest IRR may not have the highest NPV. For such mutually exclusive projects, IRR is inferior to NPV measure in ranking them. So, when projects are *mutually exclusive*, we cannot rank them by their IRRs. This is because, the IRR is independent of the size or scale of the project *(Scale-independence) i.e.,* a minute project could have a much larger IRR than a project ten times bigger. In such case, NPV should be used to choose between mutually exclusive projects.
- ☆ The IRR measure assumes that, the future cash flows will be reinvested and get the returns equal to IRR.
- ☆ IRR ignores differences in the life of the projects, the time span problem.
- ☆ The estimate of IRR is not unique, if the net cash flow into the project are non-conventional
- ☆ It is tedious to calculate.
- ☆ It says nothing about the size of the project because, one may prefer bigger project with higher NPV than a small project with low NPV, but higher IRR.
- ☆ The IRR of individual projects cannot be added or averaged to derive the IRR of a combination of projects.

Comparison between NPV and IRR

- ☆ NPV measure takes the interest rate as a known factor, where as IRR takes it as an unknown factor.
- ☆ NPV measure seeks to find out the cumulative net present cash flows (PWB - PWC) of an investment at a given market rate of interest. On the other hand, IRR seeks to find out the discount factor at which the project breaks even (PWB = PWC)
- ☆ Both NPV and IRR measures proceed with the presumption that, cash inflow can be re-invested in the new project. However, NPV assume re-investment at discount rate (OCC), but IRR measure assumes the re-investment at IRR discount factor. However, re-investment of funds at the

NPV discount rate (OCC or cut off rate) is more feasible than at the IRR. This makes the NPV more reliable compared to IRR in ranking two or more capital investment projects.

- NPV measures in absolute or totals, indicates the amount by which PWB exceed (or do not exceed) PWC. But, IRR measures the rate of return in the project in terms of percentage.
- The condition for the accepting the project is when NPV > 0. The same with reference to IRR measure is, when the IRR discount rate is more than NPV discount rate.

Similarities in Results of NPV and IRR

Both NPV and IRR measures gives the same result regarding acceptance or rejection of project investments in the following cases

- If the project involves conventional cash flows *i.e.*, when an initial cash outflow is followed by a series of cash inflows
- When the projects are independent and not mutually exclusive (Independent projects are the projects, where the proposal of one project investment does not preclude the acceptance of other projects).

Conflict between NPV and IRR in Selecting Project Investment

As mentioned earlier, in case of mutually exclusive projects, there arises the conflict between NPV and IRR *i.e.*, regarding which measure should be taken into consideration for selection of mutually exclusive projects. In general, the conflicts between these two measures will arise, because of one or more of the following reasons:

- If the projects differ in their cash outlays
- If the projects differ in their duration
- If the projects have different pattern of cash flows

Regarding conflicts that may arise in the selection of mutually exclusive projects, the selection of project investment should be based on NPV criterion and not on IRR. This is because, NPV measure directly indicates the wealth maximization of the investments, whereas IRR indicates only the rate of return on the investment rather than total wealth maximization of the investment. Hence, NPV is the best measure to rank mutually exclusive projects and the project with highest NPV is desirable for investment.

Applicability of NPV, BCR and IRR

Though several measures were available for project appraisal under discounting technique as discussed earlier, the most commonly used measures include NPV, BCR and IRR for social cost-benefit analysis.

- World Bank employs discounted measures to evaluate agricultural projects.
- Among the three discounted measures, BCR and IRR indicate the rate of return in the project investment, unlike NPV.

- NPV and BCR will be used for *ex-ante* evaluation studies, while IRR will be used for *ex-post* evaluation studies.
- Neither IRR nor BCR can be adequately used to choose between two mutually exclusive projects. In such case, NPV is the best measure.
- With regard to the implementation of single project or two or more projects with the same cost structure, NPV criterion is adequate. However, when there are several competing projects with different cost structures, NPV criteria being an absolute measure is not a correct choice.
- Unlike NPV, for competing projects with different cost structures, BCR criterion is the correct choice, being a relative measure. This criterion states that:
  - In case of single project, choose it, if the BCR is >1.
  - In case of competing projects with different cost structures, choose the project with highest BCR and rank the projects in the descending order of their BCR estimates. Choose the number of projects in such a way that the given investment fund is exhausted.
  - In case of mutually exclusive projects, still NPV criterion is meritorious over BCR. Assume two projects A and B with the following values: PWC_A: 100 units; PWB_A: 130 units; PWC_B= 40 units and PWB_B= 60 units. So, NPV_A=30, BCR_A=1.3, NPV_B=20 and BCR_B=1.5. Since NPV_A is higher, go with Project A, as the two projects are mutually exclusive.
- The demerit of NPV and BCR measures is that, they depend on an externally given SRD. However, IRR enjoy the advantage of not depending on SRD at least in the initial stages of its computation. IRR criterion states that:
  - For a single project, select it, if the R>i
  - In case of competing projects, rank them in descending order their R values and choose that set of projects from the top for which R>i, until the given investment fund is exhausted.
  - Note that, 'R' can be calculated purely from the project data, whereas computation of NPV and BCR require external SRD.
  - In case of mutually exclusive projects, still NPV is preferred over IRR in selecting the project.
- In case of single project, NPV or IRR criteria holds good. But, in case of mutually exclusive projects, NPV is used as decision criterion over BCR and IRR. However, in case of rationing a given investment, BCRs of projects will be the decision criterion for ranking the projects.

Note that, whenever there is a conflict between NPV and another decision rule, always use NPV. Please see the following examples:

Example 2.17

Assume the following data for two projects (Figures in Rs. Millions), which are mutually exclusive. Which project is to be selected for investment?

Period	*Project A*	*Project B*
0	–500	–400
1	325	325
2	325	200
IRR	19.43 per cent	**22.17 per cent**
NPV	**64.05**	60.74

Solution

Since the two projects are mutually exclusive, Project A should be preferred over Project B, as Project A enjoys higher NPV (Rs.64.05 millions).

Example 2.18

From the following table, draw the conclusion, whether to accept or reject the project?

Year 0	–90,000
Year 1	132,000
Year 2	100,000
Year 3	–150,000
IRR	10.11 per cent
NPV at 15 per cent discount factor	1,770

Solution: In the above table, IRR says to reject, but NPV says to accept. So, go with NPV and select the project for investment.

iv. Modified IRR (MIRR)

Despite the deficiencies of IRR (*i.e.*, may lead to multiple rates of return in case of projects with non-conventional cash flows, may lead to incorrect decisions in comparing mutually exclusive projects etc), it is still popular in practice even more than NPV as the former appraise the project in terms of rate of return (per cent) rather than on absolute terms. Further note that, without knowing the discount rate, we cannot estimate the NPV, but still we can calculate the IRR. Say, for example, if the IRR of the project is 40 percent, then the project manager may go for implementing the project, with the presumption that, the discount rate would be still less than IRR. Though IRR enjoys superiority over NPV, it too suffers from short comings as mentioned above. This calls for a percentage measure that overcomes the shortcomings of the IRR and this is nothing but, MIRR. NPV assumes that, periodic cash ows can and will be reinvested at the NPV discount rate, either at the cost of capital or another risk adjusted discount rate; IRR assumes reinvestment at the IRR. Neither assumption is usually realistic. In addition, when evaluating projects in terms of their nancial attractiveness, the two measures may rank projects differently. This becomes important when capital budgets are limited. Finally, a project may have several IRRs, if net cash flows go from negative to positive more than once. The MIRR, discovered in the 18th century, does account for these cash ows. While the IRR assumes that, the cash flows from a project are reinvested at the IRR, the MIRR assumes that, all cash flows are reinvested at the firm's OCC. Therefore, MIRR more accurately reflects the profitability of a project.

Procedure

The procedure to compute MIRR is discussed here under.

Step 1

Compute the PWC of cash outflows using the OCC or market rate of interest as discount factor:

$$\Sigma PWC = \sum_{t=1}^{n} C_t/(1+i)^t$$

where, Ct is the cash outflows, 'i' = market rate of interest, t = time period of project cash outflows

Step 2

Compute the Terminal Values (TV) of the cash inflows expected from the project by employing the discount factor 'i'. This is where, MIRR differs from IRR, as the modified MIRR assumes that all cash flows are reinvested at the firm's cost of capital whereas, the IRR assumes that the cash flows from a project are reinvested at the IRR. The formula used for computing TV is given by:

$$\Sigma TV = \sum_{t=1}^{n} B_t/(1+i)^{n-t}$$

where, Bt is the cash inflows, 'i' = market rate of interest, n = total duration of the project

Step 3

Compute MIRR by employing the following formula:

$$\Sigma PWC = \Sigma TV/(1+MIRR)^n$$

Example 2.19

Table 2.39: Computation of MIRR

Year	*Incr Costs*	*Incr Bene-fits*	*df @ 12%*	*PWC*	*NB*	*NPVdf @12%*	*df @25%*	*NPV @25% df*	*TV @ 12% df*
0	195		1.000	195.00	–195.000	–195.000	1.000	–195.000	
1		121	0.893		121.000	108.036	0.800	96.800	$121*(1.12)^1$ = 135.520
2		131	0.797		131.000	104.432	0.640	83.840	$131*(1.12)^0$ = 131.00
				ΣPWC = 195.00		NPV= 17.468		NPV= (-14.360)	ΣTV = 266.520
						IRR = 18.66 per cent			

For the data given through the Table 2.39, MIRR is given by:

$\Sigma PWC = \Sigma TV/(1 + MIRR)^n$

$195 = 266.520/(1 + MIRR)^2$

$(1 + MIRR)^2 = 266.520/195$

$(1 + MIRR)^2 = 1.367$

$(1 + MIRR) = (1.367)^{1/2} = 1.169$

So, MIRR = 0.169 = 16.9 per cent.

It can be inferred that (in Example 2.19), the 16.9 per cent MIRR is materially lower than the IRR of 18.66 per cent. In this case, the IRR gives a too optimistic picture of the potential of the project, while the MIRR gives a more realistic evaluation of the project. Let us look at another example.

Example 2.20

Table 2.40: Computation of MIRR

Year	*Incr Costs*	*Incr Bene-fits*	*df @ 15%*	*PWC*	*NB*	*NPVdf @12%*	*df @25%*	*NPV @25% df*	*TV @ 15% df*
0	120		1.000	120.000	–120.00	–120.000	1.000	–120.000	
1	80		0.870	69.565	–80.00	–69.565	0.833	–66.667	
2		20	0.756		20.00	15.123	0.694	13.889	$20*(1.15)^4$ = 34.980
3		60	0.658		60.00	39.451	0.579	34.722	$60*(1.15)^3$ = 91.253
4		80	0.572		80.00	45.740	0.482	38.580	$80*(1.15)^2$ = 105.800
5		100	0.497		100.00	49.718	0.402	40.188	$100*(1.15)^1$= 115.000
6		120	0.432		120.00	51.879	0.335	40.188	$120*(1.15)^0$= 120.000
				ΣPWC = 189.565		NPV= 12.346		NPV= (-19.100)	ΣTV = 467.033
						IRR=16.96 per cent			

For the data given through the Table 2.40, MIRR is given by:

$\Sigma PWC = \Sigma TV/(1 + MIRR)^n$

$189.565 = 467.033/(1 + MIRR)^6$

$(1 + MIRR)^6 = 467.033/189.565$

$(1 + MIRR)^6 = 2.464$

$(1 + MIRR) = (2.464)^{1/6} = 1.162$

So, MIRR = 0.162 = 16.2 per cent.

Again, MIRR (16.2 per cent) is lower than the IRR (16.96 per cent) and this MIRR gives a more realistic evaluation of the project. Note that, MIRR is superior than IRR in measuring the true rate of return. Superior in the sense that, MIRR assumes the project cash flows are re-invested at the OCC or market rate of interest, whereas the IRR assumes that, the project cash flows are re-invested at the IRR discount factor. We know, the re-investment of cash flows of a project at OCC is more realistic and this makes MIRR more superior to IRR. Further, MIRR does not lead to multiple rates of return, unlike IRR. So, we can infer that, in ranking mutually exclusive projects of the same duration and size, NPV and MIRR leads to the same decision. However, if the mutually exclusive projects are of different duration and size, then NPV measure still outweighs MIRR. Most financial analysts consider the MIRR to be a more prudent method of evaluating the future returns for a given investment opportunity. MIRR calculations are also helpful, if the cash flows of the project go from negative to positive and back again. For example, if you run IRR on a series of numbers that have more than one change in the signs, say -500, 150, 450, -100, 575 *etc.*, you will have two unique IRRs. The rule is that, we will have as many unique IRRs as there are changes in signs. MIRR solves this problem, as negative and positive numbers are treated separately. MIRR is considered as a more accurate measure of the attractiveness of an investment alternative because, attractiveness depends not only on the return on the investment itself, but also on the return expected from cash flow it generates.

Note that, there is some confusion in choosing the year for discounting *i.e.*, Year 0 or Year 1. World Bank believes that, since investment is made and some returns may accrue from the first year, then discounting should start from 0 to first year. In this case, the initial year is Year 1. But, other international organizations use Year 0. Their argument is that, investment must take place before benefits accrue. Thus, discounting should start from the second year. So, the students can chose any convention, but be consistent. However, in the above explanation, both the cases have been exemplified, so as to make the students familiar with the analysis.

Practical Utility of Time Comparison Principle

The following points highlight the practical importance of this principle:

i. It guides the farmer in making long term investment in the production programme.

ii. It also guides the farmer in computing the present value of future income and costs or future values of present income and costs and thereby, helps the farmer in comparing the profitability of investments in the production programme over a long period of time.

The above seven principles of farm management guide the farmer in conducting farm business regarding the level of resource usage (LDR), minimization of losses in the production programme (Cost principle), cost-effective production (Principle of factor substitution), profit maximization (Principle of product substitution), efficient utilization of limited resources (Principle of opportunity costs) and planning for long term investment that have long gestation period (Time comparison principle). All these principles explain *'why'* of profitable farm management. It is essential to note that, even without the application of these farm management principles, the farmer can do good farm business, but with the application of these principles, it will refine the production plans on the farm and thereby, saves time and costs in the use of resources and production of output. However, note that, all these principles assume that, production is known with certainty in the future. But, this is not the case for farm production, as the farmer faces several risks and uncertainties in conducting farm business and the same is discussed in the Chapter 8.

3

Farm Resources Management

In a farm, the farmer manages the employment of factors of production in taking up crops and allied enterprises. We know, the factors of production include land, labour, capital and entrepreneurship and their management is so crucial, as it directly contributes to the success of managing the farm. The farmer has to take the decisions on scientific scale in managing these factors of production with a view to maximize the profits. Scientific management of farm resources strengthens the inter-relationship between farm and farm life of the farm family. The former is concerned with maximization of profits in the farm business and the latter is concerned with the farm family satisfaction through enjoying the benefits realized from the farm business through scientific management of farm resources. Let us now discuss in-detail about the managerial aspects of farm resources here under.

I. Farm Land Management

In economics, land has a different meaning. Land includes all natural resources that human being get free from air, water and land. In short, the term 'land' refers all that nature has created on the earth, above the earth and below the earth's surface. All aspects of economic life *i.e.*, agriculture, trade and industry are generally influenced by natural resources, which is called as 'Land' in Economics. That is 'land', in an economic sense, is defined as the entire material universe outside of people themselves and the products of people. It includes all natural resources, materials, airwaves, as well as the ground. All air, soil, minerals and water is included in the definition of land. Everything that is freely supplied by nature, and not made by man, is categorized as land. As a factor of production, it is quite peculiar, as it possess the following important features:

- ☆ Land is a free gift of nature
- ☆ Land is limited in area
- ☆ Land is permanent in existence
- ☆ Land lacks geographical mobility
- ☆ Land is of infinite variety

Thus, the term land has been given a special meaning in economics. It does not mean soil only, as understood in ordinary speech, but it is synonymous with all the natural resources available from air and water, from above the land surface and below it, which yield income or useful produce. In the words of Marshall, land means *'the materials and the forces which nature gives freely for man's aid, in land and water, in air and light and heat.'* Most of the economic activities of man depend directly on land even today, as in the past, such as hunting, fishing, breeding of cattle and sheep, production of agricultural produce, gardens, minerals, metals, industrial raw material, electric power, water and other natural resources. Thus, land has a wider meaning, unlike a farm. A farm includes a piece of land over which the farmer has control in taking up crops and allied enterprises and is more concerned with the soil fertility, irrigation, drainage and other enterprise producing related factors. The farm land can be put into several uses and its use may vary over a period of time (Figures 3.1 and 3.2). Considering the land area, the approved classification of farmers (size-class of farmers) is as follows: Marginal farmer: < 1 hectare; Small farmer: 1-2 hectares; Semi-medium farmer: 2-4 hectares; Medium farmer: 4-10 hectares and Large farmer: ≥ 10 hectares. The number, area of operational holdings and per capita land holding size of farmers are shown through Tables 3.1 to 3.6 and Figure 3.3.

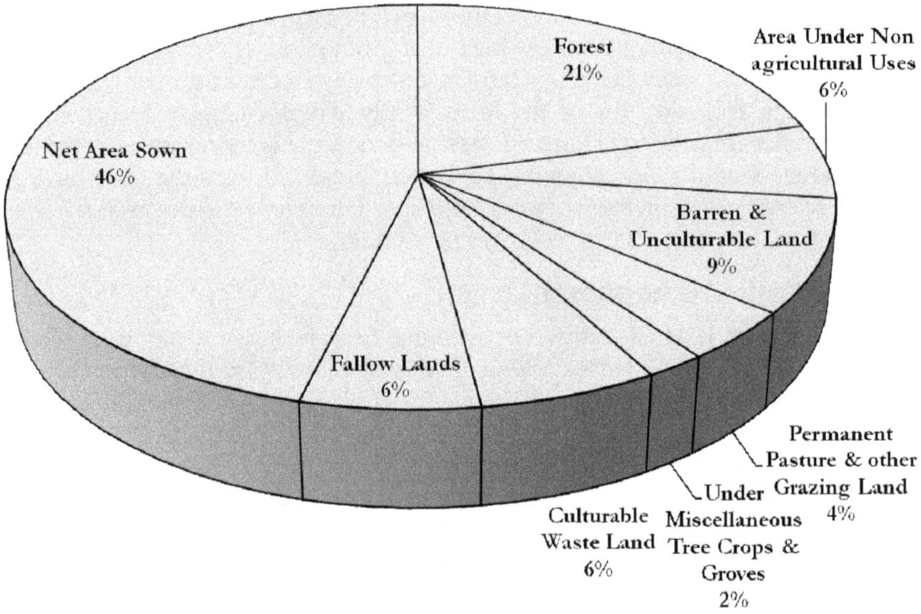

Figure 3.1: Pattern of Land Use in India (1970-71).

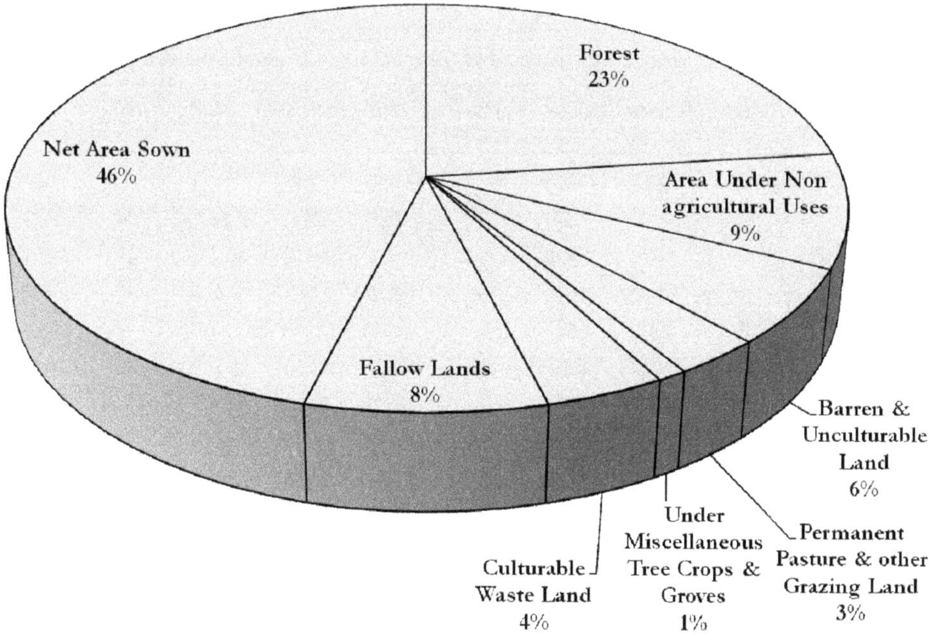

Figure 3.2: Pattern of Land Use in India (2008-09).

Table 3.1: Size Class-wise Number and Area of Operational Holdings for All Social Groups in India (2010-11)

Size Classes (In Ha.)	*Gender*	*No. of Operational Holdings('000)*				*Area Operated ('000 ha)*			
		Individual	*Joint*	*Insti-tutional*	*Total*	*Individual*	*Joint*	*Insti-tutional*	*Total*
Below 0.5	M	47596	7669	–	55265	11270	1850	–	13120
	F	8247	727	–	8974	1750	171	–	1921
	T	55843	8396	103	64342	13020	2021	20	15061
0.5-1.0	M	20606	3730	–	24336	15078	2627	–	17705
	F	3280	362	–	3642	2361	256	–	2617
	T	23886	4092	35	28014	17440	2883	25	20348
Marginal	**M**	**68202**	**11399**	**–**	**79602**	**26349**	**4477**	**–**	**30826**
	F	**11527**	**1089**	**–**	**12616**	**4111**	**427**	**–**	**4538**
	T	**79729**	**12488**	**138**	**92356**	**30460**	**4904**	**46**	**35410**
1.0-2.0	M	18594	3079	–	21672	26540	4342	–	30882
	F	2707	292	–	2999	3793	413	–	4205
	T	21300	3370	34	24705	30332	4755	49	35136
Small	**M**	**18594**	**3079**	**–**	**21672**	**26540**	**4342**	**–**	**30882**
	F	**2707**	**292**	**–**	**2999**	**3793**	**413**	**–**	**4205**
	T	**21300**	**3370**	**34**	**24705**	**30332**	**4755**	**49**	**35136**

Contd...

Table 3.1–*Contd...*

Size Classes (In Ha.)	Gender	No. of Operational Holdings('000)				Area Operated ('000 ha)			
		Individual	Joint	Insti-tutional	Total	Individual	Joint	Insti-tutional	Total
2.0-3.0	M	7253	1306	–	8559	17417	3163	–	20580
	F	909	127	–	1036	2145	307	–	2451
	T	8162	1433	18	9613	19561	3470	42	23073
3.0-4.0	M	3142	674	–	3816	10750	2315	–	13064
	F	337	65	–	402	1151	225	–	1376
	T	3479	739	10	4227	11901	2540	33	14474
Semi Medium	**M**	**10395**	**1980**	**–**	**12375**	**28166**	**5478**	**–**	**33644**
	F	**1246**	**192**	**–**	**1438**	**3296**	**531**	**–**	**3827**
	T	**11641**	**2172**	**27**	**13840**	**31462**	**6009**	**76**	**37547**
4.0-5.0	M	1807	395	–	2202	7990	1758	–	9748
	F	176	37	–	214	778	166	–	944
	T	1984	432	7	2423	8768	1924	31	10723
5.0-7.5	M	1849	433	–	2282	11133	2618	–	13752
	F	172	39	–	211	1030	235	–	1266
	T	2021	472	9	2503	12164	2854	57	15074
7.5-10.0	M	664	190	–	854	5638	1624	–	7262
	F	56	15	–	71	474	129	–	603
	T	720	205	5	930	6112	1753	46	7912
Medium	**M**	**4320**	**1018**	**–**	**5338**	**24762**	**6000**	**–**	**30762**
	F	**404**	**91**	**–**	**495**	**2282**	**531**	**–**	**2813**
	T	**4725**	**1109**	**22**	**5856**	**27044**	**6531**	**134**	**33709**
10.0-20.0	M	554	192	–	745	7223	2606	–	9829
	F	44	15	–	59	576	207	–	782
	T	598	207	9	814	7799	2813	123	10735
20.0 and Above	M	103	62	–	166	3153	2091	–	5244
	F	7	3	–	10	217	102	–	318
	T	110	66	11	187	3370	2193	1082	6644
Large	**M**	**657**	**254**	**–**	**911**	**10376**	**4697**	**–**	**15073**
	F	**51**	**18**	**–**	**70**	**793**	**308**	**–**	**1101**
	T	**708**	**273**	**20**	**1000**	**11169**	**5005**	**1205**	**17379**
All Classes	**M**	**102168**	**17730**	**–**	**119898**	**116193**	**24994**	**–**	**141187**
	F	**15936**	**1682**	**–**	**17618**	**14275**	**2210**	**–**	**16485**
	T	**118104**	**19412**	**241**	**137757**	**130468**	**27204**	**1508**	**159180**

Note: M: Male, F: Female, T: Total.

Table 3.2: Average Size per Holding for All Social Groups in Major States in India (2010-11)

States/UTs	*Gender*	*Average Size Per Holding (Ha.)*					
		Marginal	*Small*	*Semi-Medium*	*Medium*	*Large*	*All Size Groups*
Andhra Pradesh	M	0.44	1.42	2.65	5.57	14.89	1.13
	F	0.44	1.4	2.58	5.49	14.64	0.94
	T	0.44	1.41	2.63	5.56	15.5	1.08
Assam	M	0.42	1.38	2.69	5.14	16.78	1.00
	F	0.48	1.43	2.72	5.19	16.33	1.23
	T	0.42	1.38	2.69	5.15	68.11	1.10
Bihar	M	0.25	1.25	2.59	5.08	13.71	0.40
	F	0.25	1.26	2.59	5.13	12.31	0.37
	T	0.25	1.25	2.59	5.09	14.45	0.39
Chandigarh	M	0.47	1.43	2.83	5.74	11.08	1.33
	F	0.41	1.41	3.3	4.8	–	0.92
	T	0.46	1.43	2.86	5.7	11.08	1.29
Chhattisgarh	M	0.44	1.42	2.68	5.72	16.23	1.40
	F	0.41	1.42	2.66	5.66	16.02	1.06
	T	0.44	1.42	2.68	5.71	16.3	1.36
Gujarat	M	0.49	1.45	2.77	5.71	19.77	2.12
	F	0.49	1.45	2.75	5.73	16.96	1.96
	T	0.49	1.45	2.77	5.71	19.54	2.11
Haryana	M	0.46	1.47	2.87	6.09	16.57	2.19
	F	0.45	1.45	2.84	6.04	15.99	2.08
	T	0.46	1.47	2.87	6.09	17.95	2.25
Himachal Pradesh	M	0.41	1.39	2.72	5.66	14.5	1.01
	F	0.33	1.38	2.69	5.58	14.79	0.66
	T	0.41	1.39	2.72	5.66	15.44	0.99
Karnataka	M	0.49	1.41	2.68	5.69	14.12	1.61
	F	0.43	1.41	2.66	5.65	14.59	1.28
	T	0.48	1.41	2.68	5.69	14.71	1.55
Kerala	M	0.14	1.57	2.8	5.28	25.12	0.22
	F	0.12	1.56	2.77	5.39	17.9	0.16
	T	0.13	1.57	2.79	5.32	64.58	0.22
Madhya Pradesh	M	0.49	1.42	2.73	5.77	15.72	1.82
	F	0.48	1.41	2.68	5.64	14.15	1.41
	T	0.49	1.42	2.73	5.76	15.77	1.78

Contd...

Table 3.2–*Contd...*

States/UTs	*Gender*	*Average Size Per Holding (Ha.)*					
		Marginal	*Small*	*Semi-Medium*	*Medium*	*Large*	*All Size Groups*
Maharashtra	M	0.47	1.42	2.68	5.62	15.79	1.48
	F	0.48	1.4	2.61	5.55	14.97	1.26
	T	0.47	1.42	2.67	5.62	16.07	1.45
Meghalaya	M	0.56	1.57	2.7	5.41	14.83	1.35
	F	0.55	1.61	2.89	5.72	22.98	1.43
	T	0.56	1.58	2.75	5.49	17.24	1.37
Odisha	M	0.57	1.63	2.95	5.99	20.15	1.03
	F	0.53	1.62	2.92	6.02	17.05	0.96
	T	0.57	1.63	2.95	5.99	25.46	1.04
Punjab	M	0.62	1.38	2.64	5.74	14.69	3.77
	F	0.57	1.37	2.53	5.76	14.05	2.73
	T	0.61	1.38	2.64	5.74	14.75	3.77
Tamil Nadu	M	0.37	1.39	2.7	5.63	15.47	0.81
	F	0.36	1.38	2.68	5.59	15.52	0.68
	T	0.37	1.39	2.7	5.63	20.13	0.80
Uttar Pradesh	M	0.37	1.39	2.72	5.53	14.45	0.76
	F	0.35	1.37	2.69	5.37	14.17	0.59
	T	0.37	1.39	2.72	5.52	15.01	0.75
West Bengal	M	0.5	1.59	2.73	4.81	–	0.75
	F	0.35	1.38	2.57	4.62	–	0.44
	T	0.49	1.59	2.73	4.85	338.58	0.77
India	**M**	**0.39**	**1.42**	**2.72**	**5.76**	**16.55**	**1.18**
	F	**0.36**	**1.4**	**2.66**	**5.68**	**15.76**	**0.94**
	T	**0.38**	**1.42**	**2.71**	**5.76**	**17.37**	**1.16**

Note: M: Male; F: Female; T: Total (Includes institutional holdings also).

Source: Ministry of Agriculture, Govt. of India.

A. Farm Layout

It refers to the systematic planning of dividing the entire farm into fields and other fixtures like irrigation and drainage channels, farm buildings, godowns, machinery sheds, roads, fencing etc (Figure 3.4). A farm, including its land and buildings is called Farmstead. Thus, farm layout involves the compiling of physical structures on the farm and it ensures the farm manager to execute all the farm activities with high level of efficiency. The scientific farm layout will have the following features:

Table 3.3: Distribution of Number of Holdings and Area Operated in India as per Agriculture Census 2010-11

Sl. No.	Size Group	Number of holdings (in million)	Area operated (in million ha.)	Average operated area per holding (ha.)	Percentage of holdings to total holdings	Percentage of area operated to total area
1	Marginal (Below 1.00 ha.)	92.4	35.4	0.38	67.04	22.25
2	Small (1.00-2.00 ha.)	24.7	35.1	1.42	17.93	22.07
3	Semi-Medium (2.00-4.00 ha.)	13.8	37.5	2.71	10.05	23.59
4	Medium (4.00-10.00 ha.)	5.9	33.7	5.76	4.25	21.18
5	Large (Above 10.00 ha.)	1.0	17.4	17.38	0.73	10.92
	All holdings	137.8	159.2	1.16	100.00	100.00

Note: Total may not tally due to rounding off.

Source: Agriculture Census (2010-11).

Table 3.4: Size Group-wise Distribution of Average Holdings in the Country (Area in ha.)

Sl. No	Size Groups	1970-71	1976-77	1980-81	1985-86	1990-91	1995-96	2000-01*	2005-06*	2010-11P
1	Marginal (Below 1 ha.)	0.40	0.39	0.39	0.39	0.39	0.40	0.40	0.38	0.38
2	Small (1-2 ha.)	1.44	1.42	1.44	1.43	1.43	1.42	1.42	1.38	1.42
3	Semi-Medium (2-4 ha.)	2.81	2.78	2.78	2.77	2.76	2.73	2.72	2.68	2.71
4	Medium (4-10 ha.)	6.08	6.04	6.02	5.96	5.90	5.84	5.81	5.74	5.76
5	Large (Above 10 ha)	18.1	17.57	17.41	17.21	17.33	17.21	17.12	17.08	17.38
	All Size Classes	2.28	2.00	1.84	1.69	1.55	1.41	1.33	1.23	1.16

Note: Total may not tally due to rounding off. *excludes Jharkhand
P: Provisional.
Source: Agriculture Census 2010-11.

Table 3.5: Average Size of Land Holdings Across the Countries (2005-06)

Countries by Continent (Number of reproting countries is given in parenthesis)	*Average Area per Holding (Hectare)*
World Total (114)	5.5
Africa (25)	11.5
America, North and Central (14)	117.8
America, South (8)	74.4
Europe (29)	12.4
Asia (29)	1.0
India	1.23

Source: www.fao.org.

Table 3.6: FAO Recommendations on Size Classes for Tabulation of Data from Agriculture Census and their Application in India

FAO recommendations	Classifications used in India	
	For statistical purposes	**For policy purposes**
Holdings without land		
Holdings with land		
Less than 0.1 ha	*Less than 0.02 ha*	***Marginal Farmers (below 1 Ha)***
0.1 – 0.19 ha	*0.02- 0.5*	
0.2 – 0.49 ha		
0.5 – 0.99 ha	*0.5- 1.0 ha*	
1 – 1.99 ha	*1-2 ha*	***Small Farmers (1-2 ha)***
2 – 2.99 ha	*2-3 ha*	***Semi-medium Farmers (2-4 ha)***
3 – 3.99 ha	*2-4 ha*	
4 – 4.99 ha	*4-5 ha*	***Médium Farmers (4-10 Ha)***
5 – 9.99 ha	*5-7.5 ha*	
	7.5-10.0 ha	
10 – 19.99 ha	*10-20.0 ha*	***Large Farmers (over 10 ha)***
20 – 49.99 ha	*20.0 ha and above*	
50 – 99 ha		
100 – 199 ha		
200 – 499 ha		
500 – 999 ha		
1,000 – 2,499 ha		
2,500 ha and over		

Source: www.fao.org.

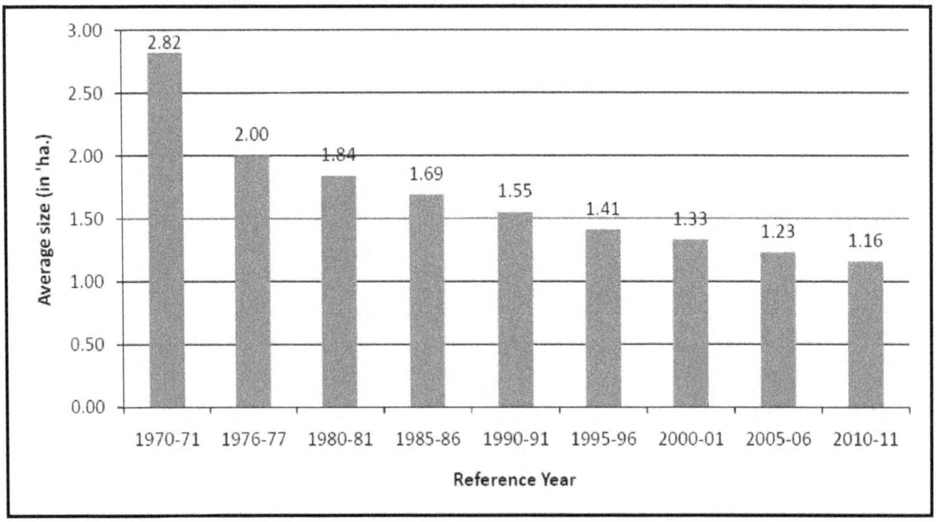

Figure 3.3: Average Size of Operational Holdings as per Different Agriculture Censuses.
Source: Agriculture Census (2010-11).

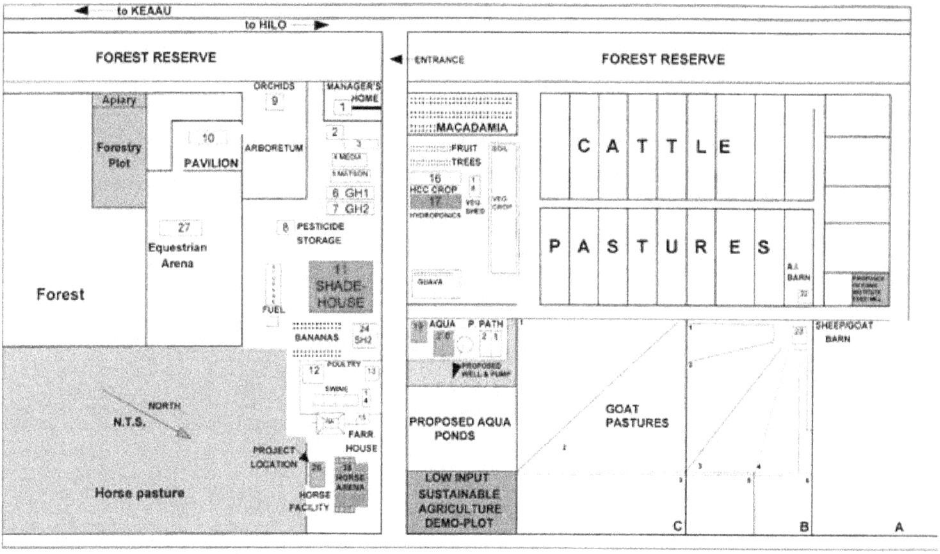

Figure 3.4: Farm Layout.
http://hilo.hawaii.edu/academics/cafnrm/farm_map.php

i. Farm fields

The following points should be taken into consideration, while planning the layout of farm fields:

- ☆ The number, size and shape of the fields should be in accordance with the topography and type of farming the farmer to be followed. Further, the number of fields should correspond to the number of years of one round of crop rotation. For example, in a three year crop rotation (say, potatoes, legumes and brassicas), the number of fields should be three and in a four year crop rotation (say, potatoes, legumes, brassicas and onions), the number of fields should be four.

Three Year Crop Rotation

- ☆ **Year one**
  Section one: Potatoes
  Section two: Legumes, onions and roots
  Section three: Brassicas
- ☆ **Year two**
  Section one: Legumes, onions and roots
  Section two: Brassicas
  Section three: Potatoes
- ☆ **Year three**
  Section one: Brassicas
  Section two: Potatoes
  Section three: Legumes, onions and roots

Four Year Crop Rotation

- **Year one**
  Section one: Legumes
  Section two: Brassicas
  Section three: Potatoes
  Section four: Onions and roots
- **Year two**
  Section one: Brassicas
  Section two: Potatoes
  Section three: Onions and roots
  Section four: Legumes
- **Year three**
  Section one: Potatoes
  Section two: Onions and roots
  Section three: Legumes
  Section four: Brassicas
- **Year four**
  Section one: Onions and roots
  Section two: Legumes
  Section three: Brassicas
  Section four: Potatoes

- If the farmer has not yet laid out his fields, obtain a contour map of his farm. This map will be useful to determine, whether there is more than one good way to lay out the fields and irrigation system. In planning the irrigation layout, assistance from an Irrigation Engineer is essential.
- Flexibility in field layout is essential depending on the slope of the land. Two or three desirable farmstead sites are to be considered and final selection of site depends upon the flexibility in field arrangement. It is usually desirable to locate the farmstead adjacent to a main traveled road. Accessibility to power and telephone lines, ease in marketing of farm products and easy supervision of farm fields are often considered in selecting the right site for farmstead. In the case of large farms, the operating efficiency that results from the farmstead being near the center of the farm usually outweighs the advantages of its being close to the road. In general, location of the farmstead near the center of the road frontage (Figure 3.4.1) is desirable especially in livestock or dairy farm. This central location provides easy access to all fields, provides maximum flexibility for change in operations and keeps field travel to a minimum. However, these advantages are not experienced by going for corner crossroads location of farmstead. In the figure, as compared to the central farmstead location, the corner location would require approximately 70 per cent more travel from the farmstead to the fields.
- Regarding the size of the fields, a smaller number of large sized fields are more preferred over large number of small sized fields, as large sized fields facilitate mechanization of farm operations.

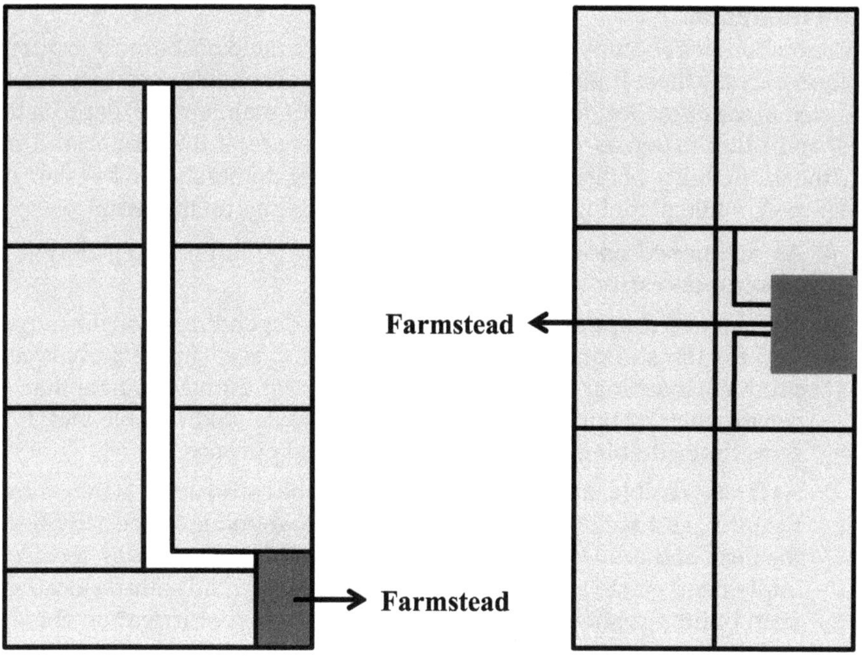

Corner Farmstead Location **Central Farmstead Location**

Figure 3.4.1: Farmstead Location.

- As far as possible, rectangular shaped fields are more preferred over square shaped fields, as the former will involve less number of turnings for the tractors and other machinery to be used in the farm. This also leads to economy of labour costs and time. As far as possible, plan the size of the field such that, it is twice as long as it is wide. Though square fields enjoy less fencing cost compared to rectangular fields, the latter is preferred for the cultivating the crops. As far as possible, ill-shaped fields should be avoided, as the cultivation in such fields consumes more labour, time and costs.
- As far as possible, each field should be uniform in its soil type.
- The size of each field may vary depending upon the availability of irrigation facilities, size of the farm, extent of farm mechanization, topography, soil fertility status, type of farming *etc.*
- The layout of farm fields should be constructed keeping in view of checking the soil erosion and conserving the soil. The fields should be extended along the contour and not down the slope, as the latter aggravates the soil erosion.

ii. Farm Buildings

As farm buildings occupy considerable space, they should not be more in number in the farm *i.e.*, only those buildings that are considered absolutely necessary must be constructed in the farm. Besides the above the reason, the maintenance, depreciation, interest and other expenses fall under working expenses of the farmer and they reduce the profitability of farm business. The following points should be taken into consideration, while planning the construction of buildings on the farm:

- ☆ As mentioned above, their number should be limited considering the absolute necessity.
- ☆ The size and shape of the buildings will vary depending upon the purpose say, for the stocking of fertilizers, pesticides, seed material, harvested produce, machinery, tools and implements *etc.* However, note that, the construction of buildings should be economical and flexible and at the same time durable enough to meet the desired purpose.
- ☆ As far as possible, the farm buildings should be constructed at the centre of the farm, as it facilitates the farm manager to monitor all the activities on the farm and easy transport of requisite materials (pesticides, fertilizers, implements etc) to all corners of the farm. However, this central location of farm buildings should not affect the construction of irrigation channels and drainage channels in the fields. Another view is to construct the farm buildings at one corner of the farm that lie nearer to the main road or highway. This facilitates to gain access to transport and communication facilities. But, in this case, the farm buildings are located at distant place from fields so that, it is difficult to transport the inputs to the fields. Another demerit is that, the trespassing animals along the roadside may spread diseases to the farm cattle. So, each location for construction of farm buildings had its own advantages and disadvantages.
- ☆ The location of farm buildings should ensure good access to power and telephone lines, ease in marketing of farm produce and the availability of a good roads to all processing factories in that locality. In the case of large farms, the operating efficiency that results from the farmstead being near the center of the farm usually outweighs the advantages of its being close to the road.
- ☆ Irrespective of the location, the construction of farm buildings should be allowed at higher elevation in the farm, so as to facilitate easy drainage. Otherwise, the stored items like fertilizers, pesticides, harvested produce *etc.*, may get spoiled due to water stagnation during rainy days. If an otherwise desirable site does not have sufficient drainage, it is often possible to do some ditching, filling or tile laying to correct the fault.
- ☆ It should be remembered to avoid the construction of farm buildings on high fertile soils.
- ☆ While constructing farmstead, the farmer should plan the cost of construction on the basis of his long term farm returns. For example, in case of storage structure, the costs incurred must be covered by the returns from

the storage (*i.e.*, Gross returns on storage = Price of the commodity at the time of destocking - Price of the commodity at the time of storage. Similarly, Net returns from storage is given by: =Gross Returns – Storage costs) in the long run. Besides construction costs, repair and maintenance, insurance premiums, taxes and interest on the investment are also to be taken into consideration. Note that, the farmer should not make excessive building costs on small farm with the expectation of getting higher returns from the business, as the farm returns are highly uncertain. So, in making the final decision before the farmer invests his capital in farm buildings, he should answer the following questions:

- ❑ Is this particular building necessary for my present farm operations?
- ❑ Would temporary construction fit my needs until farm income can be used for constructing permanent buildings?
- ❑ Would the funds spent on farm buildings bring me greater returns?
- ❑ Is this the best time to build?
- ❑ Does this building fit the long-time needs of my farm operations?
- ❑ Will the cost and size of building be in keeping with the size of my farm?
- ❑ Will the use of this building pay me a return above annual maintenance expenses?
- ❑ Will construction of this building result in the use of funds needed for the family, such as education for the children?

iii. Farm Roads

The following points should be taken into consideration, while planning the construction of farm roads:

- ☆ One wider road should be there connecting the highway or main road.
- ☆ The branches (Key approach roads) arise from the wider road should be narrow to approach the farm fields. Note that, each field need not be connected to the wider road.
- ☆ As far as possible, the number of roads should be kept minimum, but connected to all corners of the farm and fields so that, farm roads will not occupy significant area in the farm.

iv. Irrigation and Drainage Channels

The following points should be taken into consideration, while planning the construction of irrigation and drainage channels in the farm:

- ☆ Good irrigation practice is the first consideration in field layout. The layout of irrigation channels depends upon the source of irrigation. In case of canal irrigation, there should be one main irrigation channel and from this several branches (sub-channels) may arise perpendicular to main channel to connect each and every field. In case of tube well irrigation, a tube well should be installed at higher elevation in the farm and this facilitates easy flow of water to each and every field in the farm.

- ☆ As far as possible, lining of irrigation channels is to be done, so as to avoid percolation and seepage losses.
- ☆ Depending on the locality, the water and irrigation supply may be one and the same source. If the supply is not too plentiful, it is wise to locate the farmstead reasonably close to the point of water delivery. Such a location would keep the loss between point of delivery and the farmstead pond at a minimum. The crops that demand more irrigation water should be cultivated near to the source of irrigation and other crops at the corner fields in the farm.
- ☆ Like irrigation channels, construction of drainage channels on scientific lines is equally important, as they drain out excess water from the fields at times of higher rainfall. The sub-channels that arise from each field should get connected to the main drainage channel to drain out the water from the farm.
- ☆ Surface drainage channels or sub-surface drainage channels can be constructed on the farm, but the latter require huge investment on the part of the farmer, but economize the use of land.

v. Fencing

Fencing is to be provided around the farm, so as to stop encroachment of the farm land and to offer protection to the crops from trespassing cattle and wild animals. Two types of fences can be used depending on the availability of funds with the farmer *viz.*, Kaccha fencing and Pucca fencing.

- ☆ ***Kaccha Fencing (Living Fence):*** In this type, fencing is provided with shrubs by planting cactus, agave Bamboo, Casuarina, Eucalyptus spp *etc.*, and is followed, when the funds available with the farmer are limited.
- ☆ ***Pucca Fencing:*** In this type, fencing is provided around the farm by constructing a brick wall or by barbed wire. Barbed wire fencing is more common and this fencing is followed, when more funds are available with the farmer. This fencing offers more protection compared to the earlier Kaccha fencing.

Example 3.1

Compute the cost of fencing for the given data:

- ☆ Size of the farm: 5ha
- ☆ Length : Breadth of the farm : 5:2
- ☆ Length of one bundle of barbed wire : 100meters
- ☆ Weight of one bundle of barbed wire : 25kgs
- ☆ Cost of barbed wire : Rs. 50/kg
- ☆ Distance between the two poles : 3 meters, and at every 10th pole one extra pole is needed to give strength to fencing.

- ☆ Weight of one pole: 8kgs
- ☆ Size of each pit for fixing the poles : 30*30*45cms
- ☆ Cost of digging each pit : Rs.10/pit
- ☆ Cost of cement - concrete and filling : Rs.1500/cu.meters
- ☆ Cost of stretching and fixing the wires : 2 labourers are needed for every 300 meters distance
- ☆ 7 horizontal lines and 2 diagonal lines are taken for fixing barbed wire
- ☆ Cost of G.I. stapples: Rs.250
- ☆ Wage rate of labour: Rs.120
- ☆ Cost of two iron gates: 10′x 5′: Rs.6000

Now estimate the total cost of fencing of 5 ha farm.

Solution

Considering the above data, the cost of fencing to the 5 ha farm is computed and shown through the following table.

Sl.No.	Item	Total Cost (Rs.)
1.	Area of the farm = 5X*2X = 10X² = 5hA So, 10X² = 50000 Sq.mt, X = 70.71 mt So, length of the farm=5*70.71 = 355.55 mt, breadth of the farm=2*70.71=141.42 mt Perimeter of the farm = (length + breadth) * 2 = (355.55 + 141.42) * 2 = 989.94 mt	
2.	***Length and weight of the barbed wire needed:*** Given total length of the barbed wire needed, if the fencing needs 7 wires in horizontal lines and 2 in diagonal line: Total length of barbed wire: Perimeter of the farm * Number of lines: 989.94*9 = 8909.46 m Given length of one bundle barbed wire: 100m and weight of one bundle: 25 kgs So, the number of bundles required: (8909.46/100) = 89 Total weight of 89 bundles : 89*25=2225kgs	
3.	***Total cost of wire:*** Given cost of wire: Rs.50/kg, then Total cost of wire: 2225*50 = Rs.111250	111250
4.	***Cost of iron poles:*** Given distance between two poles is 3mt and at every 10th pole, one extra pole is needed to given strength to fencing. We already know that, the perimeter of the farm as 989.94mt. So, number of poles required is given by: (Perimeter/Distance between poles)+1 (*i.e.,* one in the beginning) (989.94/3)+1 = 331 poles At every 10th pole, one extra pole is required. So, extra poles required: (331/10) = 33. We need one extra pole at the beginning. So, total number of poles required: 331+33+1 = 365 Given, weight of one pole: 8kg So, weight of 365 poles = 365*8 = 2920 kgs Given, cost of each pole: Rs.50/kg So, total cost of poles: 2920*50=Rs.146000	146000

Contd...

Sl.No.	Item	Total Cost (Rs.)
5.	***Cost of digging pits:*** Given size of pit: 30*30*45 cm=0.04cu.mt Given, cost of digging each pit: Rs.10/pit So, total volume of 365 poles: 365*0.04=14.60 cu.mt Total cost of digging pits: 365*10=Rs.3650	3650
6.	Given, cost of cement-concrete+filling:Rs.1500/cu.mt Total cost of cement-concrete+filling: 14.60*1500 = Rs.23940	21900
7.	***Cost of fixing the wires:*** Given, 2 labour are needed for every 300m distance (9 lines). So, number of labour required = 989.94/300=3. Since 2 labour are required, 3*2 = 6. Given, wage rate/labour is Rs.120. So, cost of stretching and fixing wires: 6*120=Rs.720	720
8.	Given, cost of G.I. stapples to fix the wire: Rs.250	250
9.	Given, cost of two iron gates: Rs.6000	6000
	Total Cost of Fencing	**Rs. 289770**
	Cost of fencing/metre length of wire	**289770/989.94 = Rs.293**

Above all, the farmer should erect natural windbreaks by planting a grove of trees around the farm. Good soil is always desirable for the farm. This is usually a minor factor, however, unless the best farmstead site happens to be on unusually sandy or stony soil. Average soil and very often poor soil can be brought up to a highly productive level by the use of manure, commercial fertilizer, green manure crops *etc.* Thus, the farmer must balance desirable field layout with the essential factors of a good farmstead location and such a good farm layout will determine the efficiency in the use of his resources and resource services that he employs on the farm. Further, note that, while designing the farm layout, it is essential to borne in mind that, the fixtures so designed on the farm should be both economical and flexible. This is because, with the changing techniques of production and increased mechanization of farm operations, re-modeling of farm layout is inevitable. The important forms of re-modeling of farm layout include:

- Change from bullock labour to mechanization.
- Change from furrow irrigation to sprinkler irrigation.
- Change from canal irrigation to tube well irrigation or tank irrigation.
- Change from surface drainage to sub-surface drainage.
- Change from crop enterprises to allied enterprises like dairy, sheep, sericulture *etc.*

Likewise, many number of reasons will compel the farmer to remodel his farm. Two important conditions will guide the farmer to go for remodeling the farm *viz.*, initial cost of establishment of new fixture and net returns the farmer may generate after changing the layout. Besides changing the farm layout, the farmer should be vigilant in planning the cropping scheme, crop rotation, cropping pattern, soil health management, soil conservation, soil nutrient management, soil erosion control *etc.*, from time to time and he must execute these operations with prior discussions with the scientific community.

Factors Influencing Farm Layout

They include:

- ☆ Area where the farm is situated
- ☆ Availability of natural resources
- ☆ Farming practices
- ☆ Preferences of the farmer/owner
- ☆ Financial position of the owner (availability of capital)
- ☆ Farming enterprises
- ☆ Production systems used to produce a product
- ☆ Topography of the farm
- ☆ Intensity of the system
- ☆ Climatic conditions of the farm
- ☆ Product produced (Enterprises practiced)
- ☆ Rules and regulations applicable to agricultural sector.

Influences by Farm Layout

Layout of the farm can influence the following:

- ☆ *Output of enterprises:* Poor layout of the farm leads to wastage of energy and thus, can effect production adversely. Labour allotment is not effective across the enterprises and it leads to wastage of their time and energy. As a result, it slows down the production process.
- ☆ *Yield:* Poor facilities affect the hygiene on the farm and it leads to spread of pests and diseases on the crops and allied enterprise thereby, their productivity decreases.
- ☆ *Costs:* Considering the labour inefficiency and spread of pests and diseases on the enterprises leads to escalation of cost structure on the farm.
- ☆ *Quality of output:* Poor layout affects both quantity and quality of output of enterprises.
- ☆ *Cost recovery:* Due to escalation of cost structure and fall in output of enterprises, cost recovery will be poor.
- ☆ *Flexibility in use:* Proper layout of the farm will provide a greater flexibility in taking up various crops and enterprises. For example, if the farm buildings are located in the center of the farm, it provides easy transport of inputs, supervision of enterprises, easy access to all fields, provides maximum flexibility for change in operations, keeps field travel to a minimum *etc.* This arrangement further facilitates to add more buildings, if he desires.
- ☆ *Soil fertility:* Rotation of crops over the entire farm is one of the fastest means of building soil fertility. Here again, location of the farmstead in the center of the farm provides the flexibility that makes such a practice possible. A farmstead located at one remote corner of a farm would make pasturing

at the other end impracticable. Further, good farm arrangement will make it possible to carry out efficient and profitable farming practices.

B. Farm-size or Size of Land Holding

In ordinary sense, size of land holding refers to physical area of land possessed by the farmer say, in acres or hectares. But, in economic sense, size of land holding refers to either value of production or volume of production (output). Measurement of size of land holding in terms of physical area is an inadequate measure because, a hectare of land near market outlet is valued more than a hectare of land that lies away from the market outlet. Before going into the details of factors that influence the size of land holding, let us throw light on different types of land holdings:

- *Agricultural holding:* In general, agricultural holding is the total size of land holding owned by the farmer in the cultivation of crops. This is an economic unit under a single management engaged in agricultural production activities. The unit may also be engaged in non-agricultural activities so that, this concept should not be interpreted too strictly; the aim is rather to value the final production of all agricultural products. Also, establishments or specialized units, which provide agricultural services on a fee or contract basis should, in general, be included.
- *Operational holding:* Operational holding is the actual area of land holding that was put into cultivation by the farmer under single management. It is, otherwise, defined as, *'all land which is used wholly or partly for agricultural production and is operated as one technical unit by one person alone or with others without regard to the title, legal form, size or location'*. Operational holding may be greater than or less than or equal to agricultural holding.
    - Operational holding is greater than agricultural holding, if farmer takes leased in land for cultivation.
    - Operational holding is equal to agricultural holding, if the farmer puts his entire land into cultivation.
    - Operational holding is less than agricultural holding, if farmer leases out land for cultivation.

    The following is the classification of operational holdings:

    - Marginal (below 1 ha)
    - Small (1-2 ha)
    - Semi- medium (2-4 ha)
    - Medium (4-10 ha)
    - Large (10 ha or above)

    The present operation holding size in India since 1970-71 is presented here under through Table 3.7.

    Note that, operated area would include both cultivated and uncultivated area, provided part of it is put to agricultural production during the reference period. If for instance, an operational holding consists of four survey numbers out of which, one survey number is put to non-agricultural uses, the total area of the operational holding will be equal to the total geographical area of all the four survey numbers.

Table 3.7: Trends in per Capita Land Holding Size in India

Agriculture Census (Years)	*Number of Holdings (millions)*	*Area Operated (m. ha)*	*Average Area per Holding (ha)*
1970-71	71.0	162.1	2.28
1976-77	81.6	163.3	2.00
1980-81	88.9	163.8	1.84
1985-86	97.2	164.6	1.69
1990-91	106.6	165.5	1.55
1995-96	115.6	163.4	1.41
2000-01	119.9	159.4	1.33
2005-06	129.2	158.3	1.23
2010-11	137.8	159.2	1.16

Source: www.agricoop.nic.in

Operated area would also cover the land occupied by the farm buildings, including the house of the holder, provided such buildings are located within the operated area. If the farms buildings are located outside the cultivated area and are covered under abadi area (area under habitation), such buildings would not be included. Operated area would exclude Government forest land, Government waste land, village common grazing land, abadi area *etc*. If Government wasteland is allotted to an individual, then it will be included in the holding. If the entire area of the holding (the area of all the survey numbers of an operational holding) is put to non-agricultural use and/or it is under old fallow, it will not be considered as operated area. If, however, the entire area of operational holding is under current fallow during the reference year, but was cultivated in the preceding year, this would still be considered as operational holding.

In some cases, land is divided amongst all the members of the family. Where it is divided between the husband, wife and minor children and the cultivation is being done by the husband as the head of the family, the land may appropriately be treated as one operational holding. There might be cases where in the records, a holding is shown jointly in the name of more than one co-sharer, while in fact the land may have been privately divided and the co-sharers are independently cultivating. In such cases, where there is no dispute, they should be treated as many operational holdings, as the number of independent cultivators. This is necessary because, in Agricultural Census, the data is to be collected on the basis of *de facto* position rather than *de jure* position. In some cases, while from the records it would appear that, there is only one holding, but in practice, all the three or four brothers are actually cultivating the land independently of each other although there is no legal partition of land. From the Census point of view, this would constitute three or four operational holdings. For cultivated areas in the State Forests, no detailed land records are prepared. In the absence of revenue records and revenue agency such areas are excluded for Census purposes. The operated area may comprise of:

- **Land Owned and Self Operated**
  - ***Land owned:*** Land for which the cultivator has the right to permanent heritable possession would be considered as owned. This would include: land held from Government or others under grant or lease or assignment with right of permanent heritable possession with or without right of transfer and land operated under perpetual lease.
  - ***Self-operated land:*** This would include: Self cultivation, Land cultivated through members of the family, Land cultivated with the help of hired labour.

    Note that, land owned and self operated should not include land leased out to others.
  - ***Land leased in:*** Land leased in is defined as land taken on lease from others without any permanent right of possession for the lessee. Land may be leased in for: Fixed money, Fixed produce, Share of produce, Usufructuary mortgage (Ownership of the property remains with the mortgager but the possession is with the mortgagee (*i.e.* the person to whom the mortgage is made or given). Income from the property accrues to the mortgagee and the mortgage is terminated as soon as the full amount is realized).
  - ***Land otherwise operated***: This would include encroachment, land forcibly occupied, unauthorized or land in dispute *etc.*, which cannot be treated as owned or leased in, as per the definitions given above.
- ***Operational holder:*** An 'Operational holder' is the person, who has the responsibility for the operation of the agricultural holding and who exercises the technical initiative and is responsible for its operation. He may have full economic responsibility or may share it with others. The operational holding may be Individual or Joint or Institutional.
  - ***Individual holding:*** If the holding is being operated either by one person alone or by group of persons, who are the members of the same household, it will be considered as an individual holding.
  - ***Joint holding:*** If two or more persons belonging to different households, share jointly as partners in the economic and technical responsibility for the operation of an agricultural holding, such holding would be considered as joint holding.
  - ***Institutional holding:*** Holdings such as Government farms, sugarcane factories farms, cooperative farms, lands managed by trust would be treated as Institutional holding.

- ***Resident and Non-resident operational holder:*** All the cultivators residing in a particular village and cultivating some land within the same tehsil are resident cultivators of that village irrespective of the fact whether they are cultivating land in that village or not. A resident cultivator may, therefore, have either (i) entire area of the holding located in the village of his residence; or (ii) partly within the village of residence and partly outside; or (iii) entirely outside the village of residence.

  An operational holder operating area outside the tehsil in which his village of residence falls, will not be treated as a resident cultivator of the village of his residence for Agricultural Census purposes. He will be treated as a resident cultivator of the village outside the tehsil, where the area falls. If the area in a particular village is operated by a cultivator, who resides outside that village but within the same tehsil, he is a non-resident operational holder for that area. However, if this operational holder is resident of a village lying outside the tehsil in which the area is located, he will be treated as a resident operational holder (deemed resident) of the village where the area is located.
- ***Complete Holding and Part-Holding:*** A holding is said to be complete holding, if the entire operated area of that holding is located in one village. If the operated area is spread over more than one village, it would be considered as part-holding. Tehsil would be taken as the outer limit for consolidation of part holdings.
- ***Wholly Irrigated, Partly Irrigated and Wholly Unirrigated Holdings:*** If the entire net area sown in an operational holding is equal to net area irrigated, such holdings are considered as wholly irrigated holding. In case part of the net sown area is irrigated, it will be partly irrigated and if the entire sown area has not received any irrigation during the year of reference, such holding would be wholly unirrigated.
- ***Land Utilization Pattern:*** Operated area would be classified into six broad categories:
  - ***Net area sown:*** Total area sown with crops and orchards counting area sown more than once in the same year only once.
  - ***Current fallow:*** Cropped area, which are kept fallow during the current year, but was cultivated in the previous year. For example with any seeding area is not cropped in the same year, it may be treated as current fallow.
  - ***Fallow land other than current fallow:*** All lands, which are taken up for cultivation, but are temporarily out of cultivation for a period of not less than one year and not more than five years. The reasons for keeping such lands fallow may be one or more of the following:
    - Poverty of the cultivator
    - Inadequate supply of water
    - Silting of canals and rivers and
    - Unremunerative nature of farming

- ❑ ***Other uncultivated land excluding fallow land:*** This will include:
  - ❖ ***Permanent pastures and other grazing lands:*** All grazing lands, whether they are permanent pastures and meadows or not. Village common grazing lands would, however, be excluded.
  - ❖ ***Land under Miscellaneous Tree Crops:*** Cultivable land, which is not included in the net area sown, but is put to some agricultural use. Land under casuarina trees, thatching grasses, bamboo bushes and other groves for fuel which are not included under 'Orchards' would be covered under this category.
- ❑ ***Culturable waste***: All lands available for cultivation whether not taken up for cultivation or taken up for cultivation once but not cultivated during the current year and the last five years or more in succession for one reason or the other. Such lands may be either wholly or partly covered with shrubs and jungles, which are not put to any use. Land once cultivated but not cultivated for five years in succession would also be included in this category.
- ❑ ***Not available for cultivation:*** This would include Forest area under non-agricultural use, barren and uncultivable land.
  - ❖ ***Forest:*** All lands classed as 'Forests' under any legal enactment dealing with forests or administered as forests whether State owned or private and whether wooded or maintained as potential forest land. The area of crops raised in the forest and grazing land or areas open for grazing within the forests would be included under the forest area. Only private forest would be covered for the purpose of Agricultural Census.
  - ❖ ***Area under Non-Agricultural Use:*** All lands occupied by buildings or ponds or lands put to use other than agriculture will be included in this category. Only such lands within the cultivated holding should be covered in the Census.
  - ❖ ***Barren and Uncultivable Land:*** All barren and uncultivable land within the cultivated holding.

☆ ***Area sown more than once:*** This represent the area on which the crops are cultivated more than once during an agricultural year. This can be derived by deducting 'Net area sown' from 'Total cropped area'.

☆ ***Total cropped area:*** This represent the total area covered with crops in an agricultural year. It can be obtained by counting the area under each crop cultivated during the year and area sown with crops more than once in that year.

☆ ***Economic holding, Basic holding and Optimum holding:*** In agriculture, the structure of production units can be classified on the basis of size of holdings, gross or net produce, value added, capital employed, gross or net worth of the enterprise *etc.* Among all these, the size of the holding is more important because, data on size of holdings is most readily available and factors that are related to size of holdings like land utilization, cropping pattern, yield, other production factors and income differences in relatively homogeneous rural areas can be better explained by the size of land holdings than by other important variables. For describing a suitable unit of cultivation, The Agrarian Reforms Committee (1947) under the Chairmanship of Sri J.C. Kumarappa distinguished three types of land holdings *viz.*, Economic holding, Basic holding and Optimum holding.

- ***Economic holding:*** This is the size of land holding, which fulfills the following three criteria:
  - The income earned from this holding must provide a reasonable standard of living to the farm family.
  - The holding must provide full employment level to an average size of family with a pair of bullocks.
  - It might to have a bearing on other relevant factors peculiar to the agrarian economy of the region.
- ***Basic holding:*** Recognizing the fact that, many of the land holdings are smaller than the size of economic holding, the above Committee evolved the concept of Basic holding. That is, basic holding is smaller than economic holding, but larger than those holdings that are uneconomical from the point of efficient execution of farm operations.
- ***Optimum holding:*** The Congress Agrarian Reforms Committee (1951) defined 'Optimum holding' as the maximum size of holding, which an individual farmer can cultivate. The Committee opined that, with bullocks and plough techniques, an optimum holding should not be more than three times of economic holding. Thus, optimum holding > economic holding > basic holding. So, optimum holding is the size of land holding, that produces the greatest surplus with the available factors of production. In general, an optimum holding is that, average cost per hectare and cost incurred per Rs.100/- of gross income is found minimum and is as high as 30-50 acres of good irrigated land.

Note that, optimum holding will not be the same under different farming situations. It is a dynamic phenomenon and changes with the passage of time. The optimum size of land holding depends upon various factors. The optimum size of land holding varies with the type of farming practiced by the farmers. For example, the optimum size of holding will be small for cultivating rice and root crops when compared to the farms cultivating wheat, maize, gram *etc.* This is because, in case of former crops, the feasibility of use of mechanization is limited compared to the latter crops. For example, 10 acres of vegetable farm may yield more than 50 acres of paddy farm. Further, vegetable cultivation is highly intensive and even a small farm of 0.4 hectares can provide full and continuous employment to an average agricultural family. On the other hand, paddy requires larger holding. That is, in the farms, where there is more feasibility of employing machinery usage, the optimum size of land holding will be more and *vice versa*. Like type of farming, system of farming also influences the optimum size of land holding. The optimum size of land holding will be smaller in peasant farming compared to Cooperative farming, Collective farming, Capitalist farming and State farming. Similarly, presence of even topography and adoption of modern production technology will directly influence the optimum size of land holding. On the contrary, soil fertility, cropping intensity, irrigation facilities, location of the farm towards market (both factor and product markets) vicinity *etc.*, will inversely influence the optimum size of land holding.

C. Factors Influencing Size of Farm

The following are the factors that influence the size of land holding or size of farm.

- ☆ ***Physical factors:*** They include climate, rainfall, topography, irrigation water, drainage facilities, soil type, soil health *etc.* For example, if the climate is congenial in an area for crops cultivation, the farm size will be bigger and *vice versa*. Similarly, in areas, where the topography is even, the farm sizes will be bigger and in hilly areas, where the topography is uneven, the farm size is smaller.
- ☆ ***Economic factors:*** They include availability of transport facilities, communication facilities, marketing facilities, processing facilities, credit facilities, inputs supplies *etc.*
- ☆ ***Social factors***: They include accessibility to schools, hospitals, traditions, customs and habits of the people in that area.
- ☆ ***Capital investment:*** If the farmer enjoys more of capital, he can invest the same to reclaim the land (say, saline land) that is unfit for cultivation and thereby, the farm size increases.
- ☆ ***Nature of cultivation:*** If the farmer goes for intensive cultivation, the size of farm is small and if the farmer goes for extensive cultivation, the size of farm is bigger.
- ☆ ***Availability of irrigation facilities:*** Irrigation facility directly influences the size of the farm. That is, if the farmer enjoys good irrigation facilities, he can operate large size farms and *vice versa*. Similarly, source of irrigation also influences the size of farms. For example, canal irrigated farms are bigger in size than well irrigated farms.
- ☆ ***Nature of crops grown:*** The size of an orchard cultivating farm (say, mango orchard) is much bigger than the farm cultivating annual crops (say, vegetables, paddy, bajra, groundnut etc.).
- ☆ ***Managerial ability of the farmer:*** If the farmer is well-trained and with more managerial skills, he can operate large farms when compared to farmers with poor managerial ability.
- ☆ ***Law of Inheritance:*** Due to sub-division of land holdings, the size of farms becomes smaller and smaller.
- ☆ ***State Laws:*** In countries, where there is a great pressure of population on land, the Government will intervene and impose land ceiling *i.e.*, it will fix a limit on the size of the land holding the individual must possess (Table

3.8). The availability of land as a resource for agricultural production programmes must be viewed in relation to the pressure of population on it. As the population in the country increases relative to available land, competition also increases among the population for this scarce resource. The strength of this competition for agricultural land would depend on the significance of agricultural production in the country. The greater the population-land ratio, the poorer the availability of land and the smaller the average farm size.

Table 3.8: State-wise Ceilings on Land Holding in India (2004)

State	*Irrigated Land with Two Crops (Acres)*	*Irrigated Land with One Crop (Acres)*	*Dry Land (Acres)*
As Recommended in 1972 National Guidelines	10 to 18	27	54
Proposed in Agenda Notes 1985 of Regional Minister's Conference (RMC)	12	18	30
Andhra Pradesh	10 to 18	15 to 27	35 to 54
Assam	17	17	17
Bihar	15 to 18	25	30 to 45
Gujarat	10 to 18	15 to 27	20 to 54
Haryana	18	27	54
Himachal Pradesh	10	15	30 to 70
Jammu and Kashmir	9 to 12.5	9 to 12.5	15 to 23
Karnataka	10 to 20	25 to 30	54
Kerala	12 to 15	12 to 15	12 to 15
Madhya Pradesh	18	27	54
Maharashtra	18	27	54
Manipur	12	12	15
Odisha	10	15	30 to 45
Punjab	17	27	51
Rajasthan	18	27	54 to 175
Tamil Nadu	12	30	60
Sikkim	12.5	12.5	50
Tripura	10	10	30
Uttar Pradesh	18	27	45
West Bengal	12	12	17

Note: 1: The actual limits for lands in Karnataka and Uttar Pradesh are higher due to classification of land; 2: The actual ceiling limits in Himachal Pradesh and Rajasthan are higher due to hilly terrain and desert lands; 3: 1 Acre=0.404686 Hectare.

Sources: Agricultural Statistics at a Glance 2004, Ministry of Agriculture, Government of India.

- *Significance of agriculture:* In developing countries like India, majority of the population economically depends on the land. When industrialization is under progress, the significance of the agricultural sector declines and job opportunities increases in the non-agricultural sector and emigration out of agriculture will occur. This emigration will release land to be used by remaining farmers, thus increasing the per-capita farm size. That is, when employment opportunities increase in non-farm sector, it draws part of the working force away from agriculture, thereby, farm size will increase. The process of 'push' and 'pull' can be applied regarding the movement of labour force away from the agricultural sector. As mentioned above, when better employment opportunities are offered in non-farm sector through offering higher wages and better working conditions then it 'pulls' the labour force away from the agricultural sector. When the 'push' operates, the agricultural labour will move away from the agricultural sector due to substitution of machinery to labour. Among these two *i.e.*, 'pull' and 'push' factors, push process is revolutionary and its overall effect is beneficial. Though, it suffers one generation of agricultural labour, but it benefits the subsequent generations. In fact this 'push' factor is essential for solving many agricultural problems in India and other population countries.
- *Relative factor proportions:* Due to emigration of farm labour towards non-agricultural sectors for employment, wage rates of labour in agricultural sector record drastic increase. As a result, capital intensive production techniques gain importance. So, considering the relative factor prices of labour and capital, substitution takes place regarding the employment of capital for labour. More intensive use of capital inputs increases both the TFC and optimum point in the production programme is at the minimum of SRATC curve. With the employment of capital intensive techniques of production, large sized farms dominate the agricultural scenario in the country.
- *Terms of trade in agriculture:* Welfare of farmers is measured by the ratio of the index of prices received by producers to the index of prices paid by producers, which is known as 'terms of trade in agriculture'. So, as the terms of trade improves in agriculture, there will be incentives to produce more or to increase farm size.

All the above factors will make the farmer more cautious and guide him in selecting the right farm for investment.

D. Farm Size and Productivity

The relationship between farm size and productivity has been intensely debated in India. The earlier studies conducted during the 1960s and 1970s proved that, there exists inverse relationship between farm-size and productivity *i.e.*, crop productivity per unit of land declines with an increase in farm size (Sen 1962, 1964; Mazumdar 1965; Khusro 1968; Hanumantharao 1966; Saini 1971; Bardhan 1973; Berry 1972). Their view provided strong support for the implementation of land reforms, land ceil-ing and various other policies to support smallholders on ground of efficiency and growth. That is, small farms will not only lead to increase in the output, but also the employment opportunities as well. This led the majority of economists to explore the factors that contribute to the inverse relationship between farm-size and productivity. Berry and Cline 1979; Bhalla 1979; Binswanger and Rosenzweig 1986; Dong and Dow 1993; Frisvold 1994 and Raghben-dra *et al* 2000) and some of them even questioned the inverse relationship between farm size and productivity. Bhalla and Roy (1988) observed that, the inverse relation be-tween farm size and productivity weakened and disappeared when soil quality variable was included in their study. Ghose (1979) went a step ahead and opined that, with the advances and adoption of modern technology on the farm, the existence of the inverse relation-ship phenomenon will vanish. The same view was shared by Deolalikar (1981) by stating that, the inverse size-productivity relationship cannot be rejected at low levels of agri-cultural technology in India, but can be rejected at higher levels of technology and hence, there is no scope for propounding a general law regarding farm size and productivity relationship. However, Hanumantharao (1975) and Subbarao (1982) re-ported a positive relationship between farm size and productivity and attributed this to higher application of fertilizer and other cash-intensive inputs on large farms. According to Fan and Connie (2005), to increase labour productivity, and therefore, farmer's income, either land productivity has to increase or land to labour ratio has to improve. Since small farms have a lower land-labour ratio than large farms, the small farms are less productive than the latter. Dyer (1997) and Havnevik and Skarstein (1997) argue that, small farms enjoy higher land productivity in the short run, but in the long-run land productivity tends to drop. This is because, in the long run, the farmer goes for intensive cultivation of the land in order to maintain labour productivity. When more and more people need to survive on the same small area of farmland, and as the small farmers are resource-poor to invest in preserving soil fer-tility, land productivity drops. A similar reason was given by Hazell (2011) stating that, in the long run, many of the advantages of small farms like high land productivity and high labour productivity will disappear. This is because, as the per capita income rises, the economy diversifies and labour leave agriculture and then it becomes more efficient to have progressively larger and more mechanized farms.

Thus, there are divergent views regarding the relationship between farm size and productivity. This debate has assumed a renewed importance in the wake of the changes brought about by technologies, liberaliza-tion, commercialization and further sub-divisions of landholdings. Considering these recent dynamic changes, it can be viewed that, the farm size no longer directly influence its productivity, especially in the long run. The studies pertaining to this farm-size and productivity relationship are gaining much importance now, because of the following reasons:

- ✰ Increasing pressure of population on land. That is, though the share of agriculture and allied sec-tors in the Gross Domestic Product (GDP) stands at 13.7 per cent in 2012-13 at All-India level, the percent work force engaged in these sectors is more than 50.
- ✰ Sub-division of land holdings.
- ✰ Increasing disparity between per worker income in agriculture and non-agriculture sectors.

Because of these reasons, small farms were put under severe strain, so as to promote land productivity on one side and improving the income and livelihood of small farmers, who constitute more than 80 per cent of total farming households, 50 per cent of rural households and 35 per cent of total households in India. Hence, it is essential to boost the land productivity of small farms in the country. However, note that, in the earlier explanation of this topic, it was clearly mentioned that, there exists inverse relationship between size of the farm and productivity of land. But, note that, in this case of above production function, output depends upon the units of land only *i.e.,* land was the only variable factor. But, practically, with the advent of Green Revolution, it was proved that, productivity from land also depends upon technology adopted, High Yielding Varieties (HYV) seeds, fertilizers, Integrated Pest Management (IPM), Integrated Nutrient Management (INM), Integrated Water Resources Management (IWRM) *etc.,* and these factors also contribute to a remarkable increase in land productivity in producing more output. Thus, the production function now involves several factors besides land. Now, let us study, whether Green Revolution in India has led to increase in the productivity of large farms or it has helped to increase the productivity of small farms.

Considering the multi-factor production function, there exist a positive relationship between size of land and both productivity of land and value of per acre output. This is because, with increase in size of farm *i.e.,* we approach towards large-farms with strong resources position and hence, they enjoy easy access to all modern of agricultural inputs compared to small farmers. Thus, the 'Green Revolution' technology has led to abolish the traditional theory that, per acre yield of small farms is higher than that of large farms. Some economists are of the opinion that, there exists no difference between relative productivity of large farms and small farms, as both employ modern inputs in their respective production programmes after Green Revolution period. This is because, though small farms have poor resources base, the Government is making all necessary arrangement to supply modern inputs and technology at subsidized prices. So, not only big farmers, even small farmers as well are enjoying the fruits of Green Revolution. However, large farmers with their sound financial position, strong resource base, easy borrowing from financial institutions, good relations with the labour and the staff of Scientific Community and staff of Department of Agriculture, level of knowledge about modern techniques of production *etc.,* enjoy less risk or uncertainty in their production programmes compared to small farmers. Consequently, the benefits which arise due to large farms are more than those from small farms and hence, after Green Revolution, the disparities in income distribution in rural areas will increase between these two farms. However, in the long run, the small farmers could be able to use the modern inputs with the same intensity as used by the large farmers. This means that, in long run, both small farms and large farms enjoy higher land productivity and this infers that, the inverse relationship between the size of the farm and the productivity of the land can be temporarily suspended. But, still small farms enjoy higher land productivity over large farm and this can be attributed to the close supervision of farm business to realize higher resource use efficiency. The same is explained through Figure 3.5, where there is both shift and movement on a production function.

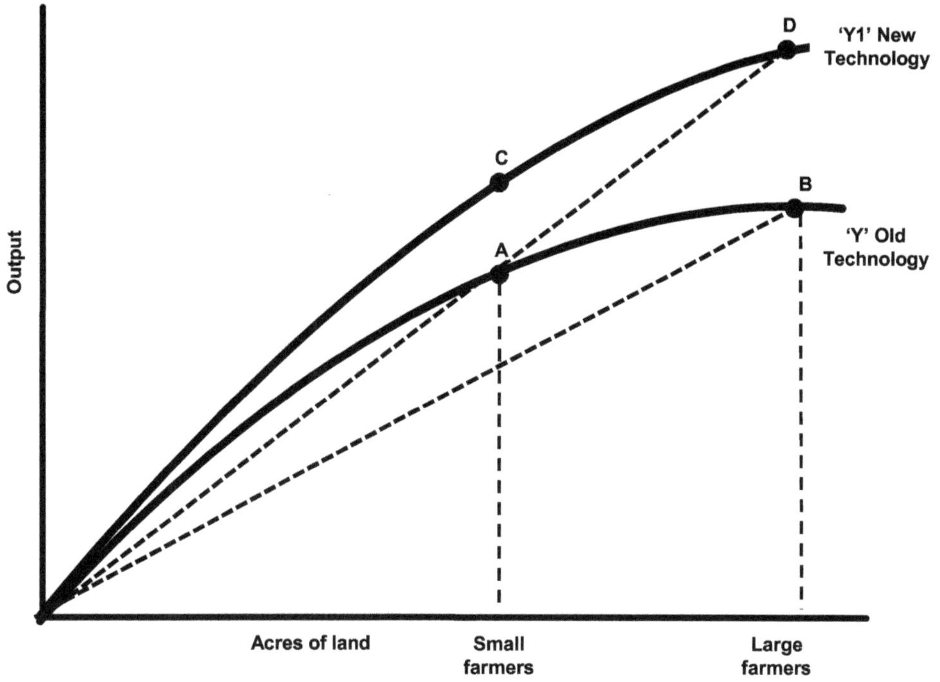

Figure 3.5: Relation between Size of Farm and Land Productivity both in Short Run and Long Run.

In the presence of old (traditional) technology, the small and large farmers are at the points 'A' and 'B' on the production function (Y). It is obvious that, the per acre yield of small farms is higher than that from the large farms. But, in short run, due to adoption of modern technology by the large farms (as they are more accessible for the reasons discussed earlier), the large farmers reach the point 'D' on the new production function Y_1. As the points 'A' and 'D' lie on the same production function indicated by the line joining these two points drawn from the origin, they show that, the output increases in the same proportion to increase in the size of land. But in the long run, even small farmers also adopt modern technology and hence, they also shift over to new production function (Y_1), as the shifting from 'A' to 'C' shows. This again denotes that, per acre yield of small farms is greater than that of the large farms. This also confirms the inverse relationship between the size of the farm and the productivity of the farm even in the long run.

Thus, the above discussion on the relationship between farm size and productivity is never ending and is continuous debate even after experiencing the Green Revolution technology. This is because of the fact that, though modern technology after Green Revolution is highly expensive, small farmers are getting in access towards these modern inputs at subsidized rates offered by the Government.

E. Large farms vis-à-vis Small farms

In general, size of farm can be broadly categorized into large farms and small farms. It is essential to note that, irrespective of the size of the farm, all the farm management principles (discussed in Chapter 2) are equally applicable to ensure successful farm management. Let us discuss in-detail about the relative advantages and disadvantages of large farms vis-à-vis small farms here under.

Advantages of Large Farms

They include:

- ☆ Large farms facilitate the farmers to go for mechanization of farm operations and thereby, the farmer can enjoy economies of large scale production.
- ☆ There is better use of land, labour, capital and management, as all these factors of production can be employed with proper coordination.
- ☆ The farmer can go for extensive farming. Even he can go for intercropping, so as to increase the profits in the business.
- ☆ The farmer can also go for taking up allied enterprises like dairy, sheep, goat etc, as the by-products from the crop enterprises can be effectively utilized.
- ☆ The fixed resources of the farm business can be fully exploited.
- ☆ The farmer can go for experimentation in his business and if the results are fruitful, he can take up them on large-scale in the business.
- ☆ Large-scale farming might be better suited when farmers must compete in international market that enforces very stringent quality requirements on products.
- ☆ Large farms enjoy greater marketable surplus compared to small farms and thereby, it can participate and demand higher prices for the products in the international market. Further, these large farms enjoy greater economies of scale in processing and marketing compared to small farms.
- ☆ In large farms, large-scale investment is inevitable, but it reduces farmers' risk through providing secure market outlets for output.
- ☆ There are advantages to increase farm size, as incomes will rise with large farm sizes as long as costs can be controlled. Therefore, larger farms will have higher net farm incomes than smaller farms, again, assuming costs can be managed.
- ☆ Land costs tend to increase on a per acre basis as farm size increases. This is because, larger farms tend to cash rent more of their farmland at higher cash rent prices.
- ☆ Note that, the tasks of management for large farms are similar to small farmers, but taken up on larger scale. That is, hiring 50 labourers is the same as hiring one labour, purchasing 50 fertilizer bags is the same as purchasing one fertilizer bag *etc.* But, on large farms, the farm operation can be organized more systematically with a scientific plan and can realize cost effectiveness. For example, by having 50 labourers, the farm activities

can be accomplished more systematically (say, through division of labour) than hiring one labour.

- The following are the factors that contribute lower per unit costs with increase in farm size:
    - The TFC are spread over a large amount of output
    - Mechanization of farm operation substitutes high labour costs
    - Specialization of farm business encourages division of labour to perform farm operations.

  As a result of the above three influences, per unit cost curves of large farms fall below compared to small farms. Note that, considering the above influences, doubling the farm size will be more than double the profits.
- One of the major advantages of large farms is that, they can employ machinery of different sizes, unlike small farms.

Disadvantages of Large Farms

They include:

- It is difficult on the part of the farmer to supervise the farm operations and thereby, the cost structure of the enterprises gets escalated.
- When the production of enterprises gets affected due to abnormal conditions, the farmer suffers from greater losses. Since the business is diversified, the losses from each enterprise would add to the total loss.
- Difficult to maintain soil fertility due to large scale operations on the farmer.
- Inputs procurement and marketing of produce of all the enterprises is difficult on the part of the farmer.
- Family operated small farms are widely accepted to be economically much more efficient than large farms (say, plantations) operated by hired (wage) labour.
- Large farms are less productive compared to small farms. One reason for the low levels of productivity on large farms is that they tend to practice monocultures. Generally, large farmers tend to plant monocultures because, they are the simplest to manage with heavy machinery. However, small farmers are much more likely to plant crop mixtures - intercropping - where the empty space between the rows is occupied by other crops. They usually go for crop diversification and mixed farming, for effective utilization of by-products and to maintain soil fertility. Such integrated farming systems produce far more per unit area than do monocultures.
- The management of large farms is extremely difficult and often less successful than that of small farms.

Advantages of Small Farms

They include:

- As discussed earlier, there exists an inverse relationship between farm size and land productivity. There are increased incentives for family members to work hard and manage their enterprises efficiently. The family labour tend to think in terms of whole jobs or livelihoods rather than number of hours of work. That is, these labour are less driven by wage rates, unlike hired labour. Small farmers exploit land, labour and capital productivities in realizing higher yields on the farm.

- Small farms employ more of labour-intensive methods rather than capital-intensive machines and thus, promote labour employment.
- The farmer can easily supervise all the farm operations and thereby, resource use efficiency will be increased.
- When the enterprise(s) gets affected due to abnormal conditions, the losses to the farmer will be small and far less compared to large farms.
- Farmer can maintain soil fertility status, as he has to manage small piece of land.
- Farmer can go for intensive farming.
- Inputs procurement and marketing of farm produce is not a tedious job, unlike in large farms.
- The farmer can realize higher productivity per unit of land. (It is essential to note that, there exists inverse relationship between land productivity and size of farm. So, small farms will enjoy more cropping intensity and higher productivity compared to large farms).
- The farmer can devote more attention both on farm production and farm family satisfaction, unlike in large farms where the emphasis is more on commercial outlook of business.
- Small farmers enjoy better knowledge of local contexts *i.e.,* they know most about local resources, possible risks in production and which technical changes are, or are not, compatible with local livelihoods compared to large farmers.
- When forward linkages are better developed, it enable small farms to grow and obtain access to markets and off-farm employment (say, in value-chains) increases as well.
- Small farms contribute towards greater food security, particularly in subsistence agriculture and in under-developed areas, where locally produced foods avoid the high transport and marketing costs associated with many purchased foods.
- Small farms also benefit by integrating crops and livestock. By practicing mixed farming, animal manure is used as fertilizer, and then the part of the crop that is not consumed by humans (say, stalks of a corn plant) is used as food for the animals. So, there is recycling of nutrients and biomass within the system. That also makes small farms more efficient and productive.
- Small farmers tend to involve more family labour on their land and the quality of this labour is much better, as for them, the future depends upon maintaining the productivity of the soil that they naturally take better care of it. That too makes small farms more productive.

- When the cultivation on large farms is made, the production is carried (mainly by hired labour) till the level that, VMP or MVP_X=MFC of labour. While on small farms, the output is produced by employing more of family labour and the production is carried out till the level that, MVP_X of last labour is zero. Thus, on the basis of per acre productivity, the small farms are more efficient.
- Small farmers utilize the small farms effectively because, such farms are the only source of their income. So, they use their farm inputs in the best possible manner. On the other hand, large farmers enjoy diversified businesses and activities.
- According to Bhagwati and Chakarwati Distress Argument, the quality of small farms is better than large farms due to demographic reasons. They opined that, when there are crop failures, droughts, floods, indebtedness *etc.*, they have to sell less important or inferior lands. These lands are purchased by Mahajans or landlords. In this way, the inferior lands are accumulated with landlords and the small farmers get rid of them. Thus, small farmers enjoy more productivity on land than landlords.
- We already know, small farms employ more of family labour than large farms. Since family labour works on domestic lands, they work with more dedication and does not have to go away in search of an alternative job. For family labour, wage rates are lower than hired labour. So, per acre yield from small farms is higher and output is produced cost-effectively compared to large-farms.
- The greater efficiency of small farms stems from their greater abundance of family labour per hectare farmed. Family workers are typically more motivated than hired workers and provide higher quality and self-supervising labour.
- Small farms typically achieve their higher productivity with lower capital intensities than large farms.
- Small farms also contribute to greater food security, particularly in areas with poor infrastructure, where high transport costs make locally produced foods less costly and less risky than many purchased foods.

Disadvantages of Small Farms

They include:

- It is difficult for the farmer to go for mechanization of farm operations.
- There is no proper coordination among the factors of production.
- Scope for inter-cropping is less compared to large scale farming.
- By-products of the enterprises cannot be effectively utilized.
- Fixed resources of the farm cannot be fully exploited.
- Fixed costs or overhead costs are high.
- The farmer cannot go for experimentation in his business.

- ☆ Farmers generally suffer from inadequacy of capital and hence, they cannot go for large-scale fixed investments.
- ☆ Majority of small farmers lack access to key inputs and services like HYV seeds, technology, machinery, credit *etc.*, and even they do not have the information or knowledge necessary to exploit beneficial technologies. This is so because, in many parts of the world, especially in developing countries, the private sector has failed to gain the requisite momentum for making investments in agriculture, as the Government sector failed to create the stable enabling environments and more over, the sector itself involve several inherent risks.
- ☆ Small-volume trading, variable and sub-standard quality products to sell, lack of adequate market information, poor links with buyers in the marketing chain, high cost of production, high transaction costs, poor access to market infrastructure like transport, processing, storage *etc.*, adversely influence both domestic and export competitiveness of commodities.
- ☆ Compared to large farmers, small farmers are more vulnerable to climatic and price risks and because of low-level of income, they enjoy limited use of modern risk-management tools. Inspite of these limitations, they still do not specialize in high-value cash crops; instead, they take a diversified and subsistence approach to their livelihood. That is, after meeting their family consumption needs, they think about marketing of any surplus produce, if they achieve.
- ☆ In the context of globalization and trade liberalization, the small farmers cannot compete in the international market, because of higher subsidies and stringent restrictions imposed by the importing countries, especially developed countries.
- ☆ In small farms, intensive farming is adopted and the tillage operations the farmers practice may cause accelerated soil erosion. Especially, when population pressure on land increases, the small farmers expand their cropland areas into unsuitable environmental situations such as steep slopes thereby, causing damage to the environment.

Ways of Increasing Size of Farm Business

Having understood the relative advantages and disadvantages of large farms and small farms, it is important to find the ways of increasing the size of farm business. They include:

- ☆ Bringing leased-in land for cultivation.
- ☆ Reclamation of lands (say, saline land) and make it fit for cultivation.
- ☆ By employing modern technology in the business so that, the operation of LDR can be delayed.
- ☆ By increasing cropping intensity. When cropping intensity is increased, it ensures cost-advantage to the farmer, as the fixed costs in the business are spread over larger output produced from 3 to 4 crops produced in the same year.

☆ With the use of HYVs, the farmer can generate more income with little capital.

☆ By following INM, IPM, IWRM *etc.*, the farmer can generate more income through cost-effectiveness.

☆ By crop diversification, the farmer can sustain the annual net income.

☆ The farmer can go for mixed farming so that, by-products can be effectively utilized.

F. Measuring the Size of Farm

There are different ways of measuring the size of the farm as listed here under.

☆ ***In terms of area i.e., Acres or Hectares:*** In this measure, size of the farm is measured in terms of physical area *i.e.*, in terms of acres or hectares. But, since the cropping intensity varies from one area to another area depending upon the availability of irrigation facilities, measurement of size of farm in terms of physical area will not give a correct picture. Further, assume that, Farm A is using 3 acres of land + 200 man days and another Farm B is using 5 acres of land + 170 man days. Thus, considering the number of acres in cultivation, Farm B is considered larger than Farm A. However, in terms of number of labour (man days) employed, Farm A is considered to be larger. For this reason, acreage does not serve as a satisfactory measure about the size of the farm. But, this measure can be used only where similar type of farming with similar cropping intensity is followed and when the farmer takes up only crop enterprises without any allied enterprises.

☆ ***Number of livestock***: This is also an useful measure, especially when the farmer practice only livestock enterprises like cows, buffaloes, poultry, sericulture *etc.*

☆ ***Total capital invested***: This is a useful measure, as it helps to compare different farms in the same region. However, with the categorization of loans into short term, medium term and long term loans and small and marginal farmers because of their poor asset position do not have much access to long term loans thereby, this measure may not give a realistic picture about size of farms.

☆ ***Productive Man Work Units (PWU or MWU):*** **It refers to** the productive work accomplished in the farm in a span of 8 hours. The total productive man work units is given by:

❑ Average of each crop * Average labour requirement for each crop

❑ Number of livestock * Average labour requirement for each livestock

So, this measure directly gives the total productive work accomplished in each enterprise in a season or a year. The sum of productive work units across all the enterprises in a farm directly gives the total PWUs for the farm. So, this measure helps to compare different farm sizes even though they take up different enterprises. Even number of labour (man days) employed will not provide satisfactory measure about size of the farm. This is so because, the labour employed across the farm are not of the same quality and productiveness.

Table 3.9: Average Number of Man-Hours Used for Producing One Quintal of Selected Crops in India (1998-99)

Crops	*Average Number of Man-Hours Used for Producing One Quintal*
Groundnut	69.3
Soyabean	34.4
Rapeseed and Mustard	34.7
Tur	72.4
Gram	31.2

Source: www.indiastat.com.

- ☆ ***Total value of production:*** This measure helps to compare the size of farms through computing the total value of all the enterprises' output in a year. This is a realistic measure, as it compares the farms of different sizes practicing similar enterprises. However, since market prices of farm outputs fluctuate from one region to another region, this measure cannot compare farm sizes in different regions.
- ☆ ***Total output of the farm:*** This is the most realistic measure in measuring the size of the farm. This measure takes into consideration the total output and thereby, productivity of each enterprise on the farm. By comparing the outputs or yields of all the enterprises across the farms, we can compare different farm sizes. Of course, this measure is suitable, when the farms under comparison take up similar enterprises only.

Thus, no single measure is perfectly realistic in measuring the size of the farm and for comparing farms of different sizes. Hence, the best measure would be the one, which combines all the criteria *i.e.*, land, labour and capital employed. However 'measuring the total output of the farm' can be considered as a meritorious measure over other measures, as it can be used to compare farm of different sizes, but practicing similar enterprises.

G. Appraising the Value of Land or Farm

It refer to the estimation of value of land at a point of time. This is a quite difficult task for agriculture land in the sense that,

- ☆ The value of land is increasing over a period of time due to increasing pressure of population on the land.
- ☆ With the advent of modern production techniques, the income from agricultural land showed continuous increase.

Besides above aspects, the appraisal of land value also considers the following factors:

- Physical factors like topography, rainfall, soil type, soil health, farming situation, availability of irrigation facilities, drainage facilities, inventory like farm buildings and other assets *etc.*
- Economic factors like marketing facilities, communication facilities, transport facilities, re-sale value of land, market rate of interest, income from the farm, rental value of land *etc.*
- Personal likes and dislikes of the individual, who wish to purchase land.

After assessing, the above three factors, the appraiser will estimate the value of land by one of the following methods: Sales Comparison Method, Income Approach or Net Income Capitalization Approach, Soil Productivity Approach and Cost Approach.

a. Sales Comparison Method

In this method, before purchasing the land, the appraiser will enquire about the known values of similar pieces of land sold earlier or in recent period in that locality. This method of appraisal will be useful in normal periods *i.e.*, when the market prices of lands are normal (*i.e.*, there is neither boom period nor depression period for land values) otherwise, there is a chance of quoting higher prices for land during boom period. So, the major premise of the Sales comparison approach is that, the market value of a land is directly related to the prices of comparable and competitive lands in that locality. Hence, this approach is otherwise called as 'Market Data Approach'. The more comparable sales that can be found, the better the final analysis of the given piece of land. Once a set of comparable sales has been identified, they are adjusted to the subjected piece of land based on the date each sale occurred, the buyer or seller motivation, the productivity of land, fixtures on land like buildings, roads *etc.* Note that, this Sales comparison approach is applicable to all types of lands, when there are sufficient recent, reliable transactions to indicate value patterns or trends in the market. When the market is weak and the number of market transactions is insufficient, the applicability of the sales comparison approach may be limited.

b. Income Approach or Net Income Capitalization Approach

This approach uses mathematical procedures (discounted cash flow analysis) to analyze a land's capacity to generate benefits (usually monetary) and convert these benefits into an indication of present value. Since value of land is created by the expectation of benefits to be derived in the future, value may be defined as the present worth of all these future benefits. This approach attempts to consider anticipated future benefits and estimate their present value. The anticipation of receiving future benefits creates value, but the possibility of losing future benefits detracts from value. Appraisers must recognize purchaser or investor's attitudes in analyzing future market for land in that area and future benefits that can be derived from that land considering these two, he has to apply capitalization procedure for estimating the value of land. We know, the purchaser of land expect to earn a higher rate of return on investments that are more risky than the investments that involve less risk. This should be reflected in the discount rate used by the appraiser. The value of land (or any other fixed asset) on its current income in relation to its prevailing rate of interest is called Capitalized value. This method is considered more reliable and quicker over the earlier method, as the farmer considers the annual income from land and the prevailing rate of interest. This method is followed differently considering the stability in annual net income derived from land.

Case 1

When the annual net income (TR-(TFC+SRTVC)) is constant, the formula used is: V=R/r

where, V = Capitalized value of land (Rs.), R = (Expected) Annual net income from land (Rs.), r = Rate of interest (per cent) or Capitalization rate

Example 3.2

Assume the annual net income from land is the 25,000 per hectare and the market rate of interest is 10 percent. Calculate the capitalized value for one hectare of land.

Solution: Capitalized value (V) = R/r = 25000/0.1 = Rs.2,50,000.

Case 2

When the annual net income fluctuates at a constant arithmetic rate, the formula used is:

$V=(R/r) \pm (i/r^2)$

where, i = Annual increase or decrease in net income per year.

Example 3.3

In the above example, if the rise in market price of output brings an increase in annual net income by Rs. 100, the capitalized value of land is given by:

$V=(R/r) \pm (i/r^2) = (25000/0.1) + (100/(0.1)^2) =$ Rs.2,60,000

Example 3.4

In the above example, if the fall in market price of output brings a decline in annual net income by Rs.100, then the capitalized value of land is given by:

$V=(R/r) \pm (i/r^2) = (25000/0.1) - (100/(0.1)^2) = 2{,}40{,}000$

In following this approach, the appraiser must take into consideration that, since future benefits cannot be known with certainty; the discounting process should weigh the near cash flows more heavily than those that will occur in the more distant future. This makes the choice of the discount rate very critical.

c. Soil Productivity Approach

In this approach, the appraiser will conduct survey in that locality and assign the best piece of land with a value of Rs. 1. Now, he will compare the rest of lands with the best value of land and express their value in terms of relative price of best value of land. In this method, the appraiser will take into consideration several aspects like type of soil, soil health, availability of irrigation facilities, drainage facilities, cropping intensity, proximity to market *etc.* The method of valuation is followed in Punjab, Himachal Pradesh and Madhya Pradesh *etc.*

d. Cost Approach

In this approach, the value of land is estimated by combining the existing value of land plus the improvements it demands for its best use. That is, initially the available piece of land is considered unimproved and there is scope for improvement for its best use. So, the value of land is given by the sum of value of initial unimproved land plus the value of improvements to be made on this piece of land for its best use. Initially, the given piece of land is considered unimproved and broken down into different classes based on physical characteristics and prevailing market values of each class of land. Then the value of improvements on each class of land is determined based on the Replacement Cost New (RCN) less depreciation (which includes both physical and functional deteriorations of land and economic obsolescence). So, in Cost approach, land and improvements on land will be valued separately. This approach will often be the highest value indication, since some of the component parts may have less value when combined with other component parts than alone. So, like the Sales comparison and Net income capitalization approaches, this cost approach to value is also based on comparison. This approach is important and advantageous over Sales comparison approach in two conditions *viz.*,

- ☆ When a lack of market activity limits the usefulness of the Sales comparison approach and
- ☆ When the physical characteristics of comparable lands differ significantly.

H. Owning the Land vis-à-vis Leasing-in for Land

i. Owning the Land

For a farmer owning of land in a village is a prestigious issue, It gives him maximum psychological satisfaction.

Merits of Owning the Land

The importance of owning the land by the farmer ensures the following advantages to the farmer:

- ☆ Enables the farmer to plan for making permanent improvements on land.
- ☆ The land can be shown as a security (mortgage) to claim credit both from institutional and non-institutional sources.
- ☆ He enjoys more freedom in practicing different enterprises on the farm.
- ☆ He can plan the business as he likes say, regarding crop rotation, water-harvesting, extent of farm mechanization *etc.*
- ☆ He puts all his efforts to the maximum, as the farming is enjoyed by the owner himself.
- ☆ Soil health and fertility are given due importance.
- ☆ Owned land serve as a property for his heirs.
- ☆ Encourage the farmer to adopt modem technology on the farm and since it is size-natural *i.e.*, even on small size farm, the technology leads to higher output.

Demerits of Owning the Land

Though owning of land involves several advantages, there are certain demerits for owning the land for agricultural purposes as listed here under.

- ☆ Since the returns from the farm bussiness are highly uncertain, they may not be in proportional with the purchased value of land.
- ☆ Illegal occupation may be there due to increasing pressure of population on land.
- ☆ Small-sized land holdings are not convenient for mechanization of farm operations.

ii. Leasing-in for Land

In India, majority of the agricultural workers are landless labourers. The landlords often practice the farming through absentee landlordism by identifying the tenants to cultivate their lands on rental basis. Some farmers also show interest in renting out some portion of their land either due to management problems or due to assured rental income they could get considering uncertainty of farm income. Not only agricultural labourers, even small and marginal farmers can also take the land for lease purpose considering their managerial ability and extent of mechanization of farm operations.

Merits of Leasing-in Land

The leasing in land by the farmer ensures the following advantages:

- ☆ By leasing in land, the tenant can supplement his annual income.
- ☆ By leasing in land, the operational holdings of small and marginal farmers will increase and this facilitates the farmers to go for mechanization of farm operations, so as to achieve cost-effective production of commodities.
- ☆ Further, crop diversification taken up by the farmer with increased size of land holding will reduce the risk of farm business.

Demerits of Leasing-in the Land

However, compared to land owner, tenant farmer faces several limitations in practicing farm business as listed here under.

- ☆ The tenant farmer cannot go for making permanent improvements on leased in land.
- ☆ The tenant farmer is not much concerned about soil health and soil fertility on leased in land.
- ☆ There is insecurity of tenure for the agricultural labourer or even small and marginal farmers, unlike in case of landowner.
- ☆ Limitations may be imposed by land owner on the tenant regarding the selection of crops and allied enterprises.

II. Agricultural Labour Management

'Labour' can be defined as any exertion of mind or body undergone partly or wholly with a view to earn some good other than the pleasure derived directly from the work. In economic sense, labour refers to any type of work performed by a labourer with an intention to earn income. As a factor of production, it is quite peculiar, as it possess the following peculiarities:

- Labour is inseparable from the labourer
- Labourer sells his services and not himself
- Labour is more perishable than any other commodity
- Labourer has not the same power of bargaining as their employers
- Labour is less efficient compared to machinery
- Labour is less mobile
- Supply is independent of demand
- Labourers differs in their efficiency

According to the Agricultural Labour Enquiry Committee, *'agricultural labour as a person who, for more than half of the total number of days, worked as an agricultural labour. An agricultural labour may be the small or marginal farmer or an artisan, but when a person derives his main earning by doing some agricultural work on others farm is called an agricultural labour'*. First Agricultural Labour Enquiry Report (1950-51), *'those people are agricultural labourers, who are engaged in raising crops on payment of wages'*. The basis of this definition was thus the quantum of hired employment during the period of any year. Accordingly, the Committee laid down that, *'those people should be regarded as 'agricultural workers', who worked for 50 percent or more days on payment of wages'*. The Committee also defined an 'agricultural labour household' as *'if the head of household or 50 percent or more of the earners report agricultural labour as their main occupation, that family should be classified as an agricultural labour household'*. According to the Second Agricultural Labour Enquiry Report, 1956-57, *'a hired labour receiving 50 per cent or more income of his total earnings from agricultural operations during the year is called an Agricultural labour'*. Thus, the Second Agricultural Labour Enquiry Committee adopted 'income' as a criterion for demarcating agricultural labour families. The Committee further opined that, *'a person was deemed to be an agricultural labourer and family agricultural household, if his or her or families major source of income during the previous year was from agricultural wage'*. This changeover, from 'work' to 'income' seemed to be more scientific. In the First Enquiry, the definition was confined to those employed for wages in the processes of crop production. In the Second Enquiry, agricultural labour has been defined to include not only labour employed in crop production, but also hired employment in other agricultural occupations like dairy farming, horticulture, raising of livestock, bees or poultry *etc.* However, these two definitions given by First and Second Agricultural Labour Enquiry Committees are not without flaws, because there is no separate class of workers in agriculture depending wholly on agricultural wages for their income. For example, many small and marginal farmers also work partly on the farms of others to supplement their income. To what extent should they be considered agricultural labourers is not easy to answer. Further, the income earned from agriculture is season-bound and the labour may not depend solely on agricultural income, and they join in non-farm activities as well to supplement income, especially in dry land areas. So, it is difficult to define the term 'agricultural labour' in precise terms.

The National Commission on Labour regarded *'agricultural labourer as one, who is basically unskilled and unorganized and has nothing but physical labour to exist. As such, the major part of the income of such a worker is derived from wages for work on land'*. Thus, agricultural workers whose main source of income is in the form of wages obtained as a result of working on land fall in this group. These workers have nothing except their labour to earn livelihood. According to the Census of India, 2001 *'a person who works on another person's land for wages in money or kind or share is regarded as an agricultural labourer. She or He has no risk in the cultivation, but merely works on another person's land for wages. An agricultural labourer has no right of lease or contract on land which she/he work'*. In developing countries like India, the share of work force engaged in Indian agriculture declined from almost 65 percent in 1993-94 to only about 53 percent in 2009. However, due to their surplus number, their demand is low (except during peak seasonal agricultural operations) thereby, their MPP is zero or almost equal to zero. This refers to Disguised unemployment of agricultural labour. However, with the introduction of new techniques of production, it is essential on the part of the labour to acquire new skills and their efficiency in turning out productive work is gaining much importance, so as to get employed in the farm business. Inefficient labour soon goes out of the business and become jobless in agriculture (Table 3.10). Before going into the details of studying the classification of farm labour and labour efficiency, let us highlight the definitions about different categories of farm labour.

☆ ***Rural Labour Household:*** A household was classified as rural labour household, if his major source of income during the last 365 days preceding the survey was more from wage paid manual labour (agricultural and/or non-agricultural) than either from paid non-manual employment or from self-employment. Rural labour households include agricultural labour households also.

Table 3.10: Utilization of Human Labour in Mechanized Farms vis-à-vis Non-mechanized Farms

Size-group (Hectares)	*Mechanized*				*Non-mechanized*			
	Permanent		*Casual*	*Total*	*Permanent*		*Casual*	*Total*
	Family	*Hired*			*Family*	*Hired*		
1. Below 6	65	20	53	138	86	35	68	190
2. 6-10	63	27	78	168	78	30	69	177
3. 10-15	53	28	108	189	67	24	85	176
4. 15-20	46	37	91	174	60	51	71	182
5. Above 20	34	36	91	161	63	56	62	181
Average	45	33	91	169	68	43	69	180

Source: Singh, Roshan and B.B Singh (1972). Farm Mechanization in Western UP: Problems of Farm Mechanization. Seminar Series Indian Society of Agricultural Economics, Feb. (Page 147).

- ☆ ***Agricultural Labour Household:*** Of the households, which are initially classified as 'Rural Labour Households, those deriving 50 percent or more of their total income from wage paid manual labour in agricultural activities are treated as Agricultural labour households.
- ☆ ***Manual Work:*** A job essentially involving physical labour is considered as manual work. However, jobs essentially involving physical labour, but also requiring a certain level of general, professional, scientific or technical education are not to be termed as manual work. On the other hand, jobs not involving much of physical labour and at the same time not requiring much educational background, are to be treated as manual work.
- ☆ ***Wage-Paid Manual Labour:*** A person, who does manual work in return for wages in cash or kind or partly in cash and partly in kind (excluding exchange labour) is a Wage paid manual labour. Salaries are also to be counted as wages. A person, who is self-employed in manual work is not treated as a wage paid manual labour.
- ☆ ***Rural Labour:*** Rural labourer is defined as one, who does manual work in rural areas in agricultural and/or non-agricultural occupation in return for wages in cash or kind or partly in cash and partly in kind. The term wages included salary also. Any person who was self employed, though in manual work, was not treated as a wage paid manual rural labourer.
- ☆ ***Agricultural Labour:*** A person was treated as an agricultural labourer, if he/she followed one or more of the following agricultural occupations in the capacity of a labourer on hire, whether paid wholly in cash or kind or partly in cash and partly in kind:
  a. farming including cultivation, tillage etc;
  b. dairy farming;
  c. production, cultivation, growing and harvesting of any horticultural commodity;
  d. raising of livestock, bee-keeping or poultry farming;
  e. any practice performed on a farm as incidental to or in conjunction with farm operations (including any forestry or timbering) and the preparation for market and delivery to storage or to market or to carriage for transportation to market of farm products).

  It might be noted that, manual work in fisheries was excluded from the purview of the category of agricultural labour. Further, carriage for transportation coming under the category (e) above, referred only to the first stage of transportation from farm to the first stage of disposal.

A. Classification of Farm Labour

Figure 3.6 show that, farm labour can be broadly categorized into:

i. ***Family (Unpaid) labour and Hired (Paid) labour*** - based on the payment they receive for performing the farm operation) and

ii. ***Skilled, Semi-skilled and Unskilled labour*** - depending upon the skills with which they perform work in the farm.

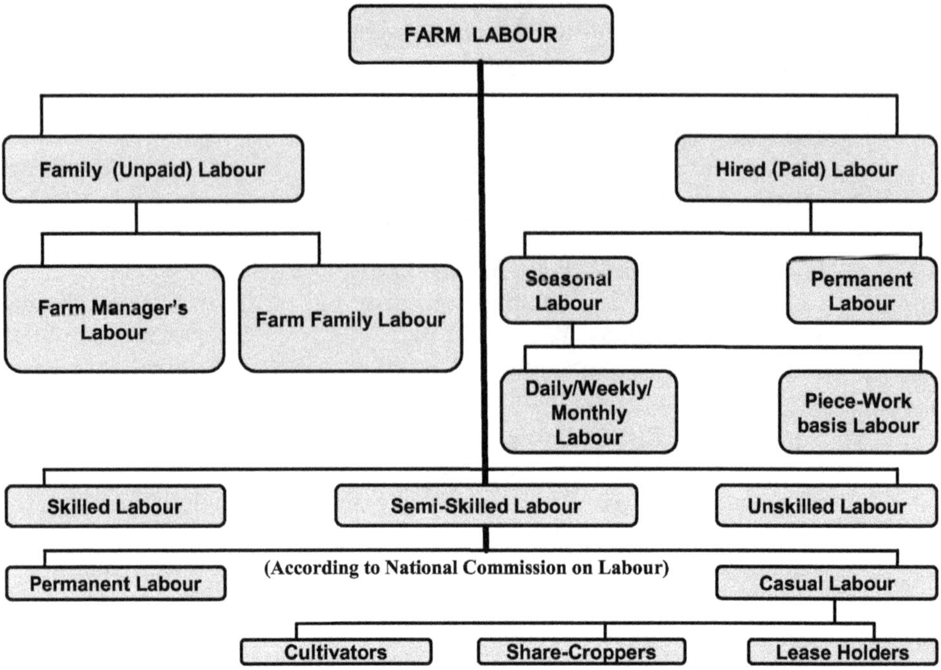

Figure 3.6: Classification of Farm Labour.

i. Family (Unpaid) Labour and Hired (Paid) Labour

a. Family Labour (Unpaid Labour)

This is the labour force that participate from the farmer's family. In India, especially on small farms, family labour perform most of the agricultural operations *i.e.*, their living and working are closely associated with the farm. This family labour is the main source of labour on Indian farms. With increase in farm size, the role of family labour to participate in performing agricultural operation decreases. Note that, if any member of the family earn significant amount of money by performing off-farm employment, he should not be considered as family labour. This form of labour generally comprises of adult males, adult females and children working on the farm. This family labour can be further categorized into Farmers' own labour and Farm family labour.

- ☆ ***Farmer's own labour:*** This is also called as Farm manager's labour. This is the labour work done by the farmer himself on his farm. This is the most common form of labour seen in Indian conditions, especially on small and marginal farms. Besides labour work, farmer himself plays three more roles *viz.*, farm entrepreneur, farm manager and capitalist. This is the best type of labour that is available on the farm, as the farmer himself renders the job works with much more dedication. He was so practical oriented and guides other farm family labour and hired labour in performing farm operations. For the work rendered by him on the farm, he is not paid for himself, but such costs on the farm represent implicit or imputed costs.

- ☆ ***Farm family labour:*** This is the main source of farm labour on Indian farms, especially on small and marginal farms. The labour comprise of all members of a farm family other than farmer himself. So, family labour comprises of adult males, adult females, children *etc.*, from the farmer's family. Like farm manager's labour, these labour costs also fall under implicit costs.

b. Hired Labour (Paid Labour)

Unlike family labour, these labour are hired for performing the farm operations and they are paid for the services rendered by them. As the farmer himself and farm family members are less skilled and less trained in performing farm operations, the employment of hired labour assumes greater importance. Further, since agricultural operations are to be performed in larger areas, the employment of hired labour is inevitable in the farm business. The necessity of engaging hired labour arises during peak season of agricultural operations like sowing, transplanting (paddy), weeding, harvesting *etc.* These hired labour are generally paid in the form of cash or kind or both. These hired labour can be further categorized into Casual labour and Permanent labour.

- ☆ ***Seasonal or Casual labour:*** These are temporary labour hired from time to time in performing farm operations. They are further sub-divided into Daily labour and Piece-work basis labour.
    - ❑ ***Daily labour:*** These are the casual hired labour that are hired on day to day basis. That is, as and when the work is to be done on a particular day, these daily labour are engaged. For example, for performing weeding operation, for spraying a pesticide, for picking cotton (kapas) *etc.*, these daily labour are engaged. These daily labour are generally employed on small farms, as the fulfillment of any particular operation will be completed in one day.
    - ❑ ***Piece–work basis labour:*** These are also the casual hired labour, but these are hired for fulfilling a particular task or operation. These labour are generally employed on large farms, as the fulfillment of any particular operation will consume more than a day. For example, for performing harvesting, threshing and winnowing of paddy, piece–work basis labour will be employed to fulfill all these operations.
- ☆ ***Permanent labour:*** These are the labour that are hired on permanent basis on the farm. Generally, these labour are hired for the entire season of an agricultural year or for the complete agricultural year depending upon the cropping intensity of the farm. The employment for these labour is generally found in large farms, unlike in small farms, where in the latter, the farmer himself performs the role of permanent labour. These labour are often paid on monthly basis and the payment may be in the form cash or kind or both.

Note that, among the categories of labour discussed above, farmer's own labour, farm family labour and permanent labour constitute permanent labour force on the farm and hence, they are regarded as fixed resources on the farm due to their general lack of mobility. However, the other category *i.e.,* hired labour (casual hired labour (daily labour, piece work basis labour)) represent temporary work force on farm and thereby, they are regarded as variable resources on the farm. The Second Agricultural Labour Enquiry,1956-57 further categorized hired labour as:

- ☆ ***Landless agricultural labour:*** These are the labour that do work on farmer's field and receive payment on daily basis.
- ☆ ***Attached labour:*** These are the labour that are attached to a farmer's family on a contract basis to perform agricultural operation for a specific period of time.
- ☆ ***Bonded labour:*** For these labour, the landlord advances loan in cash or kind and demands free service or service on nominal wages from them as long as the loan is not repaid.
- ☆ ***Forced labour:*** Forced labour is any work or service, which people are forced to do against their will under the threat of some form of punishment. Almost all slavery practices, including trafficking in people and bonded labour, contain some element of forced labour. It also refers to *'all work or service which is extracted from any person under the menace of any penalty and for which the said person has not offered himself voluntarily'.*
- ☆ ***Migratory labour:*** These are the labour that migrates from densely populated areas to scarcely populated areas is search of employment for performing agricultural operations.

Note that, in India, most of the agricultural labourers are casual labourers and landless agricultural workers. Even, marginal farmers and small farmers also work as agricultural labourers in large farms, so as to supplement their annual income. According to National Commission on Labour, agricultural labour mainly consist of two sub-categories *viz.,* landless agricultural labour and very small cultivators, whose main source of earnings, due to their small and sub-marginal holdings, is wage employment. Landless agricultural labour, in turn, can be classified into two broad categories *viz.,* Permanent labour and Casual labour. The second group *i.e.,* Casual labour can again be sub-divided into three sub-groups viz.,: Cultivators, Share-croppers and Lease holders (Tenants).

- ☆ ***Permanent (Attached) labourers:*** They generally work on annual or seasonal basis and they work on some sort of contract. They are attached to the landlord. These labour are employed for a period of times *i.e.,* on annual or seasonal basis by the assignment of lodging on the farm, who are under some sort of contract with the employers, and in whose case the mode of payment is determined by custom and tradition. They are to work for their employers and are not ordinarily free to seek employment elsewhere.
- ☆ ***Casual (Temporary) labour:*** Unlike permanent labour, casual labourers are engaged only during peak period of work. Their employment is temporary

and they are paid wages at the market rate. They are not attached to any landlord, unlike permanent labour. These labour are engaged in peak period and attend to rush work only. They are free to leave one job for another.

In most cases, the difference between the permanent labour and temporary labour is stated initially in terms of period for which a man is engaged and whether or not he receives daily wages. According to the First Agricultural Labour enquiry (1950-51), 90 percent of the total agricultural labour families were 10 percent attached and 90 percent casual workers. The corresponding figures for the Second Enquiry (1956-57) are 27 percent and 73 percent respectively. The percentage of agricultural labour in rural population was 30.4, of which 50 percent were without land at the time of First Enquiry. During the Second Enquiry, these figures were 24.5 percent and 57 percent respectively. These analytical findings also prove that, even the experts are not agreed upon the definition of agricultural labour.

The difference between the First and Second Labour Enquiries relates to the distinction between 'casual' and 'attached' labour. In the First Enquiry, *'casual' labourers were defined in one place as those who were paid at market rates,* and *'attached 'labourers as those 'who, whenever required by their master, have to work for him and are not ordinarily free to seek employment elsewhere'*. Further, *'attached' workers were those, who were 'more or less in continuous employment and are under some sort of contract with employers during the period of employment', while casual workers were those 'other than attached and employed from time to time according to exigencies of work'*. In the Report on the First Enquiry, the difference between 'casual' and 'attached[1] labour was stated in terms of the period for which a man was engaged and whether or not he received daily wages. In the Report on the Second Enquiry, all these different criteria are lumped together in the following statement: *'the classification of workers is on the basis of exigencies of farm work. Two types of labourers are required for farm operations–those who are employed for rush work to cope with nature's time-schedule for completing agricultural operations well within the season and those who attend to routine farm operations all the year round. The first category of workers is broadly known as 'casual' workers and the second category as 'attached' workers. Casual workers are employed on daily wages for specific operations, which last only for a short duration; while attached workers are often employed on contract, oral or written, extending over a period of a quarter, half-year or year as the case may be. The terms and conditions of employment of attached labourers show-considerable diversity as they vary from region to region according to local tradition and custom' (Report on the Second Enquiry, P. 38).* These casual labour can be further sub-grouped into:

- ***Cultivators:*** They include small and marginal farmers, who possess very little land and therefore, have to devote most of their time working on the lands of others as labourers.
- ***Share-croppers:*** They are those who, while sharing the produce of the land for their work, also work as labourers.

- ***Lease holders (Tenants):*** They are those, who not only work on the leased land, but also work as labourers. The Agricultural Labour Enquiry Committee also differentiated between the 'attached' and 'casual' labourers and it is already discussed earlier.

So, considering the above discussion, we must remain content with a working definition of agricultural worker as: *'all those persons, who derive a major part of their income as payment for work performed on the farms of others, can be designated as agricultural workers. For a major part of the year they should work on the land of others on wages'.*

ii. Skilled, Semi-skilled and Unskilled Labour

a. *Skilled Labour*

These are the labour, who are specially skilled for accomplishing a particular task or operation in the farm business. These labour are specially trained for the said purpose and thereby, they can fulfill the task with much more efficiency than semi-skilled and unskilled labourers. Their absence in the production programme will greatly affect the output in the business, as no other worker can effectively render the service as they can perform. In view of their importance, their wages are much more compared to semi-skilled and unskilled labourers. For example, machinery operators, tractor drivers *etc.*, fall under the category of skilled labour.

b. *Semi-skilled Labour*

These labour are not that much skilled enough like skilled labour, but comparatively more experienced over unskilled labour. These labour does not receive elabourate training like skilled labour and they are better than unskilled labour in accomplishing the given task or farm operation, as they are more experienced in that particular job activity. The wages for these semi-skilled labourers are less than skilled labourers, but more than unskilled labour.

c. *Unskilled Labour*

These are ordinary labour, who can perform only manual (physical) work and they are generally engaged for performing farm operations that does not command any skill oriented job. For these labourers, wage rate is lowest compared to skilled and unskilled labourers. Examples include, labour employed for manual weeding, cotton picking, cattle attendants *etc.*

B. Features of Indian Farm Labour

The following are the features of Indian farm labour:

- Majority of labour are unskilled or less skilled and hence, they perform the farm operations with low efficiency.
- Because of seasonality of agricultural production, these labour will enjoy only seasonal employment. National Commission on Labour has pointed out that, intensity of labour employment varies according to seasons. Shortage of labour is actually felt during peak agricultural seasons in several areas and a large proportion of labour remains unemployed or under-employed during the slack season.

- Not only they inadequately employed, their working conditions too are very bad. They have to put in very hard labour under the strong sun and in the rain. Their working hours are not strictly fixed and they have no provision for holidays.
- The income of agricultural labourers is very low and they are paid in terms of cash or kind or partly in cash and partly in kind.
- Wages paid to the farm labour are not in proportionate to the amount of work accomplished by them.
- Lack of technical know-how hampers the adoption of modern technology, modern implements and machinery on the farm.
- The vast number of agricultural labour lies scattered all over India. Due to lack of organization, they have low bargaining power and hence, they cannot demand higher wages.
- Farm labour are poor and their level of living is very low. Generally, they consume jowar, bajra and other inferior cereals. Items such as fruits, vegetables, milk, meat and other nutritive foods do not figure in their diet. They do not have even the minimum clothing, education and health facilities. They also suffer from many serious diseases. To meet these expenditures, they take loans and are driven into the clutches of moneylenders and caught in debt trap.
- They subsist in life, always face dire poverty, exploitation, misery, uncertainty and have no social status.
- Agricultural labour is migratory. He can be drawn from a distant place to the place of work during a busy season.
- There is lack of legal protection. Agricultural labour is though covered by Agricultural Minimum Wages Act, but usually they are exploited more.
- The hours of work of agricultural labour are not regulated by legislation. Hours of work vary from place to place, crop to crop and season to season. It should be noted that, the working hours of agricultural labourers are not very long. Generally, agricultural labourers work for about 8 hours a day with a break of two hours. There are few occasions when an agricultural labour has to work for longer hours, that is, during harvest season; but during this time he is not paid well.
- Most agricultural workers belong to the depressed classes, which have been neglected for ages. The low caste and the depressed classes have been socially handicapped and they had never the courage to assert themselves.
- The number of agricultural labourers being very large, their abundant supply is more in relation to demand for them. It is only during the sowing and harvesting seasons that there appears to be nearfull employment in the case of agricultural labourers. But, once the harvesting season is over, majority of agricultural workers will be jobless especially in areas, where there is single crop per year.

- There is generally direct and day to day 'contact between agricultural labourers and the landlords' on whose farm they are working. Unlike industrial workers, this direct contact between the employer and employees is a distinct feature of agriculture labourer.

The above peculiarities of farm labour along with other characteristics like paucity of non-agricultural jobs, rural indebtedness and increasing population of agricultural labourers are responsible for their poor economic condition. Inspite of the above mentioned special unwanted features of Indian farm labour, their demand is increasing in agriculture over a period of time because of the following reasons:

- High net growth rate of population in the country.
- Growth of absentee landlordism.
- Increased indebtedness makes the small and marginal farmers to convert into agricultural labourers.
- Replacement of kind payments to labour by cash payments. During the Eleventh Five Year Plan (2007-12), nominal farm wages in India increased by 17.5 per cent per annum and real farm wages by 6.8 per cent per annum, registering the fastest growth since economic reforms began in 1991. Farming being labour intensive, this rapid increase in farm wages has raised cost of production of agricultural commodities. This increase in labour wages along with rise in prices of other inputs like seeds, fertilizers, pesticides *etc.*, resulted in escalation of cost of production of commodities. Further, there is also strong influence of Mahatma Gandhi National Rural Employment Guarantee Act (MGNREGA) Scheme, started in 2006, regarding the strong 'push' in farm wages and overall scarcity of farm labour and the same is discussed in the ensuing section.
- Decline of domestic industries and handicrafts.

C. 'Pull' and 'Push' Factors of Farm Wages

The peculiarity of Indian farm labour regarding low bargaining power and low wages is not witnessed during the past one decade. Considering the volatility of prices of farm commodities, farmers' organizations have been agitating for demanding higher Minimum Support Prices (MSPs) to cover increased costs of production. Since, there was a hike in the MSPs of many of the agricultural commodities in the recent period, their cost of production showed an increase, as MSP of commodities covers COP plus an element of nominal profit. This increase in cost of production was mainly due to increase in labour wages besides increases in prices of seeds, fertilizers, pesticides *etc.* Further, with the execution of MGNREGA Scheme, started in 2006, there was a strong 'push' in farm wages. This is because, there was a shift from labour employment in agriculture towards MGNREGA Scheme thereby, causing severe scarcity of farm labour. In this context, the MGNREGA Scheme is beneficial for the farm labour, as their wage levels are pushed upwards because of their scarcity. However, farmers complain that, this Scheme is hitting them adversely, as rising costs are not fully compensated by either MSPs or market prices. So, these two are somewhat contrary feelings by the farm population and the policy makers. It is interesting to note that, the real farm wages increased by 3.7 percent per annum during 1990s compared to only 2.1 percent during 2000s. So, if real wages had followed the same trend of 1990s in 2000s, the current level of real farm wages would have been higher than what it is today with MGNREGA. However, during the 2000s, there is a sort of 'v'-shape behavior in real farm wages, declining by 1.8 percent during 2000-01 to 2006-07, and then rapidly rising by 6.8 percent during 2007-08 to 2011-12, and it is this latter half that seems to be the result of MGNREGA 'push' as well as strong growth 'pull'. In general for developing countries, as the economy prospers industrially, the labour moves out from agriculture to non-agriculture sectors. This often acts as a strong 'pull' factor raising farm wages for those who are left behind on the farms. The same is the case with India, as witnessed from the facts that, the share of work force engaged in Indian agriculture declined from almost 65 percent in 1993-94 to only about 53 percent in 2009, and that of construction works (non-agriculture) increased from 3.1 percent to 9.6 percent over the same period. So, the execution of MGNREGA Scheme acts as a strong 'push' factor and scarcity of labour in agricultural sector due to migration to non-agricultural sector act as 'pull' factor for rising farm wages.

D. Efficiency of Farm Labour or Labour Efficiency or Labour Productivity

Labour efficiency refers to the amount of productive work accomplished by the farm labour in unit time. It is, otherwise, defined as the rate of output per worker in farm business per unit of time - usually per hour. Basically, productivity is how much each labour produces per hour compared to what each labour is earning to perform the job. The efficiency of labour is important in the context of determining costs and profits in the farm business. A low productivity of labour when compared with his hours of employment in the farm implies one of the two important aspects to the farm manager *viz.*, the labour are being paid higher than the amount of work they turn out in the farm or excess labour may get employed in the farm. So, it guides the farm manager to streamline the labour force on the farm to maximize labour productivity. This, in turn, boosts the farm profits. In the modern days of farm business, cost-effective production is gaining more and more importance and this can be achieved through increasing the labour efficiency. As mentioned earlier, Indian farm labour enjoy low efficiency in producing output in the production programme, as there are largely illiterate, less skilled, under employment, lack of bargaining power *etc.* In view of this, it is essential to improve the labour efficiency in the production programme through:

- ☆ Proper supervision of work to make labour more efficient in doing farm operations.
- ☆ By employing modern tools, implements, machinery *etc.*, in the production programme.
- ☆ Promoting interest in the work through proper division of labour and allocating the works to the labour in accordance with their interests.
- ☆ Through expanding the size of business, employment can be created throughout the year and this inculcates interest among the farm labour towards fulfilling the tasks in the production programme.

- ☆ Promoting labour intensive activities in the farm (provided there is surplus of farm labour available in that area).
- ☆ By proper layout of farmstead with well planned fields without irregular shapes increases the farm labour efficiency.
- ☆ By rendering training to the farm labour in fulfilling the tasks on scientific lines.
- ☆ Daily work plan should be flexible so that, work can adjusted to changing weather.
- ☆ By planning proper enterprises combination such that, labour employment will be generated throughout the year and ensures efficient use of labour.
- ☆ By preparing a labour calendar in advance to plan labour requirement in advance.
- ☆ Work incentives should be provided to farm labour, who turns out quality work in farm.
- ☆ Working hours of labour must be reasonable, then the efficiency will be high. If the labour has to work very long, extra payment is to be provided to increase efficiency.
- ☆ By proving a healthy working environment and a good relationship between farm manager and farm labourer
- ☆ By framing strict labour laws by the Government regarding the number of hours of work, operation wise-wage payment *etc.*
- ☆ By checking references of prospective employees.
- ☆ By giving labour an opportunity for time off that fits their personal obligations
- ☆ By holding regular meetings with farm labourers to discuss farm issues, goals and operational strategies.
- ☆ By having an ideal combination of labour with other three factors of production
- ☆ Diversifying the farm business by practicing allied enterprises (that enjoy complementary or supplementary relationship) increases the labour use efficiency.
- ☆ Don't do off-season works during on-season.
- ☆ Machinery should get repaired during off season and rainy days and by the time the season commences, they should be kept ready, so as to engage skilled workers on the farm.
- ☆ Weather forecast should be kept in mind before assuming labour works.
- ☆ Comfort stay of married hired labour on the farm also improves the work efficiency.
- ☆ By doing job analysis in advance, the farm manager can analyze:
  - ❑ How best he can simplify the work process in the farm?
  - ❑ Which work is to be done and which work can be avoided?

- ❑ How best he can minimize the cost in performing an operation?
- ❑ How best he can minimize the duration of completion of an operation?
- ❑ The sequence of activities, so as to effectively utilize the farm labour?
- ❑ How to reduce travel by having farm fields and buildings close together?
- ❑ How to facilitate easy movement of carts and other transport vehicles in the farm?
- ❑ Plan to complete one operation, when another begins
- ❑ Divide the work and frame the following questions:
  - ❖ Why that work is needed?
  - ❖ When it should get completed?
  - ❖ What equipment is needed to perform that work?
  - ❖ Who should do that work?
  - ❖ What is the best way to do that work?
  - ❖ How many number and what type of labour are to be engaged to perform that work?

This job analysis enables the farm manager to simplify the work process and to accomplish the operation in a smooth manner so that, more of output can be realized with both cost-effectiveness, time effectiveness and with less energy. Hence, job analysis is, otherwise, called as Farm work simplification.

However, the promotion of labour efficiency depends on two set of factors *viz.*, 'his (labour) power to work' and 'will to work'. The former *i.e.*, 'power to work' again depends upon:

- ☆ ***Inherent qualities:*** The racial stock to which the labour belongs influences the both amount of work and efficiency of work, as some races are known to be hardier than other. These qualities are largely the outcome of climate and natural environment. Some people are suitably built to perform heavy labour, while some are very suitable for mental labour. Family background also plays very important role in this regard.
- ☆ ***Acquired qualities:*** By education and training, labour gain some technical qualities and these contribute to increase in the efficiency of the labourer.
- ☆ ***Earnings:*** If the earnings of an individual is more, he will consume quality food thereby, he enjoys sound health position and consequently, he perform more and quality work.
- ☆ ***Labour organization:*** When there is a labour organization for the labourers with constructive approach, it can improve the labour efficiency.
- ☆ ***Climatic conditions:*** Climate also plays an important role in increasing or decreasing the efficiency. Hot weather has a vital factor for the low efficiency of labour in Asia and Middle East. On the other hand, cold weather is an important element for increasing the efficiency in labour in U.S.A and Europe.

The other factor *i.e.*, 'will to work' depends upon the desire and interest of the labour in performing a farm operation. So, in accordance with the labourers' interests, works have to be assigned to them in the farm.

E. Selection of Right Employee (Labour) in the Farm

The farm manager must also note that, no two workers are alike *i.e.*, they differ in interests, capabilities, work habits, attitudes, personality, ambitions and willingness to accept responsibility. Again each farm business unit is also different in its management and labour needs. So, the farm manager must always look into:

- ☆ Finding the right employee.
- ☆ Physical and mental status of the labour.
- ☆ Updating the wage package. Every time, the farm manager has to ask himself the following questions before paying wages to the farm labour:
  - ❑ Is the wage paid by me competitive with wages paid by other farm managers?
  - ❑ What would it cost me to train and hire someone to replace a labour?
  - ❑ How should I pay the labour - by the hour, the week, or the month?
- ☆ Training the worker on modern techniques of production.
- ☆ Promoting working conditions on the farm.
- ☆ Promoting employer-employee relations.
- ☆ Offering external benefits beyond relieving work duties on the farm.
- ☆ Offering work assignments to labour as per the labour laws.

In the above selection criteria, 'finding the right employee' by the farm manager is most important, as his commitment towards the execution of farm operations counts much in turning out efficient work on the farm. But, finding such a worker has always been a difficult task for farm managers. Decline in rural population and decline in percent of workforce in agricultural sector especially with the execution of MGNREGA scheme have compounded the farm manager's difficulty in obtaining suitable workers on the farm. Traditionally, farm managers have found labour through word of mouth, but now in the days of farm mechanization, the farm managers have to employ majority of skilled labour by paying higher wages due to 'push' and 'pull' factors as discussed earlier. Once after selecting the farm labour, to make farm employment more attractive, the farm work must be flexible and farm manager must follow various measures, as discussed earlier, to improve labour efficiency. Above all, it is important to recognize that, not every prospective employee has adequate knowledge about modern techniques of farming. So, there is no problem in hiring those labour who tell they know little about modern techniques of production programme, as the farm manager can teach them. But, the problem arises, when you hire a labour who claims, but does not have, the necessary experience in performing an operation. So, choosing (selecting) the right employee is as important as finding an employee.

F. Increasing Labour Productivity: A Mixed Blessing?

Increasing labour productivity is generally hailed as a positive outcome of technological innovation. The production of more output in less span of time allows for both higher standards of living and decreased inflationary pressure, since wage increases can result from increased productivity and are not translated into higher costs for goods and services. If this increased labour productivity also results in increased labour wages, then improvement in labour productivity would be seen as a pure benefit. However, in developing countries like India, increased labour productivity has not been a boon to workers. This is indicated by the following reasons:

- ☆ Increased productivity has lead to more output and increased profits to the firms, but not resulted in higher wages.
- ☆ Increased labour productivity has also led to increased levels of unemployment and hence, the labour has to search for alternate employment opportunities. So, leisure time seems to not have come true for the majority of workers.
- ☆ Fewer workers are needed to produce the same amount of output.
- ☆ Higher labour productivity implies cost-effective production and consequent higher unemployment rates of labour may well be structural in several countries including India due to the globalization or production, increased wealth disparities, and a host of other issues.

G. Farm Wages

Wages are the remuneration paid to the 'labour' factor employed in the production programme. In Economics, 'labour' refers to *'any exertion of mind or body undergone partly or wholly with a view to earning some good other than the pleasure derived directly from the work'*. (Marshall). Thus, all types of work, whether, it is physical or mental executed by the workers, salaried persons, employees *etc.*, constitute 'labour' and the salaries or emoluments or fees or commission or bonus *etc.*, derived by them refers to 'wages' in Economics. But, in ordinary language, we generally differentiate between wage and salary, where the former is a remuneration paid to hired labour and the latter represents the remuneration for white collar job holders. Similarly, other terms like bonus, emoluments, fees, commission *etc.*, indicate only social distinction, but in the context of Economics, all the beneficiaries are said to receive 'wages'. In the words of Benham, *'a wage may be defined as a sum of money paid under contract by an employer to a worker for services rendered'*. According to Rothschild, *'wage is the price for a particular commodity viz., labour services'*.

i. Different Types of Farm Wages

Wages are paid to the labour in different modes and they are discussed here under.

- ☆ ***Time wages:*** These are the wages paid to the labour in accordance with the number of hours of work. For example, wages are paid to an agricultural labour for ploughing the land for five hours a day. The time wages are also paid daily, weekly, fortnightly, monthly *etc.*

- ☆ ***Piece wages:*** These are the wages paid to the labour in accordance with the quantity of output turned out in a production programme. For example, a worker is paid by a sugar factory in accordance with the number of quintals of sugar manufactured. If the price/unit of sugar is Rs. 1500, then the worker will be paid accordingly in terms of amount of sugar processed by him in the factory.
- ☆ ***Task wages*:** In this mode of payment, wage payment is fixed for each and every task in the production programme. For the labour, the task is allocated such that, it has to be fulfilled from the start to its end. Examples include, digging bore well in the farm, paddy transplanting in about 10 acres of land, construction of farm godown *etc.*
- ☆ ***Cash (Money) wages*:** When wages are paid to the labour in terms of liquid money, it is called Cash wages. Usually, in urban areas, the workers are paid wages in liquid cash. Money wages are also called as Nominal wages. For example, if a worker in a sugar factory is paid with Rs. 5000/month, it refers to money wages or nominal wages.
- ☆ ***Kind wages*:** When wages are paid to the labour in terms of kind component say, in terms of rice, wheat, pulses etc, it is called Kind wages. Even today, in rural areas, the agricultural labourers are often paid in terms of kind wages.
- ☆ ***Real wages*:** Nominal or Money wages does not measure the real earnings of the worker. This is because, sometimes, the worker enjoys other benefits offered by the sugar factory like free quarters, medical facilities, vehicle allowance, telephone allowance *etc.*, and all these earnings (benefits) along with the money wage the worker enjoys constitute Real wages. So, in this case, the real wages of the worker is more than money wages. Thus, nominal wages refer only to money wages of the worker, whereas, real wages represents necessaries, comforts and luxuries enjoyed by the worker in return for his services contributed in the production programme.

  The concept of real wages can also be studied from the point of view of the purchasing power the worker enjoys. The purchasing power (real wage) can be studied based on two components *viz.*, money wage and price level in the economy. This is given by, $R_W = M_W/P_L$, where, R_W = Real wage of the worker, M_W = Money wage of the worker, P_L = Price level in the economy. The following are the interesting points we can infer from the above equation:

  - ❑ With the rise in price level in the economy (inflation), the real wage of the worker falls and *vice versa*.
  - ❑ At the constancy of general price level, when the money-wage rate of the worker increases, his real wage also increases.
  - ❑ When the price level in the economy increases more than money wage, real wage of the worker will decline and *vice versa*. If this is the case in the economy, then the Government should intervene and announce

daily allowance to the worker, so as to compensate his loss in real wage.

There is another way of measurement of real wage of the worker and it is given by, $R_W = M_W/\text{Cost of living index}$. Here, cost of living index refers to the consumer's price index in the economy. Thus, the real wage determines the standard of living of the workers. Hence, compared to money wage, real wage is the true indicator of worker's prosperity. The comparison between money wages and real wages also indicates another aspect *i.e.,* it guides the worker in choosing different job alternatives. For example, if a worker finds real wages are more in one job, but money wages are less compared to another job, then the worker should choose the former job and not the latter. However, besides general price level or consumer price index, there are several factors that influence the real wages and they are discussed here under.

- ***Facilities at working place:*** If the facilities provided at the working place are good, then the worker enjoys more real wage. For example, if the workers A and B are employed in two different organizations and drawing the same salary as Rs. 10000 each, and if the worker A is provided with good facilities like infrastructure, laptop computer, air-conditioned room *etc.*, and that of the other is not equipped with such facilities, then the real wage of worker A is more compared to worker B, though they draw same nominal (money) wages.
- ***Fringe benefits:*** These are the benefits enjoyed by the worker for the service rendered by him in an organization. For example, an organization may offer several benefits to the workers like free accommodation in the quarters, free medical aid, subsidized canteen, free transport service, telephone facility, pension *etc.*, and these benefits add to the real wages of the workers.
- ***Scope for extra earning:*** If the worker has the scope to make for extra income, while rendering service in an organization or industry, then his real wage will be high. For example, a college professor can earn extra income by publishing research articles in reputed journals, publishing text books, evaluating answer sheets of students *etc.*, and thereby, he earn more than his regular salary. So, the chances of extra earning will increase the real wages.
- ***Nature of job:*** If the nature of job is more risky or seasonal, then money wage will be high, but real wage is low. For example, a worker working in coal mines, forest area *etc.*, enjoy more money wages, but real wages are low.
- ***Social prestige or status:*** Some jobs, though they carry same money wages, but in terms of social status, they greatly differ. For example, an Assistant Professor joined in the University has the same scale on par with the District Collector, but in terms of social status, District Collector is far superior compared to an Assistant Professor. So, the District Collector enjoys more real wages compared to an Assistant Professor.

- ❑ ***Timely payment of wages:*** If the workers are paid with the wages regularly and promptly, then his real wages are considered to be more than the workers, who are not paid with the wages regularly and promptly.
- ❑ ***Possibility of promotions in the job:*** If the worker has the bright chance of getting the promotion in his job duties, then his real income will be higher. If a Professor in the University has the bright chance of becoming a Vice–Chancellor of the University, then he enjoy more real wages than his money wages.
- ❑ ***Period and cost of training:*** When a job needs a long period and huge cost for training, then the real wage for the worker in that job will be lower.
- ❑ ***Trade expenses:*** When a job needs high trade expenses, then the real wages for that worker will be low. We know, a dental doctor or a surgeon has to establish and maintain their own hospitals or dispensaries, thereby, the trade expenses are very high and hence, they enjoy less real wages. In this context, an Assistant Professor in the University will enjoy high real wages compared to a dental doctor or a surgeon.
- ❑ ***Climatic conditions:*** For the workers, working under adverse or unhealthy climatic conditions, enjoy less real wages compared to the workers working under healthy environment.
- ❑ ***Nature of jobs:*** If the job is permanent, then the worker enjoys more real wages and for the worker, who is temporarily employed, the real wages are low. Similarly, compared to the real wage of a skilled worker working in a sugar factory, the real wage of a casual agricultural labour is low.

The wages offered to the farm labour vary across different farm operations and even across the sex and age-group of the labourers (Tables 3.11 to 3.16).

Table 3.11: Month-wise Average Daily Wage Rates for Agricultural Occupation : Ploughing by Sex in India (2010-11)

Month	*Men*	*Women*
July	131.36	81.33
August	132.20	74.25
September	137.31	81.50
October	140.56	86.25
November	142.70	91.25
December	144.78	93.75
January	148.16	83.18
February	151.26	88.00
March	153.07	89.55
April	154.51	83.00
May	156.63	82.27
June	153.60	109.41

Table 3.12: Month-wise Average Daily Wage Rates for Agricultural Occupation : Sowing by Sex in India (2010-11)

Month	*Men*	*Women*	*Children*
July	116.21	89.33	62.65
August	116.00	89.65	67.50
September	118.75	95.09	82.12
October	120.94	95.50	75.45
November	122.57	98.60	63.00
December	123.02	99.87	65.50
January	127.21	98.96	69.09
February	129.80	101.19	68.50
March	130.79	100.87	72.78
April	132.84	101.94	74.24
May	135.84	103.75	74.24
June	135.06	103.31	72.62

Table 3.13: Month-wise Average Daily Wage Rates for Agricultural Occupation : Transplanting by Sex in India (2010-11)

Month	*Men*	*Women*	*Children*
July	116.55	98.21	80.83
August	111.86	95.52	66.60
September	112.73	97.12	66.60
October	113.05	98.55	67.71
November	117.00	101.09	71.56
December	118.37	103.71	72.56
January	123.48	107.94	75.90
February	124.04	107.54	71.79
March	123.04	108.01	70.41
April	123.79	107.82	72.24
May	127.74	109.10	72.40
June	130.66	115.42	80.27

ii. Labour Factor vis-à-vis Other Factors of Production (Differences between remuneration paid to labour and other factors of production)

Compared to other factors of production, labour factor enjoys some distinctive features and they are discussed here under.

- ☆ Labour is inseparable from labourer himself. That means, when labour service is to be engaged in the production programme, the 'agent' (labour) must also go to the place of the work, as labour service is a human service.

Table 3.14: Month-wise Average Daily Wage Rates for Agricultural Occupation : Weeding by Sex in India (2010-11)

Month	*Men*	*Women*	*Children*
July	102.71	86.51	65.20
August	101.44	85.41	68.77
September	105.82	90.15	70.67
October	107.18	91.85	70.03
November	109.39	94.37	70.68
December	112.11	95.92	70.31
January	114.02	97.39	69.71
February	115.03	99.85	73.19
March	115.59	100.52	73.31
April	114.87	100.65	76.03
May	117.61	102.32	75.19
June	118.93	104.59	78.03

Table 3.15: Month-wise Average Daily Wage Rates for Agricultural Occupation : Harvesting by Sex in India (2010-11)

Month	*Men*	*Women*	*Children*
July	112.21	94.07	66.54
August	111.52	94.05	66.19
September	115.54	96.56	65.10
October	120.40	99.72	67.13
November	119.68	98.59	69.97
December	122.10	101.95	71.80
January	122.60	102.76	77.66
February	124.42	104.15	78.30
March	127.18	106.67	74.59
April	128.79	109.51	72.23
May	132.44	109.70	71.44
June	133.51	110.61	69.95

☆ The engagement of labour in the work depends upon the willingness, physical fitness and mental alertness of the labour. His feelings and emotions counts much towards fulfilling the assigned tasks and in turning out quality work. Besides above, the execution of labour work also depends upon the working conditions, pleasantness and monetary compensation he derives in the production programme.

Table 3.16: Occupation-wise Average Daily Wage Rates (Rs./-) in Agricultural Occupations in India (2010-11)

Year	*Ploughing*	*Sowing*	*Weeding*	*Transplanting*	*Harvesting*	*Winnowing*	*Threshing*	*Picking**	*Herdsman*	*Well-Digging*	*Cane Crushing*
2006-07											
Men	81.79	73.29	64.97	69.47	68.45	66.18	67.40	67.45	43.46	99.48	72.46
Women	42.37	51.41	52.82	56.44	55.69	51.04	54.41	51.06	34.43	53.37	47.05
Children	–	41.32	37.81	42.67	38.69	40.95	40.71	34.39	29.62	–	–
2007-08											
Men	91.38	79.28	70.07	73.79	75.24	71.06	73.50	72.46	47.64	106.96	77.92
Women	49.96	57.18	58.27	61.93	62.31	56.09	59.41	58.15	37.78	58.33	54.93
Children	–	44.72	42.35	45.70	42.54	40.79	40.18	40.90	31.40	–	–
2008-09											
Men	102.90	90.00	80.15	83.28	87.05	81.23	85.06	81.10	53.48	116.28	87.27
Women	55.43	65.00	68.02	71.43	71.58	65.08	67.66	66.37	41.32	63.47	61.23
Children	–	48.91	49.46	52.51	50.49	43.40	46.06	45.78	36.22	–	–
2009-10											
Men	120.85	104.52	92.78	98.29	102.82	96.32	100.23	96.98	62.23	140.81	98.43
Women	70.43	79.47	78.94	86.71	84.95	79.02	82.12	78.94	46.66	75.44	75.49
Children	–	58.41	58.80	58.08	61.72	48.27	53.32	51.41	42.75	–	–
2010-11											
Men	145.51	125.75	111.22	120.19	122.53	112.82	117.78	121.10	77.17	170.32	120.33
Women	87.23	98.17	95.79	104.17	102.36	94.83	97.08	101.19	60.43	93.81	89.09
Children	–	70.64	71.76	72.56	70.91	58.83	66.41	78.31	54.47	–	–

- ☆ The employment of labour in a production programme is influenced by the ethical, institutional, behavioural and sociological aspects. Further, other aspects like accommodation facilities, medical facilities in that locality, recreational facilities, security of employment, leisure hours *etc.*, also influence the employment of a labour in a farm business.
- ☆ Labour is the only factor of production, which acts as both producer and consumer of goods produced in the production programme.
- ☆ Since, supply of labour is more than their demand in farm sector, they enjoy low bargaining power thereby, they get exploited and get low wages compared to their productivity in the production programme. So, the concept of demand and supply theory will not exactly determine the price for labour factor. Further, labour is the most perishable factor of production and we know that, when the commodity is highly perishable, demand is the major force that influences price of the commodity. So, when the demand for labour (perishable factor) is less compared to the supply, their price will be low and this infers that, labour gets exploited in his employment.

☆ Pricing of labour factor involves Government intervention in the form of minimum wage level, so as to avoid their exploitation. This is because of excess supply of labour over demand and consequent, low bargaining power. Further, the labour is a perishable commodity, thereby, their exploitation is severe in the context of market imperfections and absence of trade unions. However, this concept of Government intervention in the form of minimum rent, minimum interest and minimum profits will not arise in case of other factors of production like land, capital and entrepreneur (management) respectively.

☆ Supply curve of labour will not show perfect (direct) relationship between wage rate of labour and number of working hours of labour. This is because, up to a certain level of increasing wage rate, the number of working hours contributed by the labour will increase, but at a higher level of wage rate, the number of working hours of labour will decrease, as they prefer more number of leisure hours and less number of working hours (Figure 3.7). Thus, at a higher level of wage rate, there exists inverse relationship between wage rate and number of working hours of labour and this is due to inelastic cash requirements on the part of the labour. Thus, there is no standard functional relationship between wage rate and number of working hours (labour supply) contributed by the labour. Moreover, the supply of labour depends not only on the wage rate, but also on various factors like

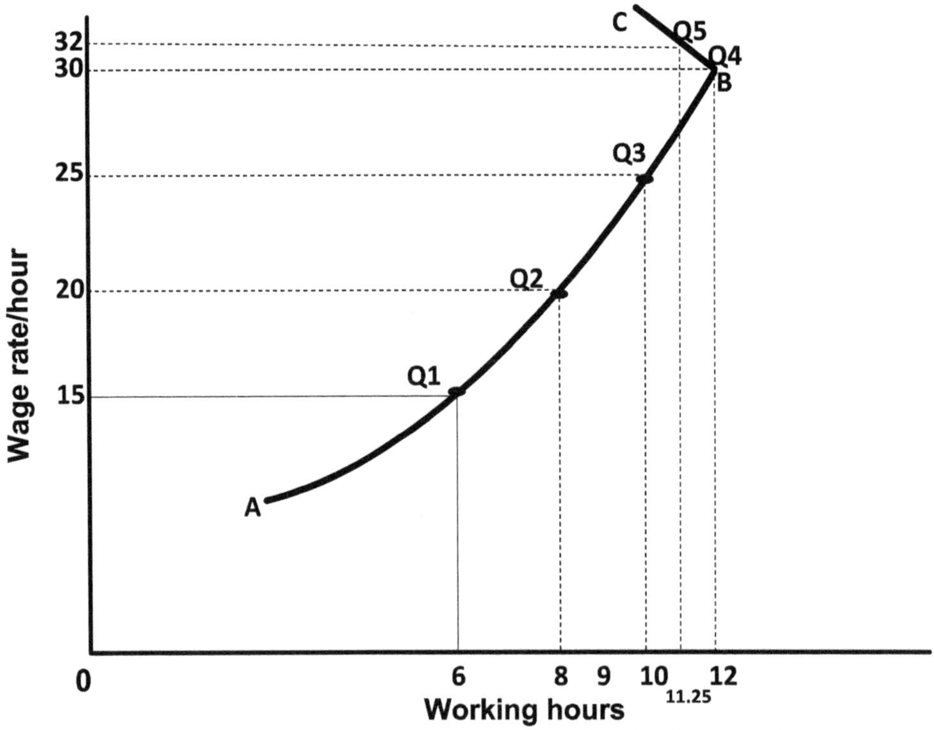

Figure 3.7: Supply Curve of Labour for an Economy as a Whole (Backward bending supply curve).

population, working age-groups, sex ratio, ethical and social considerations, desire to work by the labour *etc.* However, in case of product market, there exists direct functional relationship between price and product supply into the market.

In the Figure 3.7, when the wage rate is Rs.15/hr, the labour contributed six working hours, when the wage rate increased to Rs.20/hr, then the number of working hours are increased to eight, and when the wage rate is still increased to Rs.30/hr, the labour contributed 12 working hours. But, when the wage rate is further increased to Rs.32/hr, now the labour contributed less number of working hours *i.e.,* only 11.25 working hours. This infers that, at higher wage rates, the labour prefers more number of leisure hours compared to working hours. This is because, the labour will have inelastic cash requirements. That means, when the wage rate is Rs.30/hr, the labour contributed 12 working hours and thereby, he derived Rs. 360/- income. But, when the wage rate increased to Rs.32/hr, he contributed only 11.25 working hours and still he derives same amount of income *i.e.,* 360/-. So, the labour prefers more number of leisure hours and less number of working hours at very high wage rate, because of inelastic cash requirements.

- ☆ The bargaining power of farm labour can be increased, if they form trade union and this is not possible in case of other factors of production.
- ☆ The supply of labour is comparatively inelastic when compared to other factors of production. That means, when the demand for the labour suddenly increases, the supply of labour cannot be increased overnight or few days or few months. However, compared to labour factor, the supply of (durable) products can be increased rather quickly into the market due to increase in demand.
- ☆ The concept of bilateral monopoly *i.e.,* monopsony in the demand for labour by the entrepreneur and monopoly in the supply of labour by the labour supplier can be seen only in the labour market and not possible with reference to other factors of production. Such imperfections in the labour market are due to weak bargaining power on the part of labour, absence of trade unions, less mobility of labour, entrepreneur's may enjoy monopsonistic power, differences in skills and efficiencies of labour *etc.*

A. Marginal Productivity Concept of Farm Labour

Considering the above peculiar features of labour factor in contrast to other factors of production, it is justifiable to have a separate theory to analyze the pricing of labour factor. Let us analyze the determination of wages paid to labour through the concept of marginal productivity of labour factor. This concept emphasizes that, the entrepreneur generally employs the labour factor with higher marginal productivity and he substitute the labour with higher marginal productivity in place of the labour with lower marginal productivity. This concept is based on the following propositions:

- ☆ The marginal productivity of the labour determines the price (wage) of the labour.

- ✰ In the long run, the wages paid to the labour tends to equate to its Average Revenue Product (ARP) and Marginal Revenue Product (MRP).
- ✰ The point of optimal allocation of labour in the production programme is when the remuneration paid to the labour (MFC_X) equals the MRP.

Assumptions

This concept is based on the following assumptions:

- ✰ All the labour are homogenous, thereby, they are perfectly substitutable.
- ✰ The technology is given, though the scales and proportions of labour factor may change.
- ✰ There is perfect mobility of labour between different employments.
- ✰ There is perfect competition both in the labour market and product market.
- ✰ The marginal productivity of labour is measurable.
- ✰ The firm aims at profit maximization through efficient allocation of labour.
- ✰ This theory considers long run analysis, as the price paid to the labour tends to be equal to ARP and MRP.
- ✰ There is full employment equilibrium in the economy.
- ✰ This theory is based on the concept of LDR.
- ✰ The bargaining power of the seller and buyer of the labour service are equal.
- ✰ There is no Government intervention in the fixation of labour's remuneration like Minimum wage rate *etc.*

a. Remuneration Paid to the Labour is Equal to its Marginal Productivity

We know, a firm employs the agricultural labour, when they are productive enough to increase the output in the production programme. That means, if the agricultural labour is productive only in terms of contributing or increasing the output, then only the firm will engage and pay wages to the labour. So, in employing the agricultural labour, the firm often compares the productivity contributed by the labour with the wages it pays as remuneration to the labour and the firm continuously increase or engage the labour, so long as marginal productivity contributed by the labour is higher than wage rate paid to the labour by the firm. This infers that, the marginal productivity contributed by the agricultural labour determines his wage rate and it varies directly. The employment of the agricultural labour in a firm increases, so long as the marginal productivity contributed by the labour is greater than wage rate paid to the labour and the firm will come to equilibrium or stop employing additional labour, when the marginal productivity of labour is equal to his wage rate. To generalize the statement, a firm will engage the agricultural labour up to the point, where the MFC_X of the agricultural labour (from the firm side) or when the reward for the labour (from the factor side) is equal to his marginal productivity. At this point of equilibrium, the firm will minimize the cost in the production programme. This is because, when marginal productivity of the agricultural labour is greater than the wage rate, it implies, the firm can still engage more number of agricultural labour in the production programme. But, if marginal productivity of labour is less than the wage rate paid by the firm, it is better for the firm to remove excess labour, as they are not contributing much to the total output of the firm in proportion to the wage rate they receive, and thereby, the firm will attain equilibrium when marginal productivity of labour is equal to his wage rate. Thus, the firm will attain equilibrium in the production programme with reference to the employment of agricultural labour, when the marginal (revenue) productivity (MRP) is equal to the cost of employing additional unit of labour (MFC_X).

b. Firm's Equilibrium in the Short Run

In Figure 3.8, MRP=MVP_X or VMP is an inverted 'U' shaped curve and WW_1 refers to the wage rate paid to the agricultural labour=AFC (Average wage rate)=MFC_X (Marginal wage rate) and it is an horizontal straight line parallel to X-axis, assuming perfect competition both in the product and labour markets respectively. It is clear from the Figure 3.8 that:

- ☆ We know, MRP=VMP under perfect market competition and MRP indicates the firm's demand curve for labour.
- ☆ From the firm's view point, at a given wage rate OW, the factor's supply curve is perfectly elastic *i.e.*, WW_1.
- ☆ So, from the above two curves *i.e.*, MRP (= VMP) and WW_1, the firm can draw the information pertaining to the price of the product and wage rate of the agricultural labour.
- ☆ At point 'E', MRP=MFC_X or wage rate derived by the agricultural labour and this infers that, the firm is in equilibrium by employing ON number of agricultural labour.

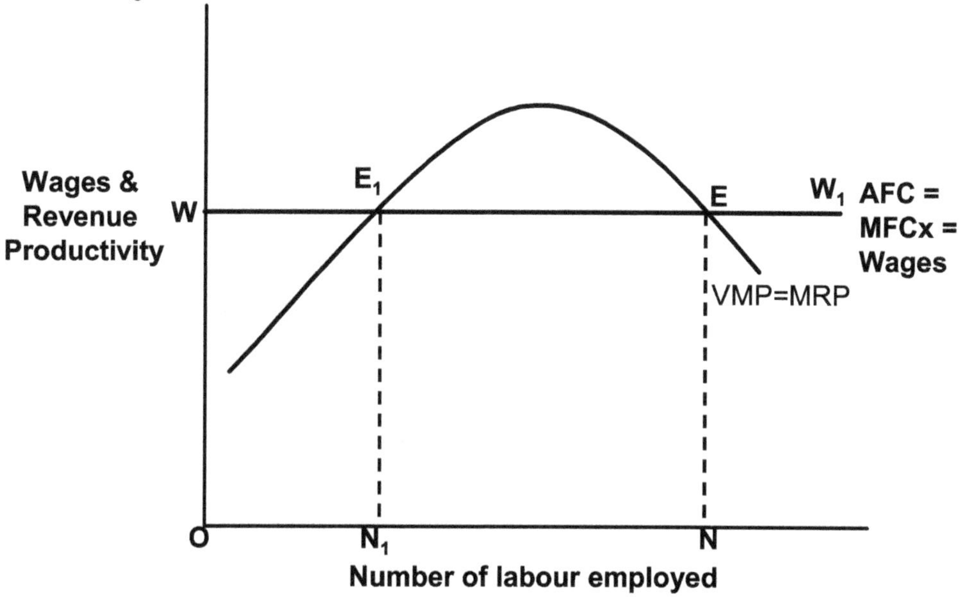

Figure 3.8: Marginal Productivity Theory of Wages – Pricing of Labour Factor Under Perfect Competitive Product and Labour Markets (Short run).

- ☆ Below ON number of agricultural labour, MRP of agricultural labour is greater than wage rate paid per labour and thereby, the firm can still employ number of labour up to ON to attain equilibrium. Even at point E_1, the firm is in short run equilibrium, where MRP= MFC_X, with reference to ON_1 level of employment of labour. But, beyond E_1, the MRP> MFC_X and thereby, the firm can still increase the employment up to ON number of labour, where MRP is again equal to MFC_X, and thereby, the firm is in equilibrium.
- ☆ If the firm employs more than ON number of agricultural labour, the MRP of agricultural labour is less than the wage rate paid per labour, thereby, the firm must necessarily reduce the number of labour to ON, so as to ensure equilibrium or minimization of costs in the production programme.
- ☆ This infers that, in a competitive market, the firm will be in equilibrium when the marginal productivity or MRP of a factor is equal to the MFC_X (or) price paid per factor with reference to employment of a factor in the short run production programme.
- ☆ So, the essential condition for firm's equilibrium in short run with respect to the employment of a factor is that, the demand curve or MRP curve must cut the supply curve of the factor or MFC_X curve from above, when MRP is falling.

c. Long Run Industry Equilibrium

When a firm is in short run equilibrium, it does not mean that, the industry is also in equilibrium with respect to employment of a factor. When the firm is in short run equilibrium, it implies MRP = MFC_X and at this point of equilibrium, the firm maximizes the super-normal profits. These super-normal profits are lucrative and thereby, new firms enter the industry. Consequently, the demand for the factor increases, and thereby, the wage rate of agricultural labour will increase. Since, new firms enter the industry, the supply of the output into the market will increase, thereby, the price of the product will fall in the market and hence, MRP falls. When MRP falls, ARP also falls. This will continue till MRP=ARP= MFC_X (=Average Factor Cost (AFC_X)=wage rate) and this is the condition of industry equilibrium in the long run (Figure 3.9). That means, in the long run, the essential condition for the firm's equilibrium with reference to employment of labour factor is MRP=ARP=MFC_X and ARP must be tangent to the MFC_X (=AFC_X=Wage rate) at the point of equilibrium. But, in short run, the essential condition for firm's equilibrium is only MRP= MFC_X. As shown in the Figure 3.9:

- ☆ With reference to point 'E', where MRP=ARP=MFC_X (=AFC_X=wage rate), the firm is said to be in long run equilibrium, by employing ON number of agricultural labour, where all the firms derive only normal profits in the industry.
- ☆ Let us suppose, OW_1 is the short run wage rate of labour and at this wage rate, the firm incurs losses, as ARP is less than OW_1 wage rate by E_1A_1. So, some firms will leave the industry, thereby, the demand for agricultural labour will decrease and the wage rate will fall from OW_1 to OW and again the firm's equilibrium is attained.

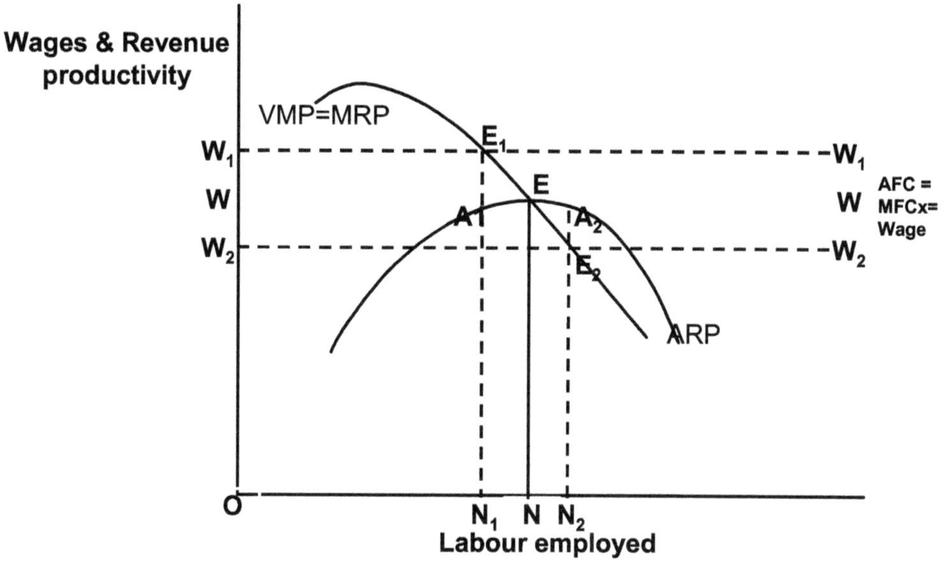

Figure 3.9: Marginal Productivity Theory of Wages – Pricing of Labour Factor Under Perfect Competitive Product and Labour Markets (Long run).

- Let us suppose, OW_2 is the short run wage rate of labour and at this wage rate the firm will enjoy super-normal profits, as ARP is higher than OW_2 by E_2A_2. New firms get attracted to these super-normal profits and enter the industry. As a result, the demand for the agricultural labour will increase, thereby, wage rate increases from OW_2 to OW. Further, with the increase in supply of the product into the market due to the entry of new firms into the industry, the price of the product will fall and thereby, ARP will fall and gets equated to OW wage rate. So, due to increase in demand for the factor and fall in demand for the product, again the firm will attain long run equilibrium, where, MRP=ARP=MFC_X (=AFC_X=OW wage rate).
- Hence, in the long run, the industry will be in equilibrium when MRP=ARP=MFC_X and ARP is tangent to MFC_X(=AFC_X=Wage rate) at the point of equilibrium, where all the firms will earn only normal profits.

However, in case of small and marginal farmers with abundant family labour, they go on employing the family labour to the point, where VMP=0. That is, below the point of intersection between VMP and MFC_X, VMP falls and up to zero VMP, TVP rises at diminishing rate. As shown through Figure 3.10 at point L_2, VMP of labour is zero and thereby, TVP of labour is maximum *i.e.*, OY_2. This implies that, when farmer engages hired labour, he will stop employing labour (OL_1), where VMP = MFC_X and thereby, he produces OY_1 output. However, when the farmer (say, small or marginal farmers with abundant family labour) employ family labour, he can employ the same up to point where, VMP of labour is equal to zero or TVP of labour is maximum. If still farmer increases family labour input beyond L_2, VMP of labour is negative, TVP of labour decreases in accordance with concept of LDR. However, in the figure, the

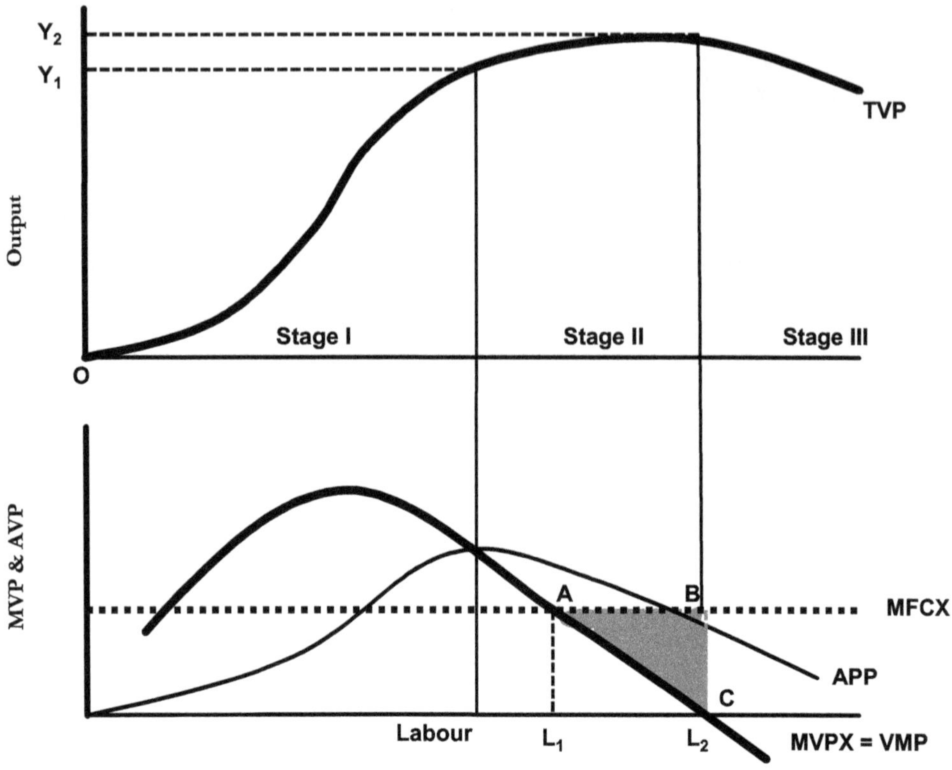

Figure 3.10: Optimum Employment of Labour (MFC_X = VMP).

shaded portion between A,B and C indicates loss to small and marginal farmers, as MFC_X is greater than VMP of labour and this has only theoretical significance.

B. Causes for Wage Differentials

Under conditions of perfect competition in the labour market, identical workers performing similar jobs will get same wage rate for their service. However, in practical sense, imperfect competition in the labour market is more common and thereby, workers derive different wages for the services rendered by them across different regions and occupations in a country and the various causes for wage differentials are discussed here under.

- ☆ ***Differences in demand conditions:*** Since, the demand for labour varies from one firm to another firm producing different goods and even among the firms that produce a homogenous good, the output levels will differ, thereby, demand level varies for the labour and accordingly, wage rates will fluctuate. The demand for labour also varies from place to place and in places, where there is abundant supply of labour, the wage rate of the labour will be low and *vice versa*.
- ☆ ***Differences in labour efficiency:*** The demand for labour also depends upon the efficiency of the labour and if the labour is more efficient and skilled, the wage rate will be more and *vice versa*.

- ☆ ***Availability of substitute*:** If a substitute (machinery) is available for labour, then the entrepreneur will substitute machinery usage for labour and thereby, demand for labour will decline and hence, wage rate will be low.
- ☆ ***Differences in labour supply*:** In some areas, the supply of labour will be more than their demand, thereby, the wage rate will be low.
- ☆ ***Degree of mobility may be low*:** Due to several factors, as discussed earlier, such as, social, cultural, ethical, economical, language barriers, family attachments *etc.*, the degree of mobility of labour may be low from one occupation to another occupation and this causes wage differentials among the workers working at different places.
- ☆ ***Differences in education, experience and efficiency*:** Workers differ in their education and experience status, thereby, they differ in working efficiency. The more is the working efficiency on the part of the workers, the more is the wage payment and *vice versa.*
- ☆ ***Permanency of the job*:** In general, the workers will be prepared to work at lower wages, provided the job is permanent. When the job assignment is purely temporary, the worker bargains for higher wages.
- ☆ ***Degree of bargaining power*:** If the trade union in a factory is strong enough for collective bargaining of high wage rates, its efforts will be fulfilled and the workers will get higher wages. On the other hand, if the trade union is weak, its efforts will be futile in increasing wage rate for the workers. So, the greater the bargaining power on the part of the workers (trade union), the higher the wage rates and *vice versa.*
- ☆ ***Risks involved*:** If the workers have to face more risk in executing the job assignment, they demand for higher wages and *vice versa*. For example, the workers functioning in forest area, local mines *etc.*, generally demand higher wages from the organization, as they have to face more degree of risk in executing their respective job duties.
- ☆ ***Future prospects*:** The future prospects of the worker vary from one occupation to another occupation. If a worker enjoys more future prospects in one job, he will accept that job even at low wage rate. On the contrary, if the worker believes less job prospects for him, he will continue in the same, if he derives a higher wage rate.
- ☆ ***Sex difference*:** This is one of the important factors that influences wage difference across the workers. In general, men workers were paid more wages compared to women workers and this is due to several reasons as mentioned below.
- ☆ The productivity contributed by women workers is low compared to men workers, as they are physically less strong compared to men.
- ☆ Women are more burdened with other duties like family care, children's care, house care *etc.*, thereby, they could not concentrate on job duties as efficiently as men.
- ☆ The areas of work for women labour are few compared to men labour.

- Women have to face many social and religious restrictions to come out of the family and to execute the jobs.
- Compared to men, the organizational power of women workers is weak, as they are burdened with other responsibilities, thereby, their bargaining power is low.
- ***Non-monetary benefits:*** The workers prefer for jobs even at low wage rates, provided they enjoy non-monetary benefits like job satisfaction, pleasantness at work, facilities provided by the organization, freedom in selecting the work schedule *etc.*
- ***Social prestige:*** Some workers desire to enjoy social prestige in rendering jobs and thereby, they even accept such jobs even at low wage rates. For example, a business man may earn more than an IAS officer, but the IAS officer enjoys more social prestige than the business man.
- ***In-born qualities:*** Some people like artists, singers, players *etc.*, have inborn qualities and thereby, they earn more remuneration compared to others.

The above discussion infers that, there are several factors that influence the wage differentials across the workers. But, the major influential factor is the difference between supply and demand forces. That means, in some occupations, demand for labour is more than their supply and in some other occupations, reverse is the case. In occupations, where demand is more than supply, the wages are more and in other occupations, where supply of workers is more than demand, wages are less. Further, differences in supply of workers across the occupations arise due to imperfect mobility of the workers. That means, workers cannot move freely across the occupations, as their occupational mobility is restricted by several factors (as discussed earlier) and this is also the major causal factor for wage differentials.

C. Fixation of Minimum Wages

In the context of exploitation of workers and wage differentials across the workers, the concept of fixation of minimum wages for the workers came into existence. In some industries, labour are not organized, as they are relatively small in number or scattered or due to illiteracy, thereby, entrepreneur exploits such labour by paying low wage rate than their MRP. Such industries are called 'Sweating industries'. So, the demand for fixation of minimum wages to the labour calls the Government to react by passing the enactments, such that, no entrepreneur should pay the wages below the prescribed minimum wages. For example, Government of India passed the 'Minimum Wages Act' in 1948. As shown in the Figure 3.11,

- OW is the equilibrium wage rate at which ON number of labour are employed.
- If the Government fixes the minimum wage rate above OW as OW_1, then at that OW_1 wage level, W_1D_1 is the demand for labour and W_1S_1 is the supply for labour, thereby, supply of labour (W_1S_1) > Demand for labour (W_1D_1) by D_1S_1.
- That means, due to fixation of minimum wage level (OW_1) above equilibrium wage level (OW), D_1S_1 is the total number of labour unemployed (observed

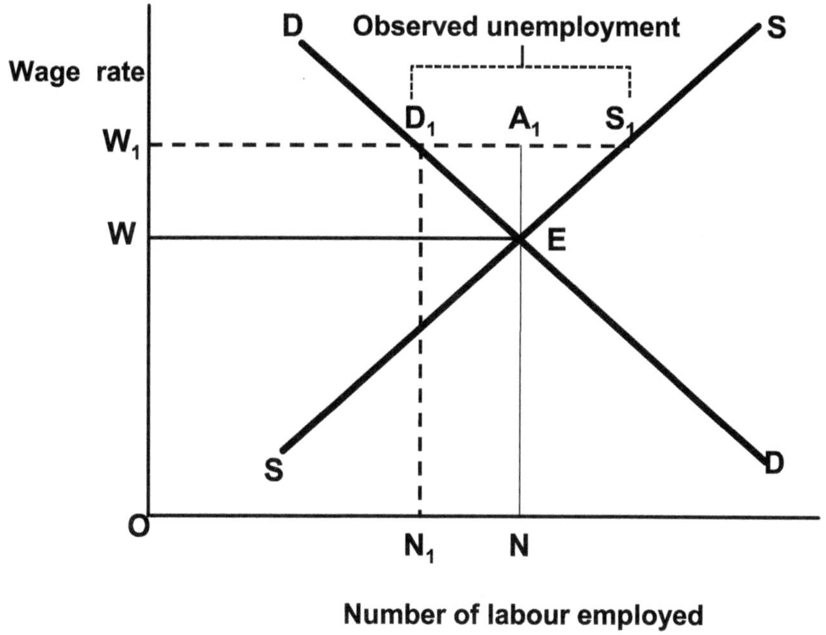

Figure 3.11: Effect of Minimum Wages on Labour Employment.

unemployment) and out of this D_1S_1 number, D_1A_1 is the decline in employment compared to equilibrium level of employment and A_1S_1 is the unemployment due to increase in number of labour supplied.

- Thus, observed unemployment D_1S_1 is higher than the reduction in employment D_1A_1 due to rise in minimum wage by the Government.

However, the extent of observed unemployment and decline in employment depends upon the relative elasticities of demand for and supply of labour force. The following are the two interesting cases:

- When the demand for labour is more inelastic than supply for labour (Panel A of the Figure 3.12), then the observed unemployment D_1S_1 is considerably higher than decline in employment N_1N due to fixation of minimum wage (OW_1) by the Government above the equilibrium wage (OW). That means, the decline in employment (N_1N) do not account much in observed unemployment (D_1S_1). Thus, at the minimum wage level, the decline in employment is low, but the supply of labour force is comparatively very high. Since, the decline in employment is at low scale, the fixation of minimum wage higher than the equilibrium wage can be justified.
- When the demand for labour is more elastic than supply of labour (Panel B of the Figure 3.12), then the decline in employment N_1N accounts much in the observed unemployment D_1S_1 due to fixation of minimum wage (OW_1) by the Government above the equilibrium wage (OW). Thus, at the minimum wage level (OW_1) the decline in employment N_1N is high and it occupies a

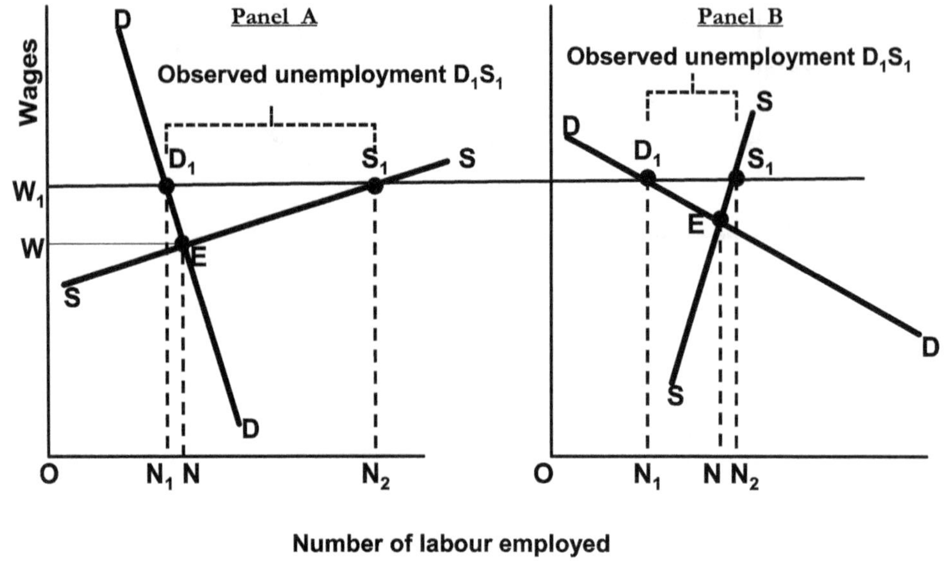

Figure 3.12: Effect of Minimum Wages on Labour Employment Depending upon the Relative Elasticities of Demand and Supply Forces.

significant share in the observed unemployment D_1S_1. Since, the decline in employment is significantly high, the fixation of minimum wage at such a high level cannot be justified.

It is important that, the minimum wage level fixed by the Government is not a fixed wage rate, but it will be fluctuating considering the inflationary pressures in the economy. So, whenever there is a change in the minimum wage level, the Government has to pass the legislation prescribing that wage level is minimum for the labour force till the new legislation is passed.

i. Merits of Fixing Minimum Wage Level

The following are the merits of fixing minimum wage level to the labour force by the Government.

- ☆ It helps the labour force to remove exploitation from the entrepreneur.
- ☆ When minimum wage is fixed above the equilibrium wage, it increases income on the part of labour, their standard of living will improve and their working efficiency will increase. When the productive capacity increases on the part of the workers, it guides the entrepreneur to update machinery and technology usage in the production programme.
- ☆ It ensures industrial peace, as trade unions has no much role to play regarding bargaining for higher wages.
- ☆ It makes the labour market perfect *i.e.,* supply curve of labour for the industry becomes perfectly elastic and it is parallel to X-axis, thereby, the industry can employ any number of labour at the minimum wage level and hence, the labour are not exploited by the entrepreneur.

- ☆ When minimum wage is fixed above the equilibrium wage, it increases income on the part of the labour, thereby, the demand for the products increases and it leads to more employment.
- ☆ It ensures equitable distribution of income among the labour force.

ii. Demerits of Fixing Minimum Wage Level

Though fixation of minimum wage level ensures benefits both to the work force and to the entrepreneurs, it too suffers from the following limitations:

- ☆ Sometimes, if the Government fixes the minimum wage level below the equilibrium wage level, the labour are greatly exploited by the entrepreneur.
- ☆ If minimum wage is fixed such that, it is same both for men and women, then it leads to total reshuffling of labour force in the production programme, as women labour are replaced by men labour, old labour may be replaced by youth *etc.*
- ☆ If minimum wages are fixed at higher level compared to equilibrium wage level, then it leads to decline in profits on the part of the entrepreneur. Further, the entrepreneur will substitute machinery for labour thereby, it leads to decline in employment of labour force.
- ☆ If minimum wages for labour are announced in one sector and not in other sector, it leads to wage-disparity or income-inequality among the wage earners.

D. Measures taken by the Government to Improve Economic Condition of Agricultural Labour

Soon after Independence, the both Central as well as the State Government have taken some measures to improve the economic condition of agricultural labour. They include:

- ☆ ***Passing of the Minimum Wage Act, 1948:*** In a labour surplus economy like India, wages couldn't be left to be determined entirely by forces of demand and supply, as it would lead to the fixation of wages at a very low level resulting in exploitation of less privileged class. Keeping this in view, the Government of India enacted the Minimum Wages Act, 1948. The purpose of the Act is to provide that, no employer shall pay wages to workers in certain categories of employments including agriculture, at a rate less than the minimum wage. In fact, the sole purpose of this Act is to prevent exploitation of sweated and unorganized labour (including agricultural labour), working in competitive market. The Act provides for fixation or periodic revision of minimum wages in employments where the labour is vulnerable to exploitation. As per this Act, every State Government was asked to fix minimum wages for agricultural labour. The minimum wages are fixed keeping in view the total costs and standard of living. Since, conditions in various parts of the country are different and even within a State, the Law allows different rates of wages to be fixed.

- ☆ ***Abolition of Bonded Labourers:*** Debt bondage in India is most prevalent in agricultural areas. Farmers taking small loans can find themselves paying interest on the loans that exceeds 100 percent of the loan per year. Debts that are not paid off in a debtor's lifetime can be passed down to their descendants, making the original debtor's family indebted to the families of rural landlords and money lenders, across multiple generations. The law dealing with bonded and forced labour was legislated by the Indian Parliament in 1976. The Bonded Labour System Abolition Act (1976) of India is quite extraordinary in that it recognizes: the overlap between forced labour and bonded labour in customary relationships, and also the manifestation of these relationships in contract labour and inter-state migration, and considers the nature of restraints suffered by the labourer as a result of the bonded/forced labour relationship, and makes all of these illegal.
- ☆ ***Providing land to landless labourers:*** Tenancy laws have been passed in most of the States protecting the interests of the tenants and labourers and enabling them to acquire the lands they cultivate. Many States have passed legislations by fixing ceiling on agricultural holdings by which the maximum amount of land which a person can hold has been fixed by law (Table 3.8). Land resettlement schemes were also executed and among these Bhoodan movement deserves special mention. This movement aimed at a solution of the problem of landless agricultural labourers by a redistribution of land on a voluntary basis. However, this movement, failed to solve the problem in a big way.
- ☆ ***Special Area Programmes:*** During the earlier seventies, Government implemented Small Farmers Development Agency and Marginal Farmers and Agricultural Labourers Development Agency Programmes *etc.*
- ☆ ***Special schemes for providing employment:*** They include:
    - ❑ Crash Scheme for Rural Employment (CSRE)
    - ❑ Pilot Intensive Rural Employment Project (PIREP)
    - ❑ Food for Works Programme (FWP)
    - ❑ National Rural Employment Programme (NREP)
    - ❑ Rural Landless Employment Programme (RLEP)
    - ❑ Drought Prone Area Programme (or Rural Works Programme)
    - ❑ Jawahar Rojgar Yojana (which come in with the merger of NREP and RLEGP)
    - ❑ Desert Development Programme
    - ❑ National Scheme of Training of Rural Youth for Self-Employment (TRYSEM)
    - ❑ Development of Women and Children in Rural Areas (DWCRA)
    - ❑ Abolition of Bonded Labourer Act

- Integrated Rural Development Programme (IRDP)
- MGNREGA Scheme

☆ ***Other measures:*** Various other measures are adopted by the Government from time-to-time to improve the living conditions of agricultural workers. For instance, promotion of cottage industries, village handicrafts and development of industrial estates in rural areas have created job opportunities for agricultural workers.

All the above measures were aimed at one or more of the following, so as to improve the socio-economic position of the agricultural labourers through:

☆ Better implementation of legislative measures
☆ Improvement of the bargaining position
☆ Creating alternative sources of employment
☆ Protection of women and child labourers
☆ Improving the working conditions
☆ Regulation of hours of work
☆ Improvements in agricultural sector
☆ Obtain credit at cheaper rates of interest on easy terms of payment for undertaking subsidiary occupation.
☆ Proper training for improving the skills of farm labourers
☆ Cooperative farming

E. Suggestions for Improving the Economic Conditions of Agricultural Labour

The following suggestions are made for improving the economic conditions of agricultural labourers:

☆ Legislative measures taken for the welfare of agricultural labour must be revised from time to time keeping the changing price trends in view.

☆ Alternative sources of employment by diversifying the enterprises on the farm must be created, so as to stabilize the annual income of agricultural labourers. The best strategy would be to promote labour intensive industries in rural areas. For this purpose facilities of power, finance and training to rural youth should be provided in the villages. This will reduce the dependence of agricultural workers on land and increase their incomes.

☆ Hours of work should be statutorily fixed and strictly enforced. In case of work beyond the stipulated hours, overtime payments should be made. Child labour should be totally banned.

☆ As the employment is season bound in farm sector, it is necessary to organize rural work programmes like construction of roads, school buildings, digging of canals, wells *etc.*, during off-season so that, employment can be provided to agricultural workers all the year round.

☆ State should provide essential food items to agricultural labourers through fair price shops to save them from purchasing at higher prices.

- ☆ Agricultural labour has no social security, no earned leave, no sick leave and no pension or gratuity. Substantial efforts should be directed in this field. Since, these labourers are not permanently attached to any employer, the task of providing social security is indeed a complex one. Thus, this responsibility has to be borne by the State.

The above measures can go a long way in solving most of the problems of agricultural labourers. In addition to the above measures, the points discussed with reference to measures for increasing farm labour efficiency also should be addressed to ensure fuller opportunities for work, better living of agricultural labourers and for increasing the efficiency of farm labour in performing farm operations. Even necessary legislative measures must be enforced to safeguard and promote the economic conditions of agricultural labourers.

F. Estimation of Demand and Supply for Agricultural Labour in a Village

The following is the procedure followed to analyze the demand supply gap of agricultural labour in a village:

- ☆ Assume total population of the village (Males+Females): 1000
- ☆ Assume potential labour in the village (16-60 years of age) : 70 percent
- ☆ So, potential labour units: (1000 x 70)/100 = 700
- ☆ Conversion factor: 2 men = 3 women (based on labour efficiency)
- ☆ Men labour units = (700 x 2)/5 = 280
- ☆ Women labour units = (700 x 3)/5 = 420

Man Working Days (MWD)

- ☆ Average number of working days in an agricultural year in any region (Single cropped area) : 130 MWD
- ☆ Average number of working days in an agricultural year in any region (Double cropped/Inter cropped area) : 190 MWD

Supply of labour

- ☆ ***Supply of labour in single cropped area:*** Total labour units available in single cropped area = 700 x 130 = 91000 MWD
- ☆ ***Supply of labour in Double/Inter cropped area:*** Total labour units available in Double/Inter cropped area = 700 x 190 = 133000 MWD

Demand for labour (Prepare for each crop)

Crops	*Area (ha)*	*MWD/ha*	*Total MWD*
Crop 1	100	120	12000
Crop 2	150	100	15000
Crop 3	90	110	9900
Total	**36900**		

Supply of labour units: 91000 MWD (Single cropped area)

Demand for labour : 36900 MWD

Surplus of labour: 54100 MWD

III. Capital Management

For most farm businesses, capital is not an infinite resource. Each farm business has a specified amount of capital and a unique blend of capital allocation based upon enterprise type or enterprises combination, scale of operation of enterprise, future plans of the farmer *etc.* Being a limited resource at the farmer's level, he has to consider its allocation and use in relation to both the operation of enterprises and future expansion of the firm. Capital is the third factor of production. It is that wealth, which assists in the production of further wealth. It is *'produced means of production'* or in other words *'man-made instrument of production'*. It includes all those goods, which are produced not for consumption, but for use in future production. Machines, tools and implements, irrigation infrastructure like drip irrigation, sprinkler irrigation, projects like canals and dams, stocks of raw materials, cash invested in business *etc.*, are some of the examples of capital. Thus, capital is the wealth which man acquires by his own labour and then uses it for producing more wealth. The above mentioned meaning of capital distinguishes it both from land and labour because, both land and labour are not produced factors, but are gifted by nature. Therefore, land and labour are called primary or original factors of production, whereas capital is man-made or produced factor of production. Capital is generally classified into working capital and fixed capital.

- ☆ ***Working Capital:*** It is important for the farmer to build and maintain an adequate level of working capital to conduct the day to day operations in the farm business. This capital is generally defined as cash and current assets that will be converted to cash within a 12 month period minus any payables and liabilities that require repayment within 12 months or in the same accounting year. For example, the expenditure incurred by the farmer towards seeds, fertilizers, pesticides *etc.*, falls under Working capital. That is, working capital comprises single-use producer goods like raw materials, which are used up on a single act of use. The costs incurred on these resources are included in variable costs and these costs should be recovered by the farmer from the TR in the same accounting year.
- ☆ ***Fixed Capital:*** Besides working capital, the farmer has to strengthen fixed capital in the farm business. Fixed capital is that portion of the total capital that is invested on fixed assets (such as land, buildings, machinery, plant and equipment, tractors, tools and implements etc) that stay in the business almost permanently, or at the very least, for more than one accounting period. Thus, fixed capital comprises durable-use producer goods, which are used in production again and again till they wear out. Fixed capital does not mean fixed in location. It is called so because, money spent upon durable-use goods like plant and machinery becomes 'fixed' for a long period, whereas money spent on raw materials (working capital) is released as soon as output produced with these raw materials is sold in the market.

Thus, fixed capital includes the resources like tractors, machinery, implements, farm buildings *etc.* These resources can be employed in the production programme for several production cycles. These resources cannot be stocked for a later period and their services are forthcoming like a flow and hence, they are considered as Flow resources. Since these resources does not get consumed in the production programme and only their services are available to the farmer for a longer period of time, the costs incurred on these resources cannot be included in TFC in producing the output. So, farmer need not recover these costs from the TR in the same accounting year. So instead of taking the original cost of an asset into consideration, only the cost of service is taken into consideration, as it is offering service for a fairly longer period to time. This cost of service is estimated indirectly. That means, if the asset is used on the farm continuously, its value will gradually decrease due to wear and tear and this declined value implies cost to the farmer. So, the farmer needs to keep some account of money aside to increase the value of asset to its original value by resorting to repairs and maintenance charges. As the years goes by, due to wear and tear, the asset value goes on decreasing. After sometime, the asset will be completely exhausted on account of use. A new asset must then be purchased requiring a large sum of money. If the whole amount of profit is withdrawn from TR each year without considering the loss on account of depreciation, necessary sum may not be available for buying the new asset. In such a case, the required money is to be collected by introducing fresh capital or by obtaining loan or by selling some other assets. Thus, to increase the value of the asset to its true value, the farmer should meet some expenses every year toward repairs and maintenance charges of the asset. This cost incurred by the farmer every year due to wear and tear of the capital equipment in the farm business is called Depreciation. So, Depreciation refers to declined value of a capital equipment or asset due to wear and tear and time in the production programme (Figure 3.13). It is, otherwise, defined as prorating the original cost of capital asset

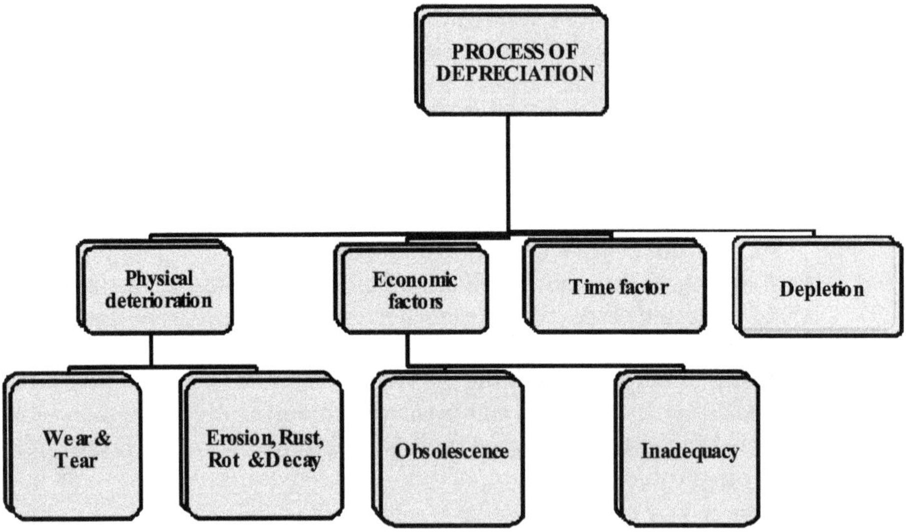

Figure 3.13: Process of Depreciation of Capital Asset.

over its lifetime. Depreciation may also be defined as the permanent and continuing diminution in the quality or the value of an asset (*William Pickles*). Depreciation is the gradual and permanent decrease in the value of an asset from any cause (*R.N. Carter*). Depreciation is charged on a continuous basis. Once the depreciation is charged, it must be charged on regular basis in the succeeding period also. Note that, depreciation is fall in the value of the fixed assets (except Land) only. Land can never be depreciated. Depreciable assets can be either tangible or intangible. Tangible depreciable assets (can readily see or touch) include livestock, machinery, buildings, dams, fences, irrigation tanks or irrigation systems. Intangible depreciable property (cannot readily see or touch) include computer software copyrights, patents *etc.*

A. Causes of Depreciation

The causes of depreciation can be due to physical deterioration, economic factors, the time factor, and depletion. These are briefly explained below:

i. Physical Deterioration

- ☆ ***Wear and Tear:*** When a machinery is used on the farm, it eventually wear out. Some machinery may last for many years, others last only a few years. This is also true for farm buildings, although some may last for a longer period of time.
- ☆ ***Erosion, Rust, Rot and Decay:*** When machinery is kept idle on the farm, its use efficiency may decrease because of rusting or corrosion. Similarly, land may be eroded or wasted away by the action of wind, rain and other elements of nature.

ii. Economic Factors

These factors make the asset to put out of use even though it is in good physical condition. These factors are related to obsolescence and inadequacy.

- ☆ ***Obsolescence:*** This is the process of becoming out of date. For example, over the years there has been great progress in the development of modern machinery with additional features. So, the old machinery will, therefore, become obsolete, and much of it will have been taken out of use by farm managers. Note that, when updated machinery is released into the market, it does not mean that the present asset used in the farm is worn out rather, it is outdated. Then the farm manager may even decide to sell this old machinery to others possibly because they cannot afford to buy new up-to-date equipment.
- ☆ ***Inadequacy:*** This arises, when an asset is no longer used because of the growth and changes in the size of the farm business. For example, a paddy thresher is operated by a farmer will become entirely inadequate, when the farmer expands the business. Then it will be found that it would be more efficient and economical to operate a combined harvester, and so the small size thresher will be put out of use by the farmer. Note that, in this case it does not mean that, the paddy thresher is neither no longer in good working condition nor that it is obsolete. It may be sold to another farmer operating small size of farm.

iii. Time Factor

Obviously time is needed for wear and tear, rusting, erosion, obsolescence and inadequacy to take place. However, there are some fixed assets to which the time factor is connected in a different way, as they enjoy legal life fixed in terms of years. For example, an entrepreneur may agree to rent a cold storage unit for ten years on lease-basis. When the years have passed, the lease is worth nothing to the entrepreneur. Similarly, if a person buys a patent, he is able to produce something. When the patent's time has finished, it then has no value.

iv. Depletion

Other assets are treated as waste, once the extraction of raw material is over from them. The extracted material can be used in the business or can be marketed outside to other businesses. Natural resources such as mines, quarries and oil wells, indiscriminate extraction of water from well etc., come under this heading.

Depreciation is otherwise called as Capital Consumption Allowance. That means. there is definite allowance on the part of capital to get consumed in the production process due to wear and tear while using the asset in use in the production programme. Depreciation is included in fixed cost because, even when there is no production programme, this cost will be incurred, as during the course of time, due to corrosion or rusting of the machinery, there will be decline in efficiency of the capital asset and thereby, its value will decrease. Thus, depreciation is a loss. Unless it is considered like all other expenses and losses, true profit or loss cannot be ascertained in the farm business. In other words, depreciation must be considered in order to work out true profit or loss of a business. Thus, depreciation must be considered as a part of the cost of production of commodities. Otherwise, the cost of production would be shown less than the true cost. Since, market price of the product is given at a point of time (assuming perfect market competition), if the cost of production of a commodity is shown less by ignoring depreciation, it may give a wrong picture that the farmer is enjoying higher profits in the business. That is, if loss on account of depreciation is not considered in determining profit (or loss) at the year end, profit will be shown more. If the excess profit is withdrawn, the working capital will gradually reduce, the business will become weak and its profit earning capacity will also fall. So, it is essential to compute depreciation of the farm asset every year and include it as one of the components of TFC in the business. While working out depreciation, the following are the important aspects needed:

- ☆ Original cost of the asset (say, machinery).
- ☆ *Number of years of useful life of asset:* It refers to the number of years of service provided by the asset to the farmer till it completely wears out.
- ☆ *Junk value/Scrap value/Salvage value:* It refers to value of the asset at the end of its useful life.

B. Methods to Compute Depreciation

There are six important methods to work out depreciation *viz.,* Straight line method, Diminishing balance method, Sum of the years digits method or Reducing fraction method, Compound interest method, Annual Revaluation method and

Machine hours basis method. Among these four methods, Straight line method is commonly followed.

i. Straight Line Method

It is a simple and most commonly followed method. This method is also known as Fixed installment method and Original cost method. In this method, the number of years of use is estimated and the total anticipated depreciation is then divided by the number of years to give the depreciation charge each year. Under this method, the amount of depreciation will be equal each year and this is the special feature of this method. If the annual depreciation is plotted on a graph paper, it will show a straight line, since the amount of depreciation is equal every year. This is why, this method is called Straight line method. The following is the formula employed to compute the annual depreciation of capital equipment:

Annual Depreciation = (Original cost – Junk value)/Number of years of useful life of asset

Original cost – Junk Value is called Total anticipated depreciation.

So, to calculate annual depreciation under the straight line method, simply divide the depreciable balance (Original cost – Junk value) by number of years of useful life of asset.

Example 3.5

Assume the following data: Original cost of the asset: = Rs. 40000, Junk value = Rs.2000, Useful life of asset = 10 years. Compute the year-wise depreciation of the asset up to its useful life.

Solution: Annual Depreciation = (40000-2000)/10 = 3800. Note that, in this method, the value of annual depreciation remains same throughout the life of the asset.

Years	*Annual Depreciation (Rs.)*	*Remaining value (Rs.)*
1	3800	40000 – 3800 = 36200
2	3800	36200 – 3800 = 32400
3	3800	32400– 3800 =28600
4	3800	28600– 3800 = 24800
5	3800	24800– 3800 = 21000
6	3800	2100– 3800 = 17200
7	3800	17200– 3800 = 13400
8	3800	13400– 3800 = 9600
9	3800	9600– 3800 = 5800
10	3800	5800– 3800 = 2000 (Junk Value)

This Straight line method is very easy to employ because of its simplicity, But, this method suffers from the limitation that, it assumes the same economic usefulness of the asset each year thereby, the repairs and maintenance expenses are essentially same each period. This is not true.

ii. Reducing Balance Method or Diminishing Balance Method

In this method, a fixed or constant rate of depreciation is used every year and applied to the value of the asset at the beginning of every year. So, in this method, junk value is not deducted and instead a fixed rate of depreciation is used every year. The fixed rate of depreciation to be charged over the useful life of the asset is computed by dividing 100 per cent with the useful life of the asset. Say, if the useful life of the asset is 10 years, then rate of depreciation will be (100/10) = 10 per cent. There is another methodology to compute rate of depreciation provided the following data are known: original cost of the asset, useful life of the asset and junk value of the asset. The formula is given by:

Rate of Depreciation 'r' = $1 - (J/O)^{1/n}$

where, n = Useful life of the asset (years), J = Junk value of the asset (Rs.) and O = Original cost of the asset (Rs.). Say, for example, an asset was acquired for Rs.1,050 with an expected useful life of five years and a junk value of Rs.50. By using the above formula, the annual rate (r) would be 45.6 per cent. Similarly, assume n = 3 years, O = Rs. 64,000 and J = 1,000,000. Then, rate of depreciation r = $1 - (64{,}000/1{,}000{,}000)^{1/3}$ = = 1 – (40/100) = 60 per cent. Since this depreciation rate per cent is applied on reducing balance of asset, this method is called reducing balance method or diminishing balance method.

According to this method, as the value of asset goes on diminishing year after year, the amount of depreciation charged every year also goes on diminishing. This method is normally applied on those assets, which demand large repair expenses and purchase and sale of assets is also very common. Also appropriate for assets, which lose value quickly in the early year, which become outdated/obsolete and enjoy higher utility in the earlier years of its life. But, the demerit of this method is that, for assets which have a short life, the percentage used to calculate depreciation is very large.

Example 3.6

Assume the following data: Original cost of the asset: 40,000/-, Fixed rate of depreciation: 20 percent, Number of years of useful life: 10 years. Compute the year-wise depreciation of the asset up to its useful life.

Years	*Value of the Asset at the Beginning of Each Year (Rs.)*	*Annual Depreciation (Rs.)*	*Remaining Value (Rs.)*
1	40000.000	(40000*20 per cent) = 8000.00	40000-8000 = 32000.00
2	32000.00	(32000*20 per cent) =6400.00	32000-6400 = 25600.00
3	25600.00	5120.00	20480.00
4	20480.00	4096.00	16384.00
5	16384.00	3276.80	13107.20
6	13107.20	2621.44	10485.76

Years	Value of the Asset at the Beginning of Each Year (Rs.)	Annual Depreciation (Rs.)	Remaining Value (Rs.)
7	10485.76	2097.15	8388.61
8	8388.61	1677.72	6710.89
9	6710.89	1342.18	5368.71
10	5368.71	1073.74	4294.97

Note: Total Depreciation (35705) + Junk value (4295) = Original cost (40000).

Straight Line Method vs Diminishing Balance Method

Following are the main points of difference between straight line method and Diminishing balance method of depreciation:

Straight Line Method	Diminishing Balance Method
Fixed amount is charged.	Fixed rate is charged.
The amount of depreciation per year remains same.	The amount of depreciation goes on reducing.
The older the asset the larger the cost of its repair. But the amount of depreciation remains the same each year. Hence, the total of depreciation and repairs increases every year. This reduces annual profit gradually.	The amount of depreciation decreases gradually, while the cost of repairs increases. So the total of depreciation and repairs remain more or less the same each year. Hence, it causes little or no change in annual profit/loss.
Computation of depreciation under straight line method is comparatively easy and simple	Depreciation can be computed without any difficulty, but it is not easy and simple

In computing annual depreciation by this method, the fixed rates of depreciation followed for different farm assets are listed here under (Dhondyal):

- ☆ **Bullocks:** 10 per cent
- ☆ **Buildings:**
  - ❑ *Pucca buildings:* 2-5 per cent
  - ❑ *Katcha buildings:* 5-10 per cent
- ☆ **Implements and Machinery**
  - ❑ *Ploughs and harrows:* 10 per cent
  - ❑ *Water lifts:* 5 per cent
  - ❑ *Tractor:* 5 per cent
  - ❑ *Harvester:* 20 per cent or 2000 crop ha. harvested
  - ❑ *Thresher:* 16 per cent or 4 M. Tonnes of grain harvested
  - ❑ *Crow bar:* 10 per cent
  - ❑ *Sickle:* 100 per cent
- ☆ **Fencing:** 5 per cent

☆ **Wells**

- ❑ *Tube well :* 10-12 per cent
- ❑ *Pucca well :* 3 per cent
- ❑ *Katcha well :* 15-20 per cent

☆ **Pucca drains :** 5 per cent

☆ **Irrigation channels :** 5 per cent

iii. Sum of the Years Digit Method or Reducing Fraction Method

In this method, the basic assumption is that, depreciation expenses will be distributed in excess in the early years of use of asset and less in the later years because, the value of the asset at later years is already low. Hence, in this method, first total anticipated depreciation is worked out and this value is multiplied with the fraction of each year of life of asset. The fraction of each year is worked out as follows:

Fraction of each year is given by the formula:

Years of life of asset remaining at the beginning of each accounting period/Sum of the years of asset

To get the sum of years of the asset, employ the formula: [n(n+1)/2], where 'n' is the number of years of useful life of asset. Thus, this method simply sums up the years in an asset's lifespan to be used as denominator, and reverses the individual year numbers to be used as numerator. It normally applied to fairly long lived assets.

Annual Depreciation = (Original cost of asset – Junk value) x Fraction of each year.

Example 3.7

Assume the following data: Original cost of the asset: = Rs. 40000, Junk value= Rs.2000, Useful life of asset = 10 years. Compute the year-wise depreciation of the asset up to its useful life.

Years	*Value of Asset at the Beginning of Each Year (Rs.)*	*Fraction for Each Year*	*Annual Depreciation (Rs.)*	*Remaining Value (Rs.)*
1	40000.00	10/55	(40000-2000)x10/55 =6909.09	33090.91
2	33090.91	9/55	(40000-2000)x9/55=6218.18	26872.73
3	26872.73	8/55	(40000-2000)x8/55 = 5527.27	21345.45
4	21345.45	7/55	(40000-2000)*7/55=4836.36	16509.09
5	16509.09	6/55	(40000-2000)*6/55=4145.45	12363.64
6	12363.64	5/55	(40000-2000)*5/55=3454.55	8909.09
7	8909.09	4/55	(40000-2000)*4/55=2763.64	6145.45
8	6145.45	3/55	(40000-2000)*3/55=2072.73	4072.73
9	4072.73	2/55	(40000-2000)*2/55=1381.82	2690.91
10	2690.91	1/55	(40000-2000)*1/55=690.91	2000.00 (Junk Value)

Years	Straight Line Method	Diminishing Balance Method	Reducing Fraction Method
1	3800.00	8000.00	6909.09
2	3800.00	6400.00	6218.18
3	3800.00	5120.00	5527.27
4	3800.00	4096.00	4836.36
5	3800.00	3276.80	4145.45
6	3800.00	2621.44	3454.55
7	3800.00	2097.15	2763.64
8	3800.00	1677.72	2072.73
9	3800.00	1342.18	1381.82
10	3800.00	1073.74	690.91

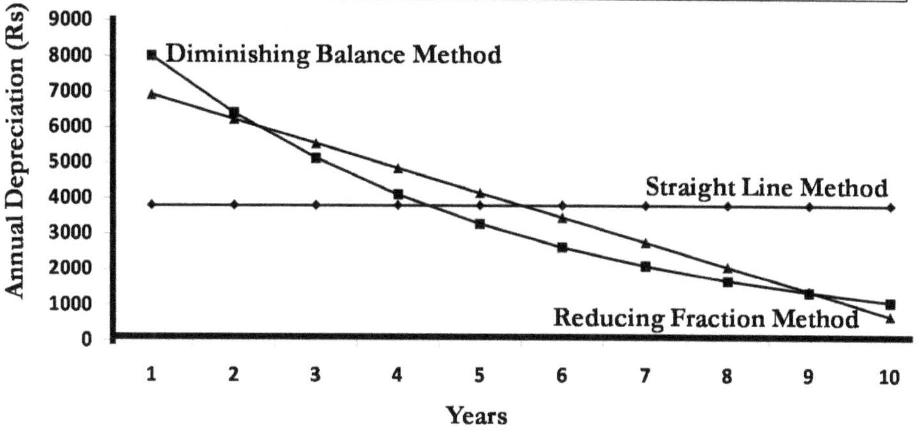

Figure 3.14: Annual Depreciation Across Three Methods – Comparative Picture.

Thus, it may be seen that (Figure 3.14), under the straight line method, equal amounts are subtracted every year, while in the sum of years digit method, the depreciation is faster during earlier years than during the later years and in diminishing balance method, the annual depreciation rate remains same across the useful years of life of asset. The diminishing balance method presupposes that, there is a scrap value for every commodity. The diminishing balance and sum of years digit methods are to be used, when the farmer expects bigger return to his investment during the first few years.

iv. Compound Interest Method

This method is also called as Depreciation fund method, as this method assumes that, depreciation fund will be re-invested in the business and this fund will grow at a compound rate of interest. So, in using the capital equipment, some fixed amount will be kept aside every year to the extent of depreciated amount to re-invest the total sum again in the business. Since, compound interest method is considered in estimating the depreciation fund every year, its value will increase every year. Any difference between the purchase price of the new asset and depreciation fund is adjusted by a debit or credit to the profit and loss account of that year. This method of computing depreciation is followed for machinery, as it provides ready money for the replacement of that asset without disturbing the financial position of the business.

Example 3.8

Assume the following data: Original cost of the asset: = Rs. 92000, Useful life of asset = 10 years, Market rate of interest: 10 per cent. Compute the year-wise depreciation of the asset up to its useful life.

Solution: With 10 per cent rate of interest, at the end of first year, the depreciation charges will be Rs.9200 (*i.e.*, 92000*0.1=Rs.9200). So, the depreciation fund for the first year will be Rs.9200. Regarding depreciation charges for the second year = Cumulative depreciation fund at the end of first year + (Cumulative depreciation fund at the end of first year * Depreciation rate) *i.e.*, 9200 + (9200*0.1)=Rs.10120. Similarly, depreciation charges for the third year = Cumulative depreciation fund at the end of first year + (Cumulative depreciation fund at the end of second year * Depreciation rate) *i.e.* (9200 + (19320*0.1)=Rs.11132. Similarly, depreciation charges for fourth year = Cumulative depreciation fund at the end of first year + (Cumulative depreciation fund at the end of fourth year*Depreciation rate) *i.e.* (9200 + (30452*0.1)=Rs.12245.20. Likewise, both depreciation and cumulative depreciation fund at the end of each year is calculated. It is clear from the Table 3.17 that, the total depreciation fund is Rs.146624 computed at a rate of interest of 10 per cent employed by compound method. This implies that, Rs.146624 is needed to replace that asset after 10 years in a farm business.

Table 3.17: Computation of Annual Depreciation by Compound Interest Method

Years	*Value of Asset at the Beginning of Each Year (Rs.)*	*Depreciation @10 per cent*	*Cumulative Depreciation Fund at the End of Each Year (Rs.)*
1	92000	9200.00	9200.00
2		(9200+(9200*0.1)=10120.00	(9200+10120)=19320.00
3		(9200+(19320*0.1)=11132.00	(19320+11132)=30452.00
4		(9200+(30452*0.1)=12245.20	(30452+12245.20)=42697.20
5		13469.72	56166.92
6		14816.69	70983.61
7		16298.36	87281.97
8		17928.20	105210.17
9		19721.02	124931.19
10		21693.12	146624.31

v. Annual Revaluation Method

In this method, the value of asset is determined both at the beginning and at the end of an accounting year and this difference in value of asset is taken as annual depreciation. That is, under this method, the assets are revalued each year. This method is normally adapted to charge depreciation on numerous inexpensive fixed assets like small tools, live stock and other assets of such nature, which are constantly changing and their period of life is most uncertain. Excess of the opening over the closing inventory thus gives the periodic depreciation expenses. However, this method has the limitation, when there are greater fluctuations in the prices of the assets. This method is also not suitable to assets like machinery, buildings *etc.*, that are not bought and sold very frequently. However, this method is useful in case of livestock in the early years of life *i.e.*, in the appreciating phase. Let us look at the following example: assume, the value of tools at the beginning of the year was Rs.25,000, and during the current year tools worth of Rs.28000 were purchased. At the end of the year, revaluation was undertaken and it amounted to Rs.50,000. Then the amount of depreciation for that year will be: [(25000+28000) – 50000] = Rs.3000. Thus, excess of the opening over the closing inventory gives the periodic depreciation expenses. This method is very simple, as the amount of loss can be ascertained very easily. But, the demerit is that, the valuation of asset year is very time consuming.

vi. Machine Hours Basis Method

This method considers the number of hours the machine runs every year and based on this, depreciation rate per hour will be calculated. In employing this method, it is essential on the part of the farmer to maintain a work hour chart for the machinery to have the information regarding the number of hours it works/runs on the farm. Let us look at the following example:

Example 3.9

Assume the following data: Original cost of the asset (machinery): = Rs. 40000, Junk value= Rs.2000, Useful life of asset = 10 years. The machinery is expected to run 1000 hours per year on an average. Compute the depreciation charges per hour of the machinery up to its useful life.

Solution: Total anticipated depreciation = Rs.40000-Rs.2000 = Rs.38000

Total working hours of machinery = 1000 * 10 = 10000 hours in a span of 10 years

So, depreciation charges per hour = 38000/10000 = Rs. 3.80/hour.

C. Points to be Remembered in Computing Depreciation

They include:

- ☆ The data on original cost of the asset should be collected as far as possible from the farm records. If the farmer do not maintain farm records, repetitive enquires should be made to ascertain the true or original cost of the asset.
- ☆ The junk value of the asset and expected useful life are purely hypothetical values and they should be obtained based on the expertise of the farmer or from the farmers using the similar assets for a fairly longer period of time. Some assets enjoy useful life more than the expected life and in such case, suitable adjustments must be made to compute the annual depreciation of the asset.
- ☆ Minor repairs like use of oils, lubricants *etc.*, need not be included under depreciation charges. However, if major repairs are performed like re-modelling of buildings, additional charges must be added to the existing value of the asset.

- ☆ In case of small tool like sickles, which are used up within one agricultural year, depreciation should be taken as 100 percent.
- ☆ In case of livestock, at breeding phase or appreciation phase, annual revaluation method will be more useful. However, when they start depreciating say, after three years, Straight line method would be more appropriate.

Note that, every method of computing annual depreciation has its own strength and weaknesses and the selection of a particular method depends upon the nature of capital asset under consideration. In most cases, Straight line method is commonly followed.

D. Depreciation vs Obsolescence of a Capital Asset

- ☆ ***Depreciation:*** It is a gradual deterioration or decrease in the value of a capital asset after using that asset in day to day farm operations or after spending of time. In this world, everything is perishable and so to compute the true value of any asset at present time, it is very necessary to compute depreciation on fixed asset and deduct from it.
- ☆ ***Obsolescence:*** When new fixed assets' quality, efficiency and capacity decrease the value and usability of old fixed assets, then it is called obsolescence of old fixed assets. In general, every new equipment decreases the value of previous equipment. Thus, obsolescence is not related to the nature and use of fixed asset and this is where, it differs from depreciation. Thus, we can say, Obsolescence of fixed assets is a process of depreciation due to technological progress. There are two forms of obsolescence: first, is the reduction in the cost of reproduction of new asset due to increased productivity in the industry that manufactures them (*i.e.*, new machinery are becoming cheaper) and the second form of obsolescence associated with the emergence of new, better and more productive analogues of existing machinery and equipment.

E. Farm Machinery Decisions

Regarding capital management, say with reference to purchase of machinery, the following are the points to be considered:

- ☆ Depreciation on capital equipment (say, machinery) occurs due to both time and use.
- ☆ The total costs of owning and using the machinery involves the sum of fixed costs and variable costs. The fixed costs of machinery include the costs, which remain constant irrespective of use of machinery such as depreciation due to time (weather conditions), obsolescence *etc.* The variable costs of machinery include the costs, which vary with the use of machinery. For example, depreciation due to use is a variable cost. Compared to fixed costs, variable costs of using machinery are small because, machinery usage generally last for about less than one month per year.

- In owning the machinery, it is essential to consider the additional costs incurred in using the machinery. However, the costs which occur even if the machinery is not brought are excluded when figuring the cost of owning the machinery. This concept can be better understood from the following examples:
  - All fuel and lubricant costs fall under added costs, so they are considered while owning the machinery.
  - If the farmer had a pair of bullocks and an implement is to be purchased to be drawn by the bullocks, the feed costs of the bullocks should not be considered in purchasing the implement, as the bullocks have to be fed, whether the farmer purchases the implement or not. On the other hand, if additional draft animals are added to drag the implements, then feed costs must be considered.
  - Repairs and maintenance charges are inescapable added costs, while owning the machinery.
  - When the farmer owns the shed to stock the machinery, the annual depreciation costs of the shed or depreciation of machinery due to weather need not be considered while owning the machinery. Otherwise, if more housing space is to be provided in the shed, then the annual costs on providing more shed space or the depreciation charges due to weather (if machinery is exposed to weather all the year) must be considered under added costs.
  - Insurance charges for machinery are always an added cost, while owning the machinery.
  - When farm manager or his family labour can themselves operate the machinery, the labour costs need not be considered as an added cost. However, if a skilled worker is to be engaged to operate the machinery, then the labour wage is to be considered as an added cost, while owning the machinery.
  - If the farmer purchases the machinery by borrowing the capital, the interest on borrowed capital is an added cost. On the other hand, if the farmer purchases the machinery from his owned capital, the opportunity cost of capital must be considered.

  In addition to the above factors, the farmer must consider the costs that he may incur in the future (*i.e.*, after owning the machinery) like accidental breakage of parts, possible obsolescence due to technological breakthrough, changes in production plans and farming practices *etc.*, while owning the machinery.

- Generally, farmer prefer to own the machinery, when its use is high or frequent on the farm thereby, the ratio of annual cost on the use of machinery to output produced or annual cost on the use of machinery to substituted labour cost is low. Since, machinery use on the farm is limited for a smaller period of time, it is essential on the part of the farmer to select the machinery that have low initial cost and preferably have more useful life.

☆ It is a known fact that, by delaying the farm operations like sowing of seeds, inter-cultivation *etc.* (due to labour shortage), the yields of crops get affected. So, the farmer should plan for desired size of machinery that brings in timeliness of farm operations. Since, the firms in the market offer different sizes of machinery, it is essential on the part of the farmer to select the desired size considering the follows factors.

- ***Initial cost of the machinery:*** Generally, farmers prefer low initial cost machinery to high cost machinery, as for the latter, the added costs like depreciation, annual maintenance, insurance charges *etc.*, will be much higher compared to the former. The higher initial cost plus higher added costs of a machinery may not contribute much to offset the saved labour costs.
- ***Annual use of the machinery on the farm:*** Annual use of machinery on the farm counts much in deciding the size of machinery to be purchased. In small farms, there is less scope for the use of machinery and hence, the farmers generally prefer small size machinery. If small farmer purchase large size machinery, its unit fixed cost per usage of machinery will be very high, unless the farmer goes for providing the machinery for hire purpose outside, joint farming with neighbouring farmers *etc.* In case of large farms, the farmer can go for large size machinery, as the higher annual use of machinery contribute to lower unit fixed costs even when compared to small farms.

- ***Number of labour displaced by the machinery i.e., capital-labour ratio:*** The number of labour displaced by the machinery counts much in selecting the size of machinery. In case of large farms, where there is more severity of labour shortage, lage-size machinery is useful. When a small farmer faces with limited capital, less annual use of machinery and ample supply of labour in that locality, it is better for the farmer to prefer small-size machinery.
- ***Relative values of capital and labour on the farm:*** Let us go through the following Table 3.18 (hypothetical data):

Table 3.18: Comparison between Total Costs of Using the different Sized Grain Drills in Two different Sized Farms

Items	*Labour @Rs.10/hour*				*Labour @ Rs.20/hour*			
	12x7 Drill		*24x7 Drill*		*12x7 Drill*		*24x7 Drill*	
Acres	10	25	10	25	10	25	10	25
Machine cost (Unit fixed cost per year)	100	50	150	80	100	50	150	80
Power cost (Only added cost)	50	50	30	30	50	50	30	30
Labour cost	70	70	45	45	210	210	100	100
Total costs/acre	220	170	225	155	360	310	280	210

It is the evident from the Table 3.18 that,

- When the labour charges are low (*i.e.,* Rs.10/hour), small sized grain drill is more economical for 10 acres of land use for year (Rs.220/acre) compared to large sized grain drill (Rs. 225/acre). However, with in this lower labour cost @Rs.10/hour, the large sized grain drill drills the grain more cheaply (Rs.155/acre) than the small sized grain drill, when the land use is 25 acres per year.
- Within the small sized grain drill, at their lower labour cost of Rs. 10/hour, when the land size is 25 acres (*i.e.,* when the annual use of grain drill is more), the total costs/acre is cheaper (Rs.170/acre) compared to 10 acres of land use per year (Rs.220/acre).
- With labour charges @Rs.20/hour, same is the case with reference to large-sized drill, which drills the grain more efficiently than the small-sized grain drill, whether the land use is 10 acres or 25 acres per year.

  This clearly infers that, the higher machinery costs of large sized grain drill is offsetted by the still higher savings of labour costs and power costs, especially when the labour wages are more and land area is more. Thus, when the farmer faces the problem of limited labour supply and ample capital, it is better to employ large-sized machinery, as it economizes the annual cost expenditure on the part of the farmer. But, on farms, where capital supply is limited, it is better to economize on size of the machinery. Thus, the availability of capital with the farmer and labour supply determine the size of machinery to be used on the farms.

☆ The farmer generally applies the principle of opportunity cost in deciding between animal power and purchase of machinery (say, tractor). So, a farmer goes for mechanization of farm operations, if the opportunity cost of investment on animal power is lower than the returns derived due to use of mechanical power on the farm. Since mechanization of farm operations calls for re-arrangement of size and shape of farm fields, these costs should also be taken into consideration for analyzing the substitution rate of mechanical power to animal power. The substitution of machinery for labour can be done in three ways *viz.,* changing methods from hand to machine, changing type of machines and increasing the size of machines.

- ***Changing methods from hand to machine:*** In this case, human labour is replaced by the employment of machinery in performing farm operations. For example, weeding by rotary weeder instead of human labour in SRI technology of paddy production, mechanical picking of cotton (kapas) instead of hand picking *etc.*
- ***Changing type of machines:*** In this case, the combinations of labour and machinery is taken into consideration in terms of substitution rate, relative prices of machinery (rental value) and labour (wage rate) and annual usage of machinery on the farm. Considering the above three

aspects, low cost combination of labour and machinery is taken into consideration for mechanization of farm operations.

- ❑ ***Changing size of machines:*** In this case, large machines are substituted for small machines and then, machinery service substitute human labour. But, this is followed, when the extent of substitution of human labour is increased with increase in size of the machine *i.e.*, the extent of labour and power saved by the large sized machine is enough to offset its higher costs.

☆ ***Application of Time comparison principle regarding the purchase of machinery to meet weather risk or uncertainty:*** We know, machinery purchased by the farmer fall under long term investment and the investment in machinery involves tie up of funds for several years. This calls for the application of time comparison principle and this suggests that, whether the farmer has to go for investment or not? Assume the case that, severe cyclone rains coincide with the harvesting of crop X in a farm area of 50 acres in Nandyal region of Andhra Pradesh. As a result of this, the farmer wishes to purchase a machinery (harvester) worth of Rs. 7,00,000 to overcome the losses of crop X. Let us now analyze, whether it is beneficial for the farmer to go for purchasing machinery or not and consider this under two situations *viz.*, when the capital is unlimited with the farmer and when the capital is limited with the farmer.

i. ***When the capital is unlimited with the farmer:*** As discussed earlier, when the capital is unlimited with the farmer, the present value of net income is discounted at market rate of interest (say, 10 per cent) and the same is through Table 3.19. The NPV of investment on machinery is Rs. 12.450 lakhs. This implies that, if the farmer can get no more than

Table 3.19: Present Value of Net Returns from a Farm (Case of Unlimited Capital with the farmer)

Years	*Net Returns (Rs.)*	*df 10 per cent*	*NPV (Rs.)*
1	1.84	0.909	1.673
2	2.16	0.826	1.785
3	1.94	0.751	1.458
4	2.21	0.683	1.509
5	1.69	0.621	1.049
6	1.96	0.564	1.106
7	1.87	0.513	0.960
8	1.74	0.467	0.812
9	1.56	0.424	0.662
10	1.91	0.386	0.736
11	1.06	0.350	0.372
12	1.03	0.319	0.328
		NPV	12.450

10 per cent of returns on money invested elsewhere, he can profitably invest to purchase the harvester at present, as it ensure timeliness of harvesting of crop soon after the forecast of cyclonic rains. Thus, this investment on machinery prevents losses of crop yield due to weather risk or uncertainty.

ii. ***When the capital is limited with the farmer:*** We already know, when the capital is limited with the farmer, the present value of net income is discounted at the rate of return obtained on the next best alternative enterprise (say, 30 per cent). The findings through Table 3.20 reveals that, NPV of investment on machinery is Rs. 6.112 lakhs at a discount factor of 30 percent. This infers that, NPV of Rs.6.112 lakhs is less than the present investment of Rs.7,00,000 and thus it is profitable for the farmer to invest on alternate enterprise (opportunity cost of present investment on harvester) rather than investing on harvester.

Table 3.20: Present Value of Net Returns from a Farm (Case of Limited Capital with the farmer)

Years	*Net Returns (Rs.)*	*df 30 per cent*	*NPV (Rs.)*
1	1.84	0.769	1.415
2	2.16	0.592	1.278
3	1.94	0.455	0.883
4	2.21	0.350	0.774
5	1.69	0.269	0.455
6	1.96	0.207	0.406
7	1.87	0.159	0.298
8	1.74	0.123	0.213
9	1.56	0.094	0.147
10	1.91	0.073	0.139
11	1.06	0.056	0.059
12	1.03	0.043	0.044
		NPV	6.112

Thus, the time comparison principle guide the farmer, whether he has to go for machinery investment considering the weather risk in that locality.

☆ ***Purchase of machinery considering the price risk:*** Not only weather risk, the farmers must also consider price risk in making investment on machinery. We already know, the total costs incurred on machinery include both fixed and variable costs. The investment made on the machinery falls under fixed cost. Other costs like depreciation, insurance, annual installment of term loan *etc.*, also fall under fixed costs, as the annual use of machinery does not influence these costs. Note that, if higher market prices and purchase of machinery coincides, the fixed costs on the machinery are also high. Even when the prices of machinery falls in the market, the fixed cost of machinery already purchased will not get altered. If this higher fixed cost on machinery is accompanied by lower outputs of the farm, then it is difficult for the farmer to cope up with the situation. However, if total costs of the machinery comprises large portion of the variable costs, then fall in prices of farm output can be adjusted through cutting back the production to reduce the costs. So, in case of price uncertainties, it is advisable for the farmer to reduce the investment on machinery or purchase low cost machinery. If farm output prices drastically fall, then it is better on the part of the farmer to postpone the machinery purchase, till market prices shoot up in the market for farm products and in the mean time, he has to carry the farm operations through custom hiring of machinery.

☆ The factors that influence the use of owned machinery (*i.e.*, purchase of machinery by the farm) vis-à-vis custom hiring of machinery are as follows:
  - ❑ Low annual use of machinery on the farm makes the farmer to hire the machinery instead of purchasing or owning the machinery.
  - ❑ Higher initial cost of new machinery to be purchased makes the farmer to hire the machinery rather than owning it.
  - ❑ If the farmer has to perform the operations timely, it is better for the farmer to go for owning the machinery rather than hiring it.
  - ❑ When the purchase of new machinery involves higher opportunity cost, it is better for the farmer to go for hiring the machinery.
  - ❑ To ensure quality work on the farm, it is better for the farmer to go for owning the machinery.
  - ❑ If custom operators have newer and efficient machines and if their service is readily available, it is better to go for custom hiring of the machinery.
  - ❑ If hiring charges of machinery are drastically higher because of its limited availability in that locality, it is better to go for owning the machinery keeping in view of its useful life.
  - ❑ Expected changes on costs and hired charges of machinery.
  - ❑ Expected changes in labour and capital supply to the farmer.

☆ Machinery management not only involve taking wise decisions regarding purchase of right type of machinery, but also involve efficient use of machinery by managing it scientifically. The management of purchased machinery must address the following aspects:
  - ❑ Use only quality fuel, lubricants and do not give emphasis for cost effectiveness.
  - ❑ Avoid overloading of machinery, as it may lead to higher repair cost.
  - ❑ Tractor speed should be maintained as per the recommendations made by the firm.
  - ❑ Machinery should be properly housed so that, depreciation on the machines due to weather is transferred from the machines to the machine shed or house.

- Pucca shed or Kaccha shed may be constructed depending upon the capital available with the farmer to protect the machinery from adverse weather, Irrespective of the type of house built, the farmer must maintain repairs workshop, so as to service the machines as and when required.

F. Farm Buildings Management

The money spent on other resources like land, labour, capital and machinery aims at bringing more returns in the farm business. In the similar way, money spent on the construction of farm buildings must aim at bringing highest returns to the farm. This farm buildings increase returns in the farm business through:

- ☆ Saving the labour costs, as building service combines with certain number of labour to produce a given level of output on the farm.
- ☆ By stocking the machinery in the buildings with repairs workshop, it helps to maintain machinery in good working condition. When the machinery is not housed properly, it takes more time to get machinery to put into operation. Further, housing of machinery in the buildings facilitates to repair them during off-season, when the labour costs are more. Thus, construction of farm buildings saves labour cost on the farm.
- ☆ Stocking the produce thereby, creating time utility.
- ☆ Stocking the inputs.
- ☆ Shelter the implements and machinery and thereby, checks the depreciation losses.
- ☆ Maintain the quality of produce and inputs.
- ☆ Prevent storage losses of farm produce due to pest, diseases, rodents *etc.*

Considering the above merits of construction and maintenance of farm buildings, the farmer should ascertain the probability of using the investment funds. Further, providing more building services must be taken into consideration as long as the added returns are greater than the average costs. But, note that, farm buildings with both capital-saving and labour-saving designs are rare in farm sector. This is because, if farmer aims at labour saving, he has to go for additional building investment.

When the farmer faces limited labour supply relative to capital, he can substitute farm buildings for labour as long as the savings of labour cost is greater than added cost of buildings. On the contrary, when labour supply is more relative to capital, it is better for the farmer to go low cost farm structures (say temporary or Kaccha buildings) and it also helps the farmer to release capital investment for the enterprises on the farm. The above discussion infers that, supply of labour relative to availability of capital enable the farmer to decide upon construction of farm buildings. The decisions regarding farm buildings management include:

- ☆ Location of buildings also counts much in the efficient use of farm labour. It is very much essential on the part of the farmer to plan for the amount of capital to be invested, type of farm buildings to be constructed (*i.e.*, Pucca or Kaccha buildings), their location on the farm *etc.*, at the beginning itself before going for actual implementation of the plan. Also note that, once designed and executed the plan, it is difficult to change the design and locality of the buildings. So, while planning the construction of farm buildings, think about flexibility *i.e.*, construct the building such that, it suits to various possible enterprises that may be planned on the farm.

- ☆ The flexibility of farm buildings not only ensure efficient use of labour, but also ensure their adaptability to more number of enterprises and ties up less capital for a shorter periods of time. When the capital is limited with the farmer and when the chances of obsolescence are great, flexibility of farm buildings assume greater importance.
- ☆ Internal re-modelling should also be considered even at the planning stage of the construction of the farm buildings. This is because, internal arrangement in the buildings influences the efficiency of labour irrespective of the location of the buildings.
- ☆ Note that, flexibility of buildings used alternatively for two enterprises may be less efficient than buildings meant for specialized enterprises. When two alternative enterprises have been taken up by the farmer, if one enterprise is expanded relative to the other, then the building may be insufficient and be less adapted for the expanded enterprise. So, the flexible building with its equipment may be less efficient than a specialized building in producing only one product, as the former will not permit easy shifting of production of one enterprise to another enterprise. However, most farm building plans offer flexibility, as by re-modelling them with a low cost, the farmer can use them for two enterprises (say, poultry and piggery). Thus, when farmer plans for the farm buildings, he should consider flexibility by considering current developments and with a little foresight to accept re-modelling, if necessary.
- ☆ Timely repairs and maintenance of farm buildings is essential for extending their life span. This means that, the depreciation losses are reduced. Adequate care must be taken to look after the drainage outlets from the buildings, otherwise pests and disease infestations may affect the survival of the enterprises and quality of inputs and produce stocked.

IV. Managerial Performance

Management of enterprises means to plan a business, to start it and run it. It means to bring all the other three factors of production *i.e.*, land, labour and capital together to undertake a business or production process. Organization implies not only running the business, but also shouldering the loss, if any. The person, who undertakes the responsibilities for organizing or managing the business is called an Organizer or Entrepreneur. The following are the important functions of an organizer:

- ☆ The organizer initiates a business or production considering the level of resources available with him.
- ☆ He organizes or combines the other three factors of production *i.e.*, land, labour and capital to start the business or production.
- ☆ He directs and supervises the production on a systematic line.

- ✰ He controls the business activities so that, they are tuned towards the achievement of desired goals and objectives.
- ✰ He bears risks and uncertainties in the farm business.
- ✰ He will plan for new innovations in the farm business.

Management is a very important resource in the production programme, as it aims at controlling the other three factors of production *i.e.*, land, labour and capital. In a farm management, the two important goals of farm manager is maximization of profits and farm family satisfaction. Under Indian conditions, the farmer plays four important roles as a farm labour, as farm manager and as a capitalist in the production programme. In general, the farmer under Indian conditions is a good agricultural labour, inefficient entrepreneur (business approach), inefficient manager and a weak capitalist. Besides controlling other three factors of production, the farm manager has to study the environmental aspects or natural factors also as they influence the business significantly. So, considering management as an important resource, farming has been mainly classified into 'Types of farming' and 'Systems of farming' on the basis of farm enterprises practiced and on the basis of the ownership and operationship of the area of the farming land respectively (Figure 3.15).

A. On the Basis of Farm Enterprises Practiced - Types of Farming

Types of farming refers to selection of enterprises, enterprise combinations, methods and practices involved in producing the enterprise, output and types of products sold in the market *etc.* Generally, an area in which many farms having

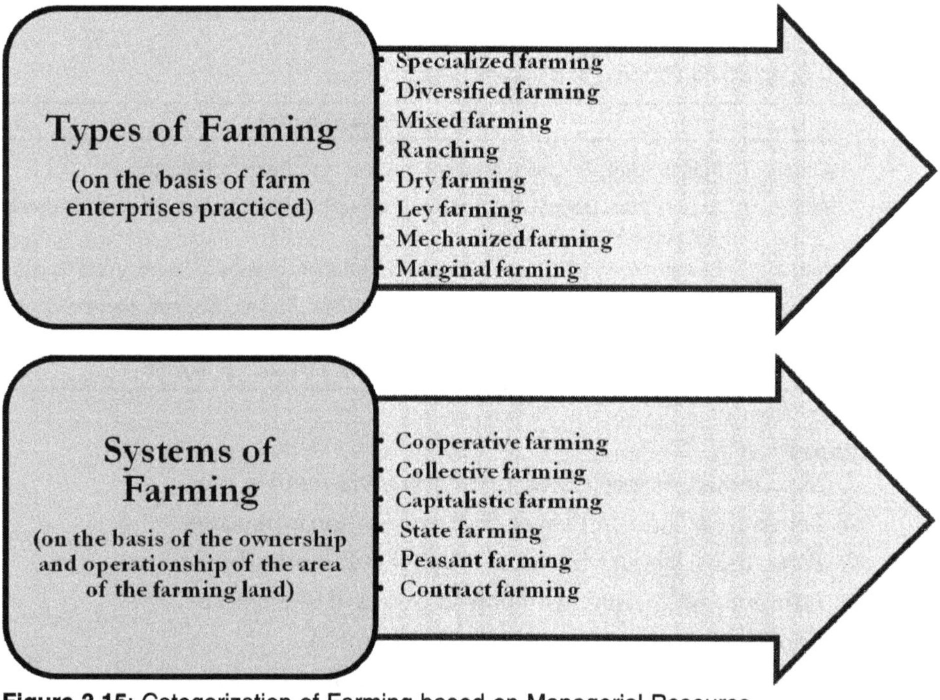

Figure 3.15: Categorization of Farming based on Managerial Resource.

similarity regarding the enterprise selected or enterprise combinations taken up, methods followed in practicing these enterprises and products sold in that area constitute types of farming. Depending upon the enterprises practiced and income earned by the farmer, there are eight important types of farming.

i. Specialized Farming

Specialized farming is a type of farming in which farmer practices one enterprise or more than one enterprise, but one enterprise will contribute more than 50 percent of total income of the farmer in a year. From the Figure 3.16 it is clear that, since paddy enterprise yields 70 percent of total income of the farmer, we can say the farmer is specializing on paddy enterprise, besides practicing maize and jowar enterprises. So, according to the definition, a farm on which 50 percent or more of the receipts are from paddy would be classified as paddy farm, and the one yielding 50 percent or more of its income from wheat would be called a wheat farm.

Table 3.21 shows the specialization of enterprises in different regions of India. Various possible reasons are given below regarding, why the farmer goes for specialized farming:

- ☆ Suitability of an enterprise in the given farming situation.
- ☆ The farmer may be having good knowledge and good managerial ability on that specialized enterprise.
- ☆ The specialized enterprise may have comparative advantage in that area in terms of costs, output, quality of output, prices, marketing outlets *etc.*
- ☆ Assured income to the farmer from that enterprise in that area because of strengthened backward and forward linkages in that area.

Table 3.21: Specialized Farming in different Regions

Sl.No.	*Crop*	*Regions of Specialization*
1.	Wheat	Punjab, Uttar Pradesh, Madhya Pradesh and Eastern Rajasthan.
2.	Paddy	Assam, West Bengal, Bihar, Eastern Uttar Pradesh, Western Ghats and Coastal belts of Odisha and Chennai.
3.	Cotton	Punjab, Madhya Pradesh, Karnataka, and some regions of Bombay and Gujarat.
4.	Sugarcane	Gangetic Plains of Uttar Pradesh and Bihar, Punjab, Madras, Karnataka and Odisha.
5.	Jute	Assam, West Bengal, Cooch-Bihar, Bihar and coastal regions.

Advantages

- ☆ Main motive of specialized farming is profit motive.
- ☆ Better use of land and hence, bulk production is possible.
- ☆ Better use of labour because of effective supervision by farm manager.
- ☆ Efficiency of labour and other resources will be increased.
- ☆ Can be taken up with small amount of capital.
- ☆ Less capital equipment and implements will be needed.

- ☆ Scientific management of enterprise(s) is possible.
- ☆ Better marketing of produce.

Disadvantages

- ☆ More risk is involved in specialized farming because, if the selected enterprise fails, the farmer's income will be greatly affected.
- ☆ By-products of the enterprise cannot be fully utilized.
- ☆ The productive resources of an enterprise cannot be fully exploited. This is because, the resources employed may be having higher opportunity cost (on other enterprises).
- ☆ Soil fertility cannot be maintained.
- ☆ Income of the farmer cannot be distributed throughout the year.
- ☆ The knowledge of the farmer may be limited to few crops only.
- ☆ More dependence on marketing conditions. That is, if the market fails to clear the volume of production, the farmer may suffer heavy losses.
- ☆ International trade may also suffer, if specialized farming suffers a set back from pests and disease incidences, escalation in cost structure *etc.*

ii. Diversified Farming

It is also called as General farming. Diversified farming is a type of farming in which no single enterprise contributes at least or more than 50 percent of total income of the farmer in the year (Figure 3.16). So, in diversified farming, there is no specific importance to a particular enterprise. The main objective of diversified farming is stabilization of annual net income of the farmer.

Advantages

- ☆ Less risk is involved in practicing diversified farming because, if one enterprise fails, the farmer gets income from other enterprise(s).
- ☆ By-products of the enterprises can be effectively utilized.
- ☆ Productive resources of the enterprises can be fully exploited.
- ☆ Soil fertility can be maintained.
- ☆ The farmer's income can be distributed throughout the year.
- ☆ The farmer can gain knowledge on a wide variety of enterprises.
- ☆ The farmer can withstand risks and uncertainties in the production and marketing of produce.
- ☆ Gives boost to international trade because, a wide variety of commodities can be exported from the country.

Disadvantages

- ☆ Since the farmer deal with a wide variety of enterprises, he has to procure large quantum of resources in advance and this may lead to resource management problems.

- ☆ This type of farming employs more number of labour and hence, labour management is a problem.
- ☆ It is difficult on the part of the farmer to supervise the business effectively because, he deals with wide range of enterprises.
- ☆ Less control on the cost of operation of enterprises.
- ☆ The farmer has to purchase more equipment and more machinery suiting to more number of enterprises.
- ☆ Since the farmer deals with a wide variety of crops, efficient marketing is also a problem.

iii. Mixed Farming

Mixed farming is a special type of diversified farming in which the farmer takes up crop enterprise along with a significant component of livestock enterprise. The main difference between diversified farming and mixed farming is that, in mixed farming, livestock enterprise is practiced as one significant component and in case of diversified farming, livestock enterprise will not be practiced. Under Indian conditions, mixed farming is a rule because, it helps the farmer in providing animals for draught purpose and also helps in maintaining soil fertility, The livestock enterprise in mixed farming contribute a minimum of 10 per cent and to a maximum of 49 per cent of the total income of the farmer. Subsistence is important objective of mixed farming (Figure 3.16).

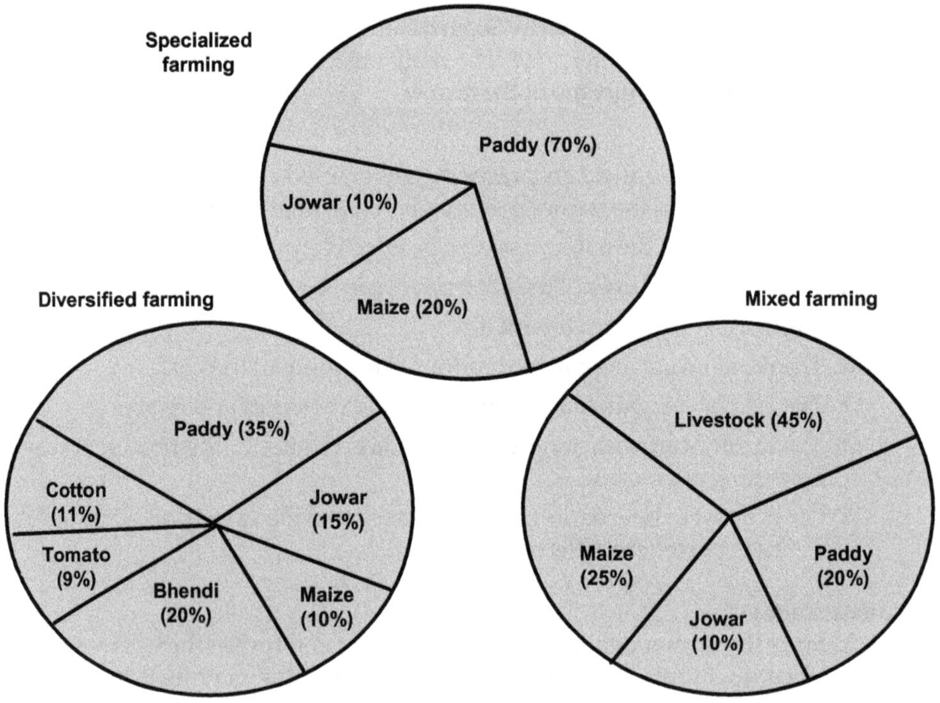

Figure 3.16: Different Types of Farming.

Advantages

- It helps in maintaining soil fertility.
- It tends to give balanced labour load throughout the year for the farmer and his family.
- It permits the proper use of farm by-products.
- It provides for greater chances of intensive cultivation.
- It often contributes higher returns on farm business.

Disadvantages

- Since the farmer deal with a wide variety of enterprises, he has to procure a large quantum of resources in advance and this may lead to resource management problems.
- Less control on the cost of operation of enterprises.
- The farmer has to purchase more equipment and more machinery suiting to more number of enterprises.

iv. Ranching

It refers to rearing of livestock on natural surroundings. That is, ranching implies, grazing and multiplication of animals on public lands or natural surroundings. These ranched lands are not fit for crop cultivation purposes. Ranching is most commonly seen in Australia and Tibet and in India, it is practiced only in hilly areas where pastures are extensively grown. In India, ranching is gradually disappearing because of the increasing pressure of population on agricultural land. Some parts of Rajasthan, ravines of river Chambal, some portions of Agra division *etc.* are the examples of this type of farming.

v. Dry Farming

It refers to cultivation of crops under rainfed conditions. Depending upon the amount of rainfall received, dry land agriculture is divided into three types of farming:

- ***Dry Farming:*** It refers to cultivation of crops, where the amount of rainfall is < 700 mm or < 20". In this farming, there will be prolonged dry spells leading to frequent crop failures.
- ***Dry land Farming:*** It refers to cultivation of crops in areas, where the amount of rainfall is between 700 – 1150 mm. Here also prolonged dry spells are common, but crop failures are less frequent.
- ***Rainfed Farming:*** It refers to cultivation of crops, where the annual rainfall is more than 1150 mm. Here, the crop failures due to dry spells is not so common, but drainage is a major problem affecting the crop production.

In dry farming and dry land farming, major emphasis is on soil moisture conservation and limited application of fertilizers (because of less soil moisture availability) and for sustainability of crop yields. In rainfed farming, major emphasis is on providing good drainage facilities, controlling of water erosion, application of higher levels of inputs to maximize the yields *etc.*

vi. Ley Farming

With increases in both human and animal populations in the Indian arid zone, the demand for grain, fodder, and fuel wood is increasing. Agricultural production in this region is low due to the low and uneven distribution of rainfall (100–400 mm/year) and the low availability of essential mineral nutrients. These demands can be met only by increasing production levels of these aridsols through adoption of farming technologies that improve physical properties as well as biological processes of these soils. So, alternate farming systems are being sought for higher sustainable crop production at low input levels and to protect the soils from further degradation. In such dry lands of India, Ley farming is practiced as a way to restore soil fertility, which involves rotations of grasses and food grains in a specific area. It is now being promoted even more to encourage organic farming, especially in the dry lands. This farming also acts as an insurance against crop failures by frequent droughts. Structurally related physical properties and biological processes of soil often change when different cropping systems, tillage, or management practices are used. Soil fertility can be increased and maintained by enhancing the natural soil biological processes. This farming provides balanced nutrition for sustainable production through continuous turnover of organic matter in the soil (Sharma, 2011).

vii. Mechanized Farming

The mechanical operation on a farm is called farm mechanization. It includes the use of manual implement, bullock drawn appliances and modern machines used in various farm operations like tractor ploughing, tube well irrigation, harvesting and threshing by reapers and threshers, spraying by sprayers and the like. In post-harvest operations, mechanization includes processing of products such as wheat or rice milling, cold storage, oil expelling, cane crushing and so on. The Agro-Industrial Corporations and some co-operative institutions provide custom service to farmers when needed.

viii. Marginal Farming

This is a type of farming, where marginal farmer does not always consider economical in practicing farming, because of his limited size of land. His first concern is to produce food on the farm to feed himself and his family members. As such, he has nothing to market except on occasions when he has to make forced sale to get some cash. Marginal farming is characterized by the following factors:

- ☆ The farms or holding are tiny with greater pressure of population on the land.
- ☆ The farmer have poor resource base and hence, he cannot give a proper direction to the allocation and utilization of resources.
- ☆ The produce is consumed directly by the farmer and his family and not exchanged in market.
- ☆ The production factors are self-employed.
- ☆ The price elasticities of production are small.

- There is a complementary relationship between enterprises, as some of them will have to be raised by utilizing the by-products of other enterprise (say, cattle maintenance without consideration for loss or profit).
- Product price fluctuations have no or marginal effect on the production of crops.

Factors Influencing Types of Farming

The factors that influence the types of farming can be broadly categorized into physical factors and economic factors. Let us discuss in-detail about these two categories of factors one by one here under.

i. Physical Factors

These are the factors, which influence the types of farming over space, but their influence does not vary significantly year by year. These factors include:

- ***Climate:*** It is the most important factor which affects the scope of type of farming. The most important climatic factor that influences the type of farming in an area is rainfall. Other factors like temperature, humidity, wind velocity *etc.*, also influence the type of farming to a certain extent.
- ***Soil:*** Both soil structure and texture determines the type of farming. For most of the crops, deep soils are most suited, as their water holding capacity is high. On the contrary, loose soils have poor water holding capacity and hence, not suitable for many crops to be cultivated. Soil fertility and health also influences the type of farming. In the case of fertile soils, manurial costs will be less, thus reduces the cost of cultivation. Soil health means, whether soils are alkaline or acidic. Slightly alkaline soils are always preferred for fodder crops.
- ***Topography:*** Soil and topography are closely related. A specific type of soil with certain fertility is usually of a single topography. Generally, plain lands are suitable for cultivating annual agricultural and horticultural crops. In areas of higher elevations, perennial horticultural crops, tea plantations, rubber plantations *etc.*, are cultivated.

ii. Economic Factors

Unlike physical factors, these factors influence the types of farming year by year considering the prospects of the farm business in each and every year. Of course, these factors influence the type of farming within the choices available as governed by the physical factors. The important economic factors that influence the types of farming include:

- ***Prices:*** This is the most important economic factor that determines the types of farming. Farmers are generally price conscious and hence, they prefer the enterprise(s) that fetches higher prices in the market. They substitute one enterprise for another enterprise considering their relative prices into account. Especially, the area and production of cash crops like cotton, tobacco, sugarcane *etc.*, are prone to change in a cyclical manner adjusting to the price fluctuations and profitability.

- ☆ ***Yield:*** Besides prices, farmer is equally conscious about yields of the crops he wishes to cultivate on the farm. Considering the yield factor and crop response to different inputs that he apply, he will select the enterprises in the production programme. He also prefer the type of farming, where the by- product of one enterprise can be effectively utilized on other enterprise.
- ☆ ***Cost of production:*** In the modern days of farm business, cost effective production is gaining more importance to boost the profitability of enterprises. So, the farmers generally prefer those crops that enjoy employment of modern technology towards cost-effective production, as such commodities have more comparative advantage in the international market. Thus, the principle of comparative advantage of commodities guides the farmer in selecting type of farming.
- ☆ ***Marketing outlets:*** In these days of commercial agriculture, efficient marketing of agricultural produce is more important. In this context, it will be more fit to say, *'a good farmer has only his hands on the plough, but both the eyes on the market'*. So, the presence of marketing outlets and processing facilities further influence the type of farming. With increased prospects for export of processed agricultural products, processing function also plays a crucial role for the selection of type of farming.
- ☆ ***Marketing costs:*** The cost of marketing of farm products and marketing problems determine what products will or should be produced. The producer's share in consumer's price also decide, what enterprises should be practiced.
- ☆ ***Availability of capital:*** When more capital is available with the farmer, he prefer to cultivate cash crops like cotton, chillies *etc.*, and further, the farmer can take more risk in the farm business. On the other hand, if the farmer is with limited capital, he cannot take more risk in the business and he may resort to those crops that yield assured returns to him (say, paddy, wheat etc). Thus, the availability of capital with the farmer decides the type of farming in the business. Further, the adoption of modern technology on the farm enterprises requires adequacy of capital with the farmer.
- ☆ ***Availability of labour:*** Some enterprises need intensive operations that are to be performed only by the employment of human labour. In such cases, the farmer selects these enterprises, when labour availability is more. In areas of labour shortage, the farmers will switch over to other enterprises, where mechanization of farm operations is feasible.
- ☆ ***Land value:*** In general, the areas with low land values attract the farmers from areas of high land values and they start a new type of farming in those areas. Due to this, the land values gradually increase in areas, where new type of farming is initiated.
- ☆ ***Competition between enterprises:*** Specialization or diversification of farming is decided by the competition among the enterprises depending upon their relative profitability and competition among the resources used.

- ☆ ***Pests and disease incidences:*** These directly affect the yields of the crops. If the pests and disease incidences occur in an epidemic fashion, the existing type of farming may ruin and a new type of farming will be started. In Guntur and Prakasam districts of Andhra Pradesh during 1984-85 and 1985-86, the attack of white fly on cotton caused a 40 per cent decrease in cotton farming area. The cultivation of pulse crops and oilseed crops emerged as a new type of farming in this cotton belt.
- ☆ ***Personal likes and dislikes:*** In a farm business, the farmer is equally interested on the profitability of enterprises on one hand and farm family satisfaction on the other. Hence, personal likes and dislikes, food habits of the farm family *etc.*, also influence the type of farming.
- ☆ ***Governmental programmes and policies:*** The type of farming to be selected by the farmer depends upon the programmes and policies formulated by the Government in the Five Year Plans. If the Government encourages the production of allied enterprises through offering more subsidies, then the farmers will go for taking up allied enterprises on specialization mode or will go for mixed farming. Further, if the Government increases the MSP for wheat, the farmer will go for specialized farming. In an alternate case, if the Government advocates the farmers not to practice certain enterprises (say, tobacco in Andhra Pradesh), the type of farming will change to alternate crops and allied enterprises.
- ☆ ***Knowledge and managerial ability of the farmers:*** The type of farming to be followed by the farmer depends on his knowledge about various enterprises and his managerial ability. If the farmer is well-versed with the scientific package of practices of more number of crops and he enjoys good managerial ability in handling several enterprises, he can go for diversified farming or mixed farming. On the contrary, if the farmer's knowledge is limited to few enterprises, he will go for specialized farming.
- ☆ ***Mechanization of farm operations:*** This greatly influences the type of farming. For example, with the mechanization of farm operations in cultivation of paddy (like paddy seed driller, paddy transplanter, paddy harvester etc), the type of farming revolves around the paddy enterprise *i.e.*, the farmer goes for specialized farming, especially in areas, where severe labour shortage is experienced.

Above these two factors (*i.e.*, physical and economic factors), Tandon and Dhondyal further opined that, social factors like traditions and customs also influences the types of farming.

B. On the Basis of the Ownership and Operationship of the Area of the Farming Land - Systems of Farming

If the farming is classified based on type of ownership and the type of operationship, it is called as systems of farming. Systems of farming also refer to combination of products sold and methods or practices involved in the production of the products. That means, the kind of major produce sold from the basis of systems of farming. The socio-economic functioning of farms also forms the basis for different systems of faming. There are six important systems of farming based on the type of ownership and operationship as given through Table 3.22.

Table 3.22: Types of Ownership and Operationship Across different Systems of Farming

Systems of Farming	Type of Ownership	Type of Operationship
i. Co-operative Farming Society		
a. Co-operative Better Farming Society	☆ Individual	☆ Collective
b. Co-operative Collective Farming Society	☆ Individual	☆ Collective
c. Co-operative Joint Farming Society	☆ Individual	☆ Collective
d. Co-operative Tenant Farming Society	☆ Collective	☆ Individual
ii. Collective Farming Society	Collective/Society	Collective/Society
iii. Capitalist Farming	Individual	Individual
iv. State Farming	State	Paid Management
v. Peasant Farming	Individual	Individual
vi. Contract farming	Individual	By the private firm in association with farmer

i. Co-operative Farming Society

Agriculture is often confronted with various problems like high pressure of population on land, sub-division and fragmentation of land holdings, primitive methods of cultivation, poverty *etc.*, thereby, affecting the prospects of agri-business. One important measure to overcome the above problems is execution of co-operative farming. Co-operative farming is a farming in which all agricultural operations or part of the operations are carried out jointly by the farmer members on voluntary basis. The farmer members will pool their land, labour and capital resources as one unit and this facilitates them to employ modern techniques of production and thereby, they enjoy the benefits of economies of large scale and large scale marketable surplus. The farmer members will elect a 'Committee' on democratic approach and based on the directions or guidance of the committee, they will take up the farming activity. The birth place of co-operative farming in the world is in the Palestine and Jews (Israel) from Palestine are the pioneers in co-operative farming. The chief distinction between individual farming on cooperative lines and cooperative farming is that, *'in the former, the individual farmer is in full possession of his land and he himself carries on the basic operations of cultivation, he joins a cooperative body only for the sake of getting those services which are beyond his individual capacity, while in the latter, the farmer transfer possession as well as ownership of his farm to a cooperative society'*. The Indian Delegation to China on Agrarian cooperatives pointed out: *'the term cooperative farming is intended to apply to joint farming and collective farming society.'* The Planning Commission of India has also pointed out, *'Cooperative farming necessarily applies to the pooling of land and joint management.'* The Working Group on cooperative farming defines cooperative farming society *'as a voluntary association of cultivators for better utilization of resources including manpower and land pooled and in which majority of the members the agricultural production employment and income.'* The working group further observed that, *'there are four types of cooperative farming societies working at present. Out of these, cooperative better farming and cooperative tenant farming societies have developed in the form of service cooperatives. But, they should be distinguished from cooperative farming because, there is no pooling of manpower and land in these societies and their members take this responsibility and risk of farm operations individually.'* The following are the four main types in which co-operative farming societies may be organized:

a. *Co-operative Better Farming Society*

This society has the following features:

- ☆ In this system of co-operative farming, both the type of ownership and operationship are individual.
- ☆ The farmers, who have small holding or limited resources join to form a society for some specific purpose (say, adoption of improved methods of cultivation, use of heavy machinery, sale of products etc). The farmer-members will elect a committee or society and this will guide the farmers in adopting improved methods of cultivation. In furtherance of its main objective, the committee may undertake or perform joint ploughing, joint pooling or assembling of produce, cleaning, grading and disposable of produce at reasonable prices. The society also provides better seeds, manures and facilities for irrigation, storage and marketing. The farmer-members retain their individual holdings, but agree to follow a plan of cultivation laid down by the society, as it is organized to introduce improved methods of farming. Each member cultivates his own land and takes his profit or bears his loss. According to the Working Group on Cooperative Farming (1959) *'for all practical purposes, a better farming society works like a multi-purpose society or service co-operative.'*
- ☆ The co-operative better farming societies are formed and run by a committee of five or more members keeping in view the size of the piece of land to be cultivated. No member loses the right of ownership of his land, but the members follow common plan of cultivation as agreed upon.
- ☆ This society forms the basis for co-operative farming in the sense that, it advocates the farmer-members to take up better farming practices or improved methods of cultivation on the land. It also conducts demonstrations and exposure visits to the farmer members to implement modern techniques of production or improved methods of production.
- ☆ The farmer members are free to follow his own crop production programme except for the purpose for which he joins the society (say, adoption of improved methods of cultivation).
- ☆ Profit is not distributed. The earnings of the members from his piece of land, after deducting the expenses, become his profit.
- ☆ The Co-operative Planning Committee recommended that, cooperative better farming societies should be organized in India, at least two in each district. State aid should be given in the form of an expert staff, long-term loans to the society for its buildings, permanent improvements of the land and expensive agricultural machinery of cattle, equipment and inexpensive agricultural machinery for the use of the members.

b. Co-operative Collective Farming Society

This society has the following features:

- In this system of farming, both type of ownership and operationship are collective. That is, under this system of farming, the right of ownership and the right of cultivation of land are pooled.
- The society gets owned land or leased land and it is collectively cultivated by the society. Sometimes, the land is also acquired free. Most of these societies are organized on Government waste lands. That means, these societies include landless workers and acquire land from Government or lands obtained after ceiling.
- Since ownership is collective, the farmers does not have right on their land and hence, no dividend is paid to individual members on the basis of ownership of land. That is, after formation of such society, the land becomes the property of the society and the members lose their individual ownership. That is, the society itself cultivates the land.
- The society owns all the agricultural implements required for productive purposes. Large scale and modern techniques of production like mechanization are employed and this is the societies most important gain. The produce is raised collectively and each member receives wages for the work done by him and a bonus is paid in proportion to the wages. The profits are worked out at the end of each year after deducting wages, costs of management and allotment for reserve fund. Members have the option to withdraw from the society, in which case they get back their capital. Net profits are distributed among members in proportion to labour and other resources contributed by them, but not on the basis of ownership of land.
- No dividend is paid on share capital. Members are entitled to claim wages for their labour and bonus too, which is distributed only in the case of profits, *prorata* their wages.
- Since members do not have a land ownership right in the society's land, three different types of collective farming societies have been noted.
  - Collective farming society, which may come into existence as a result of independent farmers transferring their land ownership right to the society in returns for shares of equivalent value. On these shares, they will be entitled for a dividend.
  - Collective farming society, which might come into existence as a result of a surrender of land ownership rights by members. Collective farms in communist countries usually conform to this pattern.
  - Collective farming society, which might obtain land from non-members either on free hold or lease hold. The members do not part with any pre-existing right of land ownership because, the society has not acquired its land through transfer from its members. Members may either be tenant or agricultural labourers leasing or buying land from Government or private land owners. Such societies in India are set up on lands made available by the Government.

c. Co-operative Joint Farming Society

To secure the advantages of large-scale farming and to solve the problem of sub-division and fragmentation of holdings, this system of farming is most suited. The land of small owners is pooled into one unit thereby, the size of the unit of cultivation increases, but proprietorship rests with individual farmer-members. This society has the following features:

- ☆ In this system of farming the type of ownership is individual and operationship is collective.
- ☆ Under the co-operative joint farming society land, labour, machinery and other farm equipment required for cultivation are pooled together. The land-holders are either owners or protected tenants, who pool the small plots of land as one unit for purposes of cultivation. They however, retain the right of ownership of land so pooled. The cultivation is undertaken by the society. That is, in this type of society, landholder (whether tenants or owners) pool their small plots of land for joint cultivation, but proprietorship of such plots rests with the owner of land. Even though the land is pooled for joint purpose the farmer will enjoy right on his own land and this pooling of land permits scientific cultivation.
- ☆ The farmer members will elect a management committee or society and based on the directions and guidance given by the society, they will execute the farm operations. That is, joint cultivation is done on the pooled land in accordance with the decisions taken by the committee elected.
- ☆ The important functions of the society includes:
  - ❑ Planning the crop production programme.
  - ❑ Joint purchase of farm inputs and joint sale of crop produce.
  - ❑ Raising of funds on the basis of security of land, crops, movable and immovable properties of the society towards making land improvements.
  - ❑ Purchase of machinery and payment of operational expenses.
- ☆ The membership is voluntary and a member enjoys the option to withdraw. The members will work jointly on the pooled land according to the programme of the society and each member will receive wages for his daily labour. As against the proprietorship of land, the owner cultivators get dividend or rent in proportion to the value of the land.
- ☆ The members are usually land-owners and protected tenants, who pool their lands for joint cultivation and such other allied purposes. The members then enter into an agreement with the society in the prescribed form. Any new entrant is required to apply for membership of the society by paying the amount of a share. A member can be expelled, if he does not observe the conditions of the membership. Every member has one vote. The society has full authority to carry on the business of the society. The society suggests for pooling of land resources from small and marginal farmers because their individual holdings are not sufficient enough to go for extensive or scientific cultivation.

- ✰ The valuation of the land so pooled is made according to the rules framed by the society with the approval of the Registrar of Co-operative Societies. This valuation serves as the basis to determine the size of income from the property to be paid to the members. The society arranges for the supply of all the agricultural requisites. The members are required to work according to the directions of the society in respect of all matters connected with production, protection and marketing of agricultural produce.
- ✰ The small owners of land are encouraged to pool their land, so as to form a large unit of cultivation. The society can also purchase or take on lease land for cultivation. Out of the proceeds received from the disposal of the produce, all the expenses of cultivation including payment for the use of land, wages and cost of management are met first. Provision for interest on borrowings and depreciation of assets is also made. The residue is then shared by members in proportion to the wages earned by each after utilizing a part thereof towards the payment of bonus to the salaried staff.
- ✰ Since ownership of land is recognized, payment of dividend will be done in proportion to the value of land contributed by each member.
- ✰ The produce raised collectively is also disposed off collectively. The proceeds, after meeting all the expenses of cultivator including payment for use of land, wages and cost of management and providing for a reserve fund are shared by the members in proportion to the work they had done.
- ✰ The co-operative joint farming gives better results due to the economic use of land and the employment of better techniques of production.
- ✰ An important agreement will be there between the member and society such that, if the society makes improvement on the land the members has to repay the cost to the society, if he desires to leave the society.

Co-operative Collective Farming Society	*Co-operative Joint Farming Society*
In cooperative collective farming society, the members do not have ownership rights on the land and land exclusively belongs to the society. The members may get the rent.	In cooperative joint farming society, members enjoy ownership rights on their individual holdings.
In cooperative collective farming society, since the member has no ownership right, he only gets an income in return for his work on the farm.	A member of cooperative joint farming society earns two kinds of income *viz.*, ✰ Income for land ownership; and ✰ Income from work in proportion to the work done.
The type of ownership is collective and hence, no dividend is paid based on the ownership of land.	Dividend is paid for the farmer-member because ownership is individual.
This society is mainly organized among landless workers on new lands or waste lands whether obtained from the Government or lands obtained after imposing ceiling.	This society is organized mostly among land holders.
In a cooperative collective farming society, both the right of cultivation and right of ownership are pooled. Lands are cultivated by members, who are paid wages.	In cooperative joint farming society, only right of cultivation is pooled.

Whether it is joint farming or collective farming on the co-operative basis, the basic idea underlying the co-operative farming is of pooling of both land and labour resources. The individual agriculturist, whether a small holder, tenant or landless agricultural labourer in India is severely handicapped by the common factors of poverty and lack of financial resources and the small size of holding, that is always uneconomic. Add to this the vagaries of rainfall and climate which produce periodical cycle of scarcity and famine with consequent misery for the masses of agriculturists and their families. Thus, where large area of land is available on lease from landlords or from the Government, co-operative collective farming societies can be organized. The co-operative collective farming society has all the features of a co-operative joint farming society except that, in the former the land belongs to the society as freehold or lease-hold, whereas in the latter the land is held by the members as owners or tenants. The lands, which are available to cooperative collective farming society may or may not be under cultivation, whereas they are under cultivation in co-operative joint farming society and the society is in a position to command resources required for cultivation.

d. Co-operative Tenant Farming Society

This society has the following features:

- ☆ In this system of farming, the type of ownership is collective and the type of operationship is individual.
- ☆ The society will have either owned land or takes the land on lease purpose, but the society does not take up farming activity.
- ☆ The society will divide the entire land area into different plots and each plot is given to different tenant members for cultivation purpose on lease basis.
- ☆ The whole area is cultivated in accordance with the plan laid out by the society. But, the manner in which the plan is executed is left to individual members. These members work as a tenant in the society on the basis of a fixed rent. A common cropping plan is followed by the members and this plan is always suggested by the society. Each member cultivates his plot and sells the produce through the society.
- ☆ The society will take up severed functions like providing credit to members, supply of seeds, manures, fertilizers, implements and also make arrangements for the sale of produce. But, it is up to the members, whether to avail these facilities or not.
- ☆ Each tenant member cultivates his own land in accordance with a programme laid down by the society. He is entitled to the produce of land and they can dispose off their produce as they like, but he has to pay a stipulated rent to the society (as they have taken the plots on lease purpose).
- ☆ The society if gets profits, after meeting the requirements of reserve fund must be distributed among the members in proportion of the rents paid by each member.

Co-operative Better Farming Society and Co-operative Tenant Farming Society	*Co-operative Collective Farming Society and Co-operative Joint Farming Society*
These societies will provide certain services to their members on joint basis such as joint purchase of seeds, manures, fertilizers, machinery *etc.* but they have separate cultivation, possession and management of land.	Here, we have joint cultivation, joint possession and joint management of land.

Table 3.23: Comparative Picture Across different Types of Cooperative Farming Societies

Item	*Cooperative Better Farming Society*	*Cooperative Collective Farming Society*	*Cooperative Joint Farming Society*	*Cooperative Tenant Farming Society*
Land ownership	Individual	Society	Individual	Society
Land cultivation (Operationship)	Individual	Society	Society	Individual
Plan of cultivation	Society	Society	Society	Society
Inputs supply	Society	Society	Society	Society
Service	Society	Society	Society	Society
Sharing of profits	Produce from individual land	Share on basis of labour	Share on size basis of plot	In proportion to the rent paid by the tenant member

Importance of Cooperative Farming in India

As Indian agriculture is the backbone of the economy, all efforts therefore, should be made to make agriculture a surplus industry and to remove the causes of low production. For stepping up agricultural production and for ensuring economic cultivation, an increase in the size of the unit of cultivation is necessary. Here, co-operative farming, which implies pooling of land and joint management, has direct relevance. Without undermining the sense of proprietorship and the incentive to industry that it gives, co-operative farming can produce all the advantages that a larger unit possesses. Government have, therefore, sanctioned a special comprehensive scheme of co-operative farming, indicating there in the main types of co-operative farming societies, which are envisaged and the scales on which financial assistance is available to farming societies. Assistance is to be provided in the form of loans at a low rates of interest and subsidy for land improvement, contribution to share capital of the society, subsidies for meeting the cost of seeds and manures during the first three years, subsidies for managerial expenses during the same period, and concession in the form of remission in land revenue on private lands pooled for co-operative farming. The concession of grant of Government waste lands available on long lease on permanent occupancy basis has also been extended to co-operative farming societies. The execution of co-operative farming is a relatively new system in India. Its goal is to bring together all of the land resources of farmers in such an organized and united way so that, they will be collectively in a position to take up enterprises on every bit of land to the best of the fertility of the land. There is an immense scope for co-operative farming in India although the movement is as yet in its infancy. The progress of co-operative financing in India has been very slow. The reasons are fear of unemployment, attachment to land, lack of proper propaganda *etc.*, are some of the important reasons. However, in the context of meeting the subsistence needs of the mounting population, farming on co-operative basis has become an important medium of the present economic upheaval (disturbances) in rural areas of the country. These cooperative farming societies are member driven organizations and work on Anti-Darwin principle. They aim at protection of weak and they survive and grow on principles of survival of weakest. This system of farming helps to mitigate the evils resulting from traditional impediments such as inequitable distribution of land, uneconomic size of holding, fragmentation and sub-division of land and the age old methods of cultivation. So, the movement of co-operative farming imbibes the sense of communal living and aims at cost-effective production of enterprises through mechanization of farm operations, which is generally beyond the capacity of small and marginal farmers. In addition, it widens the scope of employment for the agricultural labourers through subsidiary business on the farm.

Reasons for Co-operative Farming

This system of farming is gaining more importance because of the following reasons:

- ☆ Pooling of land enables the farmer-members to go for mechanization of farm operations, better use of land, soil conservation, strengthening of irrigation facilities *etc.*
- ☆ Farmers can employ modern techniques of production and can take up the farming with low risks.
- ☆ Better use of labour thereby, helps to solve the problems of under-employment and unemployment in the rural areas.
- ☆ Helps to protect the weak *i.e.*, the farmers who are weak in terms of unequal distribution of wealth and labour exploitation are protected with the development of cooperative farming societies. Thus, co-operative farming aims at self help and equality among people.
- ☆ Joint management in farming helps in better housing for livestock, larger space for crops and suitable marketing arrangements can be accomplished more economically.
- ☆ Fragmentation is eliminated through pooling of small plots of land.
- ☆ Cooperative farming aims at cost-effective production of enterprises through full and rational use of animal and human labour, mechanization of farm operations, adoption of scientific methods of cultivation, economies of large scale production *etc.*
- ☆ Cooperative farming aims at strengthening of credit, irrigation, technological and marketing facilities, which contribute to increase production on pooled large farms rather than on small farms.

- ☆ Co-operative farming is now regarded as an effective answer to the evils of sub-division and fragmentation. Thus, co-operative farming aims at the formation of economic holdings, which is an essential pre-requisite for making agriculture profitable.
- ☆ Facilitate reclamation of lands. This is possible through co-operative farming only in India, as Capitalist and State farmings have no or less scope in India.
- ☆ As the farmer-members can enjoy large scale marketable surplus, the bargaining power of the farmers under cooperative farming are strong compared to individual farming.

The report of the Food and Agricultural Organization (FAO) summed up the advantages of co-operative farming as '*there are certain obvious advantages of the completely co-operative or collective pooling of land, of which the most important are the opportunities for more intelligent management, including planning of rotation, the use of power driven machinery, the selection of different types of land for the purpose of which they are naturally.. suited, the improvement of irrigation, the abolition of boundaries and access roads which waste land, and the more economical and general use of fertilizers and pesticides. Fragmentation is automatically eliminated*'.

Considering the above meritorious grounds, it is essential to go for implementation of cooperative farming in India, We are clearly aware that, the land holdings in India have reduced in size due to the continuing process of sub-division and fragmentation for over the last several decades. This process has accelerated because of the growing pressure of population on land, absence of alternative occupation and the legal coverage provided by the law of succession. The main problem is not merely application of modern productive techniques, but the basic need is to alter agrarian structure and create units of economic size amenable for greater efficiency and productivity. So, the better alternative for fragmentation of land holdings is the introduction of co-operative farming, which is voluntary in character and constructive in approach.

ii. Collective Farming

This system of farming has the following features:

- ☆ Both the type of ownership and operationship are collective.
- ☆ The farmer-members will surrender their land, labour, capital resources, livestock and dead stock to the society and hence, the ownership rights of the land lies with society only and not with the members and each society will work under the directions of the State or Government. That is, collective farming implies the collective management of land, wherein large number of farm families residing in the same village pool their resources.
- ☆ The main objective of this collective farming is to make the farmer members enjoy the benefits of economies of large scale.
- ☆ This system of farming involves extensive use of machinery and hence, the State or Society provides up to date machinery in suitable areas.

- ☆ The labour will be divided into different groups called as 'Brigades' and they will work on group basis. Each brigade will have a brigade leader and he will supervise both the out turn and quality of work performed every day. These labour groups will be assigned works by the society in accordance with the plans laid out by the State or Government.
- ☆ If any farmer wants to dissociate from the society, he can do so, but he cannot go with his share (resource). Money is lieu of his share will be given to him.
- ☆ The main source of earnings is labour earnings. Each member is paid on the basis of work day units. That means, the society will standardize the payment for each and every operation depending upon the following aspects.
  - ❑ Total out turn of work done by the member on each day.
  - ❑ Quality of work turned out on each day.
  - ❑ Contribution of work by each member to the net output of the farm.
  - ❑ Each collective farm has to sell to the State affixed amount of produce at a fixed rate before going into the open market.
- ☆ The worst thing with this system is that the individual farmer-member has no voice. This system is not prevalent in India, but common in communistic countries of the world. This system had started in Russia.

Co-operative Collective Farming Society	*Collective Farming Society*
It is more democratic in its approach, as the society is fully managed by the members without any State or Government intervention.	Even though it appears to be democratic apparently, but there is interventions from the State or Government side regarding the plans or policies to be followed on the farm.
The land of the society is of free hold or leased hold and the membership is open to member in Co-operative Collective Farming Society. That means, if the member comes out of Co-operative Collective Farming Society he will get back his ownership rights on land along with the capital he subscribed earlier.	Even though the land originally belongs to the member, but once the farmer joins the collective farming, it will become the property of Society or State and hence, the member loses the ownership rights on his land.

iii. Capitalist or Corporate Farming

This system of farming has the following features:

- ☆ Both the types of ownership and operationship are individual.
- ☆ This system of farming is commonly seen in developed nations or capitalist countries like USA, England, Australia, Canada *etc.* These farms are not very common in India.
- ☆ The management and ownership of such farms is under rich persons or capitalists. The size of such farms is sufficiently large and the management is also quite efficient.

- This system of faming is characterized by extensive use of capital, more mechanization, employment of more number of hired labour than family labour, adoption of modern techniques of production *etc.* Resources are plenty, latest technical know-how is used and hence, they are efficient. Sugar factories farms, rubber, coffee and tea plantations are common examples of such a system.
- This system of farming is mainly profit or market oriented.
- The advantages of this farming are good supervision, strong organizational setup, sufficient resources *etc.* Its weaknesses are that, it creates socio-economic imbalances, absentee landlordism (*i.e.,* the actual cultivator is not the owner of the farm) *etc.*

iv. State Farming

This system of farming has the following features:

- In this system of farming, the ownership lies with the State but the type of operationship is through paid management.
- The farms are managed by the State.
- Supervision is done by the farm manager or farm incharge, who in turn is a government official. All the labourers are hired on daily or monthly basis *i.e.,* the main source of earnings is through paid management and they have no right in deciding farm policy. Such farms are not very paying because of lack of incentive. Farm policy is usually planned at the top and the same is executed at grass root level by the employed professionals. There is no dearth of resources in these farms, but sometimes it so happens that, they are not available in time and utilized fully.
- The state farms are provides with up to date machinery and latest production technologies and this facilitates good experimentation and research.
- In India, all state farms are managed by a single body called State Farms Corporation of India (SFCI). But, such farms are not many and they are generally attached either to some institution or they themselves are institutions for a particular work.

v. Peasant Farming

This system of farming has the following features:

- Both the types of ownership and operationship are individual.
- The farmer manages the business in his own way and he himself is the manager of the business. That is, farmer is the owner, manager and organizer of the farm. He makes decisions and plans for his farm depending upon his resources, which are generally meager in comparison to other systems of farming.
- This system of farming is characterized by:
  - Scarcity of resources at the farmer's level.

- ❑ Employment of more number of family labour.
- ❑ Family labour works for more number of hours on each day.
- ❑ Living and working are closely associated.

☆ The biggest advantage of this system is that, the farmer himself is the owner and therefore, takes all business decisions.

☆ The major weakness of this system of farming is limited resources with the farmer. Another demerit is that, because of the law of inheritance, an individual holding goes on reducing in its size, as all the members in the family have equal rights on the land.

vi. Contract Farming

This system of farming is recently emerging in India. In this system of farming, wherein the firm (say, food processing firm) enters into a contract with the farmer and promises to buy the farmer's produce at a pre-negotiated price under pre-negotiated conditions. Besides, the buyer agrees to supply the required farm inputs at the required time. Contract farming is effective to address many of the traditional ills affecting the agricultural sector and the farmers, such as fragmentation of holdings, long chain of market intermediaries, ignorance about the requirements of the buyers, low farm mechanization, inadequacy of capital and distress sales and consequent heavy losses to farmers etc (Table 3.24). In this system of farming, land is taken on long time lease basis from individual land owners (farmers). Land is remained under ownership of farmers, but they have no role to play in farm policy. They are paid rental value of land. This system of farming is commonly seen in developed countries, where holdings are large and this is also gaining popularity in India. But, in India, if the large chunk of small and marginal farmers lease out their land, they will be forced to migrate to cities in search of jobs. In long run, there are chances of landlessness also.

Table 3.24: Benefits of Contract Farming to Farmers and Contracting Agency

Benefits	*To Producer*	*To Contracting Agency*
Risk	It minimizes the price risk	It minimizes risk of raw material supply
Price	Price stability ensuring fair price	Price stability as per pre-agreed contract
Quality quality	Use of quality seeds and inputs	Get good quality produce and control on
Payment	Assured and regular payments through bank tie up	Easy handling and better control on payments
Post harvest handling	Minimizes risk and cost of handling	Control and efficient handling
New technology	Facilities in farm management and practices	For better and desired produce to meet consumer needs
Fair trade practices	Minimizes malpractices and no involvement of middle man	Better control on trade practices
Crop insurance	Reduces risk	Reduces risk
Mutual relation ship	Strengthens	Strengthens
Profit	Increases	Increases

Factors Influencing of Systems of Farming

The major factors that influences the systems of farming are discussed here under.

- ***Size of land holdings:*** If the farmer enjoys adequate farm size with sufficient number of family labour and if the farm size is regarded as optimum size, then it is better far the farmer to go for peasant farming. On the contrary, if the farm size is small or marginal, it may be better on the part of the farmer to join the cooperative farming, so as to enjoy the benefits of large scale marketable surplus.
- ***Availability of capital:*** If more amount of capital is available with the farmer, he can go for capitalistic farming through employing modern techniques of production. On the contrary, he can go for co-operative farming or collective farming.
- ***Volume of output:*** If the farmer is with small size of land holding and if he wishes to realize the benefits of large scale marketable surplus, it is better to go for cooperative farming or collective farming.
- ***Managerial ability of the farmer:*** If the farmer enjoys good managerial ability and possess knowledge on a wide range of enterprises, he can go for peasant farming. Otherwise, he has to join in a cooperative society, where the emphasis is to protect the weak.
- ***Backward and forward linkages:*** If the farmer with large size of land holding enjoys adequate credit facilities, input supplies, processing facilities, storage facilities *etc.*, he can go for peasant farming. On the other hand, with all the above backward and forward linkages, but the farmer had only small size of land holdings, it is better for the farmer to go for cooperative farming or collective farming.

C. Other Classifications of Farming Considering the Managerial Performance

There are some other ways to classify the farming in agriculture. They are discussed here under.

i. On the Basis of Agricultural Land Availability

Based on this criterion, there are two categories of farming *viz.*, extensive farming and intensive farming. We know, the farmer on given plot of land obtains more or less definite quantity of yield at any particular time. If he wants to increases his output, he can either bring more land under cultivation or by applying more inputs to the same piece of land. The former refers to extensive farming and the latter refers to intensive farming.

a. ***Extensive farming:*** When more land is available for cultivation and by increasing the cultivated area, we produce more output, it refers to extensive farming.
b. ***Intensive farming:*** When intensive cropping is practiced is the same unit area of land by employing modern technologies of production and other

facilities, then it is called intensive farming. That is, in this farming, land remains fixed in quantity, while other factors are increased.

ii. On the Basis of Number of Enterprises Practiced on the Farm

Considering the number of enterprises taken up on the farm, we can classify the farming into two categories *viz.*, Mono farming and Mixed farming.

a. ***Mono farming:*** If the farmer practices only one enterprise on the farm say, paddy or dairy or poultry or prawn culture *etc.*, over a period of time, then it is known as mono farming.

b. ***Mixed farming:*** If the farmer practices two or more than two enterprises in a farm say, paddy with dairy, paddy and black gram *etc.*, over a period of time, then it is known as mixed farming.

iii. On the Basis of Availability of Water in the Farm Area

Based on this criterion, there are two categories of farming *viz.*, rainfed farming and irrigated farming.

a. ***Rainfed farming:*** If a farm is totally dependent on rainfall for taking up the enterprises, then this type farming is known as rainfed farming.

b. ***Irrigated farming:*** If crop cultivation is practiced by irrigated water, then this type of farming is known as irrigated farming.

4

Farm Business Analysis

Farm business analysis is the process of retrieving, organizing, processing and analyzing information used in farm business decision making. This is, otherwise, defined as a technique that is employed to analyze the efficiency measures of different resources used in the production programme. This analysis serves as a critical ingredient in the management of the farm business. We know, farmer employs different resources in the production programme like land, labour, capital and management and these should be efficiently utilized for achieving cost minimization and profit maximization in farm business. After analyzing the efficiency measures for a farm, the same should be compared with the standards derived from similar types of farms in that locality *i.e.*, in the same farming situation. By comparing with the standard measures, we can ascertain, whether the farm under consideration is maintaining efficiency standards in employing various resources. Of course, the efficient use of resources of a farm reflects in the form of annual net income derived from it and thereby, the progress of net income of a farm indicates the progressiveness of a farmer in efficient use of resources. Further, farmers must be able to quickly respond to changes in the prices of the inputs they buy and the products they sell, if they are to maintain farm profitability in today's rapidly changing market environment. Thus, they are no longer isolated from changes elsewhere in the economic system. To analyze the net income of the farmer, he should have adequate information pertaining to the cost structure of enterprises, output of different enterprises, prices of commodities, marketable surplus, gross returns *etc.*, and to have access to these data, the farmer must maintain records popularly called as Farm Records. Further, he must successfully respond to changes in consumer tastes, Government regulations, and a whole host of other changes that occur in the world beyond the farm gate. Thus, detailed and accurate information is a necessary component of the farm manager's decision making process. So, farm records serve as the basic foundation of good farm management, as the farm manager must be able to use business records in day-to-day decision making. Use of these records in farm management requires ability to organize information from the records, to select the relevant from that which is less important, and to focus on the areas of the business that need attention. Before going into the details of farm business analysis, let us discuss about farm records here under.

Farm Records

These are the reports, registers and books that are maintained by farmer, so as to keep track of what is happening on the farm. Having accurate facts about the farm cost structure, output of enterprises, price trends of commodities *etc.*, in the past is essential for the farmer to plan the farm business in the future. Thus, farm records register all the transactions of a farm business, whether physical and financial that helps the farmer to know the strengths, weakness and possible improvements he can make on the farm. A good record keeping system will allow farm manager to monitor and evaluate the performance of farm business from seed to seed. If these records are maintained over a period of time, it enables the farmer to identify his mistakes if any made on the farm, draw corrective measures in advance for the subsequent years, assess the trends in profitability, growth or deterioration of farm business *etc.* Thus, farm records are essential in scientific management of farm. Note that, farm record keeping is more than just keeping track of what crop was planted in what field, and it involves dealing with all the operations on all the enterprises considered on the farm. Above this, these records also furnish the statements of facts or data about different operations performed on the farm in relevance to physical, monetary and financial aspects of the farm business. This infers that, farm records maintenance is a systematic documentation of all activities taking place in a farm over a given period of time. It is an act of writing down every activity taken up on the farm in every production season and at different stages of the production process up to the disposal of the produce to the final consumer. This system of maintaining farm records by the farmer is dealt under two different names *viz.*, Farm accounting and Farm book keeping, but the ultimate objective of maintaining the farm records is same in both the cases. Let us define these two terms.

Farm Accountancy

'It is an applied science, where in the principles of accounting are applied to the management of farm. It deals with the recording of business transactions of a farm in the books in a regular and systematic manner so that, their nature, extent and financial effects can be readily ascertained at any time in the year' (Adams).

Farm Book Keeping

'This is known as a system of records written to furnish the history of business transactions with special reference to financial side' (Adams). This is, otherwise, defined as *'the science of recording transactions involving money or money's worth in a regular and systematic manner in such a way that the books of accounting will show a true and fair state of the financial worth of a business readily at any point in time'*. So, farm book keeping highlights

the history of business transactions of a farm and this information can be used to predict to the current trends of farm business. There are advantages of the scientific book keeping:

- ☆ Avoids mistakes in conducting transactions in the farm business.
- ☆ Details of receipts and expenditure are known.
- ☆ The actual financial position of the farmer is known at the end of the year. That is, farm books are simply a record of the money the farmer spend and the money he earn in an accounting year.
- ☆ Financial position of the farmer can be compared with neighbours.
- ☆ Administration and economy are better understood and business habits are acquired.
- ☆ In case of any legal dispute, records become the sources of evidence.

Thus, book-keeping is the essential first step in organizing farm business transactions. Note that, simple maintenance of farm records or books or data will not improve the farm business, but the data recorded should be thoroughly analyzed to draw the plan for smooth conductance of farm business with a view to achieve maximum possible net income. As mentioned earlier, this analysis also enables the farmer to compare his farm with the other successful farms in that locality or similar farming situation.

A. Importance of Maintaining Farm Records

There are a number of reasons for keeping farm records in the farm business:

- ☆ It enables the farmer to know,
  - ❑ Which enterprise is more profitable on the farm compared to other enterprises?
  - ❑ Which enterprise on the farm demands more cost structure?
  - ❑ To locate the weak points in the organization of farm and in following scientific packages of practices of different enterprises.
  - ❑ Whether the farmer has to go for long term capital investment on the farm?
  - ❑ Whether the farmer has to go for specialization or diversification.
  - ❑ Which enterprise enjoys more comparative advantage in the market over the other?
- ☆ Guides the farmer in planning future decisions on the farm regarding land reclamation, strengthening of infrastructure, farm mechanization *etc.*
- ☆ The farmer can make complete diagnosis of the farm structure and thereby, he can identify the strengths and weakness of the farm.
- ☆ Critical analysis about the farm, based on the data recorded in the farm registers or records, makes the farmer more vigilant and competent enough to plan the business strategies and thus, improve his managerial ability in running the farm business.

- ☆ Farm records can also serve as a proof for the financial institutions in disbursing farm credit. That is, a good set of farm records allows the farmer to determine credit needs and support loan requests. Properly kept records provide bankers financial information they need for making credit decisions and good records also demonstrate farmer's managerial ability.
- ☆ Farm records also form the basis for the conductance of agro-economic research such as analyzing the efficiency of resource usage on the farm, profitability of farm business, break even analysis of the farm *etc.*
- ☆ Farm records enable the farmer to record policy measures guided by the Government regarding the ceiling of land, labour wages, price policies, crop insurance *etc.*, and thereby, he can act accordingly in planning the farm business.
- ☆ Farm records often serve as a guide to what extent the farmer meets the balance between the farm business and farm family satisfaction, as these two aspects are strongly inter-related in farm managerial economics.
- ☆ Farm records not only indicate the trends in cost structure, progress in crop yields and returns from farm business, but also highlight the progress of net worth of farm business over a period of time, which directly indicates the business solvency and liquidity.
- ☆ By analyzing the farm records, farmer can easily plan his inputs procurement in advance, so as to organize the farm business smoothly.
- ☆ The analysis of the data in farm records enable the farmer to go for either simple farm planning or complete farm planning, so as to maximize the net income in the farm business.
- ☆ The farm records enable the farmer to count and assign value to different farm resources to get farm inventory. These resources can be classified into assets and liabilities and thereby, annual progress in net worth of business can be analyzed. This also serves as a collateral for getting a loan.
- ☆ The farm records enable the farmer to perform accurate farm analysis in terms of preparing Net Worth Statement (NWS) or Balance sheet, Income statement and Cash flow statement.
- ☆ Some lending institutions require detailed business and personal information on everything a farmer owns, as well as the status of unpaid loans. They may also require production records and an estimate of expected sales and expenses for the next year.
- ☆ Farm owners are being asked to keep records about chemical use, livestock waste applications and irrigation water use on their farms.
- ☆ Farm records are a management tool. They allow the farmer to measure how efficiently he is using the resources and to determine whether or not he is making any money in the business.
- ☆ They help the farmer to define and evaluate success as measured by income generated for family living and other needs and desires. Financial success is measured by profitability; if the farm business is not profitable it is not sustainable.

- Miscellaneous uses of farm records include pricing products for sale, evaluating land leases, deciding whether to hire services or buy equipment and evaluating farm insurance needs.

Considering their importance, the farmer must learn about record keeping system before starting to use it. He should develop a habit of keeping the record system up to date from day one. He should do most of the business through a bank account and make notes on cheques, receipts, and deposit slips.

B. Features of Good Farm Records

Considering the importance of maintenance of farm records, it is essential that, these records must be maintained on scientific lines with the following essential features:

- Should be in a proper format that addresses each and every operational aspect on the farm.
- Should have desirable features like: Complete, Accuracy, Consistent and Timely
- Record transactions in chronological order.
- The data or information must be accurate, as they are essential for accurate analysis about the farm.
- Records must be completely filled without any information gaps. One way of making sure that records are accurate is by filling them in as soon as possible after the operation or transaction is done and by checking regularly.
- Should be clear and consistent *i.e.*, they should provide information or data about each and every operation on the farm.
- Should permit the analysis needed about the operational aspects of the farm.
- Should be maintained or updated easily.
- No overcrowding of data or information is allowed *i.e.*, adequate space should be there to record all entries.
- Information or data provided should not be repetitive.
- The data should be provided for each and every enterprise taken up on the farm.
- Ample space should be provided to record all the entries.
- All the results of record keeping should be compared with some standards, which may be the results of previous years or the results for other farms.
- The record keeping system should fit into the farm organization or framework.
- The record keeping system should include:
    - A business checking account to handle all business transactions.
    - An income ledger to record all business income by calendar month.
    - An expense ledger to record all business expenses by calendar month.

- An inventory that involves both the physical counting and valuation of farm assets.
- A depreciation schedule pro-rating the original costs of assets over more than one accounting period.
- A NWS summarizing assets and liabilities of the farm.
- An Income statement (or Profit and Loss Statement) that lists receipts and expenses in the farm business (and the result is net profit or net loss).
- A Cash flow statement showing the flow of funds into the business and the flow out of the business over the accounting period.

C. Methods of Maintaining Farm Records

There are two methods of maintaining farm records *viz.*, Hand-Written method and Computerized method.

i. Hand-Written Method

This method involves recording of transactions made for each enterprise by hand into the formats designed for the purpose. For each enterprise, the transactions will be noted down in terms of quantity purchased, quantity sold, prices, cash transactions made, date of transaction *etc.*

ii. Computerized Method

This method entails the use of different software package in record keeping. Depending upon the features needed, the software packages are available. This method also ensures to maintain all types of farm records. Compared to the earlier method, this method enjoys more accuracy, quick in tracing out and analyzing the information, but suffers from high initial cost of purchasing software programmes.

Note that, for maintaining the farm records, different accounting periods will be followed depending upon the production periods in different agro-ecological situations. In India, there are different agro-ecological situations and hence, different productions periods will be considered. In general, the period between 1st July of starting year to 30th June of next calendar year is considered as a production period for maintaining farm records in most parts of the country.

D. Limitations of Maintaining Farm Records in India

Though maintenance of farm records is considered important in the context of the farm business analysis, majority of the farmers in India do not maintain these records because of the following limitations:

- Majority of the farmers are small and marginal, and their production is more subsistence-oriented. Hence, these lies no need for maintenance of farm records.
- The farmer has to perform four roles on the farm *viz.*, as farm entrepreneur, as farm manager, farm labourer and capitalist. This increases the complexity of maintaining the farm records.

- ☆ Illiteracy among the farmers is a hindrance in realizing the importance about maintenance of farm records.
- ☆ Poor extension service has failed to educate the farmers about the importance of maintaining farm records.
- ☆ Complicated nature of farm business in view of various risks and uncertainties and these pose difficulties on the part of the farmer to address all these complications in maintaining the farm records.
- ☆ Highly fluctuating turnover of farm business adversely influences the interest of the farmer in maintaining farm records.
- ☆ Non-availability of standardized formatted record books is one major limitation for maintaining farm records.
- ☆ Illiteracy among the farmers makes them fearer about the imposition of taxes by the Government in the future, if costs and returns data are recorded in the farm registers.
- ☆ There is no strict regulation by the Government or Department of Agriculture to insist the farmers for maintaining the farm records.
- ☆ Above all, there is lack of record consciousness among the farmers, as its maintenance does not add any monetary returns to their farm business.

E. Types of Farm Records

As the farmer has to maintain recorded data for each and every operational aspect on the farm across the enterprises, for convenient sake, the farm records are classified into Physical farm records, Financial farm records and Supplementary farm records. Let us discuss one by one here under.

i. Physical (Production) Farm Records

These records are related to the physical aspects on the farm *i.e.*, about the farm stead, land utilization pattern, labour utilization aspects, machinery utilization aspects *etc.* The maintenance of these records is essential, as they form the basis for maintaining the financial farm records. These records provide useful information on production and resources used by different enterprises practiced on the farm. This is valuable in measuring production efficiency and preparing efficient alternate farm plans. The various records or registers that fall under this category include:

a. Farm Map

This record displays the important fixtures on the farm like farm layout, farm buildings, irrigation channels, drainage channels *etc.* That is, it gives the over view about the farm (Figure 3.4).

b. Soil Map

This record displays different types of soils in the farm along with their fertility status and soil health position. This record will also give the details about the soil reclamation practices taken up on the farm.

c. Land Utilization Record

This record highlights different ways for which the farm land was utilized on the farm *i.e.*, area under cereals, millets, pulses, oilseeds, vegetables, fruits, pastures *etc.*, area under buildings, area under machinery sheds *etc.*

d. Labour Utilization Record

This record indicates the number of labour employed *i.e.*, owned labour and hired labour across each operation enterprise-wise practiced on the farm. The labour details will also be given across men, women and child labour employed in the farm (Table 4.1).

e. Machinery Use Record

This record shows the extent of mechanization of farm operations-wise and enterprise-wise (Table 4.2).

f. Crop Production and Disposal Record

This record shows the extent of area allocated under each enterprise, output from each enterprise and disposal of main product and by-product (if any) from each enterprise (Tables 4.3 and 4.4).

g. Livestock Production and Disposal Record

This record shows the number of livestock, output from the livestock and disposal of livestock product from the farm (Table 4.5).

Table 4.1: Format for Labour Use Register

Crop: --------- Area : ----------- Field Survey No.--------------- Year: --------------

Date	Puddling	Duration		Labour engaged			Date	Sowing	Duration		Labour engaged			Date	Irrigation	Duration		Labour engaged		
		From	To	M	W	C			From	To	M	W	C			From	To	M	W	C

Note: M: Men, W:Women, C:Children
Courtesy: M.C. Farm, Agricultural College, Mahanandi

Table 4.2: Format for Machinery Use Register

Crop: ---- Area: ----- Field Survey No.----- Year: ----- Machinery used: --------- Size: ---------- Date of purchase: -----

Date	Operation	Duration		Fuel Consumed (Litres)					Repairs
		From	To	Previous balance	Purchased	Total Fuel Available	Consumed	Balance	

Courtesy: M.C. Farm, Agricultural College, Mahanandi

Table 4.3: Format for Crop Production Record

Crop: ---- Previous Crop: ------- Variety : --------- Area: ----- Field Survey No.----- Year: -----

Operation	No./Qty	Date	Implement used	Number of labour employed					Wage rate per unit				
				M	W	C	CPD	TP	M	W	C	CPD	TP

Note: M: Men, W:Women, C:Children, CPD: Cattle Pair Day, TP: Tractor Power
Courtesy: M.C. Farm, Agricultural College, Mahanandi

Table 4.4: Format for Crop Production and Disposal Record

Crops: --------- Year: ----------

Enterprise	Area	Output (Qtls)		Domestic retentions (Qtls)				Quantity sold (Qtls)		Market price (Rs/qtl)		GR (Rs)	Balance Quantity (Qtls)
		Main Product	By-Product	Seed	Kind payment	Feed	Total Retentions	Main Product	By-Product	Main Product	By-Product		

Courtesy: M.C. Farm, Agricultural College, Mahanandi

Table 4.5: Format for Livestock Production and Disposal Record

Name of the Farm: --------- Year: ----------

Items	Production				Disposal			Balance
	Previous Balance	Produced (Born)	Purchased (Bought)	Total	Domestic Consumption	Sold in Market	Died/Losses	
Cows local bred								
Cows crossbred								
Buffaloes								
Sheep								
Goat								
Poultry birds								
Poultry eggs								
Pigs								

Courtesy: M.C. Farm, Agricultural College, Mahanandi

h. Feed Record

This record is maintained by the farmer, who specializes on livestock rearing. This record shows the details of different types of feeds employed for rearing the livestock on the farm. The feed record is maintained enterprise-wise and the main objective of maintaining this record is to analyze the feed use efficiency (*i.e.*, output/ feed employed) on the enterprises (Table 4.6).

Table 4.6: Format for Feed Record

Name of the Farm: --------- Year: ----------

Date	Milch cows (5 numbers)			Buffaloes (2 numbers)			Poultry (1000 birds)		
	Green fodder (Kgs)	Concentrates (Kgs)	Silage (Kgs)	Green fodder (Kgs)	Concentrates (Kgs)	Silage (Kgs)	Green fodder (Kgs)	Concentrates (Kgs)	Silage (Kgs)
Total									

Courtesy: M.C. Farm, Agricultural College, Mahanandi

i. Stock/Store Record

This record show the stock of inputs and outputs in the godowns and these records are maintained item-wise (Table 4.7).

j. Poultry Record

This record shows the number of poultry birds, marketing of eggs and meat produced on from the farm.

Other physical farm records include: Family consumption record, Daily labour sheet, Animal reproduction record – Breeding and weaning records, Health record – Health problems especially treatments used, success and failure of treatments, death losses of livestock, Culling record – Date and reasons for culling, Production Record – Weight at birth, three and eight weeks of age, litter size *etc.*

Table 4.7: Format for Store or Stock Register

Name of the Farm: --------- Year: ----------

Items	Date	Opening Balance (Qty)	Purchased (Qty)	Total (Qty)	Issued (Qty)	Balance (Qty)	From whom Purchased /To whom Issued	Cost (Rs)	Bill No. with Date
Urea									
SSP									
MOP									
Gypsum									
Bio-fertilizer									
Green fodder									
Concentrates									
Bhusa									
Silage									

Courtesy: M.C. Farm, Agricultural College, Mahanandi

ii. Farm Financial Records

These records are related to the financial aspects of farm business. That is, these financial records relate primarily to money or the financial transactions of the farm. That is, these records justify or prove farm income or expense transactions. Output sales, operating expenses, equipment purchases, accounts payable, accounts receivable, inventories, depreciation records, loan balances and price information are all examples of financial records. As discussed above, Physical or Production records are items that relate to quantities of inputs and levels of production by enterprise and/or by resource type. They consist of crop yields, plant populations, calves born, litres of milk produced, death loss of animals *etc.* These physical data are converted into monetary aspects in financial records. Both production and financial records are important to the efficient management of farm business. When such information is accurately maintained and categorized, it can be used to produce useful decision-making information. The important financial records are related to:

a. Farm inventory
b. Farm financial accounts or Farm cash account
c. Classified farm cash account
d. Supplementary financial records like:
   - ☆ Cash sale register

- Credit sale or purchase register
- Capital assets sale register
- Wages register
- Funds borrowed and Repayments register
- Farm expenses paid in kind register and
- Non- farm income record.

a. Farm Inventory

It is the list of all physical assets of a farm business along with their valuation at a point of time. In analyzing the financial performance of a farm business, listing farm inventory is the first step. This farm inventory shows the list of all that a farmer owns and owes on a particular date, usually at the beginning and at the end of each production year. It has not only list of physical assets of farm business, but values of all assets and liabilities or debts. There are two steps in taking a farm inventory:

- ***Physical count of assets:*** It includes a complete listing of all physical assets, verifying weights and measurements.
- ***Value physical assets:*** After writing down the physical farm assets and liabilities or debts, it is important to value them.

1. Valuation of Farm Assets in taking Farm Inventory

The valuation of farm assets forms the basis for taking farm inventory and the same is also essential for preparing the NWS of farm business. The valuation of farm assets should be accurate otherwise, there is a chance of their over valuation or under valuation. As there are different forms of farm capital assets employed in the business, there are different methods of valuating them and they are discussed here under.

- ***Valuation of farm supplies and purchase feeds:*** The farm supplies like seeds, fertilizers, pesticides, fuel, feeds, veterinary medicines *etc.*, are valued at their cost or market price, whichever is lower. For example:

  Cost of fertilizer: Rs. 2000/unit

  Market price of fertilizer: Rs. 2200/unit

  So, value of fertilizer: Rs. 2000/unit.
- ***Valuation of crops and livestock produce:*** All assets that will be sold within a year are valued in terms of net selling price. This net selling price is given by: Market price – Total marketing costs. For example, market price of paddy is Rs.12000/qtl, total marketing costs incurred are Rs.25/qtl. So, one quintal of paddy is valued at net selling price given by: 1200-25= Rs. 1175/qtl.
- ***Valuation of machinery and breeding livestock:*** These working assets are valued based on Purchasing cost - Depreciation. While using these assets on the farm, they get depreciated every year due to wear and tear and this depreciated amount should be deducted from the value of the asset at the beginning of the year, as discussed earlier under Straight line method, to estimate the present value of asset. The same is exemplified here under.

Assume the following data: Original cost of the asset: = Rs.40000, Junk value = Rs.2000, Useful life of asset = 10 years. As per the Straight line method,

Annual Depreciation = (Original cost – Junk value)/Number of years of useful life of asset

Annual Depreciation at the end of first year = (40000-2000)/10 = 3800. So, the present value of asset at the end of first year = 40000-3800 = Rs. 36200. Similarly, the present value of the machinery at the end of second year is 36200-3800= Rs.32400. Likewise, for the subsequent years of useful life of the asset, the present values are worked out by subtracting annual depreciation from the remaining value of the asset at the end of current accounting or beginning of the new accounting year.

- ***Valuation of Farm Buildings:*** In case of valuation of farm buildings, the above methodology *i.e.*, cost minus depreciation may not serve the purpose, as the market value of farm buildings fluctuate very frequently. So, instead of (construction) cost minus depreciation, replacement cost minus (total) depreciation will be used to valuate farm buildings. Replacement cost is the cost at which the building can be reconstructed at present prices and under present methods of construction. After computing the replacement cost, deduct total depreciation to arrive at present value of building. This method of valuation can be understood from the following example:

  Example: Assume a farmer has constructed a godown for storing produce in the year, 2008. Its replacement cost on June, 2013 is Rs.400000. Find the present value of godown assuming rate of depreciation as 2 percent.

  Solution: Given, replacement cost of godown: Rs.4,00,000

  Annual depreciation rate = 2 percent

  So, annual depreciation = 400000x (2/100) = Rs. 8000.

  So, total depreciation in five years = 8000 * 5 = Rs. 40000.

  So, present value of godown in June, 2013 = Replacement cost - Total depreciation

  = 400000-40000= Rs. 360000.

  However, if the farm building is constructed only a few years back (say, one and a half year), it can be valued by cost minus depreciation method.

- ***Valuation of Land:*** As discussed earlier under section I of Chapter 3, value of land is estimated through several methods like Sales comparison method, Income Approach or Net Income Capitalization Approach, Soil Productivity Approach and Cost Approach. Among these, Income capitalization method is most commonly followed for valuating the farm land, which contributes income to the farmer over a longer period of time. However, this method of computation of value of land by income capitalization method suffers from the limitation that, the rate of capitalization (rate of interest) is difficult to determine.

The following Table 4.8 summarizes different methods of valuation followed across different types of farm assets employed in the business:

Table 4.8: Summary Statement Showing Various Methods Employed to Valuate different Farm Assets

Method of Valuation	*Farm Assets*
Cost or Market price whichever is lower.	Valuation of farm supplies like seeds, fertilizers, pesticides, fuel, veterinary medicines and feeds to livestock.
Net Selling Price (Market Price - Total Marketing Costs)	Valuation of crops and livestock produce
Purchasing Cost- Depreciation	Valuation of working assets like machinery and livestock
Replacement cost - Depreciation	Valuation of farm buildings like storage structures
Sales comparison method, Income Approach or Net Income Capitalization Approach, Soil Productivity Approach and Cost Approach	Valuation of land

2. Time of taking Farm Inventory

In general, farm inventory is listed out at two points of time in an agricultural year *i.e.*, at the beginning and at the end of an agricultural year. Since, the end point of an agricultural year, marks the beginning of succeeding agricultural year, every year at its beginning, farm inventory is listed out. That is, the closing inventory for a year is the beginning inventory for the next year. So, the best time to take a farm inventory is at the beginning of an agricultural year *i.e.*, on or near 1st July. This is so because, usually at this point of time, new crop season commences and the past agricultural year ends. Further, the retained produce and stored feed are at minimal quantities by this point of time, which makes the value measurement of inventory easier. Note that, farm inventory can be listed out at any point of time in an agricultural year, but once the time is fixed, the farmer must stick to it in the future. In general, two aspects must be considered by the farmer in fixing the time for taking the farm inventory *viz.*,

- ☆ When the farmer is having ample leisure time.
- ☆ When the stocks of produce, inputs and feed are at minimal quantities or exhausted in the farm godowns so that, the farmer can avoid value estimates of these items.

3. Preparation of Farm Inventory

This involves two aspects *viz.*, physical verification and estimation of value of farm assets. In the former, the farmer will list out all the physical assets on the farm either by counting or measurement or weighment. Note that, physical damages must be minimal, while taking the list of inventory. In case of valuation of farm assets, the famer must estimate the value considering their market price or replacement cost or net selling price *etc.*, and these methods of valuation of farm assets are discussed earlier. Note that, while estimating the value of farm assets, the farmer must be very careful, as any minor error in the valuation of any item in the inventory may lead to misleading results. For example, a farmer produced 500 quintals of paddy and he valued it at Rs.1055/quintal instead of Rs.1050/quintal, resulting in an over valuation by Rs.2500 and this increase in valuation is not an insignificant amount. This over valuation of produce will inflate the net worth of the business. This inflated opening inventory will reduce the income in the next year by the same amount. On the contrary, the under valuation of produce will deflate the net worth of the business and it will increase the income in the next year by the same amount.

4. Items Considering in Listing Out Farm Inventory

Three items are considered for preparing the list of farm inventory *viz.*, Non-depreciable assets, Depreciable assets and Cash assets and the same are shown through Table 4.9.

Table 4.9: Measurement of Change in Farm Inventory

Name of the Farm: --------- Year: ----------

Items	Beginning of Agricultural Year (1st July, 2012)		End of Agricultural Year (30th June, 2013)	
	Quantity/Number	Value (Rs)	Quantity/Number	Value (Rs)
I. Non-Depreciable Assets • Seeds • Fertilizers o Urea o DAP o SSP o MOP • Pesticides o Monocrotophos o Chloropyriphos o Imidachloprid • Marketable Produce **Sub-Total (I)**				
II. Depreciable Assets • Implements o Seed drill o Star weeder • Machinery o Tractor o Threshers o Decorticator • Farm buildings • Livestock o Milch cows o Buffaloes **Sub-Total (II)**				
III. Cash Assets • Cash in hand • Savings in bank • Shares in PACSs **Sub-Total (III)**				
Grand Total (Rs)		(I+II+III) = A		(I+II+III) = B
Change in Inventory (Rs)	B-A			

Courtesy: M.C. Farm, Agricultural College, Mahanandi

5. Importance of taking of Farm Inventory

The listing of farm inventory every year is helpful in the following aspects:

- ☆ Enable the farmer to know the growth of capital accumulated in a business over a period of time.
- ☆ Enable the farmer to know the change in value of farm assets over the last year.

- ☆ If the farmer collects the data pertaining to his liabilities in the farm business along with the inventory position, he can easily compute the net worth of the business.
- ☆ Farm inventory forms the basis to calculate income measures of the farm.
- ☆ Helps to compute depreciation of farm assets and thereby, their present value.

b. Farm Financial Accounts or Farm Cash Accounts

Unlike farm inventory which shows the financial condition (list of capital assets) at a point of time, Farm financial accounts shows the cash expenses and receipts of a farm over a period of time, usually for one crop season or one agricultural year.

c. Classified Farm Cash Account

This is an extension of Farm financial account, but the details of cash expenses and receipts are shown enterprise-wise over a period of time, usually for one crop season or one agricultural year.

Systems of Book Keeping

As defined earlier, farm book keeping refers to the systematic maintenance of farm records regarding the transactions made by the farmer in performing his business. We know, a farmer performs several transactions in farm business say, purchasing of inputs like seeds, fertilizers, pesticides, machinery, feed, veterinary medicines *etc.*, and selling of main product and by-product of the enterprise(s) practiced by him. In making these transactions, it is essential on the part of the farmer to record them in the registers systematically, as such data are important for taking future decisions on the farm. Let us now discuss in-detail about the two systems of entries of transactions in record books *viz.*, Single entry system and Double entry system.

i. Single Entry System

As the name itself indicates, only one entry is made in the record book for each transaction *i.e.*, only one account is maintained. In this entry system, only personal accounts are maintained and impersonal accounts are ignored altogether. So, the main characteristic of this system is the keeping of personal accounts only. In case of purchase or sale of a non-durable asset say, purchase of fertilizer, sale of paddy *etc.*, an operating account is maintained (Table 4.10) and in case of purchase or sale of a durable asset say, purchase of tractor or sale of mulch cow, a capital account is maintained (Table 4.11).

Table 4.10: Maintenance of an Operating Account

Date	*Description*	*Price*	*Quantity*	*Value*
1-1-2013	Sale of Paddy	Rs. 1300/qtl	50 qtls	Rs. 65,000

Table 4.11: Maintenance of Capital Account

Date	*Description*	*Number/Quantity*	*Value*
1-2-2013	Purchase of Tractor	One	Rs. 400000

Merits

The above system of making single entry in the record books will have the following merits:

- ☆ This system of entry is so simple and can be easily understood by the farmer.
- ☆ It is less time consuming thereby, farmer can easily spare his time to make the entries in the record books.
- ☆ As this system requires the farmer to make only one entry for every transaction, it keeps paperwork and math to a minimum.

Demerits

However, this single entry system suffers from the following limitations:

- ☆ No separate cash account is maintained.
- ☆ Does not provide readily the cash balance position of the farmer.

ii. Double Entry System

As the name indicates, in this book entry system, two entries are made for each and every transaction. One entry is made on the debit side and other entry is made on the credit side. Since every transaction involves two parties *i.e.*, one for giving a good and other for receiving the good, two entries are made at two places *i.e.*, on credit side and on debt side for each and every transaction. So, every debit entry must have a corresponding credit entry and every credit entry must have a corresponding debit entry. Thus, this is a two-fold aspect of transaction dealing with two parties *i.e.*, one for giving benefit and the other for receiving benefit. For example, in transacting paddy by a farmer, two entries are made *i.e.*, one for sale of quantity of paddy (*i.e.*, giving account) and other for receiving cash from sale of paddy (*i.e.*, receiving account). The former *i.e.*, giving account is written on the credit side of the entry and the latter *i.e.*, receiving account is written on debit side of the entry. Let us look at the following examples:

Example 4.1

A farmer received Rs.20000 from a trader. Here, cash is received by the farmer *i.e.*, Rs.20000 and is shown in cash account. This cash receiving account will be the debtor. The trader paid cash to the farmer. Here, cash is paid or given by the trader and this cash giving account is the creditor. So, farmer's account will be debited and trader's account will be credited.

Example 4.2

Assume a trader (Ravi Kumar) sells his machinery to a farmer (Sri Ram) at Rs.400000. Let us employ the double entry system of writing this transaction for both trader and farmer.

a. Double Entry System for Trader

Table 4.12: Capital (Trader) Selling (giving) Account for Trader (Ravi Kumar)

Debit			*Credit*		
Date	*Description*	*Value (Rs.)*	*Date*	*Description*	*Value (Rs.)*
			1-2-2013	Sale of tractor	Rs.4,00,000

Table 4.13: Cash Receiving Account for Trader (Ravi Kumar)

Debit			*Credit*		
Date	*Description*	*Value (Rs.)*	*Date*	*Description*	*Value (Rs.)*
1-2-2013	Cash received by selling tractor	Rs.4,00,000			

Like trader (Ravi Kumar), even the farmer (Sri Ram) also maintains record books and he makes the double entries as given below.

b. Double Entry System for Farmer

Table 4.14: Capital Receiving Account of Farmer (Sri Ram)

Debit			*Credit*		
Date	*Description*	*Value (Rs.)*	*Date*	*Description*	*Value (Rs.)*
1-2-2013	Tractor received by the farmer	Rs.4,00,000			

Table 4.15: Cash giving Account of Farmer (Sri Ram)

Debit			*Credit*		
Date	*Description*	*Value (Rs.)*	*Date*	*Description*	*Value (Rs.)*
		1-2-2013	Cash paid by farmer	Rs.4,00,000	

Note that, in the above transaction of tractor between trader (Ravi Kumar) and farmer (Sri Ram), if the trader offered the tractor on lease basis to farmer, then two transaction will get affected *i.e.*, cash receiving account of trader and cash giving account of farmer, as there is no monetary transaction between them. Thus, there only are two accounts *i.e.*, capital (tractor) giving account of trader and capital receiving account of farmer. These two transactions are shown here under.

Table 4.16: Capital (Trader) Selling (giving) Account for Trader (Ravi Kumar)

Debit			*Credit*		
Date	*Description*	*Value (Rs.)*	*Date*	*Description*	*Value (Rs.)*
			1-2-2013	Sale of tractor	Rs.4,00,000

Table 4.17: Capital Receiving Account of Farmer (Sri Ram)

Debit			*Credit*		
Date	*Description*	*Value (Rs.)*	*Date*	*Description*	*Value (Rs.)*
1-2-2013	Tractor received by the farmer	Rs.4,00,000			

It should be noted that, capital (tractor) receiving account of farmer means that, the account is maintained by the trader himself for personal dealing with farmer and it does not mean, the farmer has maintained this account. These examples illustrate that, in double entry system, two entries are made for each and every transaction and the amount of debit entry must be equal to the corresponding credit entry.

Merits of Double Entry System

This system of book entry of transactions is meritorious over single entry system in the following aspects:

- Double entry system provides complete record of both personal and impersonal transactions.
- The entries in the accounts can be easily cross-checked for their accuracy.
- Enable the farmer to draw comparative picture with preceding years' accounts for similar transactions.
- As both the accounts for each transaction must tally, it provides more reliable information.
- This entry system provides a permanent, systematic and complete record of financial transactions.
- Provide financial records for the value of assets and liabilities, purchases and sales, income and expenses.
- Provide records for ascertaining profit or loss made by the farmer at any given time.
- Shows the financial performance of an organization at any point of time.
- Helps in detecting fraud and other irregularities that may arise from inadequate accounting of data in the records.
- Provide basis for planning and effective control of business operations.

Single Entry System vis-à-vis Double Entry System

The following points highlight the differences between Single Entry System and Double Entry System:

- Compared to Single Entry System, Double Entry system is perfect in its arrangement and mathematically accurate
- In Single Entry System, only personal accounts are kept whereas, Double Entry System, records of both personal and impersonal accounts are kept.
- Trial and balance account is possible under double entry, unlike in Single Entry System.

☆ Double Entry system is perfect, accurate and results are more reliable compared to Single Entry System.

iii. Supplementary Farm Records

These records include:

a. Sanction register
b. Auction register
c. Rainfall register
d. Hire register
e. Stationary register

There is another way of classifying the farm records considering the nature of activity the farmer takes up in the farm business. The three basic types of farm records include:

☆ ***Resources inventories:*** We know that, in planning the farm business, first the farmer must assess his resource position. He has to arrange the important resources like land, labour, machinery, managerial resources, financial capital *etc.* The farmer has to maintain these resource inventories for planning the enterprises in the farm.

☆ ***Production accounts of operations:*** These records show the output (main product and by-product) details of each enterprise practiced on the farm. These records also furnish the domestic consumption details of the farmer and marketable surplus available in each year along with the previous year's stocked produce. These records also enable the farmer to draw the relationship between input(s) applied and output of the enterprise.

☆ ***Income and expenses records:*** These records express the physical inputs and outputs into income and expenses of various enterprises practiced on the farm.

Note that, selecting a record-keeping system should depend on the expected use of the records. There is no 'best' record keeping system available for all situations, but, at minimum, the farm records system should: provide accurate and necessary information, fit into the farm organization or framework, be available in a form to aid decision-making *etc.*, and other meritorious or desirable features as discussed earlier. The person responsible for keeping the records should develop a habit of regularly and accurately recording the transactions. So, making all financial transactions through a bank account can be useful. For an accuracy check, the monthly statement should be reconciled with the cheque book and record-keeping system.

Above all, a number of decisions need to be made about farm record systems. All the details of the farm business must be maintained say, number of enterprises included, deciding about home and living expenses and about business interests outside the farm. A decision needs to be made about the choice of accounting period *i.e.*, either on a calendar year basis or on a fiscal year? The time period selected should be the one that is the most suitable for the type of farm business. Regardless of how complicated the bookkeeping may be, the first step is to maintain a separate business and personal accounts and follow the following important rules:

- ☆ As far as possible, pay all business bills by cheques.
- ☆ Deposit all the farm income into the bank account and this serve as a good record of all farm income.
- ☆ Avoid using the business account to pay personal expenses.
- ☆ Balance the bank account every month and file the statements monthly.

F. Farm Efficiency Measures

As discussed earlier, there lies greater emphasis in maintaining farm records. These farm records enable the farmers to analyze about the performance of farm business over time and thus, guide him to plan for the future. Majority of the financial difficulties that the farmers face in executing the farm business can be solved through systematic maintenance and analysis of farm records. Note that, mere maintenance of farm records does not solve any purpose. These records must harbour vast amount of information about the farm and this information must be analyzed thoroughly to compare and discern trends in the farm business. These trends help farmers make sensible managerial decisions like *'Is this enterprise profitable?'* or *'Can I afford to purchase a new tractor?'* or *'Should I change my enterprise mix?' etc.* That is, good records do not ensure the farm to be successful, however success is unlikely without them. So, accuracy, up-to-date information and thorough analysis of these records are essential to successful farm management. Just as a doctor examines the symptoms of ill-health to judge the overall health of a patient, the farmer has to look at these farm records of a business and assess its financial health, both now and to some extent, in the future. They even resemble 'Report cards' students receive in a school, as they indicate, how well a farmer is managing the operations compared to other farmers in that locality. This financial assessment show, how the business has been doing so far and how it should be carried out in the future. Though it is obviously too late to correct what was happened in the past, but the farmer based on the analytical findings of information from farm records can plan for the future towards achieving financial objectives. This procedure is similar to a doctor telling the patient that, he was gaining weight and thereby, suggesting a dietary discipline toward a better weight in the future. Thus, farm records enable the farmer to compute different efficiency measures pertaining to the use of different resources on the farm and they are popularly called as Farm efficiency measures. These farm efficiency measures are essential to analyze the manner in which the available resources are allocated across the enterprises vis-à-vis the objectives of the farmer. This measures not only enable the farmer to know the performance of his farm business, but also facilitate to compare with standard farms in that locality. Generally, one farm is considered to be more efficient than another farm in terms of two aspects *viz.*, producing more output per unit of input employed and cost-effective production of output. Accordingly, the farm efficiency measures can be broadly categorized into Physical efficiency measures and Financial efficiency measures respectively. Both these measures can be further sub-divided into Aggregate or Absolute measures and Ratio measures (Figure 4.1).

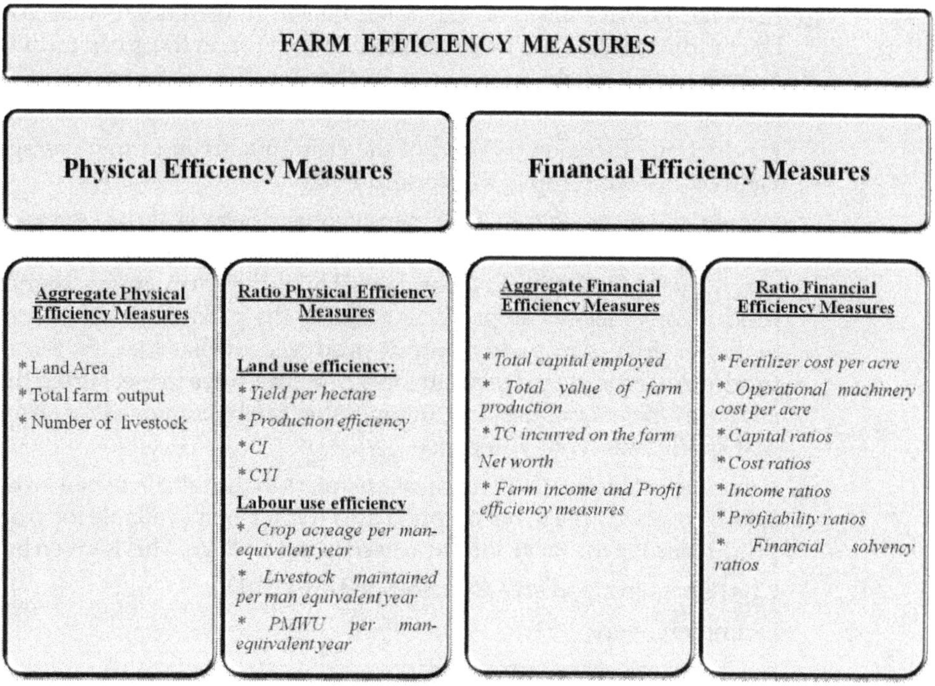

Figure 4.1: Efficiency Measures Employed in the Farm Business.

a. Physical Efficiency Measures

These measures analyze the physical (non-monetary) aspects of the farm business. They include both Aggregate and Ratio measures.

i. Aggregate Physical Efficiency Measures

These measures relate to the total production on the farm or total production units on the farm. They include:

- ☆ Total land area in terms of acres or hectares
- ☆ Total output in term of quintals or tonnes
- ☆ Total number of livestock
- ☆ Total output of milk on the farm in terms of litres

ii. Ratio Measures

These measures include:

- ☆ ***Land use efficiency:*** This can be measured in terms of
  - ❑ ***Yield per hectare:*** This refers to the ratio between total output produced to total area under the crop. This given by:

    Yield per hectare = Total output/Total area (hectares) under the crop

- ***Production efficiency:*** This can be studied with reference to each crop by computing the ratio between yield of the crop in the given farm to average yield of the same crop in that locality and expressed in percentage. This is given by:

  Production efficiency = (Yield of the crop in a given farm/Average yield of the same crop in that locality)*100

  Example: Paddy yield in Mahanandi college farm is 4t/ha. Average yield of paddy in that locality is 3.5t/ha. So, production efficiency is given by: (4/3.5)*100=114 per cent. Thus, the farm enjoys higher production efficiency in producing paddy (by producing 14 per cent higher yields) than paddy output produced in that locality. Since, production efficiency deals with only one enterprise in measuring the land use efficiency of the farm, this measure can be employed for farms that specialize on one enterprise.

- ***Cropping Intensity (CI):*** This measure refers to the ratio between gross (total) cropped area to net cropped area (or net area available for crop production) of the farm and expressed in percentage. This is given by:

  CI = (Gross cropped area/Net cropped area)*100

  Example: Given,

  1. Gross area of the farm: 100ha
  2. Area under roads: 5ha
  3. Area under buildings: 3ha
  4. Area not suitable for crop production: 2ha

  Area under different crop in the farm (2012-13)

  Kharif season: Paddy:25ha, Maize:15 ha and Turmeric: 40ha.

  Rabi season: Gram: 40ha, Groundnut: 20ha

  Solution: From items 1 to 4, we can compute, gross area available for crop production is: 100-(5+3+2) = 90ha.

  Total (Net) cropped area of the farm = Area of crops under kharif season + Area of crops under rabi season.

  =(25+15+40)+(40+20) = 140ha.

  So, CI = (140/90)*100=156 per cent

  The above calculated value of CI (*i.e.,* 156 per cent) implies that, the land cultivated in the farm for producing crop enterprises is 1.56 times the area of land available for crop cultivation.

- ***Crop Yield Index (CYI):*** This is a convenient measure, as it combines all the yields of different crops into a single figure. Hence, this measure is convenient to study the land use efficiency of the farm, when it diversify to practice several enterprises and with little emphasis on livestock rearing. The following is the procedure employed to compute CYI with reference to the example given below.

Crops	Area of Crops in Farm (ha)	Yield of Crops in the Farm (t/ha)	Avg. Yield of Crops in that Locality (t/ha)	Yield of Crops on the Farm as a per cent of locality (Production Efficiency)	Production Efficiency * Area under Each Crop
X	3	5	3	(5/3)×100=167	167×3=501
Y	7	12	9	(12/9)×100=133	133×7=931
Z	5	9	7	(9/7)×100=129	129×5=645
	15				2077

CYI = 2077/15 = 138 per cent

This implies that, the given farm is 38 percent more efficient in crop production when compared to other farms in that locality.

- ***System Index:*** This index is used for determining the rationality by which various enterprises on a certain farm are combined. It is obtained by expressing the potential net income per hectare on a farm as a percentage of the average standard net income per hectare in that locality or area. So,

  System Index = Potential Net Income per hectare on the Farm/Average Standard Net Income per hectare in that locality

Crop	Average Standard Net Income per Hectare of Enterprise in that Locality (Rs.)	Area under Units of Enterprises on the Farm (Ha)	Total Potential Net Income of the Farm (Rs.)
Crop X	1500	5	9500
Crop Y	2000	1	2200
Crop Z	1300	7	9700
Total	4800	13	21400
Average	1600		1646

If the system index is more than 100, it indicates a higher level of efficiency in combining enterprises on the farm in comparison to that by an average farm in that locality and *vice versa*. Therefore, the system index = (1646/1600)*100 = 103 per cent. However, major difficulty may be encountered in calculating this index, when the selected farmer grows crops, which are not usually grown in the locality.

- ***Labour use efficiency:*** As discussed earlier, labour is one of the essential factors employed in the crop production programme and hence, labour employment counts much in boosting output on one hand and cost effective production (if labour supply is plenty) on the other. We also know, men, women and children labour are employed in the farm to perform various agricultural operations. The standard unit employed to measure labour usage on the farm is 'man days'. A man day refers to the productive work accomplished by a labourer in a period of 8 hours per day, assuming average efficiency. Since, the farm manager employs men, women and child labour on the farm, it is essential to convert women labour and child labour into man days equivalent. The standard conversion units of women labour into man-equivalents and child labour into man equivalents are as follows: 2 men = 3 women and one man = 2 children. By using these conversation factors, women and child labour days can be converted into man-equivalent days. The sum of man equivalent days and man days (of men labour) gives the total man days worked on the farm. The ratio between total man days worked on the farm to 365 days gives man-equivalent year. Let us go through the following example:

Assume one hectare of paddy employs 70 men labour, 150 women labour and 40 child labour. Compute man-equivalent year.

Solution: Given man days (of men labour): 70

Conversion of women labour days into man-equivalent days: 150*(2/3) = 100 man-equivalent days

Similarly, conversion of child labour days into man-equivalent days: 40*(1/2) = 20 man-equivalent days

Total man days employed on the farm = 70+100+20=190 man days

So, man-equivalent year (Person year) = 190/365=0.52

Now, considering the above background, labour-use efficiency can be computed by employing the following measures:

- ***Crop acreage per man-equivalent year:*** This refers to the ratio between total crop acreage in the farm to man-equivalent year. Higher the ratio, greater is the labour efficiency in producing output of the crops.
- ***Livestock maintained per man equivalent year:*** This refers to the ratio between total number of livestock maintained on the farm to the man-equivalent year. Higher the ratio, greater is the efficiency of labour in maintaining livestock enterprises.
- ***Productive Man Work Units (PWU or MWU) per man-equivalent year:*** A 'PWU' refers to the average amount of productive work accomplished by one man in the usual 8 hours man-day. The total PWUs is measured by employing the formula:

  Total PWUs = Σ(Acreage of each crop * Average labour requirement per unit of each crop)

  This is shown below through the following Table 4.18.

Table 4.18: Computation of PWUs

Crops	*Area (Ha)*	*Average Labour Requirement per Unit of Crop*	*PWUs*
X	2	230	460
Y	4	95	380
Z	5	50	250
		Total PWUs	1090

So, PWUs/Man equivalent year can be computed as: =

$$\frac{\text{Total PWUs}}{\text{Man Equivalent Year}}$$

This measure (PWU/Man equivalent year) is meritorious in the sense that, it helps to compare farms of different sizes practicing different crop enterprises and even with varying cropping intensities.

b. Financial Efficiency Measures

These measures indicate the economic efficiency of resources usage in the farm business and finally indicate, whether the farm business is successful or failed in accomplishing its objectives. These measures are again classified into Aggregate and Ratio measures and they are discussed here under.

i. Aggregate Financial Efficiency Measures

These measures are related to the total capital employed in the farm business, total returns earned, net worth position of the farmer and other income measures.

- ☆ ***Total capital employed:*** This measure relates to both fixed capital and working capital employed in the farm business.
- ☆ ***TC incurred on the farm:*** This measure is related to the sum of fixed expenses and working expenses incurred by the farmer on the farm.
- ☆ ***Total value of farm production:*** This measure refers to the TR derived by the farmer from his farm business. Under each enterprise, the value of main product and by-product are considered to estimate the TR of the enterprise and the sum of TRs across all the enterprises constitute the total value of farm production. This measure helps to compare different farms of same sizes. The total value of farm production is computed are shown below:

Crops/ Enterprises	*Area (Ha)*	*Main Product (Qtls)*	*By-product (Qtls)*	*Price of Main Product (Rs./qtl)*	*Price of By-product (Rs./qtl)*	*TR (Rs.)*
X	5	150	25	1000	300	157500
Y	3	120	–	1200	–	144000
Z	4	80	–	1500	–	120000
	Total value of farm production					**421500**

- ☆ ***Net worth:*** This measure refers to the difference between total assets and total liabilities of the farm business. That is, if the total assets are more than total liabilities, the difference is called Net worth. On the contrary, if the total liabilities are more than total assets, the difference is called Net deficit. So,

  Net Worth (+) = Total assets – Total liabilities.

  Net Deficit (-) = Total liabilities – Total assets.

☆ ***Farm income and Profit efficiency measures***

- ❑ Net Cash Income = Total Cash Receipts – Total Cash Operating Expenses.
- ❑ Net Farm Income (NFI) = Net Cash Income ± Change in Farm Inventory in Non-Depreciable Assets and Depreciable Assets.
- ❑ Farm Earnings = NFI + Value of Farm Privileges (*i.e.*, farm produce used at home).
- ❑ Family Labour Earnings = Farm Earnings – Interest on Fixed Capital
- ❑ Returns to Management = Family Labour Earnings – Imputed Value of Family Labour.

The above measures are very useful, as they can be used to compare financial efficiency of farm business across different farms. These measures were analyzed with reference to the data given for a 5 acres farm in Nandyal region of Andhra Pradesh (Table 4.19).

Table 4.19: Computation of Farm income and Profit Efficiency Measures

Sl.No.	*Items*	*Amount (Rs.)*
1.	**Cash income from**	
	a. Sale of crops	
	☆ Groundnut	1,75,000
	☆ Maize	45,000
	b. Sale of livestock products	
	☆ Milk	37,000
	☆ Manure	10,000
	c. Sale of livestock	
	☆ Cows	47,000
	☆ Buffaloes	32,000
	d. Miscellaneous	
	☆ Rent received	12,000
	☆ Subsidies received	17,000
	Total net cash income	**375000**
2.	***Cash expenses***	
	a. Cost of material inputs like seeds, fertilizers, pesticides, feed *etc.*	50,000
	b. Labour charges	
	☆ Family labour	21,000
	☆ Hired labour	38,000
	c. Machinery labour	17,000
	Total Cash Expenses	**126000**
3.	Change in farm inventory	37,000
4.	Value of farm privileges used for family consumption	16,000
5.	Average capital investment	400000
6.	Rate of interest	10 per cent

Solution:

Net cash income = Total Cash Receipts – Total Cash Operating Expenses = Rs.375000 – Rs.126000 = Rs. 2,49,000

NFI = Net Cash Income ± Change in Farm Inventory in Non-Depreciable Assets and Depreciable Assets = Rs. 249000 + Rs. 37000 = Rs. 286000

Farm earnings = NFI + Value of Farm Privileges (*i.e.*, farm produce used at home) = Rs.286000 + Rs.16000 = Rs. 302000

Family labour earnings = Farm Earnings – Interest on Fixed Capital = Rs.302000 – Rs.40000 = Rs.262000

Returns to management = Family Labour Earnings – Imputed Value of Family Labour = Rs.26200 – Rs.21000 = Rs. 241000

ii. Ratio Measures

These measures indicate per unit costs and per unit returns of farm enterprises and this enable to compare the farm businesses even of different sizes. These measures include:

- ***Fertilizer cost per acre:*** This refers to the ratio between the total fertilizer cost incurred by the farmer and the total acreage under the crop. Lower the ratio, higher is the efficiency in using fertilizer.
- ***Operational machinery cost per acre:*** This refers to the average running cost or operational cost of the machinery per acre of each crop. Lower the ratio, higher is the efficiency in employing the machinery of the farm.
- ***Capital ratios***
    - ***Percentage return on total capital:*** The total market value of all the resources on the farm is known as total capital of the farm. It includes sum of market value of land and improvements made, if any and the value of animals, machinery, implements, grain and fodder reserves *etc.* The rate (per cent) of return on capital is calculated by expressing the annual operational profit as a percentage of the total capital. This is given by

$$\text{Percentage return on total capital} = \frac{\text{Operational Profit}}{\text{Total Capital}} \times 100$$

This rate of return on total capital does not take into account interest, loan repayments, living costs *etc.*

The Percentage return on total capital can also be computed in the following two ways:

Method 1: Percent returns to capital = [(Farm Earnings – Imputed Value of Family Labour)/Average Capital Investment] *100

=[(302000-21000)/400000]*100 = 70.25 per cent

This implies the rate of earnings in the farm is 70 percent produced by the capital invested in the business.

- ❑ ***Percentage of equity:*** A farmer's capital is sometimes expressed as a percentage of the total resources under his control and this refers to percentage of equity and this is given by

$$\text{Percentage of equity} = \frac{\text{Owned Capital}}{\text{Owned Capital} + \text{Borrowed Capital}} \times 100$$

  This ratio shows, how efficiently the farmer is operating the business with his owned capital.

- ❑ ***Capital per man equivalent per year:*** It is the ratio between total capital invested in the farm business to man-equivalent year
- ❑ ***Rate of capital turnover:*** It refers to the number of years required for the farm to cover the total capital invested through farm receipts (income). This is given by:

  = (Gross income of the farm)/(Total capital invested on the farm (or Total value of farm assets)*100

  The higher the rate, the safer is the business.

- ❑ ***Capital per unit of gross income:*** This refers to the ratio between total capital invested in the farm to the gross income derived.

☆ ***Cost ratios:*** These ratios deal with the relationship between costs and returns of farm business and they indicate, to what extent the costs of the farm-firm are absorbed by the gross income earned in the business. The measures included under costs ratios are:

- ❑ ***Operating cost ratio:*** This ratio indicates, to what extent the operating expenses of the farm are absorbed out of gross income earned in the business. This is given by:

  Operating cost ratio = Total operating expenses/Gross income

  Lower the ratio is desirable. The operational efficiency of the farm can be directly indicated by this (lower) ratio. This ratio is highly fluctuating year by year, unlike Fixed cost ratio, as both operating expenses and gross income of the farm business fluctuate every year.

- ❑ ***Fixed cost ratio (Over head ratio):*** This ratio is given by: TFC/Gross income. Again, lower the ratio is desirable. Since, TFC remains constant in the short run production programme, the fluctuations in the gross income of the farm business alone influences the magnitude of this ratio.
- ❑ ***Gross cost ratio:*** This refers to the ratio between SRTC and gross income of the farm business. This is given by:

  Gross cost ratio= SRTC/Gross income

  Lower the ratio is desirable. Both SRTC and gross income influences this ratio. This ratio directly indicates the profit margin realized by the farm.

- ***Income ratios:*** One of the important income ratios is net income per acre ratio. To compute this ratio, we need data pertaining to gross income, total expenses and number of acres cultivated in the farm. We know, net income is equal to the difference between gross income and total expenses (SRTC) of the farm. So, this ratio is given by:

  Net income per acre = Net income/Number of acres cultivated

  Higher ratio is desirable are this implies higher net profits to the farm.

- ***Profitability ratios:*** These ratios were used to compute returns to the investment made in the farm business. These ratios provide a fairly sound method of diagnosis of the financial status and overall efficiency of the farm.

  - ***Net Profit to Total Assets Ratio:*** This is the ratio of profit on total assets of the farm and their employment. An increasing trend over the years indicates the overall efficiency of the farm.

    Net profit to Total Assets Ratio = Net Profit/Total Assets

  - ***Net Profit to Net Worth Ratio:*** The ratio of net profit to net worth shows, whether profitability is being maintained or not.

    Net Profit to Net Worth Ratio = Net Profit/Net Worth

  - ***Net Profit to Fixed Assets Ratio:*** The ratio indicates whether the fixed assets are being used profitably. A decline in the ratio shows that, either the assets are being kept idle or the business conditions are bad.

    Net Profit to Fixed Assets Ratio = Net Profit/Fixed Assets

- ***Financial solvency ratios:*** These ratios directly measure the financial safety and liquidity of conducting the farm business at a point of time. These ratios are derived from NWS of farm business. The financial solvency ratios include:

  - ***Current ratio:*** This ratio measures the degree of financial solvency of farm business in the immediate or current year. This is given by:

    Current ratio= Current assets/Current liabilities

  - ***Working ratio:*** This ratio measures the degree of financial solvency of a farm business over an intermediate period of time. This is given by:

    Working ratio = (Current assets + Intermediate assets)/(Current liabilities + Intermediate liabilities)

  - ***Net capital ratio:*** This ratio measures the degree of financial solvency of a farm business over a longer period of time. This is given by:

    Net capital ratio= Total assets/Total liabilities

    Besides above three ratios, there are other financial solvency ratios like Acid-test ratio (Quick ratio), Debt Structure Ratio *etc.*, and these ratios are discussed in detail in the ensuing Chapter 5.

- ***Cost concepts:*** The CACP was basically setup as the Agricultural Prices Commission (January, 1965) to advise the Government on price policy of major agricultural commodities with a view to evolve a balance and integrated price structure in the perspective of the overall needs of the economy and with due regard to the interests of the producer and the consumer. Since March 1985, the Commission has been known as CACP. The Commission provides recommendations to the Government for announcing Minimum Support Prices (MSPs) to 25 agricultural commodities. Cost concepts defined by CACP are given below:

- **Cost A1** = Value of purchased material inputs (seed, insecticides and pesticides, manure, fertilizer),hired human labour, animal labour (hired and owned), machinery labour (hired and owned), depreciation on farm implements and farm buildings, irrigation charges, land revenue cesses and other taxes and interest on working capital.
- **Cost A2** = Cost A1 + Rent paid for leased-in land.
- **Cost A2+FL** = Cost A2 + Imputed value of family labour.
- **Cost B1** = Cost A1+ Interest on value of owned capital assets (excluding land).
- **Cost B2** = Cost B1+ Rental value of owned land (net of land revenue) and rent paid for leased-in land.
- **Cost C1** = Cost B1 + Imputed value of family labour.
- **Cost C2** = Cost B2 + Imputed value of family labour.
- **Cost C3** = Cost C2 + 10 per cent of Cost C2 (on account of managerial functions performed by farmer).
- **Cost of production** = (Cost C3-Value of byproduct)/Yield

Procedure for Imputation of Costs

Where as the valuation of purchased inputs could be made on the basis of expenditure incurred, there were problems with respect to some of the inputs used in the production of crops supplied by the farm family itself. The procedures adopted for evaluation of imputed cost of these inputs were as under:

- ☆ *Family Labour*: Charged on the basis of wages paid to attached farm labourers. Men family labour is to be charged on par with the attached servants (average wage value) of the village, while family women labour is to be imputed considering the wages paid to the women labour for the similar operation.
- ☆ *Owned Animal Labour*: In case of owned bullock labour, the per work day or per work hour cost of maintenance is to be taken into account. That is, this labour is evaluated on the basis of cost of maintenance, which included the following:
  - Cost of green and dry fodder
  - Cost of concentrates
  - Cost of labour for upkeep of livestock
  - Depreciation on animals and cattle sheds
  - Other miscellaneous expenses like veterinary medicines, vaccines *etc.*

- ☆ ***Owned Machinery Charges*:** Charged on the basis of cost of maintenance. The maintenance cost comprises: diesel, power, lubricants, depreciation, repairs and other expenses, if any. Even prevailing hire charges can also be considered. In case of hiring of machinery, actual hire charges are to be taken into consideration.
- ☆ ***Hired labour:*** The per day wage rate is to be arrived based on total wages (cash + kind + perquisites (extra payments like perks) considering the ruling price in the village at the time of operations. If the labour are permanent or attached, the per day wage rate is to be arrived based on total wages (cash + kind + perquisites) paid and the number of days of employment in the farm.
- ☆ ***Hired Bullock labour:*** In case of hired bullock labour, actual charges paid are considered.
- ☆ ***Implements*:** Cost on implements was imputed on the basis of depreciation and repairs.
- ☆ ***Farm Produced Manure*:** Evaluated on the basis of prevailing prices in the village.
- ☆ ***Interest on working capital*:** Charged at short term loan interest rate (7 per cent) on the working capital (SRTVC) for half of the duration of the crop. This is because, the application of all variable inputs on a crop roughly accounts for half of the crop period. Actual interest charges are to be considered in respect of borrowed capital.
- ☆ ***Interest on owned fixed capital*:** Charged at long term loan interest rate (10 per cent) on the present value of fixed assets (other than the land value). The total amount is to be apportioned to each crop as per the proportion of each crop in the cropping pattern on the farm.
- ☆ ***Kind payments*:** Evaluated on the basis of prevailing rates in the village at the time such payments were made
- ☆ ***Main produce and by-products*:** Imputed on the basis of post-harvest prices prevailing in the sampled villages.
- ☆ ***Allocation and Apportionment of Joint Costs*:** Some of the items of cost were applicable to the entire farm. Costs on such items were apportioned to the individual enterprise by using following methods:
  - ❑ ***Maintenance of the bullocks*:** The total cost under this was apportioned in proportion to the number of bullock pair hours used for each of the enterprise.
  - ❑ ***Depreciation, land revenue** etc.*: Allocated in proportion to the area under different enterprises.
- ☆ ***Seeds and Manures:*** If these inputs are purchased, actual charges paid are considered. If owned seed and owned manure are employed, they are to be imputed at the prices prevailed in the village at the time of their use.
- ☆ ***Depreciation:*** Depreciation on fixed assets like farm machinery, implements, buildings *etc.* (other than the value of land) should be worked out based on

Straight line method. The total amount of depreciation per year is apportioned on each crop according to the proportion of usage of assets and equipment in each crop or in proportion to the each crop acreage in the cropping pattern on the farm.

- ***Rental value of owned land:*** Local prevailing leased-out value for land is to be considered or 30 per cent of the value of output (main product plus by product) is to be considered as rental value of owned land.
- The actual costs plus transport charges are to be considered in case of other purchased inputs such as fertilizers, pesticides *etc.*

Farm Income Measures Derived from Cost Concepts

From the cost concepts discussed above, we can derive the farm income measures, which indicate the returns over different cost concepts. These income measures include:

- ***Gross returns:*** Value of main product plus by-products. The main products and by-products are to be imputed taking into account the actual market prices or the village level prices prevailed at the time of enquiry.
- ***Farm business income*** = Gross income-Cost A1
- ***Owned farm business income*** = Gross income-Cost A2
- ***Family labour income*** = Gross income-Cost B2
- ***Net income*** = Gross income-Cost C3
- ***Intensive income*** = Net income + Rental value of owned land + Interest of fixed capital
- ***Farm investment income*** = Farm business income-Imputed value of family labour
- ***Rate of Return*** = (Net returns over Cost C2/Cost C2)

5

Farm Financial Statements

Financial statements are essential documents detailing, how a farm business earns and spends its money. There are three basic types of farm financial statements *viz.*, NWS or Balance Sheet, an Income Statement and a Cash Flow Statement. The NWS provides a cross-section view of the financial side of a business. The income statement is the only tool of farm business analysis that measures profitability. Cash flow statement is an essential financial management tool for farmers. It addresses one of the most serious financial problems faced on farms today - the control of cash flow. The analysis of cash flow is largely a matter of continuous monitoring of receipts and expenditures and comparing what actually happens to projected cash flow. Thus, each type of financial statement has a specific use. Using the correct type of financial statement for the appropriate situation ensures the farm manager to analyze financial measures for making fruitful financial decisions on the farm in the future. In the last few decades, much progress has been made to standardize these financial statements in agriculture. This allows for ratios and measurements commonly used in other industries, to become standard in the farm business. Now the individual farmer can measure and understand the strengths and weaknesses of his farm business with reference to financial side. These financial statements provide excellent measurements like Liquidity, Solvency, Profitability, Repayment Capacity and Efficiency ratios. A NWS is necessary to measure 'Solvency' of farm business. In order to measure 'Profitability', 'Repayment Capacity' and 'Efficiency', a good accrual adjusted Income Statement is needed (Accrued income refers to income that is earned by a firm by selling an output or product, but has yet to be received *i.e.*, accrued income is income which has been earned, but not yet received). A Cash Flow Statement is necessary to measure liquidity of farm business. As discussed earlier, the first basic step in this process of preparation of financial statements is the establishment and maintenance of farm business records. But this is not enough. Records that are developed, but not understood or not used, make no contribution to the decision making process that is essential to successful farm management.

A. NWS or Balance Sheet

A NWS (also called Statement of financial position) is a statement that shows, what is owned, what is owed, and the owner's share or net worth of the farm business. That is, NWS organizes, what the business owns (assets) and what it owes (liabilities), which ultimately determines farm solvency. This Statement shows the best measure of a farm business's financial position. It answers the basic question, '*what is your farm business's financial position?*'. By comparing past NWSs with the present NWS, the growth or decline of assets, liabilities and net worth of a business can be determined. In a NWS, the amount of funds the owner has in the business is shown. To determine this amount, the assets owned are listed and a value is placed on them. Similarly, the total value of liabilities also is listed. The difference between total assets and total liabilities equals net worth, which represents the owner's equity in the business. This net worth is equivalent to the value that would be left, if all of the business and debt obligations were paid in full. The term '*balance*' in 'balance sheet' implies that, the value of assets must equal to the value of liabilities plus owner's equity or net worth. Thus, net worth = Total assets – Total liabilities. A balance sheet (Table 5.1) has a common set of characteristics. These are:

- ✰ It gives a snap shot picture about the net worth of the farm business at a point of time (usually at the end of the crop year) and is, therefore, a stock concept. That is, this statement pertains to a specific point of time say, on 1-2-2014. In fact, the date should be chosen such as two successive balance sheets represent the beginning and ending points of time as covered by the intervening income statement. It may correspond the agricultural year, calendar year or financial year. Thus, net worth reflects the financial position of the farm business at a point of time and will differ day to day or year to year.
- ✰ The NWS comprises of three essential components *viz.*, Assets, Liabilities and Net worth or Equity *i.e.*, the balancing entry in the account. There is no standard format for the NWS. However, there is a degree of uniformity among these statements. Regardless of the source, a balance sheet will include current assets and liabilities, intermediate assets and liabilities, long-term assets and liabilities, and net worth.
- ✰ The NWS can be prepared for a 'farm business' or for a 'farm operator's family' (includes both business and personal items). That is, a NWS may include only the farm business, or it may include household and personal assets and debts as well. For business analysis purposes, only information pertaining to the farm is needed. Thus, NWS may reflect both farm business and personal assets and liabilities or only farm business or only personal assets and liabilities. If both farm business and personal assets and liabilities are included, the result is a consolidated NWS. If only farm

business assets and liabilities are included, the document is a Farm business NWS. If the document includes only personal assets and liabilities, it is a Personal NWS.

- ☆ In the NWS, the assets are presented in the descending order of their liquidity and liabilities are arranged in the ascending order of their debt values. That is, the most liquid assets and the lowest value liabilities are presented first and the least liquid assets and the highest value liabilities are presented last.
- ☆ In a typical NWS, the assets are written on left hand side, while liabilities towards right side. Many different forms and formats exist for developing a NWS. However, all of them contain the same basic information. Completing an annual NWS is one of the simplest means available for analyzing the risk-bearing ability and financial progress of farm business.
- ☆ When total assets are greater than total liabilities, the difference is called Net worth or Equity. On the other hand, when total liabilities are greater than total assets, the difference is called Net deficit. In the Statement, the 'Net worth' or 'Net deficit' appears at the bottom part of the table. If total assets are greater than total liabilities, net worth is placed towards liabilities (right hand bottom) side to show the 'shortage of liabilities' to make the balance sheet balanced. In this case, when you add total liabilities with net worth, they will be equal to the total of the assets. If total liabilities are greater than total assets, net deficit is placed towards assets (left hand bottom) side to show the 'shortage of assets' to make the balance sheet balanced. In this case, when you add total assets with net deficit, they will equal to the total of the liabilities. Since, one side balances with the other, the tern 'Balance sheet' is given to NWS. That is, the NWS is always in balance hence, the name Balance Sheet. So, the left side – assets, equals the right side – liabilities (debts) plus equity (net worth) or the left side – assets plus net deficit equals the right side – liabilities (debts).
- ☆ NWS is a statement and not an account.

A number of definitions are in order before proceeding with a discussion of using the NWS. They are discussed here under.

a. Asset

An asset is something having economic value that is controlled by an individual or farm-firm. An asset is any tangible property, products, or inventories, *etc.*, that have value and the farm-firm either owns or is currently buying on credit. It also mean the entire possessions and property of every description, which the farmer owns at any particular date. So, an asset is, therefore, something of value, which either belongs to the farm business or is owned to it by someone else. Assets are classified into three types *viz.*, Current assets, Working assets and Fixed assets based on their extent of liquidity (*i.e.*, the length of time required to change the asset to liquid cash determines the type of asset). As shown in the NWS (Table 5.1), the statement has horizontal lines dividing the assets into these three categories followed by 'Total Farm Assets' (the total of the above).

- ***Current assets:*** Current assets consist of cash and near cash assets. These are the assets that can be converted into liquid cash easily or consumed within the single upcoming accounting year without disrupting the farm business. So, current assets are also called as Liquid assets. They include cash, accounts receivable, inventory including crops and market livestock that will be converted into cash or consumed within an accounting year. Others include: fertilizer, herbicides, fuel, feed and other input assets associated with the agricultural production. The most liquid current asset include: 'cash on hand'. Other current assets include:
  - Supplies on hand, such as seed, chemicals, fuel *etc.*
  - Pre-paid expenses such as payment made for feed to be delivered in the coming year. Show this as an asset only, if you have already paid for it or if you show the obligation to pay for it as a liability.
  - Growing crops generally should be given a value equal to the cost of cultivation already incurred.
  - Accounts receivable, such as the payment a neighbor might owe you for custom hiring or Government payments to be received for past production.

  Note that, value of crop produce is done either at current market price, or their contracted price minus marketing costs. Check with local markets or use local prices available through newspapers, radio or other sources. Value commercial feed at its purchase cost.
- ***Intermediate or Working assets or Medium term assets or Non-current assets:*** Intermediate assets have a useful life of more than one year. These assets are difficult to liquify compared to current assets, as they cannot be converted or sold for cash in short period of time. Examples include: milch and draught animals, implements, drip irrigation, sprinkler irrigation *etc.*, in the production of farm commodities. These assets normally get consumed or used up during the production process (but, they are not consumed within the year) and continue to give returns beyond one year. That is, these assets are typically held and used for several years with a life expectancy of more than one year and generally less than ten years. The livestock are valued at current market prices, minus potential marketing and transportation costs. Also check with local markets or use local prices available from newspapers, radio, television media and other sources of marketing information. Value young livestock at feeder animal prices. Value heavier livestock at their estimated weight times the current slaughter market price. Use an average of feeder and market livestock prices for animals at intermediate weights.

  Note that, when grain or livestock have been 'hedged' by selling futures contracts on a commodity exchange, value these contracts by subtracting the trading price of the contract on the date of the NWS from the original selling price (hedged price) of the contract. The result is the gain or loss that would be incurred by closing out the hedges, which sometimes could be a negative number. The physical commodity that has been hedged should be valued at its current market price, just like an unhedged commodity.

- ☆ ***Long term or Fixed assets:*** These assets are difficult to liquify to meet current obligations, as they are of permanent nature. Long term assets include those assets that have a useful life in excess of ten years and generally include assets such as land, buildings, machinery, storage godowns and other permanent improvements like, fences *etc.* They often have the largest rupee value of all the assets on the NWS.

There is often some debate over whether assets should be valued at historical cost or current market value. There are merits to both methods. Historical cost reports the value of assets at an amount of money that was actually paid to obtain the asset minus accumulated depreciation. Current market value reports asset values that reflect the changes in the assets as general price levels have changed overtime. In practice, historic cost values are most often used, and are the accepted practice. A disadvantage of the historic cost method is that, the values shown on the NWS do not always give a true indication of the value of the resources employed in the business, which may result in inaccurate measures of the efficiency of these assets. However, the current market value method suffers from fact that, market values are not always readily available, especially for infrequently traded assets, and these values may also be subject to market volatility. In general, for preparing NWS of a farm business, the accepted practice will be valuing assets at current market value and all the financial ratio benchmarks will be computed by using market value of assets.

b. Liabilities

They represent an amount, which is owed to others by the farmer, whether payable in cash, kind or services. Liabilities are what the farmer owes to his creditors for the purchase of assets or any other financial obligations. That is, liabilities include all financial obligations incurred by a farmer and are due on the date of the Statement. In a NWS, the liabilities (shown on the right hand side) are presented under three heads *viz.,* Current liabilities, Medium-term or Intermediate liabilities and Long-term liabilities and this classification is based on their maturity. That is, liabilities are usually listed according to the length of time before they become due.

- ☆ ***Current liabilities:*** These liabilities are the loans or debts due now or will come due within an operating year. That is, these are the debts, which are to be repaid or repayable by a farmer within an operating year (normally 12 months) say, crop loan. Besides this, the accrued interest (accrued interest is the amount of loan interest that has already occurred, but has not yet been paid to the lender by the borrower) on loans owed *i.e.,* medium and long term loans (*i.e.,* Term loans) in the operating year also fall under current liabilities. Current liabilities include notes payable within a year, accounts payable, accrued expenses and the current portion of term debt. Current liabilities are generally used to finance the production inputs.
- ☆ ***Medium term or Intermediate liabilities:*** There are the liabilities or obligations associated with the intermediate assets. If the outstanding

principal of a loan amount, which is due beyond 12 months and up to seven years of repayment period, it can be categorized as an intermediate liability. That is, medium term loans or liabilities are those, whose maturity is between 1 and 7 years. Loans for breeding stock, implements *etc.*, fall under this category.

- ☆ ***Long term liabilities:*** There are the liabilities or obligations associated with the long-term assets. If the outstanding principal of a loan amount, which is due beyond 7 to 15 years or more of repayment period, it can be categorized as a long-term liability. That is, long term loans or liabilities are those, whose maturity is beyond 7 years. Loans for machinery land improvements, construction of godowns and farm buildings *etc.*, usually fall under this category.

c. Net Worth or Equity

We already know, the difference between total assets and total liabilities is the net worth or equity, at the time the NWS is made. When total assets are more than total liabilities, then there is net worth or equity in the business and the business is said to be solvent. Contrarily, when total assets are less than total liabilities, then there is net deficit in the business and the business is said to be insolvent. Net worth is generally expressed in monetary terms, while the same can also be expressed as a percentage as follows:

Net worth (per cent)=[(Total Assets-Total Liabilities)/Total Assets]*100

Adding net worth to total liabilities gives a figure equal to total assets. Farm and personal net worths can be added together to find the total net worth. The term 'net worth' is most often used on financial statements of sole proprietorships. A similar term 'partners capital' is used to indicate the ownership interests of partners in a partnership. 'Shareholders' equity' is used to show the ownership interest of an incorporated entity.

Thus, a NWS is a systematic organization of everything owned and owed – at a given point in time. Once after completing the NWS, check it carefully. To begin, look at each major liability listed and see if a corresponding item can be found under the asset side. The corresponding item will usually be listed under the same section (current or fixed). If a corresponding asset cannot be found, you may have forgotten to list something or the asset originally acquired with borrowed money may have already been sold or used up before paying the corresponding liability. This is a danger sign. It means that, you must generate funds to pay this debt elsewhere in the farm business.

Influence of Changes in Assets and Liabilities on Net Worth

Net worth of a farm business may fluctuate year by year. However, an equal increase in assets and liabilities; and an equal decrease in assets and liabilities will undoubtedly affect the structure of NWS, but net worth would remain unchanged. An equal increase in assets and liabilities would arise once purchased with credit. Thus, total assets and liabilities are changed, but net worth remains unchanged. Similarly, loan payments are transactions that lead to an equal decrease in assets and liabilities, leaving the net worth unchanged. In case, if long term loans are used

Table 5.1: NWS of a Farm in Nandyal Region of Andhra Pradesh as on 1-2-2013 (Hypothetical data)

ASSETS (Rs.)		*LIABILITIES (Rs.)*	
Current Assets		***Current Liabilities***	
☆ Cash on hand	3800	☆ Accounts to be paid	5000
☆ Cash in bank	5000	☆ Operating loans + Interest	10000
☆ Accounts receivable	11000	☆ Portion of term loans due within 12 months	
☆ Crops to be sold		❖ MT loan installment (Principal+ Interest)	15000
❖ Rice	20000		
❖ Maize	9000	❖ LT loan installment (Principal+ Interest)	32000
❖ Gram	8000		
☆ Market livestock	70400		
☆ Fertilizers			
❖ Urea	5000		
❖ DAP	3000		
❖ MOP	2000		
☆ Feed	10000		
☆ Other (Marketable securities)	30000		
i. Total Current Assets	***177200***	***i. Total Current Liabilities***	***62000***
Intermediate Assets		***Intermediate Liabilities***	
☆ Livestock (Milch and Draught animals) (2+2)	50000	☆ Livestock loan	25000
☆ Machinery	40000(1)	☆ Machinery loan	15000
☆ Tube well irrigation	85000	☆ Tube well irrigation loan	40000
☆ Other depreciable property	15000	☆ Loans taken for other equipment	5000
ii. Total Intermediate Assets	***190000***	***ii. Total Intermediate Liabilities***	***85000***
Fixed Assets		***Long Term Liabilities***	
☆ Land	500000	☆ Tractor and its accessories	200000
☆ Tractor and its accessories	220000		
iii. Total Fixed Assets	***720000***	***iii. Total Long Term Liabilities***	***200000***
Total Assets (i+ii+iii) (177200+190000+720000)	***1087200***	***Total Liabilities (i+ii+iii) (62000+85000+200000)***	***347000***
		Net Worth or Equity*	***740200***
		Total Liabilities + Net Worth	**1087200**

*: Net worth is placed towards liability side, as the total assets are more than total liabilities and this makes the balance sheet 'balanced' on both the sides. Note that, if total liabilities are more than total assets, then net deficit is to be placed on the left hand side (*i.e.*, assets side), so as to make the balance sheet 'balanced' on both the sides.

to pay off the short term loans, it would result into an equal increase and decease in liabilities consequently, net worth would be unaffected since, debt has been restructured to improve the liquidity position. Note that, a single NWS does not indicate the progress or deterioration of the farm business, unless drawn overtime and net worth is compared. The NWS can be constructed on a cost basis or book value (purchase price or original cost minus depreciation) or current market value basis. Sometimes, physical data are also given to see the changes in inventory (quantity of grain or number of livestock).

Thus, the generalized structure of the NWS shows the assets are listed on the left hand side, with the current assets at the top, intermediate assets in the middle and long term assets at the bottom. Assets that are most easily converted into cash are listed at the top with less liquid assets located beneath in descending order of liquidity. The liabilities are generally listed on the right-hand side of the statement and are also divided into three categories: current, intermediate and long-term. The liabilities that mature earliest are placed or listed at the top and the liabilities that takes long time for maturity are shown at the bottom *i.e.,* the liabilities are arranged in the ascending order of their maturity.

Financial Ratios Derived from NWS of Farm Business

These ratios examine the financial structure of the farm business and thus, provide information to the banker regarding the extent of risk involved in lending to the farmer. Two types of financial ratios can be derived from the parameters of NWS *viz.,* Liquidity ratios and Solvency ratios. They are discussed here under.

i. Liquidity Ratios

Liquidity is a measure of a farm's ability to repay current debts by converting current assets into cash. Liquidity is a short run concept, since it deals with current assets and current liabilities and shows a farm's ability to meet debts when they become due, without disrupting normal operations. In general, the more cash that is available to pay current debts, the more liquid the firm is said to be. That is, 'Liquidity' can also be defined as having enough current assets on hand to cover all of the current liabilities on hand at any given point of time. Liquidity may be measured in absolute terms by Working Capital (Rupees) or in relative terms (Ratio measures) like Current Ratio, Working or Intermediate ratio, Debt Structure Ratio and Acid test ratio. These measures indicate the ability of the farmer to generate sufficient cash in order to meet the debt obligations without disrupting his farm business. These ratios are discussed here under.

- ☆ *Current ratio (Banker's Ratio or Working Capital Ratio):* This measures the ratio between current assets and current liabilities of a farm. Thus, it indicates the degree of liquidity of the farm in the short run. This ratio indicates the extent to which current assets, if liquidated, would cover the current liabilities, *i.e.,* the value of current assets for each rupee of current liability. The higher current ratio means more liquidity exists in the farm business. This is given by:

  Current ratio = Total Current Assets/Total Current Liabilities

This ratio gives an indication of a farm's ability to meet its cash obligations coming due within the next year. If the ratio is greater than 1.0, the operation is considered liquid. If the ratio is less than 1.0, the operation has some degree of cash flow risk. So, a value below one could indicate a developing cash flow problem. Having a very high value may not be desirable either, as it may indicate that, too high a level of assets are tied up in conservative investments that have lower rates of return.

Agricultural lenders generally like a current ratio of at least 1.7:1. If the ratio is 1:1, then the farm is barely liquid, and if the ratio is less than 1:1, then the firm has liquidity problems. So, a current ratio greater than 1.7 is 'Strong'; a 1.7 to 1.1 would fall in the 'Caution or Strong to Moderate' range; and less than 1.1 would be 'Vulnerable'. In the given example (Table 5.1), Current ratio = 2.86. This implies that, for every rupee of current debt, the farmer has Rs.2.86 of current assets to pay it with and this will work. This 2.86 current ratio in the above example would be in the 'Strong' range. An acceptable current ratio will depend upon the type of farm, the risks associated with its enterprises and the present amount of current debt. Enterprises like poultry, dairy *etc.*, can withstand lower current ratios because of their regular and reasonably constant cash flows (if their present current debt level is not too high). On the other hand, for business like crop enterprises, where there are greater fluctuations in annual income, they require higher current ratios to finance production over the course of the year. Note that, since the current ratio is calculated at a specific point of time (the NWS date), it will change throughout the year. The higher the current ratio, the better able the farm is to shield itself from risk. Also note that, a farm business with good overall risk-bearing ability can still have liquidity problems. This may be caused by a low income year resulting in carryover operating debt or too rapid investment of cash into intermediate and long-term assets, such as machinery or land. As mentioned above, current ratio of less than 1.0 indicates potential cash flow problems. However, this is affected by the type of farm, volume of production, and financial structure.

Some lenders prefer to look at the difference between current assets and current liabilities rather than their ratio. This difference between Total current assets and Total current liabilities is called Working capital (also refers to liquidity of farm business), and this indicates the potential cash available for meeting daily operating costs. This working capital shows, what is available in the current period after meeting debts due and money used to facilitate the operations of the farm business. That is, working capital quantifies the amount of money readily available to operate the business, being what is available after meeting debts. This indicates the ability of the farm business to meet cash obligations as they come due without having to borrow money or cash in some of its medium and long-term capitals. Working capital and current ratios have similar issues. A positive working capital value is desirable, but too large a value may indicate too many 'lazy' assets are being held.

Obviously, we need a positive figure for working capital otherwise, the farm is illiquid. That is, working capital needs to be positive for the business to be liquid. A rough guide is that, working capital should be close to expected net farm income. Otherwise, we may not be making sufficient investment in the farm. Note that, this 'working capital' is not a ratio, but is a measurement of in terms of rupees. In this example, the working capital is Rs. 115200. However, there is no standard acceptable level for 'Working Capital' in the farm business. Acceptable Working Capital will vary from farm to farm depending upon the type of farm, its size and the amount of risk associated with its production enterprises. Since Working Capital is an absolute measure of liquidity, the amount calculated will vary from farm to farm. Therefore, it is not useful in comparing one farm to another or to a benchmark for management decision making purposes. Generally, working capital should be positive, but the amount needed depends on the type and size of the operation, the time of the year, and the related seasonality of the production cycle. Remember the definition of 'Liquidity' is the ability of the farm business to generate sufficient cash flow for family living and debt payment. If the debts pile up faster than they can be repaid, liquidity is not sufficient. This does not mean that, the business failed, even the farm may be wealthy (in terms of working and fixed assets), but just not 'liquid' enough. So, a measures was designed to analyze the adequacy of working capital in the farm business and this is given by computing the 'Working capital to Gross income ratio' and it should be at least 25 percent to be considered adequate.

- ☆ ***Working or Intermediate ratio:*** Over period, both current and working assets can be converted into cash. This ratio reflects that, whether or not the cash derived in this period would be adequate to cover the liabilities of the same period. That is, this ratio measures farmers' utilization of current and working assets as reserves relative to debt claims against these assets. Thus, this ratio indicates the degree of liquidity of farm business over an intermediate period of time. Higher the ratio above one, the more is the risk-bearing ability of the farmer-borrower. This ratio is given by:

$$\text{Working or Intermediate ratio} = \frac{\text{Current assets + Intermediate assets}}{\text{Current liabilities + Intermedia liabilities}}$$

In the given example (Table 5.1), Working ratio = 2.50. So, this ratio (above 1.00) implies the surplus utilization of current and working assets of farmer relative to debt claims against these assets.

- ☆ ***Debt-structure ratio:*** This is given by:

$$\text{Debt-structure ratio} = \frac{\text{Current liabilities}}{\text{Total liabilities}}$$

Lower the value of this ratio, higher is the liquidity position of the farm business. For example, a ratio of 0.6:1 (often written as 0.6) means that, 60 percent of the total farm debt is due the following year *i.e.*, 60 percent of total business debts are in the current position (that is, are current liabilities). If total debt is small, there is nothing to worry about. But, most farms have considerable debt loads, and a debt structure ratio of 0.6 shows that, too much of the farm debt is current. In general, a ratio of 0.2 or less is safe and 0.5 or more is dangerous. In this example (Table 5.1), the debt structure ratio is 0.18. This implies that, 18 percent of the total farm debt is due the following year *i.e.,* 18 percent of total business debts are in the current position (that is, are current liabilities). This debt structure ratio indicates the part of total debt that must be repaid within one year. A ratio of 0.60 indicates that, 60 percent of total debt must be repaid within one year. The higher the ratio, the greater will be the drain on cash reserves, the more risk of being unable to repay current debt obligations on time and may indicate a need to refinance. The refinancing process typically converts part of the short-term debt to a longer-term obligation.

This ratio is often used in conjunction with Working Capital or the Current Ratio when assessing business liquidity. A high Debt Structure Ratio is desirable, if the business has positive Working Capital (or a Current Ratio greater than 1). This would indicate that, debt is being paid back in a relatively short time period. Conversely, if farms face negative working capital (or a current ratio less than 1) and an accompanying high Debt Structure Ratio, it could get benefitted by restructuring its debt so that, the amount of debt in the current position is reduced. Otherwise, liquidity can also be improved by lengthening the debt repayment time frame.

☆ ***Acid test ratio or Quick ratio:*** This ratio is a liquidity indicator that further refines the current ratio by measuring the amount of the most liquid current assets (an asset that can be converted into cash quickly and with minimal impact to the price received) there are to cover current liabilities. The quick ratio is more conservative than the current ratio because, it excludes inventory and other current assets, which are more difficult to turn into cash. Therefore, a higher quick ratio means a more liquid current position. We know, the current ratio includes all current assets, but since inventory is often difficult to turn into cash, many analysts remove it from the equation to arrive at a Acid-test ratio or Quick ratio. This Quick ratio emphasizes on current assets that are quickly convertible into cash. This ratio essentially revamps the current ratio by taking out non cash current asset items, including inventory in crops, livestock and supplies plus cash invested in growing crops from current assets and divide this numerator by current liabilities. That is,

Quick ratio = (Current assets - Inventories and supplies)/Current liabilities

The remaining assets (*i.e.,* Current assets minus inventories and supplies) are cash, marketable securities and accounts receivable. If these assets are sufficient to cover all current liabilities, the farm is decidedly liquid. So,

Quick ratio = (Cash + Marketable securities + Accounts receivable)/Current liabilities

Quick ratio = (Liquid Assets)/(Current Liabilities)

Thus, this quick ratio is the same as the current ratio, except that it excludes inventories presumably the least liquid portion of current assets from the numerator. The ratio concentrates on cash, marketable securities and account receivables in relation to current obligations and thus provide a more penetrating measure of liquidity than does the current ratio.

- ***Marketable securities:*** Marketable securities include stocks, bonds, and other securities that can quickly be converted to cash.
- ***Accounts Receivable:*** Accounts receivable are rupees due from customers. More specifically, inventory (output) is sold and shipped, an invoice is sent to the customer, and cash is collected at later time. The receivable exists for the time period between the selling of the inventory and the receipt of cash. Receivables are proportional to output sales.
- ***Inventory:*** Inventory includes unsold products that are waiting to be sold. That is, inventory is commonly thought of as the finished products a firm accumulates before selling them to end users. But, inventory can also describe the raw materials used to produce the finished goods, as they go through the production process (referred to as "work-in-progress" or WIP), or goods that are 'in transit.'

So, this quick ratio serves as a stringent indicator that determines, whether a firm has enough short-term assets to cover its immediate liabilities without selling inventory. This ratio is far more strenuous than the working capital (current) ratio primarily because, the working capital ratio allows for the inclusion of inventory assets. Furthermore, if the quick ratio is much lower than the current ratio, it means current assets are highly dependent on inventory. The traditional thinking is that, the higher the quick ratio, the better off the farm business. Greater than 2:1 for the current ratio or 1:1 for the quick ratio is good and safe; less than 2:1 or 1:1 is a sign of impending problems meeting obligations. On most farms, which already have a healthy current ratio, a quick ratio around 0.5:1 is probably reasonable. A ratio of less than 0.3:1 usually means that, the farmer has a lot of inventory and will have to take current market prices in any forced sale. That is, this ratio measures the rupee amount of liquid assets available for each rupee of current liabilities. Thus, a quick ratio of 1.5 means that, the farmer has Rs.1.50 of liquid assets available to cover each Rs.1 of current liabilities. In this example (Table 5.1), quick ratio is 0.80 and this implies that, Rs.0.80 worth of liquid assets are available for each rupee of current liabilities to cover immediate obligations.

In general, the quick ratio is lower than the current ratio, as inventories are excluded from current assets. The 'quick' ratio derives its name presumably from the fact that, assets such as cash and marketable securities are quick sources of cash. Since, inventories generally take time to be converted into cash, and if they have to be sold quickly, the farmer may have to accept a lower price than book value of these inventories. As a result, they are justifiably excluded from current assets. Thus, this ratio reflects the adequacy of cash, accounts receivable, *etc.*, to cover all current liabilities. So, the quick ratio is more conservative than the current ratio, which measures much the same thing, because the current ratio excludes the value of inventory. This is because inventory can be less liquid than other current assets. The quick ratio thus measures a farm's ability to meet obligations in a worst-case scenario.

The term 'Acid-test ratio' comes from the way gold miners would test, whether their findings were real gold nuggets. Unlike other metals, gold does not corrode in acid; if the nugget didn't dissolve when submerged in acid, it was said to have passed the acid test. That is, this ratio is often referred to as the 'acid test' because, it only looks at the farm's most liquid assets only (excludes inventory) that can be quickly converted to cash. If a farm business financial statements pass the figurative acid test, this indicates its financial integrity. Thus, acid-test ratio measures the farm's short-term liquidity. That is, it measures a farm's ability to meet its short-term obligations with its most liquid assets. For this reason, the ratio excludes inventories from current assets. This ratio is a stricter and more conservative measure of liquidity than the current ratio, as the former reflects the degree to which a farm's current liabilities are covered by its most liquid current assets *i.e.*, the kind of assets that can be converted quickly to cash.

Note that, 'liquidity' cannot totally evaluate the farm's ability to meet all cash commitments. It is only measured on the date that the NWS is created. It does not measure or predict timing or adequacy of future inflows in relation to outflows. Current assets can't always be sold immediately because of trade restrictions or more favourable price expectations and liabilities are not due instantly. Also, there are several substantial non-farm claims on cash (like family living costs) that are not accounted for in liquidity measurement.

ii. Solvency Ratios

Solvency is a measure of the firm's risk bearing ability. Solvency measures provide an indication of the firm's ability to repay all financial obligations, if all assets are sold. It also can indicate the ability as a firm to continue as a viable business after a financial adversity that would increase debt or reduce equity. Solvency is a long run concept since these measures deal with the ability of the business to survive in the future. That is, 'Solvency' can be defined as having enough value in the form of assets in the business to cover all of the liabilities of the business. So, solvency is a measure of financial security *i.e.*, what would be left in case all the assets are liquiefied (converted into cash) and debts are paid. Thus, solvency refers to the ability to pay off all debts, if the assets were liquidated. If the value of the total farm assets exceeds the value of the total farm liabilities, the farm is said to be solvent. If the sale of all the farm assets would not generate enough cash to pay off all liabilities, the farm is insolvent. The difference between the value of total farm assets and total farm liabilities, referred to as net worth or owner's equity, is the most often used measure of solvency. Thus, solvency ratios indicate the financial safety of the farm business over the debts in the long-run. They are concerned with the levels of equity and debt in the farm. They indicate the measure of risk bearing ability of the farm to carry on business after financial adversity. These ratios revolve around the relationship of the Total Assets, the Total Liabilities, and the Net Worth and they are expressed in terms of percentage. These ratios include:

- ***Net capital ratio:*** This ratio is given by: Total assets/Total liabilities. Higher the ratio is desirable, as the liqidation of farm assets would generate adequate cash to repay the total liabilities. The net capital ratio is a common measure of solvency. It measures the degree of availability of total assets to pay-off the total liabilities in the farm. This ratio is also used as a measure of risk bearing ability of the farmer. A business is solvent, if the ratio is more than one *i.e.,* there is more than one rupee of assets for each rupee of liabilities. That is, a value greater than 1.0 implies that, liquidation of the business would produce enough cash to pay-off all creditors. A financially healthy business will have a net capital ratio of approximately 2.5 or more. For example, a value of 1.4 says that, for each Rs.1 of debt, there is Rs.1.40 in assets. This means that, assets could decline by roughly 40 percent and the business would remain solvent. In this example (Table 5.1), net capital ratio is 3.13 and this implies that, for each Rs.1 of debt, there is Rs.3.13 in assets. This means that, assets could decline by roughly 213 percent and the business would remain solvent. Thus, it shows the percentage that the value of assets could decline and still cover liabilities. This ratio indicates the degree of liquidity of the farm in the long run.
- ***Debt Ratio or Debt-to-Asset Value Ratio or Solvency Ratio:*** This ratio is given by: Total liabilities/Total assets. That is, this ratio examines the proportional relationship between total liabilities and total assets. The higher the ratio, the more debt there is for each rupee of assets. That is, the higher the ratio, the greater the risk to the farm business and to those who are providing loan funds. The farmer has less flexibility to respond to adverse natural or market conditions. There is no exact standard for Debt-to-Asset Value Ratio for every farm business. However, a debt-to-asset value ratio greater than 0.50 indicates that, the owners contribute less than 50 percent of the value of the farm's assets. In this situation, creditors are often cautious about making loans. In general, if the Debt-to-Asset Value Ratio is less than 1, the business is solvent. If the 'Debt to Asset-Value Ratio' is 40 percent, it implies that the debt equals 40 percent of the assets. Another way of saying this is that, for every one rupee of assets that the farmer have, there is forty paise worth of debts. A ratio greater than 1 would indicate that, total liabilities are greater than total assets and therefore, the business is insolvent. In general, a successful farm business will have a decreasing debt ratio over time, except in years when major assets such as land are purchased with borrowed capital. A low debt-to-asset value ratio usually leads to less year-to-year variability in net farm income. A personal debt-to-

asset ratio also can be calculated, using total farm and personal asset and liability values.

Since the Debt to Asset-Value Ratio is a relative measure of solvency, it can be used for comparisons between farms. Ratios upto 40 to 50 percents are generally considered safe for the farm business. However, ratio acceptability would depend upon the nature of the farm enterprises and their income flow. Farms with regular cash flows (such as dairy) can withstand higher Debt to Asset-Value Ratio and *vice versa*. In financial analysis of a farm, Debt to Asset-Value Ratio must be used cautiously. This is because, having a favourable Debt to Asset-Value Ratio (high net worth) does not indicate debt repayment ability and therefore, can lead to a false sense of security. Repayment ability is determined by profitability and cash flow. In this example (Table 5.1), Debt to Asset-Value Ratio is 0.32 (or 32 per cent) and this implies that, the debt equals 32 percent of the assets *i.e.*, for every one rupee of assets that the farmer have, there is thirty two paise worth of debts.

☆ ***Equity-to-Asset Value ratio:*** This ratio is given by: Equity or Net worth/ Value of assets. Higher the ratio is desirable. The higher the equity-to-asset value ratio, the more capital is supplied by the farmer and the less is supplied by creditors. There is no exact standard for the equity-to-asset value ratio that should be applied to every farm business. However, as the percent equity increases above 0.50, the owner is supplying a greater percent of the total assets in the business than the creditors. This ratio should increase over time, if the owner retains farm profits and reduces debt obligations. Say, a figure of 60 percent would mean that, farmer's equity (net worth) equals 60 percent of the assets. Another way of saying this is that, for every one rupee of assets that the farmer have, he is contributing 60 paise of it, in the form of net worth. Note that, when you add the 'Debt to Asset-Value Ratio percentage' (say, 40 per cent) to the 'Equity to Asset-Value Ratio percentage' (say, 60 per cent), they will always equal to 100 percent. By looking at these ratios together, we can infer that, 'of all the assets that farmer can control, creditors are furnishing 40 percent of the capital (debt) and farmer himself is furnishing 60 percent of the capital. In this example (Table 5.1), Equity to Asset-Value Ratio is 0.68 (or 68 per cent) and this implies that, farmer's equity (net worth) equals 68 percent of the assets *i.e.*, for every one rupee of assets that the farmer have, he is contributing 68 paise of it, in the form of net worth. So, the higher the value of the ratio, the more is the total capital supplied by the owner(s) and less by the creditors.

This ratio can be calculated using either the cost or market value approach to value farm assets. This ratio is most meaningful for comparisons between farms when the market value approach is used to value farm assets. However, due to the impact of fluctuations in market value of farm assets, it is most meaningful for comparisons between accounting periods for an individual farm operation when the cost approach is used to value farm assets.

- ☆ ***Leverage ratio or Debt-to-equity ratio:*** This ratio is given by: Total liabilities / Net worth. This ratio measures the financial risk of a farm business by examining the extent to which creditors have financed the business (by liabilities) as compared to the owners (by net worth or equity). If the leverage ratio is higher (>1), the farm operator has larger claims or debts to repay in relation to the equity of farm business. That is, creditors are financing a higher proportion of the assets than is the owner. So, lower the ratio is desirable. If the ratio is less than 1, the owner is financing the majority of the assets. That is, a ratio greater than one means, assets are mainly financed with debt, less than one means equity provides a majority of the financing. If the ratio is high (financed more with debt) then the farm business is in a risky position, especially if interest rates are on the rise. This ratio is also referred to as the Leverage ratio, as it looks at how the equity capital is leveraged by using debt (non-equity) capital. Leveraging refers to increasing the use of debt relative to equity as a means of financing the business. Lenders are particularly interested in this ratio because, it shows the proportion of the risk they are taking in comparison to the farmer. Many lenders prefer the debt-to-equity ratio to be less than 1.0, with requirements varying depending on whether the liabilities are in the form of current, intermediate, or long term assets. In general, the greater the loan's risk and the longer the loan's term, the lower the lender wants the debt-to-equity ratio to be. Most lenders do not want to see leverage ratios over 1.5:1. This means that, there is Rs.1.50 of debt for every Rs.1 of net worth. The higher the ratio, the more risk the farm faces and conversely, the lower the ratio, the lower the risk. This 'Debt to Equity Ratio' is more sensitive than the 'Debt to Asset-Value Ratio' and the 'Equity to Asset-Value Ratio' in that, it jumps (or drops) in bigger increments than the other two do, given the same change in assets and debt. For example, a Debt to Equity Ratio of 75 per cent means that, for every one rupee of net worth, there is 75 per cent of debt. That is, the creditors are financing 75 paise of farm assets for every Rs.1.00 of net worth of business. In this example (Table 5.1), Debt-to-equity ratio is 0.47 (or 47 per cent) and this implies that, for every one rupee of net worth, there is 47 per cent of debt *i.e.,* the creditors are financing only 47 paise of farm assets for every Rs.1.00 of net worth of business. Lenders often refer to this ratio because, they prefer to make loans to that borrower, who has equity of 50 percent or more of total assets used in a business. Thus, lenders prefer a debt-equity ratio of less than one. This indicates that, the owner's contribution is more than that of the lender. A financially health business will generally have a debt-equity ratio of 0.67 or less. However, this can vary depending on the quality of management, enterprises taken up on the farm and the level of profits. Perhaps, the most valuable feature of this measure of solvency is the trend value - that is, the changes that occur to this ratio through time. If the ratio deteriorates through time *i.e.,* it increases in absolute size, there is reason for concern and a careful review of the farm business should be undertaken. That is, a rising debt-equity ratio means that debt is increasing.

- ☆ ***Debt Payout Ratio:*** This is given by: Total Liabilities/NFI. In this ratio, the information pertaining to NFI is obtained from 'Income Statement'. This ratio represents the number of years it would take for the farmer to reduce the debt level to zero, if all of the income of a farm could be directed towards principal reduction. It thus, relates to the ability of the farm to generate income to repay the debt.

As discussed earlier, Total assets = Total liabilities + Net worth and all the above five solvency ratios are alternative ways of expressing the overall leverage position of a farm business. An acceptable solvency position depends upon the size of the farm, enterprises taken up, managerial ability of the farmer and the measures he takes to shield the farm from risk like crop insurance, hedging, forward contracting *etc.* Like liquidity, income variability and the risks associated with production and marketing affect the farm's solvency position. Also, solvency does not measure, how wisely debt is being used. If the solvency position is strong, the possibility of paying off debt should be examined to reduce interest costs.

Solvency of a business can also be measured in terms of 'Net Worth' or 'Equity'. We already know, net worth is the difference between Total assets and Total liabilities. So, net worth is a measure of solvency because, it compares owner's equity (net worth) to borrowed capital (liabilities). If net worth is positive (total assets greater than total liabilities), the business is solvent. If net worth is negative (total assets are less than total liabilities) then the business is insolvent or bankrupt. Since net worth is an absolute measure, it cannot be used for comparing different farms.

Uses of the NWS

A NWS has many important uses and they are listed here under.

- ☆ Financial institutions use NWS to evaluate the financial position of the farmer, while sanctioning loans.
- ☆ If the farmer compare the NWSs of farm business over time, it will show how much the business net worth is increasing or decreasing.
- ☆ A NWS guide the farmer, how much funds he has to borrow for employing the same in farm business.
- ☆ The net worth position ascertained by the farmer from the NWS guide him, how best to meet liabilities. For example, if current liabilities are due for the farmer, cash will be needed to pay them. On the other hand, if the sale of current assets will not raise sufficient funds to clear the liabilities, then a long-term loan may need to be negotiated on the basis of long-term asset values.
- ☆ NWS also guide the farmer, how flexible the farm business is? That is, if the farmer enjoys more of current assets, the business is more flexible. On the contrary, if the farmer enjoys more of non-current assets (say, machinery, buildings *etc.*), he has less flexibility than one that has sufficient current assets. Note that, some flexibility in the farm business should be maintained.
- ☆ It is one of the most basic tools used in financial management and should be developed on an annual basis by every farm manager. By comparing

end-of-year NWSs from consecutive years, the manager can determine changes that are occurring in the various types of assets and liabilities. Changes in net worth, through time, can also be determined by comparison of NWSs from several years.

- NWS of a farmer facilitate him to compare the same with the earlier statements (of previous years) of the same farmer and with other farmers in that locality. The former will directly indicate the growth or decline in net worth of the business and the latter facilitate the farmer to gain evidence of weak or strong points in his farm business. Further, financial ratios computed helps to evaluate the appropriate relationship between assets and liabilities thereby, both liquidity and solvency of the business can be analyzed. Note that, in comparing NWSs across different farms, use of percentages rather than actual rupees has some advantages. This approach is called a 'Common-size statement' (Table 5.2). Each farm is put on a 'common-size' basis; *i.e.,* the various assets, liabilities, and equity are expressed as percentages within the business (Michael).
- The NWS helps to judge the ability of the farmer to pay off current debts and take on additional ones.
- The net worth of a business on a given date indicates owner's equity and is a very general indicator to a lender (financial institution) regarding the risk involved in offering a loan. If net worth is large relative to total assets in the business, the loan can be well secured and the chance of loss is small. A smaller net worth may present an obstacle to securing credit because, risk of loss to the lender is greater.
- A comparison of current assets and current liabilities from the NWS indicates the ability of the farm business to meet its cash obligations as they come due. A farm business that is able to meet its current cash obligations as they come due is said to possess more liquidity.
- The NWS of a farm business reflect a healthy financial condition, if there is an excess of current assets over current liabilities. Typically, that excess should be one-and-one-half to twice as much in current assets as in current liabilities. The excess is needed for several reasons:
  - This serves as a financial cushion in case of rapid change (say, fall) in prices of current assets. A drastic fall in prices will destroy the liquidity of a business that has barely enough current assets to cover current liabilities.
  - The excess current assets indicates good financial health of the farm business, as this excess is the source of working capital for the business. Working capital is the amount of capital required to meet the current operating expenses *i.e.,* the items that must be purchased on a day-to-day schedule to keep the business operating. If there is a deficiency of working capital, the business must borrow additional funds or it must liquidate intermediate assets to secure working capital. The procurement of additional credit often takes time. If intermediate assets

Table 5.2: Common Size NWS or Balance Sheet

ASSETS (Rs.)			***LIABILITIES (Rs.)***		
Current Assets	***Amount (Rs.)***	***Percent***	***Current Liabilities***	***Amount (Rs.)***	***Percent***
☆ Cash on hand	3800	*0.35*	☆ Accounts to be paid	5000	*0.46*
☆ Cash in bank	5000	*0.46*	☆ Operating loans + Interest	10000	*0.92*
☆ Accounts receivable	11000	*1.01*	☆ Portion of term loans due within 12 months		*0.00*
☆ Crops to be sold			❖ MT loan installment (Principal+Interest)	15000	*1.38*
❖ Rice	20000	*1.84*	❖ LT loan installment (Principal+Interest)	32000	*2.94*
❖ Maize	9000	*0.83*			
❖ Gram	8000	*0.74*			
☆ Market livestock	70400	*6.48*			
☆ Fertilizers					
❖ Urea	5000	*0.46*			
❖ DAP	3000	*0.28*			
❖ MOP	2000	*0.18*			
☆ Feed	10000	*0.92*			
☆ Other (Marketablesecurities)	30000	*2.76*			
i. Total Current Assets	**177200**	16.30	**i. Total Current Liabilities**	**62000**	5.70
Intermediate Assets			***Intermediate Liabilities***		
☆ Livestock (Milch andDraught animals)	50000	*4.60*	☆ Livestock loan	25000	*2.30*
☆ Machinery	40000	*3.68*	☆ Machinery loan	15000	*1.38*
☆ Tube well irrigation	85000	*7.82*	☆ Tube well irrigation loan	40000	*3.68*
☆ Other depreciableproperty	15000	*1.38*	☆ Loans taken for otherequipment	5000	*0.46*
ii. Total Intermediate Assets	**190000**	**17.48**	**ii.Total Intermediate Liabilities**	**85000**	**7.82**

Contd...

Table 5.2–*Contd...*

Fixed Assets			***Long Term Liabilities***		
☆ Land	500000	*45.99*	☆ Tractor and its accessories	200000	*18.40*
☆ Tractor and itsacessories	220000	*20.24*			
iii.Total Fixed Assets	**720000**	66.23	**iii. Total Long Term Liabilities**	**200000**	18.40
Total Assets (i+ii+iii) (177200+190000+720000)	**1087200**	**100.00**	***Total Liabilities (i+ii+iii)*** (62000+85000+200000)	347000	*31.92*
			Net Worth or Equity	**740200**	*68.08*
			Total Liabilities + Net Worth	**1087200**	***100.00***

are liquidated, the assets that produce income for the business have been removed and future income flow will be reduced. Thus, asset liquidation is not a viable long-term alternative.

Note that, a NWS may include only the farm business, or it may include household and personal assets and debts as well. For business analysis purposes, only information pertaining to the farming operations is needed. Information about non-farm assets and liabilities can be added in a separate section and used for analyzing debt repayment capacity. For a farm partnership, include only items owned or owed by the partnership, not by the partners individually. It is possible to develop a NWS statement at any date and as often as needed, but most farmers make out a NWS at the beginning and ending of the accounting period (*i.e.* January 1st).

B. Profit and Loss Statement

Profit and loss statement is an account otherwise called as Income statement or Income and Expense Statement or P and L Statement or Revenue Statement or Statement of Financial Performance or Earnings Statement or Operating Statement or Statement of Operations *etc.*, and is a financial statement on the income and expense of a farm business over a period of time, called the accounting period. The accounting period for most farm businesses is the calendar year. The income statement measure the profitability of the farm business over this calendar year period and what it cost to produce. The difference between these two is called the net income *i.e.*, profit or loss for the period. Thus, this statement measures the net income earned from the farm business and provides a fairly good picture of income earning and managerial ability of the farmer, in case drawn over a number of years. So, the function of profit and loss statement is to enable the farmer to ascertain the net profit or net loss resulting from the business transactions through measuring the farm's sales and expenses during a specified period of time. Thus, the function of a this statement is to total all sources of revenue and subtract all expenses related to the revenue and finally shows the farm's financial progress during the time period being examined. In farming, we call profit or loss account as 'Production or Profit and Loss A/C'. Like NWS, an income-statement can be constructed either for a farm business or of a farmer. Note that, if NWS and income statement are maintained accurately, the profit or loss shown upon the income statement will be the same as the change in net worth between two NWSs except their allowance must be made for additional investments in the business or with drawl of capital.

Points Imperative for Profit and Loss Account

They include:

- That only such item of income and expenses, which properly belong to the business are included on each side of account.
- That the items include pertaining to accounting year under review.
- The each item of income or expenditure is shown under its appropriate head.
- That there is proper grouping and classification of items.

- That the account can be constructed over a period of time and this facilitates for analyzing the profitability changes in the farm business.

Components of Profit and Loss Statement

As income and expenditure are the two major components in an income statement, each of these two components can be sub-divided into various categories as below.

i. Income Component

Usually, the income statement considers the various sources of income such as:

- Cash receipts from sale of crops, livestock and its products.
- Cash earnings from custom hiring.
- Kind income such as, value of farm produce consumed by the family.
- Rental value of farm dwellings.
- Unrealized income such as inventory changes.
- Miscellaneous sources, if any.

If income statement is to be prepared for a farm operator, the non-farm income can also be included. Normally, three income level figures, *viz.*, net cash income, NFI and returns to management, are to be considered, while preparing the income statement.

ii. Expenditure Component

Usually, the expenditure statement considers the various types of expenses such as

- Cash farm operating expenses represent those expenditures of cash, which are associated with the operations of a farm. These include: the purchases of seeds, feed, fertilizers, pesticides, wage payments, hired machinery charges/fuel expenses and draught animal charges, irrigation/electricity charges, expenses on livestock feed, veterinary medicine expenses *etc.* These variable cash expenses are incurred only, if production is undertaken.
- Fixed cash expenses like land revenue, depreciation, interest on medium and long-term loans *etc.* These expenses are incurred even in the absence of production. Note that, expenditures made on the purchase of capital assets such as tractor, bullocks, pumpsets, land reclamation *etc.*, are not considered as a cash expense because, these assets are utilized in production over a period of time. Hence, for such assets, annual depreciation is taken as an expense item.
- The current principal payment on loans is also excluded as cash expense, since repayment of principal has no effect on profit, as liabilities are reduced by an equal amount. However, the interest payments form a cash expense.

iii. Other Considerable Points for Profit and Loss Account

- ☆ The profits from the sale of farm produce held over from previous year.
- ☆ The estimated value of goods produced and still held for future sale or use on the farm.
- ☆ The value of farm produce supplied to the household of the farmer.
- ☆ The value of farm produce of the current year given as wages or fed to livestock during the year.

Table 5.3: Income Statement of a Farm in Nandyal Region of Andhra Pradesh for the year, 2012-13 (Hypothetical data)

	Items	*Amount (Rs.)*
A.	**Cash Receipts (Income Component)**	
	☆ Sale of crops	140000
	☆ Sale of livestock and livestock products	65000
	☆ Custom hiring of machinery	25000
	Total Cash Receipts or GFI	**230000**
B.	**Cash Expenses (Expenditure Component)**	
	☆ Wage payments for hired human and bullock labour	25000
	☆ Fuel charges for machinery	13000
	☆ Purchase of material inputs for crops	35000
	☆ Irrigation/electricity charges	20000
	☆ Expenses on livestock feed	10000
	☆ Veterinary and medicine expenses.	9000
	☆ Miscellaneous expenses (such as repair/upkeep of farm buildings and machinery, land revenue, depreciation on capital assets, interest on operating loans, medium and long-term loan installments plus interest there of *etc.*)	30000
	Total Cash Expenses	**142000**
C.	**Net Cash Income from farm operations** (=Total Cash Receipts (or GFI) – Total Cash Expenses)	88000
	☆ Capital Gains and Losses (Sales of Farm Capital Assets - Cost Value of Items Sold)	7000
D.	**NFI** (Net Cash Income from farm operations + Capital Gains and Losses)	95000

iv. Net Cash Income from Farm Operations

The summation of various income measures gives Total Cash Receipts or Gross Farm Income (GFI) and the summation of various expenses give Total cash expenses. These total cash farm expenses are deducted from the total cash farm revenues to get the Net cash income from farm operations. That is, Net Cash Income from farm operations (=Total Cash Receipts (or GFI) – Total Cash Expenses).

v. NFI

To derive this, for the Net cash income from farm operations so computed above, Capital Gains and Losses should be added. Note that, if there loss, it should be subtracted.

Key Measures from Income Statements

- *GFI or Total Cash Receipts:* This is the sum of the cash generated from the sale of crop produce and livestock products, custom hiring of machinery, changes in inventory *etc.*
- **Net Cash Income from farm operations:** This is given by: Total Cash Receipts (or GFI) – Total Cash Expenses
- *NFI or Net Farm Earnings:* This is given by: Net Cash Income from farm operations + Capital Gains and Losses. Note that, NFI refers to the 'Bottom line' profit that is earned (or projected to earn) by the farm business during the accounting period. The problem with NFI is that, it does not relate the income to the size of the investment. So, it is advantageous of using Rate of Return on Assets (ROA) as a measure of profitability.
  - *Rate of Return on Assets (ROA):* It is a measure of profitability, measuring the rate of return that the farm business earns on its average assets over the period. The higher the return, the more profitable the farm business. This ROA is given by:

    = (NFI + Interest Expenses - Unpaid Farm Manager's and Family Labour/Total Farm Assets

    = Return to Assets/Total Farm Assets

    This ratio represents the total income generated from the farm divided by the total assets employed to generate this income. Unpaid family labour is subtracted, as it represents a non-cash expense. This adjustment helps to compare farms, which pay family wages to those that do not. This ratio also tells, how effective the farm business in putting its assets to work. Thus, ROA is a test of capital utilization - how much profit a business earned on the total capital used to make that profit. So, ROA can also be written as: = Net profit/Assets.
  - *Rate of Return on Farm Equity (ROE):* There is another profitability measure that was employed along with ROA and this is calculated as: =(NFI - Unpaid Farm Manager's and Family Labour)/Total Farm Equity = Return to Farm Equity/Total Farm Equity. This should be higher than the ROA over the long-run. This assumes that, the farm manager is using debt leverage for an advantage. There is a trade-off here between a high return on equity and high risk as the two are positively correlated.

    Note that, if ROA > 'i' then ROE > ROA and if ROA < *'i'* then ROE < ROA, where *'i'* is the interest rate on borrowed capital. Thus, if ROA > ROE borrowed capital is earning, on average, less than the interest rate. If ROA < ROE, borrowed capital is earning, on average, more than the interest rate.

The following are the other parameters that can be derived from Income statement:

- *Gross Margin:* For a farm business, this is given by: NFI – Depreciation. Gross margin indicates funds available to cover unallocated fixed costs, returns to unpaid farm manager's and family labour and returns to owner's equity.

- *Net income:* Net income is given by:

  NFI + Off-farm income - Social security payments due on these income sources.

  Net income shows, what is available to pay for principal on past debts, new farm investments, family off-farm investments *etc.* Net income is the real bottom line of a business and is the single most important indicator of profitability. So, the last line of the income statement is 'Net Income', which tells how much profit or loss the farm experienced. If that number is positive, the farming operation made money, if it's negative, it lost money.

Uses of the Income Statement

They include:

- Financial results of the business can be ascertained for the working year.
- The true nature and extent of expenses or loss arranged under various heads and the various sources of income are known.
- It answers the basic question, *'how did the farm business do last year?*
- The income statement is a progress report of the farm business. The net income or loss shown on an income statement indicates the profitability of the farm business for a specific period of time.
- Comparing income statements over a number of periods shows the trend in profitability of farm business.
- Making comparisons of net income averages for farms of similar size can help in evaluating the efficiency of the business.
- There are two reasons to prepare a Profit and Loss Statement. One reason is that, it answers the question, *'Am I making any money?'* It is a valuable tool to monitor operations. A regularly prepared statement either quarterly or monthly for new businesses will give farm owners timely and important information regarding revenues and expenses and tell them whether adjustments might be necessary to recoup losses or decrease expenses. This statement also allows outsiders to evaluate the farm manager's ability to manage and use the farm resources. The second reason to prepare this statement is, it helps to record all business transactions and thereby, forms the basis to assess taxes on profits earned.

NWS vis-à-vis Income Statement

In financial accounting of farm business, both NWS and Income statement are the two most important types of financial statements (other being Cash flow statement). These two statements differ in the following ways:

- A NWS lists assets and liabilities of the farm at a specific point of time, *i.e.,* as of a certain date, whereas an income statement is a report for income and expenses of a farm business over a specific time period, usually an accounting year.

- A farm with strong income statements year over year will generally build a healthy NWS or balance sheet, but it is possible that, it may have a strong NWS, but weak income statement.
- NWS shows information about assets, liabilities and equity, whereas income statement shows information about sales, expenses and profits of the farm.

C. Cash Flow Statement

The 'Cash Flow Statement' examines how cash has entered and left the farm business during the financial year. This statement shows a list of cash flows that occurred during the past accounting period. Cash flow is needed to cover family living expenses, payment of debts and to make investments in farm business. Cash Flow and Net Profit are not the same thing. One could have sufficient profits, but insufficient cash flow or, one's cash flow could be adequate, but profits are lacking. A complete set of financial statements and proper analysis of them will show financial strengths and weaknesses of a farm business. To complete a 'Cash Flow Statement', one must have a good 'NWS' from the beginning of the year, another for the end of the year, and an accrual adjusted 'Income Statement' for the year. The 'Cash Flow Statement' begins by showing the farmer's 'Beginning Cash Balance' from previous year. This statement is divided into three groups *viz.*, 'Cash receipts', 'Cash expenses' and 'Cash balance' (Table 5.4). This statement is organized in terms of a calendar year, with the columns representing the sub-periods in the year. Usually the accounting period is one year, but the sub-periods can be as detailed as the farmer desires. The sub-periods can represent quarters, months and even weeks. The rows represent various categories for the beginning cash balance, cash receipts, cash expenses and the ending cash balance. Of course, the beginning cash balance for each sub-period is the ending cash balance for that sub-period of the previous calendar year. The components of Cash Flow Statement include:

a. Cash Receipts

This group include:

- ***Cash received from sale of produce:*** This is cash that is received by the farmer from selling his crops produce and livestock products.
- ***Cash received from sale of capital assets:*** This is cash that is received by the farmer from selling his capital assets like milch cattle, implements, machinery *etc.*
- ***Borrowings of farmer:*** This includes borrowings made by farmer for cultivation of crops and managing livestock enterprises.
- ***Non-farm income:*** This includes cash earned by the farmer by working elsewhere.

b. Cash Expenses

This group include:

- *Operating expenditure:* This refers to the annual expenses to be incurred on variable inputs such as, labour, fertilizer, seeds, chemicals, tractor fuel, feed purchased and electricity.
- *Capital expenditure:* This is the investment required to purchase capital items such as, machinery and livestock and to make some medium-term or long term improvements on the farm.
- *Family living and non-farm expenditure:* This is the expenditure incurred towards meeting farm family needs and other expenditure not related to farm business.
- *Payment of current year's borrowed money:* These are the expenses made towards complete repayment of ST (crop loans) borrowed in the same accounting year.
- *Interest charges:* This include interest paid for the use of term loans borrowed in the current accounting year.

Note that, many income items are also cash inflows. The sales of crops and livestock are usually both income and cash inflows. The timing is also usually the same as long as a cheque is received and deposited in farmer's account at the time of the sale. Many expense items are also cash outflow items. The purchase of fertilizer is both an expense and a cash outflow item. The timing is also the same, if a cheque is written at the time of purchase. However, there are many cash items that are not income and expense items, and *vice versa*. For example, the purchase of a tractor is a cash outflow, if the farmer pay cash from his pocket at the time of purchase. But, the expense item includes only depreciation charges incurred every year. If money is borrowed for the purchase of tractor using a LT loan, the down payment is a cash outflow at the time of purchase and the annual principal and interest payments are cash outflows each year and annual depreciation and interest payments represent expenses. However, principal payments are not an expense, but merely a cash transfer between farmer and banker.

c. Cash Balance

This is computed for the accounting year by subtracting total cash expenses from total cash receipts.

Note that, there are two types of cash flows *viz.*, Projected cash flow and Actual cash flow. Projected cash flow is completed at the beginning of the accounting period and it projects expected cash inflows and outflows for the period to estimate the liquidity reserve or ending cash balance for each month. As the accounting period progresses, keep an actual cash flow statement to record cash transactions as they take place. Then compare the actual cash flow statement with the projected cash flow statement to see, if things are going as planned, to devise remedies for solving previously unforeseen problems, or to take advantage of opportunities not anticipated. At the end of the accounting period, use the actual cash flow statement to estimate the projected cash flow for the next year. This is especially important for agricultural businesses, because of production cycles and the seasonality of the business.

Importance of Cash-Flow Statement

Note that, of all the statements that comprise a farm business plan, the cash flow statement is often the most challenging one. This is so because, this statement covers all aspects of farming *i.e.,* both receipts and expenses of the farmer throughout the year, sub-period wise and to prepare a good statement, it demands considerable amount of time, thought and commitment on the part of the farmer. However, the time spent for preparing this statement can also pay big dividends to the farmer in planning the alternate courses of action that contributes to a more profitable farm business. As this statement also guides the farmer in planning the flow of revenue into the farm business and the flow of expenditures out of the business in the future, it is also called Flow of Funds Statement or Cash Flow Budget. These flows are important because, they indicate, when cash surpluses or deficiencies will occur in the business and thereby, guide the farmer to effectively utilize the surplus income if any or meet the short fall of income during any sub-periods in the farm business. This cash flow statement is further helpful in the following aspects:

- ☆ May guide the farmer to start a new enterprise or business
- ☆ To expand the existing business
- ☆ To switch over to modern technology on the farm
- ☆ Enable the farmer to procure requisite inputs in advance
- ☆ Enable the farmer to plan credit requirements in advance
- ☆ Enable the farmer to plan for sale of products in advance
- ☆ Enable the farmer to plan for full-production period throughout the year
- ☆ A cash flow statement is not only concerned with the amount of cash flows, but also the timing of the flows, as cash flows are constructed with multiple time periods. It not only projects the cash balance remaining at the end of the year, but also the cash balance for each month.
- ☆ Preparation of this cash flow statement assumes greater importance in farm business. We know, liquid cash serves as a major ingredient that makes the business operate smoothly just as grease is the ingredient that makes a machine function smoothly. Without adequate cash, a business cannot function because, many of the transactions require cash to fulfill or complete them. By creating a cash flow budget, the farmer can project different sources and applications of funds for the upcoming time periods. He will identify any cash deficit periods in advance and thereby, he can take corrective actions now to alleviate the deficit. This may involve shifting the timing of certain transactions. It may also determine when money will be borrowed. If borrowing is involved, it will also determine the amount of cash that needs to be borrowed. Periods of excess cash can also be identified. This information can be used to direct excess cash into interest bearing assets, where additional revenue can be generated or to scheduled loan payments.

Table 5.4: Annual Cash Flow Statement of 5 Acre Farm in Nandyal Region of Andhra Pradesh

(2012-13)

Items	*June*	*July*	*Aug*	*Sept*	*Oct*	*Nov*	*Dec*	*Jan*	*Feb*	*Mar*	*Apr*	*May*	*Total*
Beginning Cash balance (beginning of themonths)	**2000**	**1500**	**1700**	**900**	**25000**	**550**	**3600**	**2700**	**2600**	**3200**	**3100**	**4500**	
Total operating sales*					17000	21000		20000		18500			**76500**
Money borrowed (Non-institutional sources)	5000					6000							**11000**
Non-farm income	3000	3000	3000	3000	3000	3000	3000	3000	3000	3000	3000	3000	**36000**
Total cash available (Rs.)	**10000**	**4500**	**4700**	**3900**	**45000**	**30550**	**6600**	**25700**	**5600**	**24700**	**6100**	**7500**	**174850**
Operating expenses**	2300	1560	2650	1120	4000	5100	2900	8000	2000	1400	2100	2800	**35930**
Capital expenditure***					29000	12000							**41000**
Family living and non farm expenditure	2500	1700	1200	1700	3500	2100	2000	3900	2100	1800	1700	2100	**26300**
Payment on current year's borrowed money	5000				6000								**11000**
Interest paid on borrowed money****			250				300						**550**
Total expenditure	9800	3260	4100	2820	42500	19200	5200	11900	4100	3200	3800	4900	114780
Ending Cash balance (end of month) in Rs.	200	1240	600	1080	2500	11350	1400	13800	1500	21500	2300	2600	

*: Operating sales is the income expected from the sales of different crops and livestock products; **: Operating expenditure refers to the annual expenses to be incurred on current inputs, such as labour, fertilizer, seeds, chemicals, tractor fuel, feed purchased and electricity; ***: Capital expenditure is the investment required to purchase some capital item, such as machines and livestock, to make some mid-term or long term improvement on the farm; ****: Interest rate at 20 per cent on Rs.5000/- and Rs.6000/- for three months each.

☆ The cash flow statement is a critical component of the business plan and will be reviewed by lenders. It answers the basic question, *'where was the cash used?'*.

Cash Flow Statement vis-à-vis Income Statement

Both cash flow statement and income statement are dynamic statements that are prepared over the accounting period and they account in between two successive NWSs (Figure 5.1). However, cash flow statement and income statement differ in the following two aspects:

☆ A cash flow statement lists cash inflows and cash outflows, while the income statement lists income and expenses.

☆ A cash flow statement shows *liquidity (It* is the ability of the farm to generate enough cash to meet financial obligations as they come due without disrupting the normal operation of the farm business), while an income statement shows *profitability (It* is the summary of all resources that have come into the farm (revenue) and all resources that have left the farm (expense). Their difference equals the net income or net loss).

☆ Cash Flow (Liquidity) records time and size of cash inflows and outflows that occur over a calendar year. Liquidity differs from profitability because, the cash flow statement only includes cash income or expenses, whereas the income statement also includes non-cash items such as depreciation and inventory adjustments.

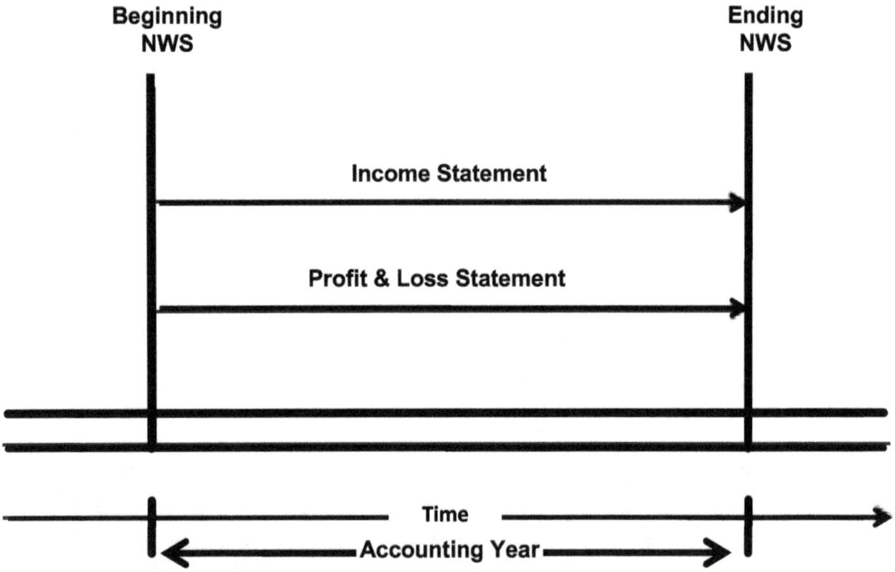

Courtesy: https://www.extension.iastate.edu/agdm/wholefarm

Figure 5.1: Integrated Farm Financial Statements.

D. Financial Ratios derived from Farm Financial Statements

The use of financial ratios in assessing, benchmarking and monitoring of farm performance has become more common over the past few years. As all production, operating and financial decisions are eventually reflected in the financial statements, analyzing them can reveal useful insights into the strengths and weaknesses of operating a farm business. These financial ratios are grouped into five areas:

i. Liquidity ratios
ii. Solvency ratios
iii. Profitability ratios
iv. Financial efficiency ratios and
v. Debt coverage ratios

i. Liquidity Ratios

Ratios in this category are designed to measure the short-run solvency of a farm *i.e.,* a farm's ability to pay its obligations in the short run. These ratios include Current Ratio, Working or Intermediate ratio, Debt Structure Ratio and Acid test ratio and these are already discussed in-detail under NWS.

ii. Solvency Ratios

Ratios in this category are designed to measure the long-run solvency of a farm. They are concerned with the levels of equity and debt in the farm. These ratios are also discussed in-detail under NWS.

iii. Profitability Ratios

Ratios in this category are designed to measure a firm's ability to generate profit. They include: ROA, ROE and Operating Profit Margin Ratio. First two ratios are already discussed under Income statement.

☆ ***Operating Profit Margin Ratio (OPMR):*** This is given by:

= (NFI + Interest Expense – Unpaid Farm Manager and Family Labour/ Value of Production (VOP) or Gross revenue

VOP = (Farm Cash Receipts + (Change in Value of Product Inventory + Change in Value of Accounts Receivable) - Livestock Purchases)

= Return to Farm Assets/Value of Production (or Gross revenue of farm)

Thus, OPMR ratio measures the proportion of gross revenues left after paying expenses. The higher the value, the more profit the business is generating per rupee of revenue. For example, if the OPMR is 0.30 it indicates that, for every one rupee of revenue, Rs.0.30 remained as profit after paying the operating expense needed to generate that rupee. Generally, farms with large investments in fixed assets such as land and few operating expenses will show a higher OPMR. Farms with more rented assets will have a higher ROA, but a lower OPMR. The range desirable for this OPMR ratio is 20 – 30 percent.

iv. Financial Efficiency Ratios

Ratios in this category are designed to measure a firm's ability to generate revenues and control costs. These ratios include:

- ***Capital Turnover Ratio:*** This is given by:

  = Value of Production/Total Farm Assets

  This ratio is a measure of capital intensity. The range desirable for this ratio is greater than 25 – 30 percent. This ratio means that, how fast the farmers that purchase assets repay their credit from their annual production. Thus, this ratio is an activity ratio, measuring how efficiently a farmer uses his assets.

- ***Operating Expense Ratio (excludes depreciation and interest):*** This is given by: =Operating Expenses (excluding interest and depreciation)/VOP

  = Operating expense-Depreciation/Gross revenue

  This ratio represents the percentage of operating expense that will consume for every Rs.1 of revenue. A useful way to view this ratio is that, the residual represents the amount of money left on a rupee of revenue that remains to:

  - debt servicing (both interest and principal),
  - provide for reinvestment in capital assets such as machinery, equipment and buildings, and
  - provide for family living withdrawals.

  For example, a 70 percent operating expense ratio would indicate that, there is 30 paise from every rupee of revenue generated left to cover debt servicing, re-investment, and family living withdrawals. The desirable range for this ratio is, it should be less than 65 percent.

- ***Depreciation Expense Ratio:*** This is given by:

  = Depreciation Expense/VOP (or Gross revenue)

  The range desirable for this ratio is less than 15 percent.

- ***Interest expense ratio:*** This is given by:

  = Interest expense/gross revenue

  The range desirable for this ratio is less than 15 percent. This ratio relates the interest expense to a farm's ability to generate income. This is a particularly useful ratio, as it can be measured accurately. This is a ratio, where the trend is vitally important. An upward trend will lead to eventual financial stress.

- ***NFI from operations ratio:*** This is given by:

  = NFI from operations/Gross revenue

  The range desirable for this ratio is greater than 15 percent.

v. Debt Coverage Ratios

Ratios in this category are designed to measure a farm's ability to generate funds to meet debt obligations. These ratios include:

- ***Interest Coverage Ratio:*** This is given by:

  =(NFI + Interest Expense)/Interest Expense

Table 5.5: Benchmarks of Farm Financial Ratios

Ratio	*Formula*	*Range Desirable for Safer Business*
i. Liquidity Ratios		
☆ Current Ratio	= Total Current Assets/Total Current Liabilities	>1.7
☆ Working Ratio or Intermediate Ratio	$\frac{\text{Current assessts + Intrermediate assets}}{\text{Curent liabilities + Intermediate liabilities}}$	
☆ Debt-Structure Ratio	$\frac{\text{Current liabilities}}{\text{Total liabilities}}$	<0.2
☆ Acid Test Ratio or Quick Ratio	= (Current assets - Inventories and supplies)/Current liabilities = Cash + Marketable securities + Accounts receivable)/Current liabilities = (Liquid Assets)/(Current Liabilities)	>0.5 with a healthy current Ratio
ii. Solvency Ratios		
☆ Net Capital Ratio	= Total assets/Total liabilities	>1.0
☆ Debt Ratio or Debt-To-Asset Value Ratio or Solvency Ratio	= Total liabilities/Total assets	<1.0
☆ Equity-To-Asset Value Ratio	= Equity or Net worth/Value of assets	>0.70
☆ Leverage Ratio or Debt-to-Equity Ratio	= Total liabilities/Net worth= [(Owned capital)/(Owned capital + Borrowed capital)]*100	<1.0
☆ Debt Payout Ratio	= Total Liabilities/Net Farm Income	
iii. Profitability ratios		
☆ ROA	= (NFI + Interest Expenses - Unpaid Farm Manager's and Family Labour/ Total Farm Assets= Return to Assets/Total Farm Assets	>5 per cent
☆ ROE	= (NFI - Unpaid Farm Manager's and Family Labour)/Total Farm Equity = Return to Farm Equity/Total Farm Equity	Look at trends and compare to other farm and non-farm investments
☆ Operating Profit Margin Ratio (OPMR)	= (NFI + Interest Expense – Unpaid Farm Manager and Family Labour/ Value of Production (VOP) or Gross revenue = Return to Farm Assets/Value of Production (or Gross revenue of farm)	20-30 per cent

Contd...

Table 5.5–*Contd...*

Ratio	*Formula*	*Range Desirable for Safer Business*
iv. Financial Efficiency Ratios		
☆ Capital (Asset) Turnover Ratio	= Value of Production/Total Farm Assets	25-30 per cent
☆ Operating Expense Ratio (excludes	= Operating Expenses (excluding interest and depreciation)/VOP	<65 per cent
depreciation and interest)	= Operating expense-Depreciation/Gross revenue	
☆ Depreciation Expense Ratio	= Depreciation Expense/VOP (or Gross revenue)	<15 per cent
☆ Interest Expense Ratio	= Interest expense/gross revenue	<15 per cent
☆ NFI from operations ratio	= NFI from operations/Gross revenue	>15 per cent
v. Debt Coverage Ratios		
☆ Interest Coverage Ratio	= (NFI + Interest Expense)/Interest Expense	
☆ Term Debt Coverage Ratio	= (NFI + Depreciation - Unpaid Farm manager and Family Labour + Term Interest)/Scheduled Annual Term Interest and Principal Payments	

This ratio is a measure of a farm's ability to meet interest payments. It is similar to the interest expense ratio, but it relates interest expense to earnings before interest. It provides a true picture of debt servicing ability than the interest expense ratio, as it accounts for expenses. As the value of the interest coverage ratio increases, the farmer's exposure to financial risk decreases. The interest coverage ratio is analogous to an asset to debt ratio taken from the balance sheet. The interest coverage ratio relates asset returns to debt obligations for a period of time, while the asset to debt ratio relates total assets to total debt at a point in time.

☆ ***Term Debt Coverage Ratio:*** This is given by:

(NFI + Depreciation - Unpaid Farm manager and Family Labour + Term Interest)/Scheduled Annual Term Interest and Principal Payments

In computing this ratio, the earnings are adjusted to account for cash flow by adding back in depreciation and subtracting out unpaid labour. Principal payments are included with the interest payments to get a clearer picture of cash flow obligations of debt. The weakness of this ratio is the estimate of unpaid labour and reduces the reliability of the values.

E. Summary Statement of Financial Ratios

Table 5.5 shows the summary statement pertaining to the benchmarks of various Farm Financial Ratios discussed above.

6

Costs and Returns of Enterprises

Agricultural Prices Commission (APC) was set up on 8th January, 1965 by the then Ministry of Food and Agriculture, Government of India with a view to evolve a balanced and integrated price structure and was mandated to advise on the price policy of 11 agricultural crops or group of crops. Although the Commission was initially set up for a period of three years, it was *'placed on permanent footing'* since 26th May, 1970. As policy paradigm changed over time, the name of the APC was also changed to 'Commission for Agricultural Costs and Prices' (CACP) on 18th March, 1985. The following are the objectives of CACP:

- ☆ To advise on the price policy of paddy/rice, wheat, jowar, bajra, maize, ragi, barely, gram, tur, moong, urad, sugarcane, groundnut, soyabean, seed, rapeseed, mustard, cotton, jute, tobacco, seasmum, niger seed, lentil (masoor), safflower, copra and such other commodities as the Government may decide from time to time, with a view to evolving a balanced and integrated price structure in the perspective of the overall needs of the economy and with due regard to the interests of the producer and the consumer.
- ☆ While recommending the price policy and the relative price structure, the Commission may keep in view the following:
  - ❑ The need to provide incentive to the producer for adopting improved technology and for developing a production pattern broadly in the light of national requirements.

- ❑ The need to ensure rational utilization of land, water and other production resources.
- ❑ The likely effect of the price policy on rest of the economy, particularly on the cost of living, level of wages, cost structure of agro-based products and the competitiveness of agriculture and agro-based commodities.

- ✰ The Commission may also suggest such non-price measures related to credit policy, crop and income insurance and other sectors as would facilitate the achievements of the objectives set out in first above.
- ✰ To recommend from time to time, in respect of different agricultural commodities, measures necessary to make the price policy effective.
- ✰ To take into account the changes in terms of trade between agricultural and non-agricultural sectors.
- ✰ To examine, where necessary, the prevailing methods and cost of marketing of agricultural commodities in different regions, suggest measures to reduce costs of marketing and recommend fair price margins for different stages of marketing.
- ✰ To keep under review the developing price situation and to make appropriate recommendations, as and when necessary, within the framework of the overall price policy.
- ✰ To undertake studies in respect of different crops as may be prescribed by Government from time to time.
- ✰ To keep under review studies relating to the prices policy and arrangements for collection of information regarding agricultural prices and other related data and suggest improvements in the same, and to organize research studies in the field of price policy.
- ✰ To advise on any problems relating to agricultural prices and other production that may be referred to it by Government from time to time.
- ✰ To effectively integrate the recommended non-price measures with price recommendations and to ensure competitive agriculture.

MSPs are currently announced for 25 commodities (Tables 6.1 and 6.2) including seven cereals (paddy, wheat, barley, jowar, bajra, maize and ragi); five pulses (gram, arhar/tur, moong, urad and lentil or masur); eight oilseeds (groundnut, rapeseed/mustard, toria, soyabean, sunflower seed, sesamum, safflower seed and niger seed); copra; raw cotton; sugar cane; raw jute and VFC tobacco. While fixing the MSPs, the Commission considers the COP of commodity (both explicit and implicit costs). The MSPs are normally announced before the commencement of sowing operations of the particular crop and have usually been remunerative and significantly higher than the COP. The MSP, by definition, becomes the floor price and farmers are assured of getting that price.

Table 6.1: MSP/Procurement Price for Crops (Crop year basis) (Rs./qtl)

Commodities	*2005-06*	*2006-07*	*2007-08*	*2008-09*	*2009-10*	*2010-11*	*2011-12*
Paddy							
☆ Common	570	580C	645H	850K	950K	1000	1080
☆ Grade 'A'	600	610C	675H	880K	980K	1030	1110
Wheat	650G	750H	100	1080	1100	1120	1285
Coarse cereals							
Jowar	525	540	600	840	840	880	980
Bajra	525	540	600	840	840	880	980
Ragi	525	540	600	915	915	965	1050
Maize	540	540	620	840	840	880	980
Barley	550	565	650	680	750	780	980
Lentil (Masur)	1535	1545	1700	1870	1870	2250	2800
Gram	1435	1445	1600	1730	1760	2100	2800
Arhar	1400	1410	1550D	2000	2300	3000L	3200L
Moong	1520	1520	1700D	2520	2760	3170L	3500L
Urad	1520	1520	1700D	2520	2520	2900L	3300L
Sugarcane (SMP)A	79.5	80.25	81.18	81.18	129.84	139.12	145M
Cotton							
☆ F-414/h-777	1760	1770E	1800E	2500B	2500B	2500B	2800B
☆ H-4 750	1980	1990F	2030F	3000J	3000J	3000J	3300J
Groundnut	1520	1520	1550	2100	2100	2300	2700
Jute(TD-5)	910	1000	1055	1250	1375	1575	1675
Rapeseed/Mustard	1715	1715	1800	1830	1830	1850	2500
Sunflower seed	1500	1500	1510	2215	2215	2350	2800
Soyabean							
☆ Black	900	900	910	1350	1350	1400	1650
☆ Yellow	1010	1020	1050	1390	1390	1440	1690
Safflower seed	1565	1565	1650	1650	1680	1800	2500
Toria	1680	1680	1735	1735	1735	1780	2425
Tobacco (per kg)							
☆ VFC F-2 (black soil)	32	32	32				
☆ L-2 (light soil)	34	34	34				
Copra (milling)	3570	3590	3620	3660	4450	4450	4525
Copra balls	3820	3840	3870	3910	4700	4700	4775
Sesamum	1550	1560	1580	2750	2850	2900	3400
Niger seed	1200	1220	1240	2405	2405	2450	2900

A: SMP upto 2008-09. Fair and Remunerative Price (FRP) from 2009-10 onwards; **B**: Staple length (mm) of 24.5-25.5 and micronaire value of 4.3-5.; **C**: An additional incentive bonus of Rs. 40 per quintal was payable on procurement between January 10, 2006 to March 31, 2007; **D**: A bonus of Rs. 40 per quintal is payable over and above the MSP; **E**: Medium staple; **F**: Long staple; **G**: An incentive bonus of Rs. 50 per quintal is payable on wheat over the MSP; **H**: An additional incentive bonus of Rs. 100 per quintal is payable over the MSP; **J**: Staple length (mm) of 29.5-30.5 and micronaire value of 3.5-4.3; **K**: An additional incentive bonus of Rs. 50 per quintal is payable over the MSP; **L**: Additional incentive @ Rs. 500/qtl of tur, urad and moong sold to procurement agencies; **M**: At 9.5 per cent recovery, subject to a premium of Rs.1.53 for every 0.1 per cent increase in the recovery above 9.5 per cent.

Source: www.agricoop.nic.in.

Table 6.2: MSPs for crops during 2010-11 and 2011-12 (Rs./qtl)

Crops	*2010-11*	*2011-12*	*Difference between 2011-12 and 2010-11 Prices*
***Kharif* crops**			
Paddy (common)	1000	1080	80
Paddy(Gr.A)	1030	1110	80
Jowar(hybrid)	880	980	100
Jowar(maldandi)	900	1000	100
Bajra	880	980	100
Maize	880	980	100
Ragi	965	1050	85
Arhar(tur)	3000	3200	200
Moong	3170	3500	330
Urad	2900	33300	400
Groundnut in shell	2300	2700	400
Sunflower	2350	2800	450
Soya bean(black)	1400	1650	250
Soya bean (yellow)	1440	1690	250
Sesamum	2900	3400	500
Niger seed	2450	2900	450
Cotton (F-414/H-777/J34)[1]	2500	2800	300
Rabi crops			
Wheat	1120[2]	1285	165
Barley	780	980	200
Gram	2100	2800	700
Masur(Lentil)	2250	2800	550
Rapeseed/mustard	1850	2500	650
Safflower	1800	2500	700

Note: An additional incentive @Rs. 500/qtl for tur, urad and moong is given to procurement agencies during the harvest/arrival period of two months.

1: Staple length (mm) of 24.5 and 25.5 and micronaire value of 4.3-5.1; 2: An additional incentive bonus of Rs.50/qtl over the MSP

Source: www.agricoop.nic.in.

Cost Concepts

As discussed under Chapter 4, the following standard cost notations are used:

Cost A1: All actual expenses in cash and kind incurred in production by owner operator

Cost A2: Cost A1+ Rent paid for leased-in-land

Cost B1: Cost A1 + Interest on value of owned capital assets (excluding land),

Cost B2: Cost B1 + Rental value of owned land (net of land revenue) and rent paid for leased-in-land

Cost C1: Cost B1+ Imputed value of family labour

Cost C2: Cost B2 +Imputed value of family labour

Cost C3: Cost C2 + 10 per cent of Cost C2 (on account of managerial functions performed by farmer)

It may be noted that, costs progressively escalate in an alphabetical order, that is to say that Ci > Bi >Ai, where i = 1 or 2. Further, costs with suffix 1 (A1, B1 and C1) exclude components of land rent/rental value while costs with suffix 2 (A2, B2 and C2) include that and therefore, A2 > A1, B2>B1 and C2 > C1. Cost of cultivation on per hectare basis and COP on per quintal basis are estimated by progressively combining various cost items in different groups. The items of costs included under each group or concept are given below:

Paid-out Costs

- ☆ Hired labour (human, animal and machinery).
- ☆ Maintenance expenses on owned animals and machinery.
- ☆ Expenses on material inputs such as seed (home grown and purchased), fertilizer, manure (owned and purchased), pesticides and irrigation.
- ☆ Depreciation on implements and farm buildings (such as cattle sheds, machine sheds, storage sheds).
- ☆ Land revenue.
- ☆ Rent paid for leased- in land.

Imputed Costs

- ☆ Value of family labour,
- ☆ Managerial input of family,
- ☆ Rent of owned land ; and
- ☆ Interest on owned fixed capital.

The reason behind making above classification of costs was to distinguish actual expenses incurred by the owner operators and tenant farmers from imputed costs, such as interest on owned fixed capital, value of family labour, rental value of owned land incurred by the farmers. This classification enables to work out range of costs within which pricing decisions could be based in a cogent manner and also allows computation of returns to land.

It is a known fact that, prices influence both domestic and export competitiveness of agricultural commodities in the market economy. In the modern era of agri-business, export competitiveness of commodities is gaining more and more significance, as it fetches more foreign exchange to the exporting country. The export competitiveness of commodities is influenced by several factors like COP, MSP and Domestic Market Price (DMP) realized for the produce/commodity, transaction costs of the commodities up to the port for placing the commodity in the international market, quality of the commodity *etc.* The same factors are also applicable for the importing countries equally to withstand stiff competition from the imported commodities. A country is said to be export competitive with respect to a commodity, if its price is less than DMP of the same commodity in the importing country. In general, the COP of the commodity helps in determining the MSP, and the DMP realized for the commodity should be higher than MSP for having competitiveness in the domestic market. If the commodity is desired to be exported, the exporter has to incur several transactions costs, insurance costs, storage costs *etc.*, up to the port till the commodity is placed in the international market. On the importing country side, the DMP of the commodity should be less than its import price (after imposition of tariffs), so as to protect the interests of domestic farmers in sustaining the production of the same commodity.

Realizing both domestic and export competitiveness for the commodities will fetch several advantages to the country like earning significant amount of foreign exchange, slowly capturing the monopoly gains in the international market, quality enhancement of the commodities, meeting consumers' tastes and preferences, profitability to the farmers, planning towards importers' need-based exports, simplification and regulation of procedural formalities at ports for making the exports at rapid pace, strengthening the exports infrastructure at ports, analyzing the tariff levels on the commodities of importing countries and accordingly fixing the export prices, strengthening the trade relationships across the countries *etc.* These advantages in the liberalized trade regime direct the Government to formulate various programmes and policies that guide the farmers to ensure both cost-effective and quality production of commodities. This also encourages the exports from the country. Further, it makes the Government to fix the MSP for the commodities considering their COP. In the liberalized trade regime, it is essential to fix the MSP for the commodity even considering its international price. We know, MSPs were recommended by the CACP to the Government based on the data collected on COP of crops at farmers' level by conducting Crop Cutting Experiments on sample basis. Based on CACP recommendations, the MSP will be announced by the Government in the ensuing season just before sowing the crop. It is disappointing to note that, the COP of commodities is increasing at rapid pace in the country due to mounting costs of seeds, fertilizers, pesticides, labour wages *etc.*, but the yield levels of the crops were more or less stable. But, in the competing countries (especially developed countries), the COP of commodities is on the decline due to excessive subsidization through Green and Blue box measures. As a result, the MSP announced by the Government based on the COP data may not reflect the realistic benefits at the farmers' level keeping in view the open trade environment and benefits due to gaining export competitiveness. This is because, sometimes, the MSP of commodities were even higher than international price. For example, the average MSP of maize during post-WTO regime (1999-00) is Rs.580.00/qtl and international price during the same period is Rs. 556.12/qtl. This clearly implies that, maize is not export competitive even at MSP level. This is because, a higher MSP announced by the Government for a commodity will indirectly encourage and support the farmers to increase the COP of the commodity up to the level of MSP. This limits the farmers in adoption of cost-effective production technologies/strategies. Hence, the MSPs should be recommended for the commodities taking into consideration not only COP, but also their international prices. Even though it may appear harsh at the farmers' level in the initial periods, but keeping in view the long term prospects and net trade position of the commodities, this must be followed and simultaneously a strong check should be imposed on inflationary price rise of inputs and other irregularities in trading the commodities.

Keeping in view the importance of price competitiveness both in domestic and international markets, the profitability analysis of enterprises is very important for several reasons. First, it analyses the COP of commodities at a point of time and even its trend. Second, it helps to assess both domestic and export competitiveness of commodities. Third, it guides the farmers to plan cost reduction measures in their production programme. Lastly, based on the trends in COP, it guides the Government to fix the MSP of crops. Above all, this profitability analysis is very important because, the trade reforms were at rapid pace in developing countries like India during the past 17 years and it is high time now to move the things in a planned manner regarding realizing the comparative advantage for the commodities in the international market. Considering this importance, now the primary objective of agricultural economists is to compute profitability of enterprises practiced on the farm and the same was discussed here under.

Procedure to Compute Cost of Cultivation of Crop Enterprises

Before going into the analysis, it is essential to note that, data are to be collected for the entire area under crop cultivation. Say, if the crop area of the farmer is 10 acres or 4.5 acres or even 70 cents, collect the data for the entire area under cultivation and not on the basis of per acre or per hectare. At the end, convert the Total Cost of Cultivation (TCOC) figure to Rs./ha. The following are the steps involved in this analysis:

- ☆ Compute only labour costs across different farm operations practiced on the enterprise (Component A).
- ☆ Compute only cost of the material or item used to perform the farm operation say, fertilizers, pesticides etc (Component B).
- ☆ Compute Interest on working capital by employing the following formula (Component C).

  = (Labour costs + Material costs) x ST loan interest rate(per cent) x (Half of crop period/12) = (Labour costs + Material costs) x (7/100) x (Half of crop period/12)
- ☆ Compute TFC incurred in the business *viz.*, land revenue, Rental value of owned/leased in land, Depreciation and Interest on owned fixed capital (Component D).
  - ❑ ***Rental value of owned/leased in land***

    = Rental value of land in that area per year x (crop period/12)
  - ❑ ***Depeciation:*** Compute annual depreciation: (Straight line method)

    =[(Original Cost – Junk Value)/Expected useful life of asset]

- ***Interest on owned fixed capital***

  = (Present value of all assets excluding land) x LT loan interest rate(per cent) or Interest on fixed deposits

  = (Present value of all assets excluding land) x 10/100

- Compute TCOC = (Component A)+(Component B)+(Component C)+(Component D)
- Compute Cost of Production (COP) (Rs./qtl) = TCOC/Total production
- ***Domestic competitiveness:*** Compare COP with MSP and Domestic Market Price (wholesale price). If the wholesale price of the commodity is higher than COP, then the commodity is said to be competitive in the domestic market.
- ***Export competitiveness:*** Compare COP with international price of the commodity. If the international price is higher than COP, then the commodity is said to be competitive in the international market
- If the commodity do not enjoy both domestic and/or export competitiveness, suggest measures, if any, to reduce Cost of Cultivation or COP of crops
- Workout cost concepts as suggested by CACP discussed in Chapter 4. The cost concepts include: Cost A1, Cost A2, Cost A2+FL, Cost B1, Cost B2, Cost C1, Cost C2 and Cost C3. Note that, TCOC should be equal to Cost C2.

Case Studies

Example 6.1

The following is a hypothetical example for computing TCOC and Cost concepts of Crop 'X' in an area of 1.25 acres.

i. TCOC

A. Labour Costs

Operations	Owned labour					Hired labour					Wage rate/labour					Amount
	TP	CPD	M	W	C	TP	CPD	M	W	C	TP	CPD	M	W	C	
Nursery								2					125			250
Land preparation						2		2			100		100			400
Transplanting				2					12					100		1400
Manures			1					2					125			375
Fertilizers			1					3					125			500
Plant Protection								2					150			300
Irrigation			1										100			100
Weeding									2					100		200
Harvesting			2					1					150			450
TOTAL LABOUR COSTS	= (1*125)+(1*125)+(1*100)+(2*150) + (2*100)= 850					= (2*100)+ (2*125)+ (2*100)+ (2*125)+(3*125)+(2*150)+(2*100) + (1*150)+ (12*100)= 3125										3975

B. Material Costs

Inputs	Quantity		Rate	Value (Rs./-)
	Owned	Purchased		
Seed	0.5 kg	1.5 kg	200/kg	400
Manures	--	2 cart loads	900/cart load	1800
Fertilizers	--	100 kg	Rs.1500/50 kg bag	3000
Plant protection chemicals	--	1.5 litres	Rs 2500/lit	3750
TOTAL MATERIAL COSTS				**8950**

C. Interest on Working Capital

= (Labour costs + Material costs) x ST loan interest rate(per cent) x (Half of crop period/12)

= (Labour costs + material costs) x (7/100) x (Half of crop period/12)

= (3975+8950) * (7/100) * (2/12)

= 150.79/-

D. Fixed Costs

Item	Formulae	Value (Rs/-)
Land revenue		200
Depreciation (of three assets Asset 1, Asset 2 and Asset 3)	(Original cost – Junk value) / Expected life of asset	**2900+1100+1000 =5000**
Rental value of owned land	= (Rental value of land per year)*(crop period/12months)	=6000*4/12 =2000
Interest on fixed capital*	(Present values of all assets of farmer excluding land) *(10/100)	**= 2800**
TOTAL FIXED COSTS		**10000**

Note: * - Interest on fixed capital (excluding land):

= (Present value of all assets excluding land) x LT loan interest rate(per cent)

= (Present value of all assets excluding land) x 10/100

Assume the farmer is having three assets, Asset 1, Asset 2 and Asset 3

***Procedure:* Asset 1**

1. **Original cost of Asset 1 :** Rs. 30000
2. **Expected life :** 10 years
3. **Years of usage:** 7
4. **Junk value :** 1000
5. **Annual depreciation:** (Straight line method)
   =[(Original Cost – Junk Value)/Expected useful life of asset]
   = (30000-1000)/10 = 2900/-
6. **Total depreciation :** = 2900 x 7 = 20300/-
7. **Present value of Asset 1 =** 30000-20300 =9700/-

Like wise, estimate present value of all other assets (Asset 2 and Asset 3) and summate all the present values. Say, it is Rs. 28000/-. So,

Interest on fixed capital = (Sum of present values of all the assets excluding land) x (10/100)

= 28000 x (10/100) = 2800

So, TCOC = (A+B+C+D) = (3975+8950+150.79+10000) = 23075.79/-

ii. Computation of Cost Concepts

For the above hypothetical example, cost concepts are worked out as shown below. Note that, the cost concepts should be expressed finally with reference to a technical unit *i.e.,* Rs./hectare.

COST CONCEPTS

COST A1 = Owned Bullock labour + Owned machinery labour + Hired human labour + Hired bullock labour + Hired machinery labour + Imputed value of owned seeds + Purchased value of seeds + Nursery + Land preparation + Transplanting + Imputed value of owned manures + Purchased manures + Fertilizers + Plant Protection + Irrigation + Weeding + Land revenue + Interest on working capital + Depreciation

Items	Value (Rs/-)
Hired human labour	2725
Hired machinery labour	400
Imputed value of owned seeds	100
Purchased value of seeds	300
Manures	1800
Fertilizers	3000
Plant protection chemicals	3750
Land revenue	200
Interest on working capital	150.79
Depreciation	3000
Total	**15425.79 = (Rs. 30851.58/ha)**

** Do not include family labour data for above operations . But, include owned bullock & machinery labour data*

Cost A2 = Cost A1 + rent paid for leased-in Land.

= **15425.79 + 0 = 15425.79/- (= Rs. 30851.58/ha)**

Cost A2+FL = Cost A2 + imputed value of Family Labour.

= **15425.79 + 850 = 16275.79/- (= Rs. 32551.58/ha)**

Cost B1 = Cost A1+ interest on value of owned (fixed) capital assets (excluding land)

= **15425.79 + 2800 = 18225.79/- (= Rs. 36451.58/ha)**

Cost B2 = Cost B1+ rental value of owned land (net of land revenue) and rent paid for leased-in land.

= **18225.79 + 4000 + 0= 22225.79/- (= Rs. 44451.58/ha)**

Cost C1 = Cost B1 + Imputed value of Family Labour

= **18225.79 + 850 = 19075.79/- (= Rs. 38151.58/ha)**

Cost C2 = Cost B2 + Imputed value of Family Labour

= **22225.79 + 850 = 23075.79/- (= Rs. 46151.58/ha)**

Cost C2 = **TCOC**

Cost C3 = Cost C2 + 10 per cent of Cost C2 (on account of managerial functions performed by Farmer).

= **23075.79 + (0.10 x 23075.79) = 25298.37/- (= Rs. 50596.74/ha)**

iii. Returns from Crop Enterprise

Table 6.3: Gross Returns from Crop 'X' (Both from main product and by-product)

Crop	*Area*	*Season*	*Main Product*		*By-Product*		*Gross Returns (Rs./-)*
			Quantity	*Value*	*Quantity*	*Value*	
X	1.25 acres	*Kharif*	50 bags (1 bag = 75 kg) =37.5 qtls	Rs.810/qtl = Rs.30375/-	2 cart loads	Rs. 500/ Cart load= Rs.1000	Rs. 31375/-

iv. Net Returns over Cost Concepts

Net returns over Cost A1 (Farm Business Income) : (Gross returns – Cost A1)

= 31375 – 15425.79 = 15949.21

Net returns over Cost A2 (Owned Farm Business Income) : (Gross returns – Cost A2)

= 31375 – 15425.79 = 15949.21

Net returns over Cost A2+FL : (Gross returns – Cost A2+FL)

= 31375 – 16275.79 = 15099.21

Net returns over Cost B1 : (Gross returns – Cost B1)

= 31375 – 18225.79 = 13149.21

Net returns over Cost B2 (Family Labour Income): (Gross returns – Cost B2)

= 31375 – 22225.79 = 9149.21

Net returns over Cost C1 : (Gross returns – Cost C1)

= 31375 – 19075.79 = 12299.21

Net returns over Cost C2 : (Gross returns – Cost C2)

= 31375 – 23075.79 = 8299.21

Net returns over Cost C3 (Net Income): (Gross returns – Cost C3)
= 31375 – 25298.37 = 6076.63

Intensive Income: (Net income + Rental value of owned land + Interest of fixed capital)

= 6076.63+4000+2800 = Rs.12876.63

Table 6.4: Break Up of Total Cost of Cultivation of Crop X (1.25 acres)

S.No	*Items*	*Rs./1.25 acres*	*Rs./ha*
	I. OPERATIONAL COSTS		
1	Seed	400.00	800.00
2	Nursery	250.00	500.00
3	Land preparation	400.00	800.00
4	Transplanting	1400.00	2800.00
5	Manures	2175.00	4350.00
6	Fertilizers	3500.00	7000.00
7	Plant Protection	4050.00	8100.00
8	Irrigation	100.00	200.00
9	Weeding	200.00	400.00
10	Harvesting	450.00	900.00
11	Interest on working capital	150.79	301.58
	TOTAL OPERATIONAL COSTS	13075.79	26151.58
	II. FIXED COSTS		
1	Land Revenue	200.00	400.00
2	Depreciation	3000.00	6000.00
3	Rental value of owned land	4000.00	8000.00
4	Interest on fixed capital	2800.00	5600.00
	TOTAL FIXED COSTS	10000.00	20000.00
	TCOC (OPERATIONAL COSTS + FIXED COSTS)	23075.79	46151.58
	GROSS RETURNS	31375.00	62750.00
	NET RETURNS	8299.21	16598.42
	RATE OF RETURN(Net returns/Total costs)	0.36	0.36

Farm investment income: Farm business income - Imputed value of family labour

= 15949.21 - 850 = Rs.15099.21

Rate of Return: (Net returns over Cost C2/Cost C2)

= (8299.21/23075.79) = 0.36.

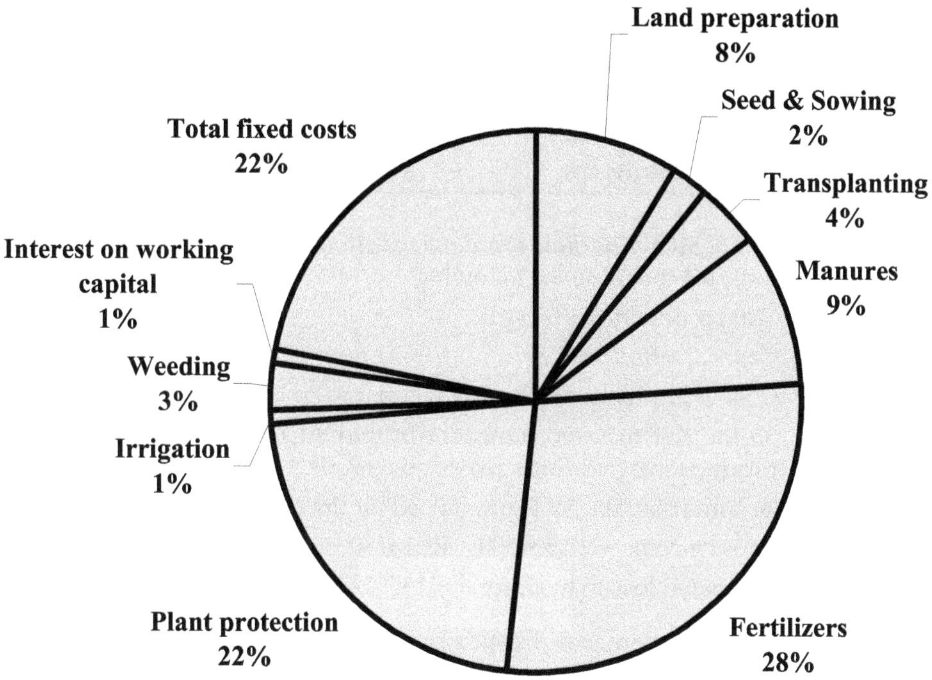

Figure 6.1: Break-up of TCOC of crop 'X'.

V. Domestic and Export Competitiveness of Commodity

It is to be noted that, if the Domestic Market Price of the commodity is higher than its COP, then that commodity is said to be competitive in the domestic market. If the Domestic Market Price is still lower than international price, then the farmer enjoys export competitiveness. It is heartening to note that, the commodity 'X' enjoys both domestic and export competitiveness (Table 6.5).

Recommendations Regarding Fixation of MSP

Farmers are under the misconception that, CACP recommends the MSP for the sake of farmers alone. But, the truth is that, this Commission tries to balance the prices for the farmers and the consumers. Unfortunately, in the recent period, the Commission fails to deliver on its mandate, as the farmers are unhappy about its recommendations. The Commission is like a lawyer for both the farmers and the consumers and tries to safeguard their interests, while fixing the MSP.

Table 6.5: Domestic and Export Competitiveness of Commodity 'X'

Sl.No.	*Item*	*Value*
1.	TCOC (Rs./1.25 acres) *i.e.*, Cost C2	23075.79
2.	Production (Qtls)	37.5
3.	Cost of Production (Rs./qtl)	615.35
	Domestic Competitiveness	
1.	Minimum Support Price (Rs./qtl)	700
2.	Support Market Price (Rs./qtl)	810
	Export Competitiveness	
1.	International price (Rs./qtl)	850

☆ ***Prof. M.S. Swaminathan's recommendation about MSP:*** From the above analysis, we conclude the following:

- ❑ Total production : 37.5qtls
- ❑ Cost C2 = Rs.23075.79
- ❑ Cost of production = Rs. 615.35/qtl

  So, the MSP to be recommended by the CACP must be above the cost of production by adding a reasonable profit.
- ❑ Assume that, the MSP announced for the crop X is = Rs.500/qtl.
- ❑ Gross income = 37.5 x 500 = Rs.18750
- ❑ Estimated loss to the farmer = 18750 - 23075.79 = – Rs. 4325.79

In the recent past, there was drastic rise in prices of resources (human labour wages, fertilizers, pesticides etc) and the same was not experienced from output side (market prices or even MSP) thereby, leading to huge losses on the part of the farmers. In view of this, Prof. M.S. Swaminathan has recommended the following formula for fixation of MSPs of agricultural commodities:

MSP = Cost of production (*i.e.*, Cost C2) + Minimum 50 per cent of cost of production

In this example, by applying the above formula, the MSP should be:

MSP = 615.35 + 307.68 = Rs. 923

So, according to Prof. M.S. Swaminathan Commission, the MSP should be fixed for the commodity 'X' at Rs. 923. By doing so, the farmer gets profits as shown below.

Gross income = 37.5 x 923 = Rs.34612.50

Profits = 34612.50 – 23075.79 = Rs.11536.71

The relevance of MSP to the farmers can be viewed from two different angles. First, the declaration of MSP should be in sufficient advance time so that, the farmer can plan the crop selection. That is, the MSPs should be announced by the Government well before the sowing season of the crops. This is not difficult because, the CACP employs the methodology in computing the MSP considering the past year data of the cost of production of commodities under consideration. It is disheartening to note that, for several years, the MSPs are not declared before decision-making about the sowing of the crops and in some years, the MSP are even announced well after sowing was completed and the farmer was committed to crop(s) sown. Second, MSP needs to provide atleast the floor level price for the crops under consideration. That is, at times of distress sale, the MSPs should provide at least cost of production incurred on the commodities. As discussed above, to safeguard the interests of the farming community and to sustain them in the agri-business, Prof. M.S. Swaminathan Commission recommended to increase the MSP to the level equal to Cost of production + Minimum 50 per cent of cost of production. Of course, this suggestion was not implemented till now.

☆ ***Bharath Krishak Samaj (BKS) (Farmers' Forum, India) recommendations:*** **According to BKS, the MSP of a produce should be 75 per cent of the price paid by the consumer.** If the Government wants to subsidize consumers, it should not be at the cost of the farmers. In addition to the above, a system of staggered procurement of food grains and increased rate of payment to the farmers with each passing month should be explored. For example:

- ❑ FCI finishes procuring wheat on 1st May and pays to the farmer for 100kgs= Value X.
- ❑ Average monthly (May) cost of storage of wheat/100kgs= Value Y.
- ❑ Average monthly (May) wastage and loss of weight while storing/ 100kgs = Value Z
- ❑ Value X + Value Y + Value Z = Value A
- ❑ Interest for one month (May) charged say, @ 12 per cent per annum on value A = Value B
- ❑ Payment to be made to the farmer in June = {X + Y (May) + Z (May)} + B (May)

  = Value A + B (May)
- ❑ Payment to be made to the farmer in July = {X + Y (June) + Z (June)} + B (June)

This can continue for nine months from date of procurement season. By this formula, without additional investment and expenditure to the Government from what the Government will save, the farmer will get an option to deliver his produce at a later date at a higher price. He will also be have a choice to sell in the open market at a later date, if the price was higher (as is mostly the case). BKS further recommends the following:

- ❑ The protein requirement of the country is fulfilled by imports. Pulses are mainly grown in rainfed areas, where the cost of production is low because, the farmer will not apply additional inputs. If the MSP for these crops was higher, the farmer could afford to apply more inputs thus, raising yields substantially.

- ❑ Farmers have great trouble in marketing crops (especially pulses) at MSPs due to less number of agencies and centers procuring crops in many areas of the country. We need to allow more organizations to procure such crops by increasing number of procurement centers.
- ❑ MSP should also be declared for essential vegetables. This will help small farmers and also help in diversification of agriculture, away from monoculture propagated by Government policies.
- ❑ The Government should offer the opportunity to the cooperatives sector to procure, store and distribute food grain in addition to the FCI. Competition will increase efficiency.

As represented earlier, unfortunately the MSP recommendations by the CACP are for the benefit of farmers and consumers alike. This is responsible for farmers being forced to subsidize the consumers. The Government should compensate or subsidize the consumers at its own cost and not at the cost of the farmers.

Cost-Effective Production Measures

In case, if the COP of commodity increases above MSP and international price, it is essential to suggest cost-effective production measures to the farmers as listed here under.

- ☆ Use farmers' own seed (of previous season) in the production programme (straight varieties).
- ☆ Adoption of seed treatment.
- ☆ Employ more of family labour (working hours) as a substitute to hired labour.
- ☆ Involvement of farm women in agricultural operations.
- ☆ Use of modern agricultural implements and machinery.
- ☆ Adoption of INM, with more emphasis on organic manures.
- ☆ Soil-test based fertilizer application (macro and micro nutrients).
- ☆ Adoption of IPM with more emphasis on biological control and use of herbal products.
- ☆ Adoption of IWRM technologies, especially micro-irrigation.
- ☆ Strengthen the cooperative farming (large-scale economies).
- ☆ Avail different production subsidies being offered by the Government.
- ☆ Avail loans from the Government financial institutions at cheaper rates of interest.
- ☆ Farmers should follow crop rotation.
- ☆ Adoption of scientific packages for cultivation of crops *viz.*, selection of good quality seed, time of sowing/planting, maintenance of optimum plant population, growing of trap crops to reduce pests and disease menace *etc.*

Table 6.6: Establishment Cost of Cashew Plantation of Selected Host Farmer (Rs./2 acres)

Sl.No.	Particulars	Unit	I Year		II Year		III Year		IV Year		Total for 4 Years	
			Qty	Value	Qty	Value	Qty	Value	Qty	Value	Rs.	per cent
I.	***Variable cost***											
A.	Labour cost											
1.	Land preparation	Pair days	2	450	2	350	1	200			1000	2.53
2.	Opening of pits	Mandays	20	1500							1500	3.80
3.	Planting and gap filling	Mandays	9	600	3	175	2	110			885	2.24
4.	Manure application	Mandays	4	250	3	190	3	200	4	250	890	2.25
5.	Fertilizer application	Mandays	4	225	4	250	4	250	4	260	985	2.49
6.	Weeding	Mandays	7	420	5	350	5	300	4	260	1330	3.37
7.	Fencing	Mandays	6	400							400	1.01
8.	Stalking	Mandays	6	400							400	1.01
9.	Spraying of chemicals	Mandays					1	50	2	100	150	0.38
10.	Watch and ward	Mandays	9	525							525	1.33
11.	Miscellaneous	Mandays	6	350		300		200		150	1000	2.53
	Total labour cost	Rupees		5120		1615		1310		1020	9065	22.95
B.	Material cost											
1.	Seedlings	Number	150	3240							3240	8.20
2.	Manure	Tonnes	3	500	3	600	3	650	4	675	2425	6.14
3.	Fertilizer	Kgs	60	1000	65	1000	70	1100	75	1175	4275	10.82
4.	Plant protection chemicals	Liters					1	85	2	200	285	0.72
5.	Others	Rupees		460		400		325		310	1495	3.79
	Total material cost	Rupees		5200		2000		2160		2360	11720	29.67

Contd...

Table 6.6–*Contd...*

Sl.No.	*Particulars*	*Unit*	*I Year*		*II Year*		*III Year*		*IV Year*		*Total for 4 Years*	
			Qty	*Value*	*Qty*	*Value*	*Qty*	*Value*	*Qty*	*Value*	*Rs.*	*per cent*
	Interest on working capital @7 per cent	Rupees		361.2		126.5		121.5		118.3	727.48	1.84
	Total variable cost	**Rupees**		**10681**		**3742**		**3591**		**3498**	**21512**	**54.47**
II.	**Fixed cost**											
1.	Rental value	Rupees		3000		3000		3000		3000	12000	30.38
2.	Land revenue	Rupees		325		325		325		325	1300	3.29
3.	Depreciation	Rupees		670		650		685		580	2585	6.54
4.	Interest on fixed capital@11%	Rupees		550		500		510		540	2100	5.32
	Total fixed cost	**Rupees**		**4545**		**4475**		**4520**		**4445**	**17985**	**45.53**
	Total cost(I+II)/2 acres	**Rupees**		**15226**		**8217**		**8111**		**7943**	**39497**	**100.00**
	Total cost/ha	**Rupees**		**19033**		**10271**		**10139**		**9929**	**49372**	

The above analysis revealed that, one hectare is taken as the unit to estimate the 'cost of cultivation' of crop, whereas one quintal is taken as the unit to work out the 'COP'. Note that, these Cost of Cultivation Studies are primarily intended for use by the CACP. In addition, these data are used by the Central Statistical Organization, Planning Commission, other Economic Ministries of Government of India as well as research organizations. These studies should continue in view of their importance in analyzing cost structure of crops, price administration of agricultural commodities, and several studies relating to farm economy. Irrespective of the agency that is assigned this work, there should be a more focused attention to proper organization and management of the studies.

Bulk Line Cost of Production

It is the cost of production at which 85 per cent production of output is covered. That is, in the above example (Table 6.5), Cost C2 is Rs.23075.79 and output produced is 37.5 qtls. So, cost of production is Rs.615.35/qtl. Regarding bulk line cost of production *i.e.*, for 85 per cent of output *i.e.*, (37.5*(85/100)) = 31.88 qtls, the cost of production is ((31.88*615.35)/37.50) = Rs.523.13/qtl. Note that, bulk line cost can be computed on crop area basis (cost covering 85 per cent of cropped area), on number of holdings or farmers' basis (cost covering 85 per cent of farmers' holdings), output basis *etc.*

Example 6.2

The following is an hypothetical example for computing Cost of Cultivation of a perennial crop (Cashew) by a large farmer. While computing the total costs, the student has to work out both establishment costs and maintenance costs.

Cashew is a perennial crop and it is grown as a sole crop. The establishment period of the crop is about four years and could be cultivated economically for about 40 years under good management conditions. So, its total life span is 40 years. Though, cashew starts yielding from the fifth year onwards, economic yields can be obtained only from ninth year onwards. The establishment and maintenance costs of the cashew plantation for a small farmer (2 acres) are presented below.

a. Establishment Cost

It is the cost incurred during the first four years of the establishment of a cashew plantation. The various items of costs incurred under the establishment of this orchard is presented through the Table 6.6.

b. Maintenance Cost

It includes all the costs incurred annually for the maintenance and production on the cashew plantation from the fifth year onwards till the end of the life span of 40 years. The various costs (per year) incurred regarding the maintenance of cashew orchard are presented through the following Table 6.7.

c. Yield and Returns

The output and prices realized by the host farmer for the cashew apples and raw nuts were used to calculate the gross returns, net returns and the returns per hectare of cashew plantation and presented through the Table 6.8.

Table 6.7: Maintenance Cost of Cashew Plantation of Selected Host Farmer (Rs./2 acres)

Sl.No.	*Particulars*	*Unit*	*Quantity*	*Value*
I.	**Variable cost**			
A.	***Labour cost***	Mandays		
1.	Application of manure	Mandays	4	250.00
2.	Application of fertilizer	Mandays	5	320.00
3.	Spraying of plant protection chemicals	Mandays	2	75.00
4.	Weeding	Mandays	5	300.00
5.	Harvesting	Mandays	19	340.00
6.	Transportation of produce	Mandays	6	200.00
7.	Watch and ward	Mandays	3	1145.00
	Total labour cost			2630.00
	a. Owned labour (Imputed) cost			750.00
	b. Hired labour cost			1880.00
B.	**Material cost**			
1.	Manures	Tonnes	4	900.00
2.	Fertilizers	Kgs		1200.00
3.	Plant protection chemicals	Liters	2	300.00
	Total material cost	Rupees		2400.00
	Interest on working capital	Rupees		176.05
	Total variable cost	**Rupees**		**5206.05**
II.	***Fixed cost***	Rupees		
1.	Rental value of owned land			3000.00
2.	Land revenue			325.00
3.	Amortized establishment cost*			987.00
4.	Depreciation			550.00
5.	Interest on fixed capital@11 per cent			600.00
	Total fixed cost			5462.00
	Total maintenance cost (Rs./2 acres)	Rupees		10668.05
	Total maintenance cost (Rs./ha)	Rupees		13335.05

* Amortised establishment cost: The total establishment cost (up to the bearing age *i.e.*, 4th year) was apportioned over a period of 40 years as the cashew plantations life span.

Computation of Cost Concepts

For the above hypothetical example, cost concepts are worked out during bearing period as shown below. As discussed earlier, note that, the cost concepts should be expressed finally with reference to a technical unit *i.e.*, Rs./hectare.

Table 6.8: Cost and Returns of Cashew Plantation of Host Farmer during Bearing Period

Sl.No.	Items	Per 2 acres	Per ha
1.	Total cost of cultivation (Maintenance cost) (Rs.)	10668.05	13335.05
2.	Output (Qtls)	10.0	12.5
3.	Cost of production (Rs./qtl)	1066.80	1066.80
4.	Gross returns (Returns from both apples and raw nuts)	40000.00	50000.00
5.	Net returns (Rs.)	40000.00-10668.05 = 29331.95	36664.95
6.	Rate of Return	29331.95/10668.05 = 2.75	2.75

Cost A1 = Hired human labour + Manures + Fertilizers + Plant Protection + Land revenue + Interest on working capital + Depreciation

= 1880 + 900 + 1200 + 300 + 325 + 176.05 + 550 = 5331.05/- (= Rs. 6663.81/ha)

Cost A2 = Cost A1 + rent paid for leased-in Land.

= 5331.05 + 0 = 5331.05/- (= Rs. 6663.81/ha)

Cost A2+FL = Cost A2 + Imputed value of Family labour.

= 5331.05 + 750 = 6081.05/- (= Rs. 7601.31/ha)

Cost B1 = Cost A1+ Interest on value of owned (fixed) capital assets (excluding land)

= 5331.05 + 600 = 5931.05/- (= Rs. 7413.81/ha)

Cost B2 = Cost B1+ Rental value of owned land (net of land revenue) and rent paid for leased-in land + amortized establishment cost.

= 5931.05 + 3000 + 987 = 9918.05/- (= Rs. 12397.56/ha)

Cost C1 = Cost B1 + Imputed value of Family labour

= 5931.05 + 750 = 6681.05/- (= Rs. 8351.31/ha)

Cost C2 = Cost B2 + Imputed value of Family labour

= 9918.05 + 750 = 10668.05/- (= Rs. 12397.56/ha)

Cost C2 = TCOC

Cost C3 = Cost C2 + 10 per cent of Cost C2 (on account of managerial functions performed by Farmer).

= 10668.05 + (0.10 x 10668.05) = 11734.85/- (= Rs. 14668.57/ha)

Net Returns Over Cost Concepts

Net returns over Cost A1 (Farm Business Income): (Gross returns – Cost A1)

= 40000 – 5331.05 = 34668.95

Net returns over Cost A2 (Owned Farm Business Income): (Gross returns – Cost A2)

= 40000 – 5331.05 = 34668.95

Net returns over Cost A2+FL : (Gross returns – Cost A2+FL)

= 40000 – 6081.05 = 33918.95

Net returns over Cost B1 : (Gross returns – Cost B1)

= 40000 – 5931.05 = 34068.95

Net returns over Cost B2 (Family Labour Income): (Gross returns – Cost B2)

= 40000 – 9918.05 = 30081.095

Net returns over Cost C1 : (Gross returns – Cost C1)

= 40000 – 6681.05 = 33318.95

Net returns over Cost C2 : (Gross returns – Cost C2)

= 40000 – 10668.05 = 29331.95

Net returns over Cost C3 (Net Income) : (Gross returns – Cost C3)

= 40000 – 11734.85 = 28265.15

Intensive Income: (Net income + Rental value of owned land + Interest of fixed capital)

= 28265.15+3000+600 = Rs.31865.15

Farm investment income = Farm business income - Imputed value of family labour

= 34668.95 - 750 = Rs.33918.95

Example 6.3

The following is an hypothetical example for computing cost of rearing of goat by small rearers (flock = 12 numbers).

Table 6.9: Investment in Goat Rearing (Rs./flock)

Item	*No./Quantity*	*Value*
Goat cost		9800
Shed/pen		3000
Equipments		
Baskets	5.49	1450
Dotties	3.92	1200
Rope		450
Sub total		3100
Total		**15900**

Note: Figures in parentheses indicates respective percentages

Small rearers: flock = 12 Nos.

Table 6.10: Costs and Returns of Rearing Goat by Small Rearers (Flock = 12 numbers)

Sl.No.	*Item*	*No./Qty (kg/yr)*	*Value*	*Per cent to Total Cost*
I.	**Fixed cost**			
1.	Amortization cost		1800	10.22
2.	Interest on fixed capital		1900	10.78
	Total fixed cost		***3700***	
II.	**Variable cost**			
1.	Feed cost	35	725	4.11
2.	Fodder cost	98	2100	11.92
3.	Medicine		375	2.13
4.	Labour	182 Man Days	10000	56.75
5.	Miscellaneous charges		250	1.42
6.	Interest on working capital		470	2.67
	Total variable cost		***13920***	
III.	**Total cost**		**17620**	**100**

Table 6.11: Returns from Rearing Goat by Small Rearers (flock=12 numbers)

Sl.No.	*Item*	*No./Quantity*	*Value*	*Per cent in Gross Returns*
1.	Sale of goat	8	22000	67.59
2.	Sale of milk(lit/yr)	60	900	2.76
3.	Sale of manure(tractor load)	2	4500	13.82
4.	Sale of meat(kg/yr)	25	5150	15.82
5.	Gross returns		32550	100.00
6.	Net Returns		32550-17620 = 14930	
7.	Rate of Return		14930/17620 = 0.85	

From the above Table 6.11, it is noted that, the returns from goat enterprise includes sale of goats, sale of milk, sale of manure and sale of meat. About 68 per cent of the total income for small rearers was from the sale of live goats. Income from sale of meat stands after the sale of animals, which accounted 16 per cent of gross returns. These are followed by the shares of sale of manure and sale of milk respectively in the gross returns. Thus, the overall income was Rs.32550 and net returns was Rs. 14930 for small rearers per flock per year.

Break Even Point (BEP)

We know, maximization of profits is one of the traditional objectives of a farm business. A farmer cannot achieve maximum profit and minimum cost at the same time. Similarly, profit maximizing output cannot be known in advance. Even if it is known, it cannot be achieved at the beginning of the programme because, in the process of production, the farmer will have to incur fixed cost even before the production starts. That is, even when output is zero, TFC will be there. But, when no unit of output is sold, then TR is zero. Thus, in the initial stages of production, SRTC remains higher than the TR. Therefore, the farmer has to bear some loss at the initial low levels of output. But, as more and more units of output are sold, TR starts increasing and it reaches to the point, where TR will cover SRTC *i.e.*, TR = SRTC. This point (at the volume or value of output), at which the TR is exactly equal to the SRTC is called BEP (Figure 6.2). So, at BEP in a farm business, there is no net profit or no loss to the farmer. It also refers to the volume of output in the farm business at which the net profit is zero. That means, the firm just 'breaks even'. BEP also refers to the volume of output, at which the farmer will be in dilemma regarding, whether he has to continue the business or not, as TR is equal to SRTC in the production programme. Note that, considering the rules presented through Table 2.14, it is advocated to the farmer to continue the production, when he faces with BEP in the business because, SRTVC<TR=SRTC. At BEP, the sales of the firm exactly cover its expenses *i.e.*, at BEP the firm sells enough units of its product to cover its expenses without making a profit or taking a loss. If it sells more beyond BEP, then it makes a profit and on the other hand, if it sells less than BEP, it takes a loss.

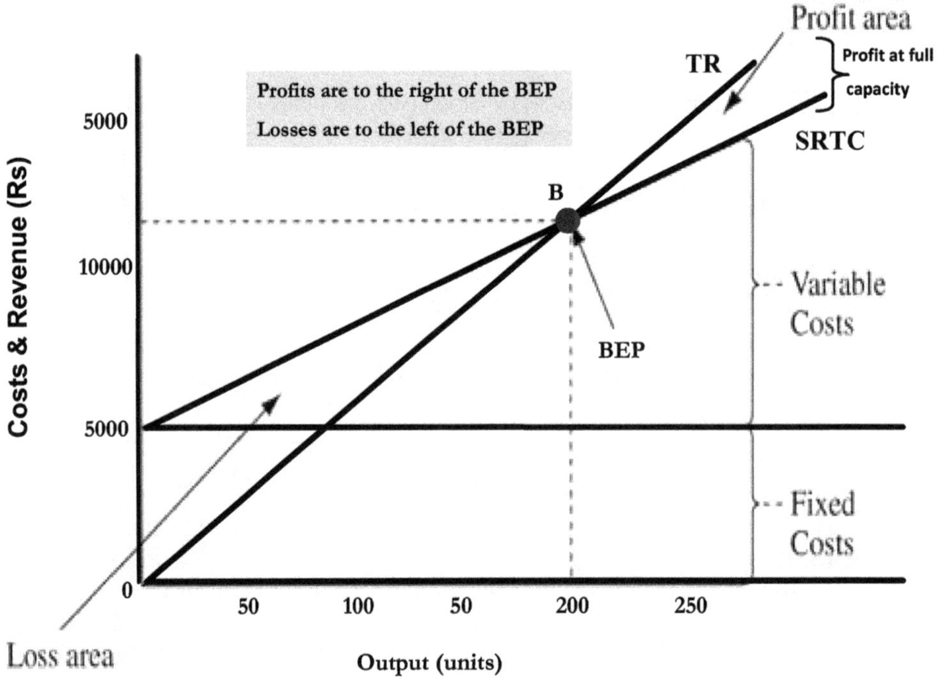

Figure 6.2: BEP in a Farm Business.

Methods of Computation of BEP

The point of beak even can be derived through the following three methods:

1. Graphical Method

Graphically, BEP is the point, where the SRTC curve meet the TR curve (Figure

6.2). Below the BEP 'B', TR<SRTC (*i.e.*, loss) and above the BEP, TR>SRTC *i.e.*, there is profit in the business and at BEP 'B', TR = SRTC (*i.e.*, no-profit and no loss).

Figure 6.2 also infers that, a business can be in any one of the following financial situations:

- ☆ ***Loss:*** This occurs, when TC exceed the TR of the business *i.e.*, up to BEP.
- ☆ ***Break-even:*** This occurs, when TR=TC in the business *i.e.*, BEP.
- ☆ ***Profit:*** This occurs, when TR exceed TC in the business *i.e.*, beyond the BEP.

2. Break-Even Formula

We know, at BEP, TR = SRTC *i.e.*, TR – SRTC = 0

We also know, SRTC = SRTVC + TFC

SRTVC = Y * Variable Cost/unit

TR = Y * Price/unit

SRTC = (Y * Variable Cost/unit) + SRFC

At BEP, TR – SRTC = 0. So,

(Y * Price/unit) – ((Y * Variable Cost/unit) + TFC) = 0

So, (Y * Price/unit) - (Y * Variable Cost/unit) = TFC

So, Y (Price/unit - Variable Cost/unit) = TFC

Y (in terms of quantity) = TFC/(Price/unit - Variable Cost/unit)

= TFC/(Sale price – SRAVC)

So, Y (Break-Even Output) = TFC/(SP – SRAVC)

= TFC/(S-V) *Equation 6.1*

where, S = Selling price/unit, V = Variable cost/unit

In the above formula (Equation 6.1): the denominator S minus V, is called the Contribution Margin per unit or Unit contribution. It refers to the amount per unit of product sold, that the firm can contribute to paying its TFC. That is, any product that makes a positive contribution to the firm will help towards paying some of the fixed costs in the business.

So, BEP = TFC/Contribution Margin per unit

Thus, BEP can alternatively be computed as the point where, Total Contribution Margin equals TFC. That is,

Total Contribution Margin = TFC

(Unit Contribution x Volume of output at BEP) = TFC

Volume of output (*i.e.*, Break even output) = TFC/Unit Contribution

The above Equation 6.1 also indicates that, to compute a firm's BEP in terms of quantity or volume of sales, we need to know the values of three variables. They include: TFC, SRTVC and selling price of the product. We already know, TFC are those, which do not change with the level of output or sales, but SRTVC do change with the level of output or sales volume. At BEP, price of the product equals the SRATC and so, below BEP, price covers both AFC and SRTVC. So, the price of the product has been set by the firm by looking at the SRATC (*i.e.*, AFC+SRAVC) and by marking it up.

The Total Contribution Margin is given by: TR – SRTVC. Contribution Margin Ratio (CMR) is the ratio between (S-V)/S. From these definitions, BEP can also be computed in terms of value (*i.e.*, Rupees) and it is given by:

BEP in terms of value (Rupees) = BEP x Sale price per unit or

= TFC/CMR

= TFC/((S-V)/S)

= TFC/(1-(V/S)) *Equation 6.2*

In the above Equation 7.13, V/S refers to Contribution Margin. So,BEP in terms of value (Rupees) = TFC/(1- Contribution Margin).

3. Tabular Method

The method uses a table to arrange data, so the BEP can be easily calculated. We already know that, at BEP, TR=TC. Let us assume that, a firm produces a processed food product with the following data particulars: TFC=Rs.5000, SRAVC=Rs.10/unit, Price per unit of product: Rs.20. With this information, the following Table 6.12 is constructed to estimate the BEP. As per the definition, BEP will be at 500 units of output of the firm, as TR=TC and hence, there will be no profit and no loss to the firm in producing and selling that product.

Table 6.12: Computation of BEP for a Firm

Output (Units	*TFC*	*SRTVC*	*SRTC*	*TR*	*Profit (Rs.)*
0	5000	0	5000	0	–5000
100	5000	1000	6000	2000	–4000
200	5000	2000	7000	4000	–3000
300	5000	3000	8000	6000	–2000
400	5000	4000	9000	8000	–1000
500	5000	5000	10000	10000	0
600	5000	6000	11000	12000	1000
700	5000	7000	12000	14000	2000

Since the BEP analysis explains the relationship between cost, production volume and returns in the business, this analysis is also known as Cost-Volume-Profit (CVP) analysis. The other names for this BEP include: Break-Even Analysis, Break-Even Formula, Break-Even Model, Expense-Volume-Profit (EVP) analysis. However, the term CVP is more appealing because, the break-even technique can be used to determine the volume of sales needed to attain a specified amount of profits in the farm business. In performing this break even analysis, the following are the important assumptions:

- ✩ Sales price per unit of output is constant.

- Variable costs per unit are constant.
- TFC are constant.
- The behaviour of both costs and revenues is linear throughout the relevant range of activity.
- Everything produced by the firm is sold *i.e.*, it assumes that the quantity of product produced is equal to the quantity of product sold.
- If the firm sells more than one product, they are sold in the same mix. That is, there is a constant product sales mix. If the sales mix changes say, from a high profit product to a low profit product, the BEP analysis must be adapted to accommodate this change.
- The cost function and revenue function are linear.
- The SRTC is divided into TFC and SRTVC.
- Prices of factors are remaining constant.
- Productivity and efficiency remains unchanged.

Example 6.4

Assume a sugar factory with TFC = Rs.10,000/year, AVC = Rs. 40/unit, Selling price = Rs. 50/unit. So, BEP (output) is given by:

We know, at BEP: $FC + VC * Y = SP * Y$

$$BEP\ (Y) = \frac{TFC}{SP - AVC} = \frac{10000}{50 - 40} = 1000 (units/year)$$

So, the entrepreneur must produce and sell at least 1000 units annually to cover TFC and SRTVC. He will have a profit after producing and selling more than 1000 units of output.

BEP in terms of value = BEP x Sale price per unit

= 1000 x 50 = Rs. 50000 or

= TFC/(1-(V/S)) = 10000/(1-(40/50)) = Rs. 50000.

Assume, the following are the sales of sugar from this factory:

Year 1: 750 units (behind 250 units)

Year 2: 1000 units (total 1750 units – still behind 250 units)

Year 3: 1250 units (total sales at the end of Year 3 = 3000 units or 1000 units per year, thus, here the factory is break even)

So, the factory will get break even at the end of the third year and would make profits after it sells 1000 units every year thereafter.

Example 6.5

Calculate the BEP in units and in sales Rupees, when sales price per unit is Rs.35, variable cost per unit is Rs.28 and TFC is Rs. 7000.

Solution: We know BEP (in terms of quantity) = TFC/Contribution Margin per unit

Contribution Margin per Unit = S-V = 35 – 28 = Rs. 7

So, BEP in terms of quantity is: 7000/7 = 1000 units

Break-even Point in Rupees = BEP x Sale price per unit or

= TFC/(1-(V/S))

= 1000 × 35 or [7000 ÷ (1-(28/35))] = Rs. 35,000.

What Happens to the BEP, if Sales Change?

Say, if the economy is in a recession, the sales of the firm will drop. Then the firm will not sell enough to make its BEP. That is, the new BEP will be less than the earlier BEP. Since, the new BEP is less now, the firm would not be able to pay all the earlier total costs. So, considering the formula for BEP discussed earlier, the entrepreneur will think about two possible solutions. First, it may either raise the price of its product and/or it find ways to reduce the TFC. So, re-writing the data in the above Example 6.4 by considering the above two possible solutions:

- ✩ ***Lowering the Fixed Costs:*** By lowering the fixed costs of the firm say, by Rs. 2000, then the TFC now becomes only Rs. 8000. So, the new BEP will now decline as given below:

$$\text{BEP (Y)} = \frac{\text{TFC}}{\text{SP} - \text{SRAVC}} = \frac{8000}{50-40} = 800(\text{units/year})$$

  So, the new BEP is only 800 units/year. From this analysis, we can say that, if the firm reduce the TFC, it can lower the BEP without having to raise the price of the product. Note that, even by reducing the SRTVC without disturbing the TFC will also reduce the BEP, as fall in SRTVC also lead to fall in SRAVC and thereby, BEP will decrease.

- ✩ ***Raising the price of the product:*** By raising the price of the product say, by Rs.5 (without disturbing the TFC), then the price now becomes to Rs. 55. So, the new BEP will now decline as given below:

$$\text{BEP (Y)} = \frac{\text{TFC}}{\text{SP} - \text{SRAVC}} = \frac{10000}{55-40} = 667(\text{units/year})$$

  So, the new BEP is only 667 units/year. From this analysis, we can see that, if the firm raise the price of the product, it can lower the BEP without disturbing the cost structure of the product.

Margin of Safety

The margin of safety is the excess of output (or value) of the firm over the break-even output (or value). Thus, the margin of safety can be expressed either in quantity of output or in value terms (*i.e.,* in Rupees) and also in percentage forms. The following are the formulae:

Margin of safety (quantity) = Actual quantity of output – Break even output

Margin of safety (quantity) = Level of demand – Break even output

Margin of safety (value) = Actual value of output (Rs./-) – Value of Break even output (Rs./-)

Margin of safety (per cent) = (Margin of safety in terms of quantity/Actual output in terms of quantity) x 100 or

= [(Actual output – Break even output)/Actual output] × 100 or

= Margin of safety in terms of value/Actual output in terms of value

Students must note that, through graphically, margin of safety can be studied only in terms of physical quantity, as volume of output is shown on the X-axis and not the value of that output (Figure 6.3). Margin of safety represents the strength of the business. It enables a business firm to know, what is the exact amount it has gained or lost and whether they are over or below the BEP *i.e.*, it indicates how safer the business is compared to the break even output. The larger the positive difference between actual output and output at BEP, the safer the firm will be in terms of earning profits, especially if there are adverse changes in the production process or marketing process or both. A positive margin of safety (or safety margin) means that, the firm makes a profit, whereas a negative safety margin means the firm makes a loss in the business.

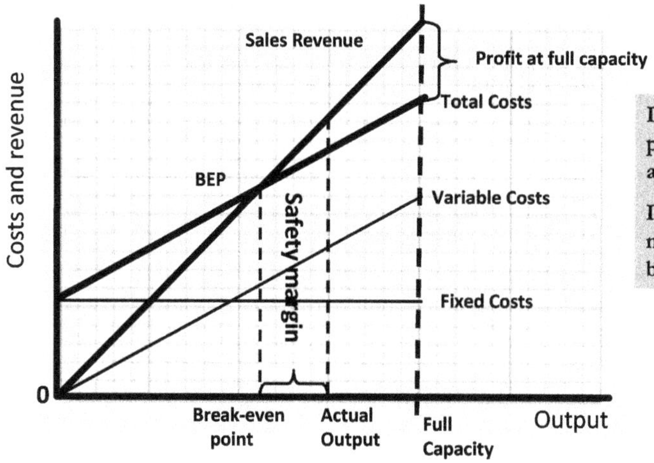

If margin of safety is positive, production is above break even.

If margin of safety is negative, production is below break even.

Margin of Safety is the amount by which the actual output exceeds the break even output. If output falls below this level, a loss will occur in the business.

Figure 6.3: Margin of Safety in a Farm Business.

Importance of Analyzing BEP

The following points indicate, why a business firm looks at the BEP in taking up the business:

- ☆ The entrepreneur can decide the margin of safety of the business and this guides him to plan the sales volume, price of the product and other transaction costs.

- BEP help the entrepreneur to gain an insight about TR from selling the output and his ability to recover the relevant production cost of that particular product.
- BEP is also helpful to the entrepreneurs in making important decisions in business like application for loans, setting prices for the products, drawing comparative picture with the rivalry firms *etc.*
- We know, break even output covers both TFC and SRTVC. This helps the managers to plan output both in short run and even used to evaluate the future demand. If, in case, the BEP lies above the estimated demand, it guides the entrepreneur to take various decisions like discontinuing the product (if the loss is very high) or planning for improved advertising strategies or re-pricing the product to increase demand in the market.
- We know, at BEP, there is no profit and there is no loss in the business. So, BEP is important for the entrepreneur, as it serves as the lower limit of profit, when prices are set and margins are determined.
- The concept of break-even analysis can be applied to a product, an investment or the entire firm's operations.
- As discussed earlier, break-even analysis is a useful tool to study the relationship between fixed costs, variable costs and returns. So, this analysis help the business manager to plan the volume of production at which price of the product necessarily covers SRATC or fix a price for the product (by using mark-up) over SRATC to achieve profits.
- As the break-even analysis explains the relationship between cost, production volume and returns in the business, the same can be extended to show, how changes in TFC-SRTVC relationships or commodity prices or in revenues will affect profit levels and BEPs.
- Break-even analysis is most useful when used with partial budgeting or capital budgeting techniques. The major benefit to using break-even analysis is that, it indicates the lowest amount of business activity necessary to prevent losses.
- If the entrepreneur has to plan and fix the price of the product, he must know how to calculate BEP.
- The BEP tells the farmer, how much money he needs to invest in the business before it starts earning actual profits. For instance, if the expenses are Rs. 1,000 per month and revenue is Rs.1,000 per month, then the farmer is at the BEP in the business. This is where, the business is making enough money to cover the total expenses, but it isn't making a profit. To increase profits in the business, the farmer must increase the contribution margin unit (say, by decreasing the SRTVC) and this decreases the BEP.
- Break-even analysis is useful because, it helps to analyze the chances of a new venture or investment succeeding in the farm business.
- BEP analysis provides a dynamic view of the relationships between costs, volume of output and profits. A better understanding of BEP say, if

expressed break-even sales as a percentage of actual sales, it helps the entrepreneur to understand when to expect to break even in his business say, in few months or in years.

- BEP analysis is important for planning and decision making, particularly in the short run. Trade-offs of fixed for variable costs or changes in variable or fixed costs and sales volume can be analyzed by using BEP analysis.
- Break-even is often a key objective of new and unestablished firms, as their viability in the future depends upon the achievement of minimum break even sales.
- BEP analysis helps to compare the profit margin of different firms.
- The concept of break even analysis provide useful answers to the following questions posed by himself by the entrepreneur:
  - A person starting a new business (say, food processing firm) often asks, 'At what level of sales will my firm make a profit?'
  - Manager of an established firm that had suffered through some rough years might have a similar question: *'At what point of sales, will I be able to draw a fair salary from my firm?'*

  The analysis of BEP will provide a thought process that may help the entrepreneur to answer the above questions and also provide useful insight as to how profits change as sales increase or decrease.

Limitations of BEP Analysis

BEP analysis suffers from the following limitations:

- In general, costs and revenue functions are non-linear and hence, the BEP analysis is more complicated.
- CVP is a short run marginal analysis *i.e.*, it assumes that, unit variable costs and unit revenues are constant. But, in the long run, all costs are variable. For longer-term analysis that considers the entire life-cycle of a product, one therefore often prefers activity-based costing.
- Achieving break-even output in the current production programme does not return the losses occurred in the past. Also it does not build up a reserve for future losses. And finally it does not provide a return on your investment (the reward for exposure to risk).
- It is best suited to the analysis of only one product at a time.
- Sometimes, predicting a precise amount of sales or profits is nearly impossible due to a firm's many products (with varying degrees of profitability), many customers (with varying demands for service), and the interaction between price, promotion and the number of units sold. These and other factors will complicate the break-even analysis.
- Break-even analysis is only a supply side concept (*i.e.*, costs only) and is not related on the demand side *i.e.*, it will not tell about, what sales are actually likely to be for the product at its various prices.

- ☆ It assumes TFC remains constant in the production programme, as it based on short run analysis. But, an increase in the scale of production in the long run is likely to cause fixed costs to rise.
- ☆ Break-even analysis is based on certain assumptions, which are assumed to be constant. This implies a static in nature. It is not applicable to the dynamic situation.
- ☆ BEP analysis fails to explain the impact of technological change, better management, division of labour, improved productivity and other factors which influence profits.
- ☆ It assumes horizontal demand curve with the constant price. It is possible only in case of perfect competition. But, this is not true in case of monopoly, oligopoly and monopolistic competitions.
- ☆ The break even analysis does not consider elements of uncertainty due to tax structure.
- ☆ Not all variable costs increase directly with output.
- ☆ Not all costs can be categorized into fixed or variable costs; some are semi-variable.
- ☆ It is unlikely that, fixed costs will not change at various output levels.

The students must note that, BEP analysis must not be mistaken for the Pay Back Period (PBP), as the latter simply indicates the time taking by the firm to recover its investment.

7

Farm Planning and Budgeting

Farm planning is a process of decision making regarding organization and operation of farm business, so as to obtain maximum possible net income. The ultimate objective of farm planning is to maximize the profits or net income of farm business. Farm planning is the fundamental or basic function of farm management and it precedes and a pre-requisite for other managerial functions like organization, direction, control, co-ordination *etc.* Farm planning is nothing but deciding in advance by the farm manager regarding what to produce, how to produce, how much to produce, where to buy and sell, when to buy and sell *etc.* Thus, a farm plan is a plan of total farm activity of the farmer drawn up in advance. Note that, the farm manager of the agricultural business should lead the initial planning with due emphasis on farm family satisfaction. That is, farm planning cannot be done in isolation from family members, particularly when goals are set for the business, the profit from which affects their standard of living in the society. So, both business and family considerations are often so interwoven in planning for farm business such that, it becomes impossible to try to separate these two. Also note that, in planning the farm business, the process is as important as the final product. This planning of farm business involves the formulation of several goals and objectives and they must be stated in a clearly understandable language, what an individual or farm family wants to achieve. The formulation of goals and objectives serves the following purposes:

- ☆ They set the direction for the future in which the farmer must proceed towards their fulfillment. Note that, the goals framed for farm business are not final and they change with circumstances. Over time, they may need to be re-evaluated and updated.

- ☆ Goals also prioritize the tasks the farmer must perform in the farm business and they serve as a reference point for the farmer to monitor, how well he is performing.
- ☆ Goals can help motivate the farmer in planning the strategies towards their accomplishment.
- ☆ Help the farmer to make a decision in the face of risks and uncertainties because, he can weigh alternatives in a decision as to how each helps him to move towards framed goals.
- ☆ Finally, goals can serve as a rallying point for the family or farm management team.

The goal-directed farm manager recognizes that, he must plan accurately so that, all the family members are generally more willing to support him and work on for achieving these goals. So, the farmer will go about determining, what crops to grow or animals to raise on their farms? and what resource or resource combinations he has to choose? The best way to make those decisions is to analyze the alternatives systematically. This is one of the first steps in the procedure called Farm planning. This farm planning provides the checklist that the farmer must follow and this refers to 'Farm plan'. This farm plan serves as a forecast for the business. This farm planning is defined in different ways by different economists as under:

- ☆ *Farm planning is a process to allocate the scarce resources of the farm to organize the farm production in such a way as to increase the resource use efficiency and the income of the farmer.*
- ☆ *Farm planning is process of deciding in the present, what to do in the future about the best combination of crops and livestock to be raised through rational use of resources.*
- ☆ *Farm planning is mainly a process of choice making or choosing from among competitive alternatives. It is concerned with various adjustments the farmer makes in the existing organizations with the purpose of making the most profitable usage of scarce resources.*
- ☆ *Farm planning is an attempt to state logically in conformity with the economic principles as to what will happen in the future of a farm business. So, farm plan serves as a blue print for the future.*

A. Importance of Farm Planning

The farm business plan is a written document that directs business decision making and is based on pre-established goals for that business. The farm planning, of course, may be annual or long range planning. Annual planning obviously is meant for ensuing agricultural year. In case of long range planning, long range objectives are involved, covering a longer period over the next 5 to 10 years. Irrespective of the range of farm planning, it ensures the following advantages to the farmer:

- ☆ Farm planning mainly aims at maximization of net income of the farm business.

- ☆ Farm planning helps the farmer to study about resources usage and possible resources combinations, so as to minimize the costs in the farm business.
- ☆ Farm planning ensures the farmer to study the best methods of resource allocation on an enterprise or enterprises combination with an objective of maximization of profits.
- ☆ Farm planning helps the farm manager in deciding, whether he has to go for specialization or diversification of farm business.
- ☆ Farm planning aims at maximization of resource use efficiency in employing limited resources in the production programme.
- ☆ Farm planning enable the farmer to plan his credit requirements and purchase or procurement of resources in advance.
- ☆ Farm planning helps to plan both production and marketing strategies against various risks and uncertainties, that may arise in the business.
- ☆ Farm planning ensures the farmer to produce and market the crops based on the principle of comparative advantage.
- ☆ Farm planning ensures minimization of wastage of scarce resources and thereby, leads to their productive utilization in the production programme. If *'necessity is the mother of invention'*, scarcity of resources is the mother of farm planning. So, when the resources are scarce with the farmer, he aims at their efficient utilization.
- ☆ Farm planning enables the farmer to plan and select various alternate courses of action with a view to maximize the profits and maximization of costs in the production programme.
- ☆ Farm planning establishes a clear direction for management and operations to execute on the farm.
- ☆ Farm planning aims at anticipating problems and thereby, takes steps to eliminate them.
- ☆ Farm planning establishes a basis for evaluating farm managerial decisions and performance of farm operations.
- ☆ Farm planning providing a management framework that will allow quick responses to changing conditions on the farm.
- ☆ Farm planning aims at improvement in the standard of living of the farmer.
- ☆ Farm planning enables the farmer to achieve his objectives in relation to his farm and family in a more organized manner.
- ☆ Farm planning helps farmer to take decisions in relation to extent of land area to be kept under cultivation, selection of crops, area under each enterprise, kind and number of livestock to be maintained, amount of inputs to be applied *etc.*
- ☆ Farm planning helps in estimating future costs and returns.

B. Features of Good Farm Planning

- ☆ Farm plan prepared should be very clear without any ambiguity or confusion on the part of the farmer. That is, farm plan should be simple, easy to understand and easily practiced by the farmer.
- ☆ Farm plan should be prepared within the available resources of the farmer.
- ☆ The farm plan prepared should suggest various alternate courses of action to the farmer in executing farm operations.
- ☆ The farm plan should ensure efficient utilization of resources in the production programme.
- ☆ The farm plan should suggest various means and methods for improving the farm income and minimization of costs.
- ☆ The farm plan should aim at improvement of soil fertility.
- ☆ The farm plan should be flexible and not rigid in its nature.
- ☆ The farm plan should help the farmer in planning the strategies towards minimization of risk and uncertainties in the farm business.
- ☆ The farm plan should employ the adoption of modern techniques of production.
- ☆ The farm plan should enable the farmers in selecting most profitable enterprise or enterprises combination relevant to the farming situation under consideration with a view to gain maximum profits.
- ☆ The farm plan should enable the farmer regarding scientific resources allocation among the enterprises under consideration.
- ☆ The farm plan should aim at maximization of resource use efficiency in the farm business with a view to get maximum profits.
- ☆ The farm plan should enable the farmer in studying various possible resources combinations in order to produce a given level of output at lowest possible cost (LCC of resources).
- ☆ The farm plan should enable the farmer for better recycling of by-products.
- ☆ The farm plan should ensure the farmer in selecting the enterprises in which he is having good managerial ability.
- ☆ The farm plan should ensure efficient marketing of farm products.
- ☆ The farm plan prepared should enable the farmer to plan his credit requirements in advance and its repayment well in time.

C. Steps in Farm Planning

To have a best farm plan, the following steps are needed to be followed, while farm planning is prepared:

- ☆ ***Define the farm's mission***: The farmer must clearly define the purpose(s) of taking the farm business. This will enable the farmer to identify the enterprises and inputs he has to employ. He further assess, what inputs are available on the farm and what are to be purchased or hired? Thus, defining farm's mission lays the foundation to establish the activities to be performed on the farm.

- ☆ ***Establishment of goals and objectives:*** These will translate the mission into concrete terms. Note that, the framed goals and objectives must be quantifiable and achievable. That is, each goal should have several characteristics *i.e.*, be 'SMART' (Specific, Measurable, Attainable, Realistic and Timed). This allows the farmer to check the progress towards the achievement of these goals and make decisions that complement the mission.
- ☆ ***Assessment of external environment:*** The farmer must assess the external environment, as every farmer faces several risks and uncertainties, threats and opportunities that are beyond his control. Even market forces may cause prices to plunge, either in the long-run or short-run. Higher output, declining consumer demand, higher tariffs on trade, changing Government policies *etc.*, are external threats that can cut profits or make business more difficult. New market opportunities are created by demographic changes, changing consumer tastes, population growth in selected regions and technological breakthroughs. So, it is important that the farm manager must clearly understand the economic, social and technological forces that will affect the farm. With this information, he can form educated guesses about what will happen to input and output prices in the immediate ensuing period over the next three to five years.
- ☆ ***Assessment of resources on the farm:*** Farm map must be drawn showing the general lay out of the farm, number and shapes of farm fields, irrigation channels, drainage channels *etc.* This also facilitates to assess the level of resources or resource position with the farmer. Rapid survey may be conducted in the farm to analyze the existing resources and their usage in current production progarmme. This will enable the farmer to analyze the farm's strengths and weaknesses. The quality and quantity of resources within the control of the farm manager is the first part of this assessment. The assessment of resources may include:
    - ❑ What are the abilities and limitations of the farm manager?
    - ❑ What skills and abilities do the farm labour have?
    - ❑ How modern and efficient is the technology?
    - ❑ How large is the resource base?
    - ❑ What are the soils on the farm?
    - ❑ What is the cash position of the farm?

    It is important that, these resources be compared against those of similar farms in that locality. Many farmers have an unrealistic view of their own resources and operations because, they do not compare themselves to others in the same business. The farmer should held frequent discussions with local farmers, scientific community and other relevant stakeholders that guides him in the best use of available resources on the farm.

- ***Recording the History of the Farm:*** It is essential to note down the history about the farm *i.e.,* what type of enterprises were practiced earlier, type of resources available in plenty in the farm, efficient use of resources, crop rotations followed previously *etc.* This will form the basis for the future planning say, regarding the type of enterprises to be followed, requirement of credit, crop rotation to be followed *etc.*
- ***Analysis of existing farm plan:*** Thorough analysis of the existing production scenario on the farm should be done *i.e.,* regarding the extent of utilization of labour, type of inputs employed, technology adopted, expected yield of the crop, actual yield of the crop in the farm *etc.* The production pattern on the farm must be compared with certain bench marks standards of model farms in that locality, so as to identify various loopholes or defects in the existing plan followed by the farmer.
- ***Interactions with scientific personnel:*** Discussions to be held with progressive farmers, scientific personnel and other related stakeholders, so as to get suitable suggestions and possible improvements on scientific scale in the new plan to be prepared.
- ***Alternate courses of action:*** The farmer must prepare various alternative courses of action taking into consideration the farmer's resource availability, farming situation, availability of different facilities like input supplies, credit, marketing *etc.* That is, the farm manager has to develop various alternative plans that describe the methods for attaining goals. Evaluation of each strategy is made according to its ability to move toward the success of one or more goals. What types of strategies can farm manager takes depends upon:
  - Cost-effective production of output
  - Profit-maximizing output
  - Increasing the quality of output
- ***Selection of final plan:*** Selection of a suitable plan for its final implementation on the farm by evaluating the alternatives available. However, there is no single method for evaluating alternatives. The following combination may be used:
  - Budgeting each alternative by Enterprise budgeting, Partial budgeting and Complete budgeting.
  - Break-even analysis.
  - Projections of balance sheet, income and cash flow statements.

D. Different Types of Farm Planning

There are two types of farm planning *viz.,* Simple farm planning and Complete farm planning.

i. Simple Farm Planning

Simple farm planning is done either for a part of the enterprise or for a part of the land in the farm business and it involves only minor changes in farm business. This farm planning is easy to understand and implement by the farmer. The process of change in the farm business always begins with simple farm planning.

ii. Complete Farm Planning or Full Farm Planning or Whole Farm Planning

Complete farm planning involves bringing scientific changes in the entire farm *i.e.,* taking farm as a unit. So, complete farm planning involves more number of changes compared to simple farm planning. This Planning is a holistic approach to farm management used to identify and prioritize various issues on a farm without compromising the farm business. Complete farm planning:

- ☆ Brings desirable changes in the cropping pattern
- ☆ Aims for taking up the crops on scientific scale with more market orientation
- ☆ Ensure specialization of farm business taking the principle of comparative advantage of the crops into consideration.

Thus, complete farm planning gives due consideration to all of the farm assets (physical and non physical); over a long period of time (perhaps several generations); with respect to all of the aims which the farmer may aspire to (say, profits, standard of living for farm family, sustainability of production, etc). Various aspects like SWOT analysis of farm, soil health, feasible enterprises, soil conservation, rate of return analysis for all possible enterprises, Government's programmes and policies *etc.*, are given due attention in complete farm planning. Above all, the farmer must evaluate each and every resource on the farm as given below.

- ☆ ***Land:***
  - ❑ What is the size of the farm?
  - ❑ How much land is under food crops, orchards, vegetables etc?
  - ❑ What is the type of soil, soil health, physic-chemical properties?
- ☆ ***Labour:***
  - ❑ How many man-working days are needed across each enterprise to be taken up on the farm?
  - ❑ How many hired labour he need across various farm operations enterprise-wise?
  - ❑ What is the demand-supply gap of labour availability in that locality?
  - ❑ How to plan division of labour on the farm?
- ☆ ***Capital:***
  - ❑ How much risk the farmer is willing to take on the enterprise(s)?
  - ❑ Whether the farmer is willing to borrow money for the investment?
  - ❑ Do neighboring farmers have machinery or equipment to get rent?
  - ❑ How long can the farmer wait before he get a return from an investment?
- ☆ ***Water:***
  - ❑ What is the source of irrigation – canal or tank or bore well etc?
  - ❑ Whether the water source is polluted?

- ❑ Whether any feasibility is there to install micro-irrigation system?
- ❑ Whether drainage facilities on the farm are on scientific lines?
- ❑ What is the water requirement of various crops to be proposed in farm plan?
- ❑ What is the demand-supply gap of water availability on the farm?
- ❑ Have your water tested for mineral content and pollution?

☆ *Equipment:*

- ❑ What are the machinery and implements available on the farm?
- ❑ Whether any scope is there to purchase new or modern machinery in the future?
- ❑ What is the extent of depreciation of machinery on the farm?

☆ *Skills:*

- ❑ What technical and managerial skills the farmer enjoy in performing farm operations?
- ❑ On which crops the farmer enjoy more expertise?
- ❑ Whether he needs any training or exposure visits to gain familiarity with the adoption of modern technology?
- ❑ What extra skills he need to take up new enterprises on the farm?

E. Farm Budgeting or Budgeting of Farm Plan

From the above discussion, it is clear that, a farmer makes plans before starting production. For example, in crop production, the farmer decides on the type of crop to be planted (say, paddy, maize, cotton, gram, chillies etc) and resources to put into production (such as land, labour, capital, technology, seed, fertilizer, manures etc). The result of the use of these inputs in a production programme results in output. Both these production inputs and output are measured in different units: inputs are measured in hectares, kilograms, litres *etc.*, whereas output is measured in quintals or tonnes or litres *etc.* So, for convenient measurement, both inputs and output are measured in monetary terms. Thus, the values of both inputs and output are expressed in monetary terms in a budget. Thus, a budget is a formal quantitative expression of farm plan on production inputs and output and it indicates type, quality, and quantity of both inputs and output. This also infers that, farm budgeting is the expression of farm plan in monetary terms *i.e.*, it involves estimation of costs, gross returns and net returns of farm business. We know, farm plan involves drawing the production activity of a farmer in advance. So, this budgeting technique aims at analyzing the farm plan for the use of resources at the command of decision maker or farmer. If farm planning is done to bring desirable changes on the farm, it should be accompanied by budgeting. Without doing farm budgeting and simply doing farm planning alone is not meaningful. The desired changes in the farm plan should be allocated with resources, so as to analyze their impact on the farm cost and income structure, and this is nothing but doing farm budgeting analysis. So farm planning and budgeting goes side by side, as farm plan forms the basis for farm budgeting. Therefore, a farm plan can be prepared without a budget, but budgeting is not possible without farm plan. The other popular definitions of farm budgeting includes:

- ☆ The expression of farm plan in monetary terms by estimation of receipts, expenses and net income is called farm budgeting.
- ☆ Farm budgeting is a process of estimating costs, returns and net profit of a farm or a particular enterprise.
- ☆ Budget is a statement of estimated income and expenditure.

So, farm budgeting enable the farmer to assess the economic viability of different farm plans and thus, guides him to select the one that is most profitable.

i. Objectives of Farm Budgeting

This include:

- ☆ To study the profitability of a farm business under the existing plan.
- ☆ To study the changes in profitability due to desirable changes made in the farm business through farm planning.
- ☆ To compare the profitability between existing plan and alternate plan of farm business.

ii. Types of Budgeting

From the definitions of farm budgeting, it is clear that, a farm budget is an attempt to predict financial performance of a farm business at a specified point of time. These budgets serve as useful tools for planning and measuring farm performance. At least, three types or levels of budgets are useful in the farm business *viz.*, Enterprise budgeting, Partial budgeting or Simple budgeting and Complete or Full budgeting. A farm manager will find a combination of all these three – not necessarily at the same time, as each one has different characteristics. These three types of budgets are discussed here under.

a. Enterprise Budgeting

We know, an enterprise refers to a crop or an allied production activity taken up in the farm business. If farm budgeting is done in terms of total costs, gross returns and net returns of an enterprise (Table 7.1), it refers to Enterprise budgeting. That is, in enterprise budgeting, each segment or enterprise of the total operation is an independent business. Each enterprise can then be examined for its contribution to profitability. So, enterprise budget estimates expenses, receipts and profits of an individual enterprise for a period of time using a specified set of production practices. This budget is generally worked out for Rs./acre or Rs./hectare or Rupees per thousand poultry birds or Rupees per hundred apiary boxes *etc.*, so that the budgetary values can be projected approximately, if such enterprises are taken up on large scale on the farm. This enterprise budget also allows comparison of profits among different enterprises on the same farm.

Table 7.1: Typical Enterprise Budget for 'Crop X' in Nandyal Region of Andhra Pradesh

Sl.No.	*Items*	*Rs./1.25 Acres*	*Rs./ha*
I.	**Operational Costs**		
1.	Seed	400.00	800.00
2.	Nursery	250.00	500.00
3.	Land preparation	400.00	800.00
4.	Transplanting	1400.00	2800.00
5.	Manures	2175.00	4350.00
6.	Fertilizers	3500.00	7000.00
7.	Plant Protection	4050.00	8100.00
8.	Irrigation	100.00	200.00
9.	Weeding	200.00	400.00
10.	Harvesting	450.00	900.00
11.	Interest on working capital	150.79	301.58
	Total Operational Costs	13075.79	26151.58
II.	**Fixed Costs**		
1.	Land Revenue	200.00	400.00
2.	Depreciation	3000.00	6000.00
3.	Rental value of owned land	4000.00	8000.00
4.	Interest on fixed capital	2800.00	5600.00
	Total Fixed Costs	10000.00	20000.00
	Total Costs (Operational Costs + Fixed Costs)	23075.79	46151.58
	Gross Returns	31375.00	62750.00
	Net Returns	8299.21	16598.42
	Rate of Return (Net Returns/Total Costs)	0.36	0.36

Merits

- ☆ An enterprise budget helps to study the input–output relationship of an enterprise *i.e.*, it indicates the resource use efficiency.
- ☆ It also indicates profitability of the enterprise under consideration in a given farming situation.
- ☆ If enterprise budgeting is done for several crops on the farm, it helps the farm manager to compare the profitability across the enterprises.
- ☆ It also helps the farmer to plan his resource requirements in advance taking the operations he wants to perform on the enterprise.
- ☆ It also helps the farmer to identify the loopholes or defects in the existing farm practices of the enterprise so that, he can make a betterment in the future.

☆ A comparison of enterprise budget taken up with old and new technology in an enterprise, will directly indicate the impact of new technology on the production programme.

Demerits

By doing enterprise budgeting alone, we start with the presumption that, each enterprise is a competitive enterprise with another enterprise and hence, it will not facilitate to study the complementary or supplementary relationships across the enterprises. Of course, by doing complete budgeting or full budgeting, we can eliminate this demerit of enterprise budgeting.

b. Partial Budgeting

We know, improvement in agricultural production technology is necessary for agricultural development. The farmers search for this modern technology to incorporate in the farm business with a view to achieve cost-effective production or higher net returns (profit maximization) or both. However, before recommending a technology to the farmers, it must be evaluated for its economic viability at the farmer's level. Of course, besides economic viability, even other factors like agro-ecological requirements, cost structure of technology, skills demanded by the technology from the farmers, possible reduction in cost of production due to adoption of technology, possible increased income due to the adoption of technology *etc.*, are to be taken into consideration. The farmer also considers the compatibility of the new technology with socio-cultural circumstances, goals and the whole farming system. Among these aspects, economic viability of technology is most important, as it directly influences the incremental income the farmer derives due to the adoption of modern technology or technological interventions made on the enterprise. Considering this importance, one of the tools in economics used to compare the economic benefits of technologies is Partial budgeting analysis. This technique serves as a basic decision-making tool on the farm. It involves the estimation of profitability on an enterprise, when relatively few modifications are made on it as per the scientific recommendations *i.e.*, when the farmer adopts for simple farm planning. That means, in partial budgeting, we estimate the increased profitability of the enterprise by fine tuning one or few operations on scientific mode. The important aspect of partial budgeting is that, we work out the profitability of the enterprise taking into consideration returns and expenses associated with the changes made on the enterprise *i.e.*, one or few operations of the enterprise. We know, in a short run production programme, some aspects of business are fixed and partial budget can evaluate changes in resource uses that are not fixed. That means, in partial budgeting, whatever the changes made on the enterprise will be accounted for to estimate the incremental income. Generally, a farmer goes for partial budgeting taking into consideration the following important factors:

☆ When there are alternative ways of performing the existing operation(s).

☆ Taking the opportunity cost or relative profitability of the alternative operation.

So, partial budgeting finally answers *'what would happen if'*. The technological changes made on the enterprise are examined to see the net effect of the following four possible changes:

- Added or Increased Returns or Income (+)
- Reduced Costs (+)
- Added Costs (-)
- Reduced Returns or Income (-)

The sum of these four possible changes will show, whether the technological change will improve or diminish profitability. If income added (directly by Increased returns or indirectly by Reduced costs) by the technological change(s) exceeds costs (directly by Added costs or indirectly by Reduced returns), then the incremental income should add to profitability. Let us define the above four possible changes on the enterprise:

- ***Added Returns:*** This refers to extra returns the farmer realizes by making desirable changes regarding the operation of the enterprise.
- ***Reduced Cost:*** This refers to reduction in cost expenditure realized by the farmer due to making desirable changes or modifications on the operation(s) of the enterprise.
- ***Added Cost:*** This refers to the extra cost incurred by the farmer due to making desirable changes or modifications on the operation(s) of enterprise.
- ***Reduced Returns:*** This refers to the declined returns from the enterprise, if the changes made on the enterprise are found futile.

Among the above four components, Added returns and Reduced costs together constitute 'Positive economic effects' or 'Total advantages' of doing partial budgeting. These two are included on credit side of partial budget (Table 7.2). The remaining two components *viz.*, Reduced returns and Added costs falls under 'Negative economic effects' or 'Total disadvantages' of doing partial budgeting. These two are included on Debit side of partial budget. As mentioned earlier, partial budgeting analysis does not determine profitability of the whole farm business rather, it only determines the 'change in profit', if an alternative or technological intervention is adopted. Also note that, even though the proposed change may enhance profit, the enterprise may still be incurring an operating loss. For example, if the farmer wishes to substitute manure for fertilizer, a partial budget analysis will reveal, whether the substitution will increase or decrease profit. But, this analysis will not reveal, whether the enterprise with fertilizer application was profitable or whether the same enterprise after going for manurial application is profitable, or whether the overall business is profitable. Similarly, if the farmer wishes to shift from one enterprise to another enterprise, a partial budget analysis will reveal, whether the shift will increase or decrease profit. But, this analysis will not reveal, whether the original enterprise was profitable, whether the alternative enterprise is profitable, or whether the overall business is profitable. Thus, the analysis will only reveal, how the level of profit will change, if the alternative is adopted.

Table 7.2: Format for Partial Budgeting Analysis to Compute Incremental Income

Positive Economic Effects (Credit)	*Negative Economic Effects (Debit)*
Added Returns (AR): What will be the new or added returns or revenues? ☆ —— ☆ —— ☆ ——	**Reduced Returns (RR):** What revenues will be reduced or lost? ☆ —— ☆ —— ☆ ——
Reduced Costs (RC): What costs will be reduced or eliminated? ☆ —— ☆ —— ☆ ——	**Added Costs (AC):** What will be the new or added costs? ☆ —— ☆ —— ☆ ——
Total Positive Effects: (AR)+(RC)	Total Negative Effects: (RR)+(AC)
Incremental Income = (Added Returns + Reduced Costs) – (Reduced Returns + Added Costs) = Credit – Debit	

Table 7.2 shows that, there are seven common components to a partial budget: Added Returns, Reduced Costs, Reduced Returns, Added Costs, Total positive effects (Added Returns + Reduced Costs), Total negative effects (Reduced Returns + Added Costs) and Incremental income or Net change (Total positive effects minus Total negative effects). So, in preparing a partial budget, only the parts of the farm business that will undergo a change, if the alternative is adopted are considered. The aspects of the business that will not be affected by the alternative made are not considered because, they will remain the same whether or not the change is made. Thus, partial budgeting is a planning and decision-making framework used to compare the costs and benefits of alternatives faced by a farm business. It focuses only on the changes in income and expenses that would result from implementing a specific alternative. However, the value of a partial budget analysis is highly dependent upon the quality of the information used in the analysis. Note that, opportunity cost is an important consideration in preparing a partial budget. For example, if the farmer adopts a modern production technology that reduces the labour requirement on the enterprise, that reduction of labour is a positive impact and must be included in the analysis as a cost saving (Reduced cost).

Examples of Partial Farm Budgeting

Example 7.1

In a farm, with reference to cultivation of crop 'X', two loopholes or defects are identified *viz.*, the host farmer has not practiced seed treatment and he is applying excess quantity of nitrogen (urea) fertilizer than the scientific recommended dosage. So, these two defects are modified as per the scientific recommendations in the alternate farm plan. With the introduction of seed treatment in the alternate plan, the pesticidal application cost will be reduced during the course of crop production programme. Further, the decline in fertilizer (urea) dosage is compensated by the slight increase in organic manure application to meet the nutrient management of the crop. The details are presented through Table 7.3 below.

Table 7.3: Existing and Alternate Farm Plans for Crop 'X' – Comparative Analysis (1.25 acres)

Operational Costs	*Existing Plan (Rs./1.25 acres)*	*Alternate Plan (Rs./1.25 acres)*
Seed	400	400
Seed treatment	---	**200**
Nursery	250	250
Land preparation	400	400
Transplanting	1400	1400
Manures	2175	**3000**
Fertilizers	3500	**2500**
Plant Protection	4050	**3100**
Irrigation	100	100
Weeding	200	200
Harvesting	450	450
Yield (qtls)	37.5	39.0

Incremental income = (Added returns + Reduced costs) – (Reduced returns + Added costs)

Added returns: Grain yield increased by 1.5 qtls + added returns from straw) = 1215+35 = Rs.1250/-

Reduced costs: Decrease in Fertilizers cost = Rs.1000/-

Decrease in Plant protection cost = Rs.950/-

Total Reduced costs = Rs.1950/-

Reduced returns: Nil

Added costs: Seed treatment : Rs.200

Manures cost: Rs.825

Total Added costs : Rs.1025

So, Incremental Income = (1250 + 1950) – (0 + 1025)

= Rs. 2175 per 1.25 acres = Rs. 4350/ha

Conclusion: By incorporating seed treatment and reduction in application of urea fertilizer in the existing farm plan, the farmer will get an incremental income of Rs. 4350/ha.

Example 7.2

Increase in Profitability of Ground Nut through Application of Fungicides for Controlling Tikka Leaf Spot

Credit		*Debit*	
Added Returnsdue to increase in output	Rs. 1500	Reduced returns	Rs. 0
Reduced cost	Rs. 0	Added costdue to application of 400 gms of Carbandezim and 500 gms of Mancozeb	Rs. 500
	Rs. 1500	Total	Rs. 500

Incremental income = (Added returns + Reduced costs) – (Reduced returns + Added costs)

$$= 1500 - 500 = \text{Rs.}1000$$

Conclusion : By using the fungicides to control the tikka leaf spot, incremental income is increased by Rs. 1000/-

Example 7.3

Substitution of Sunflower Crop for Groundnut (Hypothetical data)

Sl.No.	*Items*	*Existing Situation (Rs./ha)*	*Alternate Situation (Rs./ha)*
		Groundnut	*Sunflower*
1.	Human labour	1000	900
2.	Bullock Labour	500	400
3.	Seed cost	2000	1000
4.	Manures	800	900
5.	Fertilizers	1200	1100
	Total	11500	12000

Credit		*Debit*	
Added Returns	Rs.500	Reduced returns	--
Reduced costs			
☆ Human labour	Rs.100	Added cost	Rs.100
☆ Bullock labour	Rs.100		
☆ Seed cost	Rs.1000		
☆ Fertilizers	Rs.100		
Total	Rs.1800	Total	Rs.100

Incremental income = (Added returns + Reduced costs) – (Reduced returns + Added costs)

$$= 1800 - 100 = \text{Rs.}1700/-$$

Conclusion : By shifting from groundnut to sunflower, the income can be increased by Rs.1700/- per ha.

Other Examples

A partial budget could be prepared to ascertain the effect on net benefit of:

- ☆ Comparative economic analysis of a crop enterprise with seed treatment and without seed treatment.
- ☆ Comparative economic analysis between mechanical thinning of fruits and chemical thinning of fruits.
- ☆ Comparative economic analysis of American cotton vs Desi cotton *etc.* Note that, whether the change may be in terms of variety or a single crop in a diversified farm business, we go for partial budgeting.
- ☆ Substituting one enterprise for another without any change in the entire farmland area. For example, substituting 1 ha of paddy for 1 ha of maize.
- ☆ Changing to different levels of a single technology. For example, estimating the effect on net benefit of changing from one level of N-fertilizer application to another in maize production.
- ☆ Changing to different technology(ies). For example, changing from hand weeding to herbicide use for weed control.
- ☆ To estimate additional cost and returns from growing one hectare of two different paddy varieties.
- ☆ To estimate additional cost and returns by adopting foliar application of chemical fertilizers instead of soil application.
- ☆ When the farmer expands an enterprise (say, from 5 acres of paddy to 7 acres).
- ☆ When the farmer substitute enterprises that enjoy similar resource requirements (say, substituting 5 acres of cotton for 5 acres of chillies).
- ☆ When buying new equipment or machinery (say, buying new equipment rather than leasing or *vice versa*).
- ☆ Changing production practices (say, applying more of manure instead of indiscriminate dosage of chemical fertilizers).

Considering the above examples, a partial budget, like an enterprise budget, is based on a unit (for example, a 1 ha paddy), but it is different from an enterprise budget in the type of costs used. An enterprise budget uses total costs (variable costs plus fixed costs), while only variable input costs are used in a partial budget. Further, in partial budgeting, only those inputs and outputs that will actually change will be taken into consideration. So, partial budgeting analyze net returns from small changes or refinements to one or few farm operation(s). It focuses only on parts that change, not budget each enterprise completely, but build on enterprise budgets. Thus, in doing partial budgeting, the farmer hold all else fixed to evaluate a small change. It is also essential to decide, whether to use two enterprise budgets or a partial budgeting based on what information the farm manager wants to have when making the decision. For example, if the farm manager wants to know the revenue, costs and profit of each alternative, prepare two enterprise budgets. If the manager wants to know, how the profit of the business will be impacted by making a change in the business, prepare a partial budgeting analysis.

Steps in Partial Budgeting

After analyzing the examples of partial budgeting, it is now easier to list out the following steps involved in partial budgeting:

- Work out the enterprise budget and analyze the operations.
- Rationalize the reason for a change. That is, what is the objective of the change?
- Identify the loopholes or defects in the operation of the existing enterprise.
- Identify the possible desirable changes to be made on the enterprise.
- Search for various alternate courses of action and select the best one for use on the enterprise. Write a descriptive statement of the proposed adjustment or change to be made. Where more than one alternative exists, each alternative requires a separate budget.
- List the possible changes on the enterprises due to the technological interventions(s)
    - List the expected Added returns
    - List the expected Reduced costs
    - List the expected Reduced returns
    - List the expected Added costs
- Analyze Total positive economic effects (Added returns + Reduced Costs) and Total negative economic effects (Reduced returns + Added costs). That is, the positive effects and negative effects are added together to determine, whether the net change is positive or negative. If the net change is positive, then the proposed change would increase profitability; if the net change is negative, the proposed change would decrease profitability. Positive net changes would likely be implemented; negative net changes would likely not be implemented. The terms 'likely' and 'likely not' are mentioned here because, not all decisions are based solely on economic considerations.
- Compute incremental income (P) *i.e.* (Added returns + Reduced Costs) - (Reduced returns + Added costs).
- If incremental income is positive it implies, the desired changes are economically viable and hence the farmer may go for cash flow statement to plan his credit requirements in the future.
- Identify the possible risk factors for implementing the desired changes on the enterprise. For example :
    - Whether the farmer can get a loan for performing that operation?
    - Whether labour availability is there to perform that operation?
    - Whether the operation or desired changes fits into the overall operations of the farm structure?

- ✰ Decide whether to make the changes or not. When the farmer presumes that, the incremental income is positive and risk factors are minimum, the farmer can straight away implement the desired change(s) on the enterprise. Besides these, the farmer must also make other considerations, which are not included in the above steps. For example, whether adequate farm labour are available to execute the proposed technological interventions on the farm or how much risk is involved in practicing these interventions *etc.* So, after accounting both economic benefits and other considerations, the farmer should take the decision, whether or not to implement the change.

Merits

- ✰ All aspects of farm business that are unchanged by the decision can be safely ignored. So, partial budgeting allows the farmer to get a better handle on how a decision will affect the profitability of the enterprise, and ultimately the profitability of the farm itself.
- ✰ This partial budgeting is extremely useful to determine, how to measure incremental income in the farm business due to changes or technological interventions made with reference to operations of the enterprise. Thus, it serves as a shortcut procedure that compares profitability before and after a technological change made on the enterprise. Consequently, this technique of partial budgeting can be extremely useful for determining, whether a specific change will make an operation better off than before.
- ✰ It helps to work out the incremental income we derive from the farm business, if one or few operations are modified on scientific scale.
- ✰ Partial budgeting is a quick decision making tool of investment analysis.
- ✰ In partial budgeting, all the costs are not considered and only those costs associated with the changes made in operations are accounted for to compute incremental income and this saves lot of time on the part of farm manager.
- ✰ The results of partial budgeting are with more clarity because, they highlight the importance of technological interventions made on the enterprise.
- ✰ Partial budgeting is, otherwise, called as 'Pencil farming' because, it isolates the outcome of desirable changes made on the operations on a white paper before wasting of time, money and resources on the farm.
- ✰ Unlike complete budgeting, partial budgeting is inexpensive to use, as it deals with only minor modifications made on the enterprise and further, it can be used to assess the merits of a number of different alternatives so that, the best one can be selected. Thus, partial budget serves as the basic tool of all farm management decision making.
- ✰ Partial budgeting analysis aids scientists and extension agents in deciding, which technology to be recommend to farmers.
- ✰ Partial budgeting analysis shows the level of profitability and helps to decide, whether to adopt a new technology or not. Thus, it forces the farmer to think ahead and aids in sound decision making.

- Partial budgeting analysis can apply to all crops and cropping systems.
- Results from partial budgeting analysis assist agricultural scientists in identifying weaknesses (high cost and/or low income) of the technology being developed.
- A partial budget could be described as *'a summary of the differences between two enterprise analyses of alternative activities'*. For example, a farmer could prepare two enterprise analyses; one for the original enterprise and one for the alternative, and then compare the profitability of these two enterprises. This difference should be the same as the change in profits calculated by the partial budget analysis with references to only the changes made on one of the enterprises. Thus, there is a relationship between enterprise analysis and partial budget analysis.
- The success of the partial budgeting depends on prediction accuracy, which depends on the accuracy of the information and estimates it contains. The manager needs to collect factual data about the proposed change and provide reasonable estimates of such items as future prices, yields and gains. So, the exactness with which these data are collected, the reliability are the estimates of partial budgeting.

Demerits

- Data may not be readily available with the farmer regarding the alternate course of action. For example, if the farmer wishes to go for labour weeding instead of herbicide usage, the farmer must need the information about labour supply and labour availability data. If such data are not available, alternate course of action cannot be implemented.
- This partial budgeting does not take into consideration the managerial efficiency in increasing the income. Similarly, the alternate courses of action may also lead to other managerial problems in the farm business.
- If the incremental income derived from partial budgeting is due to one or few alternate courses of action, it may even influence the overall farm structure or organization.
- It may over simplify the problems of farm business. For example, by resorting to only few alternate courses of action, income may not be greatly increased and moreover, farm managerial problems are not so simple to address.
- Partial budgeting allows the farmer to compare two alternatives side-by-side. But, it does not indicate, whether either one of the choices is the best alternative available, only that one is better than the other.
- In partial budgeting, we deal with only few alternate courses of action even though there are several alternate course of action available to farmer pertaining to all operations.
- Partial budgeting does not always provide a complete solution to the problem. For example, threshing by machinery will involve low cost of threshing per quintal when compared to human labour threshing. But, the farmer cannot straight away implement mechanical threshing on the farm

because, he has to consider other factors before taking the decision for mechanical threshing such as:

- ❑ He need larger amount of capital resource to purchase thresher.
- ❑ It will take a significant period to achieve the BEP of mechanical thresher.
- ❑ Custom hiring for thresher may not be available in that area

- ✰ Whatever the decision taken in case of partial budgeting may not enter the complete budgeting of the farm. For example, by doing partial budgeting, it is concluded that, hybrid maize is far superior to American cotton in getting more income. But, in case of complete budgeting, both the enterprises may not find a place in the farm organization.
- ✰ The incremental income derived from partial budgeting vary from soil to soil, season to season, farming situation to farming situation, region to region *etc.*
- ✰ The success or failure of a partial budget analysis depends upon the accuracy of the estimates. If accurate estimates for the proposed change cannot be obtained, it is difficult to determine the exact influences of the technological interventions made on the enterprise. Note that, it is quite difficult to generate estimates for future unknowns, particularly prices. So, the possible outcome *i.e.*, incremental income due to desired alternate courses of action cannot be exactly quantified, if accurate data are not available with the farmer.
- ✰ This budgeting technique is restricted to evaluating *only two* alternatives.
- ✰ This budgeting technique does not take into account for the time value of money. That is, the difference in the value of cash received and/or expended now, versus its value at some future date.
- ✰ Another limitation is that partial budgeting only provides an estimate of the profitability of an alternative relative to current operations. It does not provide an estimate of the absolute profitability of the business.
- ✰ Finally, costs and returns that are not affected by an intended change are not included in the partial budget. In other words, the farmer can only use the partial budget to consider the costs and returns of a specific technological intervention. If the farmer wishes to determine all the areas (operations) that will be affected by the intended change, it might be better to use a complete budgeting to evaluate the impacts of the change.

Note that, the success of the partial budgeting depends upon prediction accuracy of the farmer, which again depends on the accuracy of the information or data predicted by the farmer regarding the four possible components discussed earlier. For getting data on these four components, the farmer must have access to data like current costs of the factors of production, costs of capital, current commodity prices or other items pertinent to the particular decision. The farm manager must estimate yields and prices to get an idea of what returns will or will not be received. Yield estimates can be obtained from several sources like production records (show the historical production levels) and prices can be estimated through analyzing the price trends of the products in that locality.

c. Complete Budgeting or Full Budgeting or Whole-Farm Budgeting or Total Budgeting

This form of budgeting is the most familiar of the three. It is also the most complete in the sense that, it includes all income and expenses in the farm business. The bottom line of the complete budgeting is assessing the profitability of the farm business by considering the entire farm as one unit. That is, complete budgeting refers to preparation of a budget for the farm as a whole. It involves extensive remodeling of the farm. That means, there is drastic change on all the operations of all the enterprises taken up in the farm and sometimes new enterprises may also come into the picture. To bring these drastic changes on the farm, first SWOT (Strength, Weakness, Opportunity and Threat) analysis has to be conducted to entire farm. So, each and every aspect of the farm must be critically evaluated for bringing the entire farm on desired scientific lines. This budgeting considers all the crops, livestock, methods of production and aspects of marketing in consolidated form and estimates costs and returns for the farm as a whole. This budget is done, when a farm plan is prepared for new farm or when drastic changes are suggested in the plan of the existing pattern on an established farm. So, complete budgeting can be defined as *'an estimation of the probable income and expenditure from a farm as a whole by considering farm as a single unit of course'*. Thus, complete budgeting is a quantitative expression of the total farm plan summarizing the income, costs, and profit (Figure 7.1). Thus, in this budgeting, the unit of analysis is the entire farm, as it deals with several enterprises. Complete budgeting can be prepared for short run (annual budget) and for long run. Complete budgeting like enterprise budgeting involves three components *viz.*, income, costs and profits. But, a complete budget is different from an enterprise budget in:

- ✰ The number of enterprises considered (only one in an enterprise budget; in a complete budget, all enterprises in the farm are included).
- ✰ The size of enterprises (a single unit for an enterprise budget, the entire farm for a complete budget).

Steps Involved in Complete Budgeting

The following are the important steps to be followed in going for complete budgeting of the farm.

- ✰ Study the objectives or goals of the farmer.
- ✰ Preparation of farm map *i.e.*, the entire farm should be clearly mapped indicating the soil type, farming situations, irrigation facilities available, drainage facilities available, problematic soils if any, land capability classification, crop rotations followed earlier in the farm *etc.*
- ✰ List out the complete farm inventory for all the valuable assets of the farmer. Besides this, it is essential to ascertain, whether these assets are in working condition or not. If they are not in working, how best the farmer plan to substitute or replace them.

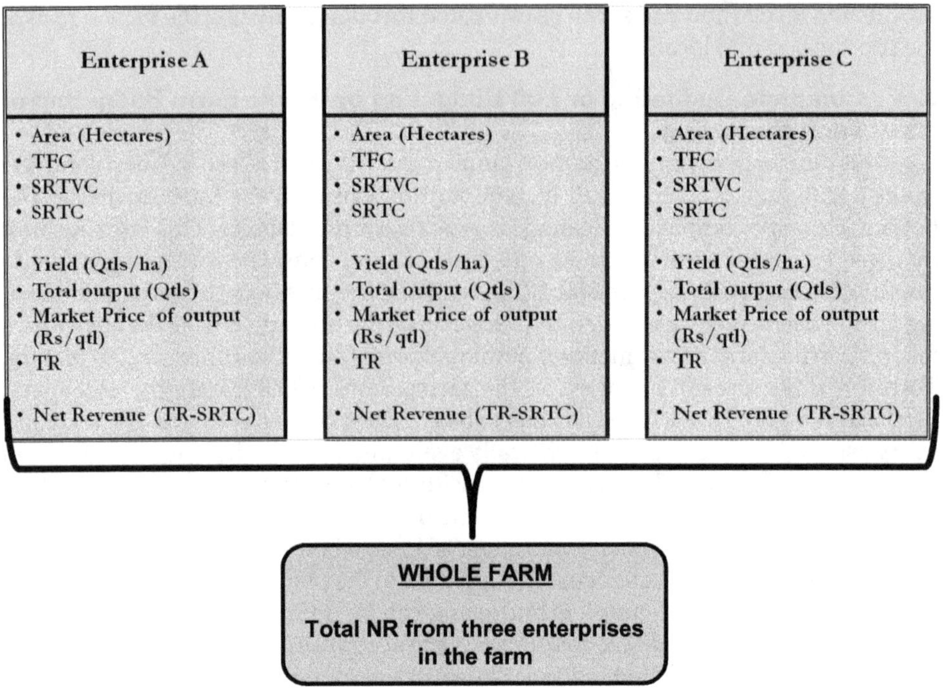

Figure 7.1: Constructing Complete Farm Budget.

- ✰ Analyze the existing weaknesses and strengths of the farm organization. The weaknesses of farm organization should be studied and they should be compared with relative strengths of the organization. For example, a farm may have various weaknesses such as lack of proper irrigation facilities, problematic soils, lack of adequate financial resources, machinery may not be available in the village for hiring purpose, no access to modern technology *etc.* The farmer should be capable of overcoming these weaknesses by studying various alternate courses of actions thereby, he can plan the entire farm organization on desired lines.
- ✰ Planning and selecting the alternate courses of action.
- ✰ When strengths outweigh the weaknesses of farm business, the farmer can plan for complete budgeting of farm organization. The selection of various alternate courses of action mainly depends upon the opportunity cost or relative profitability of the resources usage on other enterprises under consideration.
- ✰ While planning the complete budgeting, the farmer should take into consideration, farm family satisfaction besides conducting farm business. So, the farmer should try to include food crops and vegetable crops also in crop rotations to meet the farm family consumption needs and not relying exclusively on the commercial crops.
- ✰ Compute the total costs, gross income and net income of farm business (Figure 7.1).

Complete Budgeting vis-a-vis Partial Budgeting

Table 7.4 highlight the differences between Partial budgeting and Complete budgeting:

Table 7.4: Differences between Partial Budgeting and Complete Budgeting

Partial Budgeting	*Complete Budgeting*
In partial budgeting, enterprise will be taken as a base or unit and few desirable changes will be made regarding the operation(s) of the enterprise.	In complete budgeting, entire farm is taken as a unit and hence, it deals with all the enterprises on the farm.
In partial budgeting, incremental income is computed by taking into consideration only variable costs of the enterprise that too for few desirable changes made on the enterprise. So, ☆ Incremental income = (Added returns + Reduced costs) – (Reduced returns + Added costs) or ☆ Net Income = Gross Income – SRTVC	In complete budgeting or full budgeting, to estimate the net income, both fixed and variable costs will be taken into consideration. ☆ Net Income = Gross Income – Total cost
In partial budgeting, alternate courses of action will be planned taking the resource level of the farmer into consideration and that too within the existing enterprise.	In complete budgeting, both equity (owned) and non-equity (borrowed) capital resources are considered on the part of the farmer, new enterprise will be started on the farm and sometimes the farmer may also bring new land into cultivation.
In partial budgeting, only few alternate courses of action will be considered, which will not influence entire farm organization or structure.	In complete budgeting, all possible alternate courses of action will be employed on all the enterprises and hence, this will show more influence on farm structure and organization.
In partial budgeting, farm inventory analysis is not required because, only few alternate courses of action are employed.	In complete budgeting, farm inventory analysis is needed because, it employs all the possible alternate courses of actions on all the enterprises of the farm
The study on breakeven analysis of crop enterprise is not needed in partial budgeting.	The study on breakeven analysis on all crop enterprises is needed in complete budgeting.
It is practiced within the available resources structure of the farm.	All the aspects like crops, livestock, machinery and other assets are considered.
It requires relatively less efforts and time for preparation	It requires more efforts and time for preparation
Partial budgeting is more effective than the complete budgeting in determining, which technological interventions are the most profitable and which are the least profitable on an enterprise.	Complete budgeting is less effective than the partial budgeting (or even enterprise budgeting) in determining, which technological interventions are the most profitable and which are the least profitable.

Thus, a complete budget includes all the enterprises to be carried out on the farm, and projects total income and expenses instead of income and expenses per unit (enterprise budget) or the net changes in income and expenses as a result of a certain technological or management change (partial budget).

8

Risk and Uncertainity in Farm Business

We know, farmers make decisions in a risky environment every day. The consequences of their decisions are generally not known when the decisions are made. Furthermore, the outcome may be better or worse than expected. Farmers have little control over the market forces that drive commodity prices. Production levels and market supply and demand changes can cause large and unforeseen swings in prices. Variability of yields of crops and prices of commodities are the biggest sources of risk in agriculture. Furthermore, increasing global interaction in commodity markets and Governmental influences add to the uncertainty surrounding market prices. Changes in consumers' incomes, stability of the Government, trade policies and exchange rates all affect demand for commodities and, by extension, commodity prices. These and other unpredictable factors make price forecasting a difficult and volatile practice. Since, input prices translate to costs for farmers and output prices translate to revenues for farmer, unfavorable prices on either side can be devastating to an agricultural operation. Other factors like technological changes, institutional factors, legal and social concerns *etc.*, also contribute to the risk environment for farmers in farm-business. All these concerns or factors influence the farm-business in two ways: whether there is a high probability of these adverse consequences and would those adverse consequences significantly disrupt the farm-business. It is, therefore, imperative for farmers to manage risk both on the input and the output sides in order to ensure long-term profitability of the farm-business.

'Risk' and 'Uncertainty' are two terms basic to any decision making framework. Risk can be defined as an imperfect knowledge situation, where the probabilities of the possible outcomes are known. Even Uncertainty is also an imperfect knowledge situation, but the probabilities of the possible outcomes are unknown. A more common usage of these terms would state uncertainty as imperfect knowledge and risk as uncertain consequences. If a farmer says *'I am uncertain about the weather tomorrow'*, - this indicates that the person had imperfect knowledge about the future. However, if the same farmer says *'I am planning to harvest the crop tomorrow and there is a risk of rain'*, and this shows that, he is indicating preference for an alternative consequence. So, taking a risk can now be defined as *'exposing one's self to a significant chance of injury or loss'*. Risk management can then be defined as *'choosing among alternatives to reduce the effects of risk'* (Harwood, *et al*). Thus, these two terms 'risk' and 'uncertainty' indicate exposure to events that can result in losses and the lack of knowledge about the future is what is important in both risk and uncertainty. In this context, they are often used interchangeably.

I. Different Types of Risks

Risks in farm business can be conveniently classified according to whether it predominantly affects the immediate production environment, markets, or the broad institutional context in which commodities are produced and supplied. Different types of risk include:

- ☆ ***Input price risk:*** In crop agriculture, input price risk has been given considerably less attention in the literature, and has been considered less substantial than output price risk and yield risk. It normally does not translate into return variability of the same magnitude. Moreover, the time window of input price risk is shorter: fertilizer and other input costs are usually incurred within a few months of the onset of production, whereas the uncertainty around output price and yield usually remains considerably for a longer period. However, the magnitude of input price fluctuations can be significant and there is no system in place to hedge against input prices (although there is the possibility of storing some items on the farm).
- ☆ ***Yield or Output price risk:*** Regarding output price risk, it arises due to the biological lag inherent in agricultural production. Obviously, farmers must make production decisions months before they have a product to sell, before the actual crop prices are known. During this period, output prices may change dramatically in response to shocks in supply and demand. This may put farmers in a difficult situation, if commodity prices decrease drastically during the production and marketing cycle. Macroeconomic factors like variability in inflation rates, exchange rates and interest rates also impact the volatility of agricultural prices. The effect of shocks on the agriculture and food system is compounded by low elasticities of both supply and demand. Indeed, since food is an essential product with no substitute (apart from alternative foods), demand responses to price increases and decreases are typically low. Supply responses are also very low short-term, until production decisions can be made for the next season or more land brought into or taken out of production.

- ☆ ***Quantity risk:*** Quantity risk relates to reduction or loss in quantity of produce during the marketing process. For example, when produce is stored in godowns, quantity risk may arise due to fire accidents, thefts, rodent damage *etc.* Sometimes, the packing material of the produce may not be good and it may lead to physical damage. These together accounts for a large part of the loss of the produce at the individual as well as at the macro level. Such losses are loss to the society also and must be prevented to the extent possible.
- ☆ ***Quality risk:*** Quality risk relates to loss in quality of produce during marketing process, especially during storage and transportation. The produce may get spoiled with the infestation due to pests and diseases, extreme low and high temperature *etc.*
- ☆ ***Price risk:*** Regarding price risk, we know farmers generally store the produce in godowns with the anticipation that, the prices will certainly rise in the future. But, there is no guarantee, as there is equal chance of decline in the prices in future also. As a result, the farmers' income will be affected. In such a case, storage cost will become an additional burden to the farmers. Similar is the case for transportation function, that is, by the time the produce reach the distant market, the prices may fall. The prices of agricultural products fluctuate not only from year to year, but during the year from month to month, day-to-day and even on the same day. The changes in prices may be upward or downward. Price variation cannot be ruled out, as the factors affecting demand for and the supply of agricultural products change continuously. A price fall may cause a loss to the trader or farmer, who stocks the produce. Sometimes, the risks are so great that it may result in a total failure of the business, and the person who owns it may become bankrupt.

Note that, price and yield risks are the most important types of risks faced by many farmers. Yield risk varies regionally and depends on soil type, climate, the use of irrigation and other variables. In contrast, price risk for a given commodity depends on factors such as commodity stock levels and demand. Note that, crop prices tend to be more volatile than livestock prices, reflecting the yield risk inherent in crop production. The yield variability is often measured by an indicator known as the 'coefficient of variation,' which measures randomness relative to the mean (or average) value in the yield series. Price variability or risk can be measured using ratios of successive prices, Pt/Pt-1, instead of differences, Pt - Pt-1. This computation of ratio of prices offer several advantages like: it may eliminate the need to make adjustments for inflation, ratios are unit free and this facilitates comparisons among commodities and allows the comparison of volatilities estimated over time intervals of different lengths (say, the price volatility estimated with daily data for a given month can be compared with the volatility estimated for a year). Futures quotes provide a vehicle for observing price volatility changes over the growing season. The price variability changes not only within the year, but also between years due to year-to-year differences in output of crop, changes in Government's subsidies, changes in global supply and demand conditions *etc.* In contrast to prices, yields of a crop are not much volatile in a given farm locality, but they fluctuate from year to year due to varying weather conditions in different locations.

- ☆ ***Institutional risk:*** Institutional risk relates to Government price and income support programmes, trade (imposition of tariffs by the Government, large scale imports of the produce by the Government, statutory price controls etc), credit and environmental policies all of which have impacts on the operating environment. These risks may increase as firms get larger. New risks may result from new developments.

  We can also list out the following different types of risks involved in the marketing process:

- ☆ ***Time risk:*** Farmers aim at selling the produce at a profit out of anticipated raises in prices in future. During the time lag, conditions might change and the prices may fall. Thus, time risk is involved in marketing.
- ☆ ***Place risk:*** Place risk arises, when prices of the same produce is different in different places. The traders may purchase produce in a market, where prices are low with view of to sell it at other places, where the prices are high. But, prices in other market also may come down causing losses.
- ☆ ***Competition risk:*** Firms have to face risk arising from forces of competition. The competing firm may introduce modern methods of production due to which quality may be improved or cost of production may be reduced. Under such circumstances, a firm may be forced to sell at a loss which is called risk of competition.
- ☆ ***Risk of change in demand:*** The firm (say, food processor) produce products on large-scale in anticipation of increase in demand in future. But, sometimes the demand of the product may not come to expectations, resulting in losses.
- ☆ ***Risk arising from natural calamities:*** Risk from natural causes is beyond human control. These include rains, earthquake, floods, heat and cold. These risks cause heavy loss.
- ☆ ***Human risk:*** This risk arises due to adverse behaviour of human beings like theft, strikes, lockouts, heavy debts *etc.* Health problems of key individuals can severely disrupt farm performance. Furthermore, changing objectives of individuals and family members can have major effects on a farm's long run changes and viability.

Understanding risk is a key element in helping farmers to make better decisions in risky situations and also provides useful information to policymakers in assessing the effectiveness of different types of risk protection tools.

II. Knowledge Situation Available to the Farmers

Farmer generally encounters various risks and uncertainties in the farm-business. This is because, the farm production was subjected to vagaries of monsoon rains, extremely high temperatures and extremely low temperatures, floods, drought *etc.* These uncertain natural factors will pose both production and marketing problems to the farmers. This is mainly due to lack of knowledge on the part of farmers regarding the occurrence of these natural factors, which may adversely influence the farm business. So, taking the knowledge situation into consideration, Prof. Frank Knight has proposed the following classification about the knowledge situation of the farmers (Figure 8.1):

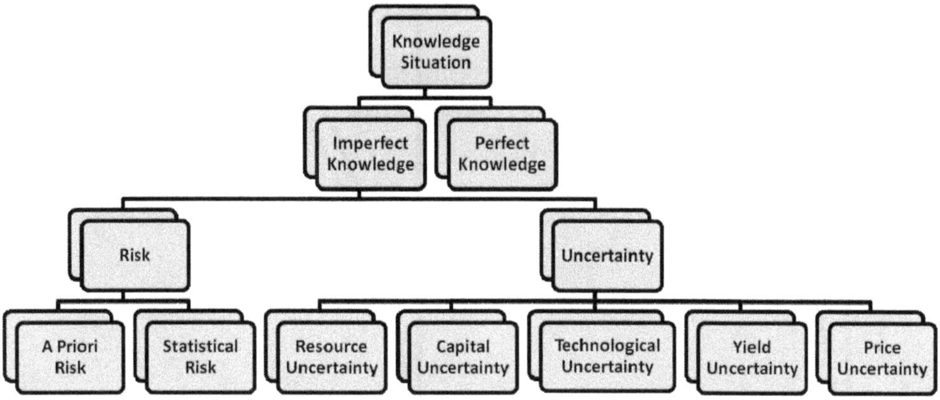

Figure 8.1: Knight's Classification of Knowledge Situation to Farmers.

A. Perfect Knowledge Situation

In this type of knowledge situation, the farmer will have perfect knowledge in advance about the occurrence of natural factors, technical efficiency of resources, price behaviour of commodities in the future, demand and supply forces *etc.* So, this will enable the farmer to plan his crop production programme with more accuracy (Figure 8.2) and for an indefinite period of time. But, this type of knowledge situation is not seen practically and hence, it should not be dealt with further.

B. Imperfect Knowledge Situation

In this type of knowledge situation, the farmer will have little or less awareness about the behaviour of natural factors, technical efficiency of resources, price behaviour of commodities in the future, demand and supply forces *etc.* So, it is not possible on the part of farmer to plan his production programme very accurately and hence, he has to face various types of risks and uncertainties in the farm business. So, this imperfect knowledge situation can be categorized into Risk and Uncertainty.

i. Risk

Risk is an imperfect knowledge situation in a farm business, where the farmer can predict the outcome of an event based on probability approach. So, we can quantify or measure the risk *i.e.*, we can measure the possible outcome of an event in the future. If this future outcome is found congenial or advantageous or fruitful, then the farmer can take up that business activity. On the other hand, if the outcome is not fruitful and it will drastically affect the business, the farmer will not take up that activity. So, the measurement of risk will guide the farmer whether to execute a particular activity or not and also help the farmer to plan alternate strategies, so as to overcome the

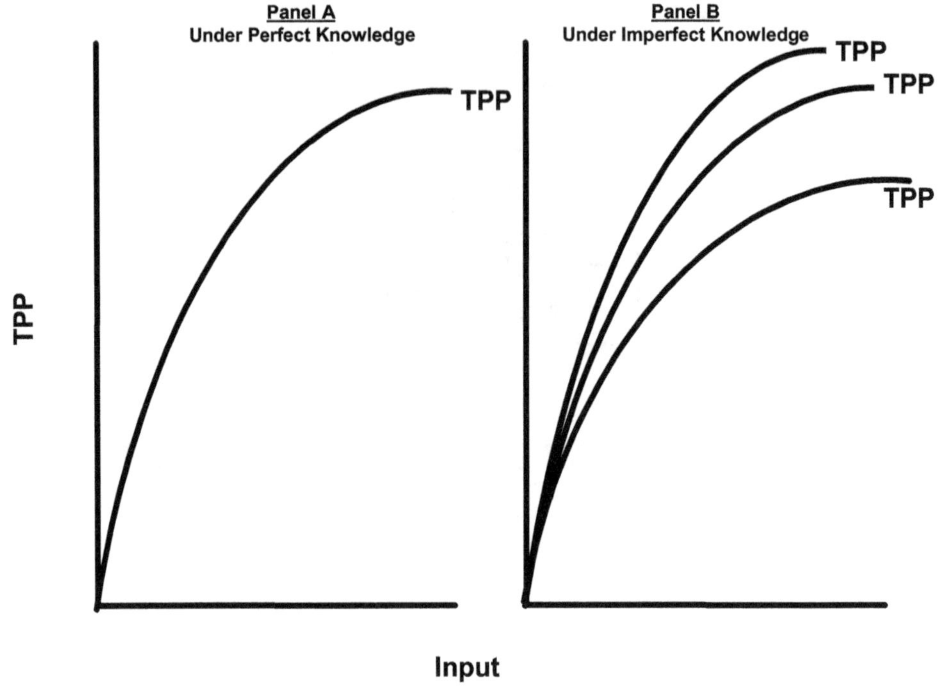

Figure 8.2: Production of Output Under Perfect and Imperfect Knowledge Situations.

adverse future event. The probability of outcome of a future event can be established in either of the following two ways:

a. *A Priori Risk*

In *A Priori* risk, sufficient information is known in advance to the farmer regarding the occurrence of a future event and based on this, he can plan the risk aversion strategies. For example, based on meteorological data (say, rainfall in a particular locality), the farmer can predict that, drought may occur once in every five years and accordingly, he can plan the cropping pattern in his farm. Other examples include:

- ☆ Theoretical probability of rolling a 2 on a standard dice is 1/6.
- ☆ Theoretical probability of choosing an ace from playing cards is 4/52.
- ☆ Theoretical probability of getting heads on a regular coin is ½.
- ☆ Empirical probability of occurrence of drought in Andhra Pradesh by 2025 is 0.60 (based on historical data).
- ☆ Empirical probability of a lifetime smoker developing lung cancer is 20 percent (based on empirical data).
- ☆ Consider how the price of a commodity or a share can change. The price can increase, decrease or remain the same. Therefore, according to *a priori* probability, we can assume that there is a 1-in-3, or 33 percent, chance of one of the outcomes occurring (all else remaining equal).

Thus, these *a priori* probabilities are most often used within the deduction method of calculating probability. This is because, the farmer must use logic to determine what outcomes of an event are possible in order to determine the number of ways these outcomes can occur.

b. Statistical Risk

In this type of risk, the outcome of an event can be determined on the basis of observations. There are many examples in agriculture like analyzing the price risk, yield risk, number of poultry eggs broken during transit, number of fruits spoiled or rotted during transit *etc.*, where outcomes involving risk are estimated by statistical tools. Two popular methods are employed *viz.*, Weighted average method and Probabilistic method.

- ***Measuring the Expectation by Weighted Average Method:*** In this method the following steps are involved:
  - List out the prices of the commodity for the past reference period under consideration (say, 2001-06).
  - Assign weights to the years under consideration. In general, more weightage is given for the recent years and less weightage is given for remote years. However experience, preferences and judgement of the decision maker will influence in assigning the weighted values to different years under consideration.
  - Compute the product between actual prices and weighted value given for that year.
  - Compute the totals of prices, weights and (Price*Weight).
  - Compute simple average and weighted average of the price of the commodity, which indicates the future price.
  - Among these two, weighted average of price is more preferred because, the future price of the commodity mainly depends upon remote years. Note that, simple average is also a weighted average, if equal weightage is given to all the years.
  - If weighted average is more than simple average, it implies that, the future outcome is favourable or less risky to the farmer and *vice-versa*.

  In the given example (Table 8.1), since the weighted average value (Rs.1425) is more than simple average value (Rs.1385), there is less price risk on the part of farmer and hence, the farmer can go for taking up this crop enterprise in the ensuring year.

- ***Measuring the Expectation by Probabilistic Method:*** Another way of measuring the future outcome or quantifying the risk is by using probability approach and this method is most commonly followed. In this method, the following steps are involved (say, for analyzing the probable yield level of a crop).
  - Assign the probability values to the possible yield levels of the crop the farmer is expecting.

Table 8.1: Price Risk of an Enterprise – Weighted Average Method

Year	*Average Annual Price (Rs./qtl)*	*Weights*	*Price * Weight*
2001	1200	1	1200
2002	1400	2	2800
2003	1300	3	3900
2004	1550	4	6200
2005	1340	5	6700
2006	1520	6	9120
Total	8310	21	29920
Simple average	1385		
Weighted average			1425

- Experience and judgement counts much in assigning these probability values because, the farmer must have a good knowledge about the variety, farming situation, resources available, managerial skills *etc.* If the farmer posses good knowledge on these aspects, he can give more probability for expecting a higher yield and *vice-versa*.
- Calculate the product between yield values and probabilities assigned. Of all the yield values, the value with highest level of probability is considered as most likely value of the yield of crop expected by the farmer.
- Compute Σ(Yield*Probability values). Also compute average expected yield of the crop.
- In the Table 8.2, the estimated future value of yield *i.e.*, 13.1 quintals/acre is less than most likely value of 14 quintals/acre, but more than average yield of the crop (13 quintals/acre) the farmer is expecting in that area. So, it is less risky on the part of the farmer to take up this crop in his farm.

Table 8.2: Yield Risk of an Enterprise – Probabilistic Method

Sl.No.	*Crop Yield (qtls/acre)*	*Probability*	*Probability * Yield*
1	12.0	0.1	1.2
2	14.0	0.4	5.6
3	13.5	0.1	1.35
4	11.0	0.3	3.3
5	12.5	0.1	1.25
	Average yield = 13q/ha		Yield = 13.1q/ha

ii. Uncertainty

Uncertainty refers to an imperfect knowledge situation, where the possible outcome of an event cannot be quantified or predicted even by a probabilistic approach. So, we can say uncertainty cannot be measured unlike risk (Table 8.3) and hence, uncertainty is also called as Non–quantifiable risk. However, these two terms are used interchangeably, as both represent imperfect knowledge situation on the part of the farmer and they indicate exposure to events that can result in losses.

Table 8.3: Risk vis-à-vis Uncertainty

Risk	*Uncertainty*
In risk, the possible outcome of an event can be predicted through a probability approach.	In uncertainty situation, the outcome of an event cannot be estimated.
The risk situation can be measured or quantified	Uncertainty is, otherwise, referred as non-quantifiable risk, as it cannot be measured.
Risk situation can be manageable (say, by insuring against it) by formulation of suitable alternate strategies.	Uncertainty cannot be managed, as the farmer cannot even predict the outcome of an event.

a. *Different Sources of Risk or Uncertainty*

☆ ***Resource uncertainty:***

- ❑ Sometimes labour may not be available in requisite number to perform the agricultural operations.
- ❑ Even though, labour is available in adequate number, they may not be skilled enough to perform technical operations.
- ❑ Even though, skilled labour are available, farm operations may not be taken up because of floods or drought in that locality.

☆ ***Capital uncertainty:***

- ❑ Capital or credit may not be available to the farmer in right time.
- ❑ Capital or credit may not be available to farmer in adequate output.
- ❑ Capital or credit may not be available to the farmer at an affordable rate of interest.

☆ ***Yield uncertainty:***

- ❑ Very high or very low rainfall and other non-congenial climatic factors may affect the yield of the crop.
- ❑ Pest and disease incidences may affect the crop growth and hence, the yield.

☆ ***Technological uncertainty:***

- ❑ Technology available to the farmer may not be suitable to his farming situation.
- ❑ Technology available to farmer may be too costlier and hence, the farmer cannot afford.
- ❑ Technology available to the farmer may be too complicated to understand and implement by the farmer.

☆ ***Price uncertainty:***

- ❑ Input prices may rise in the economy.
- ❑ Output prices may fall in the market.
- ❑ More of imports into the country may affect the prices of the domestically produced goods.
- ❑ Quality of produce may not match the international standards and hence, it will fetch low price in the international market.
- ❑ Prices of the commodity may fall due to changes in tastes, habits, incomes of the individuals *etc.*

Two theories have been developed by the economists to deal with two imperfect knowledge situations *i.e.*, risk and uncertainty in the farm business *viz.*, Game theory with regard to risk (*i.e.*, to deal with the problems of choice with known probabilities for the given situation) and Decision theory with regard to uncertainty (*i.e.*, to deal with the problems of choice in the absence of probability data for the given situation).

i. Game Theory

Strategic behaviour of firms in oligopoly competition can be analyzed by using the mathematical techniques of Game theory. This theory provides a description of oligopolistic behavior as a series of strategic moves and countermoves. This theory was developed by John Von Neumann and Oskar Morgenstern. This theory explains that, 'cooperation' rather than 'competition' between the firms can lead to a better outcome that is beneficial to both the firms in the oligopoly competition. So, this theory helps to explain mutual interdependence among the firms in the oligopolistic industry. Thus, the concept of game theory is used to analyze the behavior of the firms, who try for optimal position in the business through the use of strategic behavior, being fully aware of their mutual interdependence with the other players in the game and attempting to anticipate the decisions of those other players. In this theory, every sum of gain of one is the loss of the other and such a situation is called as two person - zero sum game. Let us look at the following examples:

Example 8.1

For example, there are only two farmers A and B involved in cultivation of crop X (duopoly situation) and suppose that, Farmer A decides to go for adoption of modern technology in production. The decision of Farmer A not only influences the profits of Farmer A, but also affects the profits of his competitive Farmer B. Now, competing Farmer B will take a counter action and he also goes for adoption of modern technology in production, which influences his profits and also affects the profits of Farmer A. Much like a game of chess, each farmer plan his moves and countermoves the strategies based on the actions or anticipated actions of competitor. Let us assume that, each farmer spends Rs.500 on their respective technology adoption. The benefits realized by each farmer in adoption of technology depend upon the actions of other farmer. The possible outcomes of this game (profits due to adoption of technology or without adoption of technology) between the two farmers in terms of adoption of technology campaign are shown through the Figure 8.3. It is evident that,

		Farmer A	
		Adoption of Technology	No Adoption of Technology
Farmer B	Adoption of Technology	I Farmer A (2500) Farmer B (2500)	II Farmer A (1500) Farmer B (4000)
	No Adoption of Technology	III Farmer A (4000) Farmer B (1500)	IV Farmer A (3000) Farmer B (3000)

Figure 8.3: Game Theory Solution for Adoption of Modern Technology by Farmers.

- ☆ *Case 1:* The lower right square (Square IV) indicates that, if neither Farmer A nor Farmer B decides to adopt the modern production technology, then each farmer receives Rs. 3000 profit. The top rectangular part in the Square IV represents the profits Rs. 3000 of Farmer A and the bottom rectangular part in the Square IV represents the profits Rs.3000 of Farmer B. So, the total profit in this case is Rs. 6000, divided evenly between the two farmers, when both farmers do not go for adoption of modern technology.
- ☆ *Case 2:* As shown through top left hand corner Square Box I, if both the farmers A and B go for adoption of technology by spending Rs.500 each, then each farmer gets Rs.2500 profit. So, the adoption of technology by each farmer effectively cancels out the profits realized by the other farmer. So, neither gains greater profits or market share, but both end up reducing profit by Rs.500 each (compared to Square Box IV). The top rectangular part in the Square Box I, represent the profits Rs.2500 of Farmer A and the bottom rectangular part in the Square Box I represent the profits Rs. 2500 of Farmer B. So, the total profit in this case is Rs.5000, divided evenly between the two farmers. That means, there is a decline in total profits of Rs.1000, when both the farmers go for adoption of technology (compared to Square Box IV), which is the total amount spent for adoption of modern technology by both the farmers.

- ✰ *Case 3:* Say, if only Farmer A adopts the modern technology, but Farmer B does not (Square Box III), then Farmer A receives Rs. 4000 profit and Farmer B receives only Rs. 1500 profit. So, Farmer A gets higher profits and Farmer B has a big drop in profits because, the adoption of modern technology by Farmer A increases the profits of Farmer A away from Farmer B. The total profit in this case is Rs.5500, which reflects the significant positive impact of Rs.500 spent in technology adoption of Farmer A.
- ✰ *Case 4:* The situation is exactly reversed, if Farmer B adopts modern technology, but Farmer A does not (Square Box II). In this case, Farmer B receives Rs. 4000 profit and Farmer B receives only Rs.1500 profit. So, Farmer B gets higher profits and Farmer A has a big drop in profits because, the adoption of technology by Farmer B increases the profits of Farmer B away from Farmer A. The total profit of both the farmers for this case is Rs.5500, which reflects the significant positive impact of Rs.500 used in technology adoption by Farmer B.

Considering the above possible cases, it is interesting to know, whether Farmer A goes for adoption of modern technology or not. What actions Farmer B might take considering the incremental income due to its adoption and possible impact, if Farmer A also goes for adoption. So, to ascertain the most profitable outcome, let us examine the following options:

- ✰ If neither farmer adopts, then total profit of both the farmers is Rs.6000 as shown in Square Box IV. If the two farmers had a mutual understanding and cooperative or collusive arrangement, then both the farmers opt not to go for adoption of technology, as this outcome maximizes the total profits (Rs. 6000) than any other option. So, each farmer can equally share the total profit. So, each avoids the Rs.500 of adoption of modern technology expenses and ends up with Rs.3000 profit. So, both the farmers are benefitted, if neither adopts modern technology.
- ✰ If both the farmers do not have a collusive arrangement, Farmer A must select the adoption strategy, which is not known to the Farmer B and the outcome selected by the Farmer A must be best for Farmer A irrespective of the decision taken by the Farmer B. Similarly, Farmer B must select the adoption strategy, which is not known to the Farmer A and the outcome selected by the Farmer B must be best for Farmer B irrespective of the decision taken by the Farmer A.

So, if both the farmers do not have collusive arrangements, then we have to ascertain the options of Farmer A and Farmer B separately considering their game in the field of adoption of modern technology, as shown through the Figure 8.3. So, based on the relative outcomes, we can decide, what Farmer A has to adopt or not to adopt and similarly, what Farmer B has to adopt or not to adopt.

Possible Options Faced by Farmer A

The following are the options faced by the Farmer A, so as to maximize his profits in the production:

- ✰ ***Option 1-Farmer B decides to adopt the modern technology:*** Then, we have two possible options for Farmer A.
- ✰ If Farmer A also adopts, then his profit is Rs. 2500 (Square Box I).
- ✰ If Farmer A does not adopt, then his profits is only Rs.1500 (Square Box II).

So, if Farmer B adopts, then it is wise or better on the part of Farmer A to adopt the modern technology, as it can earn an extra Rs.1000 profits compared to non-adoption of technology.

- ✰ ***Option 2-Farmer B decides not to adopt the modern technology:*** Then, we have two possible options for Farmer A.
- ✰ If Farmer A also does not adopt, then his profit are only Rs. 3000 (Square Box IV).
- ✰ If Farmer A adopts, then his profit is Rs. 4000 (Square Box III).

So, if Farmer B does not adopt, then it is wise or better on the part of Farmer A to adopt the modern technology, as it can earn an extra Rs.1000 profits compared to non-adoption of technology.

So, from the above two options, we can infer that, the best choice for Farmer A is, therefore, to adopt modern technology in production, regardless of the choice made by Farmer B. That means, if either Farmer B goes for adoption of technology or does not adopt technology, Farmer A definitely gets an extra profit of Rs. 1000, if Farmer A adopts the technology.

Possible Options Faced by Farmer B

The following are the options faced by the Farmer B, so as to maximize his profits in production:

- ✰ ***Option 1-Farmer A decides to adopt modern technology:*** Then, we have two possible options for Farmer B.
- ✰ If Farmer B also adopts, then his profit is Rs. 2500 (Square Box I).
- ✰ If Farmer B does not adopt, then his profit is only Rs. 1500 (Square Box III).

So, if Farmer A adopts, then it is wise or better on the part of Farmer B to adopt modern technology, as it can earn an extra Rs. 1000 profits compared to non-adoption of technology.

- ✰ ***Option 2-Farmer A decides not to adopt the modern technology:*** Then, we have two possible options for Farmer B.
- ✰ If Farmer B also does not adopt, then his profit is only Rs.3000 (Square Box IV).
- ✰ If Farmer B adopts, then his profit is Rs.4000 (Square Box II).

So, if Farmer A does not adopt, then it is wise or better on the part of Farmer B to adopt modern technology, as it can earn an extra Rs. 1000 profits compared to non-adoption of technology.

So, from the above two options, we can infer that, the best choice for Farmer B is, therefore, to adopt modern technology in production, regardless of the choice made by Farmer A. That means, if either Farmer A goes for adoption of technology or does not adopt technology; Farmer B definitely gets an extra profit of Rs.1000, if Farmer B adopts the technology.

So, the end result is that, if the two farmers are competitive, then it is better for both the farmers to decide to go for adoption of modern technology in their respective production programmes. In doing so, they end up with less profit (Rs.2500 each in Square Box I), than if they had colluded and jointly decided not to adopt the technology (Rs. 3000 each in Square Box IV). This infers that, game theory illustrates the key problem of interdependent decision-making feature between two farmers or in oligopoly form of market competition. However, in practical situation, things are not so simple, as more number of farmers may enter the competition and several other factors may also influence the decision making of a farmer. However, the concept explained above illustrates the general principle of Game theory.

Example 8.2: Let us go through the following Figure 8.4:

Case 1: If both the farmers do not modernize the cold storage structures, neither would get any profit over the normal profit (Square Box I).

Case 2: If farmer A modernizes and farmer B does not, farmer A will gain by Rs.50,000 over farmer B and farmer B loses Rs.50,000 (Square Box III).

		Farmer B	
		Do not modernize	Modernize
Farmer A	Do not modernize	I Farmer A (0) Farmer B (0)	II Farmer A (-25000) Farmer B (25000)
	Modernize	III Farmer A (50000) Farmer B (-50000)	IV Farmer A (10000) Farmer B (-10000)

Figure 8.4: Game Theory Solution for Modernization of Cold Storage Structures by Farmers.

Case 3: If farmer B modernizes and farmer A does not, farmer B will gain by Rs.25,000 over farmer A and farmer A loses Rs.25,000 (Square Box II).

Case 4: If both farmer A and farmer B modernizes, farmer A gain by Rs.10,000 over farmer B and farmer B loses by Rs.10,000, because of better technical know-how of farmer A (Square Box IV).

Now, considering these situations, now both farmer A and farmer B will go for modernization of cold storages as:

- ☆ If farmer A alone modernizes, farmer B suffers a huge loss of Rs.50,000.
- ☆ If farmer B alone modernizes, farmer A suffers a loss of Rs.25,000.

So, to avoid greater losses is not going for modernization for any one of the two farmers, both farmers will go for modernization as by doing so, farmer B suffers only a meager loss of Rs.10,000. That is, both the farmers are interested in minimization of maximum losses *i.e.,* aim at least-worst outcome. So, in Game theory, every percentage point gain of one farmer is automatically the loss of other. The total gain of both the farmers in modernization of cold storages is zero and hence, this game theory is also called as Zero-sum game.

ii. Decision Theory

Unlike in Game theory, there is no opponent for a farmer and the second competitor considered here is the 'nature' that influences the outcome. That is, the outcome of an event (say, crop production) is influenced by the nature and the farmer has to ascertain the probability of occurring an event (say, floods or drought or pest incidence etc). Let us look at the following example:

Example 8.3

A processing firm came to know that, there is declined production for product 'X' in the country. Considering the business prospects of the product X, both during slump and boom periods, he wishes to change the price of the product in the market. Based on the probability, he estimated that, there is chance of slump in prices at 60 per cent chance and only 40 per cent chance is there to get boom in prices for product X. If he leave the price alone during slump period, he would get a profit of Rs.1500 and if he increase the price, he would get a loss of Rs.1000. On the other hand, if he leaves the price alone during the bumper period, he would gain by Rs.1700 and if he increases the price, he would get a profit of Rs.10,000. Let as look at the following Table 8.4:

Table 8.4: Decision Chart for Deciding the Price of Product X

Decision taken by the Farmer	*Slump Period (P=0.6)*	*Boom Period (P=0.40)*
Leave the price alone	Rs. 1500	Rs. 1700
Increase the price	(-Rs. 1000)	Rs. 10,000

The expected gain of the outcome, as per the decision taken by the farmer is given by the formula:

$$E(\pi) = \sum_{t=1}^{n} P_t V_t$$

$$E(\pi) = P_1V_1 + P_2V_2 + P_3V_3 + \text{———} + P_nV_n$$

For the above example:

Leaves the price alone: E(π) = [(0.6)(1500)] + [(0.4)(1700)] = Rs.1580.

Increase the price: E(π) = [(0.6)(-1000] + [(0.4)(10000)] = Rs.3400

So, considering the above expected gains, it is better for the farmer to increase the price of product X.

The above discussion infers that, in Game theory, optimum strategy is derived between two competing farmers in oligopoly competition, in which one farmer wins exactly, what the other farmer loses. However, in Decision theory, the farmer will select the best course of action with the information available in terms of probability. Such a probability is also known as Binomial law (Dhondyal)

III. Decision-making in a Risky Environment

Risks can be idiosyncratic–affecting only individual farm (for example, illness of the farmer, soil salinity, pest incidence on a crop etc) or covariate–affecting many farms simultaneously (for example, droughts, floods, fluctuating market prices, epidemic diseases). Irrespective of the type of risk, it is a known fact that, making decisions would be easy, if we knew what the outcome was going to be. Look at the following probable statements:

- 'If I'd known this was going to happen, I never would have done it'.
- 'If I'd known that, paddy price was going to drop by Rs.10/quintal, I would have sold last week'.
- 'If I'd known that cotton prices were going that high, I'd have cultivated cotton'.

The above statements imply that, if the farmer is known about the possible consequences in the future, he would have made correct decisions. But, it is fact in farm business, the probable consequences of a decision are generally not known, when the decision is made. Nonetheless, decisions must be made and actions taken (taking no action is also a decision). As discussed earlier in imperfect knowledge situation, the terms risk and uncertainty are used interchangeably. To address both risks and uncertainties, the farmer must make right decisions in his production programme. Of course, decision making environment also involves attitudes toward risk or uncertainty, ability to bear them and formation of expectations about the future. This decision making process is a complex one and farmers differ both in how they make decisions and in the decisions they make. Accordingly, there are five types of individuals in the following risk-taking categories:

- ***Risk Avoiders or Averters:*** These individuals are most cautious in taking risks in farm business and they do take some risks. They expect the worst to happen and will not take the slightest chance that they can avoid. They lose because, they miss economic opportunities to profit, but they just manage to survive in the farm business. That is, these individuals will sacrifice some level of expected return in order to reduce the possibility of a loss. A person, who is considered risk averse likely will also have a low risk bearing ability. Their situation would be such that a large income loss would seriously disrupt or end the business.

- ☆ ***Daredevils:*** These individuals are exactly opposite to the Avoiders and take many unnecessary chances. Daredevils simply go ahead in taking risks without collecting any facts or probabilities of occurring an event. So, such type of farmers commonly fail because, they refuse to take precautions.
- ☆ ***Risk preferrers or Adventurers:*** These are the individuals, who enjoy taking risks. They look at the risky event and take it as a challenging one to address it. That is, they look for the chance to take risks. Many farmers and speculators fall in this category with respect to both production and marketing plans. They continue to accept the risks, as long as the farm business is financially viable. They are totally vigilant about the external environment and its influences on the farm business. So, risk preferring individuals are characterized as more adventuresome with a preference for more risky business ventures.
- ☆ ***Calculators:*** These individuals are highly calculative in taking risks in the farm business. Before making a decision or taking action, they gather information or data to analyze the possible outcome of an unknown event. So, they measure or quantify the risk to a realistic level and try to reduce risk to an acceptable level. Most farmers are Calculators, at least in the majority of their decisions.
- ☆ ***Risk Neutral:*** The risk neutral person is the limiting case between the risk averse and risk preferring individuals. This person will select the alternative with the highest expected outcome, regardless of the probabilities associated with potential gains or losses. This person will have acceptable levels of risk bearing ability such that large losses are not of concern but at the same time, achieving the highest outcome is not the focus either. The primary concern is to achieve a sustainable outcome over time.

Note that, these risk attitudes will change over time as goals, financial resources and a farm manager's experience change over time. Along with these variables, the probability and size of a gain or loss will also effect the farm manager's risk attitude. Understanding risk in farming is important for several reasons. First, most farmers are averse to risk when faced with risky outcomes. Someone, who is risk averse is willing to accept a lower average return for lower uncertainty, with the tradeoff depending on the person's level of risk aversion. Thus, strategies cannot be evaluated solely in terms of average or expected return, but also must consider risk. Second, understanding risk helps farmers and others develop strategies for mitigating the possibility of adverse events, and aids in circumventing extreme outcomes, such as bankruptcy.

IV. Information Useful for Decision Making

Since the farmer enjoys poor knowledge regarding the occurrence of risk or uncertainty situation, 'good information' serves as an useful asset to the farmer to mitigate it. There are many sources of information available to the farmer to mitigate the risk (depending upon the type of risk the farmer faces) and they are discussed here under.

i. Farm Records

These records serve as the best source of historical information about the farm. The data available in these records can be thoroughly revised and analyze to draw useful trends about the past performance of the business and thereby, future outcome can be predicted and accordingly decision-making can be initiated. For example, analysis of the past data pertaining to the crop acreages, yields, livestock production, rainfall, occurrence of pests and diseases, droughts, floods, cost information, inputs and outputs prices *etc.*, reflect the production capabilities of the farm (Tables 8.5 and 8.6). The farmer can plan the managerial strategies to both production and marketing aspects of the farm-business.

Table 8.5: Comparative Analysis of per cent Variation in COP and Prices of Major Food Grains in Kurnool District of Andhra Pradesh during Pre and Post-WTO Regimes

Commodity	*Period*	*COP*	*MSP*	*DMP*
Rice	1985-94	–	–	102.19
	1995-04#	–	–	61.65
Paddy	1985-94	–	139.44	–
	1995-04	109.38	55.56	–
Wheat	1985-94	–	122.22	136.36
	1995-04	162.33	68.42	86.49
Maize	1985-94	–	123.08	159.26
	1995-04	91.04	69.35	44.87
Sorghum	1985-94	–	115.38	93.33
	1995-04	114.79	71.67	33.75
Red gram	1985-94	–	153.33	97.92
	1995-04	103.92	73.75	73.33
Gram	1985-94	–	157.69	166.13
	1995-04	100.62	103.57	50.00

Note : #: Period after WTO; *: Data not available.

Raw Data Source: Data collected from Department of Agriculture, Kurnool district and Off-Farm Records <www.agricoop.nic.in>

Table 8.6: Comparative Analysis of CGR of COP and Prices of Selected Food Grains in Kurnool District of Andhra Pradesh during Pre and Post-WTO Regimes

Commodity	*Period*	*COP*	*MSP*	*DMP*
Rice	1985-94	–	–	9.24**
	1995-04#	–	–	4.71**
Paddy	1985-94	–	10.92**	–
	1995-04	8.39**	5.44**	–
Wheat	1985-94	–	10.92**	11.69**
	1995-04	12.98**	6.41**	5.68**
Maize	1985-94	–	10.41**	8.64**
	1995-04	6.66**	6.41**	3.51*
Sorghum	1985-94	–	9.90**	3.99NS
	1995-04	9.90**	6.66**	2.56NS
Red gram	1985-94	–	11.94**	5.93**
	1995-04	9.65**	7.15**	3.28NS
Gram	1985-94	–	12.46**	8.89**
	1995-04	8.89**	8.64**	6.41**

Note: #: Period after WTO; '–': Data not available; **: Significant at 1 per cent level; *: Significant at 5 per cent level and NS: Non-significant

Raw Data Source: Data collected from Department of Agriculture, Kurnool district and Off-Farm Records <www.agricoop.nic.in>

Beyond the above analytical information, farm records of an individual farm will also provide information about the risks faced by the business in the past like:

- Is the farm was frequently affected by drought?
- Is the farm was frequently affected by a pest say, boll worm?
- Which crops recorded the worst performance on the farm?
- Would a change in cultural practices, tillage systems or operation timing or adoption modern technology contributed to higher yields?
- Are crops always sold immediately after harvest and at profitable prices?

For these questions, the records must provide answers to mitigate these risks. The analysis should preferably provide new answers, if past decisions have not resulted in fruitful results against the risks. The records should also indicate, how successful past risk management efforts have been. Combining these historical results with the farmer's risk preferences should point out what, if any, changes in risk management should be made in the future. Of course, not all information can be generated from farm records regarding human, legal and social risks. In such case, the farmer has to refer Off-farm sources.

ii. Off-Farm Information

Information from other than farm sources should be obtained to address human, legal and social risks. These sources includes: reports, bulletins, newsletters, journals, magazines, input suppliers and other stakeholders, as they all can provide useful information to the farmer. The data generated from the sources can be used in a compatible way with the data generated from farm records. The use of these compatible sources also facilitates the farmer to know about the extent of risk in that area. For example, if the yield variability data of a crop recorded at the farmer level showed higher variation than in that district, then this is the usual situation. This is so because, as the geographic base of observations is enlarged, the variation is decreased. As it is made smaller at the farm level, the variation is increased. This is true simply because, the larger number of observations tend to even out results. Again, this emphasizes the importance of individual farm information to the management of risk for the farm business.

iii. Primary Sources

In addition to the above two sources of data or information for ascertaining various risks or uncertainties and for planning the strategies to address the same, the primary sources of information also contribute effectively. For example, the farmer can use the current market news data, quality standards, current demand for the product in the market *etc.*, for planning the sale of output. Besides marketing risk, these primary sources can be used to identify and mitigate technological, human, social and legal risks like environmental legislation, resource conservation, food safety, water quality, animal welfare, Governmental programmes and policies *etc.* Note that, the major difference between information pertaining to production and marketing risks as opposed to technical, human, social and legal risks is that, the latter is qualitative in nature. That is, the farmer can get 'hard numbers' to quantify yield and price, but the same cannot be said of the other risks.

V. Measures to Overcome Risk and Uncertainty

For an individual farmer, risk management involves finding the preferred combination of activities with uncertain outcomes and varying levels of expected returns (Harwood *et. al.*). From this point of view, risk management can be defined as choosing among alternatives for reducing the effects of risk on the farm, which in turn effects the farm's welfare position. Risk management cannot be viewed as a *'one size fits all'* action. Several key decision-making criteria that play into the risk management planning process include the goals established for the operation, the risk bearing ability of the farm and the manager's attitude towards risk. Each one of these items will be different for individual family members and each farm unit. The following are the different strategies followed by the farmer to overcome risks and uncertainties in farm business:

i. Crop Diversification

It refers to practicing more than one enterprise by the farmer in the farm business such that, no single enterprise contribute more than 50 per cent of annual net income.

The main objective of crop diversification is to stabilize the annual net income of the farmer. In case of crop diversification, if one enterprise fails, the farmer gets income from other enterprises so that, he can meet the farm family expenses and can overcome the production risk in practicing enterprises. The extent of farm diversification can be measured by using an Entropy index, which accounts for both the mix of commodities and the relative importance of each commodity (measured by its estimated value) to farm businesses (Jinkins). The entropy index ranges from 0 to 100. If the value of the index is 0, it implies complete farm specialization and a value of 100 implies a completely diversified farm with equal shares of each commodity. Many factors influence the farmers to go for crop diversification *viz.*, if they confront greater risks in farming, are relatively risk averse and face small reductions in expected returns in response to diversification. However, before diversifying the business, the farmer must note that, whether the costs of diversifying may outweigh the benefits and in such case specializing may be the preferred strategy. This is because, diversifying often requires specialized equipment and machinery, demands more capital from the farmer, the farmer may be limited by managerial expertise, labour, productive capacity of the land and the market potential in the surrounding area (Dodson). Further, diversifying requires a broader range of management expertise than does producing only one commodity, and does not typically allow for intensive management. As technologies become more complicated, such intensive management and greater farm specialization may well be increasingly important (Beneke).

ii. Flexibility

The farm plan prepared should be more flexible. That means, it should incorporate all kinds of crops such as irrigated, irrigated-dry and dry land crops. At times of adverse situations, it is easier on the part of farmer to select and adopt the best suited alternate farm plan to overcome production risks in the farm business. Further, in performing farm operations, farmers should attempt to maintain flexibility as a production response to variability. For example, increasing specialization of livestock facilities and equipment limits flexibility among types of livestock, and often there is a similar situation with respect to crops. Thus, farmers should maintain flexibility in planning acreage under crops, enterprises selection, varying output levels and provision of requisite facilities for farm production suiting to the dynamic changes in business environment.

iii. Liquidity

Instead of investing entire capital in the farm business, the farmer should maintain a significant amount of liquid cash with him. This is because, if the enterprise fails in the mid-course of its execution say, due to natural calamities or pest infestation, the liquid cash available with the farmer is sufficient to meet the family living expenses. This is important because, we generally prefer present consumption over future consumption. So, having financial reserves to provide liquidity is another financial strategy for dealing with variability. This liquidity also serves as a current asset on the farmer's balance sheet. Maintaining reserve in the form of stored grain also provide liquidity to the farmer. If an unexpected event occurs, the grain can be sold and the proceeds will be used. So, a bin of grain is better than no reserve, but the grain reserve does have some risks associated with it. If the price of grain goes down, it reduces the value of the reserve and further, stored grain earns no interest and the grain could go out of condition. So, it is essential on the part of the farmer to maintain financial reserves in the form of bank accounts, mutual funds, stocks, bonds, and other financial assets for bad times. Some farmers invest the financial reserves on non-farm activities and if these activities offer high returns, the non-farm investments can serve as financial reserves.

iv. Selecting the Enterprises that are Less Prone to Risk

The farmer should select the enterprises in his farm that are less susceptible to risk conditions. For example, the farmer has to select jowar, bajra *etc.*, in dry land areas, as they are drought resistant crops. In general, the farmer should follow the principle of comparative advantage, as this principle guides the farmer to go for regional specialization of crops and enterprises that enjoy comparative advantage in terms of output, prices, cost structure, market outlets *etc.* Moreover, farmer has to select those crops for which output or returns or prices show less amount of coefficient of variation in that locality.

v. Crop Insurance

Not all risks can be controlled or protected by traditional insurance. Price risk is one such risk. We already know, price changes of both inputs and output can have a dramatic impact on farm-business. However, insurance serves as one of the best compensation measure to overcome production risks. Most farmers use various forms of insurance to protect against specific types of losses. Crop insurance provides liquidity to replace losses due to natural calamities like floods, drought *etc.* Fire insurance provides liquidity to replace losses due to fire. Thus, the idea of insurance is to buy protection against a loss.

vi. Capital Rationing

Capital rationing refers to the allocation of capital by the farmer to the enterprise or enterprise combinations. If the farmer takes up only one enterprise, he will allocate the capital in proportion to meet the TCOC of the enterprise. If the farmer wants to take up more number of enterprises, he will go on allocating the capital among the enterprises as long as MVP_X derived is greater than MFC (of adding capital) and the point of optimality is MVP_X = MFC of capital. So, by going for capital rationing in advance, the farmer can also plan his credit requirements.

vii. Scientific Management Practices

By proper scientific managerial practices like selection of good quality seed, seed treatment, deep tillage, IPM, INM, IWRM *etc.*, these will enable the farmer to overcome production risks in farm business.

viii. Market Finance

Market finance is the finance given by the banking institutions to the farmers to overcome distress sales of produce. By taking market finance, the farmer can stock the produce when the prices are low in the market. As and when the prices rise in the market, the farmer destock and sell the produce and repay the market finance. So market finance help the farmer to overcome price risk.

ix. MSP

MSP is the price guarantee given to the farmer by the Government to overcome price risk. If price of the commodity falls below the MSP, then the Government will come forward and purchase the commodity at the announced MSP.

x. Making Forward Contracts or Futures Trade

By making the futures contracts with the prospective buyers the farmers can overcome price risk in the agri-business. The players in the futures market broadly fall into three categories *viz.*, hedgers, speculators and arbitragers depending on their attitude towards risk. In this book, let us limit our discussion to hedgers, as their main objective in practicing futures trade is to overcome price risk of commodities. Farmers, processors, importers and exporters can all be hedgers in the futures market. Hedger is a user of the futures market, who enters into futures contract to protect himself from the risk of adverse price fluctuations in respect of his existing or future product. A hedger buys/sells in the futures market to secure the future price of a commodity intended to sell/buy at a later date in the cash market. This helps the hedger to get protection from price risks. They require some people, who are prepared to accept the risk called, speculators. This process of purchase/sale of commodity in the futures market accompanied by sale/purchase of the commodity in the cash market is called Hedging. Hedging is mainly based on two assumptions:

- ☆ The purchase/sale of the commodity should be accompanied by sale/purchase of the same commodity (simultaneous transactions) and in same quantity, but in different markets (Future and Cash markets).
- ☆ Prices in both the markets (*i.e.*, Future and Cash markets) move exactly parallel *i.e.*, move up and down together so that, the loss arise in one market is offset by gain in the other market.

Thus, in hedging, the activities of buying and selling are always in opposite direction and more over, the nature and quantity of product purchased in both the markets are equal (Panels A and B of Figure 8.5). So, hedging is the practice for offsetting the price risk inherent in any cash/future market by taking an equal but opposite position in the futures/cash market. By this mechanism, the traders transfer their price risk. As the two prices both in cash and futures markets move in tandem/together, it enables the traders in the futures/cash markets to cover their price risk by taking opposite position in the cash/futures market. So, hedging is the process of protecting or safeguarding one self against the price risk in the future *i.e.*, protection against low prices for seller in the future and protection against high prices for buyer in the future. This hedging mechanism is explained through Figures 8.5 and 8.6.

Example 8.4

Assume that, on 1st June, 2012, a farmer (Ravi) wants to sell his commodity X (100 quintals) to a wholesaler (Sri Ram) at Rs. 7000/qtl (Figure 8.5) after considering its average total cost of production. But, he knows that, there is no price guarantee for

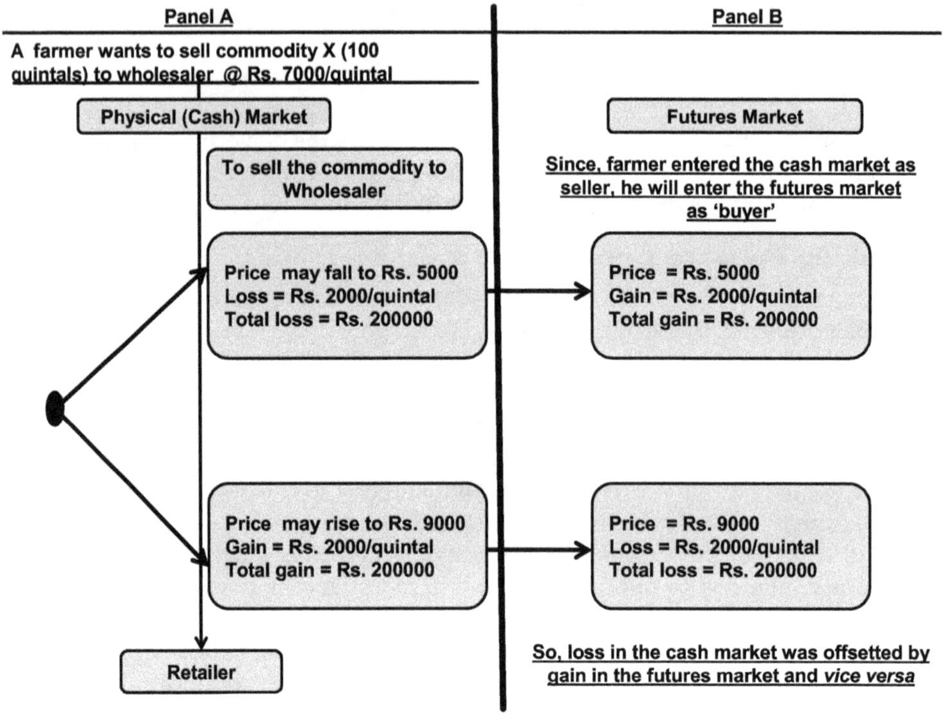

Figure 8.5: A Simple Example for Hedging Mechanism.

him, because of frequent price fluctuations in the market economy. To overcome price risk, the farmer goes for hedging mechanism in the futures market and locked the futures price with reference to 10th June, 2012 at Rs. 7000/qtl.

Case 1: Case of Price Decrease

Say, for example, in the cash market, on 5th June, 2012 the price of the commodity X is declined to Rs. 5000/qtl. So, the farmer feels that, if he waits further *i.e.,* beyond 5th June, 2012, the price may still fall and in view of this, he decides to sell the commodity in the cash market at Rs. 5000/qtl. So, he incurs a loss in the cash market to the tune of Rs. 2000/qtl (price willing to sell (Rs. 7000/qtl) – price at which commodity actually sold (Rs. 5000/qtl)) and a total loss of Rs. 200000.

However, in the futures market, the farmer gains by Rs. 2000/qtl *i.e.,* a total gain of Rs. 200000. This is because, since the farmer entered the cash market as seller, he has to enter the futures market as a buyer and so, as a buyer, he will purchase the same commodity X and in same quantity at Rs. 5000/qtl in the futures market. So, the gain is Rs. 2000/qtl (futures price locked (Rs. 7000/qtl) - price at which commodity purchased in futures market (Rs. 5000/qtl)) *i.e.,* a total gain of Rs. 200000. It is essential to note that, prices of a commodity both in cash and futures markets move in tandem *i.e.,* in the same direction with strong positive correlation. So, the loss in cash market (- Rs. 2000/qtl) is offsetted by the gain in the futures market (+ Rs. 2000/qtl) and hence, the farmer has successfully mitigated the price risk. It is also to be noted that, the entry into the cash market (as seller) on 5th June, 2012 is simultaneous with the entry in the futures market (as buyer *i.e.,* on 5th June, 2012). Further, this hedging mechanism is done only to overcome the price risk and not with the intention of gaining profits. Hence, the position of farmer on 5th June, 2012 is same as his position on 1st June, 2012.

Case 2: Case of Price Increase

Say, for example, in the cash market, on 5th June, 2012 the price of the commodity X is increased to Rs. 9000/qtl. So, it is felt appropriate by the farmer to sell away the commodity in the cash market, as he presume that, it is the maximum possible price for that commodity and beyond that date, the prices may fall. So, he decides to sell the commodity in the cash market on 5th June, 2012 in the cash market at Rs. 9000/qtl and gain Rs. 2000/qtl (price at which commodity actually sold (Rs. 9000/qtl) - price willing to sell (Rs. 7000/qtl)) and a total gain of Rs. 200000.

However, in the futures market, the farmer experiences loss by Rs. 2000/qtl *i.e.,* a total loss of Rs. 200000. This is because, since the farmer entered the cash market as seller, he has to enter the futures market as a buyer and so, as a buyer, he will purchase the same commodity X and in same quantity at Rs. 9000/qtl in the futures market. So, the loss is Rs. 2000/qtl (price at which commodity purchased in futures market (Rs. 9000/qtl) - futures price locked (Rs. 7000/qtl)) *i.e.,* a total loss of Rs. 200000. So, the gain in the cash market is offsetted by the loss in the futures market and this is nothing but, hedging mechanism.

Example 8.5

Assume that, a wholesale trader (Sri Ram) purchased commodity X (100 quintals) from farmers and he wishes to sell the same to a processor (Ravi) at Rs. 30500/tonne on 1st January, 2012 (Figure 8.6). But, the wholesaler knows that, there is no price guarantee for him, because of frequent price fluctuations in the market economy. To overcome price risk, the wholesaler goes for hedging mechanism in the futures market and locked the futures price with reference to 10th January, 2012 at Rs. 30500/tonne.

Case 1: Case of Price Decrease

Say, for example, in the cash market, on 5th January, 2012 the price of the commodity X is declined to Rs. 29500/tonne. So, the wholesaler feels that, if he waits further *i.e.,* beyond 5th January, 2012, the prices may still fall and in view of this, he decides to sell the commodity in the cash market at Rs. 29500/tonne. So, he incurs a loss in the cash market to the tune of Rs. 1000/tonne (price willing to sell (Rs. 30500/tonne) – price at which commodity actually sold (Rs. 29500/tonne) and a total loss of Rs. 100000.

However, in the futures market, the wholesaler gains by Rs. 1000/tonne *i.e.,* a total gain of Rs. 100000. This is because, since the wholesaler entered the cash market as seller, he has to enter the futures market as a buyer and so, as a buyer, he will purchase the same commodity X and in same quantity at Rs. 29500/tonne in the futures market. So, the gain is Rs. 1000/tonne (futures price locked (Rs. 30500/tonne) - price at which commodity purchased in futures market (Rs. 29500/tonne)) *i.e.,* a

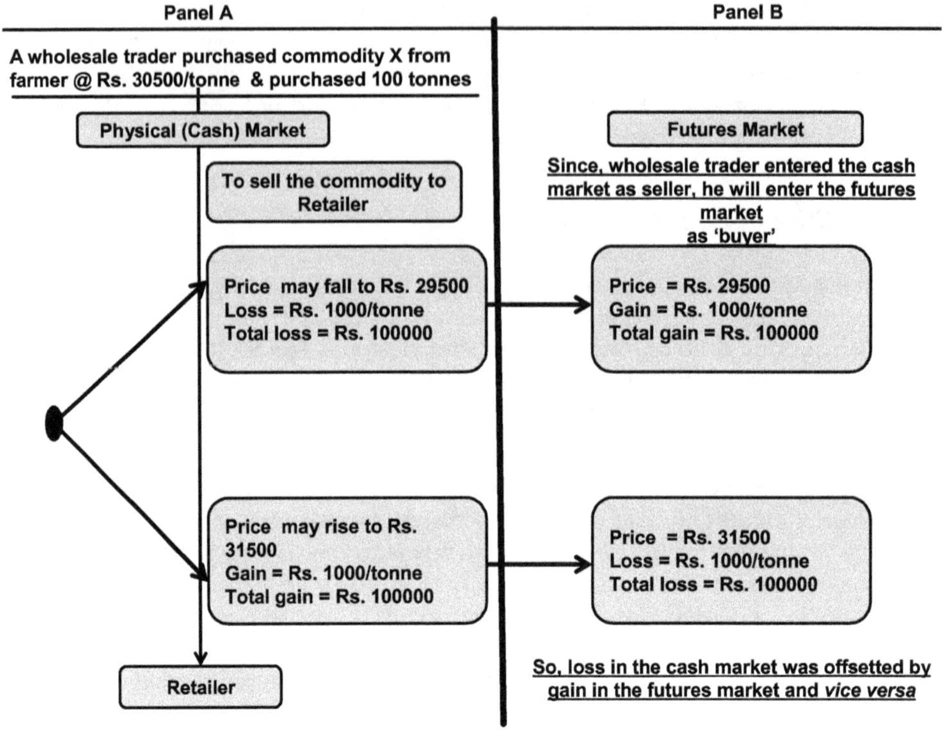

Figure 8.6: A Simple Example for Hedging Mechanism.

total gain of Rs. 100000. Since prices of a commodity both in cash and futures markets move in tandem *i.e.*, in the same direction with strong positive correlation, the loss in cash market (- Rs. 1000/tonne) is offsetted by the gain in the futures market (+ Rs. 1000/tonne) and hence, the wholesaler has successfully mitigated the price risk. It is also to be noted that, the entry into the cash market (as seller) on 5th January, 2012 is simultaneous with the entry in the futures market (as buyer *i.e.*, on 5th January, 2012). Further, this hedging mechanism is done only to overcome the price risk and not to with the intention of gaining profits. Hence, the position of wholesaler on 5th January, 2012 is same as his position on 1st January, 2012.

Case 2: Case of Price Increase

Say, for example, in the cash market, on 5th January, 2012 the price of the commodity is X increased to Rs. 31500/tonne. So, it is felt appropriate by the wholesaler to sell away the commodity in the cash market, as he presume that, it is the maximum possible price for that commodity and beyond that date, the prices may fall. So, he decides to sell the commodity in the cash market on 5th January, 2012 in the cash market at Rs. 30500/tonne and gain Rs. 1000/tonne (price at which commodity actually sold Rs. 31500/tonne - price willing to sell (Rs. 305000/tonne)) and a total gain of Rs. 100000.

However, in the futures market, the wholesaler experience loss by Rs. 1000/tonne *i.e.,* a total loss of Rs. 100000. This is because, since the wholesaler entered the cash market as seller, he has to enter the futures market as a buyer and so, as a buyer, he will purchase the same commodity X and in same quantity at Rs. 31500/tonne in the futures market. So, the loss is Rs. 1000/tonne (price at which commodity purchased in futures market (Rs. 31500/tonne) - futures price locked (Rs. 30500/tonne)) *i.e.,* a total loss of Rs. 100000. So, the gain in the cash market is offsetted by the loss in the futures market and this is nothing but, hedging mechanism.

xi. Strategic Buying and Selling

Strategic buying of inputs and selling of output can reduce the effects of marketing risk on farm profitability. Purchasing inputs for future use, when prices are relatively low and expected to increase reduces the risk of being incurring huge costs in the future. Similarly, selling output, when prices are favorable and expected to decline reduces the risk of losses in the future. So, strategic buying may necessitate storing excess inputs planned for future use that were purchased when prices were low, and strategic selling may also necessitate storing produced outputs for future sale, if current prices are unfavorable and expected to rise. So, scientific storage of both inputs and output is essential to minimize the risk. If storage of commodities is not on scientific lines, it can also introduce other types of risk (theft, spoilage *etc.*). So, the use of this tool will depend on individual farm capacity for storage and ability to manage inventory.

xii. Efficient Performance of Marketing Functions

The physical loss of a produce may be reduced by the following ways:

- ☆ Use of fireproof materials in the storage structures to prevent accidents due to fire;
- ☆ Use of improved storage structures and giving necessary pre-storage treatment to the produce to prevent losses in quality arising out of excessive moisture, temperature, attacks by insects and pests, fungus and rodents;
- ☆ Use of better and quicker transportation methods and proper handling of produce during transit; and
- ☆ Use of proper packaging material.

xiii. Minimization of Price Risks

This can be achieved through the following:

- ☆ Fixation of minimum and maximum prices for commodities by the Government and allowing movement of prices only within the defined range.
- ☆ Making arrangements for the dissemination of accurate and scientific price information to all sections of society over space and time.

xiv. Spreading Sales

The spreading of sales means, making several sales of a commodity during a year and is commonly used by farmers to overcome price risk. Dairymen and many other livestock producers are forced to spread their marketing over the entire year, because of the nature of their production. With frequent sales throughout the year, the average price received by a producer is nearly equal to the season or annual average price. But, spreading sales throughout the year essentially averages out the within year variability, it does little to reduce year to year variability.

xv: Limiting Credit and Leverage

Credit or loan limits influence the degree of leverage in a farm operation. That is, the farmer should employ more of owned capital and less of borrowed capital in the business. If the proportion of borrowed capital exceeds the owned capital, it increases the leverage in the farm business and thus, exposes the business to more risk. So, borrowed capital employed in the business must be limited in accordance with the:

- ✰ Managerial ability of the farmer
- ✰ Proportion of equity capital in the business
- ✰ Interest rate
- ✰ Frequency of occurrence risks in that locality
- ✰ Loan arrangements like the scheduling, timing, and term of loan repayments.

xvi. Off-Farm Employment

This is another financial response to risk. Many farmers and their family members have part or full time off farm jobs. which increases their capacity to bear risks. Some off-farm activities may be agriculturally related, such as weeding, harvesting, digging and lining of irrigation channels, grain hauling *etc.* Other off-farm activities may be entirely unrelated to agriculture. Though these off-farm activities are meant to supplement income for family living, but they are a significant response to risk in many instances. For many farm families, off-farm activities are the new form of diversification of enterprises.

xv. Contract Farming

Contract farming is defined as an agreement between farmers and processing and/or marketing firms for the production and supply of agricultural products under forward agreements, frequently at pre-determined prices (Eaton and Shepherd, 2001). Under this farming, farmers usually agree to deliver specific commodities in predetermined quantities and to meet predetermined quality standards, while firms agree to provide production support (*e.g.*, supply of input and provision of technologies and technical advice) and accept products at pre-determined prices. For this arrangement to work, the farmer commits himself to provide a specific commodity in quantities and at quality standards determined by the purchaser (firm). The company on the other hand agrees to support the farmer's production and to purchase the commodity. By doing so, the farmer removes the price uncertainty and the risk of a loss, if commodity prices decline, but he also forfeits the opportunity to gain if prices rise. However, note that, this forward contract require the farmer to deliver the agreed upon amount of the commodity at the agreed upon time thereby, increasing the possible negative outcomes associated with production risk. Thus, it is important to also manage production risks to ensure the ability to meet all the terms of the marketing contract.

xvi. Weather Insurance

Farmers have always been exposed to weather risks, and for a long time have developed ways of reducing, mitigating and coping with these risks (Besley, 1995 and Dercon, 2002). Traditional risk management covers actions taken both before (*ex-ante*) and after (*ex-post*) the risky event occurs (Siegel and Alwang, 1999). Examples of *ex-ante* strategies include the accumulation of buffer stocks as precautionary savings and the diversification of income-generating activities (working in farm and non-farm small businesses, and seasonal migration) or varying cropping practices (planting different crops, like drought-resistant variants, planting in different fields and staggered over time, intercropping and relying on low risk inputs). Examples for ex-post strategies range from farmers seeking off-farm employment, to distress sales of livestock and other farm assets, to withdrawal of children from school for farm labour, and to borrowing funds from family, friends and neighbours (Hanan *et al.*, 2011). While such risk management has assisted farmers in coping with weather risks (Hazell *et al.*, 1986), it has important shortfalls. These strategies are costly, as they often lower vulnerability in the short term at the expense of higher vulnerability over the longer term. For example, when a farmer diversifies he gives up higher income due to specialization in return for a lower variability of income. Similarly, when farmers seek off-farm employment in response to a natural disaster, the sudden rise in the labour supply will drive down market wages. In view of these limitations of *ex-ante* and *ex-post* risk management strategies and considering the uniqueness of weather risk or uncertainty over other production risks, the concept of 'Weather insurance' gained significance. It is nothing but the insurance cover against losses incurred due to uncertainties in climatic conditions. Basically, it is aimed to be used as hedging instrument against any vulnerability of crops or any other damage incurred in agricultural activities due to erratic and irregular weather. It is also denoted as 'weather based index insurance' and 'weather event insurance'. Note that, weather insurance is not exclusive to the agriculture alone but also applicable to industry, sports events or any other commercial events that incur loss due to the vagaries of weather. Thus, weather insurance, therefore, has broader connotation. Weather insurance has been in practice in Canada, the US and European countries. Weather insurance was formally introduced in India in 2003 as a pilot, and by 2007 the Government adopted it as an alternative to the existing yield index insurance. Around 40 crops are insured under the category for various climatic phenomena like deficit rainfall, dry-spell, excess rainfall, low temperature, high temperature, high humidity, and high wind. There has been regular mapping of the weather risks in these countries. It is likely that as agriculture being one of the largest sectors predominantly dependent on the vagaries of weather conditions, the weather insurance has been more identified with respect to agriculture or farmers. Thus, in a broader sense weather insurance protects any financial loss one may incur due to specific weather perils.

Considering the above strategies to overcome various forms of risks and uncertainties in farm business, these management strategies can be classified into three broad categories:

- ☆ ***Risk mitigation:*** These actions prevent events from occurring, limit their occurrence, or reduce the severity of the resulting losses. Examples include pest and disease management strategies, crop diversification and extension advices.
- ☆ ***Risk transfer:*** These actions transfer risk to a willing third party, at a cost. Financial transfer mechanisms trigger compensation or reduce losses generated by a given risk. Examples include: crop insurance, weather insurance, financial hedging tools *etc.*
- ☆ ***Risk coping:*** These actions help the victims of a risky event (a shock such as a drought, flood, or pest epidemic) cope with the losses it causes, and they can include Government assistance to farmers, debt restructuring, and remittances. Government and other public institutions, through their social safety net programmes play a big role in helping farmers cope with risk.

9

Linear Programming

In this chapter, let us deal with a mathematical technique called Linear Programming (LP), which can be employed to solve the farmer's problems especially when he faces with several constraints and the objective function must be optimized. As discussed earlier in Chapter 3, when the farmer's objective is to minimize the cost in the production programme in employing two resources, he chooses the LCC of resources, where MRTS of resources is inversely equal to the price ratio of two resources. Similarly, through Chapter 4, we analyzed that, when the farmer's objective is to maximize the profits in the production programme in producing two products, he chooses the OPC, where MRPS is inversely equal to the price ratio of two products. However, in practicality, the farmer often faces several constraints in the production programme *viz.*, labour constraints, capital constraints, limited land area, procurement of raw material for processing, purchase of some advanced equipment, may enter into contractual agreements regarding supply of minimum quantity of certain products *etc.*, towards optimizing the objective function (minimization of costs or maximization of profits). In solving such numerous constraints, so as to achieve optimal solution, traditional methods break down and LP must be used. So, LP is a mathematical technique aimed for solving constrained maximization and minimization problems, when there are many constraints and the objective function is to be optimized, as well as the constraints faced, are linear. LP was developed by the Russian Mathematician L. V. Kantorovich in 1939 for use during World War II to plan expenditures and returns in order to reduce costs to the army and increase losses to the enemy. Later, this technique was extended by the American mathematician G. B. Dantzig in 1947 and he first published the Simplex method to achieve optimal solution for the constraints the firm faces. The LP problem was first shown to be solvable in polynomial time by Leonid Khachiyan in 1979, but a larger theoretical and practical breakthrough in the field came in 1984, when Narendra Karmarkar introduced a new interior-point method for solving LP problems. The following points depict the short history of LP:

- ✰ In 1762, Lagrange solved tractable optimization problems with simple equality constraints.
- ✰ In 1820, Gauss solved linear system of equations by what is now call Causssian elimination. In 1866 Wilhelm Jordan refined the method to finding least squared errors as a measure of goodness-of-fit. Now, it is referred to as the Gauss-Jordan Method.
- ✰ In 1945, Digital computer emerged.
- ✰ In 1947, Dantzig invented the Simplex Method.
- ✰ In 1968, Fiacco and McCormick introduced the Interior Point Method.
- ✰ In 1984, Karmarkar applied the Interior Method to solve LP problems adding his innovative analysis.

Though LP technique involves labourious procedure in doing mathematical calculations, but with the advent of powerful computers, its acceptance and usefulness have been greatly enhanced in the recent period. The following are the popular definitions of LP:

LP, sometimes known as linear optimization, is the problem of maximizing or minimizing a linear function over a convex polyhedron specified by linear and non-negativity constraints. Simplistically, LP is the optimization of an outcome based on some set of constraints using a linear mathematical model.

LP is a mathematical method for determining a way to achieve the best outcome (such as maximum profit or minimum cost) in a given mathematical model for some list of requirements represented as linear relationships. More formally, LP is a technique for the optimization of a linear objective function, subject to linear equality and linear inequality constraints. LP is the process of finding the extreme values (maximum and minimum values) of a function for a region defined by inequalities.A LP problem is an optimization problem for which:

- ✰ *We attempt to maximize (or minimize) a linear function of the decision variables (objective function).*
- ✰ *The values of the decision variables must satisfy a set of constraints, each of which must be a linear inequality or linear equality.*
- ✰ *A sign restriction on each variable.*

The above definitions infer that, LP = Linear Algebra + Inequalities + Optimization (minimize or maximize). Also note that, LP is not a programming language like C++, Java, or Visual Basic and is just a mathematical programming that computes how best (in an optimal way) the farmer will allocate his scarce resources among the selected enterprises or select optimum combination of enterprises for the given resources, so as to ensure cost minimization and profit maximization respectively. Thus, LP deals with a class of optimization problems, where the objective function to be optimized and all the constraints are linear in terms of the decision variables. The term 'programming' in this context indicates a schedule of actions. Considering its importance, LP is one of the most widely used Operations Research.

I. Basic Terminology Used in LP Technique

☆ ***Objective function:*** The LP model that expresses, what needs to be maximized or minimized, depending on the objective of the problem is called Objective function. That is, objective function implies, what to be optimized in a given LP problem.

☆ ***Decision variables:*** These represent the quantities of each product to be produced by the farmer in order to maximize the profits or quantities of inputs to use to minimize the costs. For example, a farmer wishes to produce paddy (X_P) and maize (X_M). Unit profit of paddy is Rs.7/unit and unit profit of maize is Rs.10/unit. To simplify our discussion, let us assume, the farmer employs only two resources *viz.*, labour (man days) and fertilizer. It is necessary to employ 60 man days/acre to produce paddy and 40 man days/acre to produce maize. Similarly, the farmer requires 30 units of fertilizer per acre to produce paddy and 25 units of fertilizer per acre to produce maize. There are 350 man days of labour and 400 units of fertilizer in total with the farmer.

In the above example:

- ***What is the objective in words?:*** The farmer's wish is to maximize the profits.
- ***What are the constraints in words?***

  Labour (man days) '≤' Number of man days available

  Fertilizer '≤' Quantity (units) of fertilizer available
- ***What are the decision variables?:*** The variables Paddy (X_P) and Maize (X_M) are the decision variables
- ***Formulate the objective function:*** Max Z: $7X_P + 10X_M$
- ***Formulate the constraints:***

  Subject to

  $60X_P + 40X_M \leq 350$ ———→ *Functional Constraint for Labour*

  $30X_P + 25X_M \leq 400$ ———→ *Constraint for Fertilizer*
- ***Write the non-negative constraints:*** $X_P, X_M \geq 0$

  Thus, this LP solution for the above problem helps the farmer, how to maximize the profits in the production programme with the given resource constraints in producing paddy and maize.

☆ ***Constraints:*** **Constraints** represent, how the decision variables use resources, which are available in limited quantities. They refer to an upper limit on the availability of resources or a lower limit on the necessary levels to achieve. They are also called as Limitations or Restrictions. LP formulation can contain four types of mathematical constraints *viz.*, Maximum type (≤), Minimum type (≥), Equality type (=) and Non-constraint.

- ***Maximum Type:*** This constraint is specified as '≤'. This constraint indicates that, all uses of a particular resource across the enterprises must be less than or equal to the amount of that particular total resource available. For example: $5X_1+7X_2+4X_3 \leq 45$ Man days. In this case, '$5X_1$' refers to 5 x Man days with reference to paddy enterprise. This maximum type of constraint (specified as '≤' type) is generally included in maximization problems and it must be converted into equality type, so as to write the equation in standard LP form. To convert '≤' type of constraint into equality constraint, we add Slack Variable or Disposal activity. This slack variable or disposal activity corresponds to the amount of unused resource. This is so because, in the production programme, the farmer need not employ the entire resource that is available with him. Note that, this slack variable is non-negative, the number of slack variables depends upon the number of constraints in LP problem and the contribution of slack variables to the objective function is zero. Say, the given objective function is:

  Max Z $50X_1+25X_2+15X_3$

  Subject to:

  $X_1+2X_2+1X_3 \leq 10$ ———→ *Functional Constraint for Land*

  $5X_1+4X_2+2X_3 \leq 45$ ———→ *Functional Constraint for Labour*

  $32X_1+21X_2+15X_3 \leq 350$ ———→ *Functional Constraint for Capital*

  $X_1, X_2, X_3 \geq 0$ (Non-negativity constraint)

  The above form of LP model can be linearized by adding slack variables or disposal activities (X_4, X_5 and X_6) as given below.

  Max Z $50X_1+25X_2+15X_3+0X_4+0X_5+0X_6$

  Subject to

  $X_1+2X_2+X_3+1X_4+0X_5+0X_6 = 10$

  $5X_1+4X_2+2X_3+0X_4+1X_5+0X_6 = 45$

  $32X_1+21X_2+15X_3+0X_4+0X_5+1X_6 = 350$

  $X_1+X_2+X_3+X_4+X_5+X_6 \geq 0$

- ***Minimum Constraint (≥):*** This constraint is specified as '≥'. This constraint indicates that, all uses of a particular resource must exceed minimum amount available and hence, it is called Minimum Constraint. This minimum type of constraint (specified as '≥' type) must be converted into equality type, so as to write the equation in standard LP form. To convert '≥' type of constraint into equality constraint, we add Surplus Variable or Negative slack variable. This Surplus variable indicates the excess amount by which a particular requirement is met. Thus, surplus variable permits over fulfillment of a constraint. Note that, minimum constraint is generally included in minimization problems, the contribution of surplus variable to the objective function is zero and this surplus variable violates the non-negativity restriction or condition. To overcome this problem of violating non-negativity condition, we add another variable namely Artificial variable. Artificial variable is of mathematical convenience and has no physical meaning. Artificial variable should not find its place as basic variable (decision variable) in the optimal solution. A high cost or penalty is attached to the artificial variable in the objective function to ensure its elimination from optimal solution. High cost or penalty of artificial variable is indicated by 'M'. For example,

Min Z $3X_1+2X_2$

Subject to:

$3X_1+7X_2 \geq 45$ (Functional constraint for carbohydrates)

$7X_1+3X_2 \geq 50$ (Functional constraint for proteins)

$X_1,X_2 \geq 0$ (Non-negativity constraint)

The above standard LP model for minimization function can be linearized by adding surplus variables as given below.

Min Z $3X_1+2X_2+0X_3+0X_4+MA_1+MA_2$

Subject to

$3X_1+7X_2 -1X_3+0X_4+1A_1+0A_2 = 45$

$7X_1+3X_2 +0X_3-1X_4+0A_1+1A_2 = 50$

$X_1, X_2, X_3, X_4, A_1, A_2 \geq 0$

A_1 and A_2 are Artificial variables.

- ***Equality constraint ('='):*** This is specified as '='. This constraint implies that, all uses of particular resource across the enterprises must be equal to the amount available. It neither permits under use nor over fulfillment. Artificial variable is added to the equality constraint and is attached with high penalty or cost. For example, if a firm decides to sell all of its goods in sets (say, one razor (X_2) and two blade packets (X_1)), the new constraint is: $2X_1 = X_2$ or $2X_1 - X_2 = 0$, then constraints can take the form of an equality. The analysis of LP problem by graphical approach involving equality constraint causes all valid points to lie exactly on the constraint line.
- ***Non-constraint:*** This is in the case of objective function, where we want to derive highest or lowest possible value depending on the problem.

☆ ***Inequality Constraints:*** In LP problems, constraints are given by inequalities and hence, called as Inequality constraints. They are so called because, the farmer can employ the given inputs up to, but not more than, specified quantities of the inputs. That is, the farmer has restrictions in allocating the levels of each input. In addition, there are non-negativity constraints on the solution to indicate that, the farmer neither produce a negative output nor use a negative quantity of any input.

☆ ***Formulation:*** It is the process of translating a real-world problem into a linear program. Once a problem has been formulated as a linear program, it can be solved by graphical method or algebraic method or Simplex method or even by a computer programme, when large scale computations are to be done. The hardest part about applying LP technique is formulating the problem followed by analysis and interpreting the findings.

- ☆ ***Linear Equations:*** All of the equations and inequalities in a linear program must, by definition, be linear. A linear function has the following form:

  Max Z $a_1X_1 + a_2X_2 + a_3X_3 + ... + a_nX_n$.

  In this linear equation, the a's are called the coefficients or parameters of the equation and they are fixed values. The X's are called the Decision variables of the equation and they are allowed to take on a range of values within the limits defined by the constraints. Note that, it is not necessary to always use X's to represent decision variables and descriptive labels are more preferred.
- ☆ ***Model:*** An idealized representation of something.
- ☆ ***LP Model:*** A mathematical model, where the mathematical functions appearing in both the objective function and the constraints are all linear functions.
- ☆ ***Corner Point Property:*** An optimal solution must lie at one or more corner points.
- ☆ ***Corner-point feasible solution:*** A solution that lies at the corner of the feasible region.
- ☆ ***Feasible region:*** The geometric region that consists of all the feasible solutions.
- ☆ ***Feasible solution:*** A solution for which all the constraints are satisfied.
- ☆ ***Infeasible solution:*** A solution for which at least one constraint is violated.
- ☆ ***Optimal solution:*** A best feasible solution according to the objective function. Most LPs have only one optimal solution. However, some LPs have no optimal solution, and some LPs have an infinite number of solutions.
- ☆ ***Optimal Solution for a Maximization Problem:*** A point in the feasible region with the largest objective function value is the optimal solution.
- ☆ ***Optimal Solution for a Minimization Problem:*** A point in the feasible region with the smallest objective function value is the optimal solution.
- ☆ ***Functional constraint:*** A constraint with a function of the decision variables on the left hand side. All constraints in a LP model that are not non-negativity constraints are called functional constraints. The coefficients of the constraints are often called the Technological coefficients. The number on the right-hand side of the constraint is called the constraint's right-hand side (or RHS).
- ☆ ***Non-negativity constraint:*** A constraint that expresses the restriction that a particular decision variable must be non-negative (greater than or equal to zero).

- ☆ ***Graphical method*:** A method for solving LP problems with two decision variables on a two-dimensional graph.
- ☆ ***Sensitivity analysis:*** Analysis of how sensitive the optimal solution is to the value of each parameter of the model.
- ☆ ***Shadow price*:** The values of the slack variables in the Z-C row. A shadow price is the value of one additional unit of resource that is already being fully utilized. Assuming there are no other changes to the input parameters, the change to the objective function value per unit increase to a right hand side of a constraint is called the 'Shadow Price'.
- ☆ ***Simplex method*:** An efficient solution procedure for solving LP problems.
- ☆ ***Simplex tableau*:** A table that the tabular form of the simplex method uses to compactly display the system of equations yielding the current basic feasible solution.
- ☆ ***Additional variables used in solving LP problem:*** Three types of additional variables are used in simplex method such as:
  - ❑ ***Slack variables (S_1, S_2, S_3 etc.):*** These variables refer to the amount of left over or unused resources. It is a variable that is added to the left hand side of a less than or equal to type of constraint and thereby, transforms it to equality constraint. Slack variables are always represented by positive (+) sign *i.e.,* non-negative. These variables will have zero coefficients in the objective function. By adding slack variables, we can convert all the inequality constraints to equalities, the right hand side of the equations being non negative.
  - ❑ ***Surplus variables (S_1, S_2, S_3 etc.):*** Surplus variable is the amount of resources by which the left hand side of the equation exceeds the minimum limit. That is, it is a variable subtracted from the left hand side of a 'greater than or equal to' type of constraint, to convert it to equality constraint. It is also known as negative slack variable. In economic terms, surplus variable represent over fulfillment of the requirement. Surplus variables are always represented by negative (-) sign.
  - ❑ ***Artificial variables (A_1, A_2, A_3 etc.):*** Artificial variables are temporary slack variables, which are used for purposes of calculation, and are removed later. These are non-negative variables (coefficient of +1) introduced to facilitate the computation of an initial basic feasible solution. This variable is added on the left hand side of a 'greater than or equal to' type of constraint to convert it to equality constraint. It should be noted that, artificial variables are introduced as a computational device and does not have any physical meaning. These variables (one by one) can be removed from the simplex tableau as soon as they become non-basic. These artificial variables are introduced for equality (=) and for greater than or equal to (≥) types of constraints.

    Thus, the above variables are used to convert the inequalities into equality equations, as given below.

Constraint Type	*Variable Added*	*Format*
Less than or Equal to (≤)	Add Slack variable	+S
Greater than or Equal to (≥) Artificial variable	Subtract Surplus variable and add	–S + A
Equal to (=)	Add Artificial variable	+A

Note that, since all numbers are real values, '≤' is the same as '<' and '≥' is the same as '>'.

- ☆ ***Pivot column:*** The column with the largest negative (largest positive) entry in the shadow price row in the case of a profit maximization (cost minimization) problem.
- ☆ ***Pivot number:*** The number in a simplex tableau that currently is at the intersection of the pivot column and the pivot row.
- ☆ ***Pivot row:*** The row of a simplex tableau that is for the current leaving basic variable with lowest ratio value.
- ☆ ***Dual problem:*** The LP problem that has a dual relationship with the original (primal) LP problem of interest according to Duality theory.
- ☆ ***Basic and Non-basic variables:*** Basic variables are selected arbitrarily with the restriction that, there be as many basic variables as there are equations. The remaining variables are non-basic variables. For example:

  $X_1+2X_2+S_1 = 32$

  $3X_1+4X_2+S_2 = 85$

  This system has two equations, we can select any two of the four variables as basic variables. The remaining two variables are then non-basic variables. A solution found by setting the two non-basic variables equal to 0 and solving for the two basic variables is a basic solution. If a basic solution has no negative values, it is a basic feasible solution.
- ☆ ***Basic Solution:*** For a set of m simultaneous equations in n variables ($n > m$), a solution obtained by setting ($n - m$) variables equal to zero and solving for remaining m variables is called a 'basic feasible solution'. The variables which are set to zero are known as non-basic variables and the remaining m variables which appear in this solution are known as basic variables.
- ☆ ***Basic Feasible Solution:*** A feasible solution to LP problem, which is also the basic solution is called the 'basic feasible solution'. Basic feasible solutions are of two types;
  - ❑ ***Degenerate:*** A basic feasible solution is called degenerate, if value of at least one basic variable is zero.
  - ❑ ***Non-degenerate:*** A basic feasible solution is called 'non-degenerate', if all values of m basic variables are non-zero and positive.

- ☆ ***Optimum Basic Feasible Solution:*** A basic feasible solution, which optimizes (maximizes or minimizes) the objective function value of the given LP problem is called as 'optimum basic feasible solution'.
- ☆ ***Unbounded Solution:*** A basic feasible solution, which optimizes the objective function of the LP problem indefinitely is called unbounded solution.
- ☆ ***Transportation model:*** Transportation model is primarily concerned with the optimal (best possible) way in which a product produced at different factories or plants (called sources or supply origins) can be transported to a number of places (called warehouses or demand destinations). The objective in a transportation problem is to fully satisfy the destination requirements within the operating production capacity constraints at the minimum possible cost.

II. LP Structure or Components of LP Problem in Standard Form

LP is the most commonly applied form of constrained optimization. Constrained optimization is much harder than unconstrained optimization. In the latter, the manager or decision maker aims at the highest point (or lowest point) of an objective function. For optimization to be required, there must be more than one solution available. For example, on TPP curve, any point on the function is a solution, and because the single variable is real-valued, there are an infinite number of solutions. Some kind of optimization process is then required in order to choose the very best solution from among those available. However, in case of LP technique, which falls under constrained optimization, we aim at maximizing or minimizing a linear function that is subjected to a set of linear constraints. The constraints may be equalities or inequalities. So, in case of constrained optimization, we have to find out the best point of the function, but subjected to the limits or constraints while doing so.

The LP problem in a standard form comprises of the following components:

A. Objective Function

This is a mathematical expression that combines the variables to express the manager's or decision maker's goal. That is, it refers to the objective of the manager (say, farmer) in taking up the production programme in his farm. The typical plans of farmer revolve around two major objectives *viz.,* Maximization of profits and Minimization of costs. The goal of the farmer must be clearly specified before computations take place. In general, a LP model for maximization function and minimization function are of the following standard form:

i. Objective Function (Maximization Function)

$\text{Max } Z = a_1X_1 + a_2X_2 + a_3X_3 + \text{——} + a_nX_n \longrightarrow$ *Objective function*

Constraints (*i.e.,* subject to):

$b_{11}X_1 + b_{12}X_2 + b_{13}X_3 + \text{——} + b_{1n}X_n \leq c_1 \longrightarrow$ (*Functional Constraint of Resource* 1)

$b_{21}X_1 + b_{22}X_2 + b_{23}X_3 + \text{——} + b_{2n}X_n \leq c_2 \longrightarrow$ (*Functional Constraint of Resource* 2)

$b_{31}X_1 + b_{32}X_2 + b_{33}X_3 + \text{——} + b_{3n}X_n \leq c_3 \longrightarrow$ (*Functional Constraint of Resource 3*)

. . . .

. . . .

. . . .

. . . .

$b_{m1}X_1 + b_{m2}X_2 + b_{m3}X_3 + \text{——} + b_{mn}X_n \leq c_m \longrightarrow$ (*Functional Constraint of Resource 'n'*)

In this system of equations, 'Z' is the objective function value (Maximization of profits) that is being optimized, Xj are the decision variables whose optimal values are to be estimated, Xj ≥ 0 (Non-negativity Constraints) and a_j, b_{ij} and c_i are the constants derived. The above form of LP model can also be expressed as:

$$Max\ Z \sum_{j=1}^{n} a_j X_j$$

Subject to

$$\sum_{j=1}^{n} b_{ij} X_j \leq c_i, \qquad where, i = 1\ to\ m, j = 1\ to\ n.$$

Example 9.1

Suppose, a farmer has a piece of farm land, say 'L' acres, to be planted with either paddy or maize or some combination of the two. The farmer has a limited amount of fertilizer, F units, and pesticide, P units. Every acre of paddy requires F_P units of fertilizer and P_P units of pesticide, while every acre of maize requires F_M units of fertilizer, and P_M units of pesticide. Let S_P be the selling price of paddy per unit, and S_M be the selling price of maize per unit. If we denote the area of land planted with paddy and maize by X_P and X_M respectively, then profit can be maximized by choosing optimal values for X_P and X_M. This problem can be expressed with the following LP problem in the standard form:

Max Z: $S_PX_P + S_MX_M \longrightarrow$ *Objective function (Maximization of profits)*

Subject to:

$X_P + X_M \leq L \longrightarrow$ *Functional Constraint (Land)*

$F_PX_P + F_MX_M \leq F \longrightarrow$ *Functional Constraint (Fertilizer)*

$P_PX_P + P_MX_M \leq P \longrightarrow$ *Functional Constraint (Pesticide)*

$X_P \geq 0, X_M \geq 0$ (Non-negativity constraints)

which in matrix form becomes:

$$\begin{bmatrix} S_P & S_M \end{bmatrix} \begin{bmatrix} X_P \\ X_M \end{bmatrix}$$

Subjected to

$$\begin{bmatrix} 1 & 1 \\ F_P & F_M \\ P_P & P_M \end{bmatrix} \begin{bmatrix} X_P \\ X_M \end{bmatrix} \leq \begin{bmatrix} L \\ F \\ P \end{bmatrix}, \begin{bmatrix} X_P \\ X_M \end{bmatrix} \geq \begin{bmatrix} 0 \\ 0 \end{bmatrix}$$

ii. Objective Function (Minimization Function)

Min $Z = a_1X_1 + a_2X_2 + a_3X_3 + \text{——} + a_nX_n \longrightarrow$ *Objective function*

Constraints (*i.e.*, subject to):

$b_{11}X_1 + b_{12}X_2 + b_{13}X_3 + \text{——} + b_{1n}X_n \geq c_1 \longrightarrow$ (*Functional Constraint*)

$b_{21}X_1 + b_{22}X_2 + b_{23}X_3 + \text{——} + b_{2n}X_n \geq c_2 \longrightarrow$ (*Functional Constraint*)

$b_{31}X_1 + b_{32}X_2 + b_{33}X_3 + \text{——} + b_{3n}X_n \geq c_3 \longrightarrow$ (*Functional Constraint*)

. . . .

. . . .

. . . .

. . . .

$b_{m1}X_1 + b_{m2}X_2 + b_{m3}X_3 + \text{——} + b_{mn}X_n \geq c_m \longrightarrow$ (*Functional Constraint*)

In this system of equations, 'Z' is the objective function value (Minimization of costs) that is being optimized, Xj are the decision variables, whose optimal values are to be estimated, $Xj \geq 0$ (Non-negativity Constraints) and a_j, b_{ij} and c_i are the constants derived. The above form of LP model can also be expressed as:

$$Min\ Z \sum_{j=1}^{n} a_j X_j$$

Subjected to

$$\sum_{j=1}^{n} b_{ij} X_j \geq c_i, \qquad where, i = 1\ to\ m, j = 1\ to\ n.$$

Example 9.2

A fertilizer firm wishes to prepare special fertilizer mixture at a minimal cost by mixing two fertilizers, F_A and F_B. The mixture is to contain at least 45 units of phosphate, at least 36 units of nitrogen and at least 40 units of potassium. Fertilizer A costs the firm Rs1.00 per unit. Fertilizer B costs the firm Rs. 1.75 per unit. Fertilizer A contains

5 units of phosphate, 2 units of nitrogen and 2 units of potassium. Fertilizer B contains 3 units of phosphate, 3 units of nitrogen and 5 units of potassium. How many units of each fertilizer should the firm use in order to minimize the cost.

Min Z: $1F_A + 1.75F_B$ ———→ Objective function (Minimization of cost)

Subject to:

$5F_A + 3F_B \geq 45$ ———→ Functional Constraint (Phosphate)

$2F_A + 3F_B \geq 36$ ———→ Functional Constraint (Nitrogen)

$2F_A + 5F_B \geq 40$ ———→ Functional Constraint (Potassium)

$F_A \geq 0, F_B \geq 0$ (Non-negativity constraints)

which in matrix form becomes:

$$\begin{vmatrix} 1 & 1.75 \end{vmatrix} \begin{bmatrix} FA \\ FB \end{bmatrix}$$

Subjected to

$$\begin{bmatrix} 5 & 3 \\ 2 & 3 \\ 2 & 5 \end{bmatrix} \begin{bmatrix} FA \\ FB \end{bmatrix} \geq \begin{bmatrix} 45 \\ 36 \\ 40 \end{bmatrix}, \begin{bmatrix} FA \\ FB \end{bmatrix} \geq \begin{bmatrix} 0 \\ 0 \end{bmatrix}$$

Thus, the objective function in the above two examples indicates, how each variable contributes to the value to be optimized in solving the problem. Thus, the objective function takes the following general form:

$$Maximize\ or\ Minimize\ Z = \sum_{j=1}^{n} a_j X_j$$

where 'aj' is the objective function coefficient corresponding to the jth variable and Xj is the jth decision variable. The objective function coefficients indicate the contribution to the value of the objective function of one unit of the corresponding variable. For example, if the objective function is to maximize the profits, and 'Xj' is the jth activity in the model, then 'aj' (the objective function coefficient corresponding to Xj) gives the profits generated by one unit of activity 'j'. In case of cost minimization example, 'Xj' might be the amount of resource 'j' (say, fertilizer) used in achieving the goal. In this case, 'aj' would be the cost of using one unit of resource 'j'. Note that, the way the general objective function was written as above implies that, there is a coefficient in the objective function corresponding to each variable. Of course, some variables may not contribute to the objective function. In such case, the variable will have a coefficient of zero or the variable need not be included in the objective function at all.

The above examples also indicate that, an LP model (maximization or minimization function) comprises of the following components:

- *Decision variables*: They are the variables that appear in the objective function of the LP model and they indicate levels of activity of a firm.
- *Objective function:* A linear mathematical relationship describing an objective of the firm, in terms of decision variables - this function is to be maximized or minimized.
- *Constraints:* They are the requirements or restrictions placed on the firm by the operating environment, stated in linear relationships of the decision variables.
- *Parameters:* They refer to the numerical coefficients and constants used in the objective function and constraints.

Considering the above components, the following are the characteristics of LP problems:

- A decision amongst alternative courses of action is required.
- The decision is represented in the LP model by decision variables.
- The LP problem encompasses a goal, expressed as an objective function that the Manager or Decision maker wants to achieve.
- Restrictions (represented by constraints) refer to the maximum or minimum level of resources to be employed to achieve the objective function *i.e.*, they limit the extent of achievement of the objective.
- The objective and constraints must be definable by linear mathematical functional relationships.

B. Alternative Courses of Action

The limited resources available on the farm may be used in several alternative ways for producing different types of enterprises. That is, there must be alternative courses of action to choose from. For example, if a farmer wishes to produce three different enterprises, the farmer may use LP to decide how to allocate the limited resources among the three enterprises. If there were no alternatives to select from, we would not need LP.

C. Resource Restrictions or Constraints

These are mathematical expressions that combine the variables to express limits on the possible solutions. For example, a constraint may express the idea that the number of labour available in a processing factory is limited to operate a particular machine or that only a certain amount of fertilizer is available with the farmer for kharif season. LP problem does exist only, when the resources available with the farmer are limited. If all the resources are available in plenty on the farm, the farmer will plan the production activity that contributes to maximum profits. But, in general, the resources with the farmer are limited and hence, he has to plan the enterprises within these limits. Thus, the presence of restrictions or constraints limits the degree to which the farmer can pursue the objective function. For example, deciding how many units of each product the farmer should produce is restricted by the availability of scarce resources. So, the objective function can be maximized (or minimized) subject to limited resources (the constraints). These constraints define the possible values that the variables of a LP problem may take. They typically represent resource constraints, or the minimum or maximum level of some activity or condition. They take the following general form:

(Profit maximization objective function) subject to constraints

$$\sum_{j=1}^{n} b_{ij}X_j \leq c_i, \qquad where, i = 1 \text{ to } m, j = 1 \text{ to } n.$$

(Cost minimization objective function) subject to constraints

$$\sum_{j=1}^{n} b_{ij}X_j \geq c_i, \qquad where, i = 1 \text{ to } m, j = 1 \text{ to } n.$$

where Xj = the jth decision variable,

bij = the coefficient on Xj in constraint 'i', and

ci = the right-hand-side coefficient on constraint 'i'.

Note that 'i' is an index that runs from 1 to m and each value of 'i' corresponds to a constraint and 'j' is an index that runs from 1 to n.

Thus, the above expression represents 'm' constraints (equations or more precisely inequalities) with this form. Resource constraints are a common type of constraint. In a resource constraint, the coefficient 'bij' indicates the amount of resource 'i' used for each unit of activity 'j', as represented by the value of the variable Xj. The right-hand side of the constraint (ci) indicates the total amount of resource 'i' available in the production programme. Note that, in the earlier examples, the constraint is written as a less than or equal to constraint and greater than or equal to constraint. A greater than or equal to constraint can always be converted to a less than or equal to constraint by multiplying it by -1. Similarly, equality constraint can be written as two inequalities: a less than or equal to constraint and a greater than or equal to constraint. Besides the above two, there are also non-negativity constraints and this implies that, the variables of LP problem must always take non-negative values (*i.e.*, they must be greater than or equal to zero) and the technical reasons about the non-negativity constraints are beyond the scope of this book.

D. Linear Equations

The objective function and functional constraints in LP problems must be expressed in terms of linear equations or inequalities.

E. Variables or Decision Variables

The variables in a LP problem are a set of quantities that need to be determined in order to solve the problem; *i.e.*, the problem is solved when the best values of the variables have been identified. The variables are also called Decision variables because, the problem is to decide what value each variable should take and based on these values, the optimal solution is determined. Typically, the variables represent the amount of a resource to use or the level of some activity. In Example 9.2, Min Z: $1F_A + 1.75F_B$ is the objective function for minimization of cost and F_A and F_B are the decision variables. Note that, the values of the variables are not known when you start the problem. The goal is to find values of the variables that provide the best value of the objective function.

Thus, LP problem is an optimization problem for which we do the following:

- Identify the decision variables.
- Formulate the objective function (Maximization or Minimization function) based on the selected decision variables.
- The values of the decision variables must satisfy a set of constraints.
- Each constraint must be a linear equation or inequality.
- A sign restriction is associated with each variable. For each variable Xj, the sign restriction specifies either that Xj must be non-negative (Xj ³ 0) or that Xj may be unrestricted in sign.

Example 9.2.1

The above discussed components of LP model are shown through the following example: Assume a biscuit manufacturing company plans to produce two types of biscuits, one with a round shape and another with a square shape. The following resources are used in manufacturing the biscuits:

- Raw material, of which daily availability is 150 kg.
- Machinery, of which daily availability is 15 machine hours.
- Labour, of which daily availability is 40 man-hours.

  The resources used are shown in the following table. If the unit profit of round and square biscuits is Rs. 3.00 and Rs. 2.00 respectively, how many round and square biscuits should be produced to maximize total profit?

Resources Used

Resources	*Requirement/Unit*		*Daily Availability*
	Round Biscuits	*Square Biscuits*	
Raw material	100	115	1500 kgs
Machine	10	12	15 machine hours
Labour	3	2	40 man hours

Components of LP Problem

- ***Key Decision:*** To determine the number of round and square biscuits to be produced.

- ☆ ***Decision Variables:*** Let X_1 be the number of round biscuits to be produced daily, and X_2 be the number of square biscuits to be produced daily.
- ☆ ***Objective function:*** It is given that the profit on each unit of round biscuits is Rs. 3.00 and of square biscuits is Rs. 2.00. The objective is to maximize profits, therefore, the total profit will be given by the equation, Max Z = $3X_1+2X_2$.
- ☆ ***Constraints:*** Now, the manufacturing process is imposed by a constraint with the limited availability of raw material. For the production of round biscuits, $100X_1$ of raw material is used daily and for the production of square biscuits, $115X_2$ of raw material is used daily.

  It is given that the total availability of raw material per day is 150 kgs. Therefore, the constraint for raw material is, $100X_1 + 115X_2 \leq 150$

  Similarly, the constraint for machine hours is, $10X_1+12X_2 \leq 15$ and

  The constraint for the manpower is, $3X_1+2X_2 \leq 40$

  Since the resources are to be used within or below the daily availability level, inequality sign of less than or equal sign ($\leq$) is used. Further, we cannot produce negative number of units of biscuits which is a non-negative constraint expressed as, $X_1 \geq 0, X_2 \geq 0$

  Thus, the LP model for the given problem is,

  Maximize $Z = 3X_1+ 2X_2$

  Subject to constraints,

  $100X_1+115X_2 \leq 150$

  $10X_1+12X_2 \leq 15$

  $3X_1+2X_2 \leq 40$

  where, $X_1 \geq 0, X_2 \geq 0$

III. Assumptions in LP Technique

Since, the objective function (maximization of profits or minimization of costs) that the farmers seek to optimize as well as the constraints that they face are often linear over the relevant range of operation, LP technique is very useful. However, this technique is based on the certain assumptions. We know, an assumption is a simplifying condition taken to hold true in the system being analyzed in order to render the model mathematically tractable (solvable). The following are the important assumptions of LP technique:

- ☆ ***Linearity:*** As mentioned earlier, the objective function that the farmer seeks to optimize (*i.e.*, maximize or minimize) is linear and can be represented graphically by straight lines. This linearity applies to constraint inequalities as well, since the addition of slack and surplus variables convert all inequalities into linear equations. So, linearity implies, the objective function (*i.e.*, maximization or minimization) can be described by a linear function of the decision variables. That is, the mathematical function involves only the first powers of the variables ($3X_1$, $5X_1$) and with no cross products (say, $3X_1$*$5X_1$).

- ☆ ***Constraints set or Functional constraints:*** The constraints set can be expressed as a set of linear equations. In addition to the linear requirements, non-negativity condition state that, the variables cannot assume negative values, as negative quantity of resources and output does not have a meaning.
- ☆ ***Proportionality:*** The contribution of any decision variable to the objective function is proportional to its value. That is, the contribution to the objective function from each decision variable is proportional to the value of the decision variable. This contribution is assumed constant and independent of the variable level. Similarly, the use of each resource per unit of each decision variable is assumed constant and independent of variable level. Thus, there are no economies of scale. For example, in the profit maximization problem, the contribution from one unit of paddy area towards profit maximization is Rs. 60, from two units of paddy area towards profit maximization is Rs. 120, from three units of paddy area towards profit maximization is Rs. 180 and so on. Similarly, in diet problem, the contribution to the cost of the diet from one kilogram of apples is Rs. 30, from two kilograms of apples is Rs. 60 and from three kilograms of apples is Rs. 90 and so on. Similarly, if the net returns per unit of paddy produced is Rs. 40, then if 100 units are produced, then net returns are Rs. 4000. So, under this proportionality assumption, the total contribution of paddy enterprise to the objective function is always proportional to its level. This assumption also applies to resource usage within the constraints. For example, a farmer's labour requirement for one acre of paddy is 125 man days. If the farmer cultivates paddy in 4 acres of land, his total labour requirement will be 500 man days. Thus, the total labour man days employed in paddy cultivation is always strictly proportional to the acreage under the crop. That means, each decision variable in every equation must appear with a constant coefficient (*i.e.*, the variable is multiplied by a number and nothing else). So, in objective function, proportionality implies that, the marginal rate of contribution to the objective (maximization and minimization) of each variable is assumed to remain constant throughout the entire range of activity levels in the problem. In particular, variables cannot be multiplied or divided by other variables, cannot be raised to an exponent other than 1, or be arguments of other functional relationships (say, sin X or log X). In the functional constraints, proportionality implies that, resource usage per variable is assumed constant throughout the entire operational range of the problem.
- ☆ ***Additivity:*** The contribution to the objective function for any decision variable is independent of the values of the other decision variables. That is, this assumption deals with the relationships among the decision variables. Simply put, their contributions to an equation in objective function

must be additive. So, the total value of the objective function equals the sum of the contributions of all decisions variables in the objective function. Similarly, total resource use in the objective function is the sum of the resource use of each variable. This requirement rules out the possibility of interaction or multiplicative terms appear in the objective function or the functional constraints. For example, the total labour man days for paddy are the sum of number of man days of labour across different farm operations on paddy. In the general LP formulation, considering variables X_1 and X_2, the value of the objective function must always equal a_1 times X_1 plus a_2 times X_2. Using X_1 does not affect the per unit net return of X_2 and *vice versa*. Similarly, using X_1 does not alter the resource requirement of X_2. Thus, this assumption of additivity implies that, the combined effect of the decision variables in any one equation is the algebraic sum of their individual weighted effects. The weighting, of course, is due to the proportionality constants. That means, the variables can be added or subtracted together, but never multiplied or divided by each other. For example, total profit (or total cost) is the sum of the individual product's profits (or resources costs). In the functional constraints, additivity implies that, total resource usage is likewise the sum of individual resource usage per variable (say, product produced).

Proportionality and additivity amount to linearity. The broader implication of linearity is that, the variables are assumed to be mutually independent. In other words, the products are assumed to be neither complements nor substitutes of each other and there is no interaction between the variables. If proportionality and additivity cannot be assumed to hold, the problem would call for a non-linear programming solution approach. Thus, the objective function for an LP problem must be a linear function of the decision variables and it has two implications:

- The contribution of the objective function from each decision variable is proportional to the value of the decision variable.
- The contribution to the objective function from any decision variable is independent of the other decision variables.

☆ ***Divisibility (Continuity):*** Each decision variable is allowed to assume fractional (non-integer) values. That is, the decision variables can take on any value within a given feasible range. To make the model workable (computationally tractable), we must be prepared to accept non-integer solutions. Sometimes, the values of decision variables only make sense, if they are integers; then we need an extension of LP called Integer programming. Since we are using continuous variables, the LP model assumes that the decision variables can take on fractional variables. In many situations, the LP is being used on a large enough scale that one can round the optimal decision variables up or down to the nearest integer and get an answer that is reasonably close to the optimal integer solution. For example, if a LP model for a farmer production plan said to produce 39.992 units of paddy, we can be probably produce 40 units of paddy and be close to an optimal solution. This rounding or truncating of the optimal LP decision variables will not greatly affect the solution.

- ☆ ***Certainty:*** Each linear coefficient of the objective function and functional constraints is known with certainity and is not based on probabilistic approach. That is, the coefficients in the objective function 'aj', the coefficients in the functional constraints 'bij' and the right hand side of the functional constraints in the LP model are known as constants and they have no probabilistic elements whatsoever. So, the parameter values are known with certainty. This is technically never true in the real world; some degree of uncertainty is always present especially in long-term period. However, for short-term problems, the level of uncertainty tends to be minimal and one can often work under the assumption of complete certainty and then take small parameter variations into account with sensitivity analysis. In case of long-term problems, the aspects involve pronounced uncertainty and this call for decision making using Stochastic programming (probabilistic method) instead of standard LP. So, considering certainty assumption in this model, the values of the variables are exactly equal to the responses represented by the coefficients. As per this assumption in the given LP model (for maximization of profits), the parameters aj, bij and ci are known constants. The optimum solution derived is predicated on perfect knowledge of all the parameter values. Since all exogenous factors are assumed to be known and fixed, LP models are sometimes called non-stochastic models as contrasted with models explicitly dealing with stochastic factors. This assumption gives rise to the term 'deterministic' analysis. Thus, after developing a LP model, it is often useful to conduct sensitivity analysis by varying one of the exogenous parameters and observing the sensitivity of the optimal solution to that variation. For example, in the LP model regarding profit maximization, the profits derived from a product depends upon the quantity of resources employed, prices of resources, output, prices of products *etc.*, and all of these could be random variables.
- ☆ ***Data:*** In employing the LP technique to solve a problem, it is assumed that data are available to formulate the problem.
- ☆ Objective function is the sole criterion for choosing among the decision variables.
- ☆ The decision variables are fully manipulatable within the feasible region and are under the control of the decision maker. Further, all appropriate decision variables have to be included in the model.
- ☆ The constraints fully identify the bounds placed on the decision variables by resource availability, technology, the external environment *etc.* Thus, any choice of the decision variables, which simultaneously satisfies all the constraints, is admissible.
- ☆ Input and output prices are constant and we have constant RTS. Constant input prices and constant RTS mean that, MCs and ATCs are constant and

are linear. The production takes place with limited technologically fixed input combinations. Because of this limited technologically fixed input combinations that a farmer can use to produce output, the isoquants are not smooth and bear kinks as shown through Panel B of the Figure 9.1.

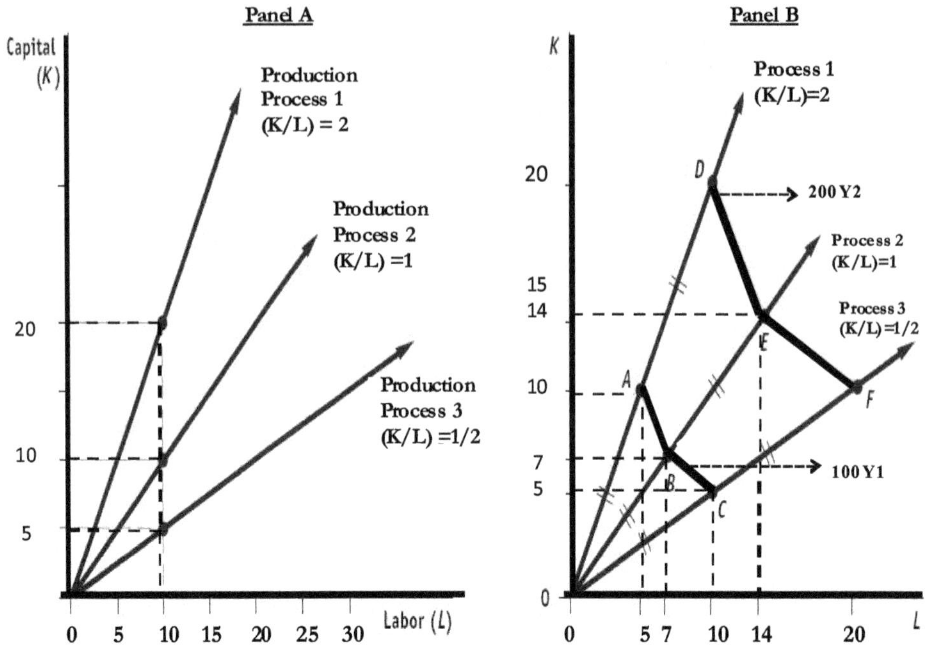

Figure 9.1: Linear Programming (Kinked) Isoquants Showing different Production Process.

IV. Production Processes in LP

Though LP technique enjoys wider applications, it is more frequently applied in taking production decisions with the objective functions *i.e.*, maximization of profits and minimization of costs. As discussed earlier through Panel E of the Figure 3.6 on LP isoquants, output can be produced with only a limited number of combinations *i.e.*, at kinks on the isoquants. The ratio of the inputs at each possible (limited) combination on an isoquant represent production process or activity and the same can be shown as a straight line ray from the origin. In Panel A of the Figure 9.1, an output of Y_1 (100 units) can be produced at three possible input ratios or production process *viz.*, K/L = 2, K/L = 1 and K/L = ½. These production processes are indicated by a ray from the origin with the slope of K/L for each respective production process. In production process of K/L = 2, it implies, for every two units of capital (K), one unit of labour (L) will be used to produce Y_1 output (100 units). In production process of K/L = 1, it implies, for every one unit of K, one unit of L will be used to produce the same Y_1 output (100 units). In production process of K/L = ½, it implies, for every one unit of K, two units of L will be used to produce the same Y_1 output (100 units). Thus, to produce the same level of output Y_1, the inputs are combined in different proportions across different production processes. This also implies that, to produce output Y_1, there are three processes, each using a particular combination of K and L. By joining these input combinations or ratios of K/L across different production process, we get an isoquant representing output Y_1 (Panel B of the Figure 9.1). Since limited production possibilities (processes) are there to produce output Y_1, the derived isoquant is not smoothly curved as in case of good substitutes (Figure 3.5), but it will have kinks indicating the points of limited production processes available to produce the same level of output. In Panel B, it is clear that, output Y_1 can be produced at three kinks or production processes (A, B and C) of different K/L ratios *viz.*, 2, 1 and ½ respectively. That is, at kink A, the farmer employs 10 units of K and 5 units of L, at kink B, the farmer employs 7 units of K and 7 units of L and at kink C, the farmer employs 5 units of K and 10 units of L and by joining these three kinks A, B and C, we get an isoquant of output Y_1 (100 units). As mentioned earlier, the isoquant so derived in not a smooth convex curve, but bear kinks indicating the three production processes that are possible to produce output Y_1. Since, the production programme experiences constant RTS, doubling both L and K exactly doubles the output (Y_2 = 200 units). Thus, isoquant Y_2 = 200 units will be produced at three kinks D, E and F with input combinations (20K + 10L), (14K + 14L) and (10K + 20L) respectively. Thus, the two isoquants Y_1 and Y_2 lie parallel to each other. Note that, the greater the number of processes available to produce a particular commodity, the less pronounced are these kinks and thereby, the isoquants approach the smooth curves.

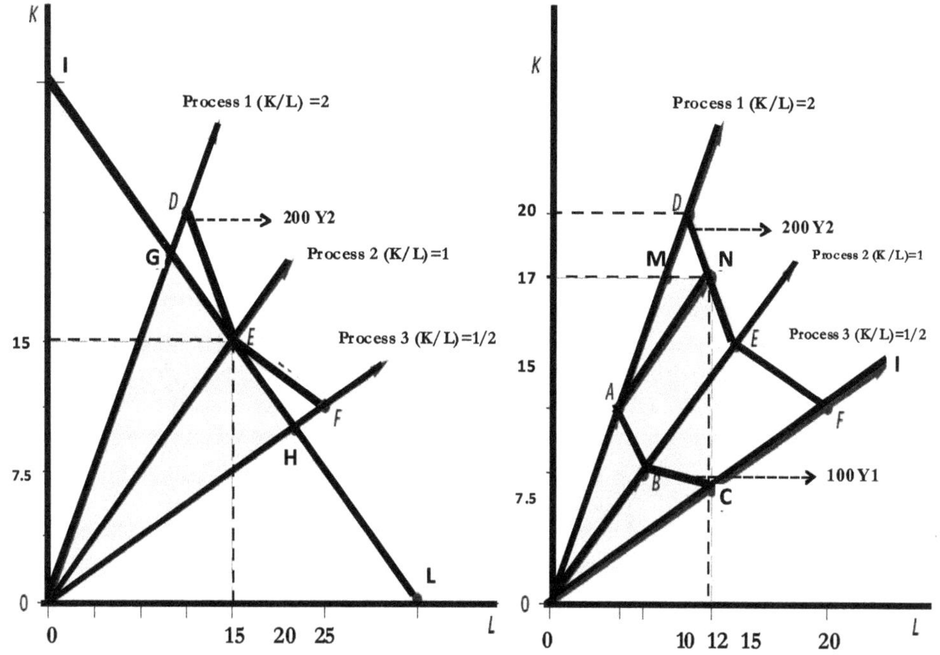

Figure 9.2: Feasible Solutions and Optimal Solutions in Linear Programming (Kinked) Isoquants.

As discussed in Chapter 3, to achieve LCC of resources, the iso-cost line should be tangent to the isoquant from below or when the slope of iso-cost line equals the slope of isoquant. The same is true for the LP analysis. In Panel A of the Figure 9.2, the iso-cost line (IL) is tangent to the kinked isoquant at point 'E' thereby, indicating the feasible region OGH for producing the output Y_2 = 200 units. The feasible region implies that, it is the area of attainable input combinations, so as to produce the given level of output and beyond that region, the combination of inputs is not possible to produce a given level of output. The same can be shown through Panel A of the Figure 9.2, as both capital intensive (which involve K/L ratio more than 2) and labour intensive (which involve K/L ratio less than ½) production programmes beyond OGH region are not possible to attain LCC of resources or optimal combination (optimal solution) of resources. Among the feasible points showing different input combinations in the feasible region OGH, the only one optimal solution is at point E, where iso-cost line lie tangent to the isoquant from below or the slope of iso-cost line equals the slope of isoquant. So, at this optimal solution (point), the farmer employs 15 units each of L and K, so as to produce the given level of output Y_2 = 200 units. However, when the farmer faces no cost-constraint, but faces a possibility of allocating only 12L and 17K inputs combination (*i.e.*, two constraints regarding allocation of two inputs), then the feasible region is given by OMNC (Panel B of Figure 9.2). That is, in this region OMNC, the feasible combinations of two inputs exist to produce a given level of output (Y_2 = 200 units). However, the optimal solution (point) is at 'N', as the farmer can employ only 12L and 17K inputs combination. To reach this point 'N', the farmer employs Production process 1 up to point A (*i.e.*, on isoquant Y_1=100 units) and remaining 100 units of output through Production process 2 (OB=AN). This implies that, given two constraints regarding the allocation levels of two inputs, the farmer can reach the maximum output of Y_2=200 units by employing two production processes. In Panel B, OA and OB are called 'vectors'. Thus, ON is equal to the sum of vectors OA and OB.

It is clear from the above discussion that, when the farmer faces cost constraint (*i.e.*, employing iso-cost line in the analysis in Panel A of Figure 9.2), he employs only one process (production process 2 *i.e.* (K/L) =1) to achieve optimal solution (LCC) in the production programme. However, when the farmer faces two constraints (Panel B of Figure 9.2 regarding allocation levels of two inputs), the farmer required two processes to reach the optimum solution. From this, we can generalize that, to reach the optimal solution, a farmer will require no more processes than the number of constraints that he faces in producing the output. Sometimes, even fewer processes will do. For example, if the farmer faces the constraints regarding allocation of only 10L and 20K (Panel B of Figure 9.2 regarding allocation levels of two inputs), the feasible region changes and now the optimum solution would be at point D, and the output Y_2=100 units can be produced by employing only production process 1. Note that, to reach any point on an isoquant between two adjacent production processes, we use the process to which the point is closer, in proportion to 1 minus the distance of the point from the process (ray). For example, if point 'N' was one-quarter of the distance DE from point D along the isoquant Y_2, the farmer would produce 1 – ¼ = ¾ of the output of 200 units *i.e.*, 150 units with production process 1 and the remaining 1/4th output (50 units) with production process 2 (Panel B of Figure 9.2). The amount of each input that is used in each process is then proportional to the output produced by each process.

Assume that, in Panel A of the Figure 9.2, if the ratio of wage rate of labour (w) to the rental price of capital (r) is increased, then the iso-cost line IL become steeper and now, the optimal solution would remain at point E as long as the new IL iso-cost (constraint) line remained flatter than the segment DE on the isoquant for Y_2=200 units. If w/r still rises, the iso-cost line IL becomes still steeper and gets coincided with segment DE on the isoquant thereby, the farmer can produce 200 units of output with production process 1 or production process 2 or any combination of production process 1 and production process 2. If w/r rose still further, the iso-cost line still becomes more steeper and the farmer would reach the optimal solution at point D on the isoquant.

V. Formulation of LP Model

As discussed above, LP is a widely used mathematical modeling technique to determine the optimal solution for the maximizing or minimizing a linear function subject to linear constraints. The constraints may be equalities or inequalities. Before going into the analytical framework for addressing an optimization problem, let us look at the basic format for formulating the LP problem for profit maximization (Table 9.1) and cost minimization (Table 9.2).

Table 9.1: Formulation of LP Model Involving the Allocation of Resources to Activities (Objective function is to maximize profits with reference to Table 9.3)

Restrictions (Resources)	*Resource Usage per Unit of Activity (Product)*				*Quantities of resources Available (Total)*
	Product 1	*Product 2*	.....	*Product N*	
1	b_{11}	b_{12}	....	b_{1n}	c_1
2	b_{21}	b_{22}	....	b_{2n}	c_2
3	b_{31}	b_{32}	....	b_{3n}	c_3
.	.	.	.	.	.
.	.	.	.	.	.
J	b_{m1}	b_{m2}	....	b_{mn}	c_m
Contribution to Max Z per unit of activity	a_1	a_2	....	a_n	

Many variants can be posed in the formulation of LP problem and this makes the LP technique to apply to a wide variety of settings. For example, the optimization problem could aim at:

- ☆ Minimizing the costs in the production programme in purchasing three inputs from different sources so that, how much of each input to buy subject to constraints on minimum and maximum levels of inputs.
- ☆ Maximizing the profits in the production programme subject to resource (labour and raw materials) constraints.

Table 9.2: Formulation of LP Model Involving the Allocation of Resources to Activities (Objective function is to minimize costs with reference to Table 9.4)

Ingredients (Resources)	*Contribution by Each Uof Activity (Product)*				*Max Limit of Ingredients (Units)*
	Activity 1	*Activity 2*	.....	*Activity N*	
1	b_{11}	b_{12}	....	b_{1n}	c_1
2	b_{21}	b_{22}	....	b_{2n}	c_2
3	b_{31}	b_{32}	....	b_{3n}	c_3
.	.	.	.	.	.
.	.	.	.	.	.
J	b_{m1}	b_{m2}	....	b_{mn}	c_m
Contribution to Min Z per unit of activity (product)	a_1	a_2	....	a_n	

- ✰ Formulation of a minimum cost transportation plan determining the amount of goods to transport across each available route subject to constraints on supply availability and demand.
- ✰ Scheduling school buses to minimize the total distance travelled when carrying students.
- ✰ Selecting the product mix in a food processing firm to make best use of machine and labour-hours available, while maximizing the firm's profit.
- ✰ Selecting the blends of raw materials in feed mills to produce finished feed combinations at minimum cost.
- ✰ Designing the distribution system that will minimize total shipping cost from several warehouses to various market locations.

Note that, in solving a constrained optimization problem by LP technique, the most difficult aspect is formulation of the problem in a LP format or framework. After formulating the problem, the actual solution to the problem is then straightforward. Simple LP problems with only a few variables can be easily solved graphically or algebraically. However, for the complex problems involving more number of variables, the use computer software programmes is inevitable. Now, let us proceed to solve LP problems based on Graphical and Simplex methods.

VI. Solutions to LP Problems

LP is an efficient way of determining optimum plan only if there are numerous (but finite) enterprises or processes and a numerous restrictions in attaining a specific objective (maximization function or minimization function). For achieving this optimal plan out of the feasible solutions, we can employ several methods like:

- ✰ Graphical method
- ✰ Analytical method or Trial and error method
- ✰ Simplex method
- ✰ Big-M method

- ☆ Two phase simplex method
- ☆ Dual simplex method
- ☆ Revised simplex method

Among the above methods, let us discuss two popular methods *viz.*, Graphical method and Simplex method.

A. Graphical Method

We already know that, LP problem is a linear function of objective function and decision variables are subjected to a number of linear inequalities. Fortunately problems of this type with just two decision variables can be easily solved by using graphical approach. So, the easiest way to solve small LP problems, when there are only two decision variables (say, units of paddy to produce and units of maize to produce) is by employing graphical solution approach. However, this method is not suitable, if the LP problem addresses more than two variables, as it is not possible to plot the solution on a two dimensional graph. Let us employ this approach to address LP problems of maximization function and minimization function.

i. Profit Maximization Objective Function

Step 1

The first basic step involved is formulation of LP problem. This refers to translating the real-world problem in the form of mathematical equations that represent the objective function, functional constraints and non-negativity constraints. This formulation of LP problem forms the crux in the research study, as it guides the researcher in collecting requisite data and subsequent steps in finding the optimal solution. This also makes the researcher to transform all the collected data into tabular form for mathematical computations.

Example 9.3

Assume a profit maximization problem, where a farmer employs two resources *viz.*, fertilizer and labour to produce two commodities *viz.*, paddy and maize. The unit profit or net income per unit for paddy is Rs.6 and for maize is Rs.8. The total quantity of fertilizer available is 300 units and total number of man days available are 110 days. To produce paddy and maize, it requires 30 and 20 units of fertilizer respectively and 5 and 10 labour man days respectively.

The above given problem contains the information for the LP problem and it can be formulated as given below.

Table 9.3: Input-output Data in Producing Paddy and Maize by the Farmer

Resources	*Amounts of Inputs Required to Produce One Unit of Output*		
	Paddy(X_1)	*Maize (X_2)*	*Total Resources Available*
Fertilizer (units)	30	20	300
Labour (man days)	5	10	110
Net income	6	8	

The above tabular form of LP problem can be conveniently expressed as mathematical equations as given below.

Max Z $6X_1+8X_2$

Subject to:

$30X_1 + 20X_2 \leq 300$ (Functional Constraint for fertilizer)

$5X_1 + 10X_2 \leq 110$ (Functional Constraint for labour man days)

$X_1, X_2 \geq 0$ (Non-negativity constraints)

Step 2

Now, the above constraint inequalities will be converted into equalities as given below.

$30X_1 + 20X_2 = 300$ (Functional Constraint for fertilizer)

$5X_1 + 10X_2 = 110$ (Functional Constraint for labour man days)

Step 3

Compute horizontal and vertical intercepts from each functional constraint equation.

$30X_1 + 20X_2 = 300$ (Functional Constraint for fertilizer)

Assume $X_1 = 0$. So, $30(0)+20X_2=300$

So, $X_2=15$ units. This 15 units of X_2 represents X_2 intercept on the graph when $X_1=0$. This implies, all the fertilizer is used to produce maize. Similarly, assume $X_2=0$. Then,

$30(X_1) + 20(0) = 300$

So, $X_1=10$ units. This 10 units of X_1 represents X_1 intercept on the graph when $X_2=0$. This implies, all the fertilizer is used to produce paddy. When these two intercepts were joined on the graph, we get a straight line (Panel A of the Figure 9.3). Similar procedure is followed to compute X_1 intercept and X_2 intercept from functional constraint for labour man days. So, from the equation: $5X_1 + 10X_2 = 110$, $X_2 = 11$ units when $X_1=0$ (this implies, all the labour are used to produce maize) and $X_1 = 22$ when $X_2=0$ units (this implies, all the labour are used to produce paddy). When these two intercepts were joined on the graph, we get a straight line (Panel B of the Figure 9.3).

Step 4

These two straight lines are now placed on the same graph (Figure 9.4). The simplest way to locate the feasible region is to plug in the coordinates of the origin (0,0) and see whether this point satisfies the constraint. If it does, then all points on the origin side of the line are feasible (valid), and all points on the other side of the line are infeasible or invalid. (If (0,0) does not satisfy the constraint, then all points on the other side and away from the origin are feasible (valid), and all points on the origin side of the constraint line are infeasible or invalid). Now feasible solution region or solution space is represented by the area on the graph that is valid for all constraints. Choosing any point in this area will result in a valid solution. *In case of maximization*

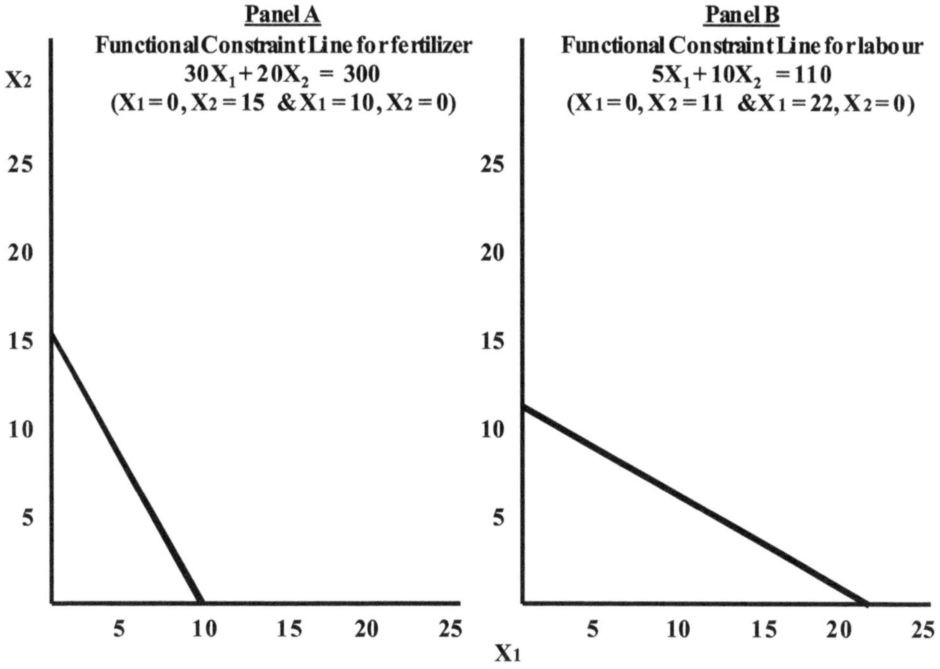

Figure 9.3: Functional Constraint Lines for Fertilizer and Labour Man Days.

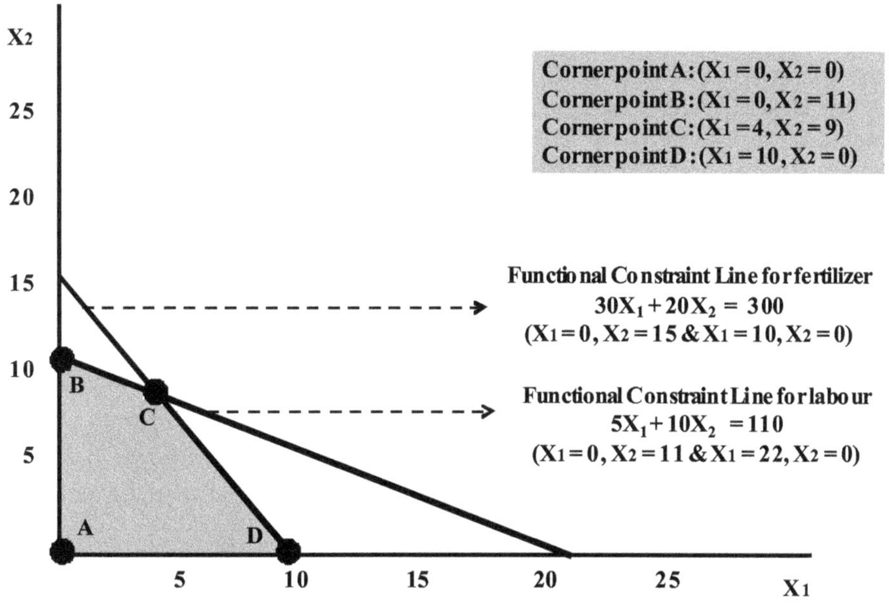

Figure 9.4: Finding Optimal Solution Based on Corner Point Approach.

function, the optimal value corresponds to the greatest value of the coordinates (in case of minimization function, the optimal value corresponds to the lowest value of the coordinates).

We will use the origin (0,0) to check the valid side (feasible region) for both constraint lines. For fertilizer constraint line, 30(0) + 20(0) is < 300 and thereby, this coordinate (0,0) is valid. For labour man days constraint line, the coordinate (0,0) is also valid, as 5(0) + 10(0) is < 110. Likewise, we can estimate the valid coordinates for the above two constraint lines and the coordinates that satisfies these two constraint lines are up to the points A, B, C and D and thereby, ABCD shaded area (Figure 9.4) is the feasible region or solution space. Let us examine now the coordinates beyond this shaded region ABCD with reference to the two constraint lines. Assume $X_1 = 10$ and $X_2 = 15$ and with reference to fertilizer constraint line: $30(X_1) + 20(X_2)$ is < 300, then: 30(10) + 20(15) is >300 and thereby, this coordinate (10,15) is not valid. Similarly, assume $X_1 = 15$ and $X_2 = 15$ and with reference to labour man days constraint line: $5(X_1) + 10(X_2)$ is < 110, then: 5(15) + 10(15) is >110 and thereby, this coordinate (15,15) is not valid. So, any coordinate outside the region ABCD is not valid to meet the functional constraints and hence, the region ABCD constitute the feasible region. There are several approaches to locate the optimal solution from the feasible region, but the two important approaches include: Corner point approach and Iso-profit line approach. Let us discuss their methodologies here under for this example.

a. Corner Point Approach

This is the simplest approach to estimate optimal solution from the feasible region ABCD shown in the Figure 9.4. In the figure, both the constraint lines for fertilizer and labour are drawn and this gives the shaded region ABCD that satisfies both the constraints. In the shaded area ABCD, 'A', 'B', 'C' and 'D' are the corner points. This approach states that, *'the optimal solution to any LP problem is at the corner point or extreme point of the feasible region that contribute to maximum profit (Maximization function) or minimum cost (Minimization function)'*. In this example, the optimal solution in the feasible (shaded) region ABCD will lie at one of the corner points *i.e.*, 'A' or 'B' or 'C' or 'D' that contribute to maximum profits. Thus, optimal solution always occurs at corners. When more than one corner corresponds to an optimal solution, each corner and all points along the line connecting the corners correspond to optimal solutions. Let us find out the values at the corner points 'A', 'B', 'C' and 'D' with reference to the objective function and the highest value at one of these four points corresponds to optimal solution in the feasible region ABCD.

Optimal solution or Profit at Corner point A: ($X_1 = 0, X_2 = 0$): $6X_1 + 8X_2 = 6(0) + 8(0) = 0$

Optimal solution or Profit at Corner point B: ($X_1 = 0, X_2 = 11$): $6X_1 + 8X_2 = 6(0) + 8(11) = 88$

Optimal solution or Profit at Corner point C: To fix the coordinates at point C, where the two constraints lines intersect each other, we follow simultaneous equations approach. We know the two functional constraints:

$30X_1 + 20X_2 = 300$ (Functional Constraint for fertilizer)

$5X_1 + 10X_2 = 110$ (Functional Constraint for labour man days)

Multiply the second equation with -2 and by adding these two equations, we get $X_1 = 4$. By substituting X_1 in any of the above two equations, we get $X_2 = 9$. So, Optimal solution or Profit at Corner point C is given by: ***(X_1 = 4, X_2 = 9):*** $6X_1 + 8X_2 = 6(4) + 8(9) = 96$.

Optimal solution or Profit at Corner point D: (X_1 = 10, X_2 = 0): $6X_1 + 8X_2 = 6(10) + 8(0) = 60$

Among the above four corner points, point 'C' contributes to highest profits *i.e.,* Rs. 96 and thereby, this is the optimal solution in the feasible region for this problem of producing 4 units of paddy and 9 units of maize. Note that, in this example, the optimal solution is at corner point 'C' *i.e.,* at the point of intersection of two constraint lines, but this is not the case always. The optimal solution can also be at the corner points bordering on the X_1 and X_2 axes *i.e.,* at point 'B' or at point 'D'. It all depends upon the values of the objective function coefficients and the angle of the iso-profit line that is discussed in the ensuing pages.

Proving the Optimal Solution

For the optimal solution to be correct, the total outputs must be equal to the total inputs available on the farm. In the above example, we obtained optimal solution at point C, where the farmer maximizes his total profits by producing 4 units of paddy and 9 units of maize. In order to determine the total amount of each input used by the farmer to produce 4 units of paddy and 9 units of maize, please refer to the columns (2) and (3) of the Table 9.3. It is shown that, to produce one unit of paddy, the farmer employs 30 units of fertilizer (F) and 5 labour man days (L) *i.e..,* 30F + 5L and to produce one unit of maize, the farmer employs 20 units of fertilizer (F) and 10 labour man days (L) *i.e.,* 20F + 10L. Since the farmer produces 4 units of paddy and 9 units of maize, the total inputs used to produce these two enterprises is shown here under.

Paddy	*Maize*
Total output x Inputs = Total inputs used	Total output x Inputs = Total inputs used
4 x 30F = 120F	9 x 20 F = 180F
4 x 5L = 20L	9 x 10L = 90L

So, the total amount of inputs used among the enterprises is given by,

Total amount of fertilizer used : 120F + 180F = 300F

Total number of labour man days employed : 20L + 90L = 110L

The last column of Table 9.3 shows the maximum amount of fertilizer available to the farmer is 300 and maximum number of labour man days available are 110. From this, we can infer that, the total amount of fertilizer available to the farmer (300 units) is equal to the total amount of fertilizer employed (300 units) and total number of labour man days available (110) are equal to the total number of labour man days employed. This infers that point 'C' in the Figure 9.4 represents the optimal solution and not at A, B or D.

b. Iso-profit Line Approach

Another approach of solving the LP problem graphically is by computing the iso-profit line in taking up two enterprises paddy and maize. This approach is comparatively quicker in estimating the optimal solution compared to the earlier approach, as it is not required to calculate profit at each and every corner point in the feasible (shaded) region. An iso-profit line is a line that indicates same level of total profit of the given objective function. So, any point on the iso-profit line indicates same profits for a given objective function. *As per this approach, the criterion for maximization of profits (minimization of costs) is when the highest iso-profit line (lowest iso-cost line) touches the highest or extreme point of the feasible region (lowest point of the feasible region).*

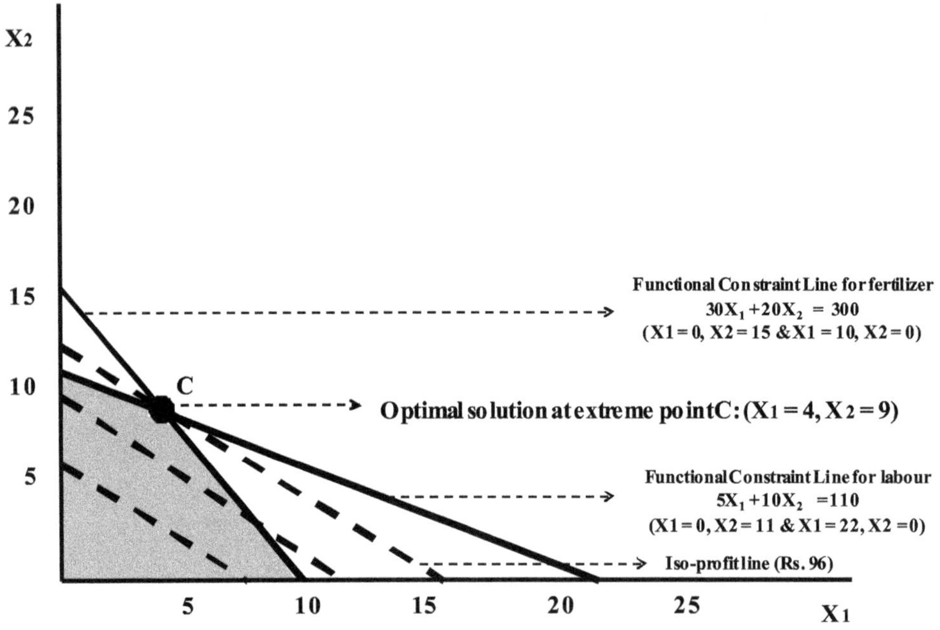

Figure 9.5: Finding Optimal Solution Based on Iso-Profit Line Approach.

Assume a profit level of Rs.48 and compute X_1 and X_2 with reference to the objective function *i.e.,*: Max Z $6X_1+8X_2 = 48$. Set, $X_1 = 0$ and then $X_2 = 6$. Now set $X_2=0$ and then $X_1=8$. Now the line connecting 8 units of X_1 and 6 units of X_2 is called iso-profit line (dotted line in Figure 9.5). As per the criterion of this approach, this iso-profit line does not touch the extreme point of the shaded region ABCD. So, again arbitrarily set another profit level say Rs. 72. Again follow the same procedure to compute X_1 and X_2 with reference to the objective function *i.e.,* Max Z $6X_1+8X_2 = 72$ and therefore, $X_1=12$ and $X_2 = 9$. Since this iso-profit line connecting 12 units of X_1 and 9 units of X_2 does not touch the extreme point of the shaded region ABCD, the optimal solution is not attained. Continuing this procedure is often labourious and time consuming and hence, draw a line that lies parallel to the previous iso-profit lines that connects the extreme point of the shaded area ABCD. This line passes through the point 'C' and (as computed in earlier approach), the coordinates at corner point C is ($X_1 = 4, X_2 = 9$). So, now with reference to the objective function (profit maximization): Max Z $6X_1+8X_2 = 6(4) + 8(9) =$ Rs.96 *i.e.*, by producing 4 units of paddy and 9 units of maize. This iso-profit line (Z=96) is drawn considering the objective function, Max Z: $6X_1+8X_2$ with $X_1=16$ and $X_2=0$; $X_2 = 12$ and $X_1=0$, as discussed above with reference to profit level of Rs.48.

Range of Optimality: Note that, the optimal solution will remain unchanged as long as

- An objective function coefficient lies within its range of optimality
- There are no changes in any other input parameters.

The value of the objective function will change if the coefficient multiplies a variable, whose value is non-zero.

ii. Dual of the Problem

With every LP problem, there is associated another LP problem, which is called the dual of the original (or the primal) problem. In the above case for maximization problem, there is a dual of minimization of cost. To formulate the dual problem for primal problem, the following points are to be noted:

- The rows and columns are inter-changed
- The direction of inequalities in the constraints is reversed. In the above case, the primal is maximization of profits and hence, the functional constraints have '≤' sign. So, in its dual (minimization of cost), the functional constraints have '≥' sign.
- The number of variables is reversed.

The following is the general relationship between primal and its dual LP problem:

Primal Problem	**Dual Problem**
Maximization function	**Minimization function**
$\text{Max } Z = a_1X_1 + a_2X_2$	$\text{Min } Z = c_1Y_1 + c_2Y_2 + c_3Y_3$
Subject to	**Subject to**
$b_{11}X_1 + b_{12}X_2 \leq c_1$	$b_{11}Y_1 + b_{21}Y_2 + b_{31}Y_3 \geq a_1$
$b_{21}X_1 + b_{22}X_2 \leq c_2$	$b_{12}Y_1 + b_{22}Y_2 + b_{32}Y_3 \geq a_2$
$b_{31}X_1 + b_{32}X_2 \leq c_3$	$Y_i \geq 0$
$X_i \geq 0$	

Let us write the dual problem now for the above studied (primal) example as follows:

Primal Problem

$\text{Max Z} : 6X_1 + 8X_2$

$\text{Subject to} : 30X_1 + 20X_2 \leq 300$

$5X_1 + 10X_2 \leq 110$

$X_{1,} X_2 \geq 0$

Dual Problem

$\text{Min Z} : 300A + 110B$

$\text{Subject to} : 30A + 5B \geq 6$ (Functional Constraint for Paddy X_1)

$20A + 10B \geq 8$ (Functional Constraint for Maize X_2)

$A, B \geq 0$

Step 1

Now, the above constraint inequalities will be converted into equalities as given below.

$30A + 5B = 6$ (Functional Constraint for Paddy X_1)

$20A + 10B = 8$ (Functional Constraint for Maize X_2)

Step 2

Compute horizontal and vertical intercepts from each functional constraint equation.

$30A + 5B = 6$ (Functional Constraint for Paddy X_1)

Assume $A = 0$. So,

$30(0)+5B=6$

So, B=1.2 units. This 1.2 units of B represents B–intercept on the graph when A=0. This implies, only labour input is employed in producing paddy X_1 and no fertilizer is employed. Similarly, assume B=0. Then,

$30(A) + 5(0) = 6$

So, A=0.2 units. This 0.2 units of A represents A-intercept on the graph when B=0. This implies, only fertilizer input is employed in producing paddy X_1 and no labour are employed. When these two intercepts were joined on the graph, we get a straight line (Panel A of Figure 9.6). Similar procedure is followed to compute A intercept and B intercept from functional constraint for maize X_2. So, from the equation: $20A + 10B = 8$, $B = 0.8$ units when A=0 (this implies, only labour input is employed in producing maize X_2 and no fertilizer is employed) and $A = 0.4$ units when B=0 (this implies, only fertilizer input is employed in producing maize X_2 and no labour is employed). When these two intercepts were joined on the graph, we get a straight line (Panel B of Figure 9.6).

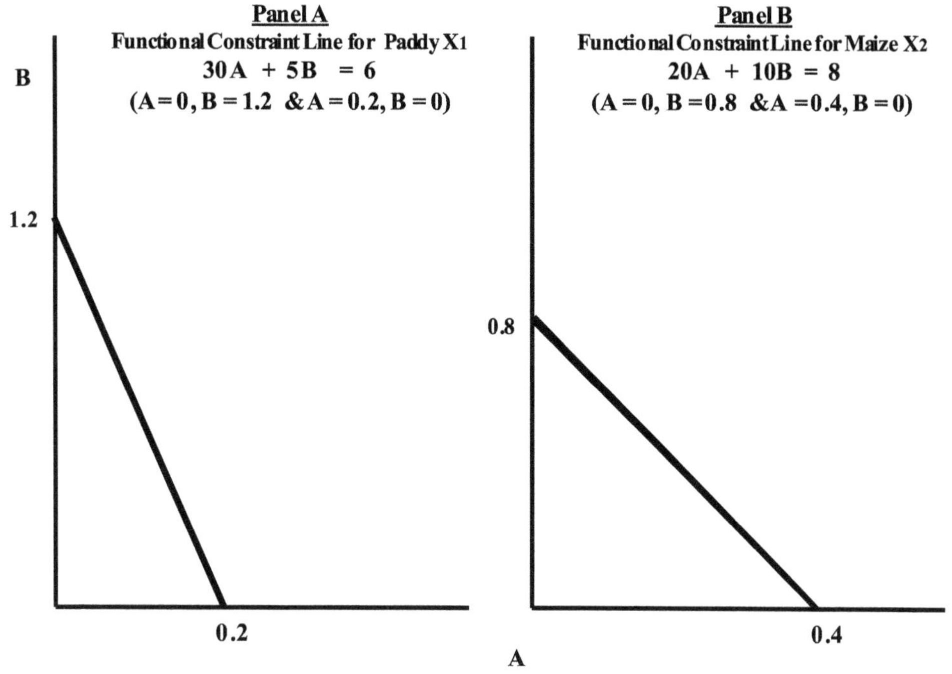

Figure 9.6: Functional Constraint Lines of Paddy X1 and Maie X2.

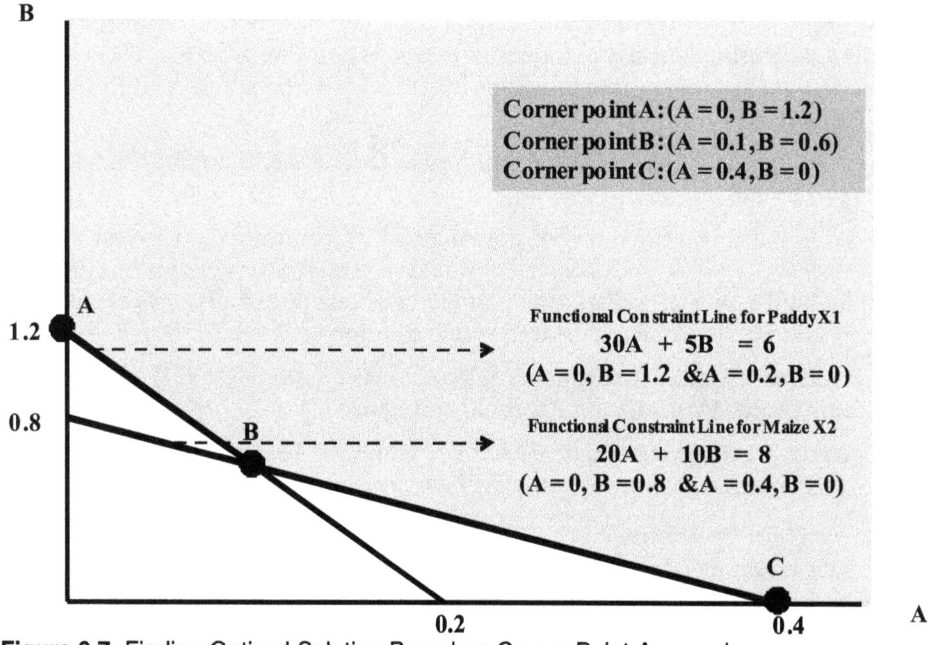

Figure 9.7: Finding Optimal Solution Based on Corner Point Approach.

Step 3

These two straight lines are now placed on the same graph (Figure 9.7). As mentioned earlier, in case of minimization function, the optimal value corresponds to the lowest value of the coordinates. We can estimate the valid coordinates for the above two constraint lines and the coordinates that satisfies these two constraint lines are beyond the points A, B and C and thereby, ABC shaded area is the feasible region. That is, any coordinate outside the region ABC is valid to meet the functional constraints and hence, the region outside ABC constitutes the feasible region. Let us follow Corner point approach to derive optimal solution for this dual problem. This approach states that, *'the optimal solution to any LP problem is at the corner point or extreme point of the feasible region that contribute to minimum cost (Minimization function)'*.

In this example, the optimal solution in the feasible (shaded) region beyond ABC will lie at one of the corner points *i.e.*, 'A' or 'B' or 'C' that contribute to minimum cost. Let us find out the values at the corner points 'A', 'B' and 'C' with reference to the objective function and the lowest value at one of these three points corresponds to optimal solution in the feasible region beyond ABC.

Optimal solution or Cost at Corner point A: (A = 0, B = 1.2): 300A+110B = 300(0) + 110(1.2) = Rs.132

Optimal solution or Cost at Corner point B: To fix the coordinates at point B, where the two constraints lines intersect each other, we follow simultaneous equations approach. We know the two functional constraints:

30A + 5B = 6 (Functional Constraint for Paddy X_1)

20A + 10B = 8 (Functional Constraint for Maize X_2)

Multiply the first equation with -2 and by adding these two equations, we get A = 0.1. By substituting A in any of the above two equations, we get B = 0.6. So, Optimal solution or Cost at Corner point B is given by: (A = 0.1, B = 0.6): 300A+110B = 300(0.1) + 110(0.6) = Rs.96.

Optimal solution or Cost at Corner point C: (A = 0.4, B = 0.0): 300A+110B = 300(0.4) + 110(0.0) = Rs.120.

Among the above three corner points, point 'B' contributes to lowest cost *i.e.*, Rs.96 and thereby, this is the optimal solution in the feasible region for this problem by employing 0.1 units of fertilizer and 0.6 units of labour. So, for all practical purposes, the primal and dual problems have the same solution *i.e.*, Max Z = Min Z. That is,

Considering solution to primal problem *i.e.*, Max Z $6X_1+8X_2$ = 6(4) + 8(9) = Rs.96 (Maximum profits in producing Paddy X_1 and Maize X_2)

Considering solution to dual problem *i.e.*, Min Z 300A+110B = 300(0.1) + 110(0.6) = Rs.96 (Minimum cost in employing fertilizer and labour).

Primal vs Dual Problems

It is clear that, the dual problem is formulated directly from the corresponding primal problem. The optimal value of the objective function of the primal problem is equal to the optimal value of the objective function of the corresponding dual problem.

This is called the Duality theorem. The characteristics of the primal problem and the dual problem can be differentiated as follows:

- ☆ If the primal problem involves maximization problem, the dual problem is minimization and *vice versa.*
- ☆ The profit constant 'aj' in the primal problem replaces the capacity constants 'cj', while writing the dual problem.
- ☆ If the primal problem involves '≤' signs (Maximization function), the dual problem involves '≥' signs (Minimization function) and *vice versa.*
- ☆ The RHS constraint inequalities of the functional constraints in the primal problem are shown as constants in the objective function of the dual problem.
- ☆ A new set of variables appear in the dual problem.
- ☆ If there are 'n' decision variables and 'm' inequalities or constraints in the primal problem, then in the dual problem there will be 'm' decision variables and 'n' inequalities or constraints.
- ☆ The 'dual of the dual' problem is the original primal problem itself.
- ☆ If the primal problem has a solution, then its dual will also have the same solution.
- ☆ If the primal problem has multiple solutions, then the dual has degenerate solution.
- ☆ If the primal problem has infeasible solution, then the dual has infeasible or unbounded solution.
- ☆ If the primal problem has unbounded solution, then the dual has infeasible or unbounded solution

  Note that, the concept of duality can be used in a wide variety of applications including:
- ☆ It may be more efficient to solve the dual than the primal.
- ☆ The dual solution provides important economical interpretation such as shadow prices, *i.e.*, the marginal values of the RHS elements.

iii. Cost Minimization Objective Function

Step 1

The first basic step involved is formulation of LP problem.

Example 9.4

Assume a cost minimization problem that, where a consumer prefer two foods Meat X_1 and Fish X_2 to derive two nutrients *viz.*, carbohydrates and proteins. The cost per unit of food X_1 is Rs.2 and for food X_2 is Rs.6. The minimum requirement of carbohydrates is 3 units and minimum requirement of proteins is 8 units. The other requisite data are shown through Table 9.4.

The above given problem contains the information for the LP problem and it can be formulated as given below.

Table 9.4: Dietary Requirements of a Consumer from Two Foods

Nutritional Elements	*Foods*		
	Meat (X_1)	*Fish (X_2)*	*Minimum Daily Requirement*
Carbohydrates(units)	1	2	3
Protein (units)	2	8	8
Unit cost	2	6	

The above tabular form of LP problem can be conveniently expressed as mathematical equations as given below.

Min Z $2X_1+6X_2$

Subject to:

$1X_1 + 2X_2 \geq 3$ (Functional Constraint for carbohydrates)

$2X_1 + 8X_2 \geq 8$ (Functional Constraint for proteins)

$X_1, X_2 \geq 0$ (Non-negativity constraint)

Step 2

Now, the above constraint inequalities will be converted into equalities as given below.

$1X_1 + 2X_2 = 3$ (Functional Constraint for carbohydrates)

$2X_1 + 8X_2 = 8$ (Functional Constraint for proteins)

Step 3

Compute horizontal and vertical intercepts from each functional constraint equation.

$1X_1 + 2X_2 = 3$ (Functional Constraint for carbohydrates)

Assume $X_1 = 0$. So, $1(0)+2X_2=3$

So, $X_2=1.5$ units. These 1.5 units of X_2 represent X_2–intercept on the graph when $X_1=0$. This implies, all the carbohydrates are derived from food X_2 and nothing from food X_1. Similarly, assume $X_2=0$. Then,

$1(X_1) + 2(0) = 3$

So, $X_1=3$ units. These 3 units of X_1 represent X_1-intercept on the graph when $X_2=0$. This implies, all the carbohydrates are derived from food X_1 and nothing from food X_2. When these two intercepts were joined on the graph, we get a straight line (Panel A of Figure 9.8). Similar procedure is followed to compute X_1 intercept and X_2 intercept from functional constraint for proteins. So, from the equation: $2X_1 + 8X_2 = 8$, $X_2 = 1$ units when $X_1=0$ (this implies, all the proteins are derived from food X_2 and nothing from food X_1) and $X_1 = 4$ units when $X_2=0$ (this implies, all the proteins are derived from food X_1 and nothing from food X_2). When these two intercepts were joined on the graph, we get a straight line (Panel B of Figure 9.8).

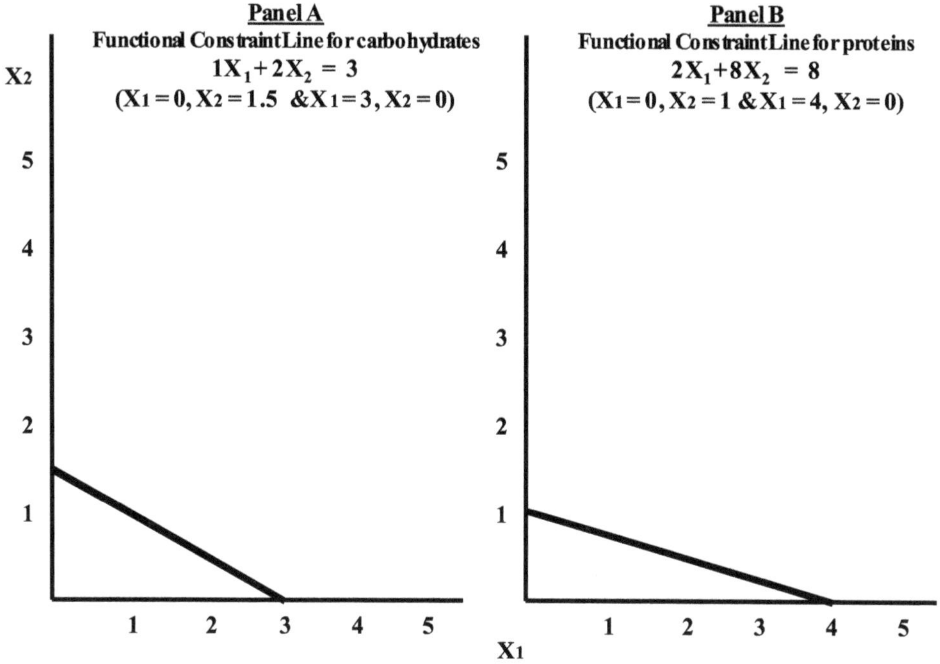

Figure 9.8: Functional Constraint Lines for Carbohydrates and Proteins.

Step 4

These two straight lines are now placed on the same graph (Figure 9.9). Feasible solution region is represented by the area on the graph that is valid for all constraints. Choosing any point in this area will result in a valid solution. In case of minimization function, the optimal value corresponds to the lowest value of the coordinates. We will use the origin (0,0) to check the valid side (feasible region) for both constraint lines. For carbohydrates constraint line, 1(0) + 2(0) is < 3 and thereby, this coordinate (0,0) is not valid. For proteins constraint line, the coordinate (0,0) is also not valid, as 2(0) + 8(0) is < 8. Likewise, we can estimate the valid coordinates for the above two constraint lines and the coordinates that satisfies these two constraint lines are beyond the points A, B and C and thereby, ABC shaded area is the feasible region. Let us examine now the coordinates in this shaded region ABC with reference to the two constraint lines. Assume $X_1 = 4.5$ and $X_2 = 0.5$ and with reference to carbohydrates constraint line: $1X_1 + 2X_2$ is ≥ 3, then: 1(4.5) + 2(0.5) is >3 and thereby, this coordinate (4.5, 0.5) is valid. Assume $X_1 = 2.5$ and $X_2 = 3$ and with reference to proteins constraint line: $2X_1 + 8X_2 \geq 8$, then: 2(2.5) + 8(3) is >8 and thereby, this coordinate (2.5, 3.0) is valid. So, any coordinate outside the region ABC is valid to meet the functional constraints and hence, the region outside ABC constitutes the feasible region. There are several approaches to locate the optimal solution from the feasible region, but the two important approaches include: Corner point approach and Iso-cost line approach. Let us discuss their methodologies here under for this example.

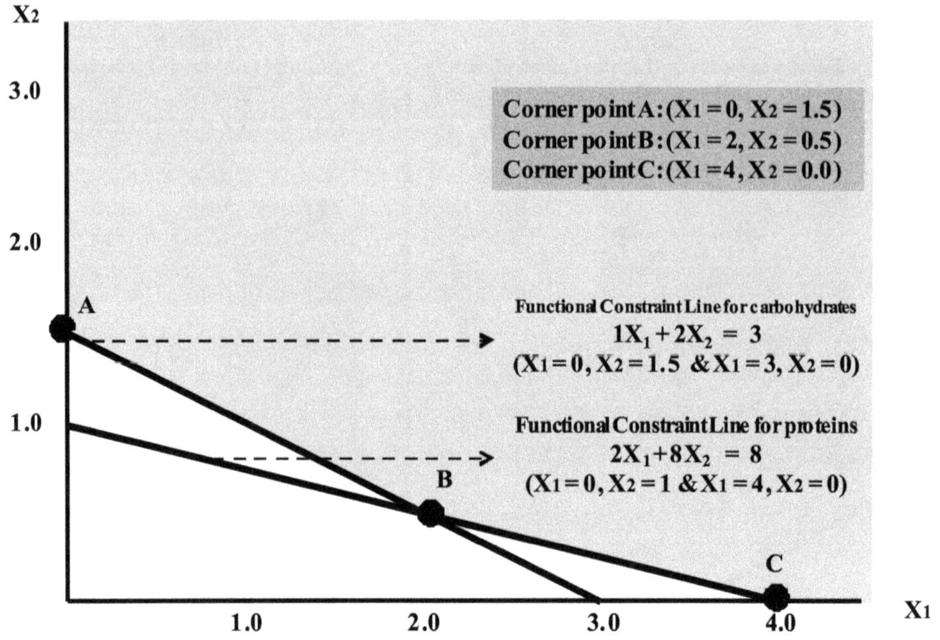

Figure 9.9: Finding Optimal Solution Based on Corner Point Approach.

a. Corner Point Approach

This is the simplest approach to estimate optimal solution from the feasible region *i.e.,* outside ABC region shown in the Figure 9.9. In the figure, both the constraint lines for carbohydrates and proteins are drawn and this gives the shaded region beyond ABC that satisfies both the constraints. In the shaded area beyond ABC, 'A', 'B' and 'C' are the corner points. This approach states that, *'the optimal solution to any LP problem is at the corner point or extreme point of the feasible region that contribute to minimum cost (Minimization function)'.* In this example, the optimal solution in the feasible (shaded) region beyond ABC will lie at one of the corner points *i.e.,* 'A' or 'B' or 'C' that contribute to minimum costs. Thus, optimal solution always occurs at corners. When more than one corner corresponds to an optimal solution, each corner and all points along the line connecting the corners correspond to optimal solutions. Let us find out the values at the corner points 'A', 'B' and 'C' with reference to the objective function and the lowest value at one of these three points corresponds to optimal solution in the feasible region beyond ABC.

Optimal solution or Cost at Corner point A: ($X_1 = 0, X_2 = 1.5$): $2X_1+6X_2 = 2(0) + 6(1.5) =$ Rs.9

Optimal solution or Cost at Corner point B: To fix the coordinates at point B, where the two constraints lines intersect each other, we follow simultaneous equations approach. We know the two functional constraints:

$1X_1 + 2X_2 = 3$ (Functional Constraint for carbohydrates)

$2X_1 + 8X_2 = 8$ (Functional Constraint for proteins)

Multiply the first equation with -2 and by adding these two equations, we get $X_1 = 2$. By substituting X_1 in any of the above two equations, we get $X_2 = 0.5$. So, Optimal solution or Cost at Corner point B is given by: ***($X_1 = 2, X_2 = 0.5$):*** $2X_1 + 6X_2 = 2(2) + 6(0.5)$ = Rs.7.

Optimal solution or Cost at Corner point C: ($X_1 = 4, X_2 = 0$): $2X_1+6X_2 = 2(4) + 6(0)$ = Rs.8

Among the above three corner points, point 'B' contributes to lowest cost *i.e.,* Rs.7 and thereby, this is the optimal solution in the feasible region for this problem by consuming 2 units of food X_1 and 0.5 units of food X_2. Note that, in this example, the optimal solution is at corner point 'B' *i.e.,* at the point of intersection of two constraint lines, but this is not the case always. The optimal solution can also be at the corner points bordering on the X_1 and X_2 axes *i.e.,* at point 'A' or at point 'C'. It all depends upon the values of the objective function coefficients and the angle of the iso-cost line that is discussed here under.

b. Iso-cost Line Approach

Another approach of solving the LP problem graphically is by computing the iso-cost line in having two foods X_1 and X_2. This approach is comparatively quicker in estimating the optimal solution compared to the earlier approach, as it is not required to calculate cost at each and every corner point in the feasible (shaded) region. An iso-cost line is a line that indicates same level of total cost of the given objective function. So, any point on the iso-cost line indicates same cost for a given objective function. *As per this approach, the criterion for minimization of costs is when the lowest iso-cost line touches the lowest point of the feasible region.*

Assume a cost level of Rs.7 and compute X_1 and X_2 with reference to the objective function *i.e.,* Min Z $2X_1 + 6X_2 = 7$. Set $X_1 = 0$ and then $X_2 = 1.1$. Now, set X_2=0 and then X_1=3.5. Now the line connecting 3.5 units of X_1 and 1.1 units of X_2 is called iso-cost line (Figure 9.10). As per the criterion of this approach, this iso-cost line passes through the extreme point B of the shaded region ABC. Any cost level beyond Rs.7 will not pass through the lowest point of the shaded region. For example, at cost level Rs. 14, considering the objective function: Min Z $2X_1 + 6X_2 = 14$. Set $X_1 = 0$ and then X_2 = 2.3. Now, set X_2=0 and then X_1=7.0. Now the points connecting 7.0 units of X_1 and 2.3 units of X_2 is called iso-cost line and this not pass through lowest point of the shaded region. So, the iso-cost line of Rs.7 passes through the lowest point 'B' of the shaded region and as computed in earlier approach, the coordinates at corner point B is ($X_1 = 2, X_2 = 0.5$). So, now with reference to the objective function, cost minimization can be achieved as: Min Z $2X_1+6X_2 = 2(2) + 6(0.5)$ = Rs.7 *i.e.,* by consuming 2 units of food X_1 and 0.5 units of food X_2.

iv. Dual Problem

Every minimization problem has its corresponding maximization problem known as the dual. The primal of the above discussed problem is:

Min Z $2X_1+6X_2$

Subject to:

$1X_1 + 2X_2 \geq 3$ (Functional Constraint for carbohydrates)

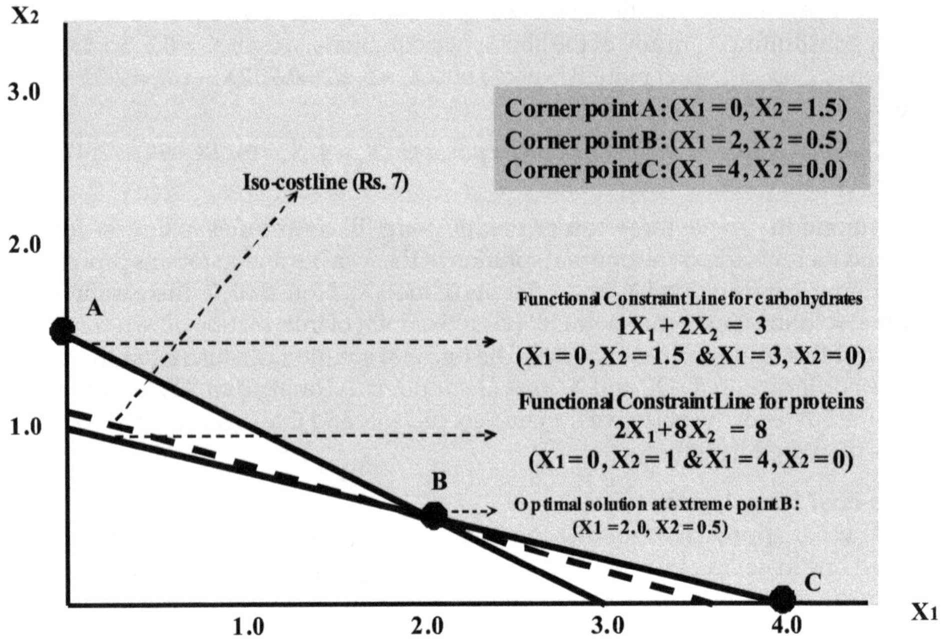

Figure 9.10: Finding Optimal Solution Based on Iso-Cost Line Approach.

$2X_1 + 8X_2 \geq 8$ (Functional Constraint for proteins)

$X_1, X_2 \geq 0$ (Non-negativity constraints)

Step 1

Let Y_1 and Y_2 be the prices of two foods X_1 and X_2 respectively. So, the objective function for the dual (maximization of value of diet) is:

Max Z $3Y_1+8Y_2$

Subject to:

$1Y_1 + 2Y_2 \leq 2$ (Functional Constraint for Food X_1)

$2Y_1 + 8Y_2 \leq 6$ (Functional Constraint for Food X_2)

$Y_1, Y_2 \geq 0$ (Non-negativity condition)

The above functional constraints imply that, the expenditure on Food X_1 ($1Y_1 + 2Y_2 \leq 2$) cannot exceed Rs.2 and the expenditure on Food X_2 ($2Y_1 + 8Y_2 \leq 6$) cannot exceed Rs.6.

Step 2

Now, the above constraint inequalities will be converted into equalities as given below.

$1Y_1 + 2Y_2 = 2$ (Functional Constraint for Food X_1)

$2Y_1 + 8Y_2 = 6$ (Functional Constraint for Food X_2)

Step 3

Compute horizontal and vertical intercepts from each functional constraint equation.

$1Y_1 + 2Y_2 = 2$ (Functional Constraint for Food X_1)

Assume $Y_1 = 0$. So, $Y_2 = 1$. This 1 unit of Y_2 represents Y_2–intercept on the graph when $Y_1=0$. This implies, all the nutrients are derived from proteins of Food X_1 and nothing from carbohydrates. Similarly, assume $Y_2=0$. Then, $Y_1=2$ units. This 2 units of Y_1 represents Y_1–intercept on the graph when $Y_2=0$. This implies, all the nutrients are derived from carbohydrates of Food X_1 and nothing from proteins. When these two intercepts are joined on the graph, we get a straight line (Panel A of Figure 9.11). Similar procedure is followed to compute Y_1 intercept and Y_2 intercept from functional constraint of Food X_2. So, from the equation: $2Y_1 + 8Y_2 = 6$, $Y_2 = 0.75$ units when $Y_1=0$ (this implies, all the nutrients are derived from proteins of Food X_2 and nothing from carbohydrates) and $Y_1 = 3$ units when $Y_2=0$ (this implies, all the nutrients are derived from carbohydrates of Food X_2 and nothing from proteins). When these two intercepts are joined on the graph, we get a straight line (Panel B of Figure 9.11).

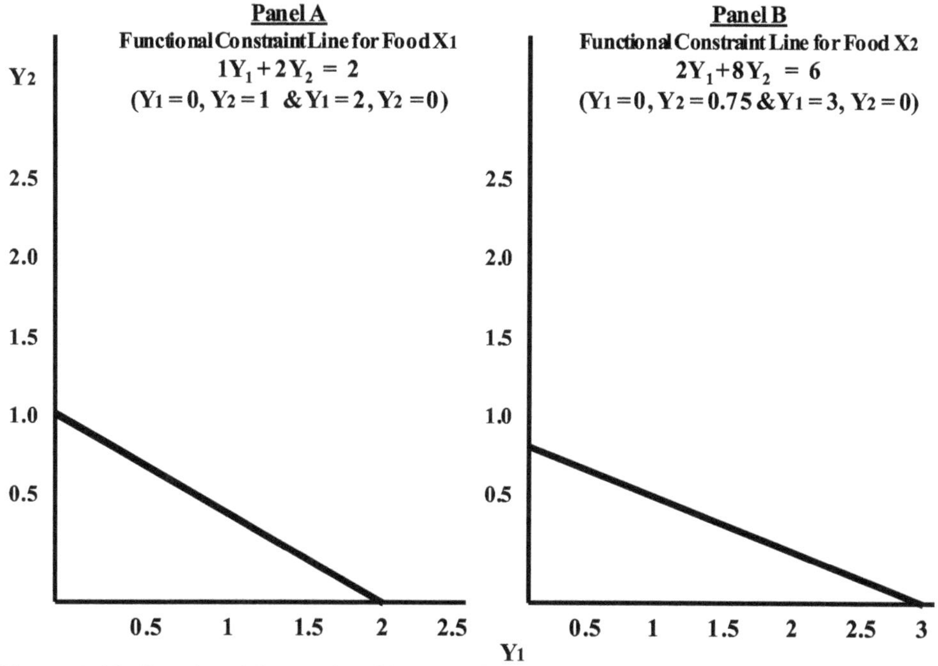

Figure 9.11: Functional Constraints Lines for Food X1 and Food X2.

Step 4

These two straight lines are now placed on the same graph. In the Figure 9.12, A, B and C are the corner points of the feasible (shaded) region. That is, both the constraint lines for Food X_1 and Food X_2 gives the shaded region below ABC that satisfies both the constraints. Let us find out the values at the corner points 'A', 'B' and 'C' with reference to the objective function and the highest value at one of these three points corresponds to optimal solution in the feasible region below ABC.

Optimal solution or Value at Corner point A: ($Y_1 = 0, Y_2 = 0.75$): Max Z $3Y_1+8Y_2 = 3(0)+8(0.75)$ = Rs.6

Optimal solution or Cost at Corner point B: To fix the coordinates at point B, where the two constraints lines intersect each other, we follow simultaneous equations approach. We know the two functional constraints:

$1Y_1 + 2Y_2 = 2$ (Functional Constraint for Food X_1)

$2Y_1 + 8Y_2 = 6$ (Functional Constraint for Food X_s)

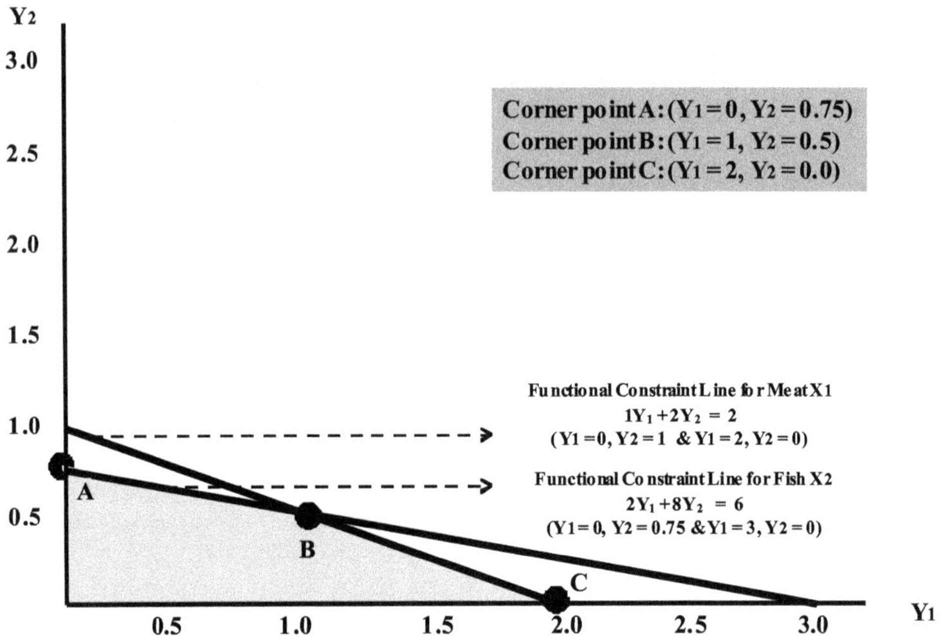

Figure 9.12: Finding Optimal Solution Based on Corner Point Approach.

Multiply the first equation with -2 and by adding these two equations, we get $Y_2 = 0.5$. By substituting Y_1 in any of the above two equations, we get $Y_1 = 1.0$. So, Optimal solution or Value at Corner point B is given by: ($Y_1 = 1, Y_2 = 0.5$): Max Z $3Y_1+8Y_2 = 3(1)+8(0.5)$ = Rs.7

Optimal solution or Value at Corner point C: ($Y_1 = 2, Y_2 = 0$): Max Z $3Y_1+8Y_2 = 3(2)+8(0)$ = Rs.6

Among the above three corner points, point 'B' contributes to highest value *i.e.*, Rs.7 and thereby, this is the optimal solution in the feasible region for this problem. So, for all practical purposes, the primal and dual problems have the same solution *i.e.*, Min Z = Max Z. That is,

Considering solution to primal problem *i.e.*, Min Z $2X_1 + 6X_2 = 2(2) + 6(0.5)$ = Rs.7 (Minimum cost of diet)

Considering solution to dual problem *i.e.*, Max Z $3Y_1+8Y_2 = 3(1)+8(0.5)$ = Rs.7 (Maximum value of diet).

So, both in primal problem and in dual problem, the consumer incurs Rs. 7 expenditure to attain optimal solution, so as to attain minimization of cost and maximum value of diet respectively.

As discussed above, in the context of LP, we call the solution region of the system of constraints as the feasible region and the points within this region as feasible points. So, the question now arises, which of all the feasible points will optimize the objective function? Testing all of the points in the feasible region would be an impossible task. So, the Fundamental Theorem of LP limits the number of points we have to test and it is given below.

- ☆ If the solution to a LP problem exists, it will occur at a corner point.
- ☆ If two adjacent corner points are optimal solutions, then all points on the line segment between them are also optimal solutions.
- ☆ LP problems with bounded feasible regions will always have optimal solutions.
- ☆ LP problems with unbounded feasible regions may or may not have optimal solutions.

v. General Procedure of Graphical Approach

The steps followed in solving LP problem based on graphical approach are listed here under.

- ☆ Express the objective function of the problem as an equation and the constraints as inequalities.
- ☆ Convert the functional inequalities into linear equalities
- ☆ Compute X-axis and Y-axis intercepts for both the functional constraints
- ☆ Plot the two functional constraints on the graph and define the feasible region. The feasible solution region or solution space is represented by the area on the graph that is valid for all constraints. In case of maximization function, the optimal value corresponds to the greatest value of the coordinates. In case of minimization function, the optimal value corresponds to the lowest value of the coordinates.
- ☆ Shade the common portion of the graph that satisfies all the constraints simultaneously. This shaded area is called the 'feasible region' (or solution space) of the given LP problem (Figure 9.13). Any point in this shaded region is called feasible solution and provides values that satisfy all constraints.
- ☆ There are several approaches to locate the optimal solution from the feasible region, but the two important approaches include: Corner point approach and Iso-profit line approach (Maximization function) or Iso-cost line approach (Minimization function). *In corner points approach, 'the optimal solution to any LP problem is at the corner point or extreme point of the feasible region that contribute to maximum profit (Maximization function) or minimum cost (Minimization function)'. In case of Iso-profit line (Iso-cost line) approach, the criterion for maximization of profits (minimization of costs) is when the highest*

iso-profit line (lowest iso-cost line) touches the highest or extreme point of the feasible region (lowest point of the feasible region). This represents the optimal solution to the problem subject to the constraints faced. Note that,

- ❑ The optimal solution cannot fall in the interior of the feasible region.
- ❑ The optimal solution must occur at a 'corner point' of the feasible region.
- ❑ In searching for the optimal solution, we only have to examine the corner points.

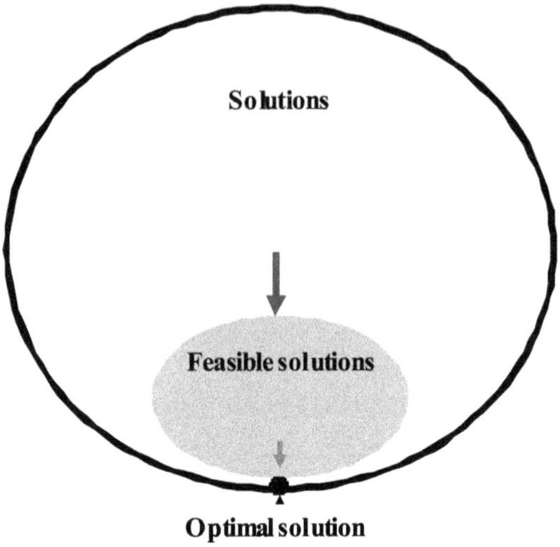

Optimal solution is the feasible solution that achieves the maximal (or minimal) objective value

Solution

- **Determine feasible region by drawing constraint lines**
- **Locate Feasible region that satisfy all coordinates of constraints**
- **Construct iso-profit lines (Maximization function) or iso-cost lines (Minimization function)**
- **Locate the optimal solution**

Figure 9.13: Generalized Graphical Approach in Solving LP Problem.

vi. Sensitivity Analysis

Farm managers are usually interested in more than the optimal solution to a LP problem. In addition to knowing the value of each decision variable and the value of the objective function, they want to know, how sensitive these answers are when parameters changes. For example, what happens, if the coefficients of the objective function and functional constraints are not exact or if they change by 10 or 15 percent? What happens if right-hand-side values of the constraints change? So, sensitivity analysis helps to test the sensitivity of the optimum solution with respect to changes of the coefficients in the objective function, coefficients in the functional constraints or the constant terms in the constraints. Because solution for a LP problem is based on the constancy of parameters or coefficients of the decision variables in objective function and the variables in functional constraints, the subject of sensitivity analysis comes into play. Hence, sensitivity analysis is also called as Post-optimality analysis. There are two approaches to perform sensitivity analysis to analyze, how sensitive an optimal solution is to changes made with respect to objective function and functional constraints. The first is simply a trial-and-error approach. This approach usually involves resolving the entire problem, preferably by computer, each time one input data item or parameter is changed. But, this approach takes a long time to test a series of possible changes. The second approach popularly called as Analytic post-optimality method, wherein after an LP problem has been solved, we determine a range of changes in the coefficients of objective function and functional constraints to analyze the optimal solution or change the variables in the solution. This is done without resolving the whole problem. LP software, such as Excel's Solver or POM for Windows will be used for this analysis. The analysis based on these two approaches is beyond the scope of this book.

vii. Special Cases in Graphical Method

a. Alternate (or Multiple) Optimal Solutions

In the above examples, for each graphical solution, there was one optimal solution (unique solution). However, in certain cases, a given LP problem may have more than one (multiple) optimal solutions. Each of such optimal solutions is termed as alternative optimal solution. This occurs, when the objective function (Z) line say, the highest iso-profit line (or lowest iso-cost line) coincides with the farthest boundary (or nearest boundary) of the solution space or feasible region, and then the problem is said to possess multiple optimal solutions. In other words, the slope of the objective function is same as that of the constraint forming the boundary of the feasible region. Consider the following examples:

Example 9.5

Max $Z = 10X_1 + 6X_2$

Subject to

$5X_1 + 3X_2 \leq 30 \longrightarrow$ *Functional constraint for fertilizer*

$X_1 + 2X_2 \leq 18 \longrightarrow$ *Functional constraint for pesticides*

$X_1, X_2 \geq 0$

Solving the above problem by graphical method (say, by iso-profit line approach), the highest iso-profit line (Rs.60) coincides with the slope of one of the functional constraint line $5X_1 + 3X_2 \leq 30$ thereby, there are alternate (or multiple) optimal solutions (Figure 9.14).

Example 9.6

Max $Z = X_1 + 2X_2$

Subject to

$X_1 \leq 80$

$X_2 \leq 60$

$5X_1 + 6X_2 \leq 600$

$X_1 + 2X_2 \leq 160$

$X_1, X_2 \geq 0$

In the Figure 9.15, there is no unique outer most corners cut by the objective function line (Iso-profit line approach). For example, all points that lie between B to C

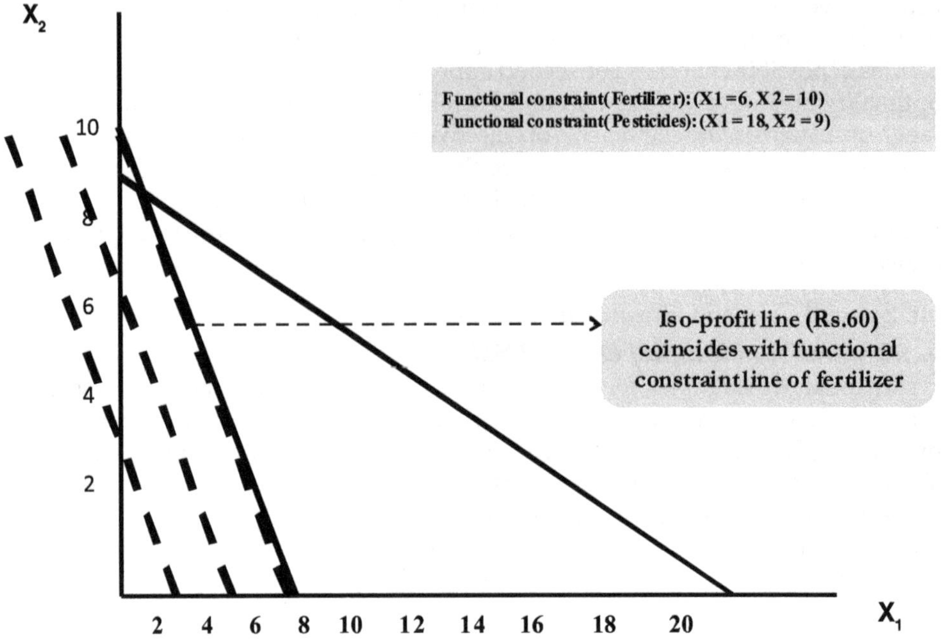

Figure 9.14: Alternate (Multiple) Optimal Solutions in LP Problem.

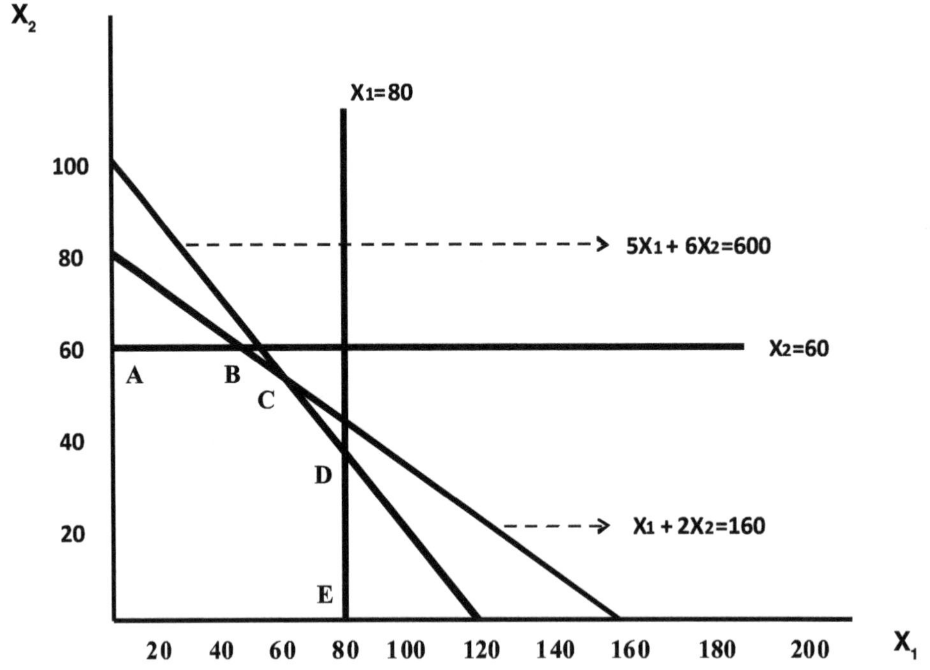

Figure 9.15: Alternate (Multiple) Optimal Solutions in LP Problem.

lying on line BC represent optimal solutions and all these will give the same optimal value (maximum profit) of Rs.160. This is given below:

- At point B, the coordinates are (40, 60) and thereby, profit is given by: Max $Z = X_1 + 2X_2 = 40 + 2(60) =$ Rs.160.
- At point C, the coordinates are (60, 50) and thereby, profit is given by: Max $Z = X_1 + 2X_2 = 60 + 2(50) =$ Rs.160.

So, every point on the line BC maximizes the value of the objective function and the given problem has multiple solutions. Thus, it is clear that,

- When more than one corner corresponds to an optimal solution, each corner and all points along the connecting line segment will correspond to optimal solutions.
- Whenever all coefficients of one equation are the same multiples of another equation's coefficients, the lines are parallel. When the objective function line is parallel to a constraint line, there are multiple optimal solutions.
- In the above Example 9.5,

  Max $Z = 10X_1 + 6X_2$ (Objective function)

  $5X_1 + 3X_2 \leq 30$ (Functional constraint)

  The ratio of X1 terms (10 and 5) is 10/5 or 2. The ratio of *X*2 terms (6 and 3) is 6/3, also 2. Thus, the two lines are parallel and multiple optimal solutions exist.

Other Examples

Multiple optimal solutions can also be derived from the following cases:

Case 1

Max $Z = 10X_1 + 12X_2$

Subject to

5X1 + 6X2 < 60 (resource one)

8X1 + 4X2 < 72 (resource two)

3X1 + 5X2 < 45 (resource three)

X1, X2 > 0

Case 2

Maximize $Z=40X_1 + 30X_2$

Subject to:

$1X_1 + 2X_2 \leq 40$

$4X_1 + 3X_2 \leq 120$

X_1, X_2 ³ 0

Case 3

Max $Z = 3X_1 + 2X_2$

subject to

$X_1 \leq 4$

$2X_2 \leq 12$

$3X_1 + 2X_2 \leq 18$

$X_1, X_2 \geq 0$

b. Unbounded Solution

Some of the LP problems may not have a finite solution. When the values of one or more decision variables and the value of the objective function are permitted to increase infinitely without violating the feasibility condition, then the solution is said to be unbounded. So, unbounded solution is a solution, whose objective function is infinite. It is to be noted that, the solution may be unbounded for maximization type of objective function with at least one of the functional constraint equations having no ≤ sign. This is because, in minimization type of objective function, the lower boundary is formed by non-negative condition for decision variables. Consider the following examples:

Example 9.7

Max $Z = 3X_1 + 5X_2$

Subject to

$2X_1 + X_2 \geq 7$

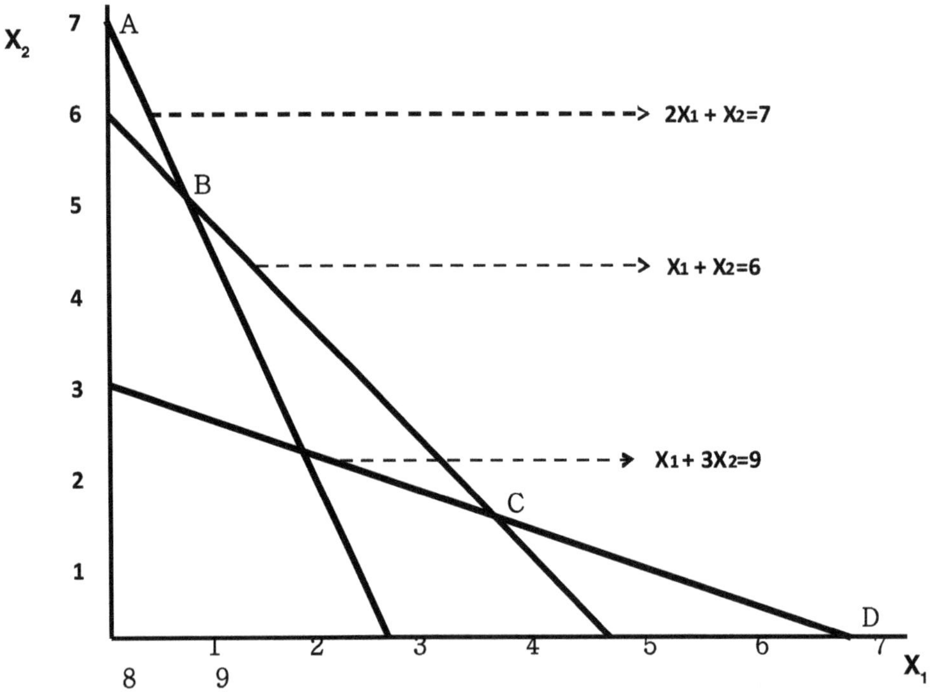

Figure 9.16: Unbounded Solutions in LP Problem.

$X_1 + X_2 \geq 6$

$X_1 + 3X_2 \geq 9$

$X_1, X_2 \geq 0$

As shown through Figure 9.16, the corner points of feasible region are A, B, C and D. The coordinates for the corner points are: A (0, 7), B (1, 5), C (4.5, 1.5) and D (9, 0). So, the objective function at A, B, C and D corner points is given by,

At corner point A: Max Z = 3X1 + 5X2 = 3(0) + 5(7) = Rs.35

At corner point B: Max Z = 3X1 + 5X2 = 3(1) + 5(5) = Rs.28

At corner point C: Max Z = 3X1 + 5X2 = 3(4.5) + 5(1.5) = Rs.21

At corner point D: Max Z = 3X1 + 5X2 = 3(9) + 5(0) = Rs.27

So, the values of objective function at corner points A, B, C and D are 35, 28, 21 and 27 respectively. But there exists infinite number of points in the feasible region, which is unbounded. The value of objective function will be more than the value of these four corner points *i.e.*, the maximum value of the objective function occurs at ∞. Hence, the given problem has unbounded solution.

Example 9.8

Max $Z = 3X_1 + 5X_2$

Subject to

$X_1 \leq 4$

$X_1, X_2 \geq 0$

The graphical solution of the above problem (Figure 9.17) reveals that, there is no closing boundary for the solution space and hence, Z will be maximum at infinite value of X_2. Hence, the solution is unbounded. So, unbounded solution occurs, when the LP problem has no feasible solution.

Other Examples

Unbounded solutions can also be derived from the following cases:

Case 1

Max $Z = 3X_1 + 2X_2$

Subject to

$X_1 - X_2 \geq 1$

$X_1 + X_2 \geq 3$

$4.5X_1 + 3X_2 \geq 9$

$X_1, X_2 \geq 0$

Case 2

Max $Z = 4X_1 + 2X_2$

Subject to

$X_1 \geq 4$

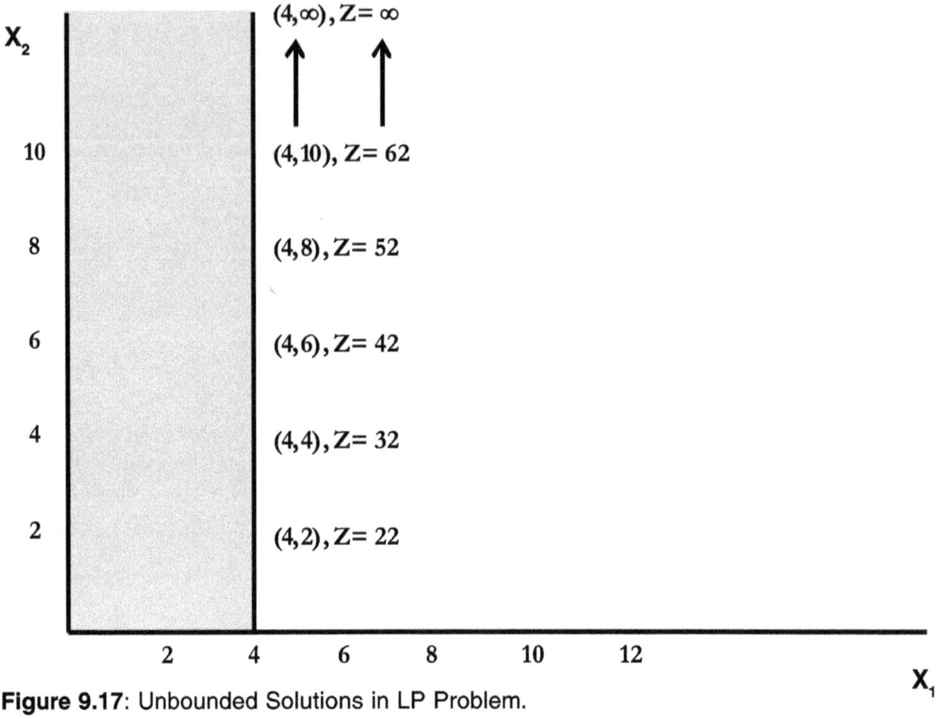

Figure 9.17: Unbounded Solutions in LP Problem.

$X_2 \leq 2$

$X_1, X_2 \geq 0$

c. Infeasible Solution

Infeasibility is a condition, when constraints are inconsistent (mutually exclusive) *i.e.*, there are no points that satisfy all of the constraints of the problem simultaneously. So, there is no unique (single) feasible region. It should be noted that, infeasibility depends solely on constraints and has nothing to do with the objective function. Consider the following examples:

Example 9.9

Max $Z = 3X_1 - 2X_2$

Subject to

$X_1 + X_2 \leq 1$

$2X_1 + 2X_2 \geq 4$

$X_1, X_2 \geq 0$

The graphical solution (Figure 9.18) reveals that, to satisfy the first constraint, the solution must lie to the left of line AB. To satisfy the second constraint, the solution must lie to the right of line CD. There is no point (X_1, X_2), which satisfies both the constraints simultaneously. Hence, this problem has no solution because, the constraints are inconsistent.

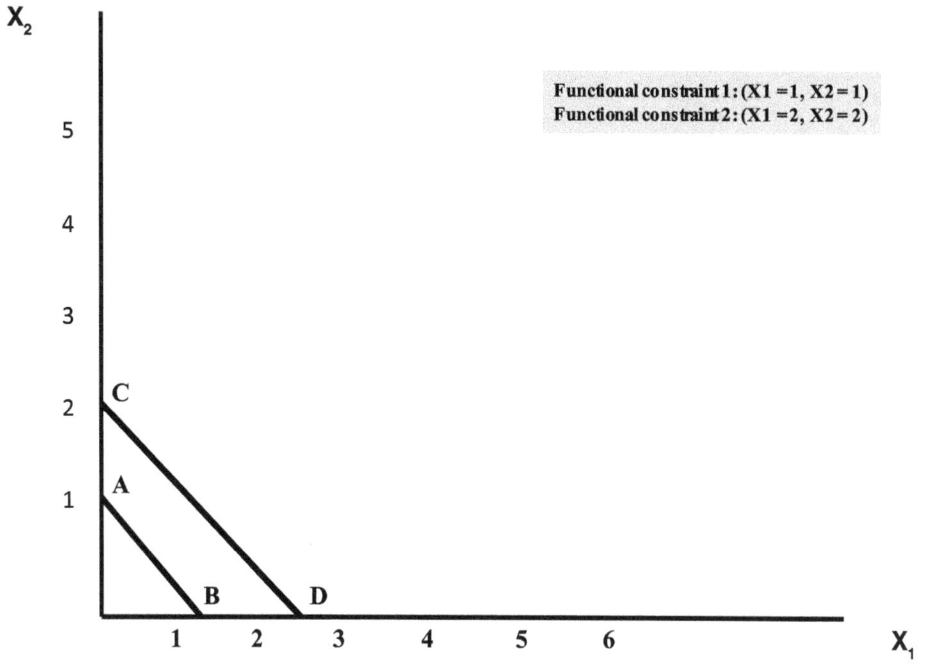

Figure 9.18: Infeasible Solutions in LP Problem.

Example 9.10

Min $Z = 200X_1 + 300X_2$

Subject to

$2X_1 + 3X_2 \geq 1200$

$X_1 + X_2 \leq 400$

$2X_1 + 1.5X_2 \geq 900$

$X_1, X_2 \geq 0$

In the Figure 9.19, the region located on the right of ABC includes all solutions, which satisfy the first and the third constraints. The region located on the left of DE includes all solutions, which satisfy the second constraint. Thus, the problem is infeasible because, there is no set of points that satisfy all the three constraints.

Other Examples

Infeasible solutions can also be derived from the following cases:

Case 1

Max $Z = 5X_1 + 3X_2$

Subject to

$4X_1 + 2X_2 \leq 8$

$X_1 \geq 4$

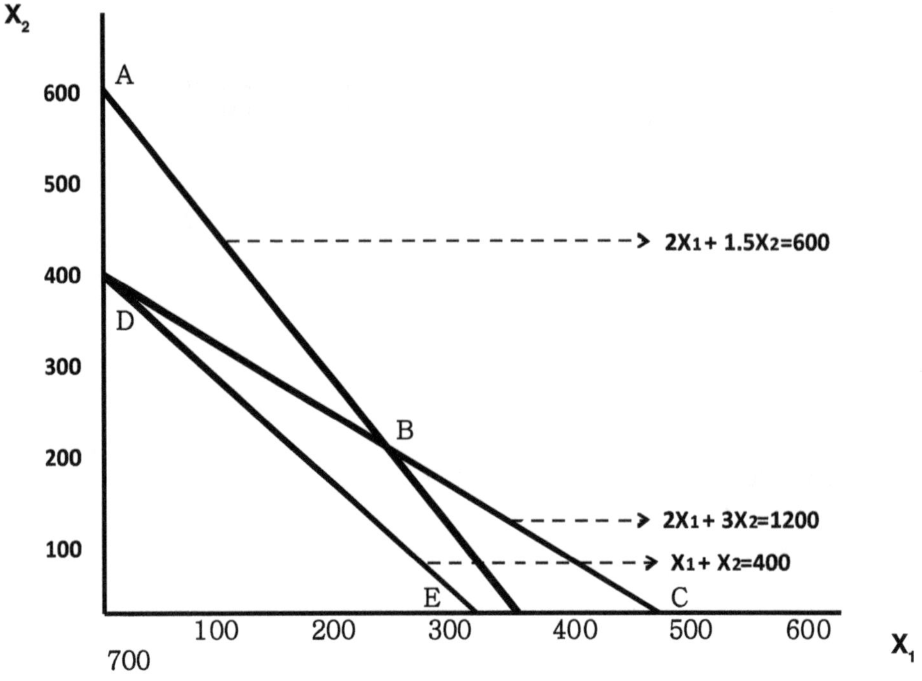

Figure 9.19: Infeasible Solutions in LP Problem.

$X_2 \geq 6$

$X_1, X_2 \geq 0$

Case 2

Max $Z = 3X_1 + 5X_2$

Subject to

$X_1 \leq 4$

$2X_2 \leq 12$

$3X_1 + 2X_2 \leq 18$

$3X_1 + 5X_2 \geq 50$

$X_1, X_2 \geq 0$

From the above discussion pertaining to the graphical approach for solving LP problem, we can conclude that,

- Alternate optimal solutions occur, when more than one point optimizes the objective function
- Unboundness occurs, when the objective function can become infinitely large (maximum) or infinitely small (minimum).

☆ Infeasibility in solution occurs, when a model has no feasible point.

☆ A Corner-Point Feasible (CPF) solution is a solution that lies at a corner of the feasible region. The LP problem must possess CPF solutions and at least one optimal solution. Furthermore, the best CPF solution must be an optimal solution. Thus, if a LP problem has exactly one optimal solution, it must be a CPF solution. If the problem has multiple optimal solutions, at least two must be CPF solutions.

B. Simplex Method

For LP problems involving only two variables, the graphical solution method discussed earlier is convenient. However, in practice, most LP problems contain more than two variables and a large number of constraints and hence, it is better to use an algebraic technique of Simplex method. In 1947, George B. Dantzig, then part of a research group of the U.S. Air Force known as Project SCOOP (Scientic Computation of Optimum Programs), developed the simplex method for solving the general LP problem. Hence, this method is also called as Dantzig's simplex method in honour of the mathematician, who devised this approach. The simplex method ensures two advantages in terms of feasibility and optimality. The search for the optimality starts from a basic feasible solution. The solution is tested for optimality and if it is optimal, then the search is stopped. The search for optimal solution is continued by designing a new and better basic feasible solution *i.e.,* if the solution is found not optimal, a new feasible solution is designed and this is continued till the optimal solution is attained. Thus, the simplex method comprises of several iterations or plans till the optimal solution (*i.e.,* maximum or minimum values of the objective function) is attained. The extraordinary computational efficiency and robustness of the simplex method, together with the availability of high-speed digital computers, have made LP the most powerful optimization method ever designed and the most widely applied in the business environment. This method is applicable to any type of problem that can be formulated in terms of linear constraints. Now, let us study addressing the LP problems through employing simplex method with reference to both profit maximization and cost minimization objective functions.

i. Profit Maximization Objective Function

Example 9.11

Assume a farmer has 12 units of land, 48 man days of labour and Rs.360 of capital. He wishes to cultivate paddy, groundnut and red gram in this farm. One unit of paddy production requires 6 man days of labour and Rs.36 of capital. One unit of groundnut production requires 6 man days of labour and Rs.24 of capital. One unit of red gram production requires 2 man days of labour and Rs.18 of capital. The net income from the production of paddy, groundnut and red gram are Rs.40, Rs.30 and Rs.20 per unit respectively. Suggest optimum production programme to the farmer considering the resource constraints.

Answer

Step 1

The above information can be conveniently presented in the form of table:

Resources	*Amounts of Inputs Required to Produce One Unit of Output*			
	Paddy(X_1)	*Groundnut (X_2)*	*Redgram (X_3)*	*Total Resources Available*
Land (units)	1	1	1	12
Labour (man days)	6	6	2	48
Capital (Rs.)	36	24	18	360
Net income	40	30	20	

Step 2

The above tabular form of LP problem can be conveniently expressed as mathematical equations. That is, translate the given data in the table into inequalities as given below.

Max Z $40X_1+30X_2+20X_3$

Subject to:

$1X_1+1X_2+1X_3 \leq 12$ units (Land)

$6X_1+6X_2+2X_3 \leq 48$ man days (Labour)

$36X_1+24X_2+18X_3 \leq$ Rs.360 (Capital)

The above expression of LP problem is said to be in 'Original form' or 'General form'. The desired largest (or smallest) value of the objective function is called the Optimal value, and a collection of values of $X_1, X_2, X_3, \ldots$ that gives the optimal value constitutes an optimal solution.The variables $X_1, X_2, X, \ldots$ are called the decision variables.

Step 3

Then, all these inequalities are to be converted into equalities by adding slack variables or disposal activities. This form of expression of LP problem represent LP problem in Standard form. So, a LP problem is in standard form, if it seeks to maximize the objective function subject to the given constraints and representing in terms of slack variables. That is, since the left-hand side of each inequality is less than or equal to the right-hand side, there must exist non-negative numbers and that can be added to the left side of each equation to produce the following system of linear equations:

$1X_1+1X_2+1X_3+X_4 \leq 12$ units (Land)

$6X_1+6X_2+2X_3+X_5 \leq 48$ man days (Labour)

$36X_1+24X_2+18X_3+X_6 \leq$ Rs.360 (Capital)

The variables X_4, X_5 and X_6 are called slack variables with respect to land, labour and capital resources because, they take up the 'slack' in each inequality. Now, the above unequal mathematical equations turn into equalities with the addition of slack variables as given below.

Max Z $40X_1+30X_2+20X_3+0X_4+0X_5+0X_6$

Subject to:

$1X_1+1X_2+1X_3+1X_4+0X_5+0X_6=12$

$6X_1+6X_2+2X_3 +0X_4+1X_5+0X_6=48$

$36X_1+24X_2+18X_3 +0X_4+0X_5+1X_6=360$

X_1, X_2, X_3, X_4, X_5 and $X_6 \geq 0$

This LP problem is called 'linear' because, the objective function to be maximized and the functional constraints (inequalities) involve the terms which are of the first degree. There is no interaction term in terms of two or more variables *i.e.*, there is no second degree (power) or more in the above equations. A linear program is said to be in Standard form or Augmented form, in which all the constraints are written as equalities. The above format can also be written as:

Max Z $40X_1+30X_2+20X_3+0X_4+0X_5+0X_6$

Subject to:

$X_4= 12 - 1X_1-1X_2-1X_3$

$X_5= 48 - 6X_1-6X_2-2X_3$

$X_6= 360 - 36X_1-24X_2-18X_3$

X_1, X_2, X_3, X_4 , X_5 and $X_6 \geq 0$

This layout is called a dictionary. Thus, setting X_1, X_2 and X_3 to zero, we can read off the values for the other variables: X_4, X_5 and X_6 as X4 = 12, X5 = 48 and X6 = 360. This specific solution is called a dictionary solution. So, dependent variables, on the left, are called basic variables and independent variables, on the right, are called non-basic variables. Note that, all the variables in the current dictionary solution are non-negative. Such a solution is called feasible solution. But, the initial dictionary solution need not be always feasible.

Initial Basic Feasible Solution

Now we assume that, nothing can be produced. Therefore, the values of the decision variables are zero *i.e.*, $X_1=0$, $X_2=0$ and $X_3=0$. When we are not producing anything, obviously we left with unused capacity *i.e.*, represented by slack variables. That means, $X_4=12$, $X_5=48$ and $X_6=360$. Thus, the current solution has three slack variables *i.e.*, X_4, X_5 and X_6 with non-zero solution values and three decision variables *i.e.*, X_1, X_2 and X_3 with zero values. Variables with non-zero values are called basic variables and variables with zero values are called non-basic variables. So, when we are not producing anything, in the above given equations, X_4, X_5 and X_6 are basic variables and X_1, X_2 and X_3 are non-basic variables. So, the basic feasible solution at the initial tableau is (0, 0, 0, 12, 48, 360) where, $X_1 = 0$, $X_2 = 0$ and $X_3 = 0$, $X_4 = 12$, $X_5 = 48$, $X_6 = 360$ and Z = 0. The solution at the initial tableau is associated to the origin point at which all the decision variables are zero. If all the variables in basic solution are *more than or equal* to zero, then it is called Basic Feasible Solution (BFS). Thus, an initial basic feasible solution is obtained by setting $X_1=0, X_2=0, X_3=0$ such that, $X_4=12$, $X_5=48$, $X_6=360$. Note that, if there are 'm' constraints in the given problem, the number of slack variables or disposal activities added will be 'm'.* In this example, there are three constraints with respect to land, labour and capital and hence, three disposal activities X_4, X_5 and X_6 are added. It is at this point, we begin applying the simplex method to solve the formulated LP problem.

Note*: ***Objective function (Maximization function):***

$$\text{Max } Z = a_1X_1 + a_2X_2 + a_3X_3 + \text{———} + a_nX_n \longrightarrow \textit{Objective function}$$

Constraints (*i.e.*, subject to):

$$b_{11}X_1 + b_{12}X_2 + b_{13}X_3 + \text{———} + b_{1n}X_n \le c_1 \longrightarrow \textit{(Functional Constraint of Resource 1)}$$

$$b_{21}X_1 + b_{22}X_2 + b_{23}X_3 + \text{———} + b_{2n}X_n \le c_2 \longrightarrow \textit{(Functional Constraint of Resource 2)}$$

. . . .

. . . .

$$b_{m1}X_1 + b_{m2}X_2 + b_{m3}X_3 + \text{———} + b_{mn}X_n \le c_m \longrightarrow \textit{(Functional Constraint of Resource 'n')}$$

After adding slack variables, the corresponding system of constraint equations is:

$$b_{11}X_1 + b_{12}X_2 + b_{13}X_3 + \text{————} + b_{1n}X_n + S_1 = c_1$$

$$b_{21}X_1 + b_{22}X_2 + b_{23}X_3 + \text{————} + b_{2n}X_n + S_2 = c_2$$

. . . .

. . . .

$$b_{m1}X_1 + b_{m2}X_2 + b_{m3}X_3 + \text{————} + b_{mn}X_n + S_m = c_m$$

where, S_1, S_2 and S_3 are the slack variables or disposal activities

Thus, a basic solution is an augmented corner point solution and it has the following properties:

- ✫ Each variable is designated as either a non-basic variable or a basic variable.
- ✫ The number of basic variables equals the number of functional constraints. Therefore, the number of non-basic variables equals the total number of variables minus the number of functional constraints.
- ✫ The non-basic variables are set equal to zero.
- ✫ The values of the basic variables are obtained as simultaneous solution of the system of equations (functional constraints in augmented form). The set of basic variables are called 'basis'.
- ✫ If the basic variables satisfy the non-negativity constraints, the basic solution is a BFS.

Step 4

In order to simplify handling the above mathematical equations in the problem, they are placed in the tabular form called Simplex tableau. The initial simplex tableau is given below (Table 9.5):

Table 9.5

Contribution	Restrictions	Restriction levels	Real (Production) activities			Slack Variables/Disposal activities		
			Paddy	Ground nut	Red gram	Land	Labour	Capital
			X_1/unit	X_2 /unit	X_3 /unit	X_4	X_5	X_6
0	Land (units)	12	1	1	1	1	0	0
0	Labour (mandays)	48	6	6	2	0	1	0
0	Capital (Rs/-)	360	36	24	18	0	0	1
	Netincome(C) (Rs/-)		40	30	20	0	0	0
	Opportunity Cost (Z)		0	0	0	0	0	0
	Shadow price (Z-C)		-40	-30	-20	0	0	0

Explanation of the Notations of the Simplex Tableau

1. In the second column, all the resources or restrictions *viz.*, land, labour and capital are given and they are known as basic variables. Note that, any variables that are not listed under the second column are not basic variables.
2. In the third column, the maximum levels of the three resources *viz.*, land, labour and capital are given and it is called as Restriction levels. So, this column indicate the values of basic variables.
3. The numbers in the 'Z' row under each variable is the opportunity cost, which indicates the value of other activity that must be sacrificed to produce one more unit of output. All values of 'Z' row in Table 9.5 are zero because, all resources are unused.
4. The difference between opportunity cost (Z) and net income (C) gives the shadow price. This row is also called as Evaluation row or Criterion row. It is the row, the Marginal Value Productivities (MVPs) are the same as those in the objective function, but with negative signs indicating the sacrifice of not including a particular activity. Although, it amounts to a positive gain by picking up the particular activity.
5. In all the disposal activities columns, enter the coefficients of slack variables as indicated in the mathematical equations.

Step 5: The above data are presented through matrices as shown below:

$$[40\ 30\ 20\ 0\ 0\ 0]\begin{bmatrix}X_1\\X_2\\X_3\\X_4\\X_5\\X_6\end{bmatrix} = \text{Max } Z$$

Subjected to:-

$$\begin{bmatrix}1 & 1 & 1 & 1 & 0 & 0\\6 & 6 & 2 & 0 & 1 & 0\\36 & 24 & 18 & 0 & 0 & 1\end{bmatrix}\begin{bmatrix}X_1\\X_2\\X_3\\X_4\\X_5\\X_6\end{bmatrix}\begin{bmatrix}=12\\=48\\=360\end{bmatrix}$$

$$\begin{bmatrix}X_1\\X_2\\X_3\\X_4\\X_5\\X_6\end{bmatrix} \geq 0$$

Now, transfer the data from the above matrix of Step 5 to the Plan I as given below.

Plan I

Contribution (Net income)	Restriction	Resource activity level	Real activities: Paddy X_1	Groundnut X_2	Red gram X_3	Disposable activities: Land X_4	Labour X_5	Capital X_6	Ratio
0	Land X_4	12	1	1	1	1	0	0	12/1=12
0	Labour X_5	48	6	6	2	0	1	0	48/6=8
0	Capital X_6	360	36	24	18	0	0	1	360/36=10
	Net income (C)		40	30	20	0	0	0	
	Opportunity cost (Z)		0	0	0	0	0	0	
	Shadow price (Z-C)		-40	-30	-20	0	0	0	

Value of programme 0

Computation Procedure

The following computational procedure is followed to derive optimal plan from the basic solution:

Opportunity Cost (Z)

In the above table (Plan I), Opportunity cost (Z) is calculated by the formula:

Σ(Contribution x Corresponding real activities of Paddy X_1, Groundnut X_2 and Red gram X_3)

(0 x 1 + 0 x 6 + 0 x 36) = 0 (For column 4)

(0 x 6 + 0 x 6 + 0 x 2) = 0 (For column 5)

(0 x 36 + 0x24 + 0x18) = 0 (For column 6)

Σ(Contribution x Corresponding disposal activity values of Land X_4, Labour X_5 and Capital X_6)

(0 x 1 + 0 x 0 + 0 x 0) = 0 (For column 7)

(0 x 0 + 0 x 1 + 0 x 0) = 0 (For column 8)

(0 x 0 + 0 x 0 + 0 x 1) = 0 (For column 9)

Ratio

To calculate Ratio, consider lowest or highest negative shadow price (*i.e.*, -40) and consider that column real activities of Paddy X_1. Divide resource activity level values of Land X_4, Labour X_5 and Capital X_6 (*i.e.*, column 3) with corresponding real activities of Paddy X_1 of lowest shadow price column (*i.e.*, column 4) *i.e.*, 1, 6 and 36 to get Ratios: *i.e.*, 12/1 =12; 48/6 =8; 360/36=10.

Value of the Programme

It is given by Σ(Contribution x Corresponding resource activity level) for each row of Land X_4, Labour X_5 and Capital X_6 restrictions *i.e.*, [(0x12)+(0x48)+(0x360)] =0

Among the computed ratio values in I Plan, consider lowest ratio (i.e, 8) and eliminate that row (*i.e.*, Labour X_5 row) in the next plan (*i.e.*, Plan II). Now, replace that row (*i.e.*, Labour X_5 row) by employing the pivot value of the column with respect to lowest shadow price column in Plan I (*i.e.*, -40 shadow price column). So, considering the Labour X_5 row and column of the lowest shadow price (-40), the pivot value is 6 *i.e.*, the intersection value of the selected row and selected column. Now, divide the entire eliminated Labour X_5 row values with the pivot value (6) and include them as Paddy X_1 row, as shown through Plan II. This is given by:

= 48/6 = 8

= 6/6 = 1

= 6/6 = 1

= 2/6 = 1/3

= 0/6 = 0

= 1/6 =(1/6)

= 0/6 = 0

Now, transfer the above calculated values as Paddy X_1 row values in Plan II. Thus, it is clear that, after computing Plan I, the row corresponding to lowest Ratio (8) is the outgoing row (Labour X_5) and it is replaced by the real activity (Paddy X_1) that corresponds to lowest shadow price or highest negative shadow price (-40) by dividing all the values of outgoing row (Labour X_5) with the pivot element of outgoing row and incoming real activity. The pivot element (or pivot number or pivot value or key number) is the common element that lies at the intersection of outgoing row and real activity column with lowest shadow price or highest negative shadow price. The row (Labour X_5) with pivot number is called Key row and other rows (Land X_4 and Capital X_6) are called non-key rows. Thus, the departing row corresponds to the smallest non-negative ratio. The entering activity or variable corresponds to the smallest (the most negative) entry in the shadow price column of the tableau. The entry or the number in the departing row and the entering activity column of the lowest shadow price or highest negative shadow price is called the pivot.

Plan II

Contribution (Netincome)	Restriction	Resource activitylevel	Real activities			Disposable activities			Ratio
			Paddy X_1	Groundnut X_2	Red gram X_3	Land X_4	Labour X_5	Capital X_6	
0	Land X_4	4	0	0	2/3	1	-1/6	0	6
40 (Paddynetincome)	Paddy X_1	8	1	1	1/3	0	1/6	0	24
0	Capital X_6	72	0	-12	6	0	-6	1	12
	Netincome (C)		40	30	20	0	0	0	
	Opportunity cost (Z)		40	40	40/3	0	20/3	0	
	Shadowprice (Z-C)		0	10	-20/3	0	20/3	0	
Value of programme		320							

Note: To calculate non-key row values in Plan II for Land X_4 and Capital X_6, the following formula is used:

N=O-(I x P), where O=Previous row value of the restriction (Land X_4 and Capital X_6) in previous Plan II, I= Incoming row value in this plan (*i.e.*, Paddy X_1 values of row 2 in this current Plan II), P=Pivot value for Land X_4 and Capital X_6 corresponding to the lowest shadow price value (-40) column in the previous I Plan (*i.e.*, 1 and 36 respectively).

So, for Land X_4 in II Plan:

N = 12-(8x1) = 4

= 1-(1x1) = 0

= 1-(1x1) = 0

= 1-(1/3 x1)=2/3

= 1-(0x1) = 1

= 0-(1/6 x1)=-1/6

= 0-(0x1) = 0

Transfer the above values for land X_4 in Plan II

Similarly, for Capital X_6 in II Plan:

N= 360-(8x36) = 72

= 36-(1x36) = 0

= 24-(1x36) = -12

= 18 -(1/3x36) = 6

= 0-(0x36) = 0

= 0-(1/6x36) = -6

= 1-(0x36) = 1

Transfer the above values for Capital X_6 in Plan II

So, the rule for transformation of non-key rows is given by the formula: N=O-(I x P). That is, subtract from the old row number in the previous plan, the product of the incoming row number (in the current plan) and pivot value for that activity in the previous plan.

After computing resource activity levels, real activities and disposal activities for Land X_4 and Capital X_6 rows, follow the same procedure as in I Plan, to compute opportunity cost values, shadow prices and ratios. That is,

Opportunity Cost (Z)

It is calculated by the formula:

Σ(Contribution x Corresponding real activities of Paddy X_1, Groundnut X_2 and Red gram X_3)

(0 x 0 + 40 x 1 + 0 x 0) = 40 (For column 4)

(0 x 0 + 40 x 1 + 0 x -12) = 40 (For column 5)

(0 x (2/3) + 40 x (1/3) + 0 x 6) = 40/3 (For column 6)

Σ(Contribution x Corresponding disposal activity values of Land X_4, Labour X_5 and Capital X_6)

(0 x 1 + 0 x 0 + 0 x 0) = 0 (For column 7)

(0 x (-1/6) + 40 x (1/6) + 0 x -6) = 20/3 (For column 8)

(0 x 0 + 40 x 0 + 0 x 1) = 0 (For column 9)

Ratio

To calculate Ratio, consider lowest shadow price (*i.e.*,-20/3) and consider that column real activities of Red gram X_3. Divide resource activity level values of Land X_4, Paddy X_1 and Capital X_6 (*i.e.*, column 3) with corresponding real activities of Red gram X_3 of lowest shadow price column (*i.e.*, column 6): *i.e.*, (2/3), (1/3) and 6 to get Ratios *i.e.*, 4/(2/3)=6, 8/(1/3)=24 and 72/6=12.

Among the computed ratio values in Plan II, consider lowest ratio (i.e, 6) and eliminate that row (*i.e.*, Land X_4 row) in the next plan (*i.e.*, Plan III). Now, replace that row (*i.e.*, Land X_4 row) by employing the pivot value of the column with respect to lowest shadow price (*i.e.*,-20/3). So, considering the Land X_4 row and column of the lowest shadow price (-20/3), the pivot value is (2/3) *i.e.*, the intersection value of the selected row and selected column. Now, divide the entire eliminated Land X_4 row values with the pivot value (2/3) and include them as Red gram X_3 row, as shown through Plan III. This is given by:

= 4/(2/3) = 6

= 0/(2/3) = 0

= (0)/(2/3) = 0

= (2/3)/(2/3) = 1

= 1/(2/3) = 3/2

= (-1/6)/(2/3) = -1/4

= (0)/(2/3) = 0

Transfer the above calculated values as row values for Red gram X_3 in Plan III.

Value of the Programme

It is given by Σ(Contribution x Corresponding resource activity level) for each row of Land X_4, Paddy X_1 and Capital X_6 restrictions *i.e.*, [(0x4)+(40x8)+(0x72)] =320

Plan III

Contribution (Net income)	Restriction	Resource activity level	Real activities Paddy X_1	Groundnut X_2	Red gram X_3	Disposable activities Land X_4	Labour X_5	Capital X_6
20 (Redgram net income)	Redgram X_3	6	0	0	1	3/2	-1/4	0
40 (Paddy net income)	Paddy X_1	6	1	1	0	-1/2	1/4	0
0	Capital X_6	36	0	-12	0	-9	-9/2	1
	Net income (C)		40	30	20	0	0	0
	Opportunity cost (Z)		40	40	20	10	5	0
	Shadow price (Z-C)		0	10	0	10	5	0

Value of programme 360

Note: To calculate non-key row values in Plan III of Paddy X_1 and Capital X_6, the following formula will be used:

N=O-(I x P), where O=Previous row value of the restriction (Paddy X_1 and Capital X_6) in previous Plan II, I= Incoming row value in this plan (*i.e.*, Red gram X_3 values of row 1 in this current plan (III Plan), P= Pivot value for Paddy X_1 and Capital X_6 corresponding to the lowest shadow price value (-20/3) column in the previous plan *i.e.*, II Plan (*i.e.*, 1/3 with reference to Paddy X_1 and 6 with reference to Capital X_6).

So, for Paddy X_1 in Plan III:

$N = O - (I \times P) = 8 - (6 \times 1/3) = 6$

$= 1 - (0 \times 1/3) = 1$

$= 1 - (0 \times 1/3) = 1$

$= 1/3 - (1 \times 1/3) = 0$

$= 0 - (3/2 \times 1/3) = -1/2$

$= 1/6 - (-1/4 \times 1/3) = 1/4$

$= 0 - (0 \times 1/3) \quad = 0$

Transfer the above calculated values as row values for Paddy X_1 in Plan III

Similarly, for Capital X_6 in Plan III:

$$N = O - (I \times P) = 72 - (6 \times 6) = 36$$
$$= 0 - (0 \times 6) = 0$$
$$= -12 - (0 \times 6) = -12$$
$$= 6 - (1 \times 6) = 0$$
$$= 0 - (3/2 \times 6) = -9$$
$$= -6 - (-1/4 \times 6) = -9/2$$
$$= 1 - (0 \times 6) \quad = 1$$

Transfer the above calculated values as row values for Capital X_6 in Plan III.

Value of the Programme

It is given by Σ(Contribution x Corresponding resource activity level) for each row of Red gram X_3, Paddy X_1 and Capital X_6 restrictions *i.e.*, [(20x6)+(40x6)+(0x360)] =360

Criteria for Stopping Computation of Plans

To arrive at the optimal solution, the criterion is that, when all the Z-C values (*i.e.*, Shadow price values) are either zero or positive. In the above Plan III, all Z-C values are either zero or positive and hence, this Plan III gives the optimal solution. Hence,

$$\text{Max } Z \; 40X_1+30X_2+20X_3$$
$$40(6)+30(X_2)+20(6)$$
$$= \text{Rs. } 360$$

Thus, considering Plan III, select Paddy X_1 and Red gram X_3 enterprises in 6 units each and by doing so, we get a maximum profit of Rs. 360/- (also indicated by Valuation of programme). Remaining Capital X_6 *i.e.*, '36' represents disposal activity and this infer the amount left over after investing on paddy and red gram. The same can be checked from the functional constraint equation of Capital X6, as given below:

$$36X_1 + 24X_2 + 18X_3 \leq 360$$
$$36 \times (6) + (24X_2) + 18(6) \leq 360$$

So, by investing on Paddy X_1 and Red gram X_3 enterprises, the maximum revenue possible is Rs. 324/- (*i.e.*, <360/-) and Rs. 36/- is left over with farmer. So, the farmer's maximizing plan includes cultivating paddy (X_1) and Red gram (X_3) in 6 units each and employing 36 man days under Paddy (X_1) and 12 man days in Red gram (X_3) as given below. The farmer is left over with Rs.36 of unused capital. Thus, the farmer's plan includes:

- ☆ All the 12 units of land should be utilized (6 units each under Paddy X_1 and Red gram X_3). That is,

  $1X_1+1X_2+1X_3 \leq 12$ units (Land)

  $1(6)+1X_2+1(6) = 12$

- All the labour will be utilized on the farm. That is,

  $6X_1+6X_2+2X_3 \leq 48$ man days

  $6(6)+6X_2+2(6) = 48$ man days (Labour).

- As calculated above, the farmer is able to use only Rs.324 of capital and remaining Rs.36 capital is unused in this plan.

Marginal Value Productivity (MVP)

It is interesting that, Z-C values under the slack variables or disposal activities of resources under optimal plant (*i.e.*, Plan III) can be interpreted as the MVP of resources under given set of conditions. So, in Plan III, under X_4, X_5 and X_6 disposal activities:

MVP_{Land} : Rs.10

MVP_{Labour} : Rs.5

$MVP_{Capital}$: Rs.0

This implies that, the farmer can pay at most Rs.10 for renting additional unit of land and Rs.5 for hiring additional labour, but nothing for rental use of additional unit of capital borrowed by him. It is evident from the values of shadow price (Z-C) that,

- The value of shadow price: 10 under X_4 (land disposal activity) in the optimal plan (Plan III) implies that, MVP_{land} = Rs.10/-. That is, if the farmer could increase one more unit of land, his net income would increase by Rs. 10/- *i.e.*, from Rs. 360 to 370. This can be easily verified with the help of marginal rates of substitution values under X_4 (disposal activity for land) in the optimal plan. The values are 3/2 for red gram X_3, -1/2 for paddy X_1 and -9 for capital X_6 indicating that, an increase in one unit of land will increase X_3 (*i.e.*, area under red gram) by 3/2 units (1.5 units), decrease paddy area (X_1) by ½ units (*i.e.*, 0.5 units) and also decrease X_6 (*i.e.*, capital) by Rs. 9. From the above information, the optimal plan for 13 units of land can be written as follows (*i.e.*, if the land area in the farm is increased from 12 units to 13 units).

  - (6) +1.5 = 7.5 units of land under red gram, X_3
  - (6) – 0.5 = 5.5 units of land under paddy X_1
  - (36) – 9 = 27 *i.e.*, capital use decreased by Rs. 9.

  The reader can check the above information, as the farmer now uses 7.5 units of land under red gram X_3, 5.5 units of land under paddy X_1 *i.e.*, 13 units of land in total and total capital use decreases by Rs. 9 *i.e.*, from Rs. 360 to Rs. 351. So, the net farm income of the new plan is:

  Max Z: $40X_1 + 30X_2 + 20X_3$

  $(40*5.5) + 30X_2 + 20(7.5)$

  $220 + 30X_2 + 150$

  = Rs. 370/-

Thus, it is proved that, the MVP of land is Rs. 10/-, as the net income from land was increased to Rs. 370/- from Rs. 360/- by increasing one unit of land in the farm cultivation.

- ☆ The value of 5 under labour X_5 disposal activity in the optimal plan (Plan III) implies that, MVP_{labour} = Rs. 5/-. That is, if the farmer could increase one more labour, his net income would increase by Rs. 5/- *i.e.*, from Rs. 360 to Rs. 365/-.
- ☆ The $MVP_{capital}$ is equal to zero, as the farmer already has Rs. 36/- in excess in implementing the optimal plan (Plan III).

Sensitivity Analysis - Shadow Prices:

The above discussion also infers that, the MVP of resources is known as Shadow prices or Accounting prices or Imputed values or Implicit values. They represent the true or intrinsic value of resources and hence, the farmer cannot pay more than these amounts for each additional units of resources. The quantities or values of these resources multiplied by their respective MVP (*i.e.*, shadow price) of each resource and their sum will indicate the TVP of resources and it will be equal to the value of the objective function of the optimal plan. In this example, TVP is given by:

$$(12x10)+ (48x5)+(360x0) = 40(6)+30(X_2)+20(6)$$

$$\text{Rs } 360/- \quad = \quad \text{Rs. } 360/-$$

(TVP from resources side) = (Value of the objective function of the optimal plan)

So, the TVP of farm resources is Rs.360.

The shadow price represents the change in optimal value of the objective function per unit increase in the right hand side of a constraint. This concept can also be better explained with reference to the Figure 9.5 through changing the right hand side of the fertilizer constraint by one unit and the same was shown through Figure 9.19.1. In the Figure 9.19.1, with increase in the right hand side of the fertilizer constraint from 300 to 301, the new X1 and X2 units are 10.03 and 15.05 respectively. So, the new functional constraint line of fertilizer does not pass through the original optimal point (corner point) 'C', but away (right side) from it. So, the new higher iso-profit line of Rs.98.6 (*i.e.*, Max Z: (6 (5.1) + 8(8.5)) = Rs. 98.6) will pass through the new optimal point (corner point) 'D' with reference to 5.1 units of X1 and 8.5 units of X2. Thus, the shadow price of fertilizer is given by: 98.6 – 96 = Rs.2.6. Thus, shadow price of fertilizer implies the change in optimal value of the objective function due to per unit increase in the right hand side of that functional constraint. This Rs.2.6 change in profits that resulted from a unit change (increase) in the fertilizer is called the Shadow price, or Dual value. That is, the value of one additional unit of a scarce resource in LP is called shadow price. This shadow price for a constraint indicates the improvement in the objective function value that results from a one-unit increase in the right-hand side of the constraint. Sensitivity analysis thus, shows the changes in the optimal value of the objective function due to per unit change in the right hand side of a constraint. This analysis also guides the farmer in various aspects like: how much should the farmer is willing to pay for additional labour hours? Is it profitable to

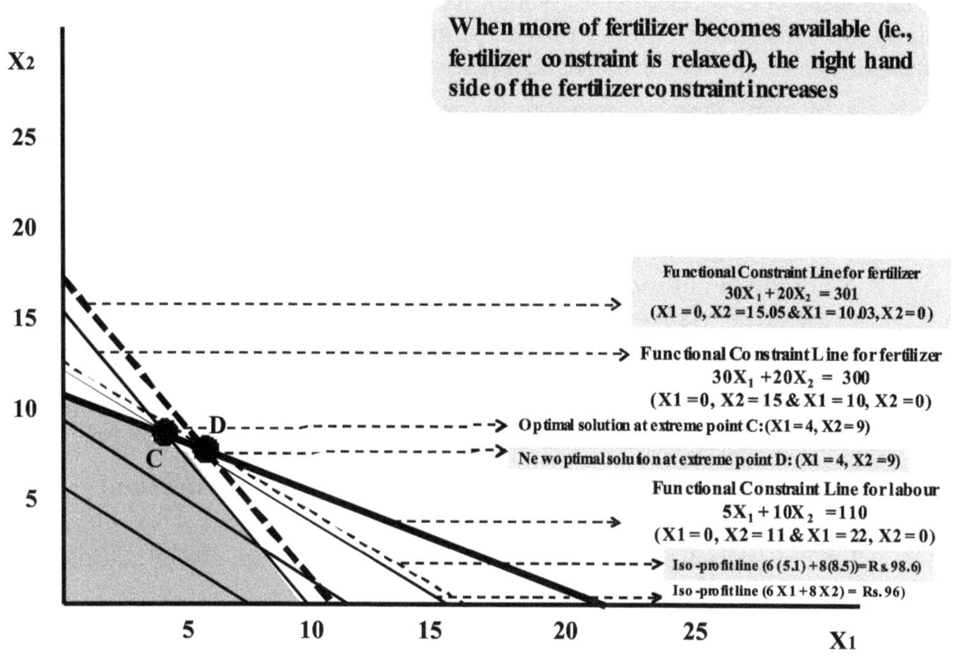

Figure 9.19.1: Finding Optiaml Solution Based on Iso-Profit Line Approach.

reduce the dosage of fertilizer? Note that, in the range of feasibility, the objective function value changes as follows:

Change in optimal value = (Shadow price/unit)(Change in the right hand side value of the constraint)

The shadow price is valid only as long as the change in the right hand side is within the Allowable Increase and Allowable Decrease values. That is, in the above example, the shadow price of Rs.2.6/unit is valid as long as the available fertilizer stays in a range within which all current corner points continue to exist. Similarly, sensitivity analysis can be worked out by changing one of the objective function coefficients. As the unit profit contribution of either product changes, the slope of the iso-profit lines also changes. The size of the feasible region, however, remains the same. That is, the locations of the corner points do not change. As in the earlier case of changing the right hand side value of the constraint, there is an allowable decrease and an allowable increase for each objective function coefficient over which the current optimal solution remains optimal. A new corner point becomes optimal, if an objective function coefficient is decreased or increased too much.

Thus, the shadow prices in a profit maximization problem indicate, how much total profits would rise per unit increase in the use of each input. Shadow prices thus, provide the imputed value or marginal valuation or worth of each input to the firm. If a particular input is not fully employed, its shadow price is zero because, increasing the input would leave profits unchanged. A firm should increase the use of the input as long as the MVP or shadow price of the input to the firm exceeds the cost of hiring the input. This shadow prices provide important information for planning and strategic decisions of the firm. Shadow prices are also used:

- ✰ by many large corporations to correctly price the output of each division that is the input to another division, in order to maximize the total profits of the entire corporation,
- ✰ by Government to appropriately price some government services, and
- ✰ for planning in developing countries where the market system often does not function properly (*i.e.*, where input and output prices do not reflect their true relative scarcity).

The computer solution of the primal LP problem also provides the values of the shadow prices. Sometimes, it is also easier to obtain the optimal value of the decision variables in the primal problem by solving the corresponding dual problem.

Generalized Procedure of Simplex Method (Maximization Function)

1. Formulate the given LP problem in Standard form.
2. Convert each inequality in the set of constraints to equality by adding slack variable or disposable activity.
3. Create the initial simplex tableau.
4. Compute opportunity cost in the Plan:
   Σ(Contribution x Corresponding real activities)
   Σ(Contribution x Corresponding disposal activity values)
5. Compute shadow price (Z-C) in the Plan
6. Compute ratio in the Plan by employing the formula:
   Divide resource activity level values with corresponding real activities
7. Compute Value of the Programme in the Plan by employing the formula:
   Σ(Contribution x Corresponding resource activity level) for each row
8. Identify the column in the Plan that corresponds lowest shadow price or highest negative shadow price.
9. Identify the lowest ratio in the Plan. Select that row and divide all the elements in that row (key row) by the pivot element *i.e.*, the element that lies at the intersection between selected lowest shadow price column are selected lowest ratio row.
10. Delete that key row in the next plan.
11. Transfer all the calculated values as above in Step 9, in the next plan for the real activity corresponding to lowest shadow price.
12. The value of elements of non-key rows are calculated by employing the formula:
    N=O-(I x P), where O=Previous row value of that resource activity in preceding plan, I= Incoming row value in the current plan, P= Pivot value in the previous plan.

13. Repeat the same procedure as above from step 4 to 12 till the optimal plan is reached.
14. The criterion for optimal plan is that, 'when all the Z-C values of the row are either zero or positive'.
15. Compute the optimal solution by employing the values of resources activity levels of enterprises/products in the objective function.
16. Verify the optimal solution with the value of the programme.

ii. Cost Minimization Objective Function

In the previous section, we demonstrated the simplex method for solving LP problem with profit maximization objective function. The steps of simplex method that are discussed at the end of the previous section are common even for minimization problem, but with slight changes and the same can be witnessed from the following example:

Example 9.12

The Vitamins A_1 and A_2 are found in two different Foods X_1 and X_2. One unit of Food X_1 contains 2 units of Vitamin A_1 and 5 units of Vitamin A_2. One unit of Food X_2 contains 4 units of Vitamin A_1 and 2 units of Vitamin A_2. One unit of Food X_1 and Food X_2 costs Rs.3 and Rs.2.25 respectively. The minimum daily requirement for a person of Vitamins A_1 and A_2 is 40 and 50 units respectively. Find the optimum mix of Foods X_1 and X_2 at the minimum cost, which makes the daily minimum requirement of Vitamins A_1 and A_2.

Solution

Step 1: The above information can be conveniently presented in the form of table as given below:

Restrictions	*Restriction Level*	*Real Activities*		*Disposal Activities*		*Artificial Variables*	
		Food X_1	*Food X_2*	*Vitamin A1 (X_3)*	*Vitamin A2 (X_4)*	*A_1*	*A_2*
Vitamin A_1	40	2	4	–1	0	1	0
Vitamin A_2	50	5	2	0	–1	0	1
Unit cost		3	2.25	0	0	M	M

Step 2: The above tabular form of LP problem can be conveniently expressed as mathematical equations. That is, translate the given data in the table into inequalities as given below.

Min Z $3X_1 + 2.25X_2$

Subject to

$2X_1 + 4X_2 \quad \geq 40$ of Vitamin A_1

$5X_1 + 2X_2 \quad \geq 50$ of Vitamin A_2

$X_1, X_2 \quad \geq 0$

Step 3: Then, all these inequalities are to be converted into equalities by subtracting surplus variables (X_3 and X_4) from the two '≥' constraints as follows:

Min Z $3X_1 + 2.25X_2 + 0X_3 + 0X_4$

subject to

$2X_1 + 4X_2 - 1X_3 + 0X_4 = 40$

$5X_1 + 2X_2 + 0X_3 - 1X_4 = 50$

$X_1, X_2, X_3, X_4 \geq 0$

X_3 and X_4 are surplus variables each for one variable X_1 and X_2 respectively *i.e.*, X_3 for X_1 and X_4 for X_2.

The surplus variables represent the extra amount of Vitamin A_1 and Vitamin A_2 that exceed the minimum requirements specified in the constraints. A surplus variable is the difference between the total value of the true (decision) variables and the number (usually, total resource available) on the right-hand side of the equation. Thus, a surplus variable will *always* have a negative value. However, the simplex method requires that, the initial basic feasible solution be at the origin, where $X_1 = 0$ and $X_2 = 0$. Testing these solution values, we have:

$2X_1 + 4X_2 - 1X_3 + 0X_4 = 40$

$2(0) + 4(0) - 1X_3 + 0X_4 = 40$

$X_3 = -40$

The idea of 'negative excess units of Vitamin A_1' is not meaningful and this also violates the non-negativity restriction of LP. To overcome this problem, we add an Artificial variable to each of the functional constraints equations of Vitamin A_1 and Vitamin A_2 as shown below.

$2X_1 + 4X_2 - 1X_3 + 0X_4 + 1A_1 + 0A_2 = 40$

$5X_1 + 2X_2 + 0X_3 - 1X_4 + 0A_1 + 1A_2 = 50$

A_1 and A_2 are Artificial variables for each surplus variable. So, one 'artificial variable' is added to each of the 'greater-than-equal-to' constraints to ensure an initial basic feasible solution. These artificial variables are 'penalized' in the objective function by introducing a large positive coefficient '*M*' for minimization problem.

Considering one of the above equations *i.e.*,

$2X_1 + 4X_2 - 1X_3 + 0X_4 + 1A_1 + 0A_2 = 40$

$2(0) + 4(0) - 0X_3 + 0X_4 + 1A_1 + 0A_2 = 40$

$A_1 = 40$

The use of artificial variable has no meaning, unlike surplus variable, as the former is simply used in the functional constraint equations only to give positive solution to the origin. That is, artificial variable is simply used to start the process of simplex method, but once the iterations were started, it has no use and thus, is discarded. These variables can be eliminated from the simplex tableau as and when they become zero (non-basic). So, the LP problem in standard form is presented as below:

Min Z $3X_1 + 2.25X_2 + 0X_3 + 0X_4 + MA_1 + MA_2$

subject to

$2X_1 + 4X_2 - 1X_3 + 0X_4 + 1A_1 + 0A_2 = 40$

$5X_1 + 2X_2 + 0X_3 - 1X_4 + 0A_1 + 1A_2 = 50$

$X_1, X_2, X_3, X_4, A_1, A_2 \geq 0$

X_3 and X_4 are surplus variables each for one variable X-$_1$ and X_2 respectively *i.e.*, X_3 for X_1 and X_4 for X_2

A_1 and A_2 are Artificial variables to bring negative value of surplus variable to positive values

Remember that, an artificial variable has no significance pertaining to the solution of the problem and it is used merely to find a solution mix in the first simplex tableau. Although artificial variables will always form part of the initial solution mix, the objective is to remove them as soon as possible by means of the simplex procedure. As long as an artificial variable still appears in the solution mix, the final solution has not yet been found. As any other variable, artificial variables are also included in the objective function, but the value attached to them creates another problem. In minimization problems, since the objective is to find the lowest cost possible, a very

The above data are presented through matrices as given below:

$$[3 \quad 2.25 \quad 0 \quad 0 \quad M \quad M] \begin{bmatrix} X_1 \\ X_2 \\ X_3 \\ X_4 \\ A_1 \\ A_2 \end{bmatrix} = \text{Min } Z$$

Subjected to:-

$$\begin{bmatrix} 2 & 4 & -1 & 0 & 1 & 0 \\ 5 & 2 & 0 & -1 & 0 & 1 \end{bmatrix} \begin{bmatrix} X_1 \\ X_2 \\ X_3 \\ X_4 \\ A_1 \\ A_2 \end{bmatrix} \begin{bmatrix} =40 \\ =50 \end{bmatrix}$$

$$\begin{bmatrix} X_1 \\ X_2 \\ X_3 \\ X_4 \\ A_1 \\ A_2 \end{bmatrix} \geq 0$$

large value is allocated to artificial variables. This value is denoted by M, where 'M' is a very large positive value.

This expression of LP problem represent LP problem in Standard form. So, a LP problem is in standard form, if it seeks to *minimize* the objective function subject to the given constraints and representing in terms of surplus variables and artificial variables. Note that, if there are 'm' constraints in the given problem, the number of surplus variables and artificial variables added will be 'm' each. In this example, there are two constraints with respect to Vitamin A_1 and Vitamin A_2 and hence, two surplus variables X_3 and X_4; and two artificial variables X_5 and X_6 are added. It is at this point, we begin applying the Simplex method to solve the formulated LP problem.

Plan I

The initial simplex tableau for a minimization model is developed in the same way as prepared under maximization model, except for one difference. That is, in Z-C row, we consider the largest positive value to select the pivot column. Note that, across the top, the decision variables are listed first, then surplus variables and finally artificial variables.

Contribution	*Resource Activity*	*Resource Activity Level*	*Real Activities*		*Surplus Variables*		*Artificial Variables*		*Ratio*
			Food X_1	*Food X_2*	*Vit A_1*	*Vit A_2*	*A_1*	*A_2*	
M	Vit A1	40	2	4	–1	0	1	0	40/2 =20
M	Vit A2	50	5	2	0	–1	0	1	50/5=10
Net income (C)			3	2.25	0	0	M	M	
Opportunity cost (Z)			7M	6M	–M	–M	M	M	
Shadow price (Z-C)			7M-3	6M-2.25	–M	–M	0	0	

In the above table:

Opportunity Cost (Z)

It is calculated by the formula:

Σ(Contribution x Corresponding real activities of Food X_1 and Food X_2)

$(M \times 2 + M \times 5) = 7M$ (For column 4)

$(M \times 4 + M \times 2) = 6M$ (For column 5)

Σ(Contribution x Corresponding disposal activity values of Vit A1 and Vit A2)

$(M \times (-1) + M \times 0) = -M$ (For column 6)

$(M \times 0 + M \times (-1)) = -M$ (For column 7)

Σ(Contribution x Artificial variable values of Vit A1 and Vit A2)

(M x 1 + M x 0) = M (For column 8)

(M x 0 + M x 1) = M (For column 9)

Ratio

To calculate Ratio, consider highest (positive) shadow price (*i.e.*,7M-3) and consider that column real activities of Food X_1. Divide resource activity level values of Vit A_1 and Vit A_2 (*i.e.*, column 3) with corresponding real activities of Food X_1 of highest shadow price column *viz.*, 2 and 5 (*i.e.*, column 4): *i.e.*, 40/2=20, 50/5=10 to workout Ratios.

Among the computed ratio values in Plan I, consider lowest ratio (i.e, 10) and eliminate that row (*i.e.*, Vit A_2 row) in the next plan (*i.e.*, Plan II). Now, replace that row (*i.e.*, Vit A_2 row) by employing the pivot value of the column with respect to highest shadow price (*i.e.*, 7M-3 shadow price column). So, considering the Vit A_2 row and column of the highest shadow price (7M-3) in Plan I, the pivot value is 5 *i.e.*, the intersection value of the selected row and selected column. Now, divide the entire eliminated Vit A_2 row values with the pivot value (5) and include them as Food X_1 row, as shown through Plan II. This is given by:

= 50/5 = 10

= 5/5 = 1

= 2/5 = 2/5

= 0/5 = 0

= -1/5 =(-1/5)

= 0/5 = 0

= 1/5 = 1/5

Transfer all the above calculated values as Food X_1 row values in Plan II.

Plan II

Contribution	Resource Activity	Resource Activity Level	Real Activities		Surplus Variables		Artificial Variables		Ratio
			Food X_1	Food X_2	Vit A_1	Vit A_2	A_1	A_2	
M	Vit A1	20*	0	16/5	–1	2/5	1	–2/5	20/(16/5) = 6.25
3	Food X_1	50/5 =10	5/5 = 1	2/5	0	–1/5	0	1/5	10/(2/5) = 25
Net income (C)			3	2.25	0	0	M	M	
Opportunity cost (Z)			3	16M/5+ 6/5	–M	2M/5+ (-3/5)	M	–2M/5+ (3/5)	
Shadow price (Z-C)			0	16M/5 – (1.05)	–M	2M/5- (3/5)	0	–7M/5+ (3/5)	

*: To calculate non-key row values in Plan II of Vit A_1, the following formula will be used:

N=O-(I x P), where O=Previous row value of that resource activity in previous plan, I= Incoming row value in this plan (*i.e.*, Food X_1 values of row 2 in this current Plan II), P=Pivot value for Vit A_1 corresponding to the highest shadow price value (7M-3) column in the previous Plan I (*i.e.*, 2).

So, for Vit A_1 in Plan II:

N = 40-(10x2) = 20

= 2-(1x2) = 0

= 4-(2/5) (2) = 16/5

= -1-(0x2)= -1

= 0-(-1/5) (2) = 2/5

= 1-(0x2)= 1

= 0-(1/5) (2) = -2/5

Transfer the above calculated values for Vit A_1 row in Plan II.

After computing resource activity levels, real activities, disposal activities and artificial variables for Vit A_1 row, follow the same procedure as in I Plan, to compute opportunity cost values, shadow prices and ratios. That is,

Opportunity Cost (Z)

It is calculated by the formula:

Σ(Contribution x Corresponding real activities of Food X_1 and Food X_2)

(M x 0 + 3 x 1) = 3 (For column 4)

(M x (16/5) + 3 x (2/5)) = (16M/5)+(6/5) (For column 5)

Σ(Contribution x Corresponding disposal activity values of Vit A_1 and Vit A_2)

(M x (-1) + 3 x 0) = -M (For column 6)

(M x (2/5) + 3 x (-1/5)) = (2M/5)+(-3/5) (For column 7)

Σ(Contribution x Corresponding Artificial variable values)

(M x 1 + 3 x 0) = M (For column 8)

(M x (-2/5) + 3 x (1/5)) = (-2M/5)+(3/5) (For column 9)

Ratio

To calculate Ratio, consider highest shadow price (*i.e.*,((16M/5)-1.05) and consider that column real activities of Food X_2. Divide resource activity level values of Vit A_1 and Food X_1 (*i.e.*, column 3) with corresponding real activities of Food X_2 of highest shadow price column *viz.*, (16/5) and (2/5) (*i.e.*, column 5): *i.e.*, 20/(16/5)=6.25, 10/(2/5)=25.

Among the computed ratio values in Plan II, consider lowest ratio (i.e, 6.25) and eliminate that row (*i.e.*, Vit A_1 row) in the next plan (*i.e.*, Plan III). Now, replace that row (*i.e.*, Vit A_1 row) by employing the pivot value of the column with respect to highest shadow price (*i.e.*,((16M/5)-1.05). So, considering the Vit A_1 row and column of the highest shadow price ((16M/5)-1.05), the pivot value is (16/5) *i.e.*, the intersection value of the selected row and selected column. Now, divide the entire eliminated Vit A_1 row values with the pivot value (16/5) and include them as Food X_2 row, as shown through Plan III. This is given by:

$= 20/(16/5) = 6.25$

$= 0/(16/5) = 0$

$= (16/5)/(16/5) = 1$

$= -1/(16/5) = -5/16$

$= (2/5)/(16/5) = 1/8$

$= 1/(16/5) = 5/16$

$= (-2/5)/(16/5) = -1/8$

Transfer all the above calculated values as Food X_2 row values in Plan III.

Plan III

Contri-bution	Resource Activity	Resource Activity Level	*Real Activities*		*Surplus Variables*		*Artificial Variables*	
			Food X_1	*Food X_2*	*Vit A_1*	*Vit A_2*	*A_1*	*A_2*
2.25	Food X_2	20/(16/5) =6.25*	0	1	–5/16	1/8	5/16	–1/8
3	Food X_1	7.5	1	0	1/8	–1/4	–1/8	1/4
Net income (C)			3	2.25	0	0	M	M
Opportunity cost (Z)			3	2.25	–0.328	–0.469	0.328	0.468
Shadow price(Z-C)			0	0	–0.328	–0.469	0.328-M	0.468-M
Value of programme				**36.5625**				

***:** To calculate non-key row values in Plan III of Food X_1, the following formula will be used:

N=O-(I x P), where O=Previous row value of that resource activity in previous plan, I= Incoming row value in this plan (*i.e.*, Food X_2 values of row 1 in this Plan III), P= P=Pivot value for Food X_1 corresponding to the highest shadow price value (16M/5 –(1.05) column in the previous Plan II (*i.e.*, 2/5).

So, for Food X_1 in Plan III:

$N = O - (I \times P) = 10 - (6.25 \times 2/5) = 7.5$

$= 1 - (0 \times 2/5) = 1$

$= 2/5 - (1 \times 2/5) = 0$

$= 0 - (-5/16 \times 2/5) = 1/8$

$= -1/5 - (-1/8 \times 2/5) = -1/4$

$= 0 - (5/16 \times 2/5) = -1/8$

$= 1/5 - (-1/8 \times 2/5) = 1/4$

Transfer all the above calculated values as Food X_1 row values in Plan III.

Value of the Programme

It is given by Σ(Contribution x Corresponding resource activity level) for each row *i.e.*, [(2.25*6.25)+(3*7.5)] = 14.0625 + 22.5 = 36.56.

Criteria for Stopping Computation of Plans

To arrive at the optimal solution, the criterion is that, when all the Z-C values (*i.e.*, Shadow price values) are either zero or negative for real activities and surplus variables (*i.e.*, Z-C row contains no positive values for real activities and surplus variables). So, Plan III gives the optimal solution. Thus, considering Plan III, select 7.5 units of Food X_1 and 6.25 units of Food X_2 and by doing so, we can minimize the cost to the tune of Rs. 36.56 (also indicated by the Valuation of programme). That is, given objective function:

Min Z $3X_1 + 2.25X_2$

$=3(7.5)+2.25(6.25)$ = Rs.36.56

To summarize, the adjustments necessary to apply the simplex method to a minimization problem are as follows:

- ✰ Transform all '≥' constraints to equalities by subtracting a surplus variable and adding an artificial variable.
- ✰ Consider highest positive shadow price to select the pivot column.

Note that, although the above discussed diet example model included only '≥' constraints, it is possible for a minimization problem to also have '≤' and '=' constraints in addition to '≥' constraints. Similarly, it is possible for a maximization problem to have '≥' and '=' constraints in addition to '≤' constraints. Problems that contain a combination of different types of inequality constraints are referred to as Mixed constraint problems. So, in case of mixed constraint problems, we have to employ slack variables, surplus variables and artificial variables and the same is discussed here under.

Thus, the simplex technique involves generating a series of solutions in tabular form, called tableaus. By inspecting the bottom row of each tableau, one can immediately tell, if it represents the optimal solution. Each tableau corresponds to a corner point of the feasible solution space. The first tableau corresponds to the origin. Subsequent tableaus are developed by shifting to an adjacent corner point in the direction that yields the highest (smallest) rate of profit (cost). This process continues as long as a positive (negative) rate of profit (cost) exists. Thus, in this method, the computational routine is an iterative process. To *iterate* means to repeat; *i.e.*, in working toward an optimum solution, the computational routine is repeated over and over, following a standard pattern. Successive solutions are developed in a systematic pattern until the best solution is reached. Each new solution will yield a value of the objective function as large as or larger than the previous solution. This important feature assures us that we are always moving closer to the optimum answer. Finally, the method indicates when the optimum solution has been reached (Sami, 2007).

Merits of Simplex Method

This Simplex method is the most widely used algebraic procedure for solving LP problems. This method is a general-purpose LP algorithm widely used to solve large scale problems. Although it lacks the intuitive appeal of the graphical approach, its ability to handle problems with more than two decision variables makes it extremely valuable for solving problems often encountered in production/operations management. Thus, simplex method offers an efficient means of solving more complex LP problems.

Complications in Simplex Method

As discussed earlier under graphical approach, a LP problem may have different type of solutions corresponding to different situations. Here, the same will be discussed in the context of Simplex method:

- ☆ Equalities instead of inequalities for constraints.
- ☆ Decision variables unrestricted in signs.
- ☆ Zero constants on the right-hand side of one or more constraints.
- ☆ Some or all decision variables must be integers.
- ☆ Non-positive constants on the right-hand side of the constraints.
- ☆ More than one optimal solution *i.e.,* multiple solutions such that, there is no unique optimal solution (Table 9.5.1).
- ☆ The constraints are such that, no feasible solution exists (Table 9.5.1).
- ☆ The constraints are such that, one or more of the variables can increase without limit and never violate a constraint *i.e.,* the solution is unbounded (Table 9.5.1).
- ☆ Some or all of the coefficients and right-hand-side terms are given by a probability distribution rather than a single value.

Limitations of Simplex Method

They include:

- ☆ Inability to deal with multiple objectives
- ☆ Inability to handle problems with integer variables

VII. LP Problems Involving Slack, Surplus and Artificial Variables

Having understood the concept of formulation of LP problem for both maximization and minimization functions, it is essential to learn to formulate the LP problem involving both slack and surplus variables. By this time we are aware that, in simplex procedure:

- ☆ All equations must be equalities.
- ☆ All variables must be present in all equations.

Table 9.5.1: Possible Complications in the Application of Simplex Method

Cases	*How to Recognize them in Simplex Tableau*
Multiple optimal solutions	If the index of a variable not contained in the solution mix is zero in the final tableau, it means that, there is more than one optimal solution. Mathematically, the inclusion of this variable in the solution mix will not change the value of the objective function.
Degeneracy	One or more constraints are redundant – as a result of this, two equally small non-negative ratios may occur in the table when the pivot row is to be identified. If the incorrect one is selected, the only problem is that, an extra iteration will be carried out. This degeneracy refers to the situation in which a LP problem has a basic feasible solution with at least one basic variable equal to zero. This can occur at formulation or if there is a tie for the minimizing value in the ratio test to determine the leaving variable. Note that, ☆ When degeneracy occurs, an optimal solution may have been attained even though some Z-C values are <0. Thus, the condition that, Z-C ≥ 0 is sufficient for optimality, but not necessary. ☆ If the number of basic variables is fewer than the number of constraints in a solution, the solution is said to be degenerate. ☆ A zero constant term for one or more basic variables in any iteration of the simplex solution would be a clear indication of a degenerate solution. Note that, the normal simplex procedure cannot solve a degenerate problem. Advanced methods are available to solve degenerate problems.
Infeasibility	This case is easily recognized, if in the final tableau, at least one of the artificial variables still exists in the solution mix, whilst all the indices indicate that an optimal solution has been found.
Unbounded solutions	When identifying the pivot row, all the ratios will be either negative or ∞. It means that, one or more variables can increase indefinitely without the constraints being exceeded in a maximization problem.

- ☆ In the case of '≤' constraints, slack variables are added to the actual variables to make the equation an equality.
- ☆ In the case of '≥' constraints, surplus variables and artificial variables are used to make the equation an equality.

Consider the following LP problem:

Min $Z = 5X_1+7X_2$

Subject to

$X_1 + X_2 = 4500$

$X_1 \leq 2000$

$X_2 \geq 800$

$X_1, X_2 \geq 0$

In the above example, there are three constraints *viz.*, one equality, one 'smaller than or equal to' and one 'greater than or equal to'. The model should now be modified as follows:

$X_1 + X_2 = 4500$

$X_1 + S_1 = 2000$

$X_2 - S_2 = 800$

$X_1, X_2, S_1, S_2 \geq 0$

where S_1 is a slack variable and S_2 is a surplus variable.

As explained earlier, the presence of a surplus variable causes a problem when drawing the first simplex tableau because of its negative value. To overcome this, we add an Artificial variable (a variable that has a positive value denoted by Ai) to the equation. The above LP model is thus rewritten before using simplex procedure.

Min Z $5X_1 + 7X_2 + 0S_1 + 0S_2 + MA_1 + MA_2$

subject to

$1X_1 + 1X_2 + 0S_1 + 0S_2 + 1A_1 + 0A_2 = 4500$

$1X_1 + 0X_2 + 1S_1 + 0S_2 + 0A_1 + 0A_2 = 2000$

$0X_1 + 1X_2 + 0S_1 - 1S_2 + 0A_1 + 1A_2 = 800$

$X_1, X_2, S_1, S_2, A_1, A_2 \geq 0$

VIII. Transportation Problem

The transportation problem is one of the sub-classes of LP problem, where the objective is to transport various quantities of a single homogeneous product that are initially produced or stored at various places (called factories or plants or sources or origins or supply origins), to different destinations (say, warehouses) in such a way that, the total transportation cost is minimum. Prof. F.I. Hitchaxic developed the basic transportation problem in 1941. However, George B. Dantzig in 1951 applied the concept of LP in solving the transportation models to ensure optimality. Thus, transportation problems or models are primarily concerned with the optimal (best possible or lowest cost) way in which a homogeneous product produced at different factories can be transported to a number of destinations (also called demand destinations). So, transportation model is basically an extension of LP model. This model can be solved by a procedure called transportation technique. The main objective in a transportation problem is to fully satisfy the destination requirements within the operating production capacity constraints at the minimum possible cost. Whenever there is physical movement of goods from the point of production to the final consumers through a variety of channels of distribution (wholesalers, retailers, distributors *etc.*), there is a need to minimize the cost of transportation, so as to increase the profit on sales. Transportation problems arise in all such cases. This model aims at providing the answer to the producer in ascertaining, how many units of a particular product should be transported from each supply origin to each demand destinations so that, the total prevailing demand for the firm's product is satisfied, while at the same time the total transportation costs are minimized.

A. Requirements of Transportation Model

They include:

- ☆ Supply at each source or origin.

- ✰ Demand at each destination.
- ✰ Unit cost of transportation of good from each source to each destination.
- ✰ Since single (homogenous) commodity is involved, each destination can receive its requirement from different sources.

B. Assumptions of Transportation Model

The important assumptions include:

- ✰ The total cost of transportation is directly proportional to the number of units of commodity shipped or transported
- ✰ Unit cost of transportation varies with the distance across each source and each destination
- ✰ The commodity transported from different sources to different demand destinations is homogeneous.
- ✰ The transportation problem applies to situations, where a single commodity is to be transported from various sources of supply **(origins)** to various demand **destinations.**

C. Formulation of Transportation Model

Mathematically a transportation problem is nothing but a special LP problem in which the objective function is to minimize the cost of transportation subjected to the demand and supply constraints. The transportation model can be presented in the form of a networking model (Figure 9.20). The line joining the source and destination represents the route through which commodity is shipped or transported. Let there be *'m'* sources of supply $S_1, S_2,$..................S_m having ai (i = 1,2,......m) units of supplies respectively to be transported to *'n'* number of destinations *i.e.*, d_1, d_2.........d_n with b_j (j = 1,2.....n) units of requirements respectively. Let C_{ij} be the cost for shipping or

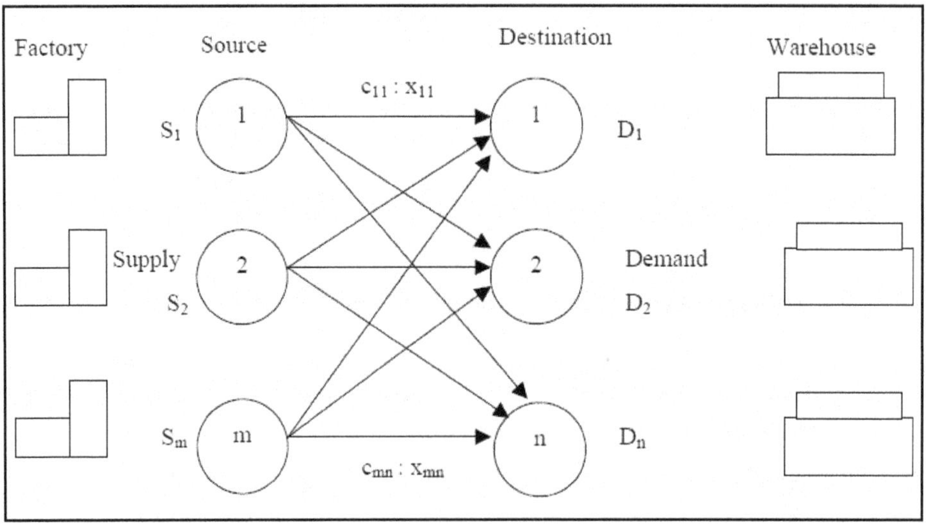

Figure 9.20: Transportation Networking Model.

transport for one unit of the commodity from source i, to destination j for each route. If Xij represents the units shipped per route from source i, to destination j, then the problem is to determine the transportation schedule, which minimizes the total transportation cost of satisfying supply and demand conditions. The transportation problem can be stated mathematically as a LP problem as below:

$$\text{Min } Z = \sum_{i=1}^{m}\sum_{j=1}^{n} C_{ij}X_{ij} \longrightarrow \text{Linear Objective Function}$$

Subject to Constraints

$$\sum_{j=1}^{n} X_{ij} \le a_i \qquad (i = 1 \text{ to } m) \longrightarrow \text{Supply constraint}$$

The above equation specifies that, the total shipments from the sources cannot exceed the supply.

$$\sum_{j=1}^{m} X_{ij} \le b_j \qquad (j = 1 \text{ to } n) \longrightarrow \text{Demand constraint}$$

The above equation specifies that, the total shipments must satisfy the demand.

$X_{ij} \ge 0 \longrightarrow$ Non-negativity constraint

$$\sum_{i=1}^{m} a_i \longrightarrow \text{Total supply from different sources}$$

$$\sum_{j=1}^{n} b_j \longrightarrow \text{Total demand from different destinations}$$

The above model infers that,

- ☆ The formulation of transportation problem is similar to LP problem formulation. Here, the objective function is the total transportation cost that is to be minimized and the constraints are the supply and demand available at each source and destination respectively.
- ☆ Let the supply at i^{th} source is a_i and demand at the destination j is b_j.
- ☆ C_{ij} is the unit cost of transporting a good from i^{th} source or origin to j^{th} destination.
- ☆ X_{ij} refers to number of units of commodity or good shipped or transported from i^{th} source to j^{th} destination.
- ☆ Linear objective function implies, total cost of transporting the product from different sources to different destinations is minimized.
- ☆ Supply constraints indicate the relationship between origin capacity of plants and product to be received by the destinations.
- ☆ The demand constraints indicate the relationship between destination requirements and product to be shipped from plants or origins.
- ☆ Non-negativity constraint implies, no negative shipment is permitted.

Keeping the above items in view, we can now formulate LP model representing transportation model assuming a firm with three plants (sources) located at different places *viz.*, Mumbai (O_1), Chennai (O_2) and Bangalore (O_3). The total output (supply) from these three plants or sources or factories is absorbed by four destinations like D_1, D_2, D_3 and D_4. In the Table 9.6, X_{11} represent number of units of commodity transported from 1st source to 1st destination. Similarly, X_{24} represent number of units of commodity transported from 2nd source to 4th destination and so on. In general, Xij represent number of units of commodity transported from ith source to jth destination. C_{12} represent unit cost incurred in transporting the commodity from 1st source to 2nd destination. Similarly, C_{24} represent unit cost incurred in transporting the commodity from 2nd source to 4th destination and so on. In general, Cij represent unit cost of transporting the commodity from ith source to jth destination.

Table 9.6: General Format of Transportation Model

Sources	Destinations				Capacity of source
	D1	D2	D3	D4	
Mumbai (O1)	C11 X11	C12 X12	C13 X13	C14 X14	b1
Chennai (O2)	C21 X21	C22 X22	C23 X23	C24 X24	b2
Bangalore (O3)	C31 X31	C32 X32	C33 X33	C34 X34	b3
Destination requirement	d1	d2	d3	d4	Σbi / Σdi

From the above information and Table 9.6, the mathematical (LP) model for transportation problem can be expressed as given below:

$$\text{Min } Z = C_{11}X_{11}+C_{12}X_{12}+C_{13}X_{13}+C_{14}X_{14}+C_{21}X_{21}+C_{22}X_{22}+C_{23}X_{23}+C_{24}X_{24}+C_{31}X_{31}+C_{32}X_{32}+C_{33}X_{33}+C_{34}X_{34}$$

Subject to

$X_{11}+X_{12}+X_{13}+X_{14} = b_1$ (Total capacity of Source O_1)

$X_{21}+X_{22}+X_{23}+X_{24} = b_2$ (Total capacity of Source O_2)

$X_{31}+X_{32}+X_{33}+X_{34} = b_3$ (Total capacity of Source O_3)

$X_{11}+X_{21}+X_{31} = d_1$ (Destination D_1 total requirement)

$X_{12}+X_{22}+X_{32} = d_2$ (Destination D_2 total requirement)

$X_{13}+X_{23}+X_{33} = d_3$ (Destination D_3 total requirement)

$X_{14}+X_{24}+X_{34} = d_4$ (Destination D_4 total requirement)

Transportation models are solved manually within the context of a *tableau,* as in the simplex method. The tableau for our wheat transportation model is shown through Table 9.7. Each cell in the tableau represents the amount transported from one source to one destination. Thus, the amount placed in each cell is the value of a decision variable for that cell. For example, the cell X_{11} at the intersection of row 2 (Mumbai Source) and column 2 (Destination, D1 (Visakhapatnam)) represents the decision variable. The smaller value within each cell (upper right hand corner in each cell) refers to the unit transportation cost for that route. For example, in the above cell at the intersection of row 2 (Mumbai Source) and column 2 (Destination, D1 (Visakhapatnam)), the value, Rs.160, is the cost of transporting one unit of product from Mumbai to Visakhapatnam. Along the outer rim of the tableau across each column and row are the total supply and total demand constraint (quantity) values, which are referred to as rim requirements.

D. Characteristics of Transportation Model

The above discussion on the formulation of transportation model reveals the following characteristics:

- ☆ A product is transported from a number of sources to a number of destinations at the minimum possible cost.
- ☆ Each source is able to supply a fixed number of units of the product, and each destination has a fixed demand for the product.
- ☆ The LP model has constraints for supply at each source and demand at each destination.
- ☆ All constraints are equalities in a balanced transportation model, where supply equals demand.
- ☆ Constraints contain inequalities in unbalanced transportation models where, demand is more than supply or supply is more than demand.

Example 9.13

The following example was used to demonstrate the formulation of the transportation model. A food processing firm has four plants at Mumbai, Chennai, Bangalore and Delhi. The product produced at these four plants is to be transported to five major destinations in India *viz.,* D_1, D_2, D_3, D_4 and D_5. Each source is able to supply the following units of product to the destinations on a monthly basis:

Plant (Source)	*Supply (Units)*
Mumbai	500
Chennai	575
Bangalore	610
Delhi	645

Each destination demands the following number of units of product per month:

Destination	Demand (Units)
D_1	410
D_2	540
D_3	390
D_4	440
D_5	550

The cost of transporting one unit of product from each plant (source) to each destination differs according to the distance and rail system. These costs are shown in the following table:

Plant (Source)	Destination				
	D_1	D_2	D_3	D_4	D_5
Mumbai	5	11	8	9	10
Chennai	7	9	10	7	9
Bangalore	6	10	12	5	8
Delhi	4	8	7	11	7

The problem is to determine, how many units of product to transport from each source to each destination on a monthly basis in order to minimize the total cost of transportation. The LP model for this problem is formulated in the equations as given below:

$$\text{Min } Z = 5X_{11}+11X_{12} +8X_{13} +9X_{14} +10X_{15} +7X_{21} +9X_{22} +10X_{23} +7X_{24} +9X_{25} +6X_{31} +10X_{32}+ 12X_{33}+5X_{34} +8X_{35} +4X_{41} +8X_{42} +7X_{43} +11X_{44} +7X_{45}$$

Subject to

$X_{11}+X_{12} +X_{13} +X_{14} +X_{15} =500$ (Total capacity of Source, Mumbai (O_1))

$X_{21} +X_{22} +X_{23} +X_{24} +X_{25}= 575$ (Total capacity of Source, Chennai (O_2))

$X_{31} +X_{32}+ X_{33}+X_{34} +X_{35}=610$ (Total capacity of Source, Bangalore (O_3))

$X_{41} +X_{42} +X_{43} +X_{44} +X_{45}=645$ (Total capacity of Source, Delhi (O_4))

$X_{11}+X_{21}+X_{31}+X_{41} = 410$ (Destination D_1 total requirement)

$X_{12}+X_{22}+X_{32}+X_{42} = 540$ (Destination D_2 total requirement)

$X_{13}+X_{23}+X_{33}+X_{43} = 390$ (Destination D_3 total requirement)

$X_{14}+X_{24}+X_{34} +X_{44}= 440$ (Destination D_4 total requirement)

$X_{15}+X_{25}+X_{35} +X_{45}= 550$ (Destination D_5 total requirement)

$Xij \geq 0$

In this model the decision variables Xij represent the number of units of product transported from each source, 'i' (where, i=1,2,3 and 4), to each destination,'j' (where j=1,2,3,4 and 5). The objective function represents the total transportation cost incurred in moving the product from different sources to different destinations. Each term in the objective function reflects the cost of the units transported for one route. For example, if 50 units of product are transported from Mumbai to Destination D1, the cost of Rs.5 is multiplied by X_{11}=50, which equals to Rs.250. The first four constraints in the above LP model represent the supply constraints at each source; the last five constraints represent the demand constraints at each destination. As an example, consider the first supply constraint and this constraint represents the units of product transported from Mumbai to all five destinations. The amount transported from Mumbai plant is limited to the 500 units of product available. Note that, this constraint (as well as all others) is an equation rather than an inequality because, all the units of product available (supply=2330 units) will be needed to meet the total demand (=2330 units). In other words, the five destinations demand, 2330 units of product, which is the exact amount that can be supplied by the four sources (=2330 units). Thus, all that can be supplied will be, in order to meet demand. This type of model, in which supply exactly equals demand, is referred to as a Balanced transportation model. This balanced model will be used to demonstrate the solution of a transportation problem.

E. Balanced and Unbalanced Transportation Models

As As mentioned above, the model in which total supply from the sources is equal to total demand by the destinations is called Balanced transportation model (Table 9.7). This is given by:

$$\text{Min } Z = \sum_{i=1}^{m}\sum_{j=1}^{n} C_{ij}X_{ij} \longrightarrow \text{Linear Objective Function}$$

Subject to Constraints

$$\sum_{j=1}^{n} X_{ij} \le a_i \qquad (\text{i} = 1 \text{ to m}) \longrightarrow \text{Supply constraint}$$

The above equation specifies that, the total shipments from the sources cannot exceed the supply.

$$\sum_{j=1}^{m} X_{ij} \le b_j \qquad (\text{j} = 1 \text{ to n}) \longrightarrow \text{Demand constraint}$$

The above equation specifies that, the total shipments must satisfy the demand.

$X_{ij} \ge 0 \longrightarrow$ Non-negativity constraint

$$\sum_{i=1}^{m} a_i \longrightarrow \text{Total supply from different sources}$$

$$\sum_{j=1}^{n} b_j \longrightarrow \text{Total demand from different destinations}$$

So, in case of Balanced transportation model:

$$\sum_{i=1}^{m} a_i = \sum_{i=1}^{n} b_j$$

Supply (from various sources) are written in the rows, while a column is an expression for the destination's demand. In general, if a transportation problem has 'm' rows and 'n' columns, then the problem is solvable, if there are exactly (m + n –1) basic (allocated or filled cells) variables. However, in reality demand may exceed the supply or supply may exceed the demand thereby, leading to unbalanced transportation. In such cases, we re-formulate the model so that, supply gets equal to the demand or demand gets equal to supply thereby, resulting in balanced transportation model.

Table 9.7: Balanced Transportation Model (Demand = Supply)

Sources	Destinations		Capacity ('000 tonnes)
	D_1 (Visakhapatnam)	D_2 (Hyderabad)	
Mumbai (O_1)	160 X_{11}	400 X_{12}	2000
Chennai (O_2)	200 X_{21}	200 X_{22}	3000
Bangalore (O_3)	204 X_{31}	136 X_{32}	2400
	4600	2800	7400 (Total Supply)
Destination-wise Demand	↓ d_1	↓ d_2	7400 (Total Demand)

i. When Demand Exceeds the Supply

In such case, a dummy plant is created (Table 9.8 and Table 9.9), so as to make it as a Balanced transportation model. The shipment of product from dummy plant to any destination is allowed. Unit cost of transportation from dummy plant to any destination is zero.

ii. When Supply Exceeds the Demand

In such case, we add dummy destination (Table 9.10 and Table 9.11). Shipment of product from the origins to the dummy destination is allowed. Unit cost of transportation from any source to dummy destination is zero.

Table 9.8: Unbalanced Transportation Model (Demand > Supply)

	Destinations		
Sources	D_1 (Visakhapatnam)	D_2 (Hyderabad)	Capacity ('000 tonnes)
Mumbai (O_1)	160 X_{11}	400 X_{12}	2000
Chennai (O_2)	200 X_{21}	200 X_{22}	3000
Bangalore (O_3)	204 X_{31}	136 X_{32}	2400
	5100 ↓	3500 ↓	7400 (Total Supply)
Destination-wise Demand ('000 tonnes)	d_1	d_2	8600 (Total Demand)

Table 9.9: Balacing Unbalanced Transportation Model (Demand > Supply) by Introducing Dummy Source (Plant)

Sources	Destinations		Capacity ('000 tonnes)
	D_1 (Visakhapatnam)	D_2 (Hyderabad)	
Mumbai (O_1)	160 X_{11}	400 X_{12}	2000
Chennai (O_2)	200 X_{21}	200 X_{22}	3000
Bangalore (O_3)	204 X_{31}	136 X_{32}	2400
Dummy source (O_4)			1200
	5100 ↓	3500 ↓	8600 (Total Supply)
Destination-wise Demand ('000 tonnes)	d_1	d_2	8600 (Total Demand)

Table 9.10: Unbalanced Transportation Model (Demand < Supply)

Sources	Destinations		Capacity ('000 tonnes)
	D_1 (Visakhapatnam)	D_2 (Hyderabad)	
Mumbai (O_1)	160 X_{11}	400 X_{12}	2000
Chennai (O_2)	200 X_{21}	200 X_{22}	3100
Bangalore (O_3)	204 X_{31}	136 X_{32}	2900
	4600 ↓	2800 ↓	8000 (Total Supply)
Destination-wise Demand ('000 tonnes)	d_1	d_2	7400 (Total Demand)

Thus, when total supply from sources equals to total demand from destinations, then it is a Balanced transportation model, otherwise it is an unbalanced model. The unbalanced model can be balanced by adding a dummy supply source (row) in case, when demand is greater than supply or by adding a dummy demand destination (column), when supply is greater than demand.

F. Things to Remember for Solving Transportation Problem

Now, let us go in-depth for solving transportation problem to obtain initial feasible solution and testing for its optimality. Before going into details, the following are the points to remember:

- ☆ The number of positive allocations in the cells of transportation matrix must be equal to (m+n-1). But, when the number of positive allocations at any stage of feasible solution is less than the required number (m+n-1), then the solution is said to be degenerate, otherwise non-degenerate.
- ☆ Cell in the transportation table having positive allocation will be called occupied cell, otherwise empty or non-occupied cell.

G. Initial Feasible Solutions in Transportation Problems

In a transportation problem, an initial feasible solution can be generated by several alternative methods. However, there are three common methods *viz.*, North-West Corner (NWC) Rule, Assignment by Inspection/Judgement or Least Cost Method (LCM) or Minimum Cell Cost Method and Vogel's Approximation Method (VAM) and they are discussed here under with reference to the following example:

Table 9.11: Balacing Unbalanced Transportation Model (Demand < Supply) by Introducing Dummy Destination

Sources	Destinations		Dummy destination	Capacity ('000 tonnes)
	D_1 (Visakhapatnam)	D_2 (Hyderabad)		
Mumbai (O_1)	160 X_{11}	400 X_{12}		2000
Chennai (O_2)	200 X_{21}	200 X_{22}		3100
Bangalore (O_3)	204 X_{31}	136 X_{32}		2900
	4600 ↓	2800 ↓	600 ↓	8000 (Total supply)
Destination-wise demand ('000 tonnes)	d_1	d_2	d_3	8000 (Total demand)

Example 9.14

A food processing firm has three plants at Mumbai, Chennai and Bangalore. The product produced at these three plants is to be transported to three major destinations in India *viz.*, D_1, D_2 and D_3. Each source is able to supply the following units of product to the destinations on a monthly basis:

Plant (Source)	*Supply (Units)*
Mumbai	150
Chennai	175
Bangalore	275
Total Supply	600

Each destination demands the following number of units of product per month:

Destination	*Demand (Units)*
D_1	200
D_2	100
D_3	300
Total Demand	600

The cost of transporting one unit of product from each plant (source) to each destination differs according to the distance and rail system. These costs are shown in the following table:

Plant (Source)	*Destination*		
	D_1	D_2	D_3
Mumbai	6	8	10
Chennai	7	11	11
Bangalore	4	5	12

The problem is to determine how many units of product to transport from each source to each destination on a monthly basis in order to minimize the total cost of transportation.

Answer

The LP model for this problem is formulated in the equations as given below:

$\text{Min } Z = 6X_{11}+8X_{12}+10X_{13}+7X_{21}+11X_{22}+11X_{23}+4X_{31}+5X_{32}+12X_{33}$

Subject to

$X_{11}+X_{12}+X_{13}=150$ (Total capacity of Source, Mumbai (O_1))

$X_{21}+X_{22}+X_{23}=175$ (Total capacity of Source, Chennai (O_2))

$X_{31}+X_{32}+X_{33}=275$ (Total capacity of Source, Bangalore (O_3))

$X_{11}+X_{21}+X_{31}=200$ (Destination D_1 total requirement)

$X_{12}+X_{22}+X_{32}=100$ (Destination D_2 total requirement)

$X_{13}+X_{23}+X_{33}=300$ (Destination D_3 total requirement)

$Xij \geq 0$

The above problem can be represented through Transportation Tableau (Table 9.12) for easy understanding and it is solved by the three methods *viz.*, NWC Rule, LCM or Minimum Cell Cost Method and VAM.

i. The North-West Corner (NWC) Rule

It is one of the simplest methods, which provide an initial feasible solution to a transportation problem. This method was developed by Dantzig and Charnes and Cooper named it as the 'NWC Rule'. The steps involved in this method (Table 9.13) are as under:

- ***Step 1:*** As the name of the rule itself suggests, first select the upper-left or the NWC cell of the transportation matrix.
- ***Step 2:*** Allocate as many units to this cell as possible considering the capacity of the source and the destination requirement. In the upper-left corner cell (*i.e.*, second row-second column (2,2)), the capacity of the source is 150 units, but the destination requirement is 200 units. So, allocate all the 150 units to the upper-left corner cell (2,2) so that, the source capacity is fulfilled,

Table 9.12: Transportation Tableau (Matrix)

Sources	Destinations			Capacity of source
	D_1	D_2	D_3	
Mumbai (O_1)	6	8	10	150
Chennai (O_2)	7	11	11	175
Bangalore (O_3)	4	5	12	275
Destination requirement	200	100	300	600 / 600

but not the destination requirement. Since destination requirement is not fulfilled, move down the same (second) column and allocate remaining 50 units in (3,2) cell so that, the destination requirement of D_1 is fulfilled. Note that, the allotment of product units should be in tune with the destination requirement. That is, the allocation is of such magnitude that, the capacity of the (first) source is exhausted or the requirement of (first) destination is satisfied or both. So, allot 200 units from the sources Mumbai and Chennai to the (2,2) and (3,2) cells as per the destination D_1 requirement.

- ☆ ***Step 3:*** After exhausting the demand for the second column, move along *i.e.,* horizontally to the next cell in the third row and third column (*i.e.,* 3,3). That is, after fulfilling the demand requirement for the second column (*i.e.* (2,2) and (3,2) cells), move horizontally to (3,3) cell *i.e.,* in the third row and third column. Then repeat the above Step 2. That is, since the destination requirement for column 2 (i.e., for D_1) was completely fulfilled, now allot 100 units (*i.e.,* 175-50=125) of second source (Chennai) to destination D_2, as per the destination requirement of D_2 (=100 units). So, by now, demand requirement of destination D_2 is completely fulfilled.
- ☆ ***Step 4:*** After exhausting the demand for the third column, move along *i.e.,* horizontally to the next cell *i.e.,* in the third row and fourth column (*i.e.,* 3,4). That is, after fulfilling the demand requirement for the third column (*i.e.* (3,3 cell)), move horizontally to (3,4) cell *i.e.,* in the third row and fourth column. Then repeat the above Step 3. That is, since the destination

Table 9.13: North-West Corner Rule

Sources	Destinations			Capacity of source
	D_1	D_2	D_3	
Mumbai (O_1)	6 **150**	8	10	150
Chennai (O_2)	7 **50**	11 **100**	11 **25**	175
Bangalore (O_3)	4	5	12 **275**	275
Destination requirement	200	100	300	600 / 600

requirement for column 3 was completely fulfilled, now allot the remaining 25 units (*i.e.*, 175-(100+50)=25) of second source (Chennai) to destination D_3, as per the destination requirement of D_3 (=300 units). So, by now, the source capacity of Chennai (*i.e.*, 175 units) was completely fulfilled.

☆ ***Step 5:*** After allotting 25 units of product to cell (3,4) now move vertically down to cell (4,4) and allot remaining 275 units from source O_3 (Bangalore) so that, both source O_3 capacity (275 units) and destination requirement of D_3 (300 units) are fulfilled.

Thus, in NWC Rule, the number of units of product allocated in the cell is the most possible, *subject to* the supply and demand constraints for that cell. The largest possible allocation is made to the cell in the upper left hand corner of the tableau, followed by allocations to adjacent feasible cells. Note that, the procedure of allocation of units of product to the cells is continued till the total quantity that is available (source capacity) is fully allocated to the various cells, as required (demand requirement).

☆ The total transportation cost of this solution is computed by substituting the cell allocations (*i.e.*, the amounts transported) into the objective function. So, total transportation cost by employing the formula:

Σ(Allocated units to each destination x Unit transportation cost incurred for transporting the product to each destination)

= Min $Z = 6X_{11}+8X_{12} +10X_{13} +7X_{21} +11X_{22} +11X_{23} +4X_{31} +5X_{32}+ 12X_{33}$
= $6(150)+8X_{12} +10X_{13} +7(50) +11(100) +11(25)+4X_{31} +5X_{32}+ 12(275)$ = Rs.5925

Thus, the methodology of this method revolves around the following two points:

- Note that, if the requirement of destination D_2 is satisfied (say, 3,3 cell), but the capacity of the source (third row, Chennai) is not exhausted, move to right in the same row and make allocation in the next cell (3,4), which exhausts the capacity of that source (third row, Chennai) or satisfy the requirement of third destination or both.
- On the other hand, if the capacity of the source (say, second row, Mumbai) is exhausted and the requirement of first destination is unsatisfied (say, 2,2), then move down the column and make second allocation (in 3,2) that satisfies the requirement of first destination or exhaust the origin capacity of second source or both.
- This process is repeated till the source capacity and destination requirement are matched.
- The number of cells occupied in the transportation matrix are equal to (m+n-1), where 'm'=number of rows (Sources) and 'n'= number of columns (Destinations). Since, there are three sources (rows) and three destinations (columns) in this example, there are (3+3-1)=5 occupied or filled cells in the transportation tableau or matrix (Table 9.13).

ii. *Assignment by Inspection or Judgement or LCM or Minimum Cell Cost Method*

This method is quicker in obtaining initial feasible solution, as it reduces the number of calculations required to be done compared to NWC rule. The following steps are involved in this method:

- ***Step 1:*** In the transportation matrix, first allocation is made to the cell having lowest shipping cost per unit.
- ***Step 2:*** The least cost cell is filled as much as possible taking the capacity of the source and destination requirement.
- ***Step 3:*** When the smallest cost is not unique *i.e.,* there are other cells having the same smallest cost, select any cell which has this smallest cost.
- ***Step 4:*** The second allocation is to be made in the same column or row to another cell having next least cost in view of the remaining capacity of source and destination requirement.
- ***Step 5:*** Eliminate that row or the column, when either the supply is exhausted or demand is satisfied.
- ***Step 6:*** Follow the same process across the columns and rows till total demand and supply are exhausted.

☆ ***Step 7:*** Compute the total transportation cost by employing the formula: Σ(Allocated units to each destination x Unit transportation cost incurred for transporting the product to each destination).

Table 9.14: Assignment by Inspection or Judgement Method or LCM

Sources	Destinations			Capacity of source
	D1	D2	D3	
Mumbai (O1)	6	8 25	10 125	150
Chennai (O2)	7	11	11 175	175
Bangalore (O3)	4 200	5 75	12	275
Destination requirement	200	100	300	600 / 600

In the given Table 9.14,

☆ The cell that enjoys lowest transportation cost per unit of product is (4,2) *i.e.,* Rs.4/unit and thereby, allocate the supply as per the destination demand *i.e.,* 200 units from source O_3 (Bangalore).

☆ Since the total destination requirement of D_1 (200 units) is fully met, now consider the next lowest unit shipping cost *i.e.,* Rs.5 in the (4,3) cell and allocate remaining 75 units from source O_3 (Bangalore) and by this allocation, the source capacity is exhausted, but destination D_2 demand is not completely fulfilled.

☆ So, now, look at the next lowest shipping cost per unit (Rs.8) in the same column 3 (*i.e.,* 2,3), as its destination demand D_2 is not completely fulfilled and thereby, allocate the supply as per the remaining destination demand *i.e.,* 25 units from source O_1 (Mumbai). Since the total destination requirement of D_2 (100 units) is fully met, now look at next lowest shipping cost per unit (Rs.10) of the fourth column *i.e.,* 2,4 (as the columns 2 and 3 destination requirements are already fulfilled).

☆ Since the total destination requirement of D_2 (100 units) is fully met, now consider the next lowest unit shipping cost *i.e.,* Rs.10 in the (2,4) cell and allocate remaining 125 units from source O_1 (Mumbai) and by this allocation, the source capacity is exhausted, but destination D_2 demand is not completely fulfilled.

☆ So, now, look at the next lowest shipping cost per unit (Rs.11) of (3,4) and thereby, allocate the supply as per the destination demand *i.e.*, 175 units from source O_2 (Chennai). By this allocation, both destination demand of D_3 (300 units) is fully met and source capacity (Chennai) is fully exhausted. Thus, the procedure of allocation of units of product is to be followed across the columns and rows till total demand and supply are exhausted.

☆ Total transportation cost can be computed by employing the formula:

Σ(Allocated units to each destination x Unit transportation cost incurred for transporting the product to each destination)

$= \text{Min } Z = 6X_{11}+8X_{12}+10X_{13}+7X_{21}+11X_{22}+11X_{23}+4X_{31}+5X_{32}+12X_{33}$

$= 6X_{11}+8(25)+10(125)+7X_{21}+11X_{22}+11(175)+4(200)+5(75)+12X_{33} = \text{Rs.}4550$

The above analysis infers that, the LCM method will provide a solution with a lower cost than the NWC solution because, the former considers lower cost in the allocation process. It is, therefore, quite natural that, a lower cost will be attained using the LCM method and is closer to the optimal solution and fewer subsequent iterations will be required to achieve the optimal solution.

iii. Vogel's Approximation Method (VAM)

This method is more accurate compared to the above two methods. This method yields a very good initial feasible solution, which sometimes may be the optimal solution. It takes into account not only least cost Cij, but also the costs that just exceed Cij. Although this method takes more time when compared to the earlier two methods in solving for initial feasible solution, but it reduces the time in reaching the optimal solution. This method is based on the concept of penalty cost or regret. If a decision maker incorrectly chooses from several alternative courses of action, a penalty may be suffered (and the decision maker may regret the decision that was made). In a transportation problem, the courses of action are the alternative routes, and a wrong decision is allocating to a cell that does not contain the lowest cost. The following is the procedure involved in this method:

Step 1: From the given data in the transportation matrix, compute penalty for the row and column data by subtracting the least cost element from the next least cost element in the same row or same column. So, penalty is the difference between the smallest and the next smallest cost in the same row and same column.

Step 2: Identify the column or row with largest penalty and in that column or row consider the least transportation cost cell. In case of a tie, select the row or column having minimum transportation cost. It, still, a tie persists, select the row or column having the maximum possible assignments or you may simply select any row or column in case of a tie without considering minimum costs *etc.*

Step 3: Allocate as much as possible to the least cost cell in the selected column (with largest penalty) from the corresponding capacity (supply) of the source.

Step 4: Adjust demand and supply by subtracting the transported units from the respective destination requirement of the selected column and respective capacity of the source of the selected row.

Step 5: Cross out the satisfied row or column.

Step 6: In the next iteration, delete that row or column for which the demand is equal to supply.

Step 7: Repeat the iterations with the same procedure discussed in the above steps till, total demand from the destinations (total destination requirement) is equal to total supply from the sources (total capacity). That is, stop the iteration, when there is only one row (source) or one column (destination).

Step 8: At the end *i.e.*, check that the total number of filled cells = (m + n–1), where 'm'=number of rows (Sources) and 'n'= number of columns (Destinations). Only then, the initial solution would be feasible.

The above discussed procedure is followed now to solve the given problem for achieving lowest possible total transportation cost for transporting the product across several destinations from different plants or sources (9.15 to 9.20). In this example, in I iteration, since the penalty is highest (considering both rows and columns) with reference to Chennai source (O_2) *i.e.*, 4, the allocation of 175 units is made in the least cost transportation cell *i.e.* (3, 2) of that row. So, in the II iteration, the Chennai source (O_2) is deleted, as for that source, the capacity is completely satisfied. In II iteration, the penalty is highest with reference to destination D_2 *i.e.*, 3 and accordingly the allocation of 100 units is made in the least cost transportation cell *i.e.*, (3, 3) of that column. Now, since the destination requirement of D_2 is completely fulfilled, that column is deleted in the III iteration. In the III iteration, the penalty is highest for Bangalore source (O_3) *i.e.*, 8 and accordingly the allocation of 25 units is made in the least cost transportation cell *i.e.*, (3, 2) of that row. Since the source capacity of Bangalore O_3 was not completely exhausted (*i.e.*, 175-25 = 150), that source was still continued in the IV iteration with the balance capacity of 150 units. In the IV iteration, since there is only column of Destination D3, the iterations were stopped and the allocations made above are shown in Table 9.20 and transportation cost was computed (Rs.5125).

In the IV iteration (Table 9.19), no more penalty can be worked out for rows (or columns in some cases) and thereby, this is the final iteration for the problem. Further, the total demand of the destination D_3 (*i.e.*, total destination requirement) is equal to total supply from the sources (total capacity).

Now, transfer all the data pertaining to allocated units into the least cost cells right from I iteration to IV iteration and the same is shown as Allocation matrix (Table 9.20). This facilitates to calculate the transportation cost by using the following formula:

Σ(Allocated units to each destination x Unit transportation cost incurred for transporting the product to each destination)

Cost of shipping = Min Z = $6X_{11}+8X_{12}+10X_{13}+7X_{21}+11X_{22}+11X_{23}+4X_{31}+5X_{32}+12X_{33}$

$= 6X_{11}+8X_{12}+10X_{13}+7(175)+11X_{22}+11X_{23}+4(25)+5(100)+12X_{33}$ = Rs.5125.

Table 9.15: Vogel's Approximation Method – Transportation Tableau (Matrix)

Sources	Destinations			Capacity of source
	D_1	D_2	D_3	
Mumbai (O_1)	6	8	10	150
Chennai (O_2)	7	11	11	175
Bangalore (O_3)	4	5	12	275
Destination requirement	200	100	300	600 / 600

Table 9.16: Vogel's Approximation Method (I Iteration)

Sources	Destinations			Capacity of source	Penalty
	D_1	D_2	D_3		
Mumbai (O_1)	6	8	10	150	8-6=2
Chennai (O_2)	7 175	11	11	~~175~~	11-7=4
Bangalore (O_3)	4	5	12	275	5-4=3
Destination requirement	~~200~~ 25	100	300	425 / 425	
Penalty	6-4=2	8-5=3	11-10=1		

Table 9.17: Vogel's Approximation Method (II Iteration)

Sources	Destinations			Capacity of source	Penalty
	D1	D2	D3		
Mumbai (O1)	6	8	10	150	8-6=2
Bangalore (O3)	4	5 100	12	~~275~~ 175	5-4=1
Destination requirement	25	~~100~~	300	325 ~~325~~	
Penalty	6-4=2	8-5=3	12-10=2		

Table 9.18: Vogel's Approximation Method (III Iteration)

Sources	Destinations		Capacity of source	Penalty
	D1	D3		
Mumbai (O1)	6	10	150	10-6=4
Bangalore (O3)	4 25	12	~~175~~ 150	12-4=8
Destination requirement	~~25~~	300	300 ~~300~~	
Penalty	6-4=2	12-10=2		

Table 9.19: Vogel's Approximation Method (IV Iteration)

Sources	Destination	Capacity of source	Penalty
	D3		
Mumbai (O1)	10	150	
Bangalore (O3)	12	150	
Destination requirement	300	300 \ 300	
Penalty			

Table 9.20: Vogel's Approximation Method – Allocation Matrix and Cost of Shipping

Sources	Destinations			Capacity of source
	D1	D2	D3	
Mumbai (O1)	6	8	10	150
Chennai (O2)	7 175	11	11	175
Bangalore (O3)	4 25	5 100	12	275
Destination requirement	200	100	300	600 \ 600

Cost of shipping = Min Z $= 6X_{11} + 8X_{12} + 10X_{13} + 7X_{21} + 11X_{22} + 11X_{23} + 4X_{31} + 5X_{32} + 12X_{33}$
$= 6X_{11} + 8X_{12} + 10X_{13} + 7(175) + 11X_{22} + 11X_{23} + 4(25) + 5(100) + 12X_{33} =$ Rs.5125

H. Criteria to Identify Initial or Basic Feasible Solution

The solution obtained by any of the above three methods must fulfill following conditions:

- ☆ The solution must be feasible, *i.e.*, it must satisfy all the supply and demand constraints. This is called Rim condition.
- ☆ The number of positive allocations must be equal to (m+n–1), where, 'm' is number of rows and 'n' is number of columns.

The solution that satisfies both the above mentioned conditions is called a non-degenerate initial (basic) feasible solution.

I. Test for Optimality

An optimality test can be performed to find whether the obtained feasible solution is optimal or not. For testing the optimality, first the feasible solution must satisfy:

- ☆ Number of allocations equal to (m+n-1), where 'm' is the number of rows and 'n' is the number of columns. In the solution derived (Table 9.14 – being the lowest transportation cost (Rs. 4550) achieved under LCM), the number of filled (allocated) cells are five in number and this is equal to (m+n-1)=(3+3-1=5). Hence, optimality test can be performed.
- ☆ Further these (m+n-1) allocations should be in independent positions. That is, a close look at the feasible solution (Table 9.14) of the problem indicates that, all the allocations are in independent positions, as it is impossible to increase or decrease any allocation without either changing the position of the allocations or violating the row and column restrictions. For example, if the allocation in cell (2,3) is changed from (25) to (35), then the allocation in cell (2,4) must be changed from (125) to (115) in order to satisfy the row restriction. Similarly the allocation in cell (4,3) must be changed from (75) to (65) in order to meet the column restriction. Likewise, the row restriction for (4,2) should also be adjusted. A simple rule for allocations to be in independent positions is that, the occupied (allocated) cells do not form a closed loop. This closed loop is not seen in the Table 9.14 of feasible region. This closed loop is exemplified through Table 9.21.

Since, the above two conditions are satisfied, now employ procedure for testing the optimality of feasible solution. Two methods are commonly used for this purpose *viz.*, Stepping-Stone Method and Modified Distribution (MODI) Method. Among the above three methods for computing the initial feasible solution, LCM yielded lowest transportation cost (Rs.4550) compared to NWC Rule Method and VAM and hence, the feasible solution derived from LCM will be considered to test for its optimality.

i. Stepping-Stone Method

Consider the Table 9.14, which gives the first feasible solution for the problem under consideration by employing LCM. Let us start with any arbitrary empty cell, say (4,4) and allocate '+1' unit to this cell (Table 9.22). In order to keep up the column 4 restriction, '-1' must be allocated to cell (3,4). In order to keep up the row 3 restriction, '+1' must be allocated to cell (3,3). Consequently, '-1' must be allocated to cell (4,3) in order to keep up the column 3 restriction. The net change in transportation cost as a

Table 9.21: Allocated Cells Forming a Loop Implying NOT a Feasible Solution

Sources	Destinations D1	Destinations D2	Destinations D3	Capacity of source
Mumbai (O1)	6	8	10	150
Chennai (O2)	7 / 124	11 / 136	11	260
Bangalore (O3)	4 / 59	5 / 110	12	169
Destination requirement	183	236	160	579 / 579

Table 9.22: Stepping Stone Method to Test for Optimality Considering LCM

Sources	Destinations D1	Destinations D2	Destinations D3	Capacity of source
Mumbai (O1)	6	8 / 25	10 / 125	150
Chennai (O2)	7	11 (+1)	11 / 175 (- 1)	175
Bangalore (O3)	4 / 200	5 / 75 (-1)	12 (+1)	275
Destination requirement	200	100	300	600 / 600

result of this perturbation is calculated as given below and this is called the Evaluation of empty cell.

= (+1x12)+(-1x11)+(+1x11)+(-1x5) = +7

The rules of thumb are:

- ☆ When there are 'm' rows and 'n' cells, the total number of empty cells is given by: (m–1)(n–1). In this case, the number of empty cells are (3-1)(3-1)=4.
- ☆ Cell evaluations must be worked out for all these empty cells. If any cell evaluation is negative, the cost can be still reduced so that, the initial feasible solution under consideration can be improved and thereby, the obtained initial feasible solution is not optimal. On the other hand, if all cell evaluations are positive or zero, the initial feasible solution obtained is considered optimal.

In the above case, the Stepping Stone method proved cell evaluation is positive (+7) and even for other empty cells and thereby, the obtained feasible solution is optimal.

ii. MODI Method

In MODI method, cell evaluations of all the occupied cells are calculated simultaneously and only one closed path for the most negative cell is traced, unlike in Stepping Stone Method, Thus, MODI method is more time-saving compared to the

Table 9.23: Step 1: MODI Method or The 'u-v- Method – Cost Matrix for Occupied Cells

Sources	Destinations		
	D_1	D_2	D_3
Mumbai (O_1)		8	10
Chennai (O_2)			11
Bangalore (O_3)	4	5	

Stepping Stone Method. The methodology involved in this method is discussed here under through the following steps:

Step 1: Set up a cost matrix (Table 9.23) with reference to the unit costs associated with the cells for which allocations have been made (*i.e.*, filled or occupied cells).

Step 2: Determination of row and column values for occupied cells: For this, in the obtained feasible solution through LCM (Table 9.14), consider the unit costs of the occupied (filled) cells with respect to each column and each row. Let 'Ui' be the row value and 'Vi' be the column value and assume, 'U1'=0, then

U2+V3=8. So, 0+V3=8 ⟶ V3=8

U2+V4=10. So, 0+V4=10 ⟶ V4=10

U3+V4=11. So, U3+10=11 ⟶U3=1

U4+V2=4. So, -3+V2=1 ⟶ V2= 4

U4+V3=5. So, U4+8=5 ⟶ U4= -3

The above calculations for each row and column are shown along the borders of the Table 9.24.

Table 9.24: Step 2 – Determination of Row and Column Values for Occupied Cells

		4	8	10
	Sources	**Destinations**		
		D1	**D2**	**D3**
0	**Mumbai (O1)**		**8**	**10**
1	**Chennai (O2)**			**11**
−3	**Bangalore (O3)**	**4**	**5**	

Step 3: Fill the empty cells with the sums of Ui+Vi. This gives the Implicit costs of empty cells.

Z22=U2+V2=0+4=4

Z32=U3+V2= 1+4=5

Z33=U3+V3= 1+8=9

Z44=U4+V4= -3+10= 7

The above calculations are shown through Table 9.25.

Step 4: Computation of opportunity cost of empty cells: This is given by:

Opportunity cost = Implicit cost – Actual cost. That is, this Step 4 includes the subtraction of empty cell values of original cost matrix (Table 9.14) from implicit cost matrix of empty cells in Step 3 (Table 9.25). The resulting matrix is called Cell evaluation matrix. So,

Z22-C22=4-6= -2

Z32-C32=5-7= -2

Z33-C33=9-11= -2

Z44-C44= 7-12= -5

The above calculations are shown through Table 9.26.

The rule of thumb is, if the opportunity cost values of all empty cells are either zero or negative (non-positive), it implies optimal solution. From the above calculations, since all the opportunity cost values of empty cells are negative, it implies an optimal solution. So, the objective function with reference to LCM *i.e.,*

$= \text{Min } Z = 6X_{11}+8X_{12} +10X_{13} +7X_{21} +11X_{22} +11X_{23} +4X_{31} +5X_{32}+ 12X_{33}$

$= 6X_{11}+8(25)+10(125)+7X_{21} +11X_{22} +11(175)+4(200)+5(75)+ 12X_{33} = \text{Rs.}4550$

is an optimal solution.

Table 9.25: Step 3 – Determination of Implicit Costs of Empty Cells

		4	8	10
	Sources	**Destinations**		
		D1	**D2**	**D3**
0	**Mumbai (O1)**	**4**		
1	**Chennai (O2)**	**5**	**9**	
–3	**Bangalore (O3)**			**7**

Table 9.26: Cell Evaluation Matrix

Sources	Destinations		
	D_1	D_2	D_3
Mumbai (O_1)	-2		
Chennai (O_2)	-2	-2	
Bangalore (O_3)			-5

J. Generalized Procedure to Solve a Transportation Problem

The solution algorithm to a transportation problem can be summarized into the following steps:

Step 1: Formulate the problem and set up in the matrix form. As discussed earlier, the formulation of transportation problem is similar to LP problem formulation. Here, the objective function is the total transportation cost that is to be minimized and the constraints are the supply available at each source and demand at each destination.

Step 2: Obtain an initial basic feasible solution. This initial basic solution can be obtained by using any of the following methods:

- ☆ NWC Rule
- ☆ LCM
- ☆ VAM

Step 3: The solution obtained by any of the above three methods must fulfill the following conditions:

- ☆ The solution must be feasible, *i.e.*, it must satisfy all the supply and demand constraints. This is called Rim condition.
- ☆ The number of positive allocations/filled cells/occupied cells must be equal to (m+n–1), where, 'm' is number of rows and 'n' is number of columns.

Step 4: Test the initial basic feasible solution for its optimality: Use the following two methods to test the optimality of obtained initial basic feasible solution:

- Stepping Stone Method
- MODI Method

If the solution is optimal then stop, otherwise, determine a new improved solution.

K. Merits of LP Technique

LP is an important branch of applied mathematics that solves a wide variety of optimization problems. This technique finds place in various applications like:

- In production planning and scheduling problems. In these problems, we determine the number of units of different products, which should be produced and sold by a firm when each product requires a fixed manpower, machine hours, labour hours per unit of product, warehouse space per unit of the output *etc.*, in order to make maximum profits.
- In aircraft and crew scheduling. The airline industry uses LP to optimize profits and minimize expenses in their business. Airlines needed to consider how many people would be willing to pay a higher price for a ticket if they were able to book their flight at the last minute and have substantial flexibility in their schedule and flight times. The airline also needed to know how many people would only purchase a low price ticket, without an in-flight meal. Through LP airlines were able to find the optimal breakdown of how many tickets to sell at which price, including various prices in between. Airlines also need to consider plane routes, pilot schedules, direct and in-direct flights, and layovers.
- LP is important in managerial decision making. The reason is that, it helps the business firm in minimizing the costs and maximizing the profits. It also guides the manager to work under limitations and conditions.
- In solving staffing problems like the number of staff needed in colleges, hospitals, mines, hotels and other types of businesses.
- In the field of marketing say, regarding the selection of the best advertising medium among a number of media.
- In solving the diet problems through minimizing the cost and this is very useful for hospitals. In these problems, we determine the amount of different kinds of constituents/nutrients which should be included in a diet, so as to minimize the cost of the desired diet such, that it contains a certain minimum amount of each constituent/nutrients.
- In addressing transportation problems. That is, we determine a transportation schedule in order to find the cheapest way of transporting a product from plants/factories situated at different locations to different markets.
- Farmers Managers LP to increase the revenue of their operations, like what to produce, how much of it and what to use it for.
- Amusement parks use LP to make decisions about queue lines.

- ☆ In other different areas such as finance (resolving situations of capital budgeting, financial planning and so on), product mix problems (problems based on blending resources to produce an item, management must decide the quantity of each product), multiple plant location studies (the new location will be, where the total production and distribution cost will be minimized), maximizing material utilization (determine the combination of cuts that will meet requirements for the amounts of the different sizes with a minimum trim loss) *etc.*

Above all these applications, another remarkable characteristic of LP technique is that, it has the adapting facility to reality, which allows solving, by computer programs, problems with thousands of variables and constraints. It also allows sensitivity analysis *i.e.*, helps to analyze, what happens to the results when we change the coefficients of the objective function and/or in the constraints. That is, the manager can ascertain, how changes affect the optimal solution to the original LP problem. (The range of values over which the current solution will remain optimal, despite the change of the coefficients, is called range of optimality).

Thus, considering the above applications of LP, it serves as an important part of operations research and continues to make the world more economically efficient.

L. Demerits or Limitations of LP Technique

Though LP enjoys wider applications across various fields like theory of firm's production, in inter-regional trade, in general equilibrium analysis, in welfare economics, in development planning *etc.*, it suffers from the following limitations:

- ☆ It involves labourious mathematical calculations to determine the given objective function. Hence, it demands analytical skills on the part of the researcher to run the computer software programme to perform huge number of mathematical calculations.
- ☆ Even if the objective function is clearly specified, it may not be so easy to find out various technological, financial, marketing and other constraints that may be operative in pursuing the given function.
- ☆ Given a specified objective function and a set of functional constraints, the latter may not be directly expressible as linear inequalities.
- ☆ LP technique is based on the assumption that, there exists linear relationship between inputs and outputs. This means that inputs and outputs can be added, multiplied and divided. But, in practicality, the relations between inputs and outputs are mostly non-linear.
- ☆ LP technique assumes perfect competition both in product and factor markets. But, perfect competition is not a reality and is only a myth.
- ☆ The LP technique is based on the hypothesis of constant returns. However, in reality, there are either diminishing or increasing returns, which a firm experiences in its production programme.
- ☆ Mostly, LP models present trial and error solutions and it is difficult to find out optimal solutions to the various economic complexities.

- ☆ LP technique assumes that, in objective function, proportionality implies that, the marginal rate of contribution to the objective (maximization or minimization) for each variable is assumed to remain constant throughout the entire range of activity levels in the problem. That is, variables cannot be multiplied or divided by other variables, cannot be raised to an exponent other than 1, or be arguments of other functional relationships (say, sin X or log X). However, this may not always hold true in the real world. Economies of scale, for instance, reflect variations in costs and profit margins as production levels change. Price discounting for certain preferred customers also violates the proportionality assumption. Similarly, in functional constraints, proportionality implies that, resource usage per variable is assumed constant throughout the entire operational range of the problem. But, in many situations, the manager might get a volume discount such that, the price per unit of product goes down, if he purchase more quantity of a product. These discounts are often nonlinear, which that a LP model is either inappropriate or is really an approximation of the real world problem.
- ☆ LP technique assumes linearity of the variables both in the objective function and in functional constraints. The broader implication of linearity is that, the variables are assumed to be mutually independent. In other words, the products are assumed to be neither complements nor substitutes of each other and there is no interaction between the variables. Clearly, this may not be the case in the actual system, in which case majority of the products are either substitutes or complements of each other and thereby, the linearity assumption would be violated.
- ☆ Factors such as uncertainty, weather conditions *etc.*, are not taken into consideration. That is, when using LP, there is no way to deal with uncertainty. We formulate the problem with the assumption that, we know all of the values for costs, profits, constraints *etc.* But, in real-life problems, these variables often are unknowns. Methods such as chance constrained programming or linear programming under uncertainty can be used in these situations.
- ☆ Only one single objective is dealt with, while in real life situations, problems come with multi-objectives.
- ☆ Parameters are assumed to be constants, but in reality they may not be so.
- ☆ As per the assumption of LP model, the solution variables can have any value, but in some cases, the variables may have only integer values. For example, if a machinery manufacturing firm aims at, how many processing machines have to be produced, then only integer values of decision variables are meaningful.
- ☆ LP model does not take into account the influence of time on both objective function and functional constraints.

To conclude, a comparative picture between *pros* and *cons* about LP reveal that, LP is the most used program in the management area, despite it has several arguments against it. There are sound reasons, which take us to select this method for solving various management problems owing to the complexity of the problems that can be handled.

M. Concept of Optimality

The earlier discussion under factor-product relationship, factor-factor relationship and product-product relationship and the discussion under LP technique commonly highlight the concept of 'optimality' in the production programme. In all the above concepts, optimality implies utilization of resources more efficiently in a production programme, so as to achieve either cost minimization or profit maximization or both. Besides the above decision making areas, the concept of optimality also arises with reference to consumer behaviour and firm's behaviour under different forms of market competition (perfect and imperfect market competitions). Let us now refresh the concept of optimality in the above decision making areas.

1. Decision Making by Consumer

a. Consumer's Equilibrium when the Commodity is Available Free of Cost to the Consumer

If the commodity is freely available to the consumer, he will not hesitate to consume the same commodity till he reaches the point of maximum satisfaction. That means, he will consume the same commodity till the point of satiety, which occurs when Marginal Utility (MU) is equal to zero or Total Utility (TU) is maximum. In case of certain commodities, the point of satiety is reached quickly, while in others, it takes more time.

b. Consumer's Equilibrium when Commodity is Priced to the Consumer

Case-1: One-commodity Consumer's Equilibrium

On the other hand, if the commodity is not available at free of cost to the consumer, which is the common practical situation, the consumer tries to attain maximum satisfaction taking into consideration several aspects like MU derived from each unit of the commodity, price of the commodity, MU of money, MU derived from the commodity in terms of money (MU derived from the commodity/MU of money), MU of expenditure (MU derived from the commodity/Price of the commodity), prices of the substitutes *etc.* So, in this case, the consumer will not consume the commodity till the point of satiety. Rather, he will go on consuming the commodity units, as long as, MU derived from the commodity in terms of money is higher than price of the commodity or MU of expenditure is higher than MU of money. The consumer will reach the point of equilibrium or attain maximum satisfaction when MU derived in terms of money is equal to the price paid for each unit of the commodity or MU of expenditure is equal to MU of money.. Since, the consumer is rational, he will not pay more for the commodity than the MU received in terms of money from each unit of the commodity. As the consumer knows, if he goes on consuming the commodity, the MU derived from each unit of the commodity diminishes, and hence, he will be very careful in allocating the resources on the commodity and he stops purchasing the commodity when the MU derived in terms of money is equal to its price. The same is explained through the Figure 9.21.

In the Figure 9.21, along X-axis, number of units of commodity and along Y-axis, price and MU derived from the commodity in terms of money are taken. As the MU diminishes continuously, due to continuous consumption of the same commodity, the MU curve (in terms of money) is a continuous downward sloping curve from left to right. Since the price of the commodity is constant at a given point of time, it is represented by a straight line 'PL' parallel to X-axis and the price is OP per unit. The consumer purchases the first five units of the commodity, since the MU derived in terms of money from each unit of the commodity is higher than the price paid for the commodity, OP. At fifth unit of the commodity, the MU derived in terms of money is VA and price paid is OP. So, he is left over with a surplus satisfaction of VW over the price paid for the commodity. At the sixth unit of the commodity, the MU derived in terms of money, BX is equal to price paid for the commodity, OP. So, this is the point of consumer's equilibrium or the point of maximum satisfaction to the consumer and at this point, there is no surplus satisfaction to the consumer. If the consumer consumes seventh unit of the commodity, he derives the MU in terms of money as CZ, but he pays the same price OP and thereby, he incurs loss of YZ, as the MU derived in terms of money from the seventh unit is less than price paid for the commodity. Since consumer is rational, he is not prepared to consume beyond sixth unit of the commodity, as the MU in terms of money still diminishes below the price of the commodity. So, the consumer reaches the point of equilibrium at sixth unit of the commodity and thereby, he stops consuming at OB units or six units of the commodity.

If the consumer consumes OA units of commodity, he is left over with surplus satisfaction of VWX. If he consumes OB unit of commodity, there is scope for realizing this left over surplus satisfaction, VWX. So, at sixth unit of commodity or consuming OB units of commodity, the consumer derives maximum satisfaction, as there is no scope for surplus satisfaction or left over satisfaction. On the other hand, if the

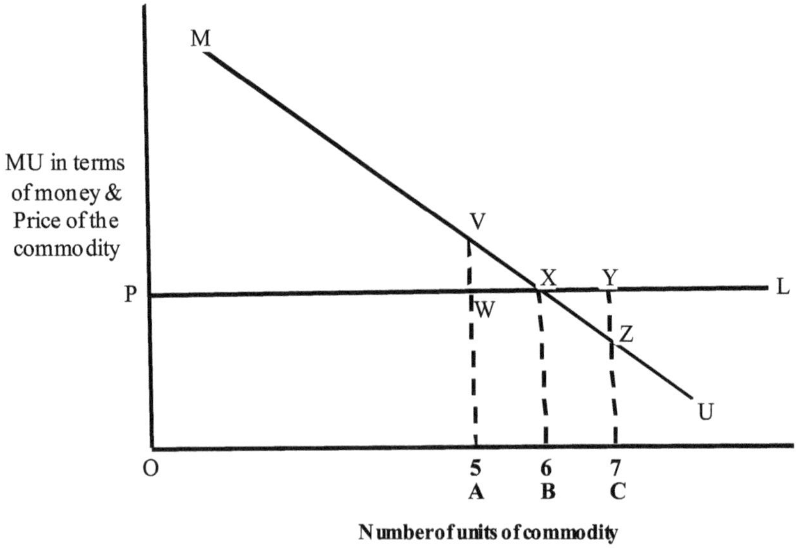

Figure 9.21: Point of Consumer's Equilibrium.

consumer consumes seventh unit of the commodity, as mentioned earlier, the price paid for the commodity is more than MU derived from the commodity in terms of money and thereby, he incur loss in satisfaction to the tune of XYZ. So, moving in either way from OB unit or from sixth unit of the commodity, will lead to diminution of total satisfaction. So consumer's equilibrium refers to the situation, in which a consumer gets maximum satisfaction for the given level of income and price of the commodity. In the words of Alfred Marshall, *'consumer's equilibrium is that state of consumer's demand, which he thinks to be the best and which he does not want to alter'*. The above explanation can be summarized in the following way:

At OA Units of Purchase of Commodity

Total satisfaction gained by the consumer =OMVA

Total cost incurred by the consumer in purchasing the commodity=OPWA

Surplus satisfaction enjoyed by the consumer=PMVW

Surplus satisfaction left over with the consumer=VWX

At OB Units of Purchase of Commodity

Total satisfaction gained by the consumer=OMXB

Total cost incurred by the consumer in purchasing the commodity =OPXB

Surplus satisfaction enjoyed by the consumer =PMX

Surplus satisfaction left over with the consumer =0 (zero)

At OC Units of Purchase of Commodity

Total satisfaction gained by the consumer =OMZC

Total cost incurred by the consumer in purchasing the commodity =OPYC

Loss in satisfaction=XYZ

So, based on the above analysis, we can derive the point of consumer's equilibrium from the formulae given below.

Method 1

The point of consumer's equilibrium is when MU of expenditure is equal to MU of money

$$\text{Consumer's equilibrium} = \frac{\text{MU of the commodity A}}{\text{Price of the commodity A}} = \text{MU of money} \qquad \textit{Equation 9.1}$$

The above equation 9.1 can be written as,

$$\text{Consumer's equilibrium} = \frac{MU_A}{P_A} = MU_M$$

In the above equation 9.1, the left side portion represents MU of expenditure or Weighted MU.

Method 2

The point of consumer's equilibrium is when MU derived in terms of money is equal to price of the commodity. So,

$$\text{Consumer's equilibrium} = \frac{\text{MU of the commodity A}}{\text{MU of money}} = \text{Price of the commodity A} \qquad \textit{Equation 9.2}$$

The above equation 9.2 can be written as,

$$\text{Consumer's equilibrium} = \frac{MU_A}{MU_M} = P_A$$

In the above equation 9.2, the left side portion represents MU derived in terms of money.

Method 3

There is another way of expressing the point of consumer's equilibrium *i.e.*, through studying the net gain in the consumption of commodity. That means, the larger the net gain between TU in terms of money and total expenditure, the greater **is** the satisfaction derived by the consumer.

Case 2: Two Commodities or More than One Commodity Consumer's Equilibrium

The same principle, as discussed above, also applies, if the consumer deals with more than one commodity to arrive at the point of consumer's equilibrium or the point of maximum satisfaction. For example, if the consumer deals with two commodities A and B, the prices of the two commodities are P_A and P_B, MUs derived from the two commodities is MU_A and MU_B and assumed constancy of MU of money is MU_M, then the point of consumer's equilibrium in case of two commodities is given by the following methods:

Method 1

If the consumer deals with more than one commodity, he will be in equilibrium when he equalizes the MU of expenditure or weighted MUs of all commodities and the consumer will go on purchasing commodities till the MU of expenditure of each commodity becomes equal to the MU of money to him.

$$\text{Consumer's equilibrium} = \frac{\text{MU of the commodity}}{\text{Price of the commodity}} = \text{MU of money} \qquad \textit{As per Equation 9.1}$$

The above equation 9.1 can be written as,

$$\text{Consumer's equilibrium} = \frac{MU_A}{P_A} = MU_M \longrightarrow \text{for commodity A}$$

$$\text{Consumer's equilibrium} = \frac{MU_B}{P_B} = MU_M \longrightarrow \text{for commodity B}$$

In the above equations, the left side portion represents MU of expenditure.

So, the point of consumer's equilibrium in dealing with both the commodities A and B is given by the formula:

$$\frac{MU_A}{P_A} = \frac{MU_B}{P_B} = MU_M \qquad \textit{Equation 9.3}$$

This is called Two commodity equilibrium or Principle of Proportionality. The above equation 9.3 implies that, in case of two commodities A and B, the consumer derives maximum satisfaction when MU of expenditure on both the commodities are equal to MU of money.

In the above equation, if $(MU_A/P_A) > (MU_B/P_B)$, then the consumer will go on substituting commodity A in place of commodity B. This results in fall in MU_A due to its excessive consumption and finally MU_A/P_A decreases and gets equal to MU_B/P_B and the consumer reaches the point of equilibrium. But, it is important that, the point of equality between MU_A/P_A and MU_B/P_B can be achieved not only once but also at different levels of expenditure. This is influenced by the size of money income with the consumer.

If the consumer deals with more than two commodities, then the point of equilibrium will be given by,

$$\frac{MU_A}{P_A} = \frac{MU_B}{P_B} = \frac{MU_C}{P_C} = \frac{MU_N}{P_N} = MU_M \qquad \textit{Equation 9.4}$$

The above equation can be expressed as

$$\frac{MU_A}{MU_B} = \frac{P_A}{P_B} \text{ and } \frac{MU_B}{MU_C} = \frac{P_B}{P_C} \text{ and so forth} \qquad \textit{Equation 9.5}$$

This indicates that, if the consumer deals with more than one commodity, he will be in equilibrium when he equalizes the ratios of MUs of commodities with the ratio of corresponding prices for each pair of commodities consumed.

Method 2

If the consumer deals with more than one commodity, he will be in equilibrium when he equalizes the MU derived from the commodities in terms of money with their respective prices.

$(MU_A/MU_M) = P_A \longrightarrow$ Consumer's equilibrium for commodity A,

where, (MU_A/MU_M) is MU derived from commodity A in terms of money.

$(MU_B/MU_M) = P_B \longrightarrow$ Consumer's equilibrium for commodity B, where, (MU_B/MU_M) is nothing but MU derived from commodity B in terms of money.

Method 3

There is another way of expressing the point of consumer's equilibrium *i.e.,* through studying the net gain across the consumption of commodities. That means, the larger the net gain between TU in terms of money and total expenditure across the commodities, the greater the satisfaction derived by the consumer.

2. Decision Making by Producer

i. Optimization of Output through Increasing Resource Use Efficiency

As discussed under Chapter 2, let us refresh once again that, Stage II is called as 'Rational stage' or 'Optimal stage' because, there is a possibility of optimization of output. At which particular point, the farmer will decide to produce depends upon the various factors like, output he would like to produce, price of the factor he has to pay, price of the product in the market *etc.* The criteria to optimize the output in this stage can be studied both from the output side and input side.

Output Side

1. MC=MR

2. MPP=Factor-Product price ratio: $[(\Delta Y/\Delta X)=(P_X/P_Y)] = MPP * P_Y = P_X$.

So, $VMP = P_X$

(where P_X = Price of factor, Fertilizer)

Input Side

$\mathbf{MVP_X=MFC_X} = [(\Delta TR/\Delta X) = (\Delta SRTVC/\Delta X)]$

Thus, the level of input usage within Stage II at which the farmer can maximize the profits is all depends upon how many units of output the farmer can sell, the price of the product, and the monetary costs of employing the variable input.

Inequality between MR and MC or MVPx (VMP) and MFCx (or P_X)

Case1: MR>MC or MVPx (VMP)>MFCx (or P_X): This case is observed in the first stage of production function and the farmer is advised to increase the input usage, so that MC or MFC_X increases and becomes equal to MR or MVPx (VMP) respectively to attain optimality in the production programme. Similarly, with increase in input usage, MPP decreases thereby, MVPx (VMP) falls and gets equal to P_X and this optimality is achieved in Stage II.

Case 2: MR<MC or MVPx (VMP)<MFCx (or P_X): This case is observed in the third stage of production function and the farmer is advised to reduce the input usage so that, MC or MFC_X decreases and becomes equal to MR or MVPx (VMP) respectively to attain optimality in the production programme. Similarly, with decrease in input usage, MPP increases thereby, MVPx (VMP) rises and gets equal to P_X and this optimality is achieved in Stage II.

ii. Cost Minimization in a Production Programme

LCC of factors can be achieved in the following two ways:

a. *Cost Minimization for a given Level of Output*

Here, the farmer tries to minimize the cost to produce a given level of output in the production programme. Three important conditions are essential to achieve point of LCC of resources:

- ☆ The iso-cost line should be tangent to the isoquant from below.
- ☆ Slope of the iso-cost line should be equal to the slope of isoquant.
- ☆ Isoquant should be convex to the origin.

Recall now the values of the slopes of these two curves. The slope of isoquant indicates MRTS of these two resources *i.e.,* $MRTS_{MF} = \Delta F/\Delta M$. The slope of iso-cost line indicates prices ratio of manure and fertilizer *i.e.,* P_M/P_F. So, the point of LCC is given by:

$$MRTS_{MF} = \Delta F/\Delta M\ (= MPP_M/MPP_F) = P_M/P_F \qquad \textit{Equation 9.6}$$

Thus, the LCC of resources occurs at the point, where the MRTS of the resources is inversely equal to the ratio of their prices or the ratio of MPP of resources is directly equal to the ratio of their prices. This simply tells the farmer that, the LCC of manure and fertilizer is such that, equal increments of output should be obtained for the last rupee spent on each of the inputs.

b. *Output Maximization for a given Cash Outlay and Prices of the Resources*

The other way of attaining the optimal combination of factors is maximizing the output for a given level of cash outlay with the farmer and for the given prices of the two resources. So, again at the point of tangency of iso-cost line and isoquant, all the three necessary conditions mentioned above are to be fulfilled for achieving optimization of resources usage.

iii. *Profit Maximization for a given Level of Resources*

Economic efficiency in product-product relationship is attained when the physical concept ($MRPS_{PM}$) is integrated with the economic concept (price ratio of products). Thus, the OPC can be determined by imposing the PPC map on iso-revenue line. Three important conditions must be fulfilled to arrive at the point of optimum combination of products. They include,

- ☆ The iso-revenue line should be tangent to the PPC from above.
- ☆ Slope of the iso-revenue line should be equal to the slope of PPC.
- ☆ PPC should be concave to the origin *i.e.,* the MRPS of paddy for maize ($MRPS_{FM}$) must be increasing at the point of equilibrium.

Recall now the values of the slopes of these two curves. The slope of PPC indicates MRPS of paddy for maize and slope of iso-revenue line indicates price ratio of two products and the point of OPC is explained below.

Slope of the PPC= $MRPS_{PM} = (\Delta M)/(\Delta P)$

Slope of the iso-revenue line = (P_P/P_M)

So, the point of profit maximization is when the slope of the PPC is equal to the slope of the iso-revenue line and this is given by,

$(\Delta M)/(\Delta P) = (P_P/P_M)$ or $MRPS_{PM} = (P_P/P_M)$ ———→ Equation 9.7

So, at the point of OPC, the slope of PPC is equal to the slope of iso-revenue line or the $MRPS_{PM}$ is inversely equal to the price ratio of paddy and maize. The point of OPC can also be stated that, the rate (MRPS) at which the farmer is willing to substitute paddy for maize is inversely equal to the price ratio between paddy and maize.

3. *Decision Making by the Firm Under Perfect and Imperfect Market Competitions*

To achieve the optimality, the firm aims at the equality of MR and MC and this will guide to optimize the output or maximize the profits. MR indicates the additional revenue the firm gets in selling additional unit of output and MC indicates the additional cost incurred by the firm in producing the additional unit of output. The rules of thumb are:

- ☆ The firm attains equilibrium, when MR=MC.
- ☆ When MR>MC, the firm should continue the production programme to increase the output, so that MC rises and thereby, the equality between MR and MC is ensured.
- ☆ When MR<MC, the firm has to reduce the output, so that MC falls and thereby, the equality between MR and MC is ensured.

The above rules of firm's equilibrium imply that, the firm will not produce an additional unit of output, which involves more MC compared to MR earned from the same. In other words, the firm will produce an additional unit of output. only when the MR earned from that unit is more than MC incurred in producing the same. So, the firm continues to produce more units of output and attains optimum level of output at the point, where MR = MC. According to Stonier and Hague, '*a firm will be in equilibrium when it is earning maximum money profits. But, the money profits of a firm will always be maximized when its marginal revenue equals the marginal cost*'. In the graphical illustration of the MR and MC approach, the equality between MRC and MC curve will not be the only sufficient condition for the firm's equilibrium, but the firm must also satisfy the second order condition *i.e.*, the MC curve should cut the MR curve from below, while MC curve is rising upward. Thus, the two important conditions for the firm's equilibrium include,

- ☆ MR= MC
- ☆ MC curve should cut the MR curve from below, while rising upward.

This approach is applicable to study the firm's equilibrium both under perfect and imperfect market competitions.

4. *LP Technique*

We already know, a LP problem consists of a linear objective function to be maximized or minimized subject to certain constraints in the form of linear equations or inequalities. The above concepts to attain optimality in the production programme are based on marginal analysis. This is where, the concept of LP technique differs from the above marginal approach and this also contribute to its superiority over them and the same can be highlighted from the following points:

- ☆ Marginalism or Marginal approach of optimality assumes continuous production function and factor inputs are substitutable. But, in case of LP technique, the decision maker chooses an finite number of production processes and they are less flexible for substitution compared to marginal analysis.
- ☆ In marginal analysis it is assumed that, the firm produces a single product, whereas the concept of LP technique can be applied to multi-factor and multi-product concepts.
- ☆ In marginal approach, the concepts of cost minimization and profit maximization are analyzed in terms of linear equalities. However, in LP technique, the functional constraints are expressed as linear inequalities to derive the values of the decision variables in the objective function.
- ☆ In the marginal approach, the graphical analysis for optimization is in terms non-linear curves. However, in LP technique, the graphical solution for optimization is studied in terms of linear curves
- ☆ Unlike marginal approach, LP technique provides corner solution for optimization in the estimated feasible region.
- ☆ Unlike marginal approach, LP technique addresses the concept of shadow price analysis.

10

Agricultural Projects Evaluation

Gittinger (1972) defined project as *'a whole complex of activities involved in using resources to gain benefits'*. He (1982) further opined that, *'project' as... an investment activity upon which resources – costs – are expended to create capital assets that will produce benefits over an extended period of time and which logically lends itself to planning, financing, and implementing as a unit. A specific activity, with specific starting point and specific ending point, intended to accomplish a specific objective. The smallest operational element prepared and implemented as a separate entity in a national plan or program. Generally unique in that it is not a segment of an ongoing program, although it may be a 'time slice' – a portion lasting several years – of a long-term program. Or, put more succinctly, 'the whole complex of activities for which money will be spent in expectation of returns'*. So, a project can be defined as an investment activity, in which the financial resources are spent, so as to create durable capital assets that provide benefits for an extended period of time. A project may also be defined as a set of activities, which aim at achieving specific objectives within a stipulated period of time and budget. While there are several definitions of project in the literature, one of the best has been offered by Tuman (1983), who states: *'A project is an organization of people dedicated to a specific purpose or objective. Projects generally involve large, expensive, unique, or high risk undertakings which have to be completed by a certain date, for a certain amount of money, with some expected level of performance. At a minimum, all projects need to have well defined objectives and sufficient resources to carry out all the required tasks.'* As defined in 'A Guide to the Project Management Body of Knowledge' (PMI, PMBOK® Guide, 2000), *'a project is a temporary endeavor undertaken to create a unique product or service. Temporary means that every project has a definite beginning and a definite end. Unique means that the product or service is different in some distinguishing way from all other projects or services'*. Declerck *et al.* (1983 and 1997), defined *'a project is a whole of actions limited in time and space, inserted in, and in interaction with a politico-socio-economic environment, aimed at and tended towards a goal progressively redefined by the dialectic between the thought (the project plan) and the reality'*. The projects are often considered as 'cutting edges of development' and 'building blocks of investment plan'.

The above definitions also infer that, the word 'project' has different connotations in different contexts. In one context, project means a location specific activity with specific objectives, time and cost limitations and of non-repetitive nature. In the context of financing and banking, a project is considered as an investment activity, in which financial resources are used for creating capital assets that produce benefits over a fairly longer period of time. In this context, cultivation of paddy, wheat, maize *etc.*, by the farmer will not represent a project, as their cultivation will not lead to the creation of durable capital assets, there is no long term investment in the production programme and the returns are not extended for a fairly longer period of time. However, if the farmer goes for mango plantation or setting up of a poultry farm, it represents a project, as it fulfills all the above three financial and banking criteria. Hence, project is sometimes called as 'Capital expenditure' or 'Capital investment' or 'Capital project'. Another term used is 'Scheme', but a scheme is smaller in scale than a project.

I. Project vs Programme

The above explanation infers, what 'Project' is. 'Programme' refers to set of projects representing various sectors of the economy for achieving overall development. For example, 'Integrated Rural Development Programme' is an anti-poverty programme that aims at alleviating poverty among rural population. To alleviate poverty among them, various activities or projects are executed representing various sectors like health, sanitation, agriculture, irrigation, electricity, education *etc.* The following points further highlight the differences between a project and a programme:

- ☆ Project is micro in its scope, whereas programme is macro in its scope.
- ☆ Project is specific in its objective(s), whereas in a programme, there are broader goals.
- ☆ Project is of shorter duration when compacted to a programme for its completion.
- ☆ Objective(s) of the project must fit into the broad frame work of the programme.
- ☆ The goals of the programme will be achieved through formulation of several projects each with specific objectives.
- ☆ Project is more precisely defined, unlike a programme.
- ☆ Unlike programme, project will have a specific clientele.

II. Project Appraisal Techniques

Project is appraised for its net benefits even before its implementation considering proposed costs and benefits. This project appraisal involves a detailed study about the project with reference to technical feasibility, economic viability and financial viability of the project investment. This appraisal is done by financing (funding) agency to ascertain, whether it has to finance for the investment or not?

- ☆ ***Technical feasibility:*** The study about technical feasibility of the project investment will be done with reference to:
  - ❑ Location of the project in the context of its access to raw materials, man power, transport facilities, communication facilities, market for the output of the project *etc.*
  - ❑ Scope for the adoption of modern technology in the project.
  - ❑ Availability of plant equipment for the project.
- ☆ ***Economic viability:*** The study about economic viability of the project investment will be done with reference to:
  - ❑ Increased net cash flows into the project.
  - ❑ Generation of employment opportunities at the country-level.
  - ❑ Contribution of the project to the National Income.
- ☆ ***Financial viability:*** The study about financial viability of the project investment will be done with reference to:
  - ❑ Cost estimates of the project.
  - ❑ Sources of the finance to the project, rates of interest *etc.*
  - ❑ Profitability of the investment (*i.e.*, earning of profits by the project should be started within reasonable period of time).
  - ❑ Repayment capability of the project investment from the cash inflow it enjoys.
  - ❑ Contribution of project investment in terms of increase in income and employment opportunities at the beneficiary (micro) level.

Broadly, there are two techniques for appraising the project *viz.*, Undiscounted technique and Discounted technique (Figure 10.1).

A. Undiscounted Technique

In this technique, time value of money is not taken into consideration in estimating the net returns and rate of return from the project during its life time. The various measures under this undiscounted technique include:

a. Ranking by Inspection

It is based on the size of the investment and duration of the project. Suppose, there are two projects with same level of investment and with same level of net benefits, then the project with longer duration is more preferred, when compared the project with shorter duration.

b. Pay Back Period (PBP)

It refers to the number of years taken by the project to completely cover its investment from the annual net cash inflows or net returns. It is, otherwise, defined as the length of time from the beginning of the project until the net value of the incremental production stream reaches the total amount of capital investment (Net

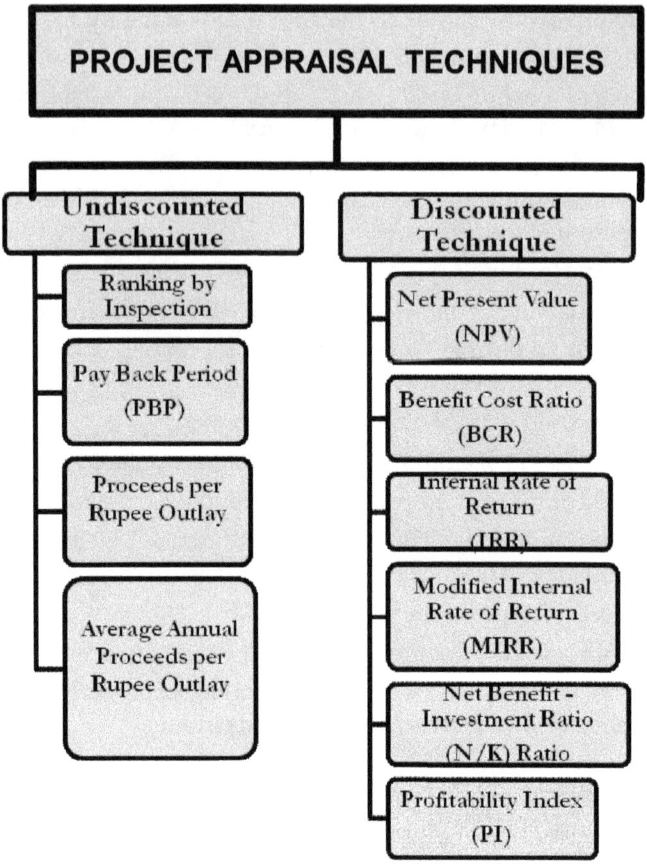

Figure 10.1: Classification of Project Appraisal Techniques.

value of incremental production = Value of incremental production less operation and maintenance cost, production cost etc). The formula used to compute PBP is given by:

P=I/R

where, P=PBP (years), I = Initial investment of the project, R = Annual net cash inflows or net returns from the project.

When two projects have same rate of return and involve same amount of risk, then the investment decision will be taken based on the PBP. In employing this measure, the projects will be ranked based on the lowest magnitude of the estimate *i.e.,* the project with lowest PBP is more preferred over the projects that have higher PBPs. This measure assess the time required for the cumulative income (arising from the investment) to equal the initial cost of the investment. This measure is used to highlight those investments that are not viable *i.e.,* investments that never achieve payback. This measure is also used to select the most appropriate source of finance. For example, investments having a short PBP would require short-term finance. Note that, PBP is a 'break-even' type measure. The decision rule is that, accept the project, if the PBP is less than some preset limit. The pay-back rule says that, *'if the calculated PBP is less than or equal to some pre-specified PBP, then accept the project, otherwise reject it'.*

Example 10.1

Two investments each needing an initial capital of Rs.10,000, but resulting in different patterns of net cash flows as shown below.

Year	*Project A*	*Project B*
0 (Investment)	(10,000)	(10,000)
1	3,000	1,000
2	3,000	2,000
3	3,000	3,000
4	3,000	4,000
5	3,000	6,000
Total	15,000	16,000
PBP (yrs)	3.3	4.0

The students must note that, if the annual net cash flow (cash inflow-cash outflow) is the same for each year of the investment, the PBP is simply calculated by dividing the amount of the investment by the annual net cash flow (Rs.10,000/Rs.3,000 = 3.3 years) *i.e.,* for Project A. On the other hand, if the annual net cash flow is irregular during each year of the investment, the PBP is assessed by taking the year, where the net cash flow is equal to the cost of the investment. In this example, for Project B, the total net cash inflow is equal to investment at 4th year *i.e.,* (1,000 + 2,000 + 3,000 + 4,000) = Rs.10,000. So, the cumulative net cash flow covers the investment in the fourth year and hence, PBP=4 years. So, Project A is preferred over Project B because, it has the shorter PBP. So, according to this criterion, the shorter the PBP for recovery of investment, the more profitable is the project.

Example 10.1.1

Assume a machine costs Rs.600,000. It produces a product such that, each unit generate a profit of Rs.5 on an output of 60,000 units per year. Compute PBP.

Solution: Given, total number of units produced/year = 60000

Also given, profit/unit = Rs.5

So, total annual profit = 5*60000 = Rs.300000

So, PBP = I/R = 600000/300000 = 2 years

Merits of PBP

They include

- PBP is a widely used investment criterion
- This method is very useful in evaluating the profits which involve high uncertainty.

- PBP helps the business firm to analyze when their capital investment will be recovered from the net cash inflows and this guides them regarding the payment of dividends.
- This measure is simple and easy to work out.
- PBP is useful measure for the firm, which suffers from liquidity crisis. This is because, such firm will be more interested in quick return of funds rather than profitability, which PBP also emphasizes.

Demerits of PBP

They include:

- It is a measure of project's capital recovery, not profitability. That is, it does not consider, how profitable a project will be, but considers how quickly the outlay will be recovered.
- Further, this method is biased against long-term projects and followed only, when capital investment is small.
- This undiscounted measure suffers from the limitation that, it ignores the cash flows arising after the PBP has occurred as well as the timing of the income flows. That is, this method considers that, the money received during earlier life of the investment is more valuable than money received later. In the above example, in investment B, the measure ignores the higher cash inflows after 4th year (*i.e.*, in 5th year). That is, this method fails to consider earnings after the PBP.
- This measure is inferior to discounted cash flow techniques because, it ignores the time value of money.

Table 10.1: Computation of Discounted PBP

Year	*Incr Costs (Rs.)*	*Incr Benefits (Rs.)*	*Net Incr Benefits (Rs.)*	*Df @ 10 per cent= $1/(1.1)^t$*	*NPV(Rs.)*	*Cumulative Net Cash Flow after Discounting*
1	10000		–10000	0.909	–9090.91	–9090.91
2		3000	3000	0.826	2479.34	–6611.57
3		3000	3000	0.751	2253.94	–4357.63
4		4000	4000	0.683	2732.05	–1625.57
5		4000	4000	0.621	2483.69	858.11
6		5000	5000	0.564	2822.37	
7		2000	2000	0.513	1026.32	
8		3000	3000	0.467	1399.52	

Discounted PBP

A variant of the PBP measure is the discounted PBP in which, the procedure is same as in undiscounted PBP discussed above, but both costs and returns are discounted considering a discount factor. For the data given through Table 10.1. For Project A, considering the undiscounted cash flow, the PBP is 4 years after starting the project. However, considering the discounted cash flows (where PWC and Present Worth of Benefits (PWB) are calculated), the PBP is between 4 and 5 years after starting the project.

Note that, PBP may be regarded roughly as the reciprocal of IRR, when the annual cash inflow is constant on the duration of the project of the is fairly long. Though discounted PBP is a useful performance indicator to appraise the project's anticipated performance, it should never be used as the sole appraisal method.

c. Proceeds per Rupee Outlay

It is the ratio between the annual net cash flow from the project and total investment of the project. The projects are ranked based on the highest magnitude of the estimate. This is given by:

Proceeds per Rupee Outlay= R/I

where, R = Annual net cash inflows or returns from the project, I = Initial investment of the project. So, the higher the proceeds per rupee of the outlay, the higher the economic viability of the project. But, this criterion however, does not take into consideration the time value of money.

d. Average Annual Proceeds per Rupee Outlay

In this method, first average annual proceeds will be worked out by dividing the TR from the project with total number of years (duration) of the project. Later, the average annual proceeds will be divided by total investment of the project, to workout average annual proceeds per rupee outlay. If average annual proceeds per rupee of outlay are high, the project will be economically justified for implementation. This is given by:

Average Annual Proceeds per Rupee Outlay= (R/N)/I

where, R = Annual net cash inflows or returns from the project, N=Number of years (duration) of project, I = Initial investment of the project.

Thus, in undiscounted technique, only absolute values of costs and returns are considered. Further, Opportunity Cost of Capital (OCC) is not taken into consideration (OCC refers to, what rate of return can the firm earns if that money was used elsewhere). So, this technique is considered less realistic compared to discounted technique.

B. Discounted Technique

In this technique, we take time value of money into consideration, unlike in Undiscounted technique. The various measures under this discounted technique include: NPV/NPW, BCR, IRR, MIRR, Net Benefit-Investment Ratio (Net Benefit-Investment Ratio (NBIR) and Profitability Index (PI): The first four discounted measures are already discussed under 'Time Comparison Principle' in Chapter 2. Let us discuss about NBIR and PI here under.

i. Net Benefit-Investment Ratio (NBIR)

This is otherwise called as N/K ratio. It is simply the present worth of net benefits divided by the present worth of investment. NBIR serves as the suitable and more convenient selection criterion for the project implementation. To calculate this measure, simply divide the sum of the present worth after the incremental net benefits-stream has turned positive by the sum of the present worth of the negative incremental net benefits in the early years (during gestation period) of the project. The reason for calculating the NBIR in this manner is that, we are interested in an investment measure that selects projects on the basis of return to investment during the initial phases of a project. If the NBIR is one or greater than one, when we are discounting at the OCC, choose the project beginning with the largest ratio value and proceed until available investment funds are exhausted. This NBIR also helps to rank projects, especially when sufficient funds are not available to implement all the projects. At any given discount rate, it is difficult to rank the project based on considering NPV, BCR and IRR ranking measures, as selection criterion vary across all these three measures. In this context, the NBIR is the only measure that can be used with confidence to rank the projects directly. This ratio computed by employing the following formula:

NBIR or N/K ratio = (Σ Present Worth of Positive NB)/(Σ Present Worth of Negative NB)

The selection criterion for the project in using N/K ratio measure must be greater than 1. Generally, for the project net incremental benefits will be negative during the gestation period because, gross returns are zero and only costs are incurred. Net incremental benefits will turn positive only after gestation period *i.e.,* when there is cash inflow into the project. This measure is often used for ranking projects especially, if rationing is in place.

Methods to make N/K Ratio = 1

If N/K ratio is more than, then it can be made equal to 1 by employing the following methods:

- ***Increasing the project investment:*** The percent by which the project investment should be increased in order to make N/K ratio = 1 is given by the following formula:

$$I(\%) = \frac{P - N}{N} \times 100$$

Where, I – Increase in project investment (per cent)

P: Sum of present worth of positive net incremental benefits

N: Sum of present worth of negative net incremental benefits

- ***By decreasing net benefits:*** The percent by which the net incremental benefits should be reduced in order to make N/K ratio = 1 is given by the following formula:

$$B(\%) = 1 - \frac{1}{N/K} \times 100$$

Example 10.12

Assume a project with the following costs and benefits (Figures in Rs. Crores). Compute the NBIR or N/K of the investment, assuming discount factor: 10 per cent.

Year	Incremental Costs (Rs.)	Incremental Benefits (Rs.)	df 10 per cent $(1/(1.1)^t$	N/K Ratio	
				Net (Incremental) Benefits (NB)(Rs.)	Present Worth of NB or NPV(Rs.)
1	2.84	0	0.909	–2.84	–2.582
2	10.25	0	0.826	–10.25	–8.471
3	11.46	0	0.751	–11.46	–8.61
4	8.37	0	0.683	–8.37	–5.717
5	4.21	0	0.621	–4.21	–2.614
6	2.09	0	0.564	–2.09	–1.18
7	2.14	6.44	0.513	4.3	2.207
8	2.51	12.32	0.467	9.81	4.576
9	3.75	16.74	0.424	12.99	5.509
10	2.91	15.45	0.386	12.54	4.835
11	1.06	30.71	0.35	29.65	10.392
12	1.03	70.26	0.319	69.23	22.059
				Sum of present worth of +ve NB	49.578
				Sum of present worth of -ve NB	–29.174
				N/K	1.699
				To make N/K equal to 1	
				Per cent Cost should be increased	69.939
				Per cent Benefits should be decreased	41.155

ii. Profitability Index

This measure allows a comparison of the costs and benefits of different projects to be assessed and thus, allow decision making to be carried out. This PI is given by:

PI = Total Present Value of Cash Inflows / Initial Capital Investment

Year	Cost (Rs.)	Cash Inflow (Rs.)	df (10 per cent)	PWB (Rs.)
0	100000		1.000	
1		30000	0.909	27270
2		50000	0.826	41300
3		60000	0.751	45060
				Total = 113630
P.I. = 113630/100000 = 1.1363 (So, accept the project)				

The PI can also be computed as follows:

PI = 1+ [NPV/Initial capital investment]

PI = 1+[13630/100000] = 1.1363

This measure is often used for government or other non-for-profit investments. It measures the benefit per unit cost, based on the time value of money. In the given example, a PI of 1.1363 suggests that, for every Rs.1 of initial investment, the project yields an additional Rs.0.1363 in value. Since, the PI is > 1, we accept the project. For mutually exclusive projects, practitioners sometimes choose the project with the highest PI. However, this approach is problematic. If there is no capital constraint, one should choose the project with the highest NPV from the mutually exclusive pool.

Merits of PI

They include:

- Investment decisions based on PI will be same as decisions made using NPV. All projects having positive NPV have PI larger than 1.0 and therefore, are acceptable.
- Since this measure is related to NPV, it generally leading to identical decisions.
- Easy to understand and communicate.
- The PI is most useful when a firm is facing capital rationing.

Demerit

However, this measure should not be used for making mutually exclusive decisions. But, between two or more mutually exclusive projects having different costs, choose project with highest PI.

Differences between Discounted and Undiscounted Techniques

The following Table 10.3 highlights the differences between discounted and undiscounted techniques:

Table 10.3: Differences between Discounted and Undiscounted Techniques

Discounting technique	*Undiscounting technique*
Time value of money is taken into consideration.	Time value of money is not taken into consideration.
OCC is taken into consideration.	It is not taken into consideration.
Projects are appraised based on discounted benefits and discounted costs.	Projects are appraised based on the absolute benefits and absolute costs.
Discounting techniques are more realistic to appraise the project for its implementation.	These techniques are relatively less realistic to appraise the project for its implementation.
Examples: NPV, BCR, IRR.	Examples: Ranking by inspection, PBP.

Merits of Discounting Technique

They include:

- ☆ Takes time value of money into consideration.
- ☆ Takes into account directly the amount of cash outflows and cash inflows over the entire project's life, unlike undiscounted measure, where simply their averages are taken.
- ☆ Gives more weight to the money values which are nearer to the present period than those which are farther from it. In case of undiscounted measures, all money units are given the same weightage, which is not realistic.
- ☆ Since discounting technique considers time value of money, it will enable to rank projects of different duration, different cash outflows and inflows etc, unlike undiscounted measures.

However, the discounting technique suffers from the limitation that, it is based on the presumption that, the cash inflows in the project can be re-invested at the discounting rate in the new investment opportunities. However, this presumption does depend upon the availability of new attractive investment opportunities.

iii. Sensitivity Analysis

In a project cycle, appraisal or analysis of the project will be done before implementation of project taking into consideration the proposed costs and benefits by employing discounted measures like NPV, BCR, IRR, MIRR, NBIR and PI and we will study the worthiness of implementing the project. If all discounted measures are found desirable as per their criteria for economic viability of the project, then the project will be selected for its implementation. But, after implementation of the project, in due course of time, both input costs and output prices, discount factor *etc.*, may fluctuate. So, accordingly the PWC and PWB of the project will change due to these variations. So, the discounted measures computed earlier before project implementation taking into consideration proposed costs and proposed benefits and the given discount factor may not give a true or realistic picture. The variations in cost and benefits and discount factor should be frequently incorporated and project data should be updated after the implementation of project and again discounted measures should be computed, so as to derive the realistic picture about the project performance for the completed period or duration and for the future period. This procedure of working out discounted measures for the project taking into consideration due changes in the costs and benefits, discount factor *etc.*, frequently after project implementation is called Sensitivity analysis. As the costs and benefits data and changes in discount factor are frequently updated in sensitivity analysis and if the results of discounted measures are still found congenial, then it is worth for continuing the project. Thus, sensitivity analysis of project will be done considering the following aspects:

- ☆ Changes in input cost.
- ☆ Changes in output prices.
- ☆ Changes in discount factor.

- ✩ Change in the length or duration of project.
- ✩ Changes in the gestation period of project.

Besides above factors, risk and uncertainty factors should also be considered to get the realistic picture about the performance of the project. One important method of analyzing the sensitivity analysis of the project is Switching value percentage method.

i. Switching Value Percentage Method

This method estimates the extent to which the percent fall in incremental benefits would make NPV = 0 at the given discount factor or OCC. This method is similar to the methodology employed in computing IRR, but here we make NPV = 0 by decreasing the incremental benefits without changing the discount factor. The procedure in this method is outlined here under.

- ✩ First, we assume a certain fall in incremental benefits of the project and we will work out present worth of net incremental benefits (*i.e.*, NPV).
- ✩ If NPV is positive, still higher percent decline in incremental benefits will be considered to estimate NPV.
- ✩ If NPV is still positive, this procedure is continued till NPV become negative.
- ✩ Between the last two successive NPVs *i.e.*, one positive NPV and one negative NPV, there is zero NPV. So, compute the percent of incremental benefits at which the NPV=0, by interpolation method through employing the following formula:

$$\text{SW per cent} = \begin{matrix}\text{Lower}\\ \text{per cent}\\ \text{fall in}\\ \text{benefits}\end{matrix} + \begin{matrix}\text{Difference}\\ \text{between two}\\ \text{per cent fall}\\ \text{in benefits}\end{matrix} \times \frac{\text{NPV at lower per cent fall in benefits}}{\text{Absolute difference between NPVs at two per cent fall in benefits}}$$

Example 10.13

Assume a project with the following costs and benefits (Figures in Rs. Crores). Compute the Switching Value percentage to make the project break even, assuming discount factor: 10 per cent (*See* Table on next page).

The switching value of 36.925 percent implies that, if benefits fall by such percentage in the project, the project will become break even. Note that, this switching value (per cent) coincides with the value of percent fall in benefits to make the project break even worked out under BCR. Likewise, the sensitivity analysis can be worked out in the project by assuming different possible changes in the project like:

- ✩ 10 per cent fall in factor prices and 10 per cent rise in output prices.
- ✩ 10 per cent rise in factor prices and 10 per cent fall in output prices.
- ✩ 10 per cent fall both in factor and output prices.
- ✩ 10 per cent rise both in factor and output prices.
- ✩ 5 per cent rise in factor prices and 10 per cent rise in output prices.
- ✩ 10 per cent rise in factor prices and 5 per cent rise in output prices.

Year	Incr Costs (Rs.)	Incr Benefits (Rs.)	df 10 per cent	NB (Rs.)	PW of NB at 10 per cent (or) NPV(Rs.)	Switching Value Per cent					
						30 per cent Fall in Benefits			45 per cent Fall in Benefits		
						Benefits after 30 per cent Fall in NB	NB (Rs.)	PW of NB at 10 per cent df (Rs.)	Benefits After 45 per cent Fall in NB	NB (Rs.)	PW of NB at 10 per cent df (Rs.)
1	2.840	0	0.909	–2.840	–2.582	0	–2.84	–2.582	0	–2.840	–2.582
2	10.250	0	0.826	–10.250	–8.471	0	–10.25	–8.471	0	–10.250	–8.471
3	11.460	0	0.751	–11.460	–8.610	0	–11.46	–8.610	0	–11.460	–8.610
4	8.370	0	0.683	–8.370	–5.717	0	–8.37	–5.717	0	–8.370	–5.717
5	4.210	0	0.621	–4.210	–2.614	0	–4.21	–2.614	0	–4.210	–2.614
6	2.090	0	0.564	–2.090	–1.180	0	–2.09	–1.180	0	–2.090	–1.180
7	2.140	6.440	0.513	4.300	2.207	4.508	2.368	1.215	3.542	1.402	0.719
8	2.510	12.320	0.467	9.810	4.576	8.624	6.114	2.852	6.776	4.266	1.990
9	3.750	16.740	0.424	12.990	5.509	11.718	7.968	3.379	9.207	5.457	2.314
10	2.910	15.450	0.386	12.540	4.835	10.815	7.905	3.048	8.4975	5.588	2.154
11	1.060	30.710	0.350	29.650	10.392	21.497	20.437	7.163	16.8905	15.831	5.548
12	1.030	70.260	0.319	69.230	22.059	49.182	48.152	15.343	38.643	37.613	11.985
				NPV	**20.404**		**NPV**	**3.826**		**NPV**	**–4.462**
						Switching value per cent			**36.925**		

iv. Shadow Price

In an economic appraisal of project, the appraiser must necessarily estimate both cash outflows and inflows. In doing this analysis, he seeks to estimate the magnitudes of both benefits and costs of a project in order to establish, whether or not going ahead with the project would increase social welfare. That is, he analyze about NPV, BCR, IRR etc., and in accordance with their bench mark criteria, he decide to accept or reject the project investment. However, not all components of costs and benefits can be quantified in the economic appraisal. For instance, regarding benefits from the project like time saving, lives saved, additional numbers of farm family children educated to particular benchmark standards etc. But to convert such flows into value forms, prices are needed. A question then arises as to which price (or prices) should be used in economic appraisal exercises. In this context, shadow pricing is often used, where the whole purpose is to capture all the variables involved in economic appraisal, and not merely those for which market prices exist. Thus, shadow prices are calculated for those items (goods and services) that do not have a market price, perhaps because, they are set by the Government. The name shadow price was so coined because, this price cannot be observed in a market economy. Dreze and Stern (1990, page 4) defined *'shadow price of a commodity is its social opportunity cost, i.e. the net loss (gain) associated with having one unit less (more) of it. The losses and gains have to be assessed in terms of a well-defined criterion or objective, which is referred to as 'social welfare'*. For example, the shadow price (the opportunity cost in this case) of one labour employed on a project is given by the reduction in social welfare that would result from his or her employment in the project. Of course, the opportunity cost would vary depending on whether the labour employed in the project was drawn from employment elsewhere or would otherwise have been unemployed. Again assume that, a project has generated one additional unit of education. The value of that additional unit of education to the recipient country is given by the increase in welfare that the society in question would obtain from that additional unit. Thus, shadow price of a commodity or resource is always expressed in terms of its social opportunity cost. Shadow price is otherwise called as Accounting price, because this price will be employed in economic analysis of the project. In general, shadow prices are considered fot three main items in a project's economic appraisal *viz.*,

i. Determining labour wage rate.
ii. Determining foreign exchange rate of currency.
iii. Determining the price of project output traded internationally.

i. Determining Shadow Wage Rate of Labour

For more populous countries like India, the labour are characterized by disguised unemployment *i.e.*, MPP_L is zero or almost equal to zero. In agricultural sector, since production is season bound, the MPP_L is zero during lean season of production and during peak season of production, slowly the marginal value product of labour will increase in the direction of prevailing market wage rate. We know, generally labour can be categorized into two types *viz.*, Unskilled labour and Skilled labour.

- ☆ For unskilled labour, the prevailing market wage rate is taken as shadow ware rate.

- In case of skilled labour, private sector wage rate is generally taken as shadow wage rate, when compared to Government sector wage rate. This is because, in private sector, the amount of wage rate received by skilled labour is in proportionate with the amount of work turned out, unlike in Government sector. Hence, private sector wage rate is taken as shadow wage rate for skilled labour.

ii. Exchange Rate of a Country's Currency

The true value of a country's currency is the price it fetches, when exchanged with other country's currency. In general, there are fixed exchange rates for exchanging one country currency with other countries currencies. However, the Government may announce official exchange rate favouring certain segments of the population in the country. Following are the examples regarding export and import scenarios of commodities:

- Indian Government will favour exporters of the country for exporting the commodities to different countries in the international market because, they are the foreign exchange earners for the country. Let us assume, the fixed exchange rate of 1$ = Rs.45. To favour the Indian exporters, Indian Government will announce the official exchange rate for exporters as 1$=Rs.50. So, the value of Indian currency is devalued and this promotes exports from the country.
- Black market rate of foreign exchange is generally lowered when compared to fixed exchange rate thereby, the Indian rupee is overvalued.
- To protect the domestic producers from large scale imports, the Government will impose import duties on imported goods. As a result, the market price of imported good will be higher than the domestically produced good and this protects the domestic producers from large scale imports.

Due to these imperfections both in import and export scenarios of commodities, it is very difficult to estimate the shadow price for foreign exchange. Hence, Gittinger opined that, the project analyst should use the shadow price of foreign exchange as suggested by the Central Planning Unit of the country.

iii. Determining of Price of Project Output Traded Internationally

Regarding project output, domestic market price is not taken as a shadow price, because of large scale imperfections in the form of Minimum Support Prices, Government subsidies to various inputs like seeds, fertilizers, electricity, water *etc.* Hence, international price of the project output will be generally taken as a shadow price, because of the prevalence of perfect market competition.

v. Differences between Financial Analysis and Economic Analysis of Project

There are important differences between financial and economic analyses of project investment. Gittinger describes these differences: '*The point of view taken in the economic analysis is that of society as a whole...... the financial analysis takes the viewpoint of the individual participants..... The methodology of comparing costs and benefits.... is the same for either an economic or financial measurement of project worth, but what is defined as a cost and what is considered a benefit are different'*. No doubt, both financial and economic analyses appraise the outcome or profit of project investment. But, the concept of financial analysis is not the same as economical analysis of project and it is discussed through the Table 10.4.

Table 10.4: Financial Analysis vis-à-vis Economic Analysis of Project

Financial Analysis	*Economic Analysis*
Financial analysis studies the increase in income and employment opportunities at the beneficiary level. So, financial analysis is micro in its scope.	Economic analysis of project indicate, how the National Income of country is increased, what extra employment is generated in the country, how best the resources are utilized in the country, what is the effect of project on foreign exchange earning of the country *etc.* So, economic analysis is macro in its scope.
Financial analysis compares benefits and costs to the project investment. That is, financial analysis studies the viability of project from the view point of beneficiaries under prevailing marketing conditions.	Economic appraisal is a more comprehensive method of analyzing project costs and benefits than financial appraisal. Economic analysis compares the benefits and costs to the whole economy. That is, economic analysis studies the viability of project from the view point of region or state or nation as a whole.
Revenue and Expenditure Statement, Balance Sheet, Source and Application of Fund Statement *etc.*, are prepared to provide most of the information needed for financial analysis.	No such statements are prepared in economic analysis.
Project costs and benefits are estimated at constant market prices to overcome the effects of inflation. These prices are called as Financial prices.	Project costs and benefits are estimated at economic prices or shadow prices by properly adjusting the financial prices with appropriate weightages.
No such information is available for financial analysis.	Economic analysis provides information on key economic variables like foreign exchange earnings, taxation revenue, employment generation in the country *etc.*
Project appraisal techniques like BCR, IRR, N/K ratio will be studied for discounting costs and benefits at constant market prices. Break even analysis and PBP are the undiscounted measures employed.	Project appraisal techniques will be studied by using economic prices or shadow prices. Nominal and Effective rate of protection are the undiscounted measures employed.
No such detailed information is needed in financial analysis.	Economic analysis deals with all types of investments and costs on infrastructure development, staff housing and transport facilities, construction of schools, hospitals *etc.* Social cost will be taken into consideration and quantified, if possible.
No shadow prices will be used in financial analysis.	Shadow price will be used to determine labour wage rate, foreign exchange rate and project output traded internationally.

Contd...

Table 10.4–*Contd...*

Financial Analysis	*Economic Analysis*
Taxes, custom duties, subsidies, welfare contributions, charitable contributions *etc.*, were included in financial analysis. Taxes in the form of excise duties, customs duties and sales taxes are considered cost, while subsidies and loan receipts are considered as benefits and are fully accounted for in the analysis. Interest payments on borrowed capital and repayment of loans are not included.	Taxes (Direct and Indirect), Subsidies, Credit Transactions and Interest are four kinds of transfer payments and they are not included in economic analysis.
In financial analysis, interest paid to external suppliers of money may be deducted to derive the benefit stream available to the owners of capital. But, interest imputed or 'paid' to the entity from whose point of view the financial analysis is being done is not treated as a cost because, the interest is part of the total return to the equity capital contributed by the entity. Hence, it is a part of the financial return that entity receives (Gittinger, 1982).	In economic analysis, interest on capital is never separated and deducted from the gross returns because, it is part of the total return to the capital available to the society as a whole and because it is that total return, including interest, that economic analysis is designed to estimate.

The purpose and objectives of financial and economic appraisals are quite different, so it will not always be the case that a project that is financially viable will be economically viable or a project that is economically viable will be financially viable. Despite these differences, both financial and economic analyses have similar features. Both estimate the net-benefits of a project investment based on the difference between the with-project and the without-project situations. However, it is to be noted that, economic and financial analyses are also complementary. For a project to be economically viable, it must be financially sustainable. If a project is not financially sustainable, there will be no adequate funds to properly operate, maintain and replace assets. As long as the project is economically viable, financial viability is not a concern, as it can be supported through government subsidies.

vi. Project Scheduling or Project Management Techniques

Project scheduling or management involves a decision making process regarding planning, organizing, control, direction and co-ordination of various activities that are performed in a project. Project manager, therefore, depends on various tools and techniques that are effective not only for acting on the desired plan, but also capable of identifying the constraints and in controlling or correcting the same. We know, a project consists of several activities that have to be completed and some of them are interdependent *i.e.*, they cannot start before the completion of some other activities. In many situations, project managers face several managerial problems in executing the project, so as to complete it on time and within the allocated budget. In this context, project management provides a number of approaches to cope up with these challenges and among them, two important approaches are Bar Charts and Net works. Bar charts are of two types *viz.*, Gantt Chart and Milestone Chart and Net works include two important techniques *viz.*, Programme Evaluation and Review

Technique (PERT) and Critical Path Method (CPM). Let us discuss about these two approaches in-detail here under.

1. Bar Charts

It is a pictorial representation of various tasks or events to be performed for accomplishment of project objectives in the form of bar diagrams. Bar charts are of two types:

i. Gantt Chart

This was developed by Henry L. Gantt in 1917. It is a system of bar charts specifying the starting time and finishing time of an event to be performed in a project. First the project is broken down into a physically identifiable and control units called 'Tasks or Events' represented by bars. These bars are spaced preferably at equi-distance on Y-axis and time element is taken on X-axis. Hence, these charts help the project manager in planning the schedule, progress and completion of events. Here, the length of the bar denotes the required time to complete the task or event and width of the bar do not have any significance.

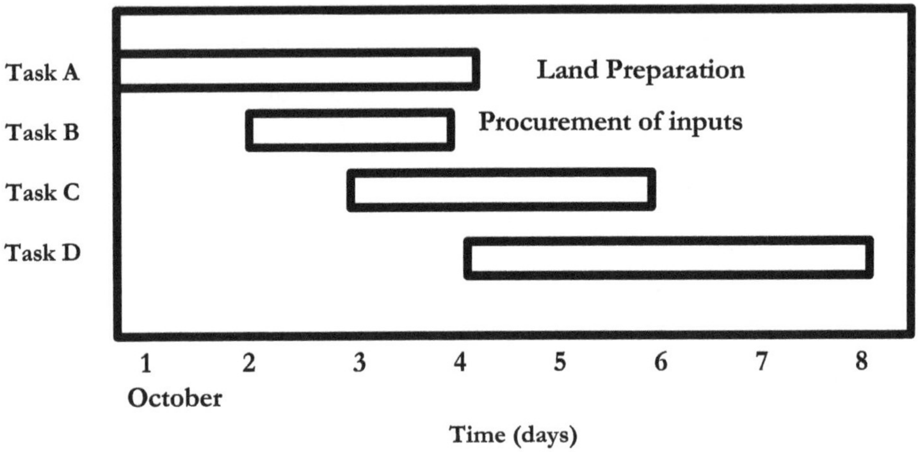

Figure 10.2: Gantt Chart Showing Schedule of Tasks or Events.

From the above Figure 10.2, it is clear that, Task A should be completed in 4 days *i.e.*, from October 1st to October 4th and another task *i.e.*, procurement of inputs will be performed simultaneously along with Task A and it should get completed from October 2nd to October 4th *i.e.*, in 3 days.

Limitations

- ☆ Difficult to handle, when more number of tasks are there in the project.
- ☆ It won't indicate the inter relationships between the tasks.
- ☆ It won't indicate the time taken for different activities within the same task. If any task is delayed or over runs time, it won't indicate, what is the impact on the project completion date.

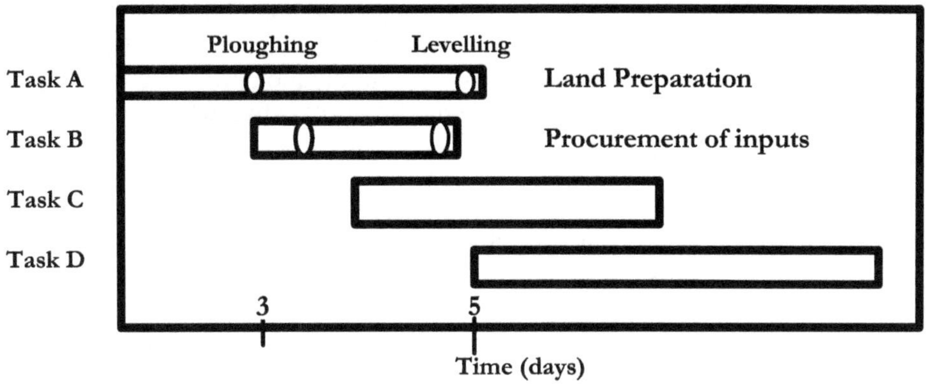

Figure 10.3: Milestone Chart Showing Schedule of Tasks or Events and Activities.

ii. Milestone Chart

This chart is an improvement over Gantt chart by introducing different milestones or activities for every task or event. This is because, from Gantt chart, it is very difficult to monitor the progress of every activity in each task. The milestones are represented by a circle in the task (Figure 1036) indicating the completion of a specific activity or milestone of the task by that time. That means, in a milestone chart, a task bar is divided into different milestones or activities and only, if these activities are fulfilled, we can say an event or task is fulfilled.

From the Figure 10.3 it is clear that, in Task A *i.e.,* land preparation, there are 2 milestones or activities *i.e.,* ploughing and leveling. Indicating a milestone on the day 3 on task bar A indicates that, ploughing activity must complete by 3rd October and leveling by 5th October.

Merits

- ☆ It helps the project manager to plan the activities accurately within a task or event so that, the entire task can be fulfilled or completed in time.
- ☆ It also helps to draw the relationship between different activities in an event.

Demerits

- ☆ It does not show any inter-dependence between different tasks or events.
- ☆ It won't indicate the interdependency of different.
- ☆ It does not indicate critical activities of the project.
- ☆ If one activity is delayed, it is difficult to analyze the impact on the project duration.
- ☆ It is very cumbersome to draw this chart for large projects.

2. Net Works

The network is a logical extension of Gantt and Milestone charts incorporating the modifications, so as to illustrate inter-relationship between different tasks and among all the milestones in an entire project. There are two important techniques of network analysis *viz.*, PERT and CPM. Both the techniques are almost similar and developed almost simultaneously during 1956-58. Both CPM and PERT provide the user with project management tools to plan, monitor, and update their project as it progresses. There are many similarities and differences between the two, however.

Similarities between PERT and CPM

These two techniques enjoy the following similarities:

- ✰ Both follow the same steps and use network diagrams to display the relationships between project activities and to help managers to address questions such as:
  - ❑ What is the total time required to complete the project (the expected total time for PERT)?
  - ❑ What are the start and the completion times for individual activities?
  - ❑ Which critical activities must be completed as scheduled to meet the estimated project completion time?
  - ❑ How much delay can be tolerated for non-critical activities without incurring a delay in the estimated project completion time?
  - ❑ What is the least expensive way to speed up a project to meet a targeted completion time?
  - ❑ PERT also provides answers to the additional questions like what is the probability of completing a project within a given time frame?, what is the variability in the project completion time?
- ✰ Both are used to plan the scheduling of individual activities that make up a project.
- ✰ They can be used to determine the earliest/latest start and finish times for each activity.

While both techniques serve the same purpose, regarding the fast and effective completion of a project, they are different in many aspects (Table 10.5):

Table 10.5: Differences between CPM and PERT

CPM	*PERT*
Developed by J. E. Kelly of Remington Raud and M.R. Walker of Dupont Company, as an application to construction project.	Developed by the US Navy Special Project Office for scheduling the R and D activities for Polaris missiles programme.
The time estimates for activities is assumed deterministic in CPM. There is only one estimate of duration. Hence, CPM is a deterministic tool, as it requires one time estimate.	The time estimates for activities are assumed probabilistic in PERT. Three time estimates are used to form a weighted average to estimate expected time based on probabilistic distribution of completion times. Hence, PERT is a probabilistic tool, as it requires three time estimates.
CPM is used where emphasis is on optimizing resource allocation. It can be used to control both time and cost of the project.	PERT is used basically for planning and control of time in the project.

Contd...

Table 10.5–*Contd...*

CPM	*PERT*
It is activity oriented because, it is built on the basis of activities and the analysis indicate the progress of activities.	It is event oriented because, it is built on the basis of events and the analysis indicate progress of events.
It allows the project manager to crash the activities, in such a way that, the project duration can be shortened at optimal cost.	It allows the project manager to schedule and coordinate various activities so that, the project can be completed in scheduled time.
The activities involved in a construction project are much more predictable, and may not need three estimated completion times. In this case, CPM may be more appropriate, since unlike PERT, CPM also allows for planners to make trade-offs between the cost of the project and the amount of time needed to complete it. So, CPM requires a single deterministic time value for each activity.	PERT is used for projects in which activity times are unknown. For example, take a R and D project, where the amount of time to complete a given task is unpredictable. In such a case, PERT is the best choice, since it allows planners to allocate three estimates for completion times – the most likely, the most optimistic and the most pessimistic. So, PERT treats activity time as a random variable.
CPM is a manual technique	PERT requires computer solutions
CPM includes the analysis of the Time-Cost Trade-off.	PERT focuses exclusively on the time variable

However, now-a-days the two techniques are used synonymously in network analysis and the differences are considered to be historical.

Basic Terms and Concepts Used in Network Analysis

i. ***Network analysis*** : This helps to indicate various events and activities to be performed in the project. In this analysis, both CPM and PERT describe the work plan of project. This analysis includes arrows and circles, which indicate the activities and events respectively in the project. The activities and events are laid in a planned sequence of their accomplishments. These activities should get completed to achieve the project objectives in time. In general, there are two types of notations used in the network diagram:

a. ***Activity-on-Arrow(AoA):*** In AoA notation, the arrow represents the work to be done and the circle represents an event. AoA network diagram are usually associated with the PERT diagram

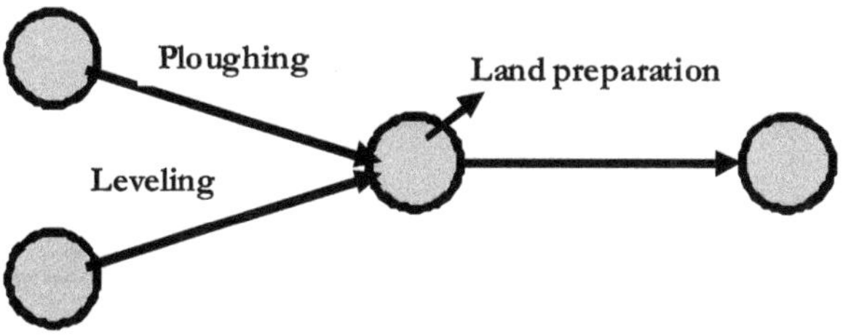

b. Activity-on-Node (AoN): In AoN notation, a box (or node) is used to show the activity to be done and the arrow simply show the sequence in which work is done. Most project management softwares usually uses AoN diagram

Terminology used in CPM and PERT

- **Event :** is defined as the starting or ending point of an activity or a group of activities. It represents a milestone and does not consume time or resources. Event is described by a circle **(O).**

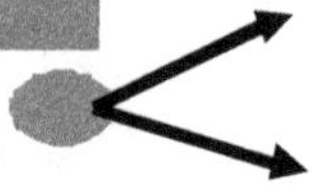

  a. Burst event : An event which gives rise to more than one activity.

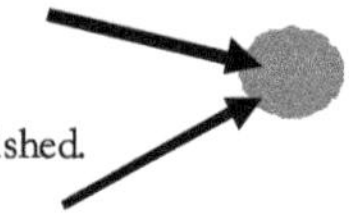

  b. Merge Event: An event which occurs only when more than one activity are accomplished.

- **Activity** : is the work required to proceed from one event to another. It, therefore, needs both time and resources for its execution and completion. It is represented by an arrow(----→). Tail represents the start and head the end of activity

- **Path :** An unbroken chain of activity indicated by arrows connecting initial event to other event

- **Critical Path:** The longest time path connecting the critical activities in the project network. The total time on this path is the longest duration of project.

- **Critical Activity:** Activities on the critical path having zero slack/float time. Also called Bottleneck activities. These activities must be started on right time and must be completed in the right time. Otherwise, project completion gets delayed.

- **Earliest Start Time (EST):** EST is the time at which the activity cannot be started earlier than this time. That means it is a waiting time to start next activity ie., the earliest possible time at which the event can occur. The EST of an activity is the time before which it cannot commence and will not affect the immediate preceding activity.

- **Latest Start Time (LST):** LST is the time, at which the starting of an activity cannot be delayed beyond this time. In other words, it includes non-waiting time. A further delay beyond this time will adversely affect the project duration. The path with shortest time among the path is considered for LST.

- **Earliest Finishing Time (EFT) :** is the minimum time required to complete/finish the activity or is the time at which the activity cannot be finished before this time.

- **Latest Finishing Time (LFT) :** is the time at which the activity must be finished or cannot be extended beyond this time, so as to complete the project in time.

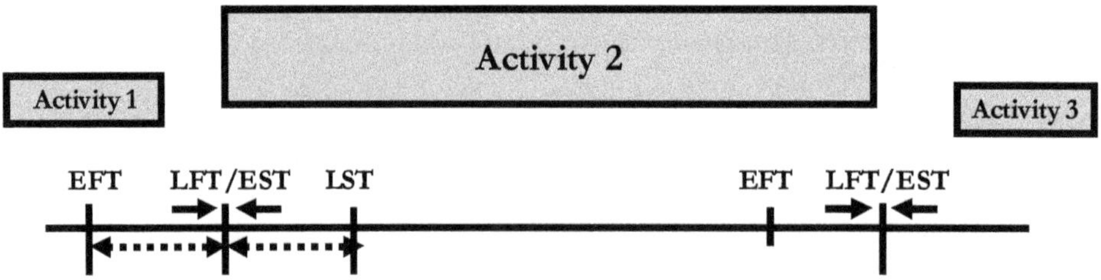

- ***Predecessor event:*** It is an event (or events) that immediately precedes some other event without any other events intervening. It may be the consequence of more than one activity.
- ***Successor event:*** It is an event (or events) that immediately follows some other event without any other events intervening. It may be the consequence of more than one activity.
- ***Fast tracking:*** Refers to performing more critical activities in parallel
- ***Crashing critical path:*** Refers to shortening the duration of critical activities
- ***Slack/Float:*** The amount of spare time available between completion of an activity and beginning of next activity or is the amount of time that a task in a project network can be delayed without causing a delay to project
  Slack/Float = LST – EST = LFT – EFT

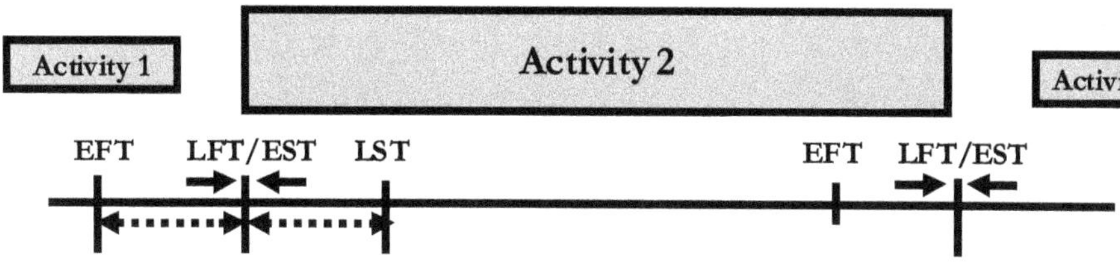

☆ ***Time of completion of activity in the project:*** PERT technique has the ability to deal with uncertainty in activity completion times. For each activity, this technique usually includes three time estimates:

- ❑ ***Optimistic time (O):*** It is the minimum possible time required to accomplish **an activity**, assuming everything proceeds better than is normally expected. This situation may occur approximately 1 percent of time.
- ❑ ***Most likely or Normal time (M):*** It is the model time/normal time required to perform an activity under normal circumstances or the time required to accomplish an activity, assuming everything proceeds as normal.
- ❑ ***Most pessimistic time (P):*** It is the maximum possible time required to accomplish **an activity** assuming everything goes wrong (but excluding major catastrophes). This situation may occur approximately one percent of time.

☆ ***Expected/Estimated time*** **(T_E):** It is the best estimate of time required to accomplish **an activity**, assuming everything proceeds as normal. That is, it is the average time the **activity** would require, if it is repeated on a number of occasions in a project or the weighted average of the estimated optimistic, most likely and pessimistic time duration of a project activity.

$T_E = (O + 4M + P)/6$

$\text{Variance}(T_E) = [(P - O)/6]^2$

Three time estimates, optimistic, pessimistic and most likely, could the decided on past experiences in execution of similar activities or from the feedback from individuals with relevant experience.

Assuming all the activities following normal distribution, the probability of completion of activity taking the 3 time periods i.e; O, M and P and the variance of computed T_E is shown through the following Figure 10.5:

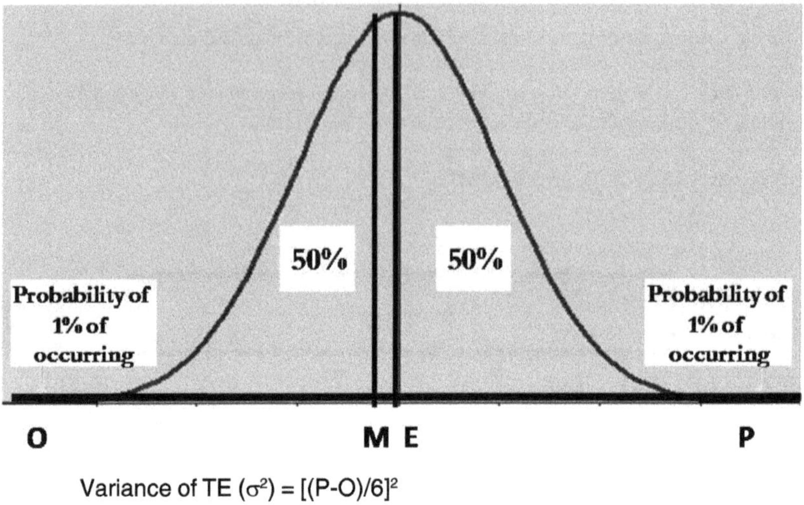

Figure 10.5: Dispersion of Variance of Expected Time Estimate (TE).

- **Network :** is a graphical representation of logically & sequentially connected events through arrows representing activities of a project. Also called as Arrow diagram
- **Network construction :** First the project is split into activities.
  Starting & Finishing events are then decided

  Then analyze the logical sequence:

  - What activities must be completed before a particular activity starts (Predecessor activities)?
  - What activities follow the particular activity (Successor activities)?
  - What activities must be performed concurrently with this activity?
  - Estimate the time for the completion of each activity. (O, M, P)

Network Rules

- Each activity must be represented by one and only arrow
- Arrow and time move from left to right.
- Arrows pointing in opposite direction must be avoided
- Arrows should be kept straight and not curved or bent
- Arrows should not cross each other. If inevitable, the following methods should be followed

Pipeline crossover **Broken arrow crossover**

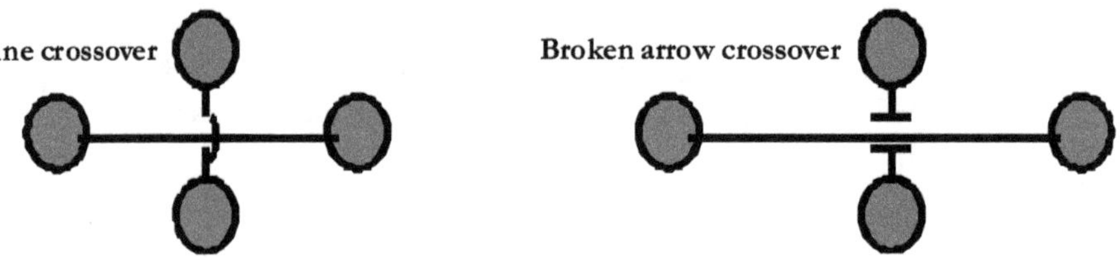

Dummy : An activity which only determines the dependency of one activity over the other, but does not consume any time refers to dummy activity. Dummies are represented by broken/dotted arrow

Assume that, start of C activity depends upon the completion of A and B activities and the start of E activity depends only on the completion of activity B. Figure A shows the wrong presentation and Figure B is the right method through introduction of dummy. No two activities have the same starting and ending event. Among Figures C and D, Figure D representation is correct.

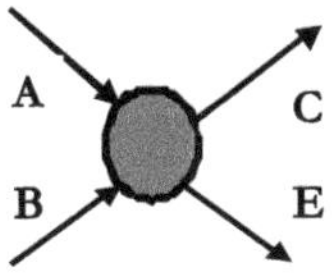

Figure A

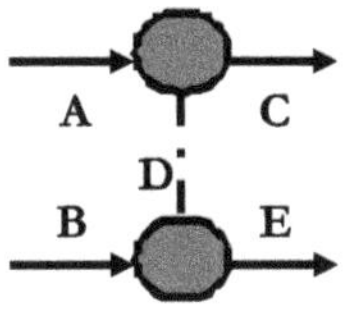

Figure B

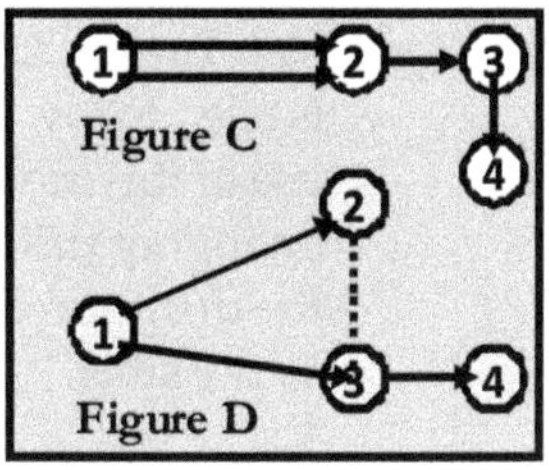

Dangling: It is the situation where events other than initial and final events do not have any successor activity. This is because, all the events except first and last of the whole project must have at least one entering and one leaving activity. By performing this dangling, it costs both time and resource on the part of project because by performing that event, it won't meet the end event. Hence, doing dangling event is merely waste of time & resources

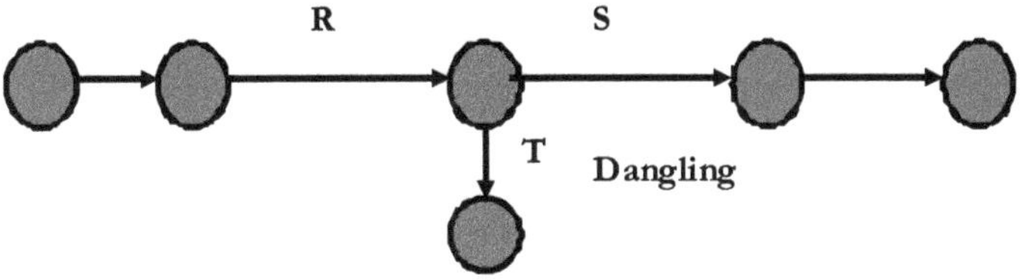

Partial dependency: In certain situations, the starting of an activity depends upon the partial completion of a predessor activity. In such cases, the predessor activity is further broken into two parts and dummy is used to make the connection. Ex: In a pipe line laying project, there are 3 activities ie., digging of 20 metres long trench, laying of 20 metre pipe and filling of the trench. Here, laying of the pipe can be started after 8 metre of trench digging and similarly after 8 metre of pipe laying, filling can be started. This is shown below:

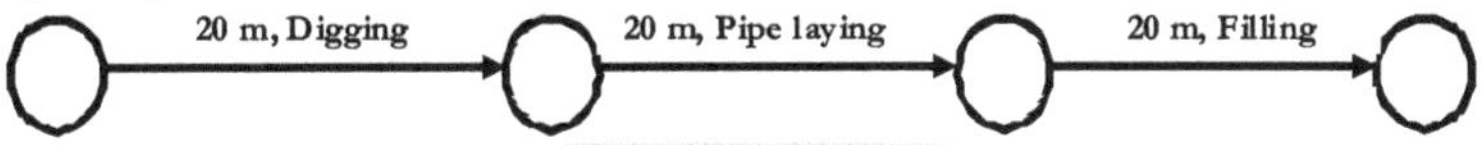

Wrong Illustration

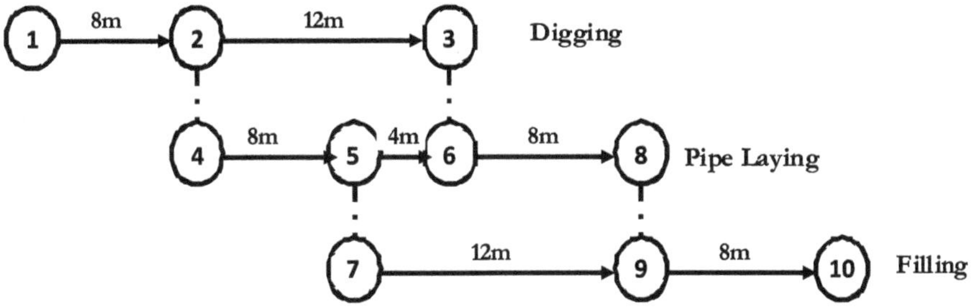

Correct Illustration

- *Crashing:* It implies. shifting resources to reduce slack time so the critical path is as short as possible. Crashing always raises project costs and is typically disruptive – a project should be crashed with caution. The goal of crashing a project is to reduce the duration as much as possible regardless of cost. It is the opposite of relaxing a project.
- *Relaxation:* The method that is the opposite of crashing a project. Relaxation is used to lower costs while extending the duration of the project. A typical use of this method is when a project may be relaxed if its resources are need on higher priority projects. This method involves deliberately lengthening the duration of the project with the specific aim of lowering costs as much as possible.

ii. Network Construction or Drawing a Network Diagram

- To draw the network diagram, first the project should be divided into different possible events and activities.
- In a project, we have to identify which is the starting event and ending event.
- Deciding starting and ending event will help the project manager to analyze the logical sequence of different activities. Logical sequence in the sense that, we have to identify 3 types of activities.
  - ***Predecessor activity:*** It is an activity, which should get completed before starting another activity.
  - ***Successor Activity:*** It is an activity, which should be started after completing an activity.
  - ***Concurrent Activity***: These are the activities, which should be executed simultaneously in the project. A project with more number of concurrent activities will have less duration for its completion. That is, concurrent activities are accomplished simultaneously. Note that, an activity may be a predecessor or successor to another activity or it may be concurrent with one or more activities.
- After identifying different activities, then assume the time duration for completion of each activity.
- In case of CPM method, we will give a single value for time period implying that it is a deterministic tool or approach.
- In case of PERT technique, we will assume 3 different time periods *i.e.*, O, M, and P for completing an activity based on weighted average and we estimate T_E values. Hence, we can say PERT technique is probabilistic tool/ approach.

iii. Steps involved in Network Analysis

They include:

1. Prepare the list of activities.
2. Define the inter-relationship among the activities.

- Each event should have a distinct (unique) number. The event number should not get replicated. An event can't occur until all the incoming activities are completed
- There should not be any loop in the project network as shown below:

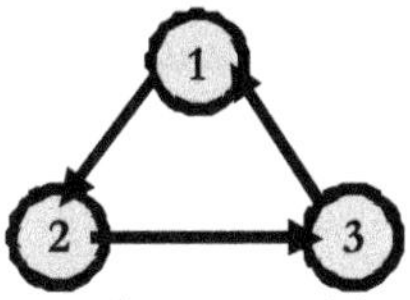

- Not more than one activity can have the same preceding and succeeding event. No two activities can be identified by the same head and tail event

Every activity, except the first and the last, must have at least one preceding and one succeeding activity

- Any number of activities may merge with an event.

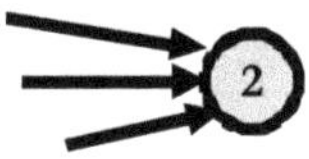

- Each activity must have a preceding and a succeeding event

3. Estimate the activity duration.
4. Assemble the activities in the form of a flow diagram.
5. Draw the network diagram.
6. Analyze the network *i.e.,* compute EST and LST; EFT and LFT, float, identify critical activities and critical path.

Step 1: Prepare the List of Activities

The project may involve a number of activities (Table 10.6) to be performed and each activity represents the work to be performed in the project, which will consume both time and resources. Once an activity is completed, an event will occur in the project. An activity in a project characterized by:

- ☆ It should be cost effective *i.e.,* consume less amount of money for its execution.
- ☆ It should have specific time period for its completion. That means, it should have a specific starting point and a specific ending point.
- ☆ The activity should be measurable (costable) or quantifiable.
- ☆ For convenient execution of the project, it an event is sub-divided into various activities and each activity is given an alphabetical symbol/code.
- ☆ When the number of activities is more, alphanumeric/multi-alphabet codes can be used.

- ☆ In a simple project, it may be easier to identify the activities. In complex projects, activities are identified and they can be split into different sub-projects. For example, the activities of a watershed project could be broken down into sub-projects such as agricultural subprojects, soil and water conservation sub-projects, afforestation sub-project *etc.* For each sub-project, again the activities will be identified. Depending on the size and nature of sub-project, they can be further divided into sub-sub projects.

Table 10.6: List of activities in the project with their codes

Sl.No.	*Activity*	*Code/Symbol*
1.	Land surveying	A
2.	Plan preparation	B
3.	Rock blasting	C
4.	Land leveling	D
5.	Drainage channel digging	E
6.	Stone pitching of drainage channel	F
7.	Digging wells	G
8.	Laying of irrigation lines	H
9.	Construction of pump house	I
10.	Procurement of pumps	J
11.	Installation of pumps	K

Step 2: Define the Inter-relationship among the Activities

After identifying the activities in a project, analyze the inter-relationship between the activities. Generally, three types of relationships will occur among the activities:

- ☆ ***Preceding activity:*** Preceding activity for an activity is its immediate predecessor. That means, a preceding activity must be completed before starting a succeeding activity or new activity. In the Table 10.7, land surveying is the preceding activity for rock blasting. That means, rock blasting is done after completing land surveying. Only terminating activity in the project will not be considered as a preceding activity and all other activities must appear at least once as a preceding activity in the project.
- ☆ ***Succeeding activity:*** Succeeding activity is one that immediately starts after the completion of preceding activity. In the Table 10.7, rock blasting is the succeeding activity for land surveying. That means, after completion of land surveying only rock blasting starts.
- ☆ ***Concurrent or Competing activities:*** These are the activities, which are performed simultaneously in a project.

The table that shows the relationship between the activities along with their preceding activities is called Precedence table (Table 10.7).

Table 10.7: Precedence Table of Activities

Sl.No	*Activity*	*Code*	*Preceding activity*
1.	Land surveying	A	--
2.	Plan preparation	B	--
3.	Rock blasting	C	A
4.	Land leveling	D	A
5.	Drainage channel digging	E	A
6.	Stone pitching of drainage channel	F	B,C
7.	Digging wells	G	B,C
8.	Laying of irrigation lines	H	E,F
9.	Construction of pump house	I	E,F
10.	Procurement of pumps	J	D,H
11.	Installation of pumps	K	G,I

Step 3: Estimate the Activity Duration

In PERT technique, we generally use three different time periods for activity completion *i.e.*, Optimistic, Most likely and Pessimistic and based on probabilities, we estimate the expected time T_E (Table 10.8). However, in case of CPM, we consider only one time period. Hence, we can say PERT is a probabilistic tool (Table 10.8) and CPM method is a deterministic tool.

Ex: Estimation of expected time for the activity 'Land surveying': For this activity, the assumed three time estimates *i.e.*, Optimistic, Most likely and Pessimistic times are 4, 6 and 8 days respectively *i.e.*, O = 4, M = 6, and P = 8. The T_E is given by:

$$T_E = [(O+4M+P)/6]=(4 + 4*6 + 8)/6 = (4+24+8)/6 = (36)/6 = 6 \text{ days}$$

Table 10.8: Computation of T_E of Activities

Activity	*Preceding Activity*	*Optimistic Time (O)*	*Most Likely Time (M)*	*Pessimistic Time (P)*	*Expected Time (T_E)(O+4M+P)/6*
A (Land surveying)	--	4	6	8	6
B	--	1	4.5	5	4
C	A	3	3	3	3
D	A	4	5	6	5
E	A	0.5	1	1.5	1
F	B,C	3	4	5	4
G	B,C	1	1.5	5	2
H	E,F	5	6	7	6
I	E,F	2	5	8	5
J	D,H	2.5	2.75	4.5	3
K	G,I	3	5	7	5

Step 4: Assemble the Activities in the Form of a Flow Diagram

Having decided on activities, their inter-relationship and duration (expected time of each activity), the next step is to draw the flow diagram (Figure 10.6) of the project based on preceding and succeeding activities.

- In a flow chart, the activity and its duration is shown in a box.
- The boxes are connected with lines based on preceding and succeeding activity relationship.
- However, the critical path for the project can be identified by comparing the various path lengths (sum of activity time from start to finish, on any path from start to end).
- The longest path in the chart is the critical path.
- The flow charts do not give details like start and completion time of each activity until unless it is super imposed on a calendar. If it is not superimposed on calendar, it does not facilitate computation of slacks.

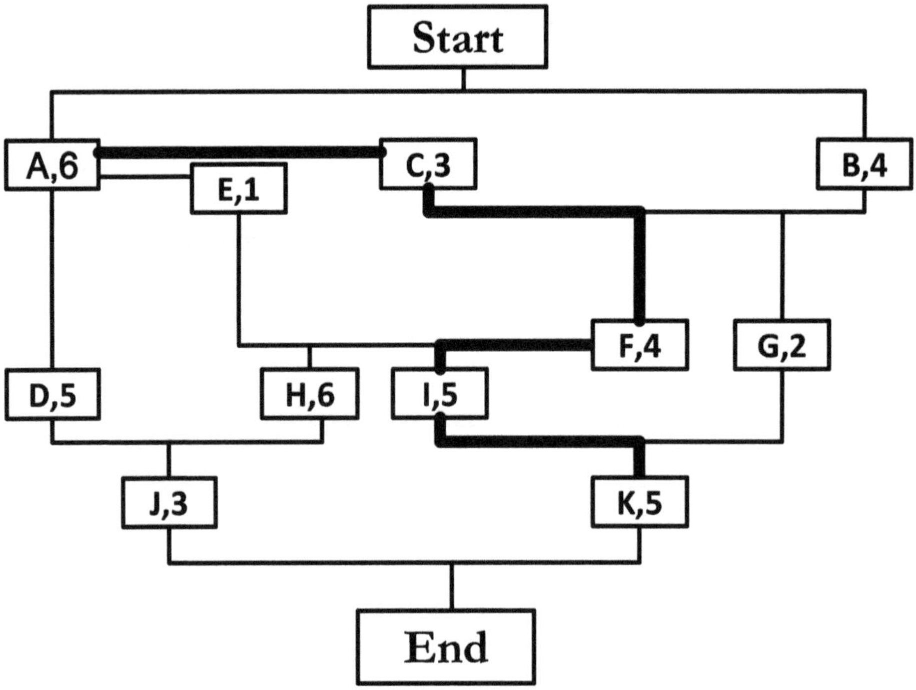

Figure 10.6: Flow Diagram.

Step 5 - Draw the Network Diagram

- Shows the precedence and successor relationship among the activities.
- An arrow generally represents activity in the diagram, while a circle represents event.
- Each activity starts with an event and end in an event. Number indicates an event and alph indicates an activity.
- Activities in a project are performed either sequentially one after another or they are undert concurrently i.e. simultaneously.
- To draw the network, it requires the knowledge of specifying which activities must be compl before other activities can be started, which activities immediately succeed other activities a which activities can be performed in parallel.

Possible combinations of activities

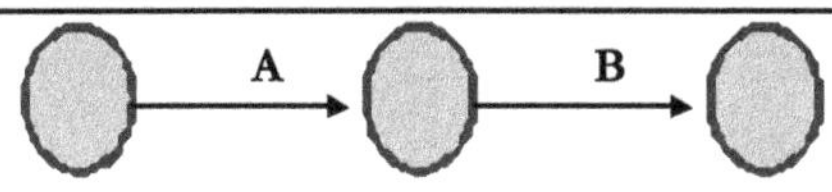	Activity "A" is preceding activity of "B". i.e activity "A" need to be completed before start of activity "B". In other words "B" starts after "A" is finished.
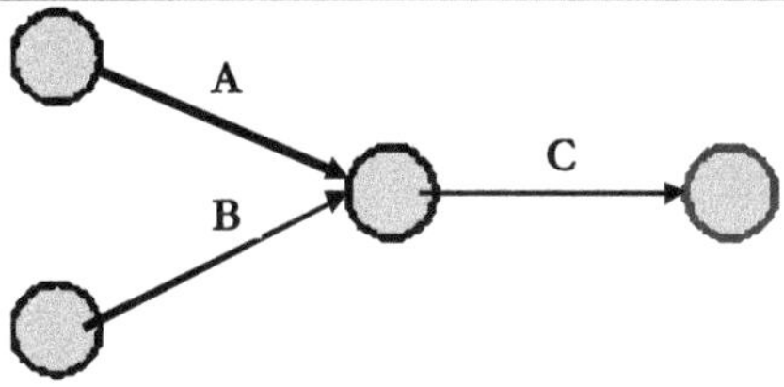	Activity "A" and "B" are concurrent. Activity "C" cannot start until both the activities "A" and "B" are completed.
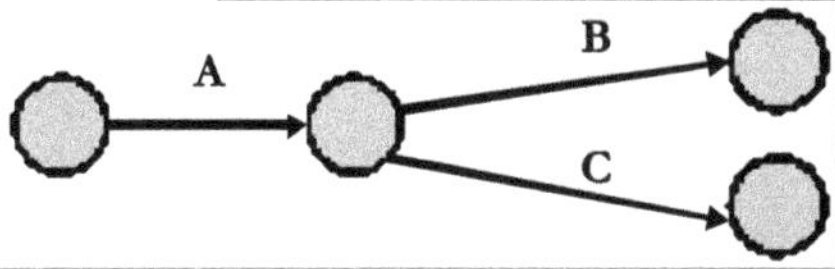	Activity "B" and "C" are concurrent activities. Any one of these cannot start until activity "A" is completed.
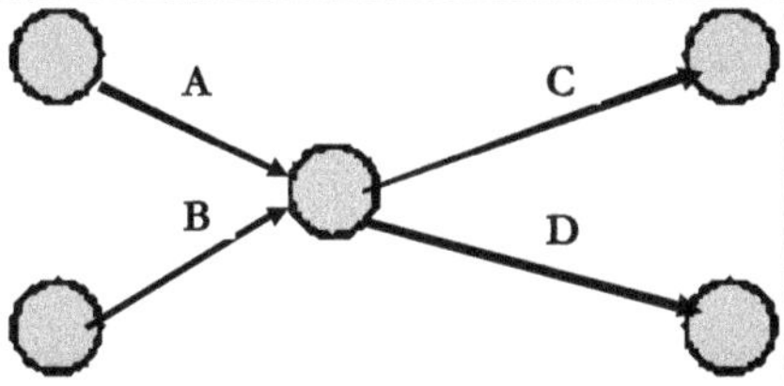	Neither activity C nor D can start until both the activities A and B are completed. But, C and D can start independently.
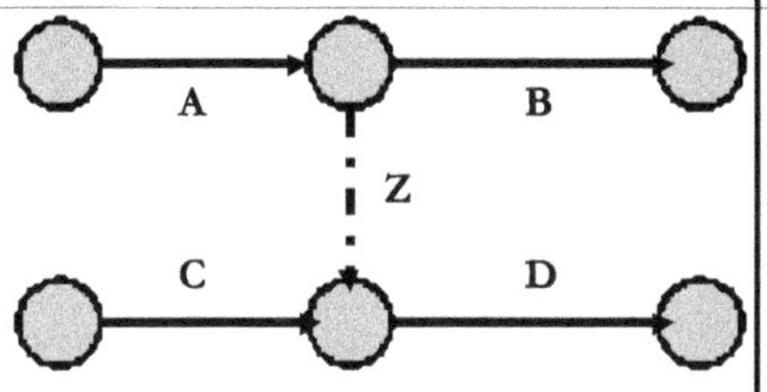	Activity D cannot begin until both A and C are completed. But B can start after A is complete. The activity Z, represented by dashed arrow, is a dummy activity. This does not consume any resource i.e., have zero time and zero cost. This only represents the logical relation among the activities.

Step 6: Analyze Network

Network analysis helps the manager to calculate start time, finishing time, slack and identify critical activities in a project and thereby, critical path of the project. The starting and finishing time for each individual activity is calculated through the network analysis. The duration of project is not necessarily the simple arithmetical sum of the individual activity durations. This is so because, several activities occur concurrently in the project. Project duration would be equal to the sum of all individual activity durations only when all the activities in the project are sequential.

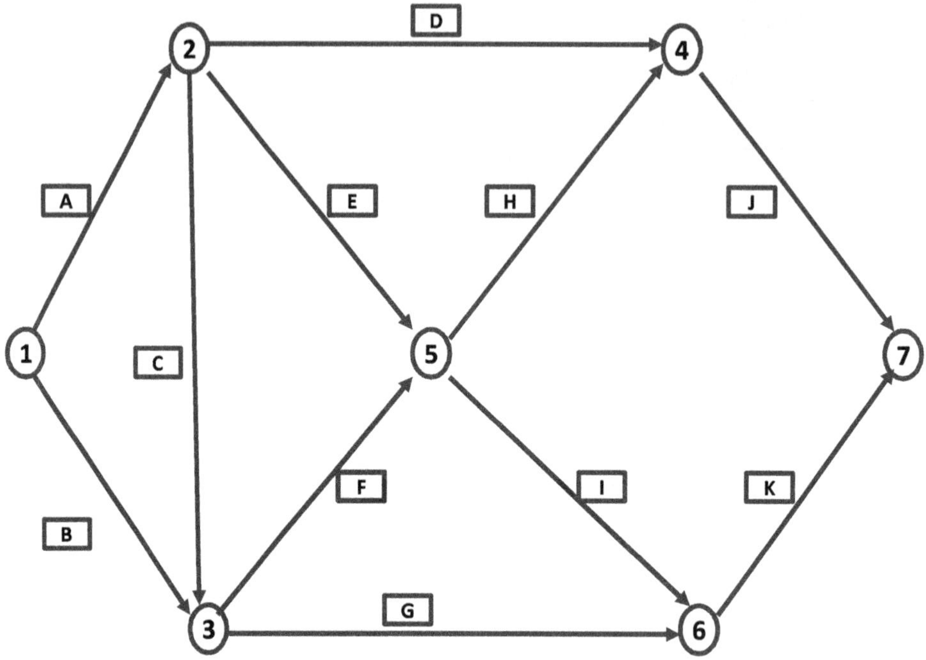

Figure 10.7: Network Diagram.

iv. Components of Network Analysis

From the network diagram (Figure 10.7) the following are the important components we can analyze:

a. Event numbering
b. Computation of the EST, EFT, LST and LFT to identify critical path
c. Computation of Slack or Float
d. Identification of critical activities
e. Identification of Critical Path and duration
f. Estimation of variance of critical activities
g. Estimation of the probability for completion of the project in right time

a. *Event Numbering*

It is very important to assign a number for every event because, they should not get repeated in the project. There are two ways of numbering the events:

- ☆ ***Sequential numbering system:*** This is suitable for small projects, where the number of events is low. In this system, the activities are sequentially numbered such that, the head event/succeeding event will bear a higher number than the tail/preceding event.
- ☆ ***Random/Skip numbering method:*** This is suitable in case of large projects or complex projects, where more number of events are involved. This system facilitates to number extra events, if they are introduced during the course of project implementation and this is not possible in case of sequential numbering system.

In sequential numbering system, if any new activity or event is to be introduced in the project during its implementation, the events succeeding after the newly introduced event should again renumbered. So, to avoid this difficulty generally Skip numbering (Figure 10.8) or Random numbering system is followed in case of large projects.

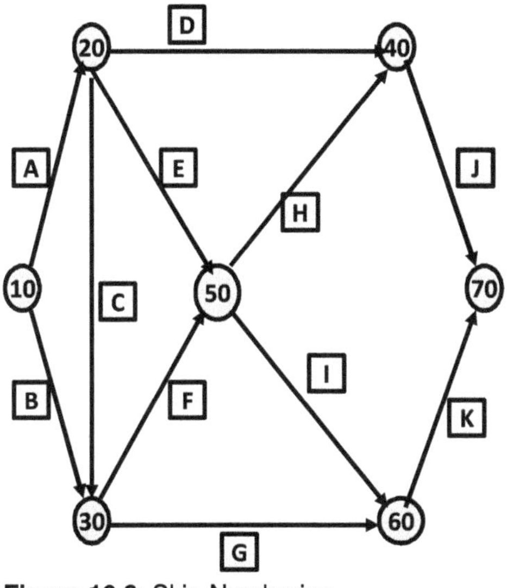

- This is not suitable when project is complex and when extra jobs have to be inserted.
- Extra job often mean extra event; when extra event was introduced, all the events following it must be renumbered.
- One way to overcome this difficulty is to use skip numbering ie., Instead of giving serial numbers 1, 2, 3 …., we use numbering in tens like 10 for the first event, 20 for the second event and so on, so that extra events if included can numbered as 12, 15, 17, 19 etc.

Figure 10.8: Skip Numbering.

Procedure to Number the Events

Fulkerson's Rule

- ☆ First identify the initial event and number it as '1' (Figure 10.9). An initial event is an event, which has arrows emerging out of it and none entering into it.
- ☆ Now delete all the arrows emerging out of that event already numbered and this will create at least one new initial event with no other arrows entering into it. If more than one initial events are created, then according to the priority assign the number.

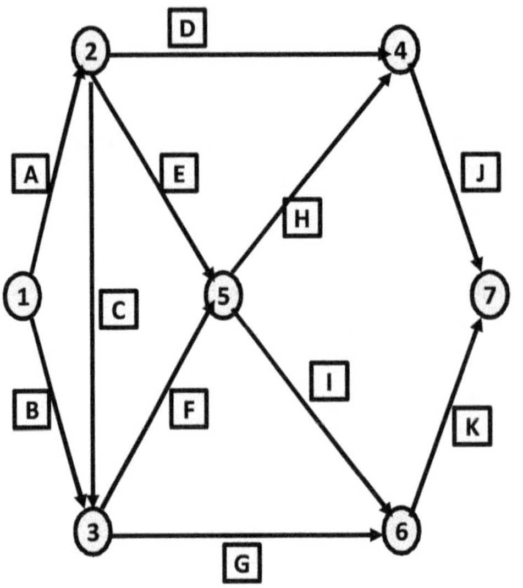

Initial event 1 is identified, as there are no incoming arrows into it

- Delete the arrows A and B. This will create one more initial event 2
- Again delete the arrows from 2 ie., C, D and E from event 2, and this will create new event 3.
- Again delete the arrows from event 3 ie., G and F and this will create new initial event 5.
- From event 5, delete H & I arrows, this will create two new initial events 4 & 6.
- Again delete J & K arrows from 4 and 6 events, and it leads to new initial event 7, which is the terminating/end event, because no arrows emerge out of it.

This sequential numbering system is convenient when project is simple & small with less number of activities.

Figure 10.9: Fulkerson's Rule.

- ☆ This procedure is continued till a final event is identified and numbered. Final event is an event, which has no arrows emerging out of it.

b. Computation of EST and EFT; LST and LFT to Identify Critical Path

- ☆ The EST is calculated first in the forward pass beginning from the start event (Table 10.9).
- ☆ For the start event, the EST is always set to zero because, there is no preceding event.
- ☆ The EST at the last event is generally considered to be the project duration *i.e.*, the minimum time required for project completion (longest duration equal to critical path duration).
- ☆ EST and LST are equal at the end event.
- ☆ LST for events is calculated through backward pass starting from the end event.

Table 10.9: Steps involved in computation EST and LST

EST	*LST*
Through forward pass *i.e.*, from first event	Through backward pass, *i.e.*, from last event
Calculation begins from start event	Calculation stars from end event
Proceeds from left to right	Proceeds from right to left
At start event, EST is Zero	At end event, LST equals to EST
Adding the activity time to EST	Subtracting the activity time from LST
At a merge event, take maximum value	At a burst event, take minimum value

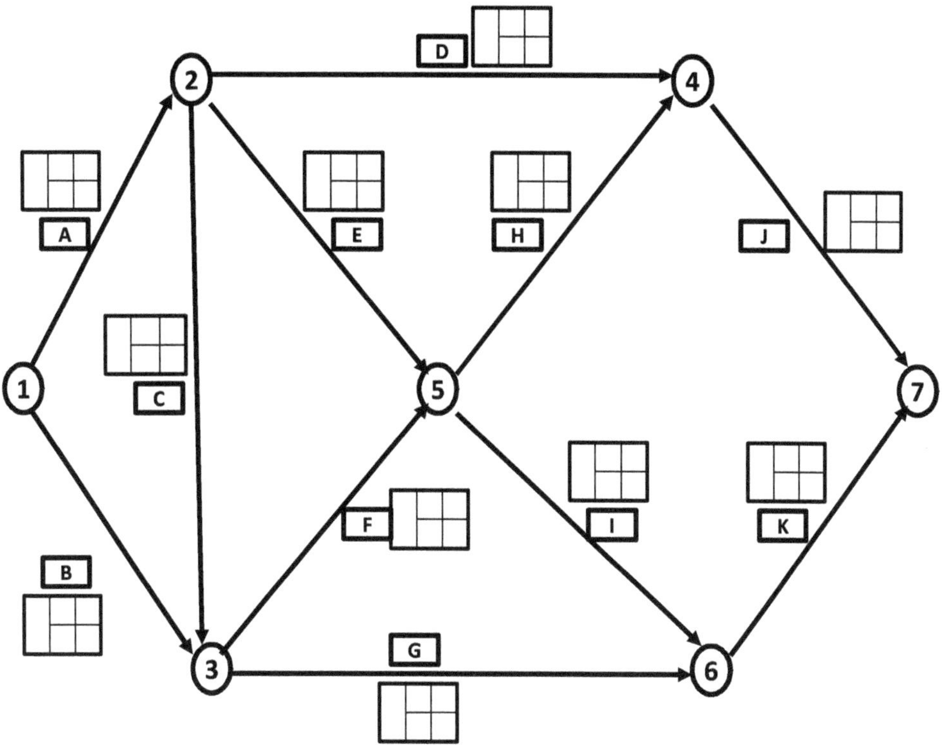

Figure 10.10: Outline of a Network Diagram.

Table 10.10: Computation of T_E for different Activities (PERT)

Activity	*Preceding Activity*	*Optimistic Time (O)*	*Most likely Time (M)*	*Pessimistic Time (P)*	*Expected Time (T_E) (O+4M+P)/6*
A	--	4	6	8	6
B	--	1	4.5	5	4
C	A	3	3	3	3
D	A	4	5	6	5
E	A	0.5	1	1.5	1
F	B,C	3	4	5	4
G	B,C	1	1.5	5	2
H	E,F	5	6	7	6
I	E,F	2	5	8	5
J	D,H	2.5	2.75	4.5	3
K	G,I	3	5	7	5

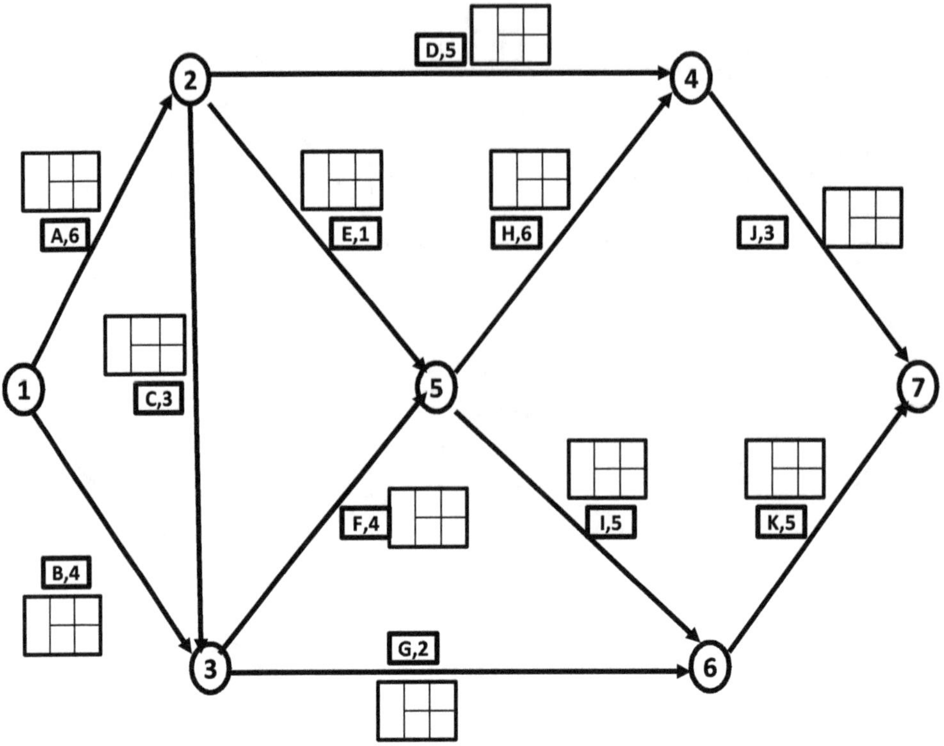

Figure 10.11: Network Diagram Showing Activities with their Respective TE.

Computation of EST and EFT

EST of an event = EST of preceding event + Activity duration

EFT of an event = EFT of preceding event + Activity duration

- ☆ EST at start activity is zero (Table 10.11 and Figure 10.12), because it is arising from the starting event and there is no preceding activity.
- ☆ To compute EFT at event number 2, add 6 to zero *i.e.*, the duration of activity A to zero. So, EST of activity A is 0 and EFT is 6. This 6 is the EST for activities C,D,E, because they arise from event 2.
- ☆ Compute EFT at event number 3, (merge event of B and C). Since, event 3 is a merge event of activities B and C, there are two EFT values *i.e.*, 4 and 9, (0+4 of Activity B and 6+3 of Activity C) and select MAXIMUM, *i.e.*, 9. This is the EST value for activities F and G, because they arise from event 3.
- ☆ Since, event 5 is also a merge event of activities E and F, there are two EFT values *i.e.*, 7 and 13, of E and F respectively and select MAXIMUM, *i.e.*, 13. This is the EST value for activities H and I because, they arise from event 5.
- ☆ Since, event 4 is also a merge event of activities D and H, there are two EFT values *i.e.*, 11 and 19, of D and H respectively and select MAXIMUM, *i.e.*, 19. This is the EST value for activity J because, it arise from event 4.

☆ Event 6 is also a merge event of activities G and I, there are two EFT values *i.e.*, 11 and 18, and select MAXIMUM, *i.e.*, 18. This is the EST value for activity K because, it arise from event 6.

☆ Event 7 is also a merge event of activities J and K, there are two EFT values *i.e.*, 22 and 23, and select MAXIMUM, *i.e.*, 23. Since event 7 is the end event of project, this EFT 23 is project's EFT.

Table 10.11: Computation of EST and EFT

Activity No.	*Activity Duration*	*EST*	*EFT*
A	6	0	6
B	4	0	4
C	3	6	9
D	5	6	11
E	1	6	7
F	4	9	13
G	2	9	11
H	6	13	19
I	5	13	18
J	3	19	22
K	5	18	23

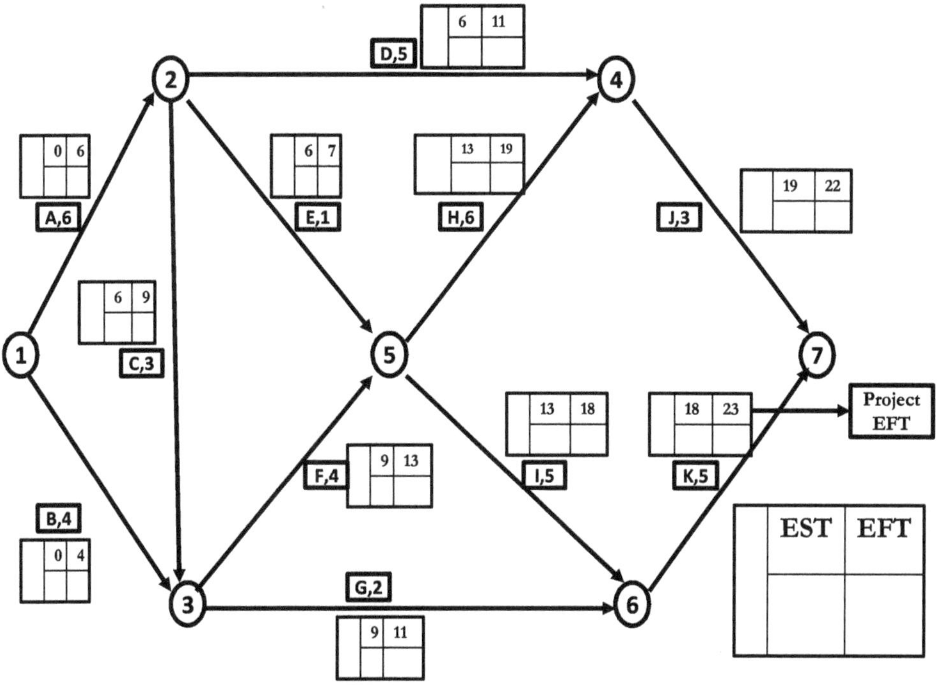

Figure 10.12: Network Diagram Showing Activities with their Respective TE, EST and EFT.

Computation of LST and LFT

LST of an event = LFT of succeeding event - Activity duration

(LST = LFT of 7th event – Activity duration)

LFT of an event = LST preceding activity + Activity duration

(LFT = LST of 6th event + Activity duration)

- ☆ To compute LST and LFT proceed from backward *i.e.,* from end event 7 (Table 10.12 and Figure 10.13). EFT of project is always equal to LFT because, project should get completed without any delay. *i.e.,* at the end event EFT = LFT
- ☆ For activities J and K, LFT is same because they leave the same event 7. LST = LFT – Activity duration *i.e.,* 20 and 18 for J and K respectively.
  - ❑ LST_J= 23-3=20, LST_K=23-5=18
- ☆ This LST 18 of K activity is the LFT for I and G activities, as they leave the same event 6.
  - ❑ LST_I= 18-5=13, LST_G=18-2=16
- ☆ The LST 20 of J activity is the LFT for D and H activities, as they leave the same event 4.
  - ❑ LST_D=20-5=15, LST_H=20-6=14
- ☆ Since event 5 is the burst event with respect to H and I activities, there will be two LST values *i.e.,* 14 and 13 for H and I activities respectively and select MINIMUM *i.e.,* 13. This forms the LFT for F and E activities leaving event 5.
- ☆ Calculate LST values for F and E *i.e.,* 9 and 12. LST_F=13-4=9, LST_E=13-1=12
- ☆ Since event 3 is the burst event with respect to F and G activities, there will be two LST values, *i.e.,* 9 and 16 for F and G activities respectively and select MINIMUM *i.e.,* 9. This forms the LFT for C and B activities leaving event 3. LST_C=9-3=6, LST_B=9-4=5.

Table 10.12: Computation of LST and LFT

Activity No.	*Activity Duration*	*LST*	*LFT*
A	6	0	6
B	4	5	9
C	3	6	9
D	5	15	20
E	1	12	13
F	4	9	13
G	2	16	18
H	6	14	20
I	5	13	18
J	3	20	23
K	5	18	23

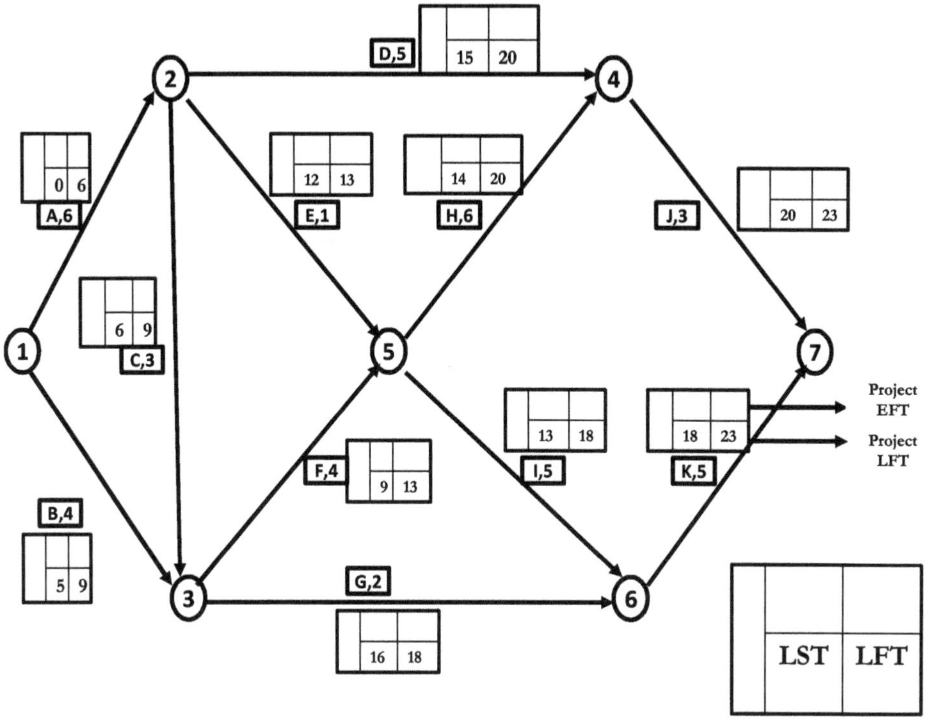

Figure 10.13: Network Diagram Showing Activities with their Respective TE , LST and LFT.

- Since event 2 is the burst event with respect to E, D and C activities, there will be three LST values *i.e.*, 12, 15 and 6 for E, D and C activities respectively and select MINIMUM *i.e.*, 6. This forms the LFT value for A activity leaving event 2.
- Calculate LST values for A and B *i.e.*, LST_A=6-6=0, LST_B=9-4=5.

Now, Table 10.13 and Figure 10.14 presents the overall picture about EST, EFT, LST and LFT of all the activities in the project.

Table 10.13: Computation of EST, EFT, LST and LFT

Activity No.	*EST*	*EFT*	*LST*	*LFT*
A	0	6	0	6
B	0	4	5	9
C	6	9	6	9
D	6	11	15	20
E	6	7	12	13
F	9	13	9	13
G	9	11	16	18

Contd...

Table 10.13–*Contd...*

Activity No.	*EST*	*EFT*	*LST*	*LFT*
H	13	19	14	20
I	13	18	13	18
J	19	22	20	23
K	18	23	18	23

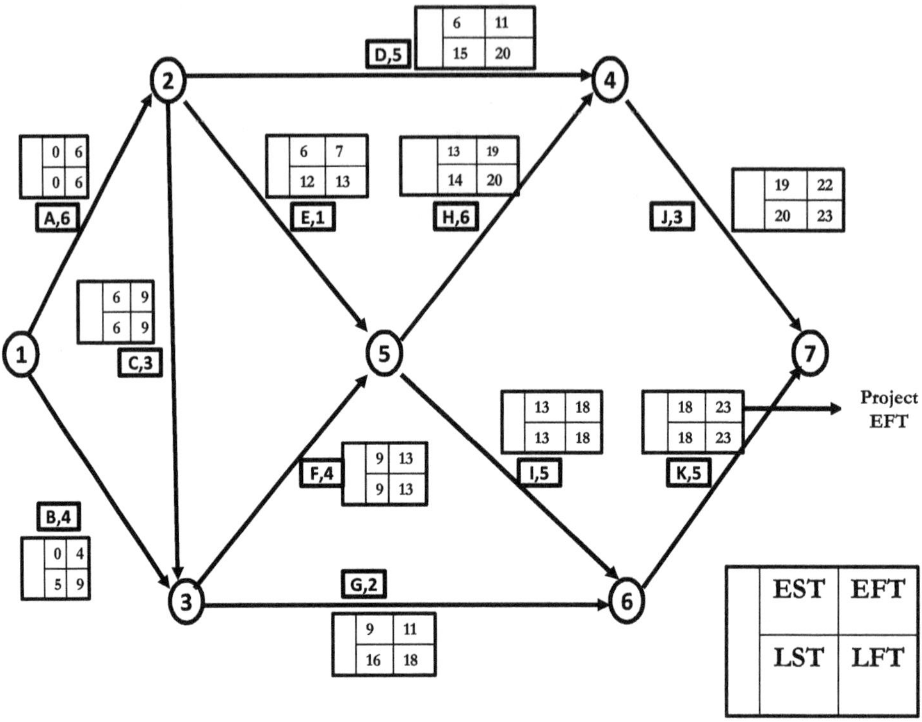

Figure 10.14: Network Diagram Showing Activities with their Respective TE , EST, EFT, LST and LFT.

c. Computation of Float/Slack/Cushion/Margin

Slack refers to the events and is used in PERT analysis. Float refers to activities and is used in CPM analysis. Slack/Float indicate the free/spare time associated with an event/activity. It is the time available for an activity in addition to its duration time. These are important for smoothening the resource utilization in a project. It is the length of time an activity can be delayed without delaying the entire project. When activities have no float time, it implies they cannot be delayed and if they are delayed, the project duration gets affected. On the critical path, there are critical activities and for these, float is zero. Since, float is zero, they must be completed in time otherwise, the total project duration will get affected. Since, every activity has different start and finishing times, there are 3 types of floats *viz.*, Total Float, Free Float and Independent Float.

- ☆ ***Total float:*** It is the amount of spare time available between completion of an activity and beginning of next activity or it is the amount of time that an event in a project network can be delayed without causing a delay to project or it is the difference between maximum time available to perform the activity and activity duration. Total Slack/Float = LST – EST = LFT – EFT
- ☆ ***Free float:*** It is the time by which an activity may be delayed or extended without delaying the start of any succeeding activity or it is the portion of total float within which an activity can be manipulated without affecting the floats of the subsequent activities.

  Free Float = EST of succeeding activity – EFT of the activity for which free float is to be calculated

  Free float = LFT – EFT for the activity

  Free float = Total float – Head event float

  Free float is found at merge events. If an activity has free float, the resources from such activity can be re-allocated to an activity on the critical path. In this way total resources and project time may remain unaffected. For dummy activity, free float will be shown as zero, even if it works out as positive value.
- ☆ ***Independent float:*** It is that portion of total float within which an activity can be delayed for start without affecting the floats of the preceding activities.

  Independent Float = EST of succeeding activity – LFT of preceding activity – Duration of the activity for which independent float is to be calculated

  Independent Float = Free float – Tail event slack

  If independent float is negative, it may be taken as zero

  So, Total Float > Free float > Independent float

  Considering the above formulae, Total Float, Free float and Independent float are calculated for all the activities and are are shown through Table 10.14 and Figure 10.15.

d. Identification of Critical Activities

Critical activities are those activities, which determine the overall duration of the project. The critical activities of the project are identified by the total slack or total float *i.e.*, the difference between LST and EST or LFT – EFT. For critical activities, this total float is zero *i.e.*, the value of LST and EST or LFT and EFT are equal. For these critical activities, there should not be any delay in the execution and completion, as they form the critical path of the project *i.e.*, these activities must be completed in time as per their activity duration. If any critical activity is delayed, it will affect the entire project thereby, entire project gets delayed. In the earlier table for activities A, C, F, I and K, the Total slack or Float is zero implying these activities are critical activities. Sometimes, critical activities are also mentioned in terms of events *i.e.*, 1,2,3,5,6 and 7

Table 10.14: Computation of different Types of Slacks/Floats

Activity (A)	*Preceeding Activity (B)*	*Time (Te) (C)*	*EST (D)*	*EFT (E)*	*LST (F)*	*LFT (G)*	*Total Slack/ Float*	*Free Float*	*Independent Float*
A	—-	6	0	6	0	6	0*	6-6=0	6-0-6=0
B	—-	4	0	4	5	9	5	9-4=5	9-0-4=5
C	A	3	6	9	6	9	0*	9-9=0	9-6-3=0
D	A	5	6	11	15	20	9	19-11=8	19-6-5=8
E	A	1	6	7	12	13	6	13-7=6	13-6-1=6
F	B,C	4	9	13	9	13	0*	13-13=0	13-9-4=0
G	B,C	2	9	11	16	18	7	18-11=7	18-9-2=0
H	E,F	6	13	19	14	20	1	19-19=0	19-13-6=0
I	E,F	5	13	18	13	18	0*	18-18=0	18-13-5=0
J	D,H	3	19	22	20	23	1	0	0-20-3=0
K	G,I	5	18	23	18	23	0*	0	0-18-5=0

Total float = LST – EST (or) LFT – EFT.

Free Float = EST of succeeding activity – EFT of the activity for which free float is to be calculated.

Independent float = EST of succeeding activity – LFT of preceeding activity – Activity duration for which IF is to be calculated.

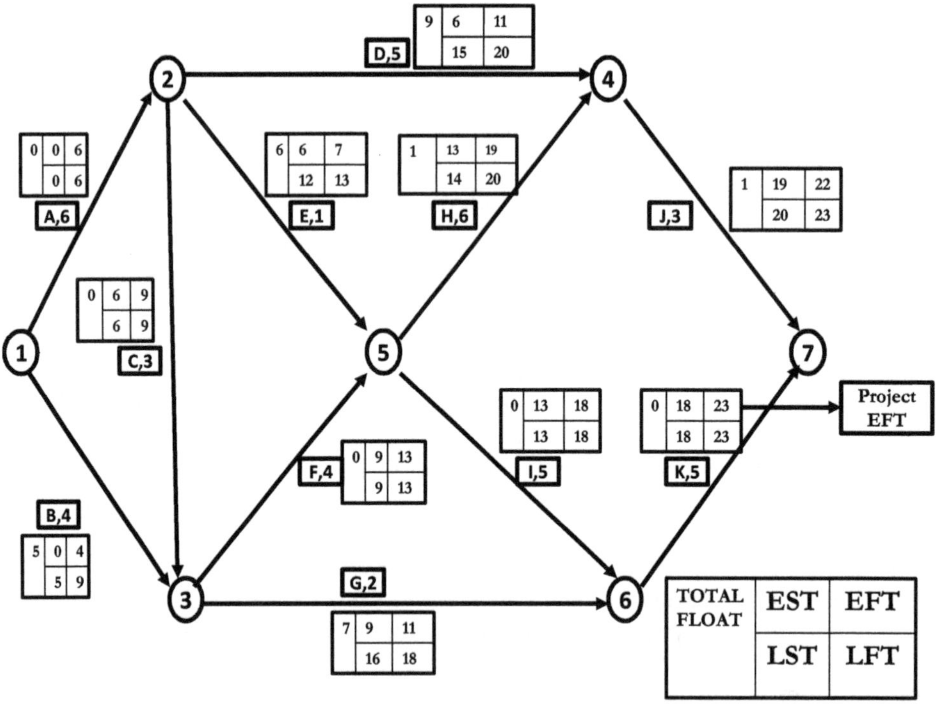

Figure 10.15: Network Diagram Showing Activities with their Respective TE , EST, EFT, LST, LFT and Total Float.

events are critical events. In the Table 10.15, for activities A,C,F,I and K, the total float is zero and hence, A,C,F,I and K represent critical activities for the project. In terms of events, 1,2,3,5,6 and 7 are the critical events (Figure 10.16).

Table 10.15: Identification of Critical Activities

Activity	*EST*	*EFT*	*LST*	*LFT*	*Total Slack/ Total Float (LST-EST) = (LFT-EFT)*	*Critical Activity*
A	0	**6**	0	6	**0***	**Critical**
B	0	**4**	5	9	5	
C	6	**9**	6	9	**0***	**Critical**
D	6	**11**	15	20	9	
E	6	**7**	12	13	6	
F	9	**13**	9	13	**0***	**Critical**
G	9	**11**	16	18	7	
H	13	**19**	14	20	1	
I	13	**18**	13	18	**0***	**Critical**
J	19	**22**	20	23	1	
K	18	**23**	18	23	**0***	**Critical**

A – C – F – I – K are the critical activities. (1,2,3,5,6,7 events).

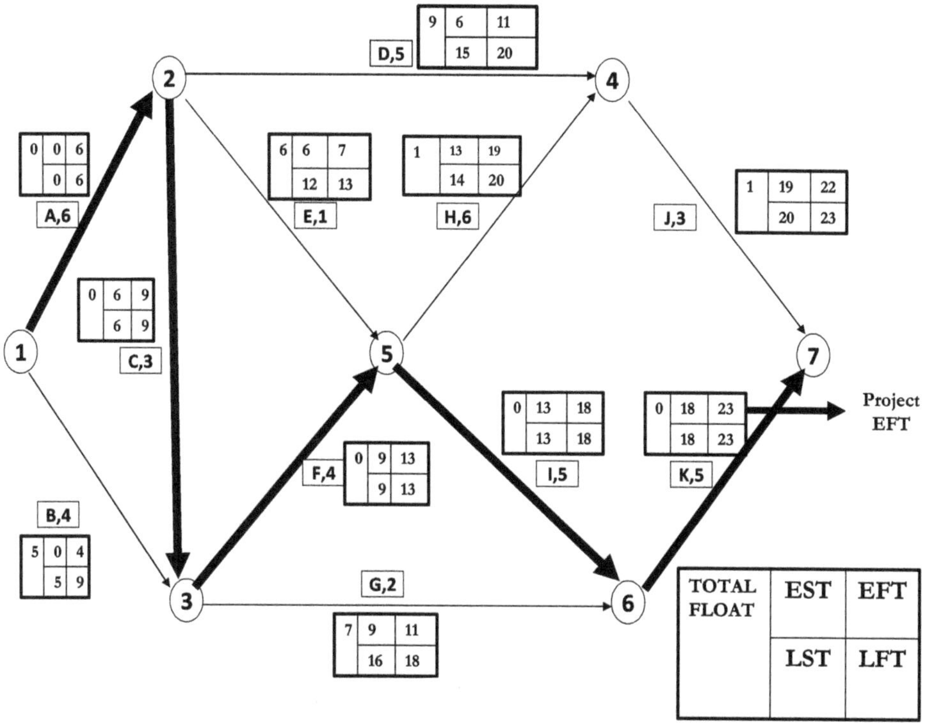

Figure 10.16: Network Diagram Showing Critical Activities (A,C,F,I and K) in the Project.

e. Identification of Critical Path and Duration

The critical path is the chain of critical activities in a network from start to end *i.e.*, the path joining all the critical events. It is also the longest path from start to end of the project network. Comparing all the possible path lengths, we can identify the critical path (Flow diagram - Figure 10.8 with longest duration).

So, if we connect all the critical activities in a network from start to end of the project, it implies critical path. So, critical path indicates the longest duration of the project and it is the minimum time required for the project from start to end *i.e.*, for its completion.

- ☆ Instead of working out EST, LST, EFT, LFT and total float for different activities of the project, critical path can also be find out by comparing all possible path lengths from start to end taking the activity duration into consideration and this information is available from the flow diagram (Figure 10.6).
- ☆ Since, A-C-F-I-K path denotes highest duration of 23 weeks, so A-C-F-I-K represent critical path of the project (Table 10.16).

Table 10.16: Identification of Critical Path and Critical Activities from Flow Diagram (Figure 10.6)

Sl.No.	*Path*	*Duration (Weeks)*
1.	A – D - J	6+5+3 = 14
2.	B – G – K	4+2+5 = 11
3.	A – C – F – I – K	6+3+4+5+5 = 23
4.	A – C – G - K	6+3+2+5 = 16
5.	A – E – I - K	6+1+5+5 = 17
6.	A – E – H - J	6+1+6+3 = 16
7.	A – C – F – H - J	6+3+4+6+3 = 22

It is clear that,

- ☆ The critical path time is the longest duration of the project. It is the minimum time required for the project for its completion.
- ☆ The critical path is denoted by denoting the critical activities on the path (A – C – F – I – K).
- ☆ The critical path of the project is denoted in terms of the event numbers (1-2 – 3 – 5 – 6 - 7).
- ☆ It is quite possible that, a project can have multiple critical paths. In such case, the duration of all the critical paths will be equal.

Importance of Critical Path

- ☆ Since there is no total slack or total float for any critical activity on the critical path, any delay in the execution of critical activity will delay the project. If any critical activity is delayed, it should be recovered during the downstream critical activities of the project and this is possible by increasing the resource usage on the downstream critical activities by resorting to project crashing.

- ☆ Since, the execution of critical activities on time is essential for the project, these activities must receive a hard look or a special attention from the project manager to complete them in right time.
- ☆ By identifying critical activities or critical path in advance, it will help the project manager to plan his resource procurement in advance for the execution of these critical activities.
- ☆ If the project manager wants to reduce total duration of the project, it is sufficient for him to concentrate only on critical activities towards going for project crashing and non critical activities need not be addressed for project crashing.

f. Estimation of Variance of Critical Activities

From the given time periods, employ the formula: Variance T_E (σ^2) = $[(P\text{-}O)/6]^2$ to compute variances of the project activities (Table 10.17).

Table 10.17: Estimation of Variance of Activities

Activity	*Preceding Activity*	*Optimistic Time (O)*	*Most Likely Time (M)*	*Pessimistic Time (P)*	*Expected Time (Te) (O+4M+P)/6*	*Variance TE (σ2) = [(P-O)/6]2*
A	—-	4	6	8	**6**	**0.444***
B	—-	1	4.5	5	**4**	**0.444**
C	A	3	3	3	**3**	**0.000***
D	A	4	5	6	**5**	**0.111**
E	A	0.5	1	1.5	**1**	**0.028**
F	B,C	3	4	5	**4**	**0.111***
G	B,C	1	1.5	5	**2**	**0.444**
H	E,F	5	6	7	**6**	**0.111**
I	E,F	2	5	8	**5**	**1.000***
J	D,H	2.5	2.75	4.5	**3**	**0.111**
K	G,I	3	5	7	**5**	**0.444***

* - Variances of critical activities.

Duration of Critical path : A – C – F – I - K (EVENTS: 1-2-3-5-6-7) = 23 weeks.

g. Estimation of the Probability for Completion of the Project in Right Time

After computing the EST, EFT, LST, LFT, Float, identification of critical activities, critical path *etc.*, then the question arises on the part of project manager, what is the probability of completing the project (*i.e.*, activities on critical path) in right time? This is because, completion of critical activities in right time is very important, as for these activities, float is zero and their duration influences the entire project duration. We already know that, in PERT, we generally assume 3 time periods *i.e.*, optimistic, most likely and pessimistic and based on these, we compute expected time (T_E) for each activity by using the following formula: $T_E = (O+4M+P)/6$.

For example, in the given Table 10.17 for activity A, which is a critical activity, the estimated activity duration is 6 weeks (T_E). But, the probability of completing this activity A in 6 weeks is only 50 per cent. This is so because, the estimated time for any activity *i.e.*, T_E will divide the area under normal distribution curve into two equal halves indicating that, probability of completing that activity in right time (T_E) is 50 per cent only. This is shown through the Panel A of Figure 10.17.

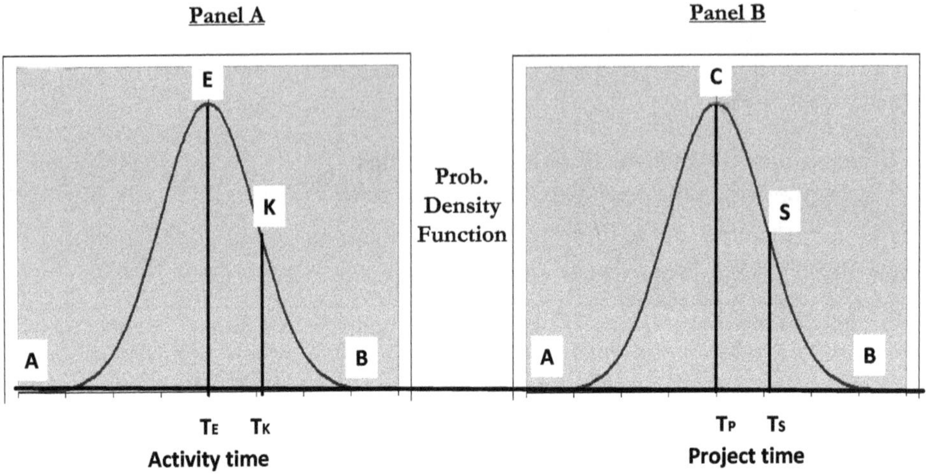

$$P(T_K) = \frac{\text{Area under AEK}}{\text{Area under AEB}} \qquad P(T_S) = \frac{\text{Area under ACS}}{\text{Area under ACB}}$$

Figure 10.17: Probability for the Completion of Activities and Project.

If the activity is completed in T_K period instead of T_E period, then the probability of completing the activity in T_K period is given by

$P(T_K) = (\text{Area under AEK})/(\text{Area under AEB})$

In a project, there will be number of activities and each activity acts as an independent random variable. Hence, we have to work out probabilities for each and every critical activity. Since, all the critical activities influence project duration, the entire project duration can also be considered as an independent variable. So, we have to work out the probability for the entire project duration also.

Let us suppose, project takes T_P time period for its completion (23 weeks in this example). If the project is to be completed in T_S time period, the probability of completing the project in that time period T_S can be known in advance from the following graph (Panel B of Figure 10.17.) *i.e.*, given by:

$P(T_S) = (\text{Area under ACS})/(\text{Area under ACB})$

The P(Ts) value depends upon the location of Ts. Taking T_P as the reference point, the distance T_P and T_S can be expressed in terms of Standard Deviation (SD). To calculate the SD for the entire project's critical path, follow the given procedure here under.

Step 1:- First, we have to work out the variance for each and every critical activity (Table 10.20) by employing the formula as given earlier *i.e.*, Variance T_E (σ^2) = $[(P-O)/6]^2$

Step 2: Work out the variance for the entire critical path by summating the variances of all the critical activities in the critical path. That is, variance of critical path = $\Sigma\sigma i^2$, where i=1 to n representing only critical activities.

Variance of all critical activities on critical path = $V_A + V_C + V_F + V_I + V_K = 1.9999$

Step 3: Compute SD for the critical path.

SD of critical path (σ) = √Sum of the variances of all the critical activities on the critical path

$$= \sqrt{\Sigma\sigma_i^2}$$

So, SD for the critical path = $\sqrt{(1.999 \approx 2)} = 1.414$

For the normal distribution curve, the SD is always equal to 1. So the above calculated SD value for the entire critical path can be taken as scale factor to study the normal deviate (Z) based on which, we assess the probability of completing the project (Table 10.18).

Normal deviate (Z) = $[(E-S)/\sigma]$

Where, E = Expected days of completion, S = Scheduled days of completion (*i.e.*, critical path duration in days), σ = S.D.

- ☆ If the Z value is +ve, it implies, the probability of completion of project by scheduled date is more than 50 per cent.
- ☆ If the Z value is -ve, it implies, the probability of completion of project by scheduled date is less than 50 per cent.
- ☆ If the Z value is zero, it implies that, the expected date of completion of project and scheduled date of completion of project are same *i.e.*, the probability of completion of project by scheduled date is 50 per cent. That is, this will happen when expected and scheduled dates of completion are equal.

Table 10.18: Probability for Completion of the Project

Specified Weeks (T_P)	*Z Value [(E-S)/σ]*	*Probability (From area under normal curve)*
20	Z =(20-23)/1.414 = -2.1216	=0.5-0.4830=0.017 = 1.7 per cent
22	Z =(22-23)/1.414 = -0.7072	=0.5-0.2612=0.2388=24 per cent
23	Z =(23-23)/1.414 = 0	=0.5=50 per cent
24	Z =(24-23)/1.414 = 0.7072	=0.5+0.2612=0.7612=76 per cent
25	Z =(25-23)/1.414= 1.4144	0.5+0.4207=0.9207=92 per cent

Let us study the possibility of completion of project in different weeks. From the Table 10.18, it is clear that, the project completion within 23 weeks is impossible. It will be completed in 23 weeks with probability of 50 percent. The project will however be completed in 25 weeks with certainty (P= 92 per cent) and in 24 weeks with certainty (P = 76 per cent). The same is shown through Figure 10.17.1.

$$Z = \left(\frac{25 \text{ weeks } - 23 \text{ weeks}}{1.414} \right) = 1.414$$

Area left of Y-axis = 050

Z	.00	.01	.02
0.0	.5000	.5040	.5080
:	:	:	:
1.4	.9192	.9207	.9222
1.5	.9332	.9345	.9357

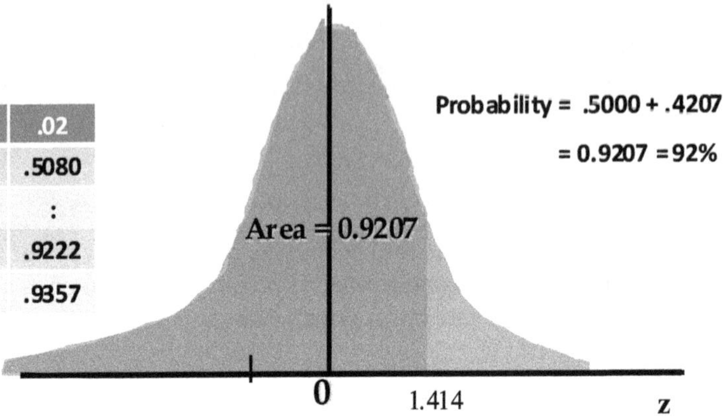

Figure 10.17.1: Probability of Completion of Project by 25 Weeks.

vii. Project Crashing and Fast Tracking

We know, there are two techniques in project management *viz.*, CPM and PERT. Among these two, CPM is a deterministic tool, where we generally assume only one time period for the completion of an activity. However, PERT is a probabilistic tool in which three different time periods are assumed and based on their weighted average, we compute T_E estimated time. Among these two techniques, CPM is a very useful tool because, it will take only one time period for the project activity and also helps to analyze the critical path of the project based on which, cost estimation can be done easily for the overall completion of the project. Generally, when the cost control outweighs the time control, CPM is the best tool. But, when time control outweighs the cost control of the project, PERT is the suitable tool. Sometimes when the selected project is running behind schedule, the project manager has to decide whether to go for 'project crashing' or 'fast tracking'. Before understanding these concepts, let's evaluate the factors, which force the management to speed-up project execution midway:

- ☆ While doing project planning, the project planners don't take into account various predictable/unpredictable risks thereby, initial time allotted to different activities in the project are too 'optimistic', but the ground realities are 'pessimistic'.

- Due to some unavoidable reasons say, non-availability of inputs, labour *etc.*, in time, the project may run behind schedule and hence, the project manager needs to complete it on time.
- Market demands the product from the project at an earlier date than expected. This demand forces the project manager to speed-up the project in order to fulfill the requirements of the market.

i. Project Crashing

As mentioned earlier, project crashing refers to the process by which duration of project is reduced by increasing the amount of resources allocated. Thus, project crashing involves time-cost tradeoffs. It is important to note that, crashing is done only to critical activities. This can be achieved by any of the following ways:

- Increasing the resource use efficiency of the current resources.
- Bringing in new additional resources to speed up the processes.
- By evaluating alternatives available and analyzing them in order to find, which one will help in compressing the duration with lowest cost.

Note that, while allocating resources to critical activities, one needs to take into consideration the slack available in non-critical activities. This will help to make sure that, crashing will not effect other activities of the project nor the project's scope. Crash cost also needs to be taken into consideration and it shouldn't be more than the penalty cost.

ii. Fast-tracking

This is another technique used in project management to compress the schedule. In fast tracking, activities that were planned to be performed in sequential order are rescheduled to be performed in parallel or partially in parallel. Examples include:

- Split long tasks into smaller chunks to squeeze more work into a shorter period of time.
- Reduce lag times between tasks.
- Reduce the scope to eliminate less important tasks.

This fast-tracking in project management, just like crashing, may lead to increase in costs and risks. Usually, the thumb rule followed by project managers while fast tracking, is to fast track the subsequent (2nd) activity after completion of 66 percent of scheduled (1st) activity.

Finally, sometimes, the best method is some combination of resource addition (project crashing) and re-schedule of activity alteration (fast-tracking). Let us now discuss in-detail about project crashing through considering an example, as it helps the students for easier understanding. Before going into the explanation note the following guidelines for crashing of the project:

- Crash only activities that are critical.
- Crash from the least expensive to most expensive.
- Crash an activity only until:

- It reaches its maximum time reduction.
- It causes another path to also become critical.
- It becomes more expensive to crash than not to crash.

The above discussion infers that, if the project manager wishes to complete the project at an earlier time than the critical path duration, he has to complete the activities at a faster pace. Generally, the project manager will concentrate only on critical activities lying on the critical path, if he wishes to reduce the duration of the project. This is because, the critical activities on the critical path represent the longest duration the project. To complete a critical activity at a faster pace, it is essential on the part of project manager to increase the level of resource usage regarding the execution of the critical activity. This process of reducing the time duration for completion of a critical activity by increasing resource usage is called Project crashing. So, in project crashing, non-critical activities are not considered. This is so because, these non critical activities do not represent the critical path duration. Even if their duration is crashed by using more of resources, critical path duration will not change and hence, it simply increases the cost of the project. Except for the fixed duration activities like crop duration, gestation period *etc.*, which cannot be altered, the project manager generally lay emphasis on critical activities only, to reduce the duration of the project by increasing the resource usage. In project crashing, there are two types of costs involved:

- ***Direct Cost:*** For these costs, there exists inverse relationship between cost expenditure and time of completion of an activity (Figure 10.18). That means, for the activities to be completed in short period of time, the resource usage or cost expenditure should be increased. Examples include: material cost, labour cost *etc.*
- ***Indirect Cost:*** These are the costs associated with the project and not with the activities. Examples include, payment of salaries for employees, depreciation on machinery, general administrative over head cost *etc.* For these indirect costs, there exists a direct relationship between cost expenditure and time of activity (Figure 10.18).

iii. Procedure for Project Crashing

Step 1: A preliminary project schedule is generated showing all the activities of the project along with their preceding activities, normal duration of each activity, normal costs incurred if the activities are completed as per their normal duration. From this, draw a network diagram, identify critical path and critical activities (Table 10.19 and Figure 10.19) as discussed earlier.

Step 2: Computation of cost slope, for each activity.

Cost slope = Cost/Time = (Crash cost – Normal cost)/(Normal time- Crash time)

Step 3: Identify the activity on the critical path for which cost slope is lowest and crash that activity first and follow the same in ascending order.

In the process of crashing the critical activity, the duration of that activity will be reduced so that, the entire critical path duration will be reduced. So, other paths having duration more than the original path after crashing the activity on the original

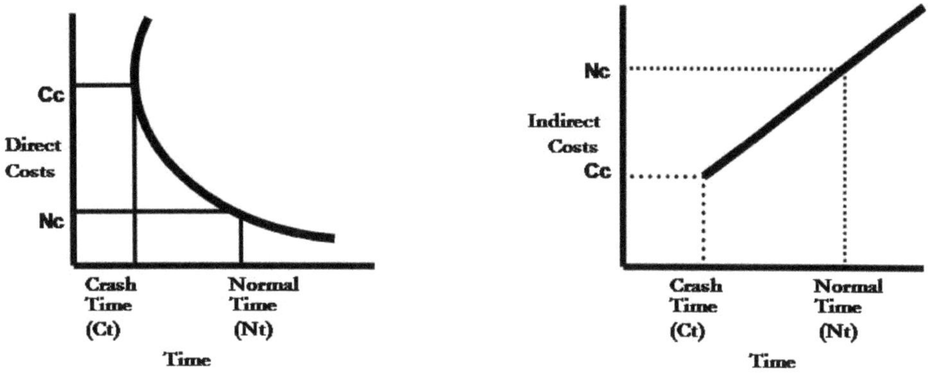

Direct costs **Indirect costs**

Figure 10.18: Direct and Indirect Costs in a Project.

Table 10.19: Project's Precedence Table Along with Activities Duration and Normal Costs

Activity	*Symbol*	*Preceding Activity*	*Normal Duration (Weeks)*	*Normal Costs*
Leveling the land	A	—	**16**	**36000**
Stone pitching	B	A	**26**	**27000**
Raising seedling	C	A	**26**	**8000**
Establishment of irrigation system	D	A	**30**	**135000**
Development of drainage system	E	C	**28**	**20000**
Making pits & transplantation	F	B	**27**	**12000**
Erection of fencing	G	D,E,F	**18**	**35000**

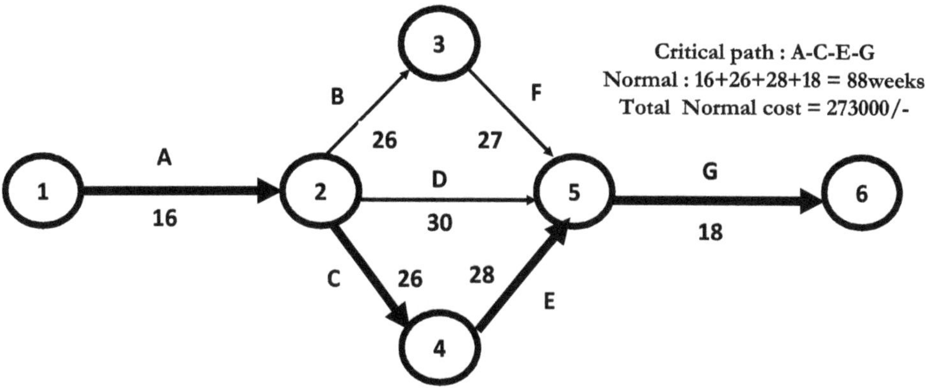

Figure 10.19: Critical Activities in a Project.

path will now become the critical path. So, due to the creation of new critical path, it implies that, the activities which are non-critical earlier will turn to critical activities. This new critical path will be crashed in the similar way by identifying an activity with low cost slope.

Step 4: If there are parallel critical paths in a project, then identify one activity each with low cost slope from each critical path and they have to be crashed at the same time.

This procedure is continued till no further crashing is possible in the project or depending upon the money resources available with the project manager.

In the above example (Figure 10.19), four critical activities are identified A-C-E-G on a critical path with duration of 88 weeks. The total normal cost of the project is Rs.2,73,000/-. Since, A-C-E-G are the critical activities, we have to consider one of the activities with lowest cost slope for project crashing. Among these four activities A-C-E-G, activity C is having low cost slope (Table 10.20) and hence, it has to be considered first for crashing. Since cost slope is Rs.180/week, this activity C is crashed for 5 weeks. So, total cost increased in the project is 5x180=Rs.900/-. So, the crash cost of activity C is increased from Rs.8000/- to Rs.8900/- and hence, the project is crashed from 26 weeks to 21 weeks. So, due to project crashing of C activity, the total cost of project is increased from 2,73,000 + 900 =2,73,900/-.

Table 10.20: Project crashing – Estimation of Cost Slope Across Activities

Activity	*Time (Weeks)*		*Cost (Rs./-)*		*Reduction in Time (Weeks)*	*Increase in Cost (Rs./-)*	*Cost Slope (Rs./week)*
	Normal	*Crash*	*Normal*	*Crash*			
A	16	11	36000	38000	5	2000	400
B	26	18	27000	33000	8	6000	750
C	26	21	8000	8900	5	900	180
D	30	23	135000	138570	7	3570	510
E	28	20	20000	22400	8	2400	300
F	27	23	12000	13700	4	1700	425
G	18	12	35000	36500	6	1500	250
	Total			273000	291070	43	18070

So, with the crashing of C activity, the total critical path duration has changed from 88 weeks - 5 weeks = 83 weeks. So, with the fall in critical path duration from 88 weeks to 83 weeks, A-B-F-G path with duration of 87 weeks now becomes the critical path (Figure 10.20). So, B and F activities, which are non-critical earlier, now turn to critical activities. This analysis further implies that, when C activity was crashed by 5 weeks in a critical path A-C-E-G, the total critical path duration was decreased by only one week *i.e.,* on new A-B -F-G critical path (87 weeks). That means, crashing of one activity by means of certain duration will not reduce the critical path duration by the same extent.

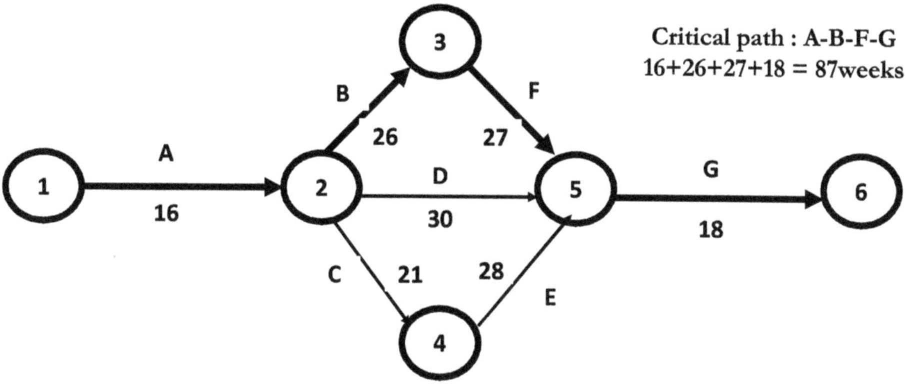

Figure 10.20: New Critical Path ABFG after Crashing C Activity.

Thus, so, in the new critical path A-B-F-G, activity G is with low cost slope *i.e.,* Rs. 250/week and it is crashed for 6 weeks. So, total extra cost incurred in the project is 6x250 = Rs.1500/- and hence, the crash cost of activity G is Rs.36,500/- increased from a normal cost of Rs.35,000/-. So, activity duration is reduced to 12 weeks from 18 weeks. Now, by crashing G activity by 6 weeks in A-B-F-G path, the critical path duration is reduced to 81 weeks.

Again a network diagram has to be drawn, compare different path lengths, identify critical path, identify activity with low cost slope, crash the same, estimate the increase in cost and reduction in time period of activity. This procedure is continued till a stage is reached, where no further crashing is possible or depending upon the available funds with the project manager. If this crashing activity is still continued in the project, the findings are shown through the Table 10.21.

Table 10.21: Project Crashing – Cumulative Reduction in Project Duration

Crashed Activity	*Crashed Time (Weeks)*	*Project Duration (Weeks)*			*Project Cost (Rs./-)*		
		Before Crashing	*After Crashing*	*Cumulative Reduction*	*Before Crashing*	*After Crashing*	*Cumulative Increase*
Normal		88			273000		
C	5	88	87	1 (1)	273000	273900	900
G	6	87	81	7 (6)	273900	275400	2400
A	5	81	76	12 (5)	275400	277400	4400
F	4	76	72	16 (4)	277400	279100	6100
E	8	72	72	16 (0)	279100	281500	8500
B	8	72	64	24 (8)	281500	287500	14500

Generally, a case will arise in a project, where there may be two or more critical paths simultaneously. If one activity is crashed on one critical path, it will not change the project duration because, there is another critical path with the previous duration. For example, as shown in the Table 10.21, after crashing F activity, there are two critical paths A-B F-G and A-C-E-G. If we crash activity E by 8 weeks, there is no reduction in project duration because, A-B-F-G- still remains as the critical path duration. So, from the Table 10.24, it is clear that, the project can be finally crashed by 24 weeks by incurring an additional expenditure of Rs.14,500/-.

So, finally project crashing implies, time cost trade off. The decision up to which the project can be crashed mainly depends upon the resources available with the project manager.

Risks of Project Crashing in Project Management

Though project crashing ensures speedy completion of project than the given critical path duration, its execution also leads to the following risk factors that the project manager must be vigilant against them:

- Various external and internal factors may lead project manager to go for crashing, but it usually affects the quality of work as the time taken (besides cost) is the major issue on his mind.
- Using additional resources does not always guarantee better results.

11

Financing the Farm Business

It is a known fact that, in developing countries like India, the agriculture sector assumes significance for a variety of reasons. It is still a source of livelihood for a majority of people in rural areas and there is a need for ensuring sustainability in these livelihoods. Recent Population Census (2011) reveals that there are 18.20 crore cultivators and agricultural workers. It is noteworthy that, the agriculture/rural sector provide demand for industrial goods and in India whenever agriculture sector has grown at the annual rate of 3-4 percent; other sectors have shown healthy growth. In fact, the required growth of productivity in agriculture means that, more capital must be invested in it. Farmers' need much more capital than they can afford to save and small and marginal farmers with meager savings require a higher input of capital. Credit is a condition that enables a person to extend his control over his ownership of resources. Indian agriculturist is not only capital starved, but faces vagaries of nature too; irrigated agriculture is roughly 33 percent of total cropped area. Agriculture, thus is, a high- risk area. It is also observed that, investments requirements in Indian agriculture fluctuate as incremental output ratios have varied significantly. In fact, it is not only the availability of credit but also the access to adequate institutional credit that matters, since most of those who are engaged in agriculture belong to the marginal and small farmer categories.

11.1. Farm Finance and its Scope

Farm finance refers to providing finance to farm sector and it is otherwise called as 'Agricultural Finance'. The scope of farm or agricultural finance varies from the 'micro concept', which involves the financing the individual farm, to the 'macro concept', such as the examination of the agricultural sector's role in the entire economy.

Both concepts are important except that one is a subset of the other. For an instance, the study of a farmer's behaviour at the micro level, can be used as the basis to understand the determinants of macro-economic outcomes in the agricultural sector. In addition, analyzing the changes in the nation's economic and financial policies may influence other related sectors of the economy say, increasing use of manufactured farm inputs, external financing and off-farm employment of farm family members. Thus, agricultural finance deals with the financial, micro and macro aspects of a farm business in an economy. Following are the important definitions of Agricultural Finance:

Agricultural Finance is considered as a branch of Agricultural Economics that deals with the provision and management of bank services and financial resources related to individual farm units.

– *Tandon and Dhondeyal* (1991)

Agricultural Finance is an economic study of borrowing funds by farmers, the organization and operation of farm lending agencies and of society's interest in credit for agriculture.

– *Murray* (1953)

Agricultural Finance is the economic study of the acquisition and use of capital in agriculture. So, it deals with the demand for, and supply of funds in the agricultural sector of the economy

– (W.F Lee, 1980)

Agricultural Finance is the study of financial intermediaries who provide loanable funds for agricultural production and that of financial markets in which these intermediaries obtain their loanable funds.

– (Penson and Lins, 1990)

From the above definitions, we can broaden the view about 'agricultural finance' as, it involves the study of all economic and financial interface between agriculture and the rest of the macro economy ; including the effects that changes in the national economic policies could have on the economic performance of agriculture as well as the financial positions of individual farm families.

As mentioned above, the study of 'Agricultural Finance' varies in scope from the 'micro perspective' to 'macro perspective'. Micro finance refers to financial management of the individual farm business units. It is concerned with the study, as to how the individual farmer considers various sources of credit, quantum of credit to be borrowed from each source, how he allocates the same among the alternative uses in his farm, the rate of interest at which the loan amount was borrowed, repayment pattern followed by the farmer etc. It is also concerned with the future use of funds. Macro finance deals with different sources of raising funds for agriculture as a whole in the economy. It is also concerned with the lending procedure, rules, regulations, monitoring and controlling of different agricultural credit institutions. Hence macro-finance is related to financing of agriculture at aggregate level. Therefore, while micro-finance refers to the financial management of individual farm business and macro-finance deals with the aspects relating to total credit needs of the agricultural sector, the terms and conditions under which the credit is available and the method of use of total credit for the development of agriculture.

From the points of view of both these perspectives, aspects of the study (scope) under individual farm units include:

i. Financial Management at Farm or Micro Level

This has to do with taking various financial decisions on the farm. These decisions determine the rate at which any farm business can grow over time and are related to both Organizational decisions and Operational decisions.

a. Organizational Decisions

These are the financial decisions taken by the farmer, which involve huge capital investment for making permanent improvements on the farm and are taken less frequently. These decisions are related to purchase of machinery, lining of irrigation canals, improvement of drainage system on the farm etc. For effective decision making, it requires a comprehensive knowledge of financial accounting system on the part of the farmer. The decisions are important for sound financial Management. Farmer would need the knowledge of keeping farm financial records and accounts like the NWS, Income Statement, Cash Flow Statement etc. These decisions also provide information on the farm's financial position as well as the efficiency and profitability of farm operations. In taking these decisions, the farmer must be aware about the concepts of time value of money, present worth of future costs and returns (*i.e.*, about discounting and compounding methods), project planning and appraisal for investment decision making etc.

b. Operational Decisions

These are the financial decisions taken by the farmer, which involve less capital investment for meeting day-to-day operations on the farm and are taken more frequently. These decisions are related to purchase of seeds, fertilizers, pesticides, engaging hired labour etc. Thus, these decisions mainly involve identification of the input-output combinations for maximization of goals like minimization of costs, maximization of profits and optimization of output in the production programme.

The nature and the number of financial decisions taken on the farm with reference to both organizational and operational aspects depends upon the following factors:

- ☆ ***Frequency:*** Frequency refers to the number of times the farmer takes the financial decisions on the farm. It depends upon two factors *viz.*, size of land holding and number of enterprises practiced by the farmer. If the size of land holding is more and if the farmer practices more number of enterprises on the farm, the number of financial decisions will be more and vice versa.
- ☆ ***Risk involved:*** If more risk is involved in executing the financial decisions, more capital is needed by the farmer and thereby, he takes less number of decisions on the farm and vice versa.

- ☆ ***Imminence:*** It refers to taking sudden and urgent decisions on farm. If the farmer notices pest or disease incidence on a crop, he immediately resort to application of pesticides. On the other hand, if a farmer wants to dig a bore well or lining of irrigation canal, he will take action rather slowly. That means, depending upon the urgency of operation on the farm, the financial decisions vary in their importance.
- ☆ ***Revocability:*** It means reversing or changing the financial decisions taken on the farm by the farmer. If the farmer feels a pesticide is ineffective against a pest, immediately he will change the pesticide. On the other hand, if the farmer digs a bore well in the farm, he cannot revoke or change the decision. This implies, the decisions, which can be changed quickly demands less capital and the decision which can't be changed, demands more capital from the farmer.
- ☆ ***Number of alternative decisions available:*** If more number of alternatives is available for a particular decision, then the farmer takes the decision rather slowly for its final implementation. On the other hand, if no alternative are available for a decision, he will execute the decision straight away.

ii. Financial Management at Aggregate or Macro Level

This involve dealing with financial aspects of agriculture and are related to:

- ☆ Determination of aggregate investment and financing behaviours of farms
- ☆ Assessing demand for money in agricultural sector
- ☆ Growth of inventories in the farm sector
- ☆ Formulation of National Economic Policy Instruments like: interest rate ceiling; concessionary rates of interest for agricultural loans; policies on microcredit financing through the Micro-Finance Institutions (MFIs) etc.
- ☆ Effects of changes in agricultural finance policies

Above all, the scope of farm finance also deals with the criteria used for Investment selection such as, economic, financial technical, social analysis of farm business et; study about financial risks; legal considerations in investment and financing decisions etc.

11.2. Farm Finance (Credit) in Agricultural Development

The word 'Credit' is derived from a Latin word *'Credo'*, meaning 'I Believe' or 'To Trust'. The Latin verb *'Credere'* means 'to repose confidence in'. Credit is a function of ability to command capital or services currently, with a promise to repay it in future *i.e.*, obtaining certain amounts of money as loan to be rapid as specified in the Agreement between the concerned parties. This is often based on confidence in the borrowers' future solvency and repayment. So, credit means the ability to command other peoples' capital in return for a promise to repay at some specified time in future. It is therefore the combination of the 'ability to borrow' and 'willingness to borrow'. It can also be regarded as an economic good to be produced, managed and marketed. Credit also means the control over money, materials, goods or services in the present in exchange for a promise to repay at some future dates. This implies that, lenders forgo the use of money or its equivalent in the current time by making loans available or extending the credit to the borrower, who promises to repay on terms specified in the loans agreement or debt Instruments. Borrowers obtain resources (credit) to use for current production/consumption purposes before generating savings that could be used to repay the borrowed sum. The following are the definitions about 'credit' and 'agricultural credit':

Credit is an advance of money or its equivalent given by a lender to a borrower for repayment at maturity, which may range from a few days to several years.

Agricultural Credit encompasses all loans and advances granted to a borrower to finance activities relating to agriculture, fisheries, forestry and for processing and distribution of products resulting from these activities.

Agricultural Credit is an important instrument for channeling funds from savers to borrowers in amount necessary to finance production expenses and capital expenditures. With the increasing mechanization of agriculture, adoption of other modern technologies and increasing costs of the inputs required to carry out farming operations, the credit requirements are on the rise to fulfill his farm production and marketing obligations. Farmers need credit to expand their scales of operations and improve on the levels of technology, as accessibility has implications for technology adoption. For the agricultural sector to perform creditably well, credit is essential for the achievements of sound economic and social development, which the nation requires. In general, farmers with poor resource-base need money to purchase their farm requirements. This could be achieved through credit supply. In this context, the following points outline the importance of agricultural credit to the farm sector:

- ☆ Suitable credit delivery and collection system will facilitate the procurement of production needs of farmers.
- ☆ Credit is needed to break the persistent vicious cycle of poverty among farmers.
- ☆ Farmers need credit to practice commercial production.
- ☆ Farm finance assumes vital role in the agro – socio-economic development of the country both at macro and micro levels.
- ☆ Farm finance plays a catalytic role in strengthening the farm business and augmenting the productivity of scarce resources.
- ☆ Use of new technological inputs purchased through farm finance helps to increase the agricultural productivity.
- ☆ Accretion to in farm assets and farm supporting infrastructure provided by large scale financial investment activities results in increased farm income levels leading to increased standard of living of rural masses.
- ☆ Farm finance can also reduce the regional economic imbalances and is equally good at reducing the inter–farm asset and wealth variations.
- ☆ Farm finance is like a lever with both forward and backward linkages to the economic development at micro and macro level.

- ☆ Credit is a unique resource that provides the opportunity to use additional inputs and capital items in the present to pay for them from future earnings.
- ☆ For adoption of modern technologies, farmers need capital. It is known that, farmer's income is seasonal, while his working expenses are usually spread over time. However, farmers' inadequate savings require some credit be harnessed to meet the increasing capital requirements. In this context, credit is a resource that helps the farmer to meet his expenses throughout the agricultural year.
- ☆ Credit not only induce profitability of current economic activities, but also shifts production from subsistence to commercial and induce employment among those who lack basic necessities to engage in productive activities.
- ☆ If the farmer plans for credit in right time,
  - ❑ He can select the best possible enterprise/enterprise combination on the farm.
  - ❑ He can start the farm operation in time.
  - ❑ He can purchase and use good quality inputs for promoting quality agriculture.
  - ❑ It ensures efficient marketing of produce.
  - ❑ It enables the farmer to take more risk in agri-business for fetching higher returns.

11.3. Requisites of Good Credit System

The following are the essentials required for a good credit system:

- ☆ All types of loans *viz.*, short term, medium term and long term should be made available to the farmers.
- ☆ Credit should be provided at the door steps of the farmers as and when needed by the farmers.
- ☆ The credit amount should be adequate to the farmers for the enterprise(s) under consideration.
- ☆ The credit should be provided in time to the farmer.
- ☆ The credit should generate savings and accelerate economic growth.
- ☆ The credit provided to the farmers should enable the farmers to adopt modern technologies.
- ☆ Besides credit supply of farm inputs and services should be made available for the farmers.
- ☆ Besides giving loans to the farmers, prompt recovery of loans from farmers is important.
- ☆ For credit recovery from the farmers, production should be linked with marketing.
- ☆ It is necessary to charge low interests from the farmers.

11.4. Problems of Agricultural Credit System in India

Some of the major problems that hamper the flow of credit to agricultural sector in India include:

- ☆ Large scale illiteracy among farmers in India makes them less awareness about different types of financial institution offering credit at cheaper rates of interest.
- ☆ The resources available with the farmer are very low and hence, they could not show any security to financial institution for availing the loans. Due to sub-division and fragmentation of land holdings, the income from agriculture is very low and hence, the farmers can't repay the earlier loans taken. As a result, the financial institution couldn't give loans further.
- ☆ Due to poor transportation and communication facilities in rural areas, the banking institutions can't operate at the farmers' level.
- ☆ Due to more subsistence nature of farming, the farmer will not maintain any assets. So, they couldn't offer any sort of security to the banks for availing loans.
- ☆ Some of the farmers are diverting the loans from productive to unproductive purposes. This was mainly due to some pressing problems in their family.
- ☆ Non-institutional sources offer credit to the farmers both in terms of adequacy and in right time without much procedural formalities, unlike financial institutions. Though the money lender is losing ground, but he is still the single largest contributor of agricultural credit. However, in recent years, rural credit scenario has undergone a significant change and institutional agencies such as Central Cooperative Banks, State Cooperative Banks, Commercial Banks, Cooperative Credit Agencies and some Government Agencies are extending loans to farmers on easy terms.
- ☆ In India, the agriculture cannot be industry, as more than 50 per cent of the cultivable land is consisted of uneconomical holdings.
- ☆ As most of the farms in India are marginal and small, they do not have major assets to show them as security for claiming loans from the financial institutions. Even if they have assets, they have go through time taking lending procedure for availing institutional loans. In such situations, they prefer to move to 'Informal Sector' for borrowings.
- ☆ The process of recovery of loans is very much low. As mentioned earlier, due to poor financial position the small farmers fail to pay back the loans. Though the banking personnel educate the farmers for prompt repayment of loans, but the process of loan recovery is limited, as the farmers hardly care for repayment of loans and arrest warrants. So, banks are shying away from rural financing. It is ironical that the recoveries position is adverse amongst rich farmers than amongst the small farmers. The political decisions of waiving off loans are further putting pressures on the financial system.

- ☆ The rural credit institutions have given overemphasis on lending financial assistance to the cultivators. While the finance is very important factor, but it should be complemented with the extension of services in form of guidance, expertise and counseling on agricultural issues.
- ☆ The rural credit structure is based on multi agency credit system, whereby there exist numerous organizations providing similar kind of financial services. But, there is a lack of coordination in this multi-agency system and thereby, commercial viability is adversely affected in this scenario.
- ☆ In order to fill the gap that occurred due to the failure of rural cooperative societies Government gave increasing role to the commercial banks. However, commercial banks lack the desired skills and expertise in the agro-credit. The banks have enough financial resources but the service consultancy is not available. Thus, there is a failure to provide complete package of assistance to the farmers. Further, financial sector reforms have put pressure on banks to improve their financial position and so these banks are now concentrating on selected clientele of large borrowers
- ☆ Despite of a large network of the institutional credit system, it has not been able to adequately penetrate the informal rural financial markets thereby, the non-institutional sources continue to play a dominant role in purveying the credit needs of the people residing in rural areas. The results of the All-India Debt and Investment Survey (AIDIS, 2002) also indicate that, the share of the non-institutional sources, in the total credit of the cultivator households, had increased from 30.6 percent in 1991 to 38.9 percent in 2002.

11.5. Promotion of Institutional Credit to the Farmers

The following are the important measures that are to be looked into, to remove the problems of agricultural credit and to promote credit flow from institutional agencies.

- ☆ The farmers should be educated about the importance of crop insurance and weather insurance programmes so that, the risk-bearing ability of the farmers can be greatly improved.
- ☆ Thorough supervision should be there to ensure the institutional loans are utilized only for productive purposes.
- ☆ The amount of loan to be sanctioned to the farmer should be in accordance with the productive efficiency of land, rather than securities offered by him.
- ☆ Instead of offering loan amount only in cash component, the loan amount should comprise both cash and kind components. This also makes the farmer-borrowers to utilize the loan for productive purposes only.
- ☆ Besides sanctioning loan amount, better advisory services should be provided to the farmer-borrower by the banking officials both for production and marketing of agricultural produce.

- ✰ The financial institutions should focus mainly in providing term loans, so as to strengthen farm infrastructure.
- ✰ Consensus should be evolved among political parties on financial discipline of rural financial institutions and should not politicize the issues like announcement of loan or interest waiver schemes, giving calls for not repaying the institutional loans etc. But, considering the risks involved in the farm-business, credit recovery system should be flexible and humane.
- ✰ As the cooperative credit societies have more rural approach, they should be strengthened. There is also a need of capacity building, human resource development of banking personnel to bring more clarity in the banking operations.
- ✰ The lending to homogenous farmer's groups needs to be organized to improve credit delivery. This would help to improve recovery because of peer pressure. Further, group lending tends to be cost-effective. Involving NGOs or rural educated youths in organizing farmers or rural families in groups, scrutinizing applications, disbursement of loan and effecting recoveries would help rural financing institutions in reducing lending costs.
- ✰ Technological improvements like computerization can be critical in building up a reliable credit information system and database on customers, reducing transaction costs and facilitating better pricing of risk, improving the efficiency of the financial system, and thereby increasing the access of un-banked rural people in an efficient manner.
- ✰ Credit counseling, awareness and financial education regarding the benefits of institutional financing are important for effective expansion of financial services in rural areas. To do this, banks may utilize the services of NGOs, village youth clubs, village panchayats, farmer clubs and self-help groups into confidence.

11.6. Different Sources of Credit to (Indian) Farmers

Credit provided to the farmer is as important as other inputs being used in agricultural production. Technical inputs can be purchased and used by farmer, only if he has adequate capital or money with him. But, the owned (equity) capital with the farmer is largely inadequate and he needs outside finance or credit. In India, till 1935, private money lenders were the only source of credit to farmers. They used to charge unduly high rates of interest, but still the farmers depended upon them because of two reasons: adequacy and timeliness of credit supply. But, at times of poor harvest and crop failures, these lenders insisted the farmers to clear their debts mercilessly. As a result, farmers were heavily burdened with debts and many of them perpetuated debts. They even resorted to distress sales of produce and even forced to sell their fixed assets to clear their debts. With the passing of Reserve Bank of India Act 1934, District Central Co-operative Banks Act and Land Development Banks Act, agricultural credit received impetus and there were improvements in agricultural credit. A powerful alternative agency came into being *i.e.,* institutional loans. So, large-scale credit became available with reasonable rates of interest at easy terms, both in terms of granting loans and recovery of them. Although the co-operative banks started financing agriculture with their establishments in 1930's, real impetus was received only after Independence when suitable legislations were passed and policies were formulated. Thereafter, bank credit to agriculture made phenomenal progress by opening branches in rural areas and attracting deposits.

Till 14 major commercial banks were nationalized in 1969, co-operative banks were the main institutional agencies providing finance to agriculture. After nationalization of commercial banks again in 1980 (6 more banks), it was made mandatory for these banks to provide finance to agriculture as a priority sector. These banks undertook special programmes of branch expansion and created a network of banking services throughout the country and started financing agriculture on large scale. Thus, agriculture credit acquired multi-agency dimension. Development and adoption of new technologies and availability of finance go hand in hand. In bringing 'Green Revolution', 'White Revolution' and 'Yellow Revolution', agricultural finance has played a crucial role. Now the agriculture credit, through multi agency approach has come to stay. Thus, the sources, which offer finance to the farmers can be broadly categorized into: Non-institutional or unorganized or Informal agencies, and Institutional or Organized or Formal agencies. It is a fact that, agriculture has been financed by non-institutional agencies for a long time and institutional agencies were started functioning only during the early part of this century.

a. Non-Institutional Sources of Finance

Non-institutional sources include private money lenders, traders and commission agents, landlords and friends and relatives. These sources provide loans to farmer-borrowers directly on personal basis, especially where they are familiar with some level of confidence in one another. The methods of obtaining the loans are relatively easier and there is rare tendencies for administrative delays. There is non-insistence on security/collaterals by lenders. Let us discuss about one by one about these sources:

i. Private Money Lenders

There are two types of money lenders in rural areas *viz.*, Agricultural money lenders and Professional money lenders. Agricultural money lender's main occupation is farming and money lending is a subsidiary one. But, for Professional money lenders, the main profession is money lending. It is essential to note that, although the dependency on money lenders by (resource poor) farmers declined over the years, the credit disbursed by money lenders still forms a major portion of the total credit obtained by the farmers. The following are the major reasons for the popularity of moneylenders in financing the agri-business:

- ☆ They meet demands of farmers both for productive and unproductive requirements
- ☆ Compared to institutional financing, these money lenders are easily approachable at odd hours
- ☆ The lending procedures are very simple for advancing loans to the farmers compared to institutional financing.

However, money lenders charge a very high rate of interest for the loans advanced by them, as they take advantage of the urgency of the farmers in carrying out farm business (time-bound) activities. Of course, over the years, a need for regulation of money lending has been felt. But, due to lack of ease of access for institutional credit, certain sections and areas had facilitated unhindered operation of money lending. The other demerits of borrowing from money lenders include:

- ☆ They deceive the farmers through manipulating bonds and promissory notes obtained from debtors and enter large sum than actually lent.
- ☆ They give no receipt for repayments and often they deny such repayments.
- ☆ Since, they give loans for both productive and unproductive purposes, it results in indebtedness

Merits

- ☆ Unrestricted supply of credit for any purpose.
- ☆ Easy access to farmers, as money lenders maintains close relationship with rural families.
- ☆ Lending procedures adopted are simple and flexible.
- ☆ Credit is available both in terms of adequacy and in right time.
- ☆ Knowledge on local conditions and experience of money lender facilitate his business.
- ☆ Money lenders do not insist upon any particular type of security for the grant of loans.
- ☆ Flexibility is associated regarding repayment schedule (but, with high rates of interest)

ii. Traders and Commission Agents

Traders and commission agents advance both crop loans and marketing loans to the farmers (*i.e.*, for productive purpose), but put a condition to the farmers that, they have to purchase inputs and sell the produce to or through their shop or agency respectively. So, it often becomes obligatory for farmers to buy inputs and sell output through them. Though the rate of interest charged by them is not as high as charged by the money lenders, they charge more in the form of concessions and service chages, making it exploitative in nature. These agents mostly finance for cash crops like cotton, tobacco, onion, sugar cane and groundnut.

iii. Landlords

Especially Small and marginal farmers and tenants rely on landlords for finance to meet out their productive and unproductive expenses. This source of finance has all the demerits associated with private money lenders. Interest rates are exorbitant. In extreme cases say, frequent crop failures, the small and marginal farmers are forced to sell out their lands to these landlords and they become land less labourers and bonded labourers.

iv. Friends and Relatives

This is the simplest source of non-institutional credit, as all farmers are living under similar socio-economic conditions. From these sources, less amount of loans are borrowed for meeting day to day expenses on the farm and normally, no interest is paid on such loans.

Note that, although, the non-institutional agencies satisfy some of the criteria of a good system of credit, the loans taken were usually diverted towards unproductive purposes. This is because, the lenders never care about the end use of the loan extended and thereby, the loans are mis-utilized. In this context, the loans offered by institutional agencies are more productive, as they insist or check, whether the farmers are using the loan amounts for productive purposes or not. Further, they disburse the loan amounts (especially term loans) in phased manner to avoid diversion of loans towards unproductive purposes. So, the institutional agencies discourage the provision of credit for consumption purposes. But, the need for consumption loan in rural households continues to persist. As the institutional agencies deny consumption loans to farmers, the non-institutional agencies continue to dominate the rural credit system. Therefore, the private credit agencies should be brought under a more realistic system of state regulation. Otherwise, the rural people would continue to suffer from indebtedness in spite of various efforts taken by the government to uplift their economic conditions.

b. Institutional Sources of Finance

As compared to the quantum of credit requirement and the financial strength of institutions to meet these credit demands under multiagency system, it is impossible to completely wipe out the non-institutional agencies from the farm sector. The Banking Committee, (1931) and the Banking Commission (1972) offered suggestions to get over the evil aspects of non-institutional lending agencies and bring them under sound credit system. The major institutions supplying credit to agricultural sector include: Government, Co-operative banks, Commercial banks, Regional Rural Banks (RRBs), Farmers Service Societies (FSSs), Self-Help Groups (SHGs) etc (Table 11.1). Let us discuss about one by one about these sources:

i. Government

The Government offers both short term as well as long term loans. These loans are popularly known as 'Taccavi loans', which are generally advanced in times of natural calamities. The rate of interest charge is low. But, it is not a major source of agricultural finance. The source of finance offered by the Government can also be categorized as both Direct and Indirect finances to farm sector. Regarding Direct finance, the Government provides taccavi loans. Land Improvement Act of 1883 and the Agriculturists Loans Act of 1984 were enacted to extend long and short term financial assistance to farmers for agricultural development and also relief measures during distress sales. Regarding Indirect finance, the Government offers loans and allocates subsidized fertilizers to States according to their needs. The price stabilization schemes for various crops also fall under this category. Further, in consultation with the Reserve Bank of India (RBI), the Government prescribes the rates of interest to be charged on loans granted to weaker sections of rural areas and also contributes to the share capital and debentures of co-operatives. Thus, in indirect finance, instead of playing direct role in providing farm credit, the Government plays a vital role in creating conditions or infra-structural facilities to the promotion of institutional credit. For both these finances, loans are granted for a longer period of time that too at low rate of interest. The Government offers a flexible or convenient repayment plan through a series of annual installments. But, the demerit of these loans is that, it is more biased towards large farmers than small and marginal farmers, as the quantum of loan is determined on the basis of value of security offered, loan amount is inadequate, the landless labourers were neglected, inordinate delay in sanctioning of loan, imposition of irrelevant conditions for sanctioning loans, no convenient recovery methods etc. In view of these demerits, it was recommended to channelize these loans through establishing co-operative banks.

ii. Co-operative Banks (Cooperative Credit Societies)

The history of cooperative movement in India dates back to 1904 when first Cooperative Credit Societies Act was passed by the Government. The scope of the Act was restricted to establishment of primary credit societies and non-credit societies were left out of its purview. The shortcomings of the Act were rectified through passing another Act called Cooperative Societies Act 1912. The Act gave provision for registration of all types of Cooperative Societies. This made the emergence of rural cooperatives both in the credit and noncredit areas, though with uneven spatial growth. In subsequent years a number of Committees were appointed and recommendations implemented to improve the functioning of the cooperatives. Soon after the independence, the Government of India following the recommendations of All India Rural Credit Survey Committee (1951) felt that cooperatives were the only alternative to promote agricultural credit and development of rural areas. Accordingly, cooperatives received substantial help in the provision of credit from Reserve Bank of India as a part of loan policy and large scale assistance from Central and State Governments for their development and strengthening. Many schemes involving subsidies and concessions for the weaker sections were routed through cooperatives. As a result cooperative institutions registered a remarkable growth in the post-independence India. The detailed structure of the cooperative credit system is given in Figure 11.1.

Primary Agricultural Cooperative Credit Societies (PACS)

Following the 'Raiffeisen Model', PACS came to existence after the enactment of First Cooperative Credit Societies Act, 1904. PACS functions on the basis of cooperative principles of voluntary participation, democratic control, limited area of operation and limited liability. These societies work at the village level and are meant for the farmers regarding provision of requisite short term and medium term loans. Supply of agricultural inputs and other essential commodities is also taken up by these societies. In addition to these PACS also helps in formulation and implementation of agricultural development plans for the welfare of its members. The PACS are associated with following functions:

- They borrow adequate and timely funds from dccbs and help the members in financial matters;

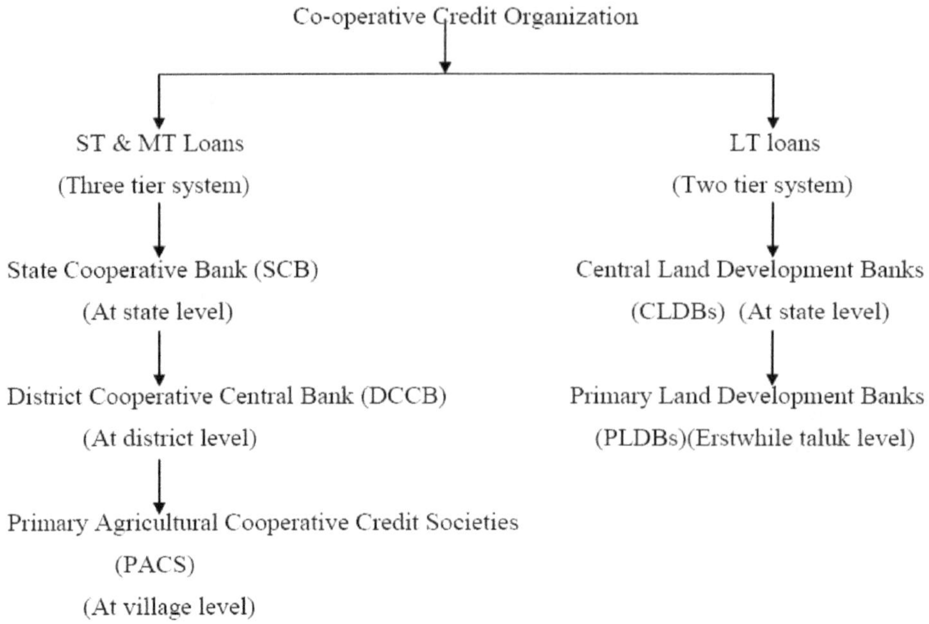

Figure 11.1: Detailed Structure of the Cooperative Credit System.

- ☆ They attract local savings in the form of share capital and deposits from the villagers, thereby inculcating the habit of thrift;
- ☆ They supervise the end use of credit;
- ☆ They make available fertilizers and insecticides etc. To the needy farmers;
- ☆ They provide machinery on hire basis to the farmers;
- ☆ They associate with the programmes and plans meant for the socio-economic development of the village;
- ☆ They are also involved in the marketing of farm produce on behalf of the farmer-borrowers;
- ☆ They provide storage facilities and marketing finance; and
- ☆ They supply certain consumer goods like rice, wheat, sugar, kerosene, cloth etc. At fair prices.

District Central Cooperative Banks (DCCBs)

DCCBs function as a link between the PACS and State Cooperative Banks (SCBs). They are basically meant for meeting the credit requirement of PACS. They also undertake banking business such as accepting deposits from public, collecting bills, cheques, drafts etc. and providing credit to the needy persons. The area of operation varies from taluk to district but in most of the states their operations are confined to the taluk level. Membership of the DCCBs is open to individuals and societies working in its area of operation. Marketing societies, consumer societies, farming societies, urban banks and PACS are usually enrolled as members of this bank. The specific functions of the bank are:

- ☆ To supervise and inspect the activities of PACS and help the credit societies run smoothly;
- ☆ To maintain close and constant contact and guide the primary societies and provide leadership to them;
- ☆ To undertake non-credit activities like supply of seeds, fertilizers besides sugar, kerosene and other consumer goods;
- ☆ To provide requisite funds to societies under their control; and
- ☆ To accept deposits from the member societies as well as from public.

State Cooperative Bank (SCB)

SCBs are at the apex of the cooperative credit organization present at the state capitals. They perform the same functions for the DCCBs as the latter does for the PACS. The membership comprises of DCCBs and individuals. Being at the apex level, this bank mobilizes and deploys financial resources among the various sectors. It finances and controls the working of the DCCBs in the state. It also serves as a link between the RBI and DCCBs. The Specific functions of SCBs:

- ☆ SCBs perform as the banker's bank for the DCCBs;
- ☆ SCBs banks facilitate the respective Sate Governments to draw up cooperative and other development plans as well as their implementation;
- ☆ They act as a link between the DCCBs and the RBI;
- ☆ They supervise, control and guide the activities of DCCBs;
- ☆ These banks also perform normal banking operations;
- ☆ They grant subsidies to DCCBs for development of cooperative activities;
- ☆ They formulate and implement uniform credit policies; and
- ☆ These banks coordinate their own policies with those of the cooperative movement of the Government.

Primary Land Development Banks (PLDBs)

The establishment of the Land Mortgage Bank (LMBs) on cooperative lines dates back to the year 1920 in Punjab. Later during the period 1920-29, a number of LMBs were established in the states of Punjab, Madras, Mysore, Assam and Bengal. After that not much growth was observed in the number of LMBs till 1945. However, during 1945-53 a rapid growth was observed in the number of these banks. During this period only rich and affluent farmers derived benefits of these banks and small and marginal farmers remained untouched of the developments. LMBs got massive support from the RBI, SBI, LIC and Agricultural Refinance Corporation. As a result LMBs had to reorient its lending policies in favour of marginal and small farmers. LMBs were renamed as Land Development Banks (LDBs) in 1974. Primary LDBs are generally organized to serve the farmers at Taluk level. Its specific functions are:

- ☆ To provide long term finance to the needy farmers for the development of land, increasing production and productivity of land;
- ☆ To provide long term loan for minor irrigation and for redemption of old debts and purchase of land;
- ☆ To provide long term finance for purchase of tractors, machinery and equipments and construction of farm structures; and
- ☆ To mobilize rural savings.

Central Land Development Bank (CLDBs)

In many states PLDBs are federated into CLDBs. Branches of CLDBs, PLDBs and individual entrepreneurs are the members of the CLDB. National Bank for Agriculture and Rural Development (NABARD) and Life Insurance Corporation (LIC) subscribe for its debentures in large amounts. In fact, NABARD is the refinance agency of CLDBs. It acts as a link between NABARD and the Government in long-term business transactions. It supervises and guides the PLDBs. It inculcates the practice of thrift among member banks by mobilizing savings and stimulating capital formation. The CLDBs provides loans to member banks for the redemption of old debts, improvement, reclamation and development of land, purchase of agricultural machinery and equipment and development of minor irrigation.

Till 1987 the farmers in Andhra Pradesh depended on primary agricultural credit societies functioning under three - tier structure for short-term and medium-term credit requirements and on primary land development banks functioning under two-tier structure for ling-term credit needs. It means that the farmers have to obtain their total credit requirements from two different cooperative institutions. In addition to this the performance of PLDBs was not satisfactory. In marketing their farm produce also, farmers faced many difficulties in getting marketing services from PACS in three- tier structure. Against this backdrop, to make cooperatives render their meaningful services, the Government of A.P thought to bring some appropriate organizational changes in the working of cooperatives in the state. Subsequently, a committee under the chairmanship of Sri. Mohan Kanda, an IAS officer was constituted to bring out some meaningful and practicable alternatives in the structure of cooperatives. The committee submitted its report in May, 1985 and recommended the establishment of 'Single Window System' and a bill was passed for its establishment in the Andhra Pradesh state assembly in January, 1987. The main intention and idea of introducing the single window system is to supply all types of agricultural credit needed by the farmers through PACS and provide adequate marketing facilities to farm produce through District Cooperative Marketing Societies (DCMS). Single window system is a three-tier structure in cooperative credit and two tier structure in cooperative marketing as shown in Figure 11.2

iii. Commercial Banks

Previously Commercial Banks (CBs) were confined only to urban areas serving mainly to trade, commerce and industry. Their role in rural credit was meagre *i.e.*, 0.9 per cent in 1951-52 and 0.7 per cent in 1961-61. The insignificant participation of CBs in rural lending was explained by the risky nature of agriculture due to its heavy

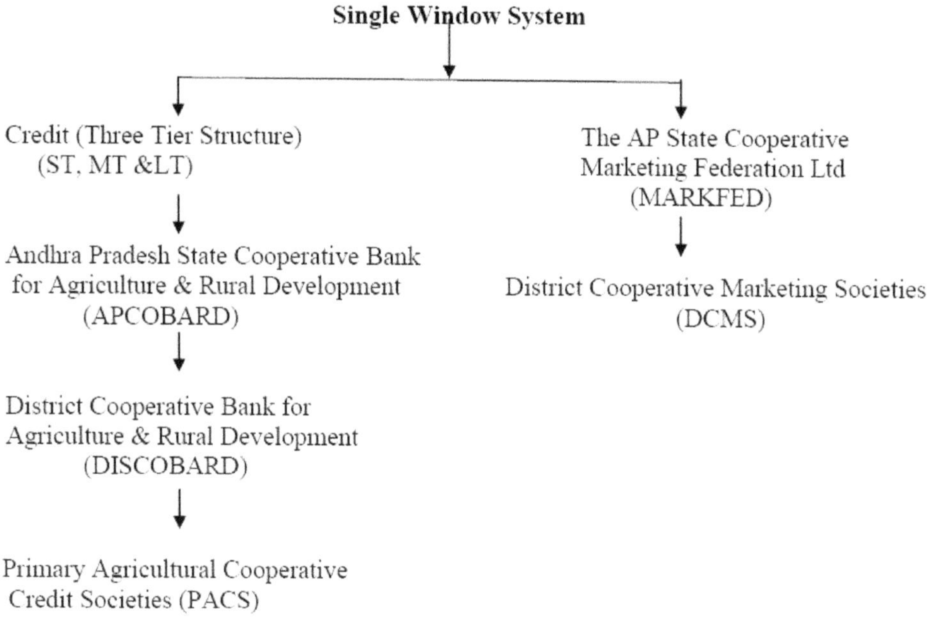

Figure 11.2: Single Window System .

dependence on monsoon, unorganized nature and subsistence approach. A major change took place in the form of Nationalization of CBs in 19th July, 1969 and CBs was made to play an active role in agricultural credit as per the ordinance called 'The Banking companies Ordinance 1969' (Acquisition and Transfer of Undertakings). Under this Act, 14 commercial banks having deposits of more than Rs. 50 crores each were nationalised and they include: Central Bank of India, Bank of India, Punjab National Bank, Bank of Baroda, United commercial Bank, Canara Bank, United Bank of India, Dena Bank, Union Bank of India, Allahabad Bank, Syndicate Bank, Indian Bank, Bank of Maharashtra and Indian Overseas Bank. Since then, CBs were made to play an active role in agricultural credit. Encouraged by the success of First spell of Nationalization of banks in 1969, six more banks in the private sector, having deposits more than Rs.200 crores were nationalized on 15th April, 1980. The six banks nationalized in the Second spell include: Punjab and Sind bank, Andhra Bank, New Bank of India, Vijaya Bank, Oriental Bank of Commerce and Corporation Bank. At present, they are the largest source of institutional credit to agriculture.

iv. Regional Rural Banks (RRBs)

RRBs were set up in those regions where availability of institutional credit was found to be inadequate but potential for agricultural development was very high. However, the main thrust of the RRBs is to provide loans to small and marginal farmers, landless labourers and village artisans. These loans are advanced for productive purposes. The RRBs combine the features of both commercial and co-operative banks in the sense that, commercial banks have more financial strength because, they are profit motive, but suffer from the limitation of limited coverage of area due to lack of rural approach, high cost of lending operation, more lending's to urban areas etc., and on the other hand, co-operative banks have less financial strength and less managerial competence, but possess a realistic rural approach. So, to combine the meritorious features of these two banks, RRBs came into existence. Further, All-India Rural Credit Review Committee in 1969 revealed that, over the large parts of the country, small farmers are neglected in having good access to credit. Accordingly, the Government of India appointed a committee under the Chairmanship of Sri. M. Narasimham and he recommended the establishment of RRBs, which came into existence on 2nd October 1975. The main purpose of establishing RRBs is to have an institutional agency in rural areas with more business outlook, which the commercial banks possess and to understand the rural problems which the co-operative banks possess and to serve the farming community with much more dedication. These banks were conceived as low cost ones, which uplift the rural economy for financing rural agriculture and trade in general, small and marginal farmers, agricultural labourers, rural artisans in particular.

v. Farmers' Service Societies (FSSs)

The National Commission on Agriculture (NCA) observed that, the existing institutional structure was unable to meet the special needs of the weaker sections of farmers, agricultural labourers and rural artisans. Hence, the Commission recommended for the organization of FSSs in 1971 to provide an integrated credit service to them. The FSS is a registered cooperative body with bye-laws to ensure autonomy, efficiency and freedom from political intervention. Each society is treated as an independent primary cooperative society for getting funds at concessional interest rates and subsidy. The FSS is sponsored and affiliated to the largest commercial bank in the area of FSS or could form part of the cooperative credit system. These FSS provide technical service to farmer members including the supply of essential inputs required for raising crops and livestock products

vi. Microfinance

Microfinance through Self Help Groups (SHGs) has assumed prominence in recent years. SHG is group of rural poor who volunteer to organize themselves into a group for eradication of poverty of the members. They agree to save regularly and convert their savings into a common fund known as the Group corpus. The members of the group agree to use this common fund and such other funds that they may receive as a group through a common management. Generally, a SHG consists of 10 to 20 persons. However, in difficult areas like deserts, hills and areas with scattered and sparse population and in case of minor irrigation and disabled persons, this number may range from 5-20. As soon as the SHG is formed and a couple of group meetings are held, an SHG can open a Savings Bank account with the nearest Commercial or Regional Rural Bank or a Cooperative Bank. This is essential to keep the thrift and other earnings of the SHG safely and also to improve the transparency levels of SHG's transactions. Opening of savings bank account, in fact, is the beginning of a relationship between the bank and the SHG. The RBI has issued instructions to all banks permitting them to open savings bank accounts in the name of registered or unregistered SHGs.

Table 11.1: Break-up of Institutional and Non-Institutional Rural Credit in India

(Per cent)

	1951	*1961*	*1971*	*1981*	*1991*	*2002*
Institutional Agencies	7.2	14.8	29.2	61.2	64.0	57.1
Government	3.3	5.3	6.7	4.0	5.7	2.3
Co-op. Society/bank	3.1	9.1	20.1	28.6	18.6	27.3
Commercial bank incl. RRBs	0.8	0.4	2.2	28.0	29.0	24.5
Insurance	—	—	0.1	0.3	0.5	0.3
Provident Fund	—	—	0.1	0.3	0.9	0.3
Others institutional agencies*	—	—	—	—	9.3	2.4
Non-Institutional Agencies	92.8	85.2	70.8	38.8	36.0	42.9
Landlord	1.5	0.9	8.6	4.0	4.0	1.0
Agricultural Moneylender	24.9	45.9	23.1	8.6	6.3	10.0
Professional Moneylender	44.8	14.9	13.8	8.3	9.4	19.6
Traders and Commission Agents	5.5	7.7	8.7	3.4	7.1	2.6
Relatives and Friends	14.2	6.8	13.8	9.0	6.7	7.1
Others	1.9	8.9	2.8	4.9	2.5	2.6
Total	*100*	*100*	*100*	*100*	*100*	*100*

*: includes financial corporation/institution, financial company and other institutional agencies.

Note: Percentage share of different credit agencies to the outstanding cash dues of the households as on 30th June.

— Denotes not available.

Source: All India Rural Credit Survey (1954); All India Debt and Investment Survey, Various Issues.

Thus, over time, spectacular progress has been achieved in terms of the scale and outreach of institutional framework for agricultural credit in India during post-independence period. It implies, India has been widening the spread of institutional machinery for credit and thereby, there is decline in the role of non-institutional sources. The share of institutional credit, which was little over 7 per cent in 1951, increased manifold to over 66 per cent in 1991, reflecting a remarkable decline in the share of non institutional credit from around 93 per cent to about 31 per cent during the same period. However, the latest NSSO Survey (2002) reveals that the share of non-institutional credit has taken a reverse swing which is a cause of concern (Table 11.1). Similarly, over time, the flow of credit to agriculture and rural sector has expanded impressively (Table 11.2). The ground level credit flow had registered an increase from Rs. 1675 crore in 1975-96 to Rs.86891 crore in 2003-04 and further to Rs.203297 crore in 2005-06. This rate of growth was even higher than the growth rate of GDP originating in agriculture. Despite this growth, the credit needs of agriculture have not been met fully and overwhelming numbers of farm households have not been able to borrow from institutional sources. While short-term credit has remained the dominant component of total credit, its relative importance declined from 70.3 per cent in 1975-76 to 58.1 per cent in 2006-07.

Table 11.2: Institutional Credit Flow to Agriculture Sector in India (Rs. crore)

Agency	*1975-76*	*1983-84*	*1993-94*	*2001-02*	*2002-03*	*2003-04*	*2004-05*	*2005-06*	*2006-07*	*2007-08**
Cooperatives	1186	2938	10117	23524	23636	26,875	31231	39404	42480	33070
RRBs	2	263	977	4854	6070	7581	12404	15223	20435	15925
Scheduled Commercial Banks	405	1885	5400	33587	39774	52441	81481	125477	140382	88765
Other Agencies	82	185	0	80	80	84	193	382	NA	NA
Total Credit	**1675**	**5244**	**16494**	**62045**	**69560**	**86981**	**125309**	**180486**	**203297**	**137760**

* Up to November 2007.

Source: All India Debt and investment Survey and NSSO.

Regarding agency-wise credit flow in India, the analysis revealed that, the cooperative banks were the major source of agriculture credit in 1975-76 constituting around 71 percent of the total ground level credit flow followed by commercial banks at 24.2 percent and regional rural banks at 4.9 percent. Though cooperative banks had dominated agriculture credit supply till the early reform period, commercial banks and RRBs recorded impressive growth rates. As a result, in 2006-07, the share of cooperative banks in the total institutional credit flow receded to 20.1 percent and that of commercial banks advanced to 69.1 percent. Although the quantum of disbursement from cooperative banks increased, it could not keep pace with commercial banks in enhancing credit flow due to several reasons including its poor financial health, dual control, lack of internal controls and corporate governance norms and excessive dependence on other financial institutions. Although the share of cooperative credit is now much lower than that of commercial banks, the reach of cooperative credit societies is much wider. Cooperative credit societies have more than twice the number of rural outlets and four times more accounts than those of scheduled commercial banks and RRBs put together. Low recovery rates and mounting over dues have clogged the process of recycling of credit by cooperatives, impaired their ability to avail of refinance facilities from (NABARD), increased transaction costs and more importantly, have deprived potential borrowers of the opportunity to avail of credit facilities from the cooperatives. As a result, cooperatives have been losing their capacity to meet the growing credit needs of agriculture. Regarding size-wise credit flow, despite impressive growth in direct credit to farmers from the scheduled commercial banks between 1991-92 and 2003-04, contrary to expectation, credit disbursement to small and marginal farmers has not been encouraging. Though the number of accounts increased for small farmers, yet the credit flow favoured the richer farmers. In view of this, RRBs, FSSs and LAMPS came into existence and their importance was already discussed earlier.

This discussion revealed that, rural credit systems have under gone several changes during the last decade. There has been an increasing trend towards institutional financing. The financial institutions are under stress, particularly since the financial sector reforms of 1992-93. The credit policy should continue to emphasize small borrowers. The commercial banks have started feeling shy of lending to agricultural sector and rural poor. The provisions of mandatory lending for priority sector and the agricultural activities should continue. The banks should take the help of NGOs and local formal institutions in their lending programmes to reduce the transaction costs and improve recoveries. The financial cum consultancy approach needs to be followed. For meeting the credit needs of the poor, the programmes like linking of self-help groups (SHGs) with lending agencies are to be further strengthened.

11.7. Types of Farm Credit

We already know, credit refers to the temporary transfer of wealth or capital from a person who has to other who has not, but with the promise that the latter (borrower) will repay the loan amount to the lender at a later date. Credit is broadly classified based on various criteria:

i. Based on Purpose

Based on purpose, credit is classified into four types:

a. Production Loans

These are the loans given to the farmer-borrower towards cultivation of crops. These loans are also called as Crop loans or Short Term (ST) loans or Seasonal Agricultural Operations (SAO) loans. The repayment period for this loan is 6-18 months. Example: Loans given for cultivation of crops like paddy, maize, cotton etc.

b. Investment Loans

These loans are also called as Term loans. These loans are mainly given for making permanent improvements on the farm. Examples: Loans given for purchase of machinery, installation of irrigation system, drainage system etc.

c. Marketing Loans

These loans are given to the farmers to overcome distress sales (market price of the commodity < cost of production) of the produce. The banks will sanction marketing loan to the farmer to the extent of 75 per cent of the value of produce after stocking it in a warehouse godown at times of drastic fall in price of the commodity. As and when the prices rise in the market, the farmer will destock the produce to market it and repay the loan amount.

d. Consumption Loans

Any loan advanced to the farmer-borrower other than for production, investment and marketing falls under the category of consumption loan. The provision of consumption loans may appear unproductive, but indirectly it is productive because, it will not allow the farmer to divert the production loans towards unproductive or undesirable purposes. These loans will be mainly provided to the farmer-borrowers, who are hard hit by natural calamities like floods, drought, famines etc. The maximum loan amount offered under this category of loan is Rs.500 at an annual rate of interest of 11 per cent.

ii. Based on Approach

Based on approach, credit is classified into three types:

a. Individual Approach

As per this approach, loans are advanced to the potential farmer borrower. Examples: Crop loans, dairy loans etc.

b. Area Approach

Loans given to the persons falling under given area for specific purpose will be categorized under this. Example: Drought Prone Area Programme (DPAP) loans

c. Differential Interest Rate (DIR) Loans

In this approach, loans will be given to the weaker sections of the farming community, SC and ST farmers, artisans etc., at the low rate of interest of four per cent per annum.

iii. Based on Security

Based on security, credit is classified into the following categories:

a. Unsecured Loans

In this category, the farmer-borrower need not show any security to the lender, but based on the confidence between farmer-borrower and lender, the loan will be given to the farmer borrower.

b. Secured Loans

In this category, the farmer-borrower has to show the security for availing loan from the banking institution. There are different types of securities as listed below:

- ☆ *Personal security:* In this form of security, the farmer borrower himself stands as security for the loan amount taken from the banking institution. Example: Promissory note.
- ☆ *Collateral security:* In this form of security, the movable properties of the farmer-borrower were shown as security for collecting loan from the financial institutions. Examples: LIC Bonds, fixed deposit bonds, warehouse receipts, machinery, livestock etc.
- ☆ *Mortgage:* In this form of security, immovable properties were shown as security for the loan amount taken from the banking institution. The person who is creating the charge of mortgage is called mortgagor (borrower) and the person in whose favour it is created is known as the mortgagee (banker). Examples: lands, buildings etc. This form of security can be divided in two types *viz.*, Simple mortgage and Equitable mortgage.
    - ❑ *Simple mortgage:* Simple mortgage is followed, when the property is inherited from the ancestors. For availing the loan from the banking institution, the farmer-borrower has to register this property on his name to show it as a security. The registration charges should be born by the farmer borrower.
    - ❑ *Equitable mortgage:* This mortgage will be followed, when the property is self- earned or self-acquired. So, there is no need of registration by the farmer-borrower to show it as a security and hence, there are no registration charges.
- ☆ *Chattal loans:* These are the loans taken from the pawn brokers by pledging movable properties like gold and silver ornaments, utensils etc. These pawn brokers will lend money at higher rates of interest.
- ☆ *Hypothecation:* Hypothecation is mainly seen in case of tractor loans, machinery etc. The person, who creates the charge of hypothecation is called as hypothecator (borrower) and the person in whose favor it is created is known as hypothecate (bank) and the property, which is denoted as hypothecated property. Hypothecated loans again are of two types *viz.*, key loans and open loans.
    - ❑ *Key loans:* At times of drastic fall in prices of the produce, the produce is kept in the godown under the control of Agricultural Market

Committee or warehouse and based on the receipt issued by these agencies, marketing loan was advanced to the farmer borrower to an extent of 75 per cent of value of produce. This will facilitate the farmer to overcome distress sales in the villages. As and when the prices shoot up in the market, the farmer will identify the buyer, clear the loan amount and sell the produce. So, when the prices are low in the market, the produce is kept under the control of an agency (Agricultural Market Committee or Warehouse) and the farmer has no control over the produce till the loan amount was cleared. Hence, the name key loan was given for this type of hypothecation.

- ***Open loans:*** Unlike key loans, in open loans, the physical position of the asset (say, tractor or machinery) lies with the farmer-borrower, but the ownership rights lie with the financial institutions. As and when the farmer clears off the loan amount, he can sell the machinery as he likes. Since the physical position of asset is with the farmer borrower even though the legal ownership remains with the financial institution, the name open loan was given for this type of hypothecation.

iv. Based on Time

Based on time, credit is classified into the following categories:

a. Short Term (ST) Loans

These loans are mainly given for crop production purpose or carrying out seasonal agricultural operations on the farm. Hence, these loans are also called as Crop loans, Operational loans or SAO loans or Production loans. The repayment period for ST loans is 6-18 months.

b. Medium Term (MT) Loans

These are the loans given towards purchasing implements, electric motors, milk cattle, sheep, goat etc. The repayment period for MT loans is 16 months to 5 years.

c. Long Term (LT) Loans

These are the loans given for making permanent improvements on the farm like purchase of machinery, installation of irrigation system, drainage system, lining irrigation channels etc. The repayment period for LT loans is 5-20 years and sometimes more than 20 years. Medium and long term loans together called as Term loans or Investment loans.

v. Based on Contact with the Farmer

Based on this criterion, credit is classified into two categories:

a. Direct Loans

These are the loans given to the potential farmer-borrower directly. Examples like loan given for paddy, maize, dairy etc.

b. Indirect Loans

These loans were not given directly to farmers, but indirectly benefit the farming community. Examples include, loans given to the fertilizer companies, pesticide companies, establishment of agro-based industries etc.

vi. Based on Liquidity

Based on this criterion, credit is classified into two categories:

a. Self-liquidating Loans

If the income derived from the loan amount is sufficient enough to clear off the entire loan amount in the same accounting year, it is called self-liquidating loan. Example: Crop loan

b. Partially–liquidating Loan

It is also called as Non-liquidating loan. If the income derived from the loan amount is not sufficient enough to clear off the entire loan amount in the same accounting year, it is called partially-liquidating loan. Hence, the farmer clears the loan amount in a series of installments. Example: Term loans

vii. Lender's Classification

Based on this criterion, credit is classified into two categories:

a. Institutional Credit

Here are loans are advanced by the institutional agencies like co-operative banks, commercial banks etc. Examples: Co-operative loans and commercial bank loans.

b. Non-institutional Credit

Here, the farmer-borrower avail loan from non-institutional agencies like private money lenders, traders and commission agents, friends and relatives etc.

viii. Borrower's Classification

This classification has equity considerations. Based on this criterion, credit is classified as flows:

- ☆ ***Based on the business activity:*** It include, crops cultivating farmers, dairy farmers, poultry farmers, apiculture farmers, rural artisans etc.
- ☆ ***Based on size of the farm:*** It include, agricultural labourers, marginal farmers, small farmers, semi-medium farmers, medium farmers and large farmers.
- ☆ ***Based on location***: It include, wet land farmers, dry land farmers, plain farmers, hill farmers or tribal farmers etc.

11.8. Economic Feasibility Tests of Credit

With the technological advancements in agriculture, the credit requirements to farmers were increased. Lending loans to the borrower by a financial institution is a two-way approach *i.e.*, from the farmer's side, he has to submit securities to banking institution and from the institution side, it has to study the economic viability, technical feasibility and credit worthiness of the farmer-borrower. Economic viability and technical feasibility are related to the technology being implemented by the farmer in his farm, whereas credit worthiness of farmer-borrower depends on the following three aspects popularly called as 3 'R's of credit, 5 'C's of credit and 7 'P's of credit.

i. 3 'R's of Credit

These include: Returns from the proposed investment, Repayment capacity the investment generates and Risk- bearing ability of the farmer-borrower. These 3Rs of credit are considered as sound indicators of credit worthiness of the farmers.

a. Returns from the Proposed Investment

Returns are nothing but the income earned by the farmer-borrower from farm business. The banker will give loan to the farmer, only when the expected returns are greater than the loan amount invested such that, the farmer can easily repay the loan amount. The returns from farm business mainly depends upon selection of farm enterprises, managerial ability of farmer, technology adopted, marketing facilities available in that area etc. We already know, loan is nothing but the additional investment made by the farmer borrower along with his own capital in the farm business. Hence, it is very important to study the marginal returns derived from that loan amount. The credit worthiness of farmer-borrower will be more, when MR is greater than MC. So, the incremental income due to the loan amount can be studied with the help of partial budgeting technique and the incremental income can be calculated as follows:

Incremental income = (Added returns +Reduced cost) - (Reduced returns + Added costs)

b. Repayment Capacity the Investment Generates

It refers to the capacity of farmer-borrower regarding the repayment of the loan amount back to the financial institution. This is important because, before repaying the loan amount, the farmer has to meet the family living expenses + working expenses on the farm in the next year etc. Hence, the incremental income should sufficiently cover the farmer's needs *i.e.*, both family needs and working expense. So, the incremental income should be sufficient enough to repay the entire loan amount. Then only, the farmer borrower is said to be credit worthy. The repayment capacity of farmer-borrower depends upon various factors and the mathematic expression is given below.

RC = f(R,S,M,E,WE,FE,- - - - - - - - - - - *etc.*)

Where, RC =Repayment capacity

R= Gross returns from the enterprise (+)

S = Size of holding(+)

M = Managerial ability of farmer (+)

E = Education status of farmer borrower (+)

WE = Working expenses of borrower (-)

FE = Family expense of the farmer borrower (-)

Note that, repayment capacity of the farmer borrower varies with the crop loan and term loans or varies between self liquidating loans and partially liquidating loans or non liquidating loans. They are given here under.

Repayment capacity for crop loans (self liquidating loans) = Gross income - [Crop loan due + Working expenses on the farm + Family living expenses of farmer + Other loans due, if any with friends or relatives + Miscellaneous expenditure]

Repayment capacity for term loans or partial liquidating or non liquidating loans or investment loan):

= Gross Income - [Annual installment due for term loan + Crop loan due + Working expenses on the farm + Family living expenses of farmer + Other loans due, if any with friends or relatives + Miscellaneous expenditure]

Causes of Poor Repayment Capacity of Farmers in India

- Small size land holding due to sub-division and fragmentation.
- Low prices of produce and frequent fluctuations in market prices.
- Higher working expenses on the farm due to increase in prices of inputs.
- High family expenditure.
- More borrowings from local or private money lenders at higher rates of interest
- Diverting credit for unproductive purposes.
- Due to illiteracy, there is less adoption of modern technology.
- Poor management of farm resources.
- Low productivity and production of crop produce due to vagaries of natural factors.

Measures to Improve Repayment Capacity

- Adopting enterprises according to farming situations.
- Adopting modern technology, which will increase production at cost effectiveness.
- Timely supply of resources or inputs and their efficient utilization.
- Improving managerial ability of farmers by providing skill oriented training programmes.
- Proper planning of repayment plans in accordance with the flow of income from the business.
- Diversification of crop enterprises.
- Practicing risk management techniques such as crop insurance, cattle insurance, machinery insurance, buy-back arrangement to farm produce.
- Improving net worth of farmer borrower.

c. Risk Bearing Ability

Risk in agri-business is inevitable because of excess dependence on natural factors. As a result, there will be greater fluctuations in yields and income of the farmer-borrower. The financial institution will take into consideration the risk factors associated with the farm business and quantify them, so as to assess their impact on yields and income of farmer-borrower. Variations in yields and income of farmer-borrower over a period of time can be studied by Coefficient of variation. This process of adjusting the farmer's income considering its coefficient of variation is called Deflation. So, while studying the repayment capacity of farmer borrower under risk conditions or assessing the risk bearing ability, the gross income is to be deflated. This deflated gross income is worked out by the formula as given below:

Deflated gross income = Gross Income - [Gross Income x Coefficient of Variation]

For example, the farmer borrower's gross income is Rs. 50000 on a farm and Co-efficient of variation of income in that area (say, village) is 20 per cent, then

Deflated Gross Income= 50000 –(50000 x 20 per cent) = 50000-(50000 x 0.20) = Rs. 40000.

The repayment capacity of farmer-borrower under risk conditions can be studied both for crop loans and terms loans and they are estimated by the formula, as given below.

Repayment capacity for crop loans (self liquidating loans) under risk conditions = Deflated Gross income - [Crop loan due + Working expenses on the farm + Family living expenses of farmer + Other loans due, if any with friends or relatives + Miscellaneous expenditure]

Repayment capacity for term loans or partial liquidating or non liquidating loans or investment loan) under risk conditions = Deflated Gross Income - [Annual installment due for term loan + Crop loan due + Working expenses on the farm + Family living expenses of farmer + Other loans due, with friends or relatives + Miscellaneous expenditure]

Note that, if the repayment capacity under risk conditions is positive *i.e.,* if deflated gross income is higher than the gross expenses of the farm business, it implies two important aspects:

- ☆ Repayment capacity of farmer borrower is higher even under the risk situations.
- ☆ The farmer borrower has good managerial abilities to with stand risk and uncertainity situations in practicing agri-business.

Measures to improve risk bearing ability of the farmer borrower:

- ☆ Improving the farmers' net worth in the business.
- ☆ Promoting the moral character *i.e.* honesty, integrity and feeling responsibility on the part of farmer borrower to avoid unproductive use of credit.
- ☆ Reducing unnecessary family and non-farm expenditure.
- ☆ Taking up or practicing stable and reliable enterprise which is less prone to risk.

- Encouraging crop diversification *i.e.* if one enterprise fails such that other enterprise contributes income.
- Encouraging savings on the part of farmer borrower to face any adverse risk and uncertain situations.
- The farmer should go for cattle insurance, crop insurance and buy back arrangement of crop produce.

ii. Five 'C's of Credit

Beside 3 'R's of credit, the economic feasibility of the proposed investment activity can also be studied by the banker from 5 'C's of credit. These include: Character, Capacity, Capital, Condition and Common sense

a. Character

Character of farmer borrower is with reference to moral character of farmer. It implies the genuenity of the farmer, his attitude towards farm business, relation with co-farmers, friends and relatives in the village, his commitment etc. If these aspects are positive, the banker will lend loan to the farmer-borrower.

b. Capacity

Capacity is synonymous with repayment capacity of the farmer-borrower. So, this capacity is a function of income obtained from the farm business. This is given by: $C=f(Y)$, where $Y=$ Gross income. When the farm income is more, his repayment capacity will be more and *vice versa*.

c. Capital

Capital refers to the equity or net worth of a farm business. It assures that, funds are available to repay loans, if character and capacity proved to be inadequate. Capital also represents one of the cornerstones for measuring the risk bearing ability of the borrower.

d. Condition

Besides assessing the moral character of farmer-borrower by the banking institution and after getting satisfied with his repayment capacity and risk bearing ability, the banking institution also impose some conditions on him regarding the submission of following certificates:

- ***10-1 Certificate:*** It indicates the farmer's ownership on land.
- ***Adangal certificate***: It indicates the cropping pattern to be followed by the farmer.
- ***Encumbrance certificate***: This shows the land mortgage details of the farmer-borrower.

If the bank satisfies with the geneunity of all the above certificates, then it will disburse loan to the farmer borrower.

e. Common Sense

It is nothing but the common understanding between the banker and the farmer-borrower regarding the disbursement of loan amount and its utilization for productive purpose. Of course, this is the *prima-facie* for sanctioning the loan amount by the bank to farmer-borrower.

iii. Seven 'P's of Credit

These include:

a. Principle of productive purpose
b. Principle of personality
c. Principle of productivity
d. Principle of phased disbursement
e. Principle of proper utilization
f. Principle of payment
g. Principle of protection

a. Principle of Productive Purpose

The farmers avail different types of loans like ST, MT and LT loans for their farm business. Besides these loans, especially small and marginal farmers are also provided with another type of loan called Consumption loan. This is because, they may divert the sanctioned ST and term loans for unproductive purposes, if they suffer from frequent crop failures. But, the banking institutions will not show much interest in advancing these consumption loans to the farmers because, no income can be derived from such type of loans. Hence, this principle states that, the loan amount advanced to the farmer should yield more incremental income than the loan amount invested. To make ST loans more productive among small and marginal farmers, they should also be provided with term loans to start allied enterprises on the farm like dairy, poultry, sheep, sericulture, apiculture etc. This is so because, if the crop enterprise(s) fail on the farm, the farmer may get the income from these allied enterprises and thereby, the farmer can repay the loan amount.

b. Principle of Personality

It states that, the farmer borrower should have more trust worthiness both in utilizing the loan amount and also in repaying the loan amount. If the farmer borrower's credit worthiness is good, the banker will lend the loan to the farmer. But, over the years of lending, the banker will also study the trust worthiness of the farmer-borrower besides his credit worthiness. If the farmer borrower couldn't repay the loan amount due to failure of his crop production programme because of natural calamities, he is not a willful defaulter. On the other hand, if the farmer gets more income in the business and still if he do not repay the loan amount, he will be considered as a willful defaulter. This character reflects the dishonesty on the part of the farmer-borrower in the banking transactions. If more number of large farmers are found to be willful defaulters, then the functional efficiency of a bank will gets affected. So, the functioning of of the bank not only depends upon the securities offered and credit worthiness of the farmer borrower, but also on his personality. Thus, the personality of farmer-borrower and functional efficiency of the bank are more inter-linked.

c. Principle of Productivity

This principle states that, loan amount offered to the farmer should be adequate and productive enough in selecting the best combination of enterprises and also in engaging the other factors of production towards ensuring more resource use efficiency. Thus, the production on the farm will be increased and it will make the farmer to be more credit worthy in the future.

d. Principle of Phased Disbursement

This principle states that, the loan amount should be disbursed by the bank to the farmer-borrower in different installments or phases instead of giving full amount in the beginning. This phased disbursement of loan ensures

- ☆ More productive use of loan by the farmer borrower
- ☆ Facilitates easy supervision by the banker till the end use of credit.
- ☆ Avoids diversion or misuse of credit for unproductive purposes.

e. Principle of Proper Utilization

The principle states that, the loan amount disbursed by the bank should be properly utilized for the productive purpose. However, the proper utilization of loan amount depends upon several factors *viz.*,

- ☆ Availability of inputs in the village both in terms of adequacy and time
- ☆ Technical expertise available to the farmers from the line departments, agricultural experts, veterinary experts, scientific community, farmers service centre etc.
- ☆ Infrastructural facilities available in the village say, storage facilities, processing facilities etc

If all these facilities are available in the village, then the farmer can take up the desired cropping pattern on scientific lines and thereby, the loan amount will be utilized properly.

f. Principle of Payment

This principle deals with the planning of repayment schedule by the banking institution for the loans advanced or disbursed by it. Generally, for crop loans the loan amount will be repaid in lump sum, as they fall under self-liquidating loans. For these loans, the repayment schedule will start 2-3 months after harvesting period because, immediately after harvesting, the price will be low in market due to glut (more supply than demand) in market. In case of term loans, the number of installments (as they are non-liquidating loans) will depend upon the incremental income earned from the loan amount. If more amount of incremental income is derived from the loan investment, then the number of installments will be less and *vice versa*. When the crop fails due to unfavorable weather conditions, the repayment period of loans will be extended *i.e.*, from short term to mid term loans and even the banker may still lend the loan to farmer to continue the farm business.

g. Principle of Protection

This principle aims at checking the willful-defaulters from purposefully avoiding repayment of loan back to the financial institution. Hence, the banker will insist the farmer=-borrower for submission of requisite securities to the bank before lending loan to him. Besides collecting securities, the bank also resort to some other protection measures like:

- ☆ *Insurance Coverage*: The banker will encourage the farmer to go for insurance for crops and also allied enterprises. In case of any eventuality or unforeseen calamities, particularly small and marginal farmers cannot repay their loan amounts. So, if the enterprises are insured against risk factors, the insurance companies will pay indemnity to the farmer-borrower depending upon the extent of losses. From the compensation the farmer receives, the bank will collect the loan amount.
- ☆ ***Linking credit with marketing***: By linking credit with marketing, the banker will be safe position in collecting the loan amount from the farmer borrower. For example, a bank has given a loan amount to a sugarcane farmer. After harvest, the sugarcane farmer will supply the cane to the sugar factory and in the mean time, the banker will provide the loan particulars of the farmer to the authorities of sugar factory. When the farmers sell the produce in sugar factory, the factory authorities will deduct the loan amount and remaining amount will be given to the farmer. Later the sugar factory authorities will deposit the loan amount in the bank on behalf of the farmer borrower.
- ☆ ***Provision of finance against warehouse receipt (Marketing loan):*** At times of drastic fall in prices of the produce, the produce is kept in the godown under the control of Agricultural Market Committee or warehouse and based on the receipt issued by these agencies, marketing loan was advanced to the farmer borrower to an extent of 75 per cent of value of produce. This will facilitate the farmer to overcome distress sales in the villages. As and when the prices shoot up in the market, the farmer will identify the buyer, clear the loan amount and sell the produce. So, when the prices are low in the market, the produce is kept under the control of an agency (Agricultural Market Committee or Warehouse). and the farmer has no control over the produce till the loan amount was cleared. Hence, the name key loan was given for this type of hypothecation. This procedure of advancing loan by taking warehouse receipt as security is a symbiotic process, where the farmer gets higher returns and the bank can collect full loan amount.
- ☆ ***Covering Credit under Small Loan Guarantee Scheme of Deposit Insurance and Credit Guarantee Corporation of India (DICGC):*** When the bank fail to recover the loans from weaker sections of farming community, the Small Loan Guarantee Scheme of DICGC will repay the loans to the bank on behalf of farmer-borrowers especially during adverse situations.

☆ ***Taking Securities:*** The banks will advance loans to the farmer borrower based on the hypothecation or mortgage of assets. If the farmer borrower is a willful defaulter, the bank will liquefy these assets, after repeated warnings and remainders and later recovers the loan amount.

11.9. Repayment Plans

Generally for Short term loans or self-liquidating loans, the repayment plan concept will not arise because, these loans will be cleared off in lumpsum in the same accounting year. However, in case of term loans or investment loans, which are partially liquidating or non- liquidating in nature, the repayment of loan amount will extend to several years. That is, the farmer cannot repay entire loan amount in same production year but he will clear off of loan in a series of installments various repayment plans are existing for clearing off the teem-loans and they all listed below.

a. Straight-end Repayment Plan
b. Partial Repayment Plan or Balloon Repayment Plan.
c. Amortized Repayment Plan
o Amortized Decreasing Repayment Plan
o Amortized Even Repayment Plan
d. Variable Repayment Plan
e. Optional Repayment Plan.
f. Reserve Repayment Plan or Future payment Repayment Plan

a. Straight-end Repayment Plan

It is also called as Single Repayment Plan or Lumpsum Repayment Plan. As the name itself indicates, the farmer-borrower, will repay the principal amount in lumpsum when the loan matures, while the interest component is paid every year. Since the principle amount is paid in lumpsum at the end of repayment period, it is also called as Lumpsum repayment plan.

b. Partial Repayment Plan or Balloon Repayment Plan

In this type of repayment plan, the repayment of loan will be done partially over several years. Hence, the name Partial Repayment Plan. In this mode of repayment, the installment amount gradually decreases till the end of repayment period, but the last installment amount will be large, hence the name Balloon Repayment Plan.

c. Amortized Repayment Plan

It is nothing but an extended version of Partial Repayment Plan. Repaying the entire loan amount in series of installments is called Amortization. The term 'amortization' implies, 'Killing by degrees'. This Repayment Plan is of two types:

☆ ***Amortized Even Repayment Plan:*** In this repayment plan, the total installment amount remains same throughout the repayment period. Principal component gradually increases throughout the repayment period, while interest component gradually declines (Panel A of Figure 11.3). This repayment plans is followed for term loans like digging wells construction of godowns, dairy, mango orchards etc. The annual installment in case of amortized even repayment plan can be worked out with the following formula:

$I = B[i/(1-(1+i)^{-n})]$

I= Annual installment, B= Principal amount borrowed by the farmer, i=rate of interest,

n=number of years/repayment period

- ✰ ***Amortized Decreasing Repayment Plan:*** In this repayment plan, the principal component remains same throughout repayment period, while interest component decreases. Hence, the total installment decreases till the end of repayment period (Panel B of Figure 11.3). This type of repayment plan is followed in case of machinery.

d. Variable Repayment Plan

As the name indicates, the total installment amount paid by the farmer borrower varies depending on level of income from farm business. At times of good harvest, the farmer pays higher installments and at times of poor or bad harvest, farmers pay less amount of installment. Generally, the banking institutions will not follow this type of repayment plan and only private money lenders follow this plan.

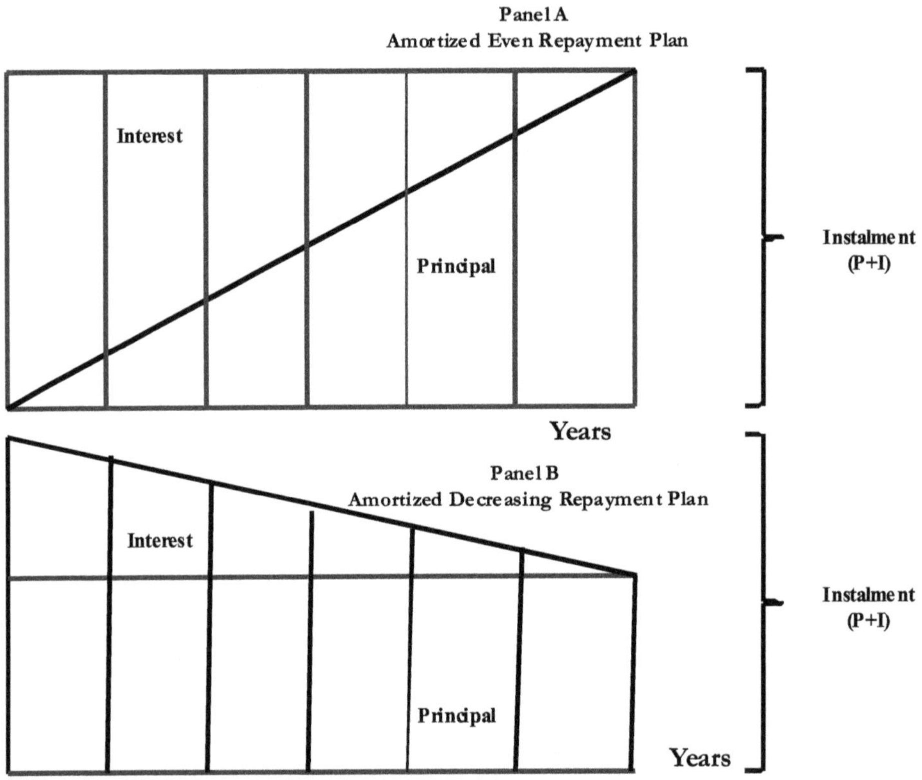

Figure 11.3: Amortized Repayment Plans.

e. Optional Repayment Plan

In this method of repayment plan, option was given to the farmer borrower to pay the principal amount depending upon the income from farm business, but interest component must be paid every year (or) regularly.

f. Reserve Repayment Plan or Future Payment Repayment Plan

This method of repayment plan followed in areas, where the agri-business income shows higher degree of variability. At times of good harvest, the farmers income will be high and banks will give option to the farmer borrower to clear off the installment, not only for the current year, but also for future years or future installments. This is because, the income is highly fluctuating in that area. If the farmer could not reap good harvest, he need not clear the installments in that year because, he had already paid the installments in advance at times of good harvest in the past. This also facilitates the farmer and borrower to maintain integrity is credit transactions.

Examples

1. Partial Repayment Plan

The loan amount taken by the farmer-borrower is Rs. 10000. Time period for repayment is 6 years, Rate of interest is 12 per cent. The principal amount was given in the following table: Workout the procedure to compute installment paid by the farmer borrower in clearing the loan amount taken.

Year	*Principal*	*Interest*	*Installment (P+I)*	*Balance Amount*
1	1000	10000 x 0.12=1200	2200	10000-1000=9000
2	1000	9000 x 0.12=1080	2080	9000-1000=8000
3	1000	8000 x 0.12=960	1960	8000-1000=7000
4	1000	7000 x 0.12=840	1840	7000-1000=6000
5	1000	6000 x 0.12=720	1720	6000-1000=5000
6	5000	5000 x 0.12=600	5600	5000-5000=0
	10000	5400	15400	

2. Amortized Decreasing Repayment Plan

The loan amount taken by the farmer-borrower is Rs. 10000. Time period for repayment is 6 years, Rate of interest is 12 per cent. Workout the procedure to compute installment paid by the farmer borrower in clearing the loan amount taken.

Year	*Principal*	*Interest*	*Installment (P+I)*	*Balance Amount*
1	1666.67 = [10000/6]	10000 x 0.12=1200	2866.67	10000 - 1666.67=8333.33
2	1666.67	8333.33 x 0.12=999.99	2666.66	8333.33 - 1666.67=6666.66
3	1666.67	6666.66 x 0.12=799.99	2466.66	6666.66 - 1666.67=4999.99
4	1666.67	4999.99 x 0.12=599.99	2266.66	4999.99 - 1666.67=3333.32
5	1666.67	3333.32 x 0.12=399.99	2066.66	3333.32 - 1666.67=1666.65
6.	1666.67	1666.65 x 0.12=199.99	1866.66	1666.65 -1666.67 = 0

3. Amortized Even Repayment Plan

The loan amount taken by the farmer-borrower is Rs. 10000. Time period for repayment is 6 years, Rate of interest is 12 per cent. Workout the procedure to compute installment paid by the farmer borrower in clearing the loan amount taken.

Ans. We know, Annual Installment is calculated by using the formula: $I = B[i/(1-(1+i)^{-n})]$

I= Annual installment, B= Principal amount borrowed by the farmer, i=rate of interest, n=number of years/repayment period

I = 10000 [0.12/(1-(1.12)-6)] = Rs. 2432.32

Year	Principal	Interest	Installment (P+I)	Balance Amount
1.	2432.25-1200= 1232.25	10000 x 0.12= 1200	2432.25	10000-1232.25 = 8767.75
2.	2432.25-1052.13= 1380.12	8767.75 x 0.12= 1052.13	2432.25	8767.75-1380.12 = 7387.63
3.	2432.25-886.51= 1545.74	7387.63 x 0.12= 886.51	2432.25	7387.63-1545.74 = 5841.89
4.	2432.25-701.02= 1731.23	5841.89 x 0.12= 701.02	2432.25	5841.89-1731.23 = 4110.66
5.	2432.25-493.27= 1938.98	4110.66 x 0.12= 493.27	2432.25	4110.66-1938.98 = 2171.68
6.	2432.25-260.60= 2171.65	2171.68 x 0.12= 260.60	2432.25	2171.68-2171.65 = 0.03
	10000.00		14593.50	

11.10. Procedural Formalities followed by the Bankers for Sanctioning and Recovery of Loans

When the farmer applies for bank loan, the financial institution is vested with the full powers either to accept or reject the loan application. This is nothing but the appraisal of farm credit proposals or procedures and formalities followed in the processing of loans. The following are the steps followed by the bankers for sanctioning and recovery of loans:

i. Interview with farmer borrower by the banking officials.
ii. Submission of loan application by the farmer borrower
iii. Scrutiny or verification of records
iv. Visit of bankers to the farmers field
v. Criteria for loan eligibility
vi. Sanction of loan
vii. Collection of requisite documents
viii. Disbursement of loan

ix. Post-credit follow up measures

x. Recovery of loan

i. Interview with Farmer Borrower by the Banking Officials

Interview with farmer-borrower by banking officials is not a mere formality because, it enables the banker to analyze or judge the farmer's honesty, integrity, frankness, progressive thinking, mental ability etc. While discussing with the farmer borrower, the banker will study about the purpose of loan, where the loan amount is invested and he will explain the farmer borrower under which terms and conditions the bank will sanction loan to him. If the farmer gets satisfies with these conditions, the banker will given loan application to the farmer.

ii. Submission of Loan Application by the Farmer Borrower

After thorough understanding of terms and conditions imposed by the banker, the farmer borrower will fill the application in which the information like name of the farmer, village map, location of field, survey no, village, purpose of loan, type of loan, quantum of loan, farm budget, financial statements etc., will be filled. Besides these details, the farmer has to submit 10-1 certificate indicating ownership rights of land, Adangal certificate indicating cropping pattern followed by the farmer, encumbrance certificate (land mortgage details) etc. Along with these details, a passport size photo of the farmer is to be affixed to loan application form.

iii. Scrutiny or Verification of Records

The details submitted by the farmer borrower will be verified by banker by interacting with village revenue officials, whether these details, assets and securities shown are genuine are not.

iv. Visit to the Farmer's Field by Bank Officials

After scrutiny of records by bank officials, the field officer of bank will visit the farmer's fields to get first hand information about the details mentioned by the farmer in his application form. This visit by the field officer helps in identifying the farmer and guarantor, locate the boundaries of land as per the map, assess the managerial ability of farmer, farmer attitude and progressiveness in farm business, economics of crops and other enterprises being practiced by the farmer, feasibility of loan investment, farmers financial position, other source of funds to farmers (say from non-institutional agencies) etc. This visit also helps the banker to verify both credit worthiness and trust worthiness of farmer borrower. These details will be included in a report and the field officer will submit it to the branch manager for taking final decision regarding sanction of loan.

v. Criteria for Loan Eligibility

After thorough analysis of the reports by the branch manager, he will fix certain criteria for judging the eligibility of farmer borrower to sanction the loan. The criteria include:

- He should have sound character, integrity and credit worthy.
- He should have proper dealings with friends, neighboring farmers and other financial institutions in the village.

- ☆ He should not be a willful defaulter in the past.
- ☆ He must have progressive outlook and receptive of modern technology.
- ☆ He should ensure proper use of credit for the desired purpose and should not divert the loan for unproductive purposes.
- ☆ The securities provided by the farmer should be free from litigation.

If all the above criteria were found positive with respect to the farmer borrower, then the branch manager will decide for sanctioning the loan.

vi. Sanction of Loan

Before sanctioning loan, the branch manager will study the technical feasibility, economic viability of investment, repayment capacity, risk bearing ability of farmer borrower etc. If the loan amount for investment is beyond the sanctioning power of branch manager, the application of farmer borrower will be forwarded to the head office incorporating his recommendations. If the authorities get satisfied with the proposed investment, they will decide to sanction the loan and the same will be communicated to the farmer-borrower.

vii. Collection of Requisite Documents

After sanctioning the loan amount to farmer-borrower, the following documents will be collected by the financial institution from the farmer borrower.

- ☆ Demand promissory mote
- ☆ Guarantee letter
- ☆ Installment letter
- ☆ Authorization letter especially during when credit was linked with marketing
- ☆ Mortgage deeds *etc.*

viii. Disbursement of Loan

After receiving the documents from farmer borrower, the loan amount is credited to his account. The loan will be disbursed in a phased manner so that, it will ensure productive use. The latter installments will be disbursed only, when the earlier installments are spent properly. A realistic (suitable) repayment plan will be framed by bank officials and hand over the same to the farmer borrower, keeping in view the income flow from the investment.

ix. Post-credit Follows up Measures

The Branch Manager or Agricultural Officer of the bank will pay visits to farmer's fields frequently to ascertain the proper use of credit by him. These visits also help the farmer borrower in developing good rapport with the banking officials and also helps him in seeking technical advices from them. Further, it promote close rapport between banker and farmer borrower and this indirectly make the latter feel more responsible for repayment of loan. These visits may also facilitate the farmer borrower to request for additional loan for the investment and if it is genuine, the banker will still extend the loan amount.

x. Recovery of Loans

The bankers will frequently remind the farmer borrower in advance about the repayment of loan in time. If needed, the bankers will arrange village meetings and advice the farmer to repay the loan amount. If the farmer borrower couldn't repay the loan amount, the bankers will ascertain, whether he is a willful defaulter or not. If he is not, the banker may also postpone the repayment schedule. To recover the loans promptly from farmer borrower, the bankers will advice the farmers to go for insurance of crops, link credit with marketing, provide market finance etc. If the farmer borrower is a willful defaulter, stringent measures will be taken through the court of law by prosecuting the farmer's assets.

References

Alberta Agriculture, Food and Rural Development, "Comparative Financial-Ratio Analysis for Alberta Farms", Production Economics Branch; Farm Business Management Branch, March 31, 1996.

Anil Kumar Soni and Harjinder Pal Singh Saluja, 'Financial Ratio Analysis of DCC Bank Limited Rajnandgaon - A Case Study', *International Journal of Accounting and Financial Management Research (IJAFMR)*, ISSN 2249-6882, Vol. 3, Issue 1, Mar 2013, 93-106.

Anonymous (2004). Internal Rate of Return: A Cautionary Tale. Tempted by a project with high internal rates of return? Better check those interim cash flows again. The McKinsey Quarterly, McKinsey and Co.

Anonymous, 'Comprehensive Guide To Farm Financial Management', Module 4: Net Worth Statement, Analysis, Saskatchewan Ministry of Agriculture.

Anonymous, Factors affecting the size of agricultural farms in Greece, Anastasios V. Semos, MEDIT 4/93.

Anonymous, Farm Planning and Enterprise Selection, 'Exploring the Small Farm Dream' USDA Department of Agriculture, National Commission on Small Farms, 1998.

Anonymous, Implement Integrated Farm Layout and Site Selection, Learner Guide, Primary Agriculture, Farm layout and Site selection, NQF Level:4 US No: 116309.

Anonymous, Partial Budgeting : A Financial Management Tool, USDA, Northeast Region, Sustainable Agriculture for Research and Education (SARE) in Cooperation with Rutgers Cooperative Extension of Salem County.

Ashok Gulati, Surbhi Jain and NidhiSatija, 'Rising Farm Wages in India-The 'Pull' and 'Push' Factors', Discussion Paper No. 5, CACP, 2013.

Bardhan, P K (1973). "Size, Productivity and Returns to Scale: An Analysis of Farm-level Data in India Agriculture", *Journal of Political Economy*, Vol 81 (6): 1370-86.

Ben Beale, Shannon Dill and Dale Johnson, *Farm Business Planning*, University of Maryland. Cooperative Extension.

Beneke, Raymond R. "Progress Comes Dressed in Strange Clothing," *Choices* (First Quarter 1998): 42-44.

Berry, R A (1972)."Farm Size Distribution, Income Distribution and the Efficiency of Agricultural Production: Colombia", *American Economic Review*, Vol 62 (1): 403-08.

Berry, R A and W R Cline (1979). Agrarian Structureand Productivity in Developing Countries (Baltimore: John Hopkins University Press).

Besley, T. (1995). "Saving, Credit, and Insurance." in: J. Behrman and T. N. Srinivasan, *Handbook of Development Economics* 3.A: 2123-2207, (Amsterdam: North Holland).

Bhalla, S (1979). "Farm Size and Productivity and Technical Change in India Agriculture" in R A Berry and W R Cline (ed.), *Agrarian Structure and Productivity in Developing Countries* (Baltimore: John Hopkins University Press), pp. 141-93.

Bhalla, S S and P Roy (1988). "Mis-Specification in Farm Productivity Analysis: the Role of Land Quality", *Oxford Economic Papers*, Vol 40 (1): 55-73.

Binswanger, Hans P and Mark R Rosenzweig (1986). "Behavioural and Material Determinants of Production Relations in Agriculture", *Journal of Development Studies*, Vol 22(3): 503-39.

Boehlje, Michael D., Vernon R. Euidman 1984). *'Farm Management'*, New York: John Wiley and Sons, Inc.

Cary, David and Dunn, Michael (1997). Adjustment of modified internal rate of return for scale and time span differences, *Proceedings of the Academy of Accounting and Financial Studies*, 2(2).

Chahal G.S. - Agricultural Cooperation, Finance and Business Management - *Agricultural Co-Operation.*

Chandy K. T. 'Cooperative Farming', Booklet No. 72, *Agricultural Cooperation*: ACS-10.

Chandy K. T., 'Agricultural Labour', Booklet No. 501, Agricultural Situation in India: *ASJS* – 2.

Chase, C. 2006b."Using enterprise budgets to make decisions." Ames, Iowa: Iowa State University, University Extension Service, Bulletin FM-1875.

Coelli, T.J., Rao, D.S. O'Donnell, C.J. and Battese, G.E. (2005). *An Introduction to Efficiency and Productivity Analysis*, Second Edition, Springer Science + Business Media, New York, USA.

Damodaran, H. (2012). 'An alternative 'theory' of Inflation,' June 12, 2012 *The Hindu.*

Daniel Thorner (1956). The Agricultural Labour Enquiry: Reflections on Concepts and Methods, *The Economic Weekly*, June 23.

Dean Dyck (2000). *Alberta Agriculture.* Alberta Feedlot Management Guide.

Delton C. Gerloff and Robert W. Holland, 'Establishing and Using a Farm Financial Record-Keeping System', The University of Tennessee Agricultural Extension Service, PB 1540.

Dennis Kaan, 'Defining Risk and a Framework for Moving Towards Resilience In Agriculture', Article 1.3, Colorado State University.

Deolalikar (1981). "The Inverse Relationship between Productivity and Farm Size: A Test Using Regional Data from India", *American Journal of Agricultural Economics,* Vol 63 (2): 275-79.

Dercon, S. (2002). "Income Risk, Coping Strategies and Safety Nets", World Institute for Development Economics Research Discussion Paper 2002/22, Oxford.

Dhondyal S.P., '*Farm Management – Economic Approach*', Aman Publications, Meerut.

Dodson, Charles B. (1993). "Farm Diversification–Still a Problem?" Agricultural Income and Finance Situation and Outlook Report.AFO-50. U.S. Dept. of Agr., Econ. Res. Serv., September, pp. 44-46.

Dong Xiao-Yuan and Gregory K Dow (1993). "Monitoring Costs in Chinese Agriculture", *Journal of Economy*, Vol 101 (3): 539-53.

Dyer Graham (1997). Class, State and AgriculturalProductivity in Egypt: A Study of the Inverse Relationship between Farm Size and Land Productivity (London: Frank Cass Publishers).

Eaton, C. and Shepherd, A.W. (2001). Contract farming: Partnership for Growth. *FAO Agricultural Services Bulletin* 145, Rome, Italy.

Elavia B. M., The Study of Co-operative Development Bank in Gujarat, Baroda: Baroda, M. S. University of Baroda.

Eta Takele and IhabSharabeen, (2005). 'Financial Ratios for Analyzing the Farm Business', Farm Business Briefs - November.

Fan Shenggen and Connie Chang-Kang (2005). "Is Small Beautiful? Farm Size, Productivity and Framework", World Bank Social Protection Discussion Paper 9926, Washington, DC.

Farrell, M.J. (1957). "The Measurement of Productive Efficiency". *Journal of Royal Statistical Society*, Vol.120, No. 30, pp. 253-290.

Frisvold, George B (1994): "Does Supervision Matter? Some Hypothesis Tests Using Indian Farm Level Data", *Journal of Development Economics*, Vol 43 (2): 217-38.

Gadgil, D. R., and V. R. Gadgil (1940a). "The Application of The Survey Method to Farm Business Studies in India" in Proceedings of the First Conference held at Delhi, February 24th and 25th, 1940, Indian Society of Agricultural Economics.

Gadgil, D. R., and V. R. Gadgil (1940b).A Survey of Farm Business in WaiTaluka, Publication No.7, Gokhale Institute of Politics and Economics, Poona.

Gary A. Hachfeld, David B. Bau, and C. Robert Holcomb, 'Balance Sheet', Agricultural Business Management, Extension Educators.

Gary A. Hachfeld, David B. Bau, and C. Robert Holcomb, 'Income Statement', Agricultural Business Management, Extension Educators.

Gary A. Hachfeld, David B. Bau, and C. Robert Holcomb, Statement of Cash Flows Financial Management Series #4 7/2013, Agricultural Business Management.

George F. Patrick, 'Managing Risk in Agriculture', NCR-406, Cooperative Extension Service, Purdue University, West Lafayette, IN 47907.

George F. Patrick, 'Risk Analysis for Agricultural Production Firms: Concepts, Information Requirements and Policy Issues', Department of Agricultural Economics, University of Illinois, AE-4574, July 1984, pp. 197-236,.

George F. Patrick, 'Risk Perceptions and Management Responses: Producer-Generated Hypotheses for Risk Modeling,' *Southern Journal of Agricultural Economics*, Vol. 17, No. 2, December 1985, p. 231-238.

Ghose, A K (1979). "Farm Size and Land Productivity in Indian Agriculture – A Reappraisal", *Journal of Development Studies*, Vol 16 (1): 27-49.

Government of India (1990). Report of the Expert Committee for Review of Methodology of Cost of Production of Crops, Department of Agriculture and Cooperation, Ministry of Agriculture.

Government of India (1990). Report of the Expert Committee for Review of Methodology of Cost of Production of Crops, Department of Agriculture and Cooperation, Ministry of Agriculture.

Government of India (1996). Cost of Cultivation of Principal Crops in India, Department of Agriculture and Cooperation, Ministry of Agriculture.

Government of India (2000). Cost of Cultivation of Principal Crops in India: February - 2000, Department of Agriculture and Cooperation, Ministry of Agriculture.

Government of India (2001). Report of the National Statistical Commission: Volume II.

Gulati, A., and Shweta Saini (2013). 'Taming Food Inflation in India', Discussion paper No. 4, CACP.

Hanan Jacoby, Rabassa, Mariano and Skoufias, Emmanuel (2011)."Distributional implications of climate change in India," *Policy Research Working Paper Series* 5623, The World Bank.

Hanumantha, Rao C H (1975). *Technological Change and Distribution of Gains in Indian Agriculture.* Macmillan, New Delhi.

Hardaker, J. Brian, Raud B.M. Huirne, and Jock R. Anderson (1997). *'Coping With Risk in Agriculture'*, New York: CAB International.

Harwood, J.R. Heifner, K. Coble, T. Perry, and A. Somwaru (1999). 'Managing Risk in Farming: Concepts, Research and Analysis', Agricultural Economic Report No. 774, Market and Trade Economic Division and Resource Economics Division, Economic Research Service U.S. Department of Agriculture. March.

Havenevik, J Kjell and Rune Skarstein (1997). "Land Tenure, State-Peasant Relations and Productivity in Tanzanian Agriculture" in Amit Bhaduri and Rune Skarstein (ed.), *Economic Development and Agricultural Productivity* (Cheltenham: Edward Elgar), pp 183-212.

Hazell, P., C. Pomareda, and A. Valdes (1986). *Crop Insurance for Agricultural Development: Issuesand Experience,* (Baltimore: The John Hopkins University Press).

Hazell, Peter (2011). "Five Big Questions about Five Hundred Million Small Farms", keynote paper presented at the *IFAD conference on New Directions for Smallholder Agriculture,* 24-25 January, International Fund for Agricultural Development, Via Paolo Di Dono, 44, Rome 00142, Italy.

Headey, D., Bezemer, D. and Hazell, P. (2010). Agricultural employment trends in Asia and Africa: Too fast or too slow, *World Bank Research Observer* 25, 57-89.

Heady E.O and Jensen R.Harald (1960). *'Farm Management Economics'*. Prentice - Hall INC, Engle Wood Cliffs, N.J.

http://agriinfo.in.

http://ajae.oxfordjournals.org.

http://economicsexposed.com/green-revolution-and-size-productivity-relationship-2/

http://extension.psu.edu/courses/meat-goat/financial-information/farm-business-analysis/balance-sheet-analysis.

http://nsdl.niscair.res.in/bitstream/123456789/498/1/

http://nsdl.niscair.res.in/dspace/bitstream/123456789/498/1/PDF+revised+Agricultural+Finance-corrected.pdf.

http://old.iita.org/cms/details/trn_mat/irg65/i65.pdf.

http://www.accountingexplanation.com.

http://www.cash4wealthng.com/how-important-are-these-ratios-to-your-business.html.

http://www.cfo.com/printable/article.cfm/3304945 (accessed on 14 Aug 2009).

http://www.fsa-micasa.com/images/formulas.html.

http://www.ictinagriculture.org/sourcebook/module-11-ict-applications-agricultural-risk-management.

http://www.morgancc.edu/abm/curric/reference/Ratios/EquityToAsset.html.

http://www.slideshare.net/Timothy212/introducing-farm-business-analysis.

http://www1.agric.gov.ab.ca/$department/deptdocs.nsf/all/econ2198.

http://www1.agric.gov.ab.ca/$department/deptdocs.nsf/all/sis14155.

https://e-uczelnia.uek.krakow.pl/mod/resource/view.php.

https://www.disnat.com/en/knowledge/ratios/debtequity.asp.

https://www.extension.iastate.edu/agdm/wholefarm/html/c3-14.html.

ISAE (1953). Problems of Farm Costs in Indian Agriculture: A Study in Methodology, *Indian Society of Agricultural Economics*, Bombay.

Jack, J. C. (1927). *The Economic Life of a Bengal District: A Study* by J. C. Jack, Oxford University Press, London.

Jinkins, John (1992). *"Measuring Farm and Ranch Business Diversity," Agricultural Income and Finance Situation and Outlook Report*. AFO-45. U.S. Dept. Agr., Econ. Res. Serv., May, pp. 28-30.

John D. Black, Marion Clawson, Charles R. Sayre and Walter W. Wilcox (1953). *Farm Management*, The Macmillan Company, New York.

Joseph OlumideOseni, Farm Records and Accounting, AEC 306, Department of Agricultural Economics and Extension, Federal University of Technology, PMB 704, Akure, Ondo State, National Open University of Nigeria.

Kandarp Patel and Swetha Kolluri, 'A Success Story of Gambhira Cooperative Farming Survival of the Weakest Through Anti Darwinian Principle', (http://www.cress-rhone-alpes.org/cress/IMG/pdf/Patel_abs.pdf).

Khusro, A M (1968). *"Returns to Scale in Indian Agriculture."* In: A.M. Khusro (ed.), Readings in Agricultural Development (New Delhi: Allied Publishers).

Kim B. Anderson and John E. Ikerd, 'Risk Rated Management Strategies for Farm and Ranch Decisions,' Extension Circular E-841, Oklahoma State University Cooperative Extension Service.

Kohl, David, and Troy Wilson (1997). "Understanding Key Financial Ratios and Benchmarks", Northwest Farm Credit Services, Business Tools Bulletin, Spokane, Washington, 1997.

Kulamani Padhi (2007). *'Agricultural Labour in India - A Close Look'*, Odisha Review, February-March.

Lucia Wegner and GineZwart (2001). *Who Will Feed the World? - The Production Challenge*, April.

Mahmood Hassan Khan, *'Economics of Green Revolution in Pakistan'*.

Mazumdar, Dipak (1965). "Size of Farm and Productivity:A Problem of Indian Peasant Agriculture", *Economica*, Vol 32, May, pp 161-73.

Michael R. Langemeier (2001). Balance Sheet – A Financial Management Tool, Farm Management Guide MF-291, Financial Management 6–Revised November.

Norm Dalsted, *'Partial Budgeting', Agriculture and Business Management*, Department of Ariculture and Resource Economics, CSU.

Oseni J.O. Farm Business Organization, AEM 451, Department of Agricultural Economics and Extension, Federal University of Technology, PMB 704, Akure, Ondo State, Nigeria.

Pandey, U.K. *'Agricultural Cooperation, Finance and Business Management'*, Course Material, CCS Haryana Agricultural University, Hissar.

Peter Hazell (2011). Five Big Questions about Five Hundred Million Small Farms, Paper presented at the IFAD Conference on New Directions for Smallholder Agriculture, 24-25 January.

Peter J. Sander and Janet Haley, *'Financial Strength Ratios for Investment Analysis'*, Value Investing For Dummies, 2nd Edition.

Peter McGuire and Peter Allsopp, 'SmartCane Principles of Farm Business Management', SmartCane Best Management Practice Booklet, BSES Limited, CANEGROWERS and the State of Queensland.

Poverty in Asian Agriculture", *Agricultural Economics*, Vol 32 (Supplements-1): 135-46.

Pulliam, A.L. (1948). Farm Layout and Farmstead, Federal Cooperative Extension Service Oregon State College, Corvallis, Extension Bulletin 685 January.

Raghbendra, J., Chitkara, P. and Gupta, S. (2000). "Productivity, Technical and Allocative Efficiency and Farm Size in Wheat Farming in India: A DEA Approach", *Applied Economic Letters*, Vol 7(1): 1-5.

Raj, K.N. (1961). Second Agricultural Labour Enquiry - A Futile and Misleading Investigation, *The Economic Weekly*, March 25.

Ramesh B. Golait and Narayan C. Pradhan (2008). 'Relevance of Weather Insurance in Indian Agriculture, CAB CALLING January-March.

Ramesh Chand, P A Lakshmi Prasanna, Aruna Singh (2011)., 'Farm Size and Productivity: Understanding the Strengths of Smallholders and Improving Their Livelihoods', *Economic and Political Weekly Supplement* EPW June 25, vol xlvi nos 26 and 27.

Ramkishen, Y. (2006). *Management of Cooperatives*. Jaico Publishing House, Mumbai (2007).

Richard W. Carkner (1904). *'Farm Business Records: An Introduction*. Farming West of the Cascades series.

Saini, G.R. (1971). "Holding Size, Productivity and Some Related Aspects of Indian Agriculture", Economic and Political Weekly, *Review of Agriculture*, Vol VI (26): A 79-A85.

Sarah Roth, Dairy Alliance, and Jeffrey Hyde, 'Partial Budgeting for Agricultural Businesses', Penn State College of Agricultural Sciences.

Sayana, V.V. (1949). *The Agrarian Problems of Madras Province*, The Business Week Press, Madras.

Sen, A K (1962). "An Aspect of Indian Agriculture", *The Economic Weekly*, Vol 14 (4-6): 243-46.– (1964): "Size of Holdings and Productivity", *The Economic Weekly*, Vol 16 (5-7): 323-26.

Sen, Abhijit, and Bhatia, M. S. (2004). "Cost of Cultivation and Farm Income", Volume 14, in *State of the Indian Farmer: A Millennium Study*, Academic Foundation in association with Department of Agriculture and Cooperation, Ministry of Agriculture, Government of India.

Sen, Amartya (1962). "Some Aspects of Indian Agriculture", *The Economic Weekly*, Annual Number, February.

Shah, C. H. (1971). *A Survey of Research in Agricultural Economics in India*, Department of Economics, University of Bombay.

Sharma, Arun K. (2011). *"The Potential for Organic Farming in the Drylands of India."* Arid Lands Newsletters. 2005. Web. 20 October 2011.

Sidhu R. S. and Gill, S.S. (2006). - Agricultural Credit and Indebtedness in India: Some Issues. *Indian Journal of Agricultural Economics*, Vol. 61, No. 1.

Siegel, P., and J. Alwang, 1999. *"An Asset-Based Approach to Social Risk Management: A Conceptual.*

Singh R.K., (2006). *Farm Management and Natural Resource Economics, Farm Record Maintenance and Cost Analysis.*

Singh, S. Pratap (1940). "Some Observations On the Cost of Production of Crops in *The Principal Sugarcane Tracts of Punjab*", in Proceedings of the First Conference held at Delhi, February 24th and 25th, 1940, Indian Society of Agricultural Economics.

Subbarao, K (1982). "Technology Gap and the Emerging Size-Productivity Relationships Following the Adoption of New Technology: An Analysis of Evidence from North-West and Eastern India", unpublished paper, University of California at Berkeley, Department of Agriculture and Resource Economics.

Subba Reddy, S. and P. Raghu Ram (2005). *Agricultural Finance and Management*, Oxford IBP publishing Company, New Delhi.

Surjit, V. (2008). Evolution of the Study of Cost of Cultivation In India, Foundation for Agrarian Studies, Studying Village Economies in India, A Colloquium on Methodology, December 21 to 24, 2008.

Thomas, P. J and K. C. Ramakrishnan (1940). *Some South Indian Villages: A Resurvey*, University of Madras.

Thorat, Y.S.P. (2006). Rural Credit in India: Issues and Concerns. *Indian Journal of Agricultural Economics*, Vol. 61, No. 1.

Thorner, D. (1980). *The Shaping of Modern India*, Allied Publishers, New Delhi.

Ulrich Hess, Kaspar Richter, Andrea Stoppa, *'Weather Risk Management for Agriculture andAgri-Business in Developing Countries'*, IFC, World Bank and Procom Agr, Rome.

Van Blokland P.J. *Introducing Farm Business Analysis*, Circular 655, IFAS Extension, University of Florida.

William Edwards, Your Net Worth Statement, *Ag Decision Maker*, File C3-20.

Working, E.J.. *Crop-Yield Index Numbers*, Unversity of Illinois.

www.agric.gov.ab.ca/$department/deptdocs.nsf/all/econ2198.

www.agric.gov.ab.ca/$department/deptdocs.nsf/all/sis14155.

www.extension.iastate.edu/agdm/wholefarm/pdf/c3-20.pdf.

www.extension.psu.edu/courses/meat-goat/financial./balance-sheet-analysis.

www.planningcommission.nic.in/plans/planrel/fiveyr/1st/1planch10.html.

www.publish.csiro.au/?act=view_file and file_id=9780643095168.

www.tnau.ac.in/eagri/eagri50/AECO342/lec14.pdf.

www.ingramcontent.com/pod-product-compliance
Lightning Source LLC
Chambersburg PA
CBHW070250260926
51849CB00001BA/102
* 9 7 8 9 3 8 6 0 7 1 1 7 0 *